An Intellectual
and Cultural History
of the Western World

CONTRIBUTING AUTHORS FOR VOLUME THREE

Art	JOHN C. GALLOWAY BERNARD MYERS
Biology, Physiology	HOWARD A. SCHNEIDER
Chemistry	O. THEODOR BENFEY
Economics	JOHN FRED BELL
Geology	CARROLL LANE FENTON
Literature	EDWARD HUBLER ANTHONY NETBOY WALTER B. SCOTT WILLARD THORP
Mathematics, Cosmology	JAGJIT SINGH
Medicine	THOMAS E. KEYS
Music	MARTIN BERNSTEIN SAUL NOVACK
Philosophy, Religion	GEORGE DENNIS O'BRIEN
Physics	BANESH HOFFMANN
Psychology	RICHARD D. WALK
Soviet Culture	DONALD W. TREADGOLD

An Intellectual
and Cultural History
of the Western World

by

HARRY ELMER BARNES

THIRD REVISED EDITION

IN THREE VOLUMES

VOLUME THREE

From the Nineteenth Century to the Present Day

Dover Publications, Inc., New York

Published in Canada by General Publishing Company, Ltd., 30 Lesmill Road, Don Mills, Toronto,
Ontario.
Published in the United Kingdom by Constable
and Company, Ltd., 10 Orange Street, London WC 2.

This Dover edition, first published in 1965, is a
revised and enlarged republication of the second
edition published by Reynal and Hitchcock, Inc.
in 1941. The first edition of this work was published
by the Cordon Company, Inc., in 1937. The work,
originally in one volume, now appears in three
volumes.

International Standard Book Number: 0-486-21277 7
Library of Congress Catalog Card Number: 63-21675

Manufactured in the United States of America
Dover Publications, Inc.
180 Varick Street
New York, N. Y. 10014

TABLE OF CONTENTS
VOLUME THREE
Part Five: The Dawn of Contemporary Thought and Culture

Part Six: Contemporary Civilization and the Future of Man

Part Five

THE DAWN OF CONTEMPORARY THOUGHT AND CULTURE

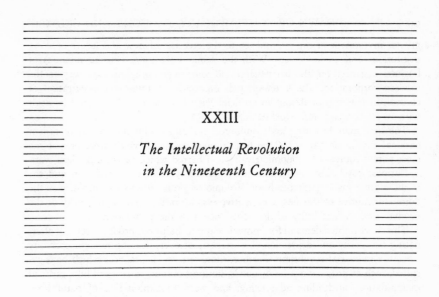

XXIII

The Intellectual Revolution in the Nineteenth Century

I. INTRODUCTION: THE INSTITUTIONAL FRAMEWORK

The Industrial Revolution.—While the main currents of thought down to the nineteenth century primarily reinterpreted medieval ideas in terms of the new natural sciences, from the nineteenth century on, economic factors sweepingly transformed man's outward life and increasingly absorbed his inward life. The most striking changes affected material culture and were associated with the "Industrial Revolution" which may be divided into three main phases: (1) revolutionary changes in the methods of manufacturing, transportation, and communication; (2) the rise of the factory system—a new type of industrial organization and labor discipline; and (3) general economic, social, and cultural results introduced by the new technology and factory system.

The first phase consisted primarily in the transition from handicraft to machine production following 1750. One invention created the need for another, and gradually they completely transformed methods of manufacturing, transportation, communication, farming, and everyday living. With the increased rapidity of inventions, contemporary civilization assumed a dynamic character.

Among the institutional by-products of the mechanical age, the factory system, perhaps, had the most far-reaching results. It represented a novel method of organizing and applying labor to productive processes. The transition from the domestic or putting-out system to the factory system was made necessary by the introduction of machinery.

The factory system brought a new and rigorous discipline to the industrial worker, and it also uprooted the older intellectual perspective and social attachments developed over tens of thousands of years.

The unparalleled expansion of manufacturing and commerce required a much

947

greater investment of capital, and led to the creation of new and larger banking institutions and credit devices. With the demand for more efficient methods of business organization, the partnership and joint-stock company gave way to the modern corporation. The latter offered important advantages: concentration of control, increased capital, and an artificial legal personality which could be dealt with in court apart from stockholders.

The new manufacturing and commerce, combined with the revival of ardent national sentiment, promoted the high protective tariffs which were one of the most potent sources of economic rivalry and hatred which produce modern wars.

Business psychology underwent a revolutionary change. Materialism and the profit motive made great headway. Volume of profit, immediate profit, was the dominant motive of this new competitive system, rather than high quality of the product or its adaptability to the actual needs of the population.

This short-sighted demand for immediate profits helped to produce cycles of alternating prosperity and depression characteristic of every leading modern economy since the industrial revolution. Further, those anti-social practices which have resulted, such as producing inferior goods, limiting output, stock gambling, railroad manipulation, misleading advertising, and wasteful exploitation of natural resources, actually prevented society from making the most of its mechanical and industrial achievements. The pecuniary gains produced by the efforts of the scientists and technicians who provided the mechanical foundations of contemporary existence were mainly diverted to the business men who exploited these achievements.

The economically and socially disastrous theory of business enterprise adopted by the employers finally permeated and dominated industrial workers, particularly strongly organized skilled laborers, who demanded high wages for short hours of what might be indifferent and relatively unproductive labor. To be sure, the workingman could hardly be blamed for learning a lesson from his employer.

With the coming of the machine technique and the factory system, so large an amount of capital was required to conduct modern business activities that, to an increasing degree, the class which controlled manufacturing and commercial activities became sharply differentiated from labor. Ultimately, a marked differentiation also developed within the controlling class. Active management of industry passed to the promoter, the factory superintendent, and the technical expert, while the possessor of great wealth often had little direct concern with production, although he supplied industry with funds.

The early capitalists regarded labor as an impersonal commodity entering into the process of manufacturing and commerce. Aristocratic ideals still dominated society, and the urban worker occupied much the same lowly social position that the peasant had earlier. The ruling industrial classes looked upon the factory worker as a distinctly inferior being. There was a tendency to perpetuate the older notion that one's status in society is a true criterion of one's ability and that both God and nature approved of the existing social and economic hierarchy. The urban worker found himself almost entirely dependent on large-scale industry, with little opportunity to go back to the farm. Extended unemployment often meant nothing short of the threat of starvation.

Through labor organizations, democratic political movements, and radical programs of social reform, the laboring class endeavored to improve its status and increase its power. Its efforts resulted mainly in a betterment of conditions rather than in emancipation, which could be achieved only if labor were able to affect vitally the control of industry and commerce.

Social Changes.—The mechanical technique and the factory system wrought tremendous alterations in social conditions. Perhaps the most notable change was the rise of factory towns and the development of urban civilization. City life subjected man to a new set of circumstances and experiences for which he was imperfectly prepared. To the degree in which a nation had been affected by the industrial revolution, it passed from an agrarian to an urban state. There was also a general shift in population away from settlements based on agricultural opportunities to places which offered special industrial advantages in natural resources.

Equally striking were the net gains in population in the states thoroughly affected by the industrial revolution. Probably the most significant cause was the development of modern medicine, particularly public hygiene and preventive medicine, which enormously reduced the death rate. Another important factor in the nineteenth century was the real incentive to breed large families—an incentive stimulated by the indiscriminate charity, child labor conditions, and frontier life of the period. This tendency towards excessive increase of population, together with the development of modern genetics and a more secular attitude towards family and sex, led to the modern birth-control movement. This represented a desire to increase population according to social considerations rather than the theological imperative to "be fruitful and multiply." Many of the older conceptions and practices relating to sex and the family were gradually undermined by the growing secularism of modern life.

One of the most significant of the population changes was the migration from more backward industrial countries to those where economic conditions for the working classes were somewhat better. This created the "immigration problem" in modern society.

A highly significant social change was the triumph of the bourgeoisie, and the expansion in numbers and power of the proletariat—the latter was to constitute the first serious threat to bourgeois power in advanced industrial states.

Among the bourgeois contributions to modern civilization were unquestionably many of the striking improvements which characterize contemporary material culture; on the other hand, middle-class ascendancy was accompanied by much exploitation, suffering, and misery. Even the fair-minded capitalist must admit the inadequacy of a socio-economic system based mainly on the criterion of immediate pecuniary profits.

The economic and social changes created by the industrial revolution produced an unparalleled diversification of social classes and groups, among employers, employees, and the professional class—a grouping with a new basis, the bond of mutual interest through identity of profession or trade. This occupational or vocational tie became the dominant factor in social groupings throughout the Western World and not only began to remold the economic organization of society, but also was to raise serious problems in regard to group and national loyalties.

The Psychology of the Modern Industrial Order.—The psychological results of the industrial revolution and the modern business order have been far-reaching. First, the medieval attitude—a striving for a universal synthesis and a monistic interpretation of life—was all but destroyed. In the modern era pluralism and pragmatism were to become the rule. Another result of the industrial revolution was the increasing range of information acquired by the average citizen. In the modern age, the individual was affected by a far greater range of stimuli—resulting from city life, the modern urban factory, and new methods of communication—than were known to the peasant of the eighteenth century. But urban and factory conditions were destined to increase mental and nervous diseases.

Another significant psychological change was the increasing demand that culture, aside from our fundamental institutions, should show the same characteristics that were observed in the machine process. Cultural products must be "practical," related to the immediate present, and capable of evaluation in concrete terms as to demand, characteristics, and cost.

This naturally produced a growing tendency to insist upon a standardization of cultural products and values, paralleling standardization in the industrial world. Such a spirit tended to stultify art, literature, drama, and music.

The main way to achieve distinction was to spend more money than others—to indulge in "conspicuous consumption." This "pecuniary standard of taste," as Thorstein Veblen called it, was a part of the deference to wealth and the social classification of people according to their income.

Along with the cultural and psychic standardization, there thus came about a specific deference towards great wealth, thus accepting what Veblen called the "theory of the leisure class," and a consequent conferring of high esteem and prestige on the various forms of conduct and attitudes which great wealth carries with it. Such types of conduct were manifested in the ability to waste huge sums of money on non-social and non-productive enterprises—ostentatious dress, elaborate entertainment, grotesquely pretentious dwellings, and, above all, almost complete abstinence from manual labor.

Not only was there this fulsome respect for great wealth but the wealthy themselves sought to emphasize the servility of the laboring classes. The latter were marked off by the necessity of manual labor, in the same way that the wealthy were characterized by their general withdrawal from all laborious physical effort. It was possible, in this way, to make the industrial proletariat defer to standards of the wealthy and more readily accept their lowly status for many decades.

Plans for a New Social Order.—The industrial revolution stimulated many plans for a new type of social order. The first of these, "economic liberalism," was formulated chiefly by followers of Adam Smith. Smith's theories were exploited by business men and sympathetic economists in order to break down earlier limitations on business and to provide authoritative resistance to any social legislation designed to advance the interests of the industrial proletariat.

Thomas Robert Malthus (1766-1834) held that remedial legislation was not only harmful but could not improve the conditions of the poor. The proletariat caused its own misery through an excessively high birth rate. David Ricardo (1772-1823) opposed legislation to increase wages since, he alleged, higher wages would increase the population sufficiently to absorb the temporary gains. Moreover, higher wages would lower profits, curtail industrial initiative, increase unemployment, and extend poverty. James Mill (1773-1836) supported Ricardo. John R. McCulloch (1789-1864), while believing in trade-unionism, felt that only a specific and limited sum could be diverted into wages without wrecking the whole industrial order. Nassau W. Senior (1790-1864) opposed even mild legislation, such as reducing the hours of labor, holding that this would eliminate profits and destroy industry. The ideas of these economic writers were eagerly adopted in England by Richard Cobden, John Bright, and the other members of the Manchester School, and by the new Liberal party. The bourgeois entrepreneur became the object of supreme social and political admiration.

In France, Jean Baptiste Say (1767-1832) stressed the great social contributions of manufacturing and industrialists. For Frédéric Bastiat (1801-1850) the function of the state was solely to maintain "order, security, and justice," and guarantee freedom of trade.

In England, the chief effects of economic liberalism were (1) the growth of free trade; (2) the abolition of slavery in the colonies; (3) the elimination of the Test and Corporation acts; (4) the increase in the political powers of the middle class through the famous Reform Bill of 1832; (5) the repeal of the savage criminal code; (6) the poor law of 1834; (7) public health legislation; and (8) a more liberal policy of imperial government.

Economic liberals were aided by the political philosophy of romanticism and by the political individualism set forth by Wilhelm von Humboldt (1767-1835). After about 1850, both economic liberalism and the individualistic attitude gained impetus from Herbert Spencer's declaration that social evolution, like biological evolution, is a natural process with which man should not interfere. Human welfare is best assured by letting evolution take its course.

John Stuart Mill (1806-1873) was the first to break with extreme forms of economic liberalism. His views opened the way for limited legislation regulating the distributive process in matters relating to wages, interest, rent, and profits.

The abuses and inequalities of the new capitalistic system suggested programs designed to terminate capitalistic ascendancy and to install the proletariat in a position of control over the economic order. The three most important programs were Marxian Socialism, Anarchism, and Syndicalism.

Karl Marx (1818-1883) and Friedrich Engels (1820-1895) were largely responsible for the origins of modern revolutionary socialism. Marx's views owed much to Hegel, Feuerbach, Ricardo, Rodbertus, Ricardian socialists (especially William Thompson), Louis Blanc, Proudhon, Weitling, and Sismondi. Marx synthesized three main currents of thought: (1) Hegelian philosophy; (2) utopian and French transitional socialism; and (3) classical economics.

The Communist Manifesto (1848) contained the essence of Marxian socialism. In this document it was contended that a class struggle between the proletariat and the capitalists must arise because labor is cheated out of its earnings by the capitalists. The proletariat will become progressively stronger through economic solidarity, party organization, and the electoral franchise. When the proletariat is strong enough it will forcibly expropriate its oppressors and institute a regime of collectivism, which, in its first stages, will be a dictatorship of the proletariat. Revisionists hold that Marx favored constitutional methods for taking power; Communists contend he advocated violent overthrow of capitalism.

The enduring theoretical contributions of Marx were his materialistic interpretation of history and his criticism of individualistic industrialism. Marx has been regarded by some as the father of "institutional economics"—the study of economic processes as they actually take place. Marx was also instrumental in establishing socialism as a political force in Europe. Marxism's greatest success was to follow the first World War. Communism in Russia was the application of Marxian principles to the problems of economic, social, and political reconstruction.

Whatever the validity of socialist plans for economic revolution, there could be little doubt of its penetrating critique of capitalism and of its valid aspiration to anchor production to the motive of social service rather than of private profit.

Modern anarchism was a revolt against oppression by either the agrarian or the capitalistic state. It advocated the abolition of both private property and the state.

Michael Bakunin (1814-1876), for whom the state was the main engine of human oppression, regarded as his chief task the teaching of hatred for the state and private property. Prince Peter Kropotkin (1842-1921), the leading constructive writer on modern anarchism, conceived his ideal as the non-coercive community free from private property, functioning effectively through mutual aid or cooperation.

The attitude of the anarchist toward property is not very different from that of the socialist, but his political ideals are diametrically opposed. The socialist urges a vast increase in state activity (it is true that Lenin said that under true communism the state would "wither away"), the anarchist seeks the complete extinction of political authority. Anarchism—because of the imperfection of the human race—seems far ahead of its time. Anarchism's contribution was this: it emphasized the oppression resulting from autocratic rule, both political and economic, and stressed the potentialities of cooperation.

Originally a French labor movement, syndicalism, like socialism, wished to end the present capitalistic order. Like labor-unionism, it believed that labor organization is the chief instrument for uniting and disciplining the proletariat. Unlike socialism, it rejected the efficacy of political activity. Unlike conservative labor-unionism it favored the industrial rather than the craft union. When socialism split into factions and was further discredited by the unfavorable governmental acts of former socialists, French syndicalism prospered. The systematic theorist of syndicalism was an aristocratic philosopher, Georges Sorel (1847-1922).

The syndicalists rejected any permanent terms with their capitalistic employers. They aimed frankly—by "direct action": "sabotage" and "general strike"—at conducting a class war which would drive the capitalist from industry and overthrow his political defense—the modern national state. The syndicalists advocated a cooperative communistic society and an administration based on industrial-unionism.

Political Developments.—Liberalism, constitutionalism, democracy, nationalism, and imperialism—all political trends of the nineteenth and twentieth centuries encouraged by the industrial revolution—reflected the economic and social ambitions of the capitalist classes. The policies of the latter were chiefly firm legal protection of property, enforcement of contract, and a large degree of industrial and commercial freedom. They opposed most types of social legislation designed to protect the working classes.

Liberals—since many of them were Protestants and even dissenting Protestants —advocated tolerance and freedom of thought to avoid persecution by Catholics and others. Liberalism championed civil liberties, economic freedom, representative government, and nationalism. In the economic realm, liberalism supported complete freedom of business activity. Wilhelm von Humboldt held that unlimited freedom of individual expression was indispensable to the progress of civilization. The state—a necessary evil—should only provide security for the individual, and should never attempt to promote human welfare by legislation, or even by public education. John Stuart Mill in his *On Liberty* (1859) argued that the state should act cautiously in seeking to promote either public or private welfare. Alexis de Tocqueville demanded liberty and independence for associations as well as for individuals. True liberty is possible only in a democracy.

Towards the close of the nineteenth century, a new type of liberals tended to abandon extreme forms of *laissez-faire.* A so-called "new liberalism" arose, best exemplified by Lloyd George and the English Liberal party in the years before the first World War, and by the "Progressive" movement of Theodore Roosevelt and his associates, and the "New Freedom" of Woodrow Wilson, in the United States. These liberals felt that considerable state activity must be tolerated in order to forestall more sweeping proletarian plans like socialism.

Bourgeois political ideas manifested themselves most directly in the form of constitutional governments—mainly since about 1775. A constitution is the organic instrument of government which not only determines the political institutions of a particular nation, but also creates the rights and immunities of its citizens. The great value of a constitution to the middle-class business man was that it gave relative fixity to the political and legal system and protected his business from arbitrary governmental interference, and, in some cases, from the effective opposition of labor organizations. In general, the bourgeoisie favored the republican form of government because monarchy had so often involved or symbolized arbitrary taxation and extensive interference with their business.

The very economic forces which made the bourgeoisie dominant also created a new social class—the industrial proletariat. The great majority of the working classes before the industrial revolution had been peasants, essentially illiterate, stable, conservative, and docile. The new industrial proletariat, subjected to common abuses, developed considerable solidarity and early began to conceive of the practical value of the ballot or right to vote. At the opening of the nineteenth century the masses were excluded from the right to vote in every modern state; at its close they had gained this privilege in nearly every progressive country in the Western World. Female suffrage, first adopted in New Zealand in 1893, spread subsequently to Australia, the United States, England, and most of the democratic governments of Europe after the first World War.

Democracy was formulated before the existence of scientific knowledge about man's political behavior and before there had been significant experience with representative government and majority rule. Democracy of the nineteenth century rested upon the following general conditions and basic assumptions: (1) a simple, unchanging agricultural society; (2) rudimentary political problems; (3) the local nature of political issues; (4) the *laissez-faire* theory of government, which contended that the best government was that which governed least; (5) the dogma of the real intellectual equality of men; (6) the equal fitness of all to vote and hold political office; (7) ardent popular interest in politics and the right of suffrage; (8) the capacity and inclination of the people to scrutinize platforms before casting their ballots; and (9) a belief in the unique capacity of the masses for eradicating injustice and reforming society.

By various methods of organization, manipulation, and subterfuge, the bourgeoisie were able to frustrate actual majority rule. By dominating political parties, monetary expenditure, psychological devices such as party program, party names, party shibboleths, they prevented the masses from thinking for themselves. In some states the landed aristocracy played a comparable role. The very fact that, after a century of universal male suffrage, true democracy has not yet been established is in itself a very severe challenge to the theory of democracy. Furthermore, since suffrage without economic and social equality means little, the working classes tried to use the vote to secure legislation which would advance their economic status and social interests. They accomplished relatively little down to the first World War. Not until the revolutions following that war were the masses able to gain even temporary control of their political system. And this gain was soon more than offset by the rise of dictatorship and totalitarianism.

Another important result of the industrial revolution was the growth of nationalism. Prior to 1750 even national wars attracted little popular attention, since armies were manned chiefly by mercenaries. There was little or nothing of modern patriotism. The industrial revolution changed all this. With world news readily available, designing politicians and editors could readily play upon the national pride through public statements, news items, and editorials which were immediately brought to every citizen's attention. Free public education played its role. Local isolation was destroyed, psychological unity developed and a national self-consciousness brought about; but, so rudimentary was the level of thought and social interests on the eve of the industrial revolution that the development of rapid means of communication tended to create the same self-satisfied provincialism on a national scale which had earlier prevailed on a local basis.

Nationalism defeated the Revolutions of 1848 in Europe, it stimulated the unification of Germany and Italy, and encouraged imperialism and aggressive foreign policies. It was to help bring about the first World War, and in 1919, to prevent a constructive and abiding peace.

On the other hand, the industrial revolution introduced counterforces, such as world commerce and communication, which tended to stimulate internationalism. Many phases of our economic and intellectual life became international but the first World War was a definite proof that nationalism was still far stronger than internationalism. Events after 1918 and even after 1945 fully confirmed this.

The dangers of extreme nationalism brought about a movement for the creation of international organizations strong enough to curb wars. The League of Nations was anticipated by many suggested projects. Among them were plans for the unity of Christendom in Europe, numerous projects for the federation of Europe, programs to achieve arbitration, and plans for limitation of armaments. Among the earlier statesmen, philosophers, and humanitarians who hoped to rid the world of the menace of war were the following: Dante in his *De monarchia,* and Pierre du Bois in the Middle Ages; after the Thirty Years' War (1618-1648), Emeric Crucé, Hugo Grotius, and Sully; after the dynastic wars of Louis XIV, William Penn, Abbé de St. Pierre, and Leibnitz; after the Seven Years' War, Voltaire and Rousseau; after the American Revolution, Jeremy Bentham in his *Plan for a Universal and Perpetual Peace;* after the wars of the French Revolution, Immanuel Kant in his *Perpetual Peace* (1795); and after the Napoleonic period, the Holy Alliance of Tsar Alexander I.

The first working arrangement, the Concert of Europe, under the guidance of Lord Castlereagh, grew out of the Quadruple Alliance of Russia, Prussia, Austria, and England following the defeat of Napoleon. It provided for the periodic assembly of the major European states to take common action against the threat to peace in the revolutionary movements emanating from France. The Concert of Europe remained in more or less active force from 1815 until 1913. After the first World War it was supplanted by the League of Nations. This failed because it refused to modify the Versailles settlement of 1919.

The accumulation of commodities which resulted from the improved mechanical techniques and the factory system encouraged a feverish search for markets and raw materials. Capital, too, sought lucrative finan̈cial investments abroad. The net result was the growth of imperialism. By imperialism is meant the control of capitalistic states over undeveloped countries and weaker peoples. To accomplish their ends powerful states resorted to armed intervention.

In 1800 about four-fifths of the land area of the world had not been explored by civilized man, and as late as 1870 nearly half of the habitable surface of the earth had not been seriously touched by Europeans. By the beginning of the twentieth century virtually the whole planet outside of the extreme polar regions had been traversed by the white man, and its material resources and potentialities catalogued.

Imperialism was more than a matter of territorial acquisition and economic exploitation. It was also a state of mind—a moral rationalization of the harsh economic policies pursued. On the assumption that they represented a far higher civilization than the natives, the Western capitalistic countries assumed that they fulfilled a moral obligation by bringing the natives the blessings of industrial civilization. This theory, which sanctioned the unspeakable barbarities and oppression which often accompanied the actual progress of modern imperialism, is usually known as "the white man's burden." Mussolini was to use this argument as late as 1935 to justify his Ethiopian venture.

There was, however, another side to imperialism. Considerable scientific progress emanated from the great laboratory of nature opened by oversea exploration. In geography, the field of cartography was perfected, physical geography developed, and the study of the influence of physical environment on man's social institutions promoted. Astronomy advanced through wider and more accurate observation of the heavens in all parts of the globe. In biology, the data collected overthrew the systems of classification of Linnaeus, Buffon, and Cuvier. The observation of plants and animals in different parts of the world enabled Darwin, Huxley, and Wallace to formulate the chief biological concept of the nineteenth century—evolution. Chemistry and medicine were enriched beyond measure by discoveries made during oversea expansion. Quinine was used as a remedy for malaria, many other drugs were introduced, and the revolutionary inoculation with malaria germs in the treatment of syphilis and paresis was first experimented with by French doctors in Indo-China and the West Indies.

No less significant was the reaction of oversea discoveries on social sciences. Without the data supplied by the observation of diverse cultures and races there could have been no such sciences as anthropology, ethnology, comparative philology, comparative religion, comparative jurisprudence, descriptive sociology, and comparative politics and economics. This expansion also provided data and motives for the use of philosophy, literature, music, and art. Oriental poems and tales abounded. The list of European writers profoundly influenced by the new lands would be long. Thomas Moore, Prosper Mérimée, Théophile Gautier, Rudyard Kipling, and Gérard de Nerval were a few. Operas with Oriental backgrounds appeared—Puccini's *Madame Butterfly*, Verdi's *Aïda*, Meyerbeer's *L'Africaine*. Hindu ideas influenced European philosophy—the *Bhagavad-Ghita*, for example, affected the doctrines of Schopenhauer and Nietzsche.

These little recognized but important cultural effects of the European expansion must be set off against its detriments when one attempts to assess modern imperialism.

II. INTELLECTUAL IMPLICATIONS OF THE THEORY OF EVOLUTION

1. *The Higher Criticism Undermines the Special Creation Theory*

The outstanding intellectual achievement of the nineteenth century was the triumph of the doctrine of evolution. This victory was won, in the main, through the vindication of the philosophical and biological propositions involved, but it was enormously aided by the simultaneous decline in the authority of the biblical concept of a special creation. There is no rational basis for believing in the doctrine of creation save for the biblical sanctions surrounding it. Therefore, progress in undermining belief in the revelation of Scriptures helped to discredit creation and to make evolution more plausible.

We have already traced the development of biblical criticism as far as the work of Karl David Ilgen at the end of the eighteenth century. In the century following Ilgen, the difficult problems of Old Testament authorship began to be solved. Among the leading names associated with this textual scholarship are W. M. L. De Wette, Hermann Hupfeld, Bishop John William Colenso, Abraham Kuenen, Bernhard Duhm, and Julius Wellhausen (1844-1918). Wellhausen brought Old Testament criticism near to perfection and is usually looked upon as the master scholar in this field. Splendid work has also been done in the last generation by such men as T. K. Cheyne, S. R. Driver, and B. W. Bacon.

These men revealed the true nature and authorship of the Bible. Whatever its excellencies as a repository of religious doctrine, moral precepts and literary masterpieces, it is still a human product. The scholars mentioned above have shown us what types of men wrote the books of the Bible, when they were written, and under what auspices. They have also made it clear that the ancient Jews were liberal indeed in altering, editing, and even abandoning certain of their religious writings. The authors or editors of the Bible did not seem to think that they were dealing with the revealed word of God. Few, if any, of the biblical books now exist as originally written down and some have been lost altogether.

The critical process has been carried beyond the study of the Old Testament text. The brilliant Cambridge professor, William Robertson Smith, in his famous *Religion of the Semites* (1889), pointed out that there is little which is unique about the Jewish religion and indicated many points of similarity between the religion of the ancient Hebrews and that of other Semitic peoples. Pursuing this line of investigation more thoroughly and precisely, scholars such as Delitzsch, Winckler, and Rogers exposed the profound influence of Babylonian mythology and religious tradition upon the Hebrews, particularly in the Hebrew adoption of the Babylonian cosmology, creation tales, and early historical myths, such as the legends of the garden of Eden, the tower of Babel, and the Deluge. James Henry Breasted has indicated that the Hebrews borrowed moral doctrines and the messianic hope from the Egyptians. Such writers as M. N. Dhalla and R. H. Charles have proved the Indo-Persian derivation of the later Jewish conceptions of the devil, heaven, and hell, afterwards borrowed by the Christians. It is today evident that the Bible is a purely secular product, quite as much as the Gilgamesh Epic, the Code of Hammurabi, the Homeric poems, Pliny's epistles, Vergil's *Aeneid,* or Dante's *Divine Comedy.* The following quotation from Professor Shotwell illuminates the character of the Bible as viewed by modern scholarship:

> Let us imagine, for instance, that instead of the Jewish scriptures we are talking of those of the Greeks. Suppose that the heritage of Hellas had been preserved to us in the form of a Bible. What would be the character of the book? We should begin, perhaps, with a few passages from Hesiod on the birth of the gods and the dawn of civilization mingled with fragments of the *Iliad* and both set into long excerpts from Herodotus. The dialogues of Plato might be given by Homeric heroes and the text of the great dramatists (instead of the prophets) be preserved interspersed one with another and clogged with the uninspired and uninspiring comments of Alexandrian savants. Then imagine that the sense of their authority

was so much obscured as centuries passed, that philosophers—for philosophers were to Greece what theologians were to Israel—came to believe that the large part of this composite work of history and philosophy had been first written down by Solon as the deliverance of the oracle of Apollo at Delphi. Then, finally, imagine that the text became stereotyped and sacred, even the words taboo, and became the heritage of alien peoples who knew nothing more of Greek history than what this compilation contained. Such, with some little exaggeration, would be a Hellenic Bible after the fashion of the Bible of the Jews. If the comparison be a little overdrawn there is no danger but that we shall make sufficient mental reservations to prevent us from carrying it too far. Upon the whole, so far as form and structure go, the analogy holds remarkably well.[1]

No informed and reasonable person, therefore, can expect the Bible to possess greater reliability as history or science than the ideas of the civilization which produced it. The recognition of this fact was of deep significance for the acceptability of the doctrine of evolution. It undermined the chief obstacle to its espousal. There could be no serious objection to the evolutionary philosophy in the Western World were it not for the rival doctrine of special creation. Once scholars understood that this dogma was the product of men far less equipped to render authoritative judgments on such matters than our astronomers, geologists, and biologists, the special creation stumbling-block was destroyed.

2. The History of the Theory of Evolution

There are two phases or aspects of evolutionary doctrine. One is the general philosophical conception of naturalistic development, which seeks to explain the origins and evolution of the whole cosmos, our solar system, the earth, organic life, man and human culture. The other is the more restricted and precise field of biological investigation which endeavors to trace the rise and growth of organic life on our planet. It is especially concerned with the origins and mutations of species and with the laws of heredity which explain both the continuity and the variations of plant and animal species. These two phases of evolutionary doctrine are often confused, with the result that evolutionary biologists are frequently given credit for achievements which they have not claimed and which should be assigned to philosophers.

The theory that change and development are the basic processes of the physical universe was first enunciated, so far as we know, by Heracleitus, Empedocles, and Anaxagoras. The best surviving classical statement of this point of view is contained in Lucretius' great cosmological poem, *On the Nature of Things*. Here we find a sweeping conception of evolution, covering the development of the universe, life, man, society, and culture. The systematic Epicurean philosophers, perhaps, produced still more comprehensive and technical statements of the theory of evolution, but if so, they have been lost.

There was no decisive advance beyond Lucretius until the eighteenth century, when the philosophy of evolution was revived and elaborated by Buffon, Diderot, the German philosophers of nature, and some of the romanticist philosophers

---

[1] J. T. Shotwell, *Introduction to the History of History*, Columbia University Press, 1922, pp. 82-83.

like Herder. In the nineteenth century, Herbert Spencer developed a comprehensive system of evolution based on the remarkable progress in natural science from Copernicus to his own day. Spencer believed that everything in nature from the cosmos to human institutions evolved according to a specific formula, namely, the passage from an incoherent, disorganized homogeneity to a welldifferentiated and thoroughly coördinated heterogeneity. Differentiation, specialization, and coördination are the master processes of evolution in Spencer's system. Spencer introduced the evolutionary formula into every phase of human knowledge in his voluminous *System of Synthetic Philosophy* (1860-1896).

It was, therefore, Herbert Spencer, not Charles Darwin, who made evolution an integral element in the intellectual equipment of every educated man of the twentieth century. Spencer's particular applications of his formula may have been premature, crude, inadequate, and often erroneous, but he must be given credit for popularizing the most momentous idea in the history of human thought. Other thinkers, from John Fiske to John Dewey, H. G. Wells, George Dorsey, and James Harvey Robinson, have carried on this task of clarifying the evolutionary doctrine and applying it to human thought and social problems.

The other phase of the history of evolution, that which relates to the development of organic life on our planet, has an equally ancient heritage. The question at issue here is the nature and origin of species. The biblical view is that all species of plants and animals were created by God once and for all about six thousand years ago—that from the moment of creation, these species have remained fixed and immutable. The evolutionary hypothesis declares that all exist ing species descended from earlier and simpler forms of life during a vast perioc of time—that no species is fixed and changeless. The history of the biological theory of evolution is the record of man's gradual perception of the mutability of species.

Aristotle believed in an ascending scale of organic life, proceeding from simple to complex types. He had at least a rudimentary notion of the facts of human reproduction, but he denied the sexuality of plants. In the Middle Ages, Albertus Magnus and other biologists revived and tested the Aristotelian view. In early modern times, Francis Bacon and Leibnitz both expressed their belief in variation and the mutability of species, thus breaking with the biblical dogma of specially created and immutable types. Joachim Camerarius demonstrated the sexuality of plants. Kant thought that widely differentiated species could be traced back to a common parent. Linnaeus worked out the first great scheme for the classification of organic life. This suggested the common parentage of different species, although Linnaeus himself believed in fixed and changeless species. Buffon clearly understood some of the broader implications of evolution, especially the relation between environmental influences and the slow differentiation of species.

The concept of adaptation to environment was developed more thoroughly by Erasmus Darwin (1731-1802), the grandfather of Charles Darwin. Malthus' law of population emphasized the importance of the struggle for existence. The poet-philosopher, Wolfgang von Goethe (1749-1832), anticipated many of the basic conceptions of organic evolution, such as adaptation to environment, vital force, vestigial organs. Sir Charles Lyell brought together in his *Principles of Geology* (1830-1833) rich geological evidence supporting the evolutionary rather than the creation hypothesis. Finally, Jean Lamarck (1744-1829) enunciated a definite doctrine of organic evolution in which the theory of mutability was based on the inheritance of acquired characteristics. Any changes in the body of a man or animal, so runs this doctrine, become by hereditary processes the starting-point for the next generation. Lamarck's classic illustration was, as we have noted, the giraffe, which, he thought, developed its long neck by stretching to reach high leaves and branches, handing on to its progeny the slight gains in length in each generation. Most of these early contributions to the biological theory of evolution were brought together in an excellent and popular book by a layman, Robert Chambers, *Vestiges of the Natural History of Creation* (1844).

These pre-Darwinian theories made a more plausible case for evolution than the traditionalists could make for creation, but it was Charles Darwin, more than any other man, who vindicated the doctrine of organic evolution and established it as the outstanding contribution of biology to human knowledge and enlightenment. He occupies much the same position in the development of the biological theory of evolution that Spencer holds in the history of the philosophical conception. Charles Darwin (1809-1882) was for a time the naturalist on a chartered ship, the *Beagle,* which enabled him to study plant and animal life in various parts of the globe, and develop many ideas about the differentiation and adaptation of species. Darwin was familiar with his grandfather's views, and was especially impressed with the Malthusian idea of the struggle for existence created by the pressure of organic life on the means of subsistence. Further, Darwin made many experiments in animal-breeding, especially with pigeons. At the same time, Alfred Russel Wallace was studying the evidence for evolution in the Malay Archipelago. He sent a somewhat hesitant and discouraging résumé of his conclusions to Darwin, with the result that the latter felt compelled to publish his epoch-making work *On the Origin of Species* (1859).

The chief significance of Darwin's book was: (1) It systematized the doctrine of the origin and development of species on the basis of his own and preceding work; (2) he marshaled the evidence for evolution; (3) he gave general currency to the notion that existing forms of plants and animals are descended from earlier and, in most cases, more rudimentary types; (4) he dealt in technical detail with certain leading processes and factors of evolution, such as the struggle for existence, the survival of the fittest, natural selection, sexual selection, and the like; (5) he proved the basic interrelationships of organic life; and (6) he applied this reasoning not only to the lower animals but also to man himself.

Many of the specific details in Darwin's explanations of evolution have been abandoned or seriously modified as the result of subsequent biological research. But his general evolutionary thesis is even more firmly established today than it was in 1859. Indeed, since Darwin, evolution has passed from a working hypothesis to a well-established fact. This answers the frequent assertion of religious critics of evolution that "Darwinism is dead." Some of Darwin's minor theories such as sexual selection are, indeed, dead, and even his doctrine of the survival of the fittest is questioned, but his evolutionary hypothesis has enduring validity and significance. Darwin occupies much the same position in biology that Newton does in the history of physics and astronomy. His work is no more dead than Newton's *Principia*.[2]

Darwin's book, undermining and assailing as it did the biblical theory of the origin of species, met with bitter resistance from nearly all clergymen, the present type of reconciling modernist being a rare individual eighty years ago. But he was warmly supported by Wallace, Haeckel, Romanes, Huxley, and others, although some of them differed with him in regard to the details of evolution. Huxley's *Man's Place in Nature* (1863) ranks next to the *Origin of Species* in its influence on the theory of evolution. The period from 1860 to 1900 was characterized by further research and bitter polemics. By the dawn of the present century the battle to establish evolution on a sound basis had been won, and the student of biology is rarely called upon today in civilized areas to enter the lists against its straggling enemies.

The outstanding phases of the progress of evolutionary biology since Darwin have been: (1) Weismann's hypothesis of the continuity of the germ plasm and the final disproof of the transmission of acquired characteristics, as originally set forth by men like Lamarck; (2) De Vries's establishment of mutations or "sports" as the source of many new species; (3) the discovery and elaboration of Mendel's ingenious law of heredity; (4) the organization of extensive and well-controlled research facilities for the study of the problems of heredity by T. H. Morgan and others; and (5) the development by Galton, Pearson, Ammon, Davenport, and others, of eugenics, a science which attempts to apply the recently discovered laws of heredity to the improvement of the human race.

3. Intellectual Applications of Evolutionary Doctrine

The most striking implication of evolution is the complete revolution in our time perspective. Instead of assigning a very brief period for the age of the earth and all living matter, we must reckon with a chronology that defies both the human imagination and conventional standards of measurement. We must assume the earth to be from three to five billion years old and we know that the sun had passed its maximum radiance before the earth originated. When one thinks of the probable amount of time involved in the evolution of the cosmos, the conceptions and standards which prevail in measuring time for earthly purposes seem trivial and inadequate. Astrophysicists have made it clear that attempts to estimate the age of the cosmos are futile. Indeed, we may have to admit that in the new cosmic perspective the very notion of time, as we understand it, is nothing more than a convenient geocentric illusion. The epoch of human life in this new time perspective, instead of being coexistent with the origin of the earth, must be

---

[2] J. H. Robinson, "Is Darwinism Dead?" *Harper's Magazine*, June, 1922. Cf. C. C. Nutting, "Is Darwin Shorn?" *Scientific Monthly*, February, 1920; and J. S. Huxley, "Where Darwin's Theory Stands Today," *New York Times "Magazine,"* March 1, 1931.

regarded as only an infinitesimal fragment, to say nothing of its utter insignificance in terms of cosmic history.

The second major implication of evolution is the dynamic notion of change as the universal principle of cosmic development. Instead of the older static ideas of a perfect creation a few thousand years ago, with but slight subsequent alterations in the nature of the heavenly bodies, the earth, and organic life, we have to recognize that change appears to be the most vital principle in cosmic development, and that there is no such thing as a static condition in the universe. Everything is in a state of alteration; some changes manifest development and progress, while others definitely indicate disintegration and decline. We have, then, the conception of a dynamic and ever-changing universe in the place of the static notions of a century ago.

A third vital implication of evolution is that man is a biochemical entity—a "colloidal aggregate." There seems to be nothing about human life or behavior that cannot be explained according to naturalistic laws and principles. This implication, combined with the two previously noted aspects of evolution, proved as disruptive of the accepted views of man as of the older beliefs concerning creation. The scientific facts—in contrast to the older views—reveal man as neither a "worm" nor a unique being a little lower than the angels. He is, at least so far as science can say, the leading member of the primate group, and therefore, for the time being, the dominant species in the animal kingdom.

In addition to these three outstanding aspects of the cultural and intellectual impact of the doctrine of evolution, there are a number of other results which are treated more in detail elsewhere in this book. The discovery of evolution meant that in the half-century following 1860 the biological sciences temporarily supplanted the mathematical and physical sciences in popularity. The idea that change is a very characteristic process of nature tends to undermine the absolutist concepts of some romanticist and idealist philosophers. Absolutes, and the notion of final and ultimate truth, no longer possess the validity they had in the days of Schelling. Truth appears to be merely a relative and changing product of evolution rather than the outcome of a divinely guided dialectic. It is something that can be pragmatically tested only through experience. The notion of progress can, seemingly, be supported on cosmic and biological as well as historical grounds. And the demonstration that biologists can control, in part, the course of biological development suggested to sociologists that they might find a way of intelligently guiding and directing social evolution. Progress may be consciously controlled, bearing mankind towards higher levels of happiness and well-being.

The view of man as an animal, which we noted as the third important implication of evolution, has been extremely repellent to many traditionalists, but there is little logical ground for such an attitude, once it is understood what is really meant by the inclusion of man in the animal kingdom. From a scientific and common-sense point of view one must recognize that the animal kingdom represents the highest order of life on the planet; that is, the highest known level of organic development. Therefore to be the temporary leader of the animal world is the highest achievement to which man could rationally aspire.

Further, not only is the concept that man is an animal a demonstrated fact in no way humiliating to the human race; it also has much practical significance. For, once we recognize the fact that man is an animal, we immediately have the rich fields of comparative anatomy, physiology, and psychology to draw upon. From these we may find a sure and illuminating approach to the study of human nature and behavior. These branches of science reveal man as a supersimian, and the study of simian psychology, as summarized in such books as those by Kohts, Köhler, Yerkes, and Hooton, is an example of the practical value of this approach to human behavior.

The anthropologists and the sociologists have made it clear that the evolutionary process applies not only to the physical development of the animal world and the human race, but also to the growth and differentiation of human institutions as well. The traditional argument for the idea of a special creation of the physical and organic world upheld the idea that all our social institutions—the family, property, the state, law, religion, and morals—are likewise the product of divine fiat. God revealed to man his decisions about the perfect type of family, religion, law, and so on.

The historians and the social scientists dealt as severely with this hypothesis as the astronomers, geologists, and biologists did with the dogma of special creation. They amply demonstrated that every human institution, religious, economic, political, legal, educational, or moral, has been the product of naturalistic influences. Our culture is an outgrowth of trial, error, and accident, controlled by broad evolutionary processes. Man has faced nature under widely different circumstances. His efforts to perpetuate life in all sorts of environments have impelled him to attack the problems of existence in a variety of ways. The result has been an impressive diversity of human institutions. In the struggles of communities, nations, and races these competing institutions and ideas have been subjected to the struggle for existence, and those relatively best adapted to a given people, time, and place have tended to survive. The others have perished or linger in remote or protected areas where superior institutions could not penetrate successfully. All of our so-called sacred human institutions are thus the naturalistic product of man's age-old struggle with nature to perpetuate his kind, and to protect them against suffering or extinction. It is, of course, recognized that even races with the most creditable institutions and beliefs have preserved a vast baggage of archaic and mostly worthless convictions and folkways which clutter up the social scene, produce inertia, and lessen human welfare.

The writer to whom we are indebted, more than to any other, for the forceful statement of this thesis is Herbert Spencer. Beginning with his *First Principles,* published in 1862, he devoted his life mainly to an application of the evolutionary hypothesis to all types of institutions and to every aspect of our mental life. A group of sociologists who followed him went to extremes and claimed that there is a complete identity between the processes of biological and social evolution. They asserted that society is an organism and that the same factors are at work in it as in the biological world. Though this contention is not widely accepted today, there are some interesting analogies between organic and social evolution.

The most ambitious effort to work out a system of social evolution was made by an American anthropologist, Lewis Henry Morgan, in his *Ancient Society* (1877). Morgan's general assumption of social evolution was more accurate than most of his special interpretations of the evolution of primitive groups and social institutions. Elaborate descriptive material on the evolution of human institutions and ideas was contained in the famous *Folkways* (1907) of William Graham Sumner. His disciple, A. G. Keller, has presented a discriminating appraisal of the applicability of Darwinian evolution to social institutions in his *Societal Evolution* (1915, revised 1931), and has given us Sumner's ideas in full in *The Science of Society* (1927).

The recognition of the secular origin of our institutions encouraged urbanity and tolerance. It is less easy to be ferocious in the enforcement of a custom that we know to be of ancient and fallible human origin than of one we believe to be divinely revealed. We can no longer imagine that we are forcing the will of God on our neighbors. The evolutionary point of view has also stimulated social optimism. If man produced our present defective institutions, he surely may, by the application of more complete knowledge, supplant them with far better ones without offering an affront to God. The social philosophy of the deists, physiocrats, classical economists, and Spencerian individualists, falls to pieces in this new perspective.

Another important implication of the doctrine of evolution is its illumination of the fact that, for all practical purposes, "man is the measure of all things." Evolution clarifies this notion in a far more thoroughgoing way than the early modern humanists, or even the later deists and reformers perceived.

While more resolute humanists tended to glorify humanity, they had no scientific knowledge of man. Hence, their tests were aesthetic only. They had no grasp of biological or social science which would enable them to know just what this creature, man, who is the measure of all things, is actually like. Poetry and art are extremely valuable, but they fall far short of being adequate guides to human values and conduct.

The deists and reformers also elevated man, but their views were strongly tinged with religion. Most of them believed in immortality and looked upon the future life as more important than earthly life. Moreover, while they used such biological and social science as existed, they had few reliable facts at hand.

The evolutionary perspective and natural and social science not only stressed the importance of man as man, but also enabled us to understand the real nature of man and to know what will make him happiest. These advances in our knowledge also emphasized the fact that life here on earth is the only life to which man may confidently look forward. Hence, it implied that our efforts should be concentrated on achieving the "good life" here and now.

III. OUTSTANDING ACHIEVEMENTS IN NINETEENTH-CENTURY SCIENCE

1. *New Trends in Natural Science*

One of the most striking aspects of contemporary scientific progress has been its increased scope, rapidity and complexity. In 1700 a versatile scientist, like Leibnitz or Newton, could and did master the outstanding facts of all natural science. In 1875 an able scholar might still have under control the complete development of a single major branch of science such as physics or chemistry. Today, it is difficult for one human mind to keep abreast of the discoveries in a single subdivision of physics or chemistry. This means that natural science today requires coöperation between nations, the several departments of science, and those engaged in work in each special field of a given department.

Another important point to be noted is the vast improvement in the organization and support of scientific research. Early modern natural science arose for the most part outside the universities in coöperative societies of enthusiastic amateurs of differing degrees of competence and training. By the second half of the nineteenth century natural science had secured an established place in the institutions of higher learning. Most of the eminent scientists of that period were university professors who added to research the burdens of teaching. Laboratories were established within university walls, one of the first of which was the chemistry laboratory opened at the University of Giessen by the great German chemist, Justus von Liebig, in 1826. In the last half-century extensive provision has been made, especially in the United States, for endowed scientific foundations. These provide ample facilities for scientific research, leaving investigators free from all responsibility save that of penetrating more intensively into the mysteries of nature. Science also became increasingly international with the rise of better means of communication. Savants in many countries could more easily pool their results.

A third novel aspect of contemporary scientific progress has been the increasing rapidity with which discoveries are exploited in technology and industry. A century ago, scientific discoveries, which have since proved of untold practical significance, were often left relatively untouched for generations by those interested in the progress of technology and economic enterprise. Today, the findings of science are eagerly awaited and are immediately applied in the appropriate field. Indeed, some of the best scientific research of our day is subsidized by great industrial concerns in laboratories connected with their factories, mines, or transportation lines. The links between science, technology, industry, and art have become increasingly direct and effective.

The progress of science in the nineteenth century was even more striking and extensive than it had been in the seventeenth and eighteenth. The main reason for this was that science was now able to build upon the foundations laid by many patient workers, extending over the centuries between Copernicus and Lavoisier. These earlier contributions acted as a sort of springboard from which nineteenth-century scientists were able to leap to unprecedented heights of achievement. Especially important were the earlier mathematical developments, which became indispensable to the progress of many natural sciences, especially astronomy and physics. The practical application of mathematics to physical science had already been set forth by Lagrange in his *Analytical Mechanics.*

In the seventeenth century the most remarkable achievements were made in astronomy and astrophysics. Chemistry stood out particularly in the eighteenth. In the nineteenth century the most revolutionary developments occurred in biology, with physics running a close second. In the twentieth century, the most startling results have been obtained in astronomy and physics, particularly in electromechanics.

2. *Mathematics and Astronomy*

In spite of remarkable achievements in the three previous centuries, mathematics in the nineteenth century made revolutionary progress. The limitations of the older algebra and geometry were transcended. Augustin Cauchy (1789-1857) opened the field of infinite functions and residual and imaginary calculus, developed later by Professor Weierstrass of Berlin. Niels Abel (1802-1829), the most precocious genius in the history of mathematics, revealed the limitations of algebra in solving the higher equations and extended our knowledge of the theory of functions. Nicholas Lobachevsky (1793-1856) and Janos Bolyai (1802-1860) further indicated the restricted nature of Euclidean geometry and improved non-Euclidean and hyper-geometry. Karl Jacobi (1804-1851) extended the theories of Abel, developed the field of elliptical functions, and advanced our knowledge of the theory of numbers. George Riemann (1826-1866) contributed to non-Euclidean geometry, and did important work in the theory of functions and the geometry of curved surfaces, fields of investigation followed by Felix Klein (1849-1925). Karl Friedrich Gauss (1777-1855) was not only a versatile mathematician but also contributed greatly to the application of higher mathematics to scientific problems, particularly to astronomy, the theory of terrestrial magnetism, and statistical methods. More than ever before, mathematics became an indispensable tool of natural science and made possible spectacular progress in other fields of scientific endeavor.

Astronomy made considerable progress in the nineteenth century. Better telescopes and observatories were constructed. New astronomical instruments—particularly the spectroscope—were invented. The spectroscope enabled astronomers to study light more scientifically and to determine the chemical composition of celestial bodies. Friedrich Wilhelm Bessel (1784-1846) succeeded for the first time in measuring the parallax of a star (1838). This astronomical phenomenon was so infinitesimal that previous astronomers had been unable to prove its existence. Its vindication confirmed the heliocentric theory and, in particular, enabled astronomers to compute the distance of the nearer stars. Neptune, the most remote of our planets,[3] was discovered in 1846 as the result of better astronomical instruments and more accurate computations. The discovery of Neptune gave additional prestige to the Newtonian system. J. C. Adams and

---

3 Excepting the little planet Pluto, discovery of which was announced in 1930.

Urbain Leverrier had predicted the existence and location of a new planet on the basis of Newtonian principles. Whereupon, J. G. Galle (1812-1910), a Berlin astronomer, turned his telescope on the indicated spot in the heavens and found the planet. Far and away the most important advances in astronomy in the nineteenth century, however, were those discoveries and investigations made possible by the spectroscope. This instrument first permitted a thorough study of celestial chemistry, spectrum analysis, and astral velocities and movements. We shall describe the invention of the spectroscope in connection with the review of nineteenth-century physics. Further progress in astronomy had to await the development of eleetromechanics and celestial photography in the latter part of the nineteenth century.

3. Nineteenth-Century Physics

The outstanding developments in nineteenth-century physics were the establishment of modern conceptions of the nature of heat, sound, light, and electricity, and their unification in the broader domain of electromechanics through the use of advanced mathematical calculations. This mathematical synthesis of physical nature by Clerk Maxwell, Willard Gibbs, and others was perhaps the most notable intellectual feat of the century.

Down to the nineteenth century the prevailing theory of heat was that it is a mysterious and imponderable quality transmitted from body to body. The discovery of the actual character of heat was the result of the work of Benjamin Thompson (Count Rumford, 1753-1814) and Sir Humphry Davy (1778-1829). In 1789-1799 they showed that friction generates heat in proportion to the amount of work expended. Rumford discovered that in boring out a brass cannon both the cannon and the shavings became intensely hot. Davy found that two blocks of ice could be melted simply by rubbing them together, even though the surrounding atmosphere was kept below the freezing-point.

The study of heat was carried still further by the last great amateur English scientist, James Prescott Joule (1818-1889). He worked out (1843) the principle of the mechanical equivalent of heat, namely, the mechanical energy required to raise the heat of a given body to any given extent. This suggested to others how energy might be converted into heat and furnished the key to the formulation of the important principle of the conservation of energy. Joule showed that the amount of work (friction) necessary to produce a given amount of heat is invariable.

The principle of the conservation of energy—a fundamental fact of modern physics—was confirmed between 1840 and 1850, the decade in which Joule's experiments were carried on. In 1842, J. R. von Mayer suggested the possibility that heat might be converted into work, or work into heat, something that was proved to be true by Joule's experiments. In 1842, also, W. R. Grove defended the idea of the interrelation of physical forces, a doctrine which he elaborated in a book four years later. This conception had been anticipated in part by a French scientist, Sadi Carnot (1796-1832), approximately twenty years earlier. It remained, however, for the most encyclopedic physicist of the nineteenth century, Professor

Hermann von Helmholtz (1821-1894) of Berlin, to set forth a systematic presentation of the principle of the conservation of energy based upon his own independent experiments as well as those of his contemporaries. His monograph on the subject appeared in the year 1847. A modern historian of science has put the matter concisely:

> The law of conservation of energy means that the sum total of the energy of the universe is a constant quantity. We cannot destroy energy and we cannot create it, we can only turn it from one form to another. It may be potential or it may be kinetic, but all the potential energy plus all the kinetic energy is a constant quantity.[4]

The concepts underlying the conservation of energy were linked with electromechanics a generation later by Clerk Maxwell and Heinrich Hertz. Maxwell's elaboration of the kinetic theory of gases extended our knowledge of the fundamentals of the physics of heat.

The scientific study of the character of heat and its mechanical equivalent not only led to the discovery of the conservation of energy; it also directly promoted the development of thermodynamics. The first law of thermodynamics was implicit in the conclusions of Joule. It was first enunciated by Helmholtz in 1847: "When during any transformation of one form of energy into another heat is produced, the amount is always the same for the same amount of energy, whatever its form, and if heat disappears, exactly the same amount of some other kind of energy will appear in its place." This is only another way of stating the principle of the conservation of energy.

Even more dramatic was the famous second law of thermodynamics, which relates to the dissipation and degradation of energy. According to this second law, while the total amount of energy in the universe theoretically remains constant, the amount of actually useful energy is always diminishing through its progressive transformation into non-useful or dissipated heat. If this be true, it means that the supply of useful energy in the universe will ultimately be exhausted and that the universe will gradually run down. The discovery of this second law of thermodynamics is attributed to Carnot (1824) and to Rudolf Clausius (1847), a German professor of physics. First systematically explained by William Thomson (Lord Kelvin) in 1852, it was carried over into physical chemistry in what is known as the phase rule, by Josiah Willard Gibbs (1839-1903), probably the most profound American scientist of the nineteenth century. In the second quarter of the twentieth century this second law of thermodynamics provoked a vigorous controversy among astronomers (for example, Jeans vs. Millikan) regarding its bearing on the destiny of the physical universe as a whole.

The first important work in the physical investigation of sound was done by Chladni and Bernoulli in the eighteenth century. They established the fact that sound is a phenomenon of waves generated in the air by a vibrating body. The fundamental character of such vibrations and of the resulting waves was not, however, fully understood until sound-waves were linked with the conception of

---

[4] R. J. Harvey Gibson, *Two Thousand Years of Science*, 2nd ed., rev., Macmillan, 1931, p. 131.

electromagnetic waves as a result of the work of Hertz and others in the last quarter of the nineteenth century.

A scientific understanding of the character of light was first attained in the nineteenth century. The earliest wave theory of light had been anticipated by two seventeenth-century scientists, Hooke and Huygens, but was rejected by Sir Isaac Newton. It was revived, however, and Newton's objections explained away, by an English and a French scientist at the opening of the nineteenth century. Thomas Young (1773-1829) and A. J. Fresnel (1788-1827) were the first to state the wave theory of light in its modern form. A half-century later (1863), Clerk Maxwell showed that light seems to behave like electromagnetic waves, and thus advanced the ultimate synthetic interpretation of heat, sound, light, and electricity. Maxwell's theories were carried further by a brilliant German physicist, Heinrich Hertz (1857-1894). The wave theory has, of course, undergone considerable modification since 1905 as a result of the development of the quantum theory and the resulting corpuscular notion of light emission, a matter we shall discuss in a later chapter.

Next in importance to the establishment of the electromagnetic theory of light was the discovery of the spectroscope and the development of spectrum analysis. The latter means the study of the radiations emitted by various substances. Newton had founded spectrum analysis. Kirchhoff, in 1858, laid down its three fundamental principles: (1) solid and liquid bodies and gases under high pressure give off a continuous spectrum, crossed by neither dark nor bright lines; (2) gases under low pressure emit a discontinuous spectrum crossed by bright lines; and (3) when a white light passes through a gas we have a discontinuous spectrum crossed by dark lines.

The first important work in spectrum analysis after Newton was executed by an English doctor, William Hyde Wollaston (1766-1828), and a German optician, Joseph von Fraunhofer (1787-1826). In the first quarter of the nineteenth century they independently called attention to the dark lines (since called Fraunhofer lines) crossing the colored bands in the visible spectrum. Fraunhofer also demonstrated the fact that starlight is independent of sunlight.

The modern science of spectrum analysis was, however, created by two German professors at Heidelberg, Robert Bunsen (1811-1899) and G. R. Kirchhoff (1824-1887). They invented the spectroscope and laid the basis for modern spectroscopy in 1859. Not only was this an important contribution to the physics of light; it also enabled physicists and astronomers to estimate accurately the movement and velocity of heavenly bodies and to discover the chemical constitution of distant celestial objects. An important practical result of the spectroscope was the discovery of helium gas by Lockyer and Ramsay. This non-inflammable gas is an indispensable, though expensive, substitute for hydrogen in the inflation of balloons and dirigibles.

The nineteenth century did much to advance our knowledge of electricity. In 1801, Wollaston, more completely than Volta, demonstrated the identity of "galvanism" and electricity. In 1819, H. C. Oersted (1777-1851), a Danish scientist, noted the agitating effect of an electric current on the needle of a compass. A. M.

Ampère (1775-1836) further studied this phenomenon and not only reduced it to a law but also worked out the elementary laws of the interaction of electric currents (1820). A further contribution was made by a German scientist, G. S. Ohm (1789-1854). He gave us our first important practical information about the nature of electric conductors and provided methods of measuring mathematically the degree of resistance in the conduction of electric currents (1827). He thus put the laws of electromotive force in mathematical terms, showing that the intensity of an electric current is directly proportional to the electromotive force impelling it.

Perhaps the outstanding figure in the study of electricity in the nineteenth century was Michael Faraday (1791-1867). He showed that electric currents produce a magnetic field, elucidated the laws governing the flow of electric currents, investigated the mediums through which electromagnetic force is produced, and described the principles of electromagnetic induction. His investigation of the induction of electric currents permitted the invention of the dynamo. Faraday was almost the sole distinguished physicist of the nineteenth century who was not a master of higher mathematics.

Building on previous work, Maxwell brought forth a mathematical statement of the principles involved in electromagnetic waves. Not only was this in itself an important contribution to electromechanics, but it also formed a basis for the mathematical synthesis of physical nature in terms of electromagnetism. The next important development in electromechanics consisted of the quantum theory and investigations of radioactivity, which will be described in the chapter on twentieth-century science. But before the nineteenth century had ended William Röntgen had discovered X-rays in 1895, and J. J. Thomson had studied cathode rays in 1897.

4. Chemistry in the Nineteenth Century

Important early nineteenth-century developments in chemistry extended our knowledge of quantitative chemistry, which began with Lavoisier's demonstration of the conservation of mass at the close of the eighteenth century. The first outstanding chemical innovation of the century was the formulation of what is known as the law of multiple (or definite) proportions in the combination of chemical elements. The man who discovered and presented this law was an English scientist, John Dalton (1766-1844). Dalton was able to make use of the earlier suggestion of two French chemists, Proust and Berthollet. Dalton took hydrogen, the lightest element, as his unit. He showed (1805) that when one element unites with another, the weight ratios are some simple multiple of the lowest unit. The combining weight of an element is the weight of that element relative to that of the other elements. A French chemist, Joseph Louis Gay-Lussac (1778-1850), formulated in 1808 the law of the combination of gases, namely, that when gases combine they do so in volumes bearing a simple and direct ratio to each other. This law was supplemented in 1811 by the Italian chemist, Count Amadeo Avogadro (1776-1856), who maintained that, at the same temperature and pressure, equal volumes of gases contain an equal number of molecules.

Dalton was not only famous for his law of multiple proportions but also for his atomic theory (1808)—the first practical application of the general ideas of Democritus, although interpreted in a more restricted and precise fashion. Dalton contended that every element is composed of extremely minute particles or atoms absolutely incapable of division, a doctrine greatly modified in recent years as a result of our study of electromechanics and quantum physics. But Dalton's theory encouraged a Swedish chemist, Baron Berzelius (1779-1848), to undertake an elaborate study of atomic and molecular weights, which he estimated for about two thousand substances.

Between 1869 and 1871 a Russian chemist, D. I. Mendelyeev (1834-1907), announced his famous periodic law, which showed that the elements, when arranged in the order of their atomic weights, fall into definite series or octaves. In this arrangement, the eighth element above any one in the series possesses characteristics similar to the one from which the count was started. The properties of the elements, therefore, stand in what is known as periodic dependence upon their atomic weights. Mendelyeev thus showed that the properties of elementary atoms depend on their mass and that their variations are due mainly to differences in structure and arrangement. Mendelyeev's thesis enabled chemists accurately to predict the existence of chemical elements which had not yet been isolated.

The foremost American contribution to theoretical chemistry was Willard Gibbs's above-mentioned "phase rule," a complete mathematical statement of the fundamental principles of chemical equilibrium. In our day, this conception has had very important practical applications in the realm of synthetic chemistry.

Next to the laws of quantitative chemistry, the most notable advances in the nineteenth century were connected with organic chemistry. It had been widely maintained that there is an impassable gulf between inorganic and organic matter. This illusion was shaken in 1828 when a German chemist, Friedrich Wöhler (1800-1882), synthetically created urea out of inorganic materials. In 1832, Wöhler and Justus von Liebig began to unravel the structures of organic compounds. At the same time, Berzelius showed that organic substances obey the same quantitative laws that had been established for the behavior of inorganic materials. The artificial synthesis of urea started organic chemistry on the road towards its marvelous later achievements in the artificial production of a large number of interesting and valuable chemical compounds. The discoveries of the German chemist F. A. Kekulé (1829-1896) gave a powerful impetus to these developments, especially his contribution to the theory of valency and his comprehensive analysis (in 1865) of the benzene ring and carbon compounds. The unique substance, carbon, enters into the composition of all organic compounds, and the chemical analysis of carbon and its combinations was indispensable to modern synthetic chemistry. In 1887, Emil Fischer was able to prepare synthetic sugar; and Adolph von Baeyer prepared synthetic indigo in 1897 and revolutionized the dye industry. These were only the prelude to many remarkable achievements in "creative chemistry."

5. *Biological Discoveries in the Nineteenth Century*

The most important advance in biology during this century was the apprehension and elucidation of the theory of organic evolution which we have already discussed. We may call attention here, however, to the important doctrines of heredity set forth by Mendel, Weismann, and De Vries.

Gregor Mendel (1822-1884) was an Austrian monk who in 1865 set forth the law of heredity that is most generally accepted by modern biologists. His views were not widely known at the time of his death and were not revived and accepted until the twentieth century. In 1885, August Weismann (1834-1914), a German biologist, challenged the popular view of the inheritance of acquired characteristics. According to Weismann, a blacksmith, for example, cannot hand down to his children a tendency towards larger biceps. The germ plasm that carries our hereditary traits seems to be inappreciably affected by external anatomical changes during the individual life span or any succession of life spans that can be observed. Hugo De Vries (1848-1935), a Dutch botanist, proclaimed at the opening of the twentieth century his famous doctrine that new species arise through sudden mutations or sports rather than as the result of slowly accumulated changes.

Next to the doctrine of evolution, perhaps the most important biological innovation of the nineteenth century was the elucidation of the cellular nature of organic life by Theodor Schwann (1810-1882) and Matthias Jakob Schleiden (1804-1881) in 1838-1839. They thereby founded what is known as cytology or the scientific study of the cell. They were greatly aided by the invention of the compound microscope in 1835. The significance of their achievement for the clarification of biological problems is thus summarized by Sir J. Arthur Thomson:

> As we have seen, not a few of the early microscopists made attempts to define the minute elementary parts that build up living creatures; but it was not till 1838 that the idea of the cell as a structural and functional unit was clearly focused in the Cell-Theory or, better, Cell-Doctrine (*Zellenlehre*) of Schwann and Schleiden. Its three propositions may be recalled. First, there is the *morphological* statement, that all living creatures have a cellular structure, and that all but the simplest, that is to say all that have what may be called a "body," are built up of cells and modifications of cells. Second, the Cell-Theory includes the *physiological* statement, that the activity of a many-celled organism is the sum of the activities of the component cells. This idea requires to be safeguarded by the fact of correlation, for the life of the whole cannot be described without recognising that it is more than the life of all its parts, just as the behaviour of a group of men with a common purpose cannot be adequately described merely in terms of the movements of the individuals. Third, the Cell-Theory includes the *embryological* statement, that the individual many-celled organism begins its life, in all ordinary cases, as a fertilised egg-cell, which divides and re-divides to form an embryo. In other words, developing and growing imply cell-division. Cellular structure is a condition of differentiation.[5]

[5] Sir J. A. Thomson and Patrick Geddes, *Life: Outlines of General Biology*, 2 vols., Harper, 1931, I, 701.

As soon as the cell theory was formulated, the cell was studied much more thoroughly. Karl von Nägeli and Hugo von Mohl examined carefully the contents of cells and in 1844 von Mohl gave the name protoplasm to the plastic nitrogenous living matter within the walls of the cell. Soon after, Max Schlutze declared (1863) that this protoplasm forms the physical basis of life. Not only healthy but diseased tissues were made the subject of scientific study. The science of pathology was revolutionized by the two ablest pathologists of the nineteenth century, Rudolf Virchow (1821-1902) of Berlin, who founded cellular pathology, and Louis Pasteur (1822-1895) of Paris, who was preeminently responsible for our present understanding of bacteriology.

The science of embryology, or the study of the organism between fertilization and birth, did much to clarify the processes of heredity. Down to the nineteenth century it was commonly held that the fertilized egg (ovum) contains the complete mammal in miniature. This notion was overthrown by the Russian biologist, Karl Ernst von Baer (1792-1876), who founded the modern science of embryology. The doctrine that the development of the individual organism between fertilization and birth roughly recapitulates or reproduces the whole biological history of the species was set forth by J. F. Meckel (1781-1833), and greatly elaborated by the famous German biologist, Ernst Heinrich Haeckel (1834-1919). While this principle is only partly true, it cast much light upon both biology and psychology and greatly stimulated the study of organic evolution and genetic psychology.

The growth of both biological and chemical knowledge helped to place the study of physiology, or the dynamics of human life, on a scientific basis. At the opening of the century François Bichat (1771-1802), the first great histologist, had contended that the whole life of the organism is the result of the combined lives of the constituent tissues. The notion that life is primarily a matter of chemical processes acquired some degree of thoroughness and scientific precision. In addition to a more complete understanding of the processes of nutrition and metabolism, the physiologists discovered that animal heat is not an innate quality, but the result of chemical combustion within the body.

Of the many men who contributed to the systematization of scientific physiology in the nineteenth century, the Frenchman, Claude Bernard (1813-1878), was probably the foremost, but we cannot overlook the work of the eminent German physiologist, Johannes Müller (1801-1858), who brought together all the existing physiological knowledge of his day in his *Outlines of Physiology*. Distinguished disciples of Müller, like Emil Dubois-Reymond and Karl Ludwig, carried on his work. Dubois-Reymond rivaled Huxley as a brilliant expositor of scientific naturalism.

In the related field of botany the most important developments were the modification and improvement of Linnaeus' classification of plants and the application of the theory of evolution to botany. In providing a new and more satisfactory system of botanical classification the main contributor was Augustin de Candolle (1778-1841), who gave us the still generally accepted "system of nature." The man who showed that evolutionary principles apply comprehensively to the plant kingdom, and did it, for the most part, independently of Darwin, was

W. F. B. Hofmeister (1824-1877), the outstanding botanist of the century. Hofmeister also made important contributions to our knowledge of plant cytology and the fertilization of plants. Further important cytological studies were carried on by von Nägeli.

6. The Rise of Scientific Psychology

The increasing knowledge of the human body that resulted from progress in biology, anatomy, and chemistry enabled scientists to obtain their first rudimentary notions of the human mind. Even the most eminent early scientists had grotesque conceptions of the mind. Aristotle, for example, believed that we think with our hearts and that the brain exists solely to pump phlegm to the heart to prevent it from overheating in moments of intense thought. In spite of this, however, Aristotle worked out a passable type of behavioristic psychology. Most studies of the mind between Aristotle and the nineteenth century were metaphysical and philosophical, with a large tincture of theology thrown in. This approach slighted both biology and chemistry. This was true of even such rationalistic writers as Hume or Condillac.

The first truly scientific study of the brain and its functions was made by Franz Josef Gall (1758-1828), an Austrian physician. He carefully dissected the brain, described its real structure, and differentiated between the functions of the gray and white matter. Some of his associates and successors debased his work by building upon it the pseudo science of phrenology. Yet it was Gall who founded the scientific study of the brain which we now know as neurology and which constitutes the starting-point of all truly scientific psychology.

The science of physics was drafted to aid the establishment of a science of the mind. Two German scholars, Ernst Heinrich Weber (1795-1878) and Gustav Theodor Fechner (1801-1887), did much to create scientific and experimental psychology by exact experimental studies of sensation and perception. Fechner coined (1860) the term "psychophysics" to describe this line of work. It reached its highest development in the twentieth century in the laboratory of E. B. Titchener of Cornell University, a student of Wundt.

The Darwinian theory of evolution exerted a considerable influence on the study of psychology, particularly in the work of Huxley and G. Stanley Hall (1846-1924). The latter used evolutionary biology to establish genetic psychology, which later became of great significance in the science of education. Genetic psychology applied evolutionary conceptions to the mind as well as the body.[6]

In the earliest important nineteenth-century efforts towards a systematic study of psychology scholars brought together the existing scientific knowledge in biology, physiology and psychology, and in its light they tried to study their mental processes through the method of informal introspection. The most influential figures in this stage of psychological development were Alexander Bain (1818-1903) and Herbert Spencer (1820-1903).

This useful but rather elementary investigation of the human mind was surpassed in the experimental laboratory of the great German psychologist, Wilhelm

[6] See above, pp. 39 ff.

Wundt (1832-1920) of Leipzig, far and away the outstanding figure in nineteenth-century psychology. The scientific approach of Wundt was accepted by Hall and William James (1842-1910) in the United States, and even more completely developed by Titchener. James wrote with great charm, and his *Principles of Psychology* (1891) was in every way the most popular and competent summary of psychological knowledge at the close of the nineteenth century.

Not only was there impressive progress in the study of the normal mind; attention was also given to abnormal mental states by men like Maudsley, Ribot, Charcot, and Bernheim. The idea of diabolism was finally ousted by the scientific theories of insanity.

It is hardly an exaggeration to say that we passed in this single century from relative ignorance of the nature of the mind to a reasonably clear comprehension of mental processes. The psychologists were not content with merely investigating the human mind, but turned to a comparative study of the mind of man and the other animals. This tendency was greatly stimulated by the growing popularity of the doctrine of evolution.

7. The Progress of Medical Science in the Nineteenth Century

The progress of physical, chemical, and biological knowledge quite naturally had a revolutionary effect upon medical science. The century began auspiciously with the epochal discovery of the theory of immunity to disease by the English physician, Edward Jenner (1749-1823), who introduced vaccination for smallpox. Jenner, as we have seen, performed his first public vaccination for smallpox in the year 1796.

The most important contribution of physics to medicine in the nineteenth century consisted in the invention of the stethoscope by Hyacinthe Laennec (1781-1826). Through the concentration of the sense of hearing afforded by this instrument a physician can detect many abnormalities of the heart and chest. It taught physicians to pay attention to chest noises. Another outstanding contribution of physics to medicine was the application of electricity to medical diagnosis and treatment, but this did not become very important until the twentieth century.

Chemistry made many helpful contributions to medicine. Perhaps the most important was the development of surgical anesthesia, or the use of chemicals (chloroform, ether, and nitrous oxide) to make surgery relatively painless. The honor of having first utilized a really effective anesthetic must be assigned to a Boston dentist, William T. G. Morton, who demonstrated the use of ether in October, 1846.[6a] Sir James Simpson of Edinburgh used chloroform and did much to popularize anesthetic surgery. It is doubtful if any other human discovery has done more to reduce pain and death. Outstanding, also, was the preparation of effective chemical germicides, especially after Lister's reforms in surgery.

The old theory that disease is caused by evil spirits was banished for all time by the announcement of the germ theory of disease in 1876. It was the work of Dr. Robert Koch (1843-1910), a brilliant German pathologist who used the important earlier experiments of Pasteur in bacterial fermentation. In 1882 Koch dis-

[6a] It is claimed by some authorities that Dr. Crawford W. Long of Georgia used ether in an operation as early as 1843.

covered the tuberculosis bacillus. This germ theory of disease, with which the names of Pasteur and Virchow are most intimately associated, revolutionized the sciences of bacteriology and pathology. The usual method of killing micro-organisms in milk still bears Pasteur's name. His work on silkworm diseases saved the silk industry of France. His studies of anthrax helped to combat this dreaded animal disease, while he was also the first to give us a successful vaccine against hydrophobia.

If Morton and his successors made surgery more painless, Lord Joseph Lister (1827-1912) made it safer against infection through his introduction of antiseptic surgery. This meant the careful cleansing of the hands and surgical instruments, and the treatment of wounds with the proper germicides. Previously surgeons had been scandalously negligent about even ordinary cleanliness, and a high death rate from infection had resulted. Pus was still frequently left on wounds. One source of a frightfully high death rate from infection was puerperal, or childbed, fever. The man who discovered, in 1843, that this deadly malady is produced by unnecessary infection, due to lack of cleanliness, was a Boston physician, better known in literature than in medicine, Oliver Wendell Holmes (1809-1894). A Hungarian physician, Ignaz Philipp Semmelweiss (1818-1865), applied Holmes's discovery to obstetrics, and thus saved the lives of countless thousands of mothers. Semmelweiss' brave struggle against the inertia, jealousy, and malice of his fellow physicians constitutes one of the more stirring chapters in the history of medicine. It was his fight, however, that thoroughly established this important new development in medical practice. Women of our day owe more to Semmelweiss than to any other human being who ever lived.

While artificial germicides are extremely important in safeguarding us from infections, the body itself provides powerful shock troops in the battle against deadly germs. This fact was first demonstrated by the eminent Russian scientist I. I. (Elie) Mechnikov (1845-1916), who showed that the function of the white corpuscles (called leucocytes or phagocytes) in the blood is primarily to fight off germs and to prevent infection and disease. The pus in an infected wound is mainly composed of the dead white corpuscles that have made the "supreme sacrifice" in our behalf.

The man who, perhaps, best summarized in his personality, knowledge, and attitudes the content and spirit of mature nineteenth-century medicine was Sir William Osler (1849-1919), an Englishman who taught for a time in the famous Johns Hopkins medical school in Baltimore.

These various lines of medical progress—diagnosis, antisepsis, anesthesia, pathology—made truly scientific surgery possible for the first time in human history. It is usually conceded that the foremost surgeon of the nineteenth century was Theodore Kocher (1841-1917) of Switzerland, although he had many close rivals. Kocher was especially famous for performing the then difficult goiter and thyroid operation.

Medicine was applied not only to our bodies but also to our minds in the related fields of psychiatry and neurology. In the latter part of the nineteenth century, psychologists and physicians such as Henry Maudsley (1835-1918), T. A. Ribot (1839-1916), Jean Charcot (1825-1893), Hippolyte Bernheim (1840-1919),

Auguste Forel (1848-1931), Pierre Janet (1859-1947), S. Weir Mitchell (1829-1914), Morton Prince (1854-1929), and others, raised the study of mental and nervous disease from the depths of witchcraft and diabolism to the level of respectable science. The stage was set for Sigmund Freud (1856-1940) and the development of psychoanalysis. Suggestion and hypnotism were developed as therapeutic techniques.

Progress in medical science between Jenner and Osler was certainly much more impressive than between Hippocrates and Jenner. This fact is usually obscured, at least by implication, even in our better medical histories, since they devote greater space to the largely irrelevant, if curious and interesting, medical lore before 1800. Aside from the work in anatomy, medical developments before 1800 are chiefly of antiquarian interest.

8. Geology and Geography

We noted in an earlier chapter that in his *Theory of the Earth* James Hutton supported the scientific and historical view of the origins of the earth, in opposition to the orthodox biblical version of creation. In the half-century following the publication of Hutton's book in 1785 a great deal of important knowledge was accumulated concerning the age and structure of the earth, particularly by the extensive study of fossils by William Smith (1769-1839), Cuvier, and Lamarck. All of this geological information was collected by Sir Charles Lyell (1797-1875) in his monumental *Principles of Geology,* published in 1830-1833.

With the appearance of Lyell's work, geology attained the rank of a true science and students were henceforth able to form precise notions of the origins, age, and structure of the earth. The two other masterpieces in geology during the century were the work of Albert Heim (1849-1937) on structural geology, especially the formation of mountains, and, even more notable, the monumental three-volume treatise of Eduard Suess (1831-1914), *The Face of the Earth,* which dealt with the dynamics of geological formations in all the main regions of the earth. Cuvier and Lamarck, through their painstaking investigation of fossils, enriched that branch of geology known as paleontology, a study developed by Alcide d'Orbigny (1802-1857), James Hall (1811-1898), and others. Cuvier did not, however, accept the logical implication that these fossils upset the doctrine of a special creation, but Lamarck did espouse evolution wholeheartedly.

Since the time of Lyell, geology has progressed mainly in the way of providing wider information and more exact description. It has also profited by exploiting chemistry and zoölogy. In the latter part of the century special attention was given to the study of glaciation by James Geikie (1839-1915), Penck, and Brückner.

Towards the end of the nineteenth century the geologists, no longer satisfied merely to describe the growth of the earth, set forth theories as to its origin which rejected Laplace's nebular hypothesis. Geology also came to have an important practical and economic value in the assistance it gave to the iron, coal, oil, and other extractive industries.

The science of geography progressed to a comparable degree during this century. Knowledge of physical geography was promoted in the first half of the century by such travelers and scholars as Baron Alexander von Humboldt (1769-

1859) and Karl Ritter (1779-1859). The physical features of the earth were described in detail in a special branch of geography known as physiography. Geographical knowledge was vastly extended after 1850 as a result of the extensive explorations of David Livingstone, Henry M. Stanley, Paul Belloni Du Chaillu, Gustav Nachtigal, Nikolai Prjevalsky, Baron Ferdinand von Richthofen, and others.[7] This matched the growth of geographical information in the earlier period of discoveries after 1492.

Certain geographers became interested in the effect of geographical factors—such as climate, altitude, fertility, topography, and routes of travel—upon man himself. They thus founded what is called the science of anthropogeography, or human geography, and put on a scientific plane a type of thought which had existed since the days of Hippocrates as a crude combination of geography, astrology and the philosophy of history. The foremost anthropogeographers of the century were Karl Ritter and his disciple, Friedrich Ratzel (1844-1904). The latter's doctrines were introduced into the United States by his student, Miss Ellen C. Semple. The eminent philosophical anarchist, Elisée Reclus (1830-1903), a French refugee in Switzerland and Belgium, also contributed notably to the sciences of descriptive geography and anthropogeography.

9. Science and Industry

There is an intimate connection between the growth of science and technological changes. More and more, technological progress became dependent upon antecedent developments in the physical sciences. James Hargreaves, a hundred seventy years ago, could invent the spinning jenny without an esoteric knowledge of physics or chemistry. The automobile, the airplane, radio, television, and other contemporary mechanisms depend, however, very decisively on many previous discoveries in highly technical phases of physical science.

We often fail to realize that great practical significance may ultimately reside in the most abstruse achievements of pure science. Willard Gibbs's erudite paper on "The Equilibrium of Heterogeneous Substances" has been described by a great scientist as "one of the mightiest works of genius the human mind has ever produced." It was so abstract and difficult that even his fellow American physicists and chemists could hardly comprehend its significance at the time of its appearance (1867). In our day, however, it has been said of Gibbs's memoir that "never has an abstract investigation so influenced the fundamental basis of industry as the treatise of Gibbs on heterogeneous equilibrium." It has been widely exploited in the development of physical and commercial chemistry.

A few illustrations of how science has directly helped to produce the technological wonders of today will quickly dissipate an often expressed belief that there is little connection between research in pure science and progress in technology.

The steam engine depended for its perfection upon the study of gases by Boyle and Mariotte, research into the physics of heat by Black and Carnot, and the investigation of the conservation of energy by Joule, Mayer, and Helmholtz. Without the elaborate experimentation of Faraday on the physical basis of electricity and magnetism we would not have had the dynamo or the electric motor. Re-

---

[7] See *Cambridge Modern History,* Vol. XII, chap. xxv.

search in gases and electricity combined to produce the internal-combustion engine and modern projectiles. Chemistry lies behind the remarkable developments in the iron and steel, rubber and petroleum industries, chemical dyes, the manufacture of explosives and the infinite utilization of by-products. Modern methods of communication likewise have a complicated scientific background. The researches of Oersted and Ampère produced the telegraph. Only extremely advanced work by Clerk Maxwell and Heinrich Hertz in mathematics and electrical physics enabled Marconi to invent the wireless telegraph. Development of the radio depended not only upon research in electromechanics but also upon the invention of the thermionic valve, derived from a study of the release of electrons from heated bodies. The following statement of a few years ago remains pertinent today:

> The pure scientists are the advance guards of civilization. By their discoveries, they furnish to the engineer and industrial chemist and other applied scientists the raw material to be elaborated into manifold agencies for the amelioration of the conditions of mankind. Unless the work of the pure scientist is continued and pushed forward with ever increasing energy, the achievements of the industrial scientists will diminish and degenerate. Many practical problems now confronting mankind cannot be solved by the industrial scientist alone, but must await further fundamental discoveries and new scientific generalizations.[8]

10. Science and Popular Thought

Remarkable progress in natural science in the nineteenth century induced many to believe that mankind suddenly became scientific-minded and that an altogether new intellectual age had blossomed forth by the time of the American civil war. Nothing of the sort occurred.

The mass of mankind in the Western World were, it is true, profoundly though indirectly affected by the progress of nineteenth-century science. They were provided with all kinds of wonderful devices and conveniences, which vitally altered their lives. They were more surely and more frequently healed of diseases and operated upon by surgeons more successfully and painlessly. In popular magazines and newspapers they read superficially about the wonders that modern science had uncovered. They looked through better telescopes, and more powerful microscopes at the vast wonders of the heavens and the minute wonders of the animal and vegetable worlds.

In spite of all of this, however, the thinking of most men in the Western World was but slightly altered by the direct impact of science. To be sure, the perspective of a man who has traveled across a continent in a railroad train must be somewhat different from that of a person whose travels have been limited to an oxcart within a rural township. But a transcontinental railroad trip may not prevent a person from thinking about the fundamental problems of life and society much as his grandfather did.

Such was the case with Western civilization as a whole. In their conceptions

[8] G. E. Hale, "Science and the Wealth of Nations," Harper's Magazine, January, 1928, p. 243.

of God, the world, man, politics, law, wealth and economics, education, and the problems of right and wrong, the overwhelming majority were as dominated by custom, tradition, folklore, and habit in 1885 as in 1685. The power of the supernatural over human thought was lessened but little by scientific progress. Tradition and emotion, rather than fact and logic, still dominated. Prejudices reigned supreme.

Even the scientists themselves, at least down to the close of the century, rarely thought scientifically outside their laboratories. They usually rejected scientific discoveries in other fields if these challenged their personal prejudices or religious convictions. Even so eminent a scientist as Pasteur, at the close of the nineteenth century, never accepted the theory of evolution or allowed his orthodoxy to be shaken in the slightest. An able English biologist, St. George Mivart, opposed evolution until his death in 1900. Among the scientists a Haeckel or a Huxley was the exception rather than the rule, and such men were generally frowned upon by other members of the scientific fraternity.

Civilization in the year 1900 was, thus, intellectually speaking, a greedy and unappreciative parasite, thriving on the discoveries of a few score outstanding scientists since 1500. In any popular sense, nothing approaching a scientific and skeptical age had yet dawned.

11. The Impact of Natural Science on Thought and Religion

While nineteenth-century natural science had little effect on the thinking of the masses, it had as revolutionary an influence on the thought of the scholarly classes as did the remarkable scientific advances from Copernicus to Newton upon thinkers of that age. The notion of a "world-machine" best summarizes, perhaps, the general intellectual reaction to the new scientific discoveries. Astronomy in the days of Newton had emphasized the elements of law and order in the physical world and had identified natural law with divine law. God was pictured as standing behind the physical universe as the author of the invariable laws of nature. Nineteenth-century science elaborated this conception of the physical universe as a vast and complicated machine obeying immutable laws. Moreover, the doctrine of evolution, as applied to astronomy and thermodynamics, produced a conception of the universe as a machine in motion on a much grander and more complicated scale than the Newtonian system. The idea of the universe as a dynamic mechanism almost completely triumphed among those whose thinking was at all attuned to science.

The new scientific approach to intellectual problems postulated an invariable cause-and-effect relationship between physical phenomena. As Max Planck describes it, the nineteenth century regarded causation "as an expression of inviolable regulation which inheres in events, and is therefore a necessary framework in which experience comes to us, and without which experience is incomprehensible." In every field of nature, if one had a complete understanding of the causes, so it was believed, he could predict and describe the effects that would follow. This scientific conception of causal relationships was, of course, derived in considerable degree from the metaphysical theories of cause and effect of Hume,

Kant, and other philosophers. Cause-and-effect relationship occupied much the same position among nineteenth-century scientists that God, the perfect being, occupied in the perspective of Descartes. The latter had also believed in the reality of certain definite categories of knowledge; so, likewise, the nineteenth-century scientists felt positive that they could fall back upon certain definitely established realities, such as indivisible atoms, the transformation of energy, the conservation of energy, and the laws of radiant energies. A good statement of the way in which cause-and-effect dominated nineteenth-century thought is offered by Professor Kirtley F. Mather:

> In Joshua's World anything could happen. Magic played a most important part in everyday life. Happenings were determined by the caprice of ruling powers whose whims and intentions varied from day to day. Ours is a world of law. Effect follows cause with unvarying relations. Order and regularity reign where formerly magic and caprice held sway. The law of gravity operates relentlessly, the same yesterday, to-day and to-morrow, regardless of bribe or entreaty.[9]

In this prevailing air of certainty, man was looked upon as capable of discovering the ultimates in the realm of science. He might not, as Spencer admitted, be capable of mastering the elusive ultimates in religion and philosophy—the unknowable—but he could be sure of handling with precision and accuracy the facts of the physical world. Such assumptions were conceded to the scientists even by many philosophers who held that science was quite incapable of dealing with ultimate realities. Kant and his successors granted that science was competent to describe and understand those facts of the phenomenal world which could be discerned through sense perception. In short, they admitted that man could master scientific data, however much he might fall short of understanding and interpreting the ultimate or noumenal world.

Scientific discoveries in the nineteenth century also had, as we have hinted above, a marked influence upon the theory of progress which had been so popular in the previous century. The doctrine of evolution seemed to offer a complete scientific confirmation of the dogma of progress. Further, it gave the notion of progress greater precision. In the past, man had turned primarily to history to get evidence to confirm the doctrine of progress. Now he could have recourse to physical and biological science. Progress no longer seemed merely a matter of opinion. It was regarded as a universal law. Moreover, it applied not only to man, culture, and things of this world, but involved the whole physical universe. Man possessed a dynamic affinity with the cosmos as a whole.

Not only did scientists embrace such ideas as these; the more advanced students of religion, especially near the end of the nineteenth century, received them with open arms. So far as the physical universe was concerned, they were inclined to accept what the scientists taught. They might, following Kant and Schleiermacher, hold that faith is superior to reason, and that the scientist never touches the world of ultimate reality. In the realm of physical phenomena, however, the modernists in religion were inclined to take science and its dogmas at their face value without any serious questioning.

[9] Mather in *World Unity*, October, 1927, pp. 36-37.

IV. RELIGIOUS TRENDS IN THE NINETEENTH CENTURY

The nineteenth century was extremely important in the history of religion. We have already referred to the remarkable progress in biblical criticism. There were significant developments within the Christian church, and this century also witnessed the rise of the first extensive attack upon supernaturalism as a whole. The earlier rationalists, including even Voltaire and Thomas Paine, had been supernaturalists. With the exception of a few atheists, such as Baron d'Holbach, they all believed ardently in God. They merely asked that supernatural religion should be reasonable and urbane. In the nineteenth century, many critical thinkers demanded that all forms of supernaturalism be rejected, even though many of them did not deny that God may possibly exist.

The first striking development in religion in the nineteenth century was, however, a marked revival of religious fervor and pietism. For a number of reasons, there was a far wider popular enthusiasm for religion in 1850 than in 1750. The very attacks leveled against orthodoxy by rationalists from Bayle to Voltaire and Thomas Paine brought about a natural reaction and a swing of the pendulum to the other extreme. We have already noted how the "Christian evidences" movement got under way in Paley's effort to combat rationalism. The French Revolution had been in part an antireligious, and especially an anti-Catholic, movement. Therefore, the political reaction after 1815 brought an increase in the fervor of Catholicism, especially French Catholicism. The writings of Chateaubriand were a product of this reaction. Kant, Schleiermacher, and their disciples, gave a new moral depth and philosophical dignity to Protestantism. Above all, the rise of evangelical sects that appealed more to human emotions than reason helped to increase the hold of religion on the masses. Methodism had taken the lead in the eighteenth century and other evangelical Protestant sects followed.

These popular new sects also gained strength among the common people because they took an active part in attacking the bad working and living conditions which followed the industrial revolution. Such religions appealed to the American frontiersmen, eking out a living on the borders of civilization.

Pending real social reforms, which did not come until the middle of the nineteenth century, Methodism offered a valuable release for the more sensitive element among the proletariat, who were hopelssly beaten down in the competitive struggle. The Little Bethels with their congregations of sorely burdened weavers present a touching picture. It is easy to deride the "pie in the sky" motive, but this consolation was very real, given the conditions of the time and type of mind involved. At least these poor unfortunates were offered a means of transcending their earthly lot.

Rationalism thus received a notable setback. It required the doctrine of evolution, biblical criticism, cultural history, anthropology, and psychology to put it back on its feet again near the end of the nineteenth century.

Within Protestantism, the most notable development, perhaps, was the tendency to split up into rather antagonistic sects. There were only a half-dozen leading branches of Protestantism, for example, in the seventeenth century, consisting of the followers of Luther, Calvin, Zwingli, Knox, and others. By the close of the nineteenth century there were nearly three hundred Protestant sects, thus fulfilling the gloomy Catholic prophecy of Bishop Bossuet in the seventeenth century that a break with Catholic authority would lead to endless sectarianism.

Although sectarianism may have weakened Protestantism, the latter was simultaneously strengthened in a number of ways. Protestantism gained a new moral fervor as the result of the works of Immanuel Kant and his followers. Though Kant lived in the eighteenth century, his religious influence was felt chiefly in the nineteenth. His influence on Protestantism has probably been exceeded only by that of Martin Luther. In his *Critique of Pure Reason,* as we have seen, Kant demolished all arguments for the existence of God. He showed that in the phenomenal world the idea of duty is nonsensical, since everything is inevitably determined by natural causes. Science gives man no justification whatever for a moral terminology. In his *Critique of Practical Reason,* however, Kant reversed his emphasis and declared that the assumption of God, freedom, and immortality helps to make moral conduct appear rational and to make the categorical "ought" universally binding. Kant's religious influence was, as we have seen, exerted mainly through the *Critique of Practical Reason,* and his chief disciples were Schleiermacher, Harnack, Constant, Maurice, and McGiffert. His influence was also apparent on the doctrines of Ritschl which we shall analyze later.

Another source of Protestant strength in the nineteenth century was the growth of foreign missions. The Catholics had proselytized among "foreigners" ever since the days of Paul. But the first important Protestant missionary activity is associated with the Society for the Propagation of the Gospel in Foreign Parts, founded in 1701, and the Baptist Foreign Missionary Society, established in 1792. Other Protestant sects, in turn, founded missionary societies and proselytized extensively among the "heathen," particularly in Asia and Africa. This activity not only gained new converts overseas, but also stimulated moral and religious fervor at home among contributors to this missionary enterprise. The Protestant missionary activity naturally stirred the Catholics to a new zeal in promoting their faith in foreign lands.

Inevitably the church, both Protestant and Catholic, came into sharp conflict with the scientific trends of the nineteenth century, especially with the theory of evolution and the higher criticism of the Bible. Evolution and criticism were merged in scholarly fashion in the ninth edition of the *Encyclopaedia Britannica,* edited by T. S. Baynes following 1875. This great publication was the best summary of nineteenth-century rationalism, fairly comparable to Diderot's rationalistic *Encyclopédie,* which had appeared a century earlier.

Certain Protestant sects, particularly evangelical groups, rejected both evolution and the higher criticism root and branch. They clung to the literal word of the Bible and defended the inspiration theory and special-creation doctrine. These thoroughly devout and orthodox religionists came to be known, at the close of the century, as Fundamentalists. Some liberal Protestants were inclined to accept evolution and the findings of biblical scholarship. They made a real effort to reconcile the essentials of Christianity with modern science and criticism. This school of Protestant thought came to be known as devout modernists. They resembled the Christian deists of the preceding century. While accepting the idea that the universe, the earth, and its inhabitants were produced by evolutionary processes, and conceding that the Bible was written without direct supernatural inspiration, the devout modernists vigorously maintained their belief in God and the divinity of Jesus Christ. They laid special emphasis upon the importance of Jesus as a religious teacher and revived the old deistic distinction between historical (conventional) Christianity and the vital teachings of Jesus. They were about evenly divided for and against the belief in a future life.

Nowhere within Protestantism during the nineteenth century was there a marked tendency to reject both the belief in God and the divinity of Jesus. There were two important humanistic religions, however, which did reject orthodox ideas of God and Jesus, but they were formed outside of conventional religious circles. The first of these was the so-called Positivism of Auguste Comte. Comte proposed a religious system which would be devoted to the worship of humanity and in which the priests would be sociologists. It was espoused and warmly recommended by the English historian and essayist, Frederic Harrison. Other English scholars favorably impressed by Positivism were John Stuart Mill, George H. Lewes and Harriet Martineau. The other outstanding humanistic cult was the Ethical Culture Society, founded in New York City in 1876 by Felix Adler, a high-minded Jewish professor of philosophy and ethics. It aimed to bring together the best moral teachings from the earliest times to our own day. Recognizing the teachings of Jesus as an important contribution to our moral tradition, the ethical culturists studied his sayings respectfully. But they insisted upon regarding Jesus as a strictly human teacher. The Ethical Culture Society gained a considerable following in both the United States and England, but it never became a major religious movement. It appealed chiefly to urbane intellectuals.

In contrast to the large number of Protestant sects, the Catholic church maintained its unity unimpaired from the time of the counter-reformation. This unified discipline gave it a strength and coherence even out of proportion to its large number of communicants, and it accounts mainly for the remarkable vitality of Catholicism in our own day.

But the Roman Catholic church was not wholly free from inner struggles. The papacy of Pius IX (1846-1878) was characterized by a policy of reaction along many lines. At first it was hoped that Pius IX would support liberal, if not revolutionary, political principles in Europe. In France the liberal Catholic sentiment was expressed by Alphonse de Lamartine (1790-1869), who tried to line up Catholicism behind republican tendencies, and by Robert de Lamennais, a former reactionary, who endeavored to harmonize Catholicism and the democratic principles of the French Revolution. But Pius IX soon decisively condemned revolution and democracy, and ranged himself on the side of political reaction and absolutism. The revolutionary movements of the day, the revival of skepticism, and the growth of evolutionary doctrines, as well as his own difficulties in Rome, encouraged Pius IX to espouse many reactionary religious policies.

The dogma of the immaculate conception was affirmed in 1854. This doctrine should be distinguished from that of the virgin birth which asserts that Christ was born of a virgin without sexual intercourse. The dogma of immaculate conception contends that the Virgin Mary "from the first instant of her conception, was . . . preserved from all stain of Original Sin, is a doctrine revealed by God, and therefore to be firmly and steadfastly believed by all the faithful." The next great reactionary event was the papal encyclical, *Quanta cura* and the *Syllabus of Errors,* both promulgated in 1864. In effect, the syllabus was a cogent summary of modern thought, and as such is of value to a student of modern intellectual progress. The irony of the situation is that all this effort to bring together a synthesis of intellectual progress was expended for condemnatory purposes. In the encyclical and the syllabus, all manifestations of "naturalism," not only in biology but in all forms of human thought and action, were roundly denounced.

In 1870 another backward step was taken with the announcement of the dogma of papal infallibility by the Vatican Council of 1869-1870. This dogma means, in effect, that when the pope speaks *ex cathedra* on matters of faith and doctrine he is to be regarded as infallible. This was carrying the papal power to a most extraordinary, but thoroughly logical, conclusion, and the step was not taken without considerable opposition within the church.

Such famous historians and liberal Catholics as Lord Acton in England and Ignaz von Döllinger in Germany, calling themselves the Old Catholic party, firmly opposed this papal move; a second group of moderates considered the occasion decidedly inopportune without objecting to the idea; while a third group, composed largely of Spanish and Italian Jesuits, firmly supported the pope. The council, which finally approved the dogma of infallibility, lasted for many months and the success of the party favoring it was won by a process of intellectual attrition, the history of which is hardly creditable to the church. Ultramontanism and obscurantism triumphed in Catholic scholarship under the leadership of Hefele, Hergenröther, Janssen, Pastor, and Denifle.

Leo XIII (pope, 1878-1903) was a more amiable personality than Pius IX. On social and economic matters he took at least a mildly liberal position. He was also more compromising in his attitude towards the Third French Republic, and made his peace with most civil governments outside of Italy. But he condemned just as logically and just as relentlessly as had Pius IX all the progressive intellectual tendencies of his day, even protesting vigorously against the erection of a monument to Giordano Bruno in Rome. In his encyclical, *Aeterni patris,* Leo reasserted the primacy of the theology of Thomas Aquinas and reaffirmed the doctrines of the encyclical and syllabus of 1864.

The next struggle within the Roman Catholic church took the form of a clash with science and scholarship within its own membership. Theoretically, the Catholics are better prepared than Protestants to reckon with advances in knowledge. On principle, the Protestants are compelled to follow the literal word of the Bible, which is fixed once and for all and cannot be modified. In abstract

Catholic theory, on the other hand, the pope may reinterpret Catholic doctrine so as to harmonize it with the findings of science and scholarship. In practice, however, the Catholic church did not readapt its dogmas to scientific advances in the nineteenth century, whereas, as we have seen, many Protestants abandoned the literal word of the Bible and accepted many scientific findings concerning religion, man, and the universe.

From the beginning to the end of the century, the Catholic church stood firmly against evolution, biblical scholarship, and all other phases of the new learning which directly challenged Catholic dogmas. It did not, however, oppose science where the latter in no way conflicted with religious interests. Therefore, it freely permitted Mendel to study the hereditary characteristics of the pea vine, allowed Pasteur to study bacteriology and pathology, and offered no objections to the work of Mivart in natural history and comparative anatomy. But the Catholic church opposed promptly and vigorously those scientific discoveries which cut at the roots of Catholic doctrines. Works which were deemed in any way dangerous were placed upon the index of forbidden books.

The Christian churches increased their popularity in the nineteenth century by entering directly into social reform and thereby earning the gratitude of the masses. Conspicuous in this respect was the Christian socialist movement led by the Anglicans Kingsley and Maurice, and by Catholics like Buchez in France. The evangelical Protestants, in particular, attacked the evils of the factory system and Negro slavery in the English colonies. The Society of Friends (Quakers) took a leading part in prison reform in the early nineteenth century. They were responsible for the famous Pennsylvania system of prison discipline. The other outstanding influence in prison reform in the early nineteenth century was a devout American clergyman, Louis Dwight, who was impelled towards prison reform as a result of impressions received while distributing Bibles to prisoners. He was chiefly responsible for the spread of the Auburn prison system, the great rival of the Pennsylvania system. By and large, evangelical Protestantism also strongly supported the democratic movement of the nineteenth century. Catholicism, as well, advocated moderate democracy under Pope Leo XIII, who also reasserted the economic doctrines of Aquinas. In his famous encyclical, *Rerum novarum* (1891), Leo put the Catholic church behind traditional labor-unionism and social justice. In Germany, Bishop von Ketteler powerfully espoused reform, while in the United States Cardinal Gibbons, with great courage for the time, defended the Knights of Labor and the right of workers to organize freely and unhampered.

While the main religious developments of the nineteenth century occurred within Catholicism and Protestantism, three rather important new religions came into being in Western civilization during this period. The first was Mormonism (the Church of the Latter-day Saints), founded by Joseph Smith and Brigham Young in the second quarter of the nineteenth century. The Mormons regard themselves as the religious descendants of the lost ten tribes of Israel, who, according to Mormon tradition, migrated to America by way of the Bering Straits. One of the last and greatest of the prophets of these mythical immigrants, Mormon, is reputed to have written an account of their wanderings. This makes up a large part of the *Book of Mormon*—the Mormon Bible. The latter was transcribed on golden plates (which were buried) in 400 A.D. by Moroni, son of Mormon. In 1823 an angel revealed their location to Joseph Smith, a young man deeply influenced by the revivalistic religion of his era. Smith alleged that he dug up the golden plates near Palmyra, New York, in 1827, and translated them from hieroglyphics by aid of miraculous spectacles buried with the plates. Smith published his translation of the *Book of Mormon* in 1830, and founded his new religion at Fayette, in central New York, on April 6, 1830. Smith was killed in Carthage, Illinois, after a riot (1844), but his followers, under his successor, Brigham Young, a man of great physical force, resolution, and statecraft, migrated to Utah in 1847.

Rapidly increasing their numbers both by missionary enterprise and the practice of polygyny (polygamy), the Mormons built up a great religious and economic commonwealth in Utah and surrounding states. They also proselytized considerably in Europe and other foreign lands. With certain important modifications, the Mormons accept the Jewish and Christian Bible, and the points of similarity to Judaism and Christianity are far more numerous than the differences. In general, they accept the Christian epic, modified only in detail by the historical episodes of the *Book of Mormon,* the Christian Trinity, and the Christian eschatology. Indeed, the technical title of Mormonism is the Church of Jesus Christ of the Latter-day Saints.

The second important new religion of the nineteenth century was Christian Science, founded by Mary Baker Eddy (1821-1910). Mrs. Eddy, though a nervous invalid, was a person of great zeal and determination. In the autumn of 1862 she was treated by Dr. P. T. Quimby of Portland, Maine, a mesmerist and faith-healer. Somewhat of a philosopher, he was particularly interested in the ancient Stoics and in the metaphysician, Bishop George Berkeley, who, as we have seen, denied the reality of material substance. Quimby was as well a Christian and a constant Bible reader. His therapeutic "system" intermingled Stoicism, transcendentalism, mesmerism, amateurish psychological suggestion, and Christianity. It was Quimby who coined the term "Christian Science."

Mrs. Eddy's health was greatly improved as a result of her contact with Quimby. Her faith in his technique was confirmed after a seemingly miraculous recovery from a bad fall on the ice in 1866. His ideas absorbed her completely; and drawing freely upon them, she devoted herself for nearly twenty years to the composition of what became the Christian Science "Bible." After preliminary editions had appeared (the first in 1875), she submitted it for final literary polishing to a Boston writer, Mr. James H. Wiggin, and it appeared in 1890 under the title *Science and Health.*

Mrs. Eddy's creed is a remarkable admixture of Christian doctrine, abstract metaphysics, and "new thought." She made the widest use of allegory since the Dark Ages. To the uninitiated her book seems quite unintelligible. At any rate, while considerable Christianity is intertwined with the metaphysics, there is certainly no science in her book, in any reasonable interpretation of the term "science."

A great "Mother Church" was constructed in Boston and the movement spread much more rapidly than Mormonism. Unlike evangelical religion, which made its chief appeal to the lower orders of the cities and to rural types, Christian Science is primarily a religion for the urban middle class. It is optimistic and eupeptic, and marvelously efficacious for business men. Not a few predicted that Christian Science would become the great American religion.

The power of Christian Science to attract converts appears to have been based upon two fundamental advantages. In the first place, by its "Father-Mother-God" symbolism, it makes to both sexes an emotional appeal comparable to that of the Catholic church. In the second place, it presumes to relieve physical and mental diseases—in fact, regards both as mainly imaginary. Through its power of suggestion, Christian Science probably does help thousands of primarily neurotic patients with imaginary disorders. That there is a real power of the mind over the body, modern psychiatry has made clear, especially in its study of the so-called "conversion neuroses." Christian Science makes practically no intellectual demands, which is one reason why it easily outdistanced the far more scientific Emmanuel Movement, founded in Boston in 1906 by Dr. Elwood Worcester in an effort to link religion and scientific psychiatry. Christian Scientists appear unusually healthy, efficient, and optimistic—traits which appeal particularly to an aggressive capitalistic civilization such as the United States had become by the close of the nineteenth century. The affinity between Christian Science and the "American dream"—i.e., frontier optimism and buoyancy—also helped the popularity of the new religion.

Christian Science has been especially noted for its decided and unconventional attitude towards medicine and disease. It denies the reality of matter, evil and disease. The latter is believed to be the result of the operation of a malignant principle, namely, "malicious animal magnetism." Christian Science trains its own practitioners, who apply their faith-cures according to these curious notions of pathology. In its earlier days the cult was bitterly attacked by the medical profession, but with the rise of newer psychological techniques, that hostility has somewhat abated. At the same time the Christian Scientists have disclaimed jurisdiction over surgical and obstetrical cases and bowed to public authority in such matters as vaccination and quarantine.

The third important new religious movement of the nineteenth century was the Salvation Army, founded by General William Booth (1829-1912). The Salvation Army has been compared by some writers to the Franciscans of the Middle Ages, with their passion for serving the poor. Their quasi-military organization is more reminiscent of the Jesuits, but they lack the intellectual interests of the Jesuits. They resemble somewhat the Methodists of a century earlier, in that both appealed at the outset especially to poverty-stricken Englishmen.

Booth founded the Christian Mission in the London East End in 1865. He was originally a Methodist evangelist of great persuasiveness, but he became convinced that even more sensational methods were necessary to attract the churchless masses. Hence he abandoned Methodism. Aided by his wife, Catherine Booth, the ablest woman preacher of the century, he gradually developed the "army" organization and formally established the Salvation Army in 1878. This has since grown into an international organization with headquarters in London. Its work has spread to more than sixty countries. It has nearly 10,000 posts, about 25,000 officers and nearly 30,000 brass bandsmen. The growth of the organization after 1878 owed much to the energy of William's son, General Bramwell Booth. The Army makes its appeal not only through preaching but also by band music and quasi-military tactics and uniforms. Its meetings are often held in streets, in the attempt to attract idle pedestrians, stragglers, and others who have no religious affiliations.

The Army gained added strength from the fact that it insisted from the beginning upon the equality of women and men in preaching and leadership. Like Christian Science, it has made wide use of lay preachers and personal testimony. Its religious doctrine is of the most orthodox, emotional, and informal variety.

The strength of the Salvation Army resulted not only from its sensational preaching methods, but also from its relief and reform work. It early allied itself with the temperance movement and made total abstinence a condition of membership. It was thus able to convert and reclaim drunkards effectively. It has also worked in the slums with prostitutes and discharged convicts. It took a leading part in bringing religion into prisons and has helped to care for released convicts. Its extensive contact with the urban poor has made it a powerful adjunct of public relief, especially in England and the United States. From the Salvation Army came Gipsy Smith, the leading English evangelist of modern times.

It was inevitable that aggressive scientists and others deeply affected by scientific discoveries would attack Christianity directly. Herbert Spencer contended in his *First Principles* that those ultimate issues connected with God and religion are unknowable to the human mind and hence may be ignored even if they cannot be disproved. Spencer's friend, Huxley, a much abler natural scientist, was rather more aggressive than Spencer in his assault upon religion. A brilliant debater and public speaker, he gloried in assaulting orthodoxy on the public platform, where he debated gaily with the greatest churchmen of England, as well as with the prime minister, W. E. Gladstone, a staunch pietist. Even more extreme and scathing in his attack upon Christianity was the eminent German biologist, Ernst Haeckel.

Anti-religious scientists did not lack allies in the world of affairs. Because the Catholic church had opposed the Third French Republic, the leaders of the latter were anticlerical. Georges Clemenceau, for instance, openly assaulted Christianity and the church. In the opening years of the twentieth century, this French anticlericalism led to the complete separation of church and state. In the United States, antireligious forces were headed by Colonel Robert G. Ingersoll, one of the foremost lawyers of his generation, a prominent Republican politician and an outstanding orator. He spread the gospel of evolution and the discoveries of biblical criticism before vast enthusiastic audiences in all parts of the country. A prominent statesman and educator, President Andrew D. White of Cornell University, exercised a wide influence in behalf of free thought among the learned classes in the United States through his notable work, *The History of the Warfare of Science with Theology* (1896). The Anarchist movement was based upon a frank repudiation of God as well as of the state. It maintained an attitude of bellicose atheism.

Organizations such as the Rationalist Press Association, started by Charles A. Watts in England, were founded chiefly to publish and distribute important books and pamphlets attacking orthodox religion. Organized opposition to religion appeared in the International Freethinker's League founded in 1880, with many national branches. Leaders of the movement were Friedrich Büchner, Haeckel, Clemenceau, C. J. Holyoake, Charles Bradlaugh, Ingersoll, and Lester F. Ward.

Next to evolution and biblical criticism, the greatest excitement in religion in the nineteenth century was created by the critical studies of the life of Jesus. Most deists and rationalists, while rejecting historical Christianity, united in accepting the divinity of Jesus. They regarded "true Chrstianity" as wholly the work of Jesus. The nineteenth century developed a much more critical and qualified view of Jesus, and some great scholars questioned not only his divinity but also his very historicity (i.e., they denied that he had ever lived).

The central figures in this controversy were a group of scholars at the University of Tübingen in Germany, led by Ferdinand Christian Baur (1792-1860). They were influenced by Hegel and attempted to interpret the development of Christianity in terms of Hegelian dialectic. According to Baur, Jewish Christianity (that of Peter) was the thesis; Gentile Christianity (that of Paul) was the antithesis; and the Roman Catholic church of the age of Constantine was the synthesis. For the first time, Paul's overwhelming influence in the rise and spread of Christianity was fully recognized. Baur's main work was a classic life of Paul (1845). Jesus was held to be relatively unimportant in Christian origins, save as an earnest religious teacher who launched the movement in an exceedingly favorable intellectual environment. The known facts about Jesus were considered few and simple. Baur believed that the gospel stories were written in the second century and were chiefly mythical.

These ideas were elaborated by a student of Baur, David Friedrich Strauss (1808-1874), who startled the learned world in 1835 by his precocious *Life of Jesus*. He stressed even more than Baur the mythical elements in the accounts of Jesus in the Synoptic Gospels and asserted that the Jews of Jesus' generation read into his career their own messianic ideas. In a second edition of his work, published in 1864, Strauss contended that the Gospel stories about Jesus were not myths but deliberate falsifications. Finally, in his *Old and New Faith* (1872), Strauss flatly repudiated Jesus and Christianity and contrasted the Christian view of life with the modern evolutionism and materialism which he espoused. He joined Comte in deifying humanity.

Less devastating than the works of Baur and Strauss but even more popular was the *Life of Jesus* (1863) by Ernest Renan (1823-1892), the eminent French Semitic scholar. Renan presented in popular language many of the views of German critics. He rejected entirely Jesus' claim to divinity as well as any supernatural revelation in connection with his life and work. He composed a brilliant but largely imaginary account of the life and mission of Jesus, whom he interpreted as "a pure, high-minded Galilean peasant" who accepted the fatherhood of God. The work was a rationalistic reconstruction; Jesus became as much a creature of Renan's brilliant and urbane imagination as an actual historical figure.

The most extreme stand was taken by Bruno Bauer (1809-1882), a professor at Bonn, who wrote an elaborate work on the historicity of the Synoptic Gospels. He contended that they were not to be taken seriously as history. Their authors were pure myth-makers like Homer and Hesiod. Bauer not only denied the divinity of Jesus, he even denied that Jesus ever lived. His work led to his dismissal from Bonn.

The religionists were not slow in organizing a defense and carrying the battle into the enemy's territory. To counteract the contention that there is little ground for the special-creation hypothesis, there developed what was known as the Christian evidences movement, which we described earlier. It retained its strength until the close of the century. Another form of opposition to rationalism appeared in the application of certain doctrines of Immanuel Kant, which we mentioned in another connection in this chapter. The critical biographies of Jesus were answered by swarms of pious biographies, among the best-known of which were those by Neander, Pressensé, Farrar and Geikie.

If Kant and Schleiermacher supplied the major impulse to a reinvigorated Protestantism in the first half of the nineteenth century, the chief stimulus in the last half of the century came from another German theologian, Albrecht Ritschl (1822-1899). Since he sought to free religion from all dogmatic theology his ideas came at an opportune moment. Evolution, biblical criticism, and the history of religion had severely challenged Christian dogmas by 1874, when Ritschl's famous work, *The Christian Doctrine of Justification and Reconciliation,* appeared. But Ritschl sought to render religion independent of the conventional facts of the Christian epic and of the dogmas of traditional theology. He would make it rest on experience and have it devoted to practical work for moral betterment. Following Kant, he held that we can never obtain any theoretical knowledge of reality. Taking his next cue from Schleiermacher, he maintained that religion must be, so far as the personal aspect is concerned, a matter of experience. We can never know God, but we can feel conscious of him in our experience. In our experience of God he seems to stand to us in the relation of a father to his children. This gives us the sense of a greater power outside of ourselves, in cooperation with which we can work rationally for moral progress and the betterment of the world. Religion must be eminently practical, a sincere devotion to a deep moral purpose. Christ was the supreme example of a religious leader thus devoted to moral progress. If we accept his doctrine of Love, we may become one with him and, ultimately, with God.

To contemporary historical and psychological students of religion, Ritschl's religious ideas seem a rationalization of the dogmas which he rejected as systematic theology. Yet they appeared to many sincere religionists of the latter half of the nineteenth century to be a sure means of salvaging Christianity from the inroads of history, science, and critical thought. His views were brought into the

United States by Walter Rauschenbusch (1861-1918) and made the basis for a powerful movement in American Christian socialism.

Evolution and critical scholarship in the nineteenth century alarmed mainly the Christian intellectuals. They did not seep down to the pious masses. But in the twentieth century the latter awoke to the challenge and organized the "Fundamentalist" movement which we shall describe later.

V. NINETEENTH-CENTURY PHILOSOPHY

The philosophy of the nineteenth century may be fairly divided into two types— (1) that which represented a hangover from eighteenth-century romanticism and idealism, and (2) that which reflected new developments in nineteenth-century thought, especially science, evolution, and industrialism.

Hegel's philosophy, with its emphasis on the "knowability" of reality, the identification of reality with philosophic speculation, and the rationality of the universe, was ascendant in the early nineteenth century. But a serious reaction against it set in. A number of philosophers believed that Hegel's contention that philosophical thought could grasp fundamental reality was both presumptuous and untrue. So they established a "back to Kant" movement which limited human knowledge to the phenomenal world and denied it any command over the ultimate world of "things-in-themselves." Kant's doctrines had been expounded and popularized by Karl Reinhold (1758-1823) and his son, Ernst Reinhold (1793-1855). The Kantian stronghold was the University of Jena, where Kant was glorified by Jacob Friedrich Fries (1773-1843). Later leaders of this "back to Kant" movement were the popular teacher of the history of philosophy, Professor Ernst Kuno Fischer (1824-1907) of Heidelberg, who, though deeply influenced by Hegel, sounded a call about 1860 for the return to Kant; and Friedrich Albert Lange, who wrote his *History of Materialism* in 1867. Men like Friedrich Paulsen (1846-1908) in Germany, and Charles Bernard Renouvier (1818-1903) in France, joined in reviving the Kantian tradition.

Others thought that Hegel had been too aristocratic and was not sufficiently concerned with social justice for the masses. He had nothing to say about relieving the "miseries of those with whom the Idea had not seen fit to concern itself." This led to what has been called the revolt of the "Hegelians of the left," under the leadership of Ludwig Feuerbach (1804-1866), who moved in the direction of materialism and suggested that man can never be truly good or happy unless he is free from material worries. Another Hegelian of the left, Karl Marx, offered a historic plan for providing this freedom from economic insecurity—a plan (socialism) which we have already analyzed. The materialistic trend in Feuerbach's thought was elaborated in Friedrich Büchner's *Force and Matter* (1855) and in Ernst Haeckel's *The Riddle of the Universe* (1899)—the classic statements of nineteenth-century materialism.

For the most part, vestiges of the conservative philosophy of the late eighteenth century were either a revival of romanticism, as with Lotze, Schopenhauer, Nietzsche and von Hartmann, or eclectic syntheses of Kant, Hegel, and the lesser

German romanticists and idealists. Such syntheses of Germanic philosophies were made by Wilhelm Dilthey, Wilhelm Windelband and Heinrich Rickert in Germany, all of whom tended towards critical idealism; Victor Cousin in France; Sir William Hamilton, Edward Caird, Thomas Hill Green, F. H. Bradley and Bernard Bosanquet in Britain; and Josiah Royce, G. S. Morris, W. T. Harris, J. G. Hibben, and J. G. Schurman in the United States. We may profitably examine a little more in detail the doctrines of some of the more important of these philosophers.

Even the romanticists were compelled to take account of scientific discoveries and to reason away any challenge to romanticist tenets that seemed to be embodied in the scientific method. Representative of this type of thought were the writings of Rudolf Hermann Lotze (1817-1881), who attempted to reconcile the new mechanistic theories with the dogmas of romanticism and idealism. He conceded that cause-and-effect relationships prevail in the mechanical realm of nature and suffice to explain scientific problems. But beyond and superior to the physical world lies the world of value, characterized by a spiritual unity which is absent from purely material phenomena. In exploring this world of spiritual values, the soul leads man to discover truth. By his emphasis on value, Lotze became one of the founders of the so-called "value philosophy," technically known as axiology. The term is derived from a Greek word meaning "things worthy," or of value. Others have explained it as justified by the fact that it is axiomatic that value and reality are identical.

One important outgrowth of Lotze's spiritualistic philosophy has come to be known as personal idealism (personalism). Its most influential representative, the German philosopher, Rudolph Eucken (1846-1926), opposed both materialism and absolutist idealism. He was himself mainly interested in the problems of spiritual redemption and personal adjustment to the cosmos. A popular American expositor of personalism was Borden Parker Bowne (1847-1910). The theories of Eucken and Bowne strongly influenced liberal Protestantism.

Lotze's conclusions were basically optimistic. Those of Arthur Schopenhauer (1788-1860) were decidedly pessimistic. Schopenhauer, like Lotze, held that natural science can investigate and explain the realm of external phenomena—the world as idea. Only intuition, however, can enable us to get at reality. When we follow intuition we discover that the ultimate reality is will. This absolute will is, however, irrational, and from this conclusion we must deduce an inescapable and all-pervading pessimism. Human wants, which motivate the will, outrun human satisfactions both in number and in duration. The worst possible evil that can befall us is to be born. It is utterly futile to strive for happiness. The only relief that man can secure from the irrational world of will is to be found in art, in the pure contemplation of ideas, and in an ascetic repression of natural impulses which gradually enables us to approach the Nirvana, or unconsciousness of the world and its problems. Schopenhauer had been impelled towards this last conclusion by his studies of Hindu mysticism.

Eduard von Hartmann (1842-1906) sought, as a follower of Schelling, to effect a synthesis of Hegel and Schopenhauer. His *Philosophy of the Unconscious* (1869)

was immensely popular. He laid great stress on the importance of the unconscious in both cosmic history and human thought. From Hegel he derived his
theory that civilization is advancing and culture evolving. But as culture im-
proves man himself becomes more miserable, thus demonstrating the truth of
Schopenhauer's pessimistic views. Evolution and pessimism are thus the twin
products of cultural progress and human experience.

In France, Victor Cousin (1792-1867) attempted a broad, eclectic synthesis not
only of Germanic philosophy but also of Cartesian thought. He was fairly successful in creating a systematic philosophy out of his many sources. He did much
to stimulate interest in the history of philosophy in France. In Britain, Sir William Hamilton (1788-1856), a Scotchman, replied to Hume's skepticism in his
Philosophy of the Unconditioned (1820) by reviving Kantian metaphysics and
ethics. Thomas Hill Green (1836-1882), in his introduction to Hume's philosophy
and his *Prolegomena to Ethics,* popularized in England an idealistic philosophy
based on Kant and Hegel. Francis Herbert Bradley (1846-1924) tried to effect
a synthesis of German idealism and the empiricism of Locke and Hume in his
Appearance and Reality by seeking reality in experience as revealed by personal
feeling. In his religious thought Bradley exhibited affinity with Hume's agnos-
ticism. Bradley held that to realize the self fully, it must be merged in the higher
and more complete life of the community. Bernard Bosanquet (1848-1923) returned to Hegelianism and acclaimed the power of philosophy to encompass reality and to give its attributes a logical formulation. Bosanquet was an influential
political philosopher. His *Philosophical Theory of the State* popularized in England the Hegelian theory of the state. He also made an important contribution
to the philosophy of aesthetics.

G. S. Morris introduced both Kant and Hegel to the United States, while
W. T. Harris, also famous as an educational reformer, championed Hegelian
thought. But far and away the most influential American expositor of German
idealism was the distinguished Harvard professor, Josiah Royce (1855-1916),
whose doctrines were set forth in his *Spirit of Modern Philosophy* (1892) and
The World and the Individual (1900). Royce reminds one in a way of Anselm,
who held that the very arguments of the atheist prove the existence of God.
Royce similarly contended that skepticism demonstrates the correctness of
idealism. In its assertion that human knowledge beyond the self (i.e., personal
experience) is impossible, Royce maintained that skepticism thereby demonstrates
the existence of a unique being in the universe, namely, God. Moreover, experience becomes intelligible only when interpreted as part of a divine plan in the
universe. Royce adopted the Hegelian position that ultimate reality is knowable
if viewed as a universal consciousness individuated into selves through the action
of the will. Royce agreed with Bradley that the most complete realization of the
self is its identification with a higher loyalty to the community and the state.

These doctrines are representative illustrations of the aftermath of German
romantic and idealistic philosophy. We may now turn to a brief consideration
of the more novel philosophies of the nineteenth century which reflected current
developments in science and social experience.

The first important philosophical synthesis of the nineteenth century was Auguste Comte's Positivism. His significant works were *The Principles of Positive Philosophy* and *The Principles of a Positive Polity*. Comte revived the Baconian idea of the importance of science in human life and social relationships, and tried to formulate laws for the various branches of science. These he crowned with a supreme new science, sociology, that drew upon all the other sciences in its effort to remold society. In aspiring to create a new social order, Comte combined the scientific outlook with the idealism which characterized social reformers. The latter wished to devise a plan which would take advantage of the benefits of industrialism while escaping its miseries. We have already described the nature of Comte's program of social reconstruction.

Another popular type of mid-nineteenth-century philosophy devoted to social reform was Utilitarianism, which we have already mentioned. It was given a substantial psychological and philosophical foundation by James Mill and his son, John Stuart Mill. The latter introduced into utilitarianism a considerable element of German idealism.

Of all the philosophies promoted by industrialism and the quest for social reform, Marxism was destined to become the most persistent and influential. We shall have more to say about it in a later chapter.

The most important contribution of natural science to nineteenth-century philosophy was the concept of evolution. We have already noted that Herbert Spencer was the chief protagonist of evolution. He set forth the basis of his system in his *First Principles* and applied his doctrines to the whole realm of human knowledge and social institutions in his many volumes on *Synthetic Philosophy,* covering biology, psychology, sociology, political science, ethics, and education. Spencer contended that ultimate reality—God, final causes and the like—is unknowable, and contented himself with showing how evolution governs the realm of the knowable. Spencerian evolutionism was amplified and popularized by his American disciple, John Fiske, in his widely read *Outlines of Cosmic Philosophy* (1874).

The extraordinary progress of natural science in the nineteenth century seemed to demand a basic work on scientific methodology, and John Stuart Mill attempted to supply this need in his *System of Logic* (1843). He aimed to complete the attack made upon deductive logic and scholasticism by Francis Bacon, and to fashion a satisfactory body of inductive and experimental logic as a basis of scientific philosophy. He took a broader view of the scientific process than Bacon did by allowing more room for hypotheses and deduction. While it contains incongruities and contradictions, Mill's book was probably the most influential English contribution of the century to the philosophical bases of the scientific method. The interrelations of natural science and the mental sciences, including philosophy and social science, were carefully studied by Dilthey, Windelband and Rickert. They gave special attention to the limitations and qualifications involved in any valid application of the principles and methods of natural science to the social sciences.

Several important American philosophers attempted to harmonize the new scientific attitudes with philosophical formulations. Among them were Charles S. Peirce (1839-1914), William James (1842-1910), and John Dewey (1859-1952). Peirce doubted the absolute character of scientific laws and suggested that our main criterion of truth is experience tested by experiment. James was not only well read in science but was also the foremost American psychologist of the nineteenth century. Hence, he was the first important philosopher who approached the problems of knowledge equipped with passable information about man's thinking machinery. He believed that human thought is primarily a tool for action, thus suggesting what has come to be known in Dewey's hands as the philosophy of instrumentalism. Recognizing that the human mind cannot fathom ultimates and arrive at any absolute assurance of reality, James accepted a practical test known as pragmatism, already suggested by Kant and Peirce. This, in a general way, means that the validity of an idea is to be tested by whether it seems to work out in practice. James rejected any attempt to achieve either a spiritual or a materialistic unity. He abandoned monism in favor of what he called pluralism, roughly resembling, in a more developed form, Montaigne's "hunch" that diversity is the rule of nature.

John Dewey was greatly affected by James' pragmatism and pluralism, but he differed from James in approaching philosophy from the logical and social point of view, whereas James's interests had been religious, ethical, and individualistic. Dewey went far beyond James in developing the theory of instrumentalism, which he made the real foundation of his philosophical system. He possessed much more social consciousness than James and aimed to put his philosophy to work in education, politics and society. He was a staunch supporter of democracy and was the most potent influence upon American education in the first quarter of the twentieth century. Dewey was also an enthusiastic Darwinist. Down to his day evolution had made its way into philosophy chiefly in the form of Spencerianism. Dewey clearly indicated the bearing of Darwinism on the reconstruction of philosophy. We shall have more to say about Dewey in dealing with twentieth-century philosophy. James's pragmatic views found an English protagonist in Ferdinand C. S. Schiller (1864-1937), whose most important works are *Humanism* and *Logic for Use*. Schiller called his variety of pragmatism, humanism. James's doctrines also attracted a great deal of attention in France.

One of the most interesting products of nineteenth-century philosophy was the system of thought propounded by the Frenchman, Henri Bergson (1859-1941). It was an original synthesis of certain aspects of German romanticism and idealism, with some regard for the scientific advances of the century. Bergson based his philosophy on the conception of a vital impulse—the *élan vital*—which is fundamental to all activity and to the creative spirit of the world-process. He stressed the element of time, change, and evolution to an even greater degree than Hegel did. Our consciousness is a continuous memory of the past, and the past is always impelling us to create new forms of thought and culture.

Thought, even scientific thought, is only a practical instrument for serving transient human needs. A knowledge of the phenomenal world, as studied by science, is necessary for our daily convenience and for guiding our conduct. But thought cannot lead us to reality. Bergson agreed with Schopenhauer that the only key to reality lies in intuition. Yet, to Bergson, intuition is more refined and precise than it was to Schopenhauer. It must reckon with science as its starting-point, and in due time intuition will come to be regarded as the highest form of empirical reasoning. As such, intuition is to human (scientific) thought much as the sun illuminating the world is to a glimmering lantern in a dark tunnel. Consistency with his general philosophy impelled Bergson into mystical flights, such as his conception of a vitalistic monism and his dogma that the consciousness of man, as an unbroken heritage from the past, must survive the death of individuals.

Friedrich Nietzsche (1844-1900) was one of the most provocative philosophers of the nineteenth century. He combined the axiology (value philosophy) of Lotze with the voluntarism (will philosophy) of Schopenhauer. He made value the fundamental concept in his philosophy and proposed a reconsideration of values. Whereas many, especially the utilitarians and the democrats, sought the supreme value in the work of the masses, Nietzsche held that the finer values can come only from individual heroes. Hence, the *Herrenmoral,* the ethical values of the aristocrat, is on a different and higher plane from the *Sklavenmoral,* the ethical values of the masses. This conception of values conducted Nietzsche to voluntarism, expressed in his notion of the "will to power," the basic impulse which guides the superman in his effort to create the highest values. Nietzsche was highly critical of Christianity, which he looked upon as embodying the essentials of the despised *Sklavenmoral.*

As a result of his approval of the ruthless triumph of the strong over the weak, Nietzsche has often been regarded as espousing a perverted form of Darwinism. This is not accurate, for Nietzsche did not accept evolution in either the Spencerian or the Darwinian sense. His view of progress was a curious combination of evolution with the antique theory of cycles of development. In each cycle we go through an evolutionary process, but in due time we return to the same starting-point. In this respect, there is a resemblance between Nietzsche's philosophy of history and that of Oswald Spengler which became very popular in the pessimistic period after the first World War.

VI. EDUCATIONAL TRADITION AND PEDAGOGICAL PROGRESS IN THE NINETEENTH CENTURY

Education in the nineteenth century became more extensive and diversified. Among the outstanding features of educational development were the secularization of education and teaching, and the introduction of universal education. Down to the nineteenth century education had been, in considerable part, in the hands of the church and hence religion was a prominent part of its content. The Protestant revolution had weakened the power of the Catholic church in education in Protestant lands. Protestantism, indeed, tended to encourage state control of education. But even in Protestant countries ecclesiastical forces were prominent in education until well along in the nineteenth century, when education became increasingly a state function and was concerned with economic and political life, as well as with secular literature and art.

Perhaps no single force exerted a greater influence in secularizing education than industrialism. Industrialism stimulated democracy, which created a self-conscious proletariat determined to secure educational advantages for their children, and it encouraged the introduction of more practical and technical subjects into the curriculum. The class interests which it produced gave rise to the more important educational controversies, and to many battles over academic freedom. The urbanization which industrialism created deeply affected educational movements, since most of the educational innovations were urban developments.

The declining influence of the church in education was logically paralleled by the increasing prominence of the state. During the nineteenth century there was unprecedented agitation for free, universal, and compulsory education. This was stimulated by the growth of democracy, but even monarchical states promoted public education. In fact, the first important step towards public education was taken by the benevolent despot, Frederick the Great, in 1763, when he published a decree establishing a public school system and making attendance compulsory. It required over thirty years to execute this plan because of opposition from the clergy and other conservative forces. A law of 1794 conclusively set up compulsory education in Prussia, and in 1811 the school system was put under the direction of the great geographer, Alexander von Humboldt. Prussian schools were expanded and strengthened by subsequent legislation, particularly the laws of 1825, 1854, and 1872.

The French revolutionists at the close of the eighteenth century were enthusiastic about public education, and started an excellent school system, later distorted by Napoleon. A national normal school and a number of secondary schools were, however, established in 1794, and the University of France was created in 1806 to control public education in the land. Elementary public education began in France in 1833, mainly as a result of the support received from the eminent historian François Guizot (1787-1874), who was then minister of public instruction. The Third Republic was especially favorable to public education, and free compulsory primary education was provided in 1881-1882. Jules Ferry took the lead in organizing French education at this time. The law of 1886 thoroughly centralized French public education. From then on, public schools rapidly superseded church schools, and early in the twentieth century most French church schools were closed by hostile legislation.

During the nineteenth century little was achieved in England in the way of establishing a real system of free education. Not until 1833 did the government begin to support education. In that year, the government began to make grants for educational purposes to church and other private educational foundations. This policy was pursued with increasing liberality during the rest of the century. The first elementary schools were provided in the education act of 1870, proposed by William E. Forster, but they were for a long time far outnumbered by the private schools that enjoyed state aid. Compulsory education was introduced by an act of 1876. In 1899 a central board of education was created. Not until 1918, however, was a passably adequate public school system set up in England. In the United States, though Thomas Jefferson had advocated public education, it made little headway until the era of Andrew Jackson. The most important figures in the struggle for free public education in the United States were James Gordon Carter (1795-1849), Horace Mann (1796-1859) and Henry Barnard (1811-1900). The first law providing for free public education was passed in Pennsylvania in 1834. In the following half-century free compulsory public education was established in most American states. Mann created a model school system in Massachusetts following 1837. Education ceased to be a privilege of the few and became the right of every child, however humble his economic circumstances. Some enlightened states also aided the movement for public education by laws restricting the working-hours of children in industry.

In Catholic countries the church still exerts a dominant control over all but higher education, wisely deciding that this is the surest way to maintain the fidelity and loyalty of its flock. Even in Protestant countries like the United States, where full religious freedom exists, there are, however, numerous parochial schools.

Another important educational innovation of the nineteenth century was the establishment of a thoroughly graduated school system covering the entire educational evolution of the individual, the kindergarten for the pre-school child, the elementary school, grammar school, and secondary or high school. If fortunate, a boy might proceed to college, where he could obtain a bachelor of arts degree based on a so-called liberal curriculum. Towards the end of the nineteenth century graduate schools were created in great universities, where young scholars might advance from college work to specialized study under experts. The development of graduate schools first became notable in Germany early in the nineteenth century and were then introduced into other countries, especially the United States. Higher education was also slowly opened to women in the last half of the nineteenth century.

With the increasing importance of public education, a real need arose for professionally trained teachers. To meet this demand, special teacher-training schools were created. At first they were somewhat superficial "normal schools" with relatively short terms of instruction. But in due time respectable teachers' colleges were established, which provided thorough instruction in the theories and methods of education. The first state normal school was opened in Albany, New York, in 1844. Education also became a department of instruction in universities, schools of education being frequently set up within them.

Until the end of the nineteenth century elementary and grammar schools were chiefly devoted to rudimentary subjects such as reading, writing, arithmetic, and grammar. But in the secondary schools, and especially in the colleges and universities, the curriculum was considerably modified during the century. In the year 1800 the curriculum in the institutions of higher learning reflected primarily the influence of medievalism and humanism. That is, instruction was chiefly limited to grammar, rhetoric, logic, Greek and Latin literature, and mathematics. Attacks on religion in the latter part of the eighteenth century had also stimulated the creation of courses in "Christian evidences," the character of which we have already described.

The first important changes in the curriculum consisted of instruction in vernacular languages and literature. Next came a gradual introduction of natural science, often established as accessory to departments of mathematics. Germany took the lead in making a place for natural science, while English colleges and universities were most stubborn in resisting this trend. Latest of all came history and the social sciences, such as economics, politics, sociology, anthropology, and ethics. While adequate courses in these subjects had been established in Germany by the time of the American civil war and had gained some headway in France at this period, English and American higher education neglected them until the closing decades of the nineteenth century. Indeed, no sociology course was offered in any English college or university until the first decade of the twentieth century.

In spite of concessions to new studies, the older subjects which came down from the Middle Ages and the era of humanism were given distinct advantages in the curriculum. Students were required to devote most of their time to them. Natural or social science, even if taught, played a minor rôle. Although Thomas Jefferson advocated a modernization of the curriculum when he founded the University of Virginia, it was not until 1869 that the so-called elective system, giving the student some freedom of choice, was introduced at Harvard by President Charles W. Eliot in the face of severe and even malicious criticism. But even under the elective system large doses of traditional subject matter were required for the bachelor of arts degree. Hence, in spite of these evidences of a growing discontent with the old system of education and with traditional subjects, higher education still had little relation to everyday life at the end of the nineteenth century. Nobody made this clearer than Thomas Henry Huxley, who delivered the following stinging indictment of English education:

Now let us pause to consider this wonderful state of affairs; for the time will come when Englishmen will quote it as the stock example of the stolid stupidity of their ancestors in the nineteenth century. The most thoroughly commercial people, the greatest voluntary wanderers and colonists the world has ever seen, are precisely the middle classes of this country. If there be a people which has been busy making history on the great scale for the last three hundred years,— and the most profoundly interesting history,—history which, if it happened to be that of Greece or Rome, we should study with avidity—it is the English. If there be a people which, during the same period, has developed a remarkable literature, it is our own.

If there be a nation whose prosperity depends absolutely and wholly upon their mastery over the forces of nature, upon their intelligent apprehension of and obedience to, the laws of creation, and distribution of wealth, and of the stable equilibrium of the forces of society, it is precisely this nation. And yet this is what these wonderful people tell their sons:

"At the cost of from one to two thousand pounds of our hard-earned money, we devote twelve of the most precious years of your lives to school. There you shall toil, or be supposed to toil; but there you shall not learn one single thing of all those you will most want to know directly you leave school and enter upon the practical business life. You will in all probability go into business, but you shall not know where, or how, any article of commerce is produced, or the difference between an export and an import, or the meaning of the word 'capital.' You will very likely settle in a colony, but you shall not know whether Tasmania is part of New South Wales, or *vice versa*. . . . Very probably you may become a manufacturer, but you shall not be provided with the means of understanding the working of one of your own steam engines, or the nature of the raw products you employ; and, when you are asked to buy a patent, you shall not have the slightest means of judging whether the inventor is an impostor who is contravening the elementary principles of science or a man who will make you as rich as Croesus. You will very likely get into the House of Commons. You will have to take your share in making laws which may prove a blessing or a curse to millions of men. But you shall not hear one word respecting the political organization of your country; the meaning of the controversy between free traders and protectionists shall never have been mentioned to you; you shall not so much as know that there are such things as economical laws. The mental power which will be of most importance in your daily life will be the power of seeing things as they are without regard to authority; and of drawing accurate general conclusions from particular facts. But at school and at college you shall know of no source of truth but authority; nor exercise your reasoning faculty upon anything but deduction from that which is laid down by authority. You will have to weary your soul with work, and many a time eat your bread in sorrow and in bitterness, and you shall not have learned to take refuge in the great source of pleasure without alloy, the serene resting place for worn human nature,—the world of art."

Said I not rightly that we are a wonderful people? I am quite prepared to allow that education entirely devoted to these omitted subjects might not be a completely liberal education. But is an education which ignores them all a liberal education? Nay, is it too much to say that the education which should embrace these [neglected] subjects and no others would be a real education, though an incomplete one; while an education which omits them is really not an education at all, but a more or less useful course of intellectual gymnastics? [10]

Throughout the nineteenth century there was considerable talk about the so-called liberal education in the higher institutions of learning. But the word "liberal," as thus used, in no way meant progressive, free, or flexible education. It referred to the seven liberal arts, to which were added classical languages and higher mathematics. A liberal education, in this sense, was then and still is the very negation of liberalism as the term is used outside of educational jargon.

The nineteenth century was also notable for the establishment of various types of professional schools offering such courses as law, medicine, engineering, fine arts. Of course, schools of theology, law, medicine, and business existed in the Middle Ages, and in many areas these continued into modern times. In the nineteenth century these professional schools became more numerous, more adequate and better equipped.

The importance of applied science and machinery demanded efficient technical

---

[10] Cited in Monroe, *Text-book in the History of Education*, pp. 690-91. See also the observations on English education in the latter half of the nineteenth century by H. G. Wells in his *Experiment in Autobiography*, Macmillan, 1934.

education. The earliest engineering instruction was given mainly in military schools as a phase of army engineering. Military academies providing some engineering training were established in Vienna in 1747, at Mézières in France in 1749, at Berlin in 1764, and at West Point in 1802. The first nonmilitary engineering school was established in Brunswick, Germany, in 1745, and another was opened in Freiburg in 1765. In the nineteenth century many civilian engineering schools were created, and by the end of the century these became fairly numerous and highly efficient. The first general engineering school devoted solely to civilian engineering was the Rensselaer Polytechnic Institute, opened in 1824 at Troy, New York. A number of specialized schools devoted to the fine arts appeared during the century, the first and most famous being the *École des Beaux Arts,* opened in Paris in 1793.

The industrialization of modern society created intensive economic rivalry between nations. Therefore alert countries quickly saw the value of giving vocational training which would produce more efficient workers. In the nineteenth century, instruction in manual training, needlework, cooking, agriculture, horticulture, and commerce was introduced into both public and private schools. Night schools were established to make these advantages available to those who work during the day. Continuation schools were set up to allow students to supplement their academic education with vocational training.

Natural science, which exerted so wide an influence upon nineteenth-century religion and philosophy, also affected education. The doctrine of evolution was introduced into psychology and pedagogy. It was shown that the human race underwent mental as well as physical evolution, and that we have mental as well as physical affinities with other animals.

Apprehension of the fact that every person passes through an impressive mental evolution from the blank mentality of the newborn infant to the fully developed adult mind led pedagogues to emphasize the child's mind and to recognize certain parallelisms between the evolution of the human mind in general and that of the individual. An American scholar, G. Stanley Hall, whom we have already discussed in this chapter in connection with the development of psychology in the nineteenth century, was chiefly responsible for linking evolutionary biology with psychology and education.

Though science made but slow headway against the stubborn resistance of the humanities, by the end of the nineteenth century scientific subjects had been thoroughly installed in most institutions of higher learning. Interestingly enough, the United States took the lead in this respect, owing, probably, to the fact that in a new country vested educational interests had less of a stranglehold upon pedagogy. As early as 1642 Harvard University offered instruction in astronomy and botany, and in 1690 in physics. Liberal concessions were made to natural science in Columbia University (King's College) in 1755, and in the University of Pennsylvania in 1756. The normal school established in Paris in 1794. provided some instruction in mathematics and physics. It was not until 1825, however, that a scientific (chemical) laboratory was opened even in a German university—the laboratory of Professor Justus von Liebig at the University of Giessen.

Courses in science were not established at Oxford or Cambridge until 1869, although scientific instruction was offered in the technical schools founded in England in the middle of the century.

The United States also took the lead in introducing science into the secondary schools. Scientific subjects were taught in many American academies before the American Revolution. Science was introduced into German secondary education in 1816. Some English secondary schools welcomed scientific subjects around 1835, before they could get a real footing in either Oxford or Cambridge. In no country, however, did natural science assume a position of equality with the older "disciplinary" and literary subjects in either higher or secondary education.

Important advances were made in educational theory. The earliest nineteenth-century pedagogical doctrines were an outgrowth of the theories of Rousseau and Basedow which we noted in an earlier chapter. Heinrich Pestalozzi (1756-1827) "made positive and concrete the negative and general educational principles enunciated by Rousseau." He believed that the pedagogue should follow nature and pay attention to the normal development of a child's personality. He defined education as "the natural, progressive and harmonious development of all the powers and capacities of the human being." Pestalozzi was, however, a somewhat eccentric character and not an "accepted scholar," and therefore his principles were resisted by those who demanded "soundness" and erudition in educational leadership.

This difficulty was remedied by Johann Friedrich Herbart (1776-1841), who brought Pestalozzi's doctrines into accord with reputable learning and with such psychological principles as existed. Herbart thus established Rousseau's doctrines in formal pedagogy, but he still viewed educational problems primarily from the standpoint of the teacher. He laid special stress on "apperception," holding that pupil interest could not be aroused or sustained unless the material presented was related to the student's previous knowledge and interests.

These ideas were adopted with important modifications by Friedrich Froebel (1782-1852), who was especially influenced by Pestalozzi. The great pedagogical revolution that we associate with Froebel was his insistence that the child rather than the teacher must constitute the starting-point of education, thus reversing Herbart's point of view. Froebel believed, like Rousseau, that successful education consists of a shrewd, intelligent, and tolerant guidance of the spontaneous tendencies of the child. Froebel thus placed logical emphasis upon education of the emotions as well as the intellect. He looked upon the educational process as successfully directed self-activity. He established the first kindergarten (1839) and organized the first experimental school. No other man of his day was so influential in assaulting the older cut-and-dried disciplinary education. In short, Froebel transformed Rousseau's vague aspirations into a formal system of education. Froebel's own work was limited chiefly to the theory of kindergarten instruction, but his doctrines were later extended to all stages of education.

Froebel's theories were vitally supplemented by the development of biology and reliable child psychology, particularly by G. Stanley Hall and his disciples.

This gave us a better knowledge of the true child personality, thus eliminating much of Rousseau's romantic idealism.

Another outstanding influence upon educational theory was derived from the teachings of sociology in the work of Comte, Spencer, Lester F. Ward, F. H. Giddings, and others. These sociologists laid great stress upon the social basis of human life and the way in which group life creates our ideas, customs, and institutions. Sociologists looked upon education as the only available means of attaining rational social control, and viewed it as a medium through which social traditions may be criticized, sorted, and transmitted. Finally, Lester F. Ward and his followers believed that education would enable man artificially to control the course of social evolution and create a happier world. In this way sociology, while not ignoring the individual teacher or pupil, laid the necessary emphasis upon the social basis of the life of both teacher and student.

The democratic movement in the nineteenth century was closely linked to education. The first ardent champion of free education was James Gordon Carter, who prepared the way for the work of Horace Mann. Of the latter, Joy Elmer Morgan writes:

> Mann was convinced that "in a Republic ignorance is a crime." So clearly did he visualize the school system which would develop educated citizens that for more than a century the states have moved more or less steadily in the direction he indicated. He knew that sanitary and comfortable buildings were necessary to the health of the children. Teachers who had been given special preparation for their work were essential in the improvement of the curriculum. Statewide supervision was the first step in the provision of equal opportunities for all children. Finally, the people themselves must be won to the support of the whole enterprise. Step by step, he worked to carry out his plan.[11]

The critical date in Mann's career—and in American education as a whole—was 1837, when he became secretary of the newly established Massachusetts board of education, which Carter had created. Mann worked out a school system ideal for the time. It was widely imitated by other states and foreign countries.

Mann's work was supplemented by Henry Barnard. Though Barnard took a prominent part in practical educational reforms and held responsible administrative positions, such as state superintendent of schools in Connecticut—he was also the first United States commissioner of education—his most important contribution was the foundation of the *American Journal of Education* in 1855. Realizing that American education could not progress as it should without full knowledge of what was being done in the whole educational field, he used his journal to give a complete account of educational developments in both Europe and America. Meanwhile, Carter agitated for normal schools to train teachers.

Democratic theorists asserted that apparent differences in ability and success are due primarily to differences in opportunity. If educational opportunity were equalized, children would show equal ability and achieve relatively uniform success. Education thus seemed the logical avenue to the speedy attainment of

[11] I. E. Morgan, *Horace Mann: His Ideas and His Ideals*, National Home Library, 1937, p. 19.

utopia. While this optimism was subsequently modified, the democratic movement is responsible for providing free public instruction from elementary schools to colleges and universities. In the twentieth century, the democratic educational ideals were linked up with scientific psychology and pedagogy by John Dewey and his associates.

These are only the main aspects of educational progress in the nineteenth century. In spite of it, archaic tradition, pompous pedantry, specious "good taste," and solemn formalism were all too powerful even in the year 1900. But a decisive breach had been made in tradition, and education was started on its way towards becoming a technique for the rational and successful control of human life.

VII. THE DIFFERENTIATION, EMERGENCE, AND DEVELOPMENT OF THE SOCIAL SCIENCES

The nineteenth century not only witnessed incomparable developments in the natural sciences, it also ushered in our social sciences, which are devoted to the accurate study of human relationships. From this time onward social analysis no longer had to depend upon either guesswork or revelation.

The importance attached to social science has varied with the emphasis laid upon man as a member of a secular group. Before the Greeks, supernaturalism was too powerful to allow for a matter-of-fact study of man and society. Nor was there any knowledge available for such study. The highly developed Greek centers of civilization achieved a remarkable degree of secularism. The Greek skeptics rejected supernaturalism and became interested in man as man. The Sophists, Plato, Aristotle, the Stoics, and Lucretius made many valuable contributions to the analysis of social relationships. But they did not possess enough scientific knowledge to go very far towards establishing real social sciences. The classical attitude towards man and his problems, much like that of the rationalists of the eighteenth century, did, however, encourage the study of man and society. Moreover, the Greek and Roman writers created political philosophy, which embraced all the social sciences down to the end of the eighteenth century. Plato's *Republic,* Aristotle's *Politics,* and Cicero's *De republica* and *De legibus* represent the most distinguished products of antique political philosophy.

With the triumph of Christianity, interest in social science declined rapidly. Man was of importance as the custodian of an immortal soul and not as a gregarious being. This attitude persisted for almost fifteen hundred years. Theology occupied the place held today by social science. Man's social relationships were important mainly as they affected salvation in the world to come.

A number of factors contributed to a changed attitude and the rise of the social sciences between 1700 and 1850. The deists stressed the dignity of man. The humanitarians, from the Abbé de Saint-Pierre to Helvétius and Bentham, concentrated their interests upon the good life here and now. Psychology, biology, and anthropology inaugurated the scientific study of human behavior and institutions. The theory of progress challenged the special-creation hypothesis and the Christian epic, and emphasized the dynamic factors in civilization. The industrial revolution dislocated social institutions, and attracted special attention to a study of these changes and their consequences.

In the nineteenth century the social sciences split off from their parent stem, political philosophy. From Plato to Saint-Simon, the study of the state, economics, international relations, ethics, and the like, was comprised in the body of subject matter known as political philosophy. Plato's *Republic,* Aristotle's *Politics,* Marsiglio's *Defensor Pacis,* Dante's *De monarchia,* Bodin's *Commonwealth,* and Pufendorf's *Law of Nature and of Nations* are good examples of this traditional but comprehensive subject.

The need for a broad fundamental social science was first thoroughly recognized by Saint-Simon at the very opening of the nineteenth century. He saw that some scientific method must be provided to determine the validity of the various programs of social reform suggested by the miseries of the industrial revolution. His disciple, Auguste Comte, established such a science and called it sociology, or the science of social life. Comte was deeply concerned with social reform, and projected an ideal society, in which intellectual direction would be furnished by sociologists, practical control by business men, and moral stimulus by women.

The most influential sociologist of the nineteenth century was Herbert Spencer. He used the evolutionary hypothesis to explain the nature and history of human society, and argued vigorously against conscious attempts to shape the future of humanity. He declared that social progress must be an automatic process of evolution. Man will only muddle matters and delay progress if he attempts to interfere. His ideas were warmly embraced by the American sociologist, William Graham Sumner. Spencer's theory that social progress must be spontaneous was vigorously attacked by Lester F. Ward, the outstanding American sociologist of the century. Ward believed that the chief purpose of social science is to guide our efforts to create a more satisfactory social order.

Biology and the doctrine of evolution had a profound influence upon nineteenth-century sociology. One school, known as the organicists, devoted itself mainly to describing the alleged similarities between human society and the individual biological organism. The foremost members of this school were a Russian, Paul von Lilienfeld, and a German, Albert Schäffle. Another group of writers, led by the Polish sociologist, Ludwig Gumplowicz, misapplied Darwin's theory of the struggle for existence and contended that physical conflict (warfare) is the chief positive factor in human progress. This doctrine was vigorously attacked by a Russian sociologist, Jacques Novicow. He held that the struggle for existence should, as mankind advances, pass from physical warfare to cultural competition.

The doctrine of evolution was instrumental in creating another social science—anthropology, or the study of the development of the human body and the cultural evolution of the human race. As Professor R. R. Marett had defined the subject: "Anthropology is the whole history of man as fired and pervaded by the doctrine of evolution. Man in evolution—that is the subject in its full reach." Once Darwin and others had proved that man has evolved from lower organic types, scientists attempted to trace human evolution in detail. Physical anthropologists like Huxley, Broca, Topinard, and Haeckel studied human skeletons of widely varying age and structure and sought to reconstruct from these remains the story of the bodily evolution of man. Others, interested in the so-called prehistoric period, unearthed and classified man's stone, bone, copper, bronze, and iron artifacts, and designated by their use the early cultural ages. The most important pioneers in this field were Boucher de Perthes, Sir John Lubbock, and Gabriel de Mortillet. Herbert Spencer, Charles Letourneau, Lewis H. Morgan, E. B. Tylor, Julius Lippert, William Graham Sumner, and others, studied in detail the evolution of human ideas and social institutions.

The beginnings of the science of economics, or the study of man's wealth-getting and wealth-using activities, have been described in earlier sections on mercantilism and liberalism. The first important nineteenth-century economists were the so-called classical economists, Malthus, Ricardo, Senior, and James Mill, disciples of Adam Smith, who defended the new capitalism and the manufacturing class. They were fond of formulating abstract economic laws—since called "pecuniary logic"—which often had little relationship to actual economic facts, and usually favored the rising capitalist class. The classical economists were criticized by the German historical school, which emphasized the necessity of studying the evolution of economic institutions and of paying close attention to current economic life. An even more direct attack came from the welfare economists, led by Sismondi. Such writers held that economics should be a science of welfare, rather than of wealth, devoted to promoting the prosperity of the whole state, not merely of the capitalist class. Not until the latter part of the nineteenth century, when economists made thorough use of the statistical and historical methods, were they able to make their subject truly scientific. Far and away the most influential synthesis of nineteenth-century economic doctrine was the *Political Economy* of John Stuart Mill. While based primarily on the classical economics of Ricardo, it gave some attention to other trends, such as historical studies, social reform and statistical investigation.

As is usually the case in the development of a science, the first steps in the growth of political science involved definitions and classifications: (1) concentration upon the definition of political terms; and (2) classifications of states, forms of government and types of political institutions. Before institutional political history and the functional analysis of the state could proceed very far, it was necessary to have a uniform nomenclature and a clear understanding of political forms and types.

While this morphological stage may be legitimately criticized as formal and sterile, offering little insight into political processes and no guidance for political practice, we must not overlook its very real importance in the development of the subject.[12] Nevertheless, we should not mistake this preliminary stage of definition and classification for the mature perfection of political science.

[12] Among the writers most influential in forwarding work of this type should certainly be mentioned Jeremy Bentham, John Austin, J. K. Bluntschli, Robert von Mohl, J. G. Droysen, Paul Laband, Georg Jellineck, Heinrich Marquardsen, Francis Lieber, Theodore Dwight Woolsey, John W. Burgess, and W. W. Willoughby.

While the professional political scientists were thus absorbed, practical states-men like the Americans James Madison and John C. Calhoun suggested, in par-ticular, that government is fundamentally an adjustment between conflicting social and economic interests. The function of the government is to act as umpire in the conflict and see that justice is done. Much later, sociologists like Gustav Ratzen-hofer, A. W. Small, and A. F. Bentley emphatically supported views similar to those of Madison and Calhoun.

The first important step beyond formal classification and definition was a de-tailed description of contemporary political life, as in Alexis de Tocqueville's famous study of *Democracy in America,* published over a century ago. A half-century later appeared the more comprehensive *American Commonwealth* by the eminent English publicist, James Bryce.

Quite naturally, the question of the merits and the possibilities of democracy received wide attention. By and large, European political scientists in the last century assailed democracy and American writers defended it. There were, of course, exceptions, for democracy was not without European champions and American critics. Among the leading critics of democracy were Nietzsche, Henry Sumner Maine, W. E. H. Lecky, and Émile Faguet. It was defended by men like James Russell Lowell, E. L. Godkin, and Franklin Henry Giddings. As the nineteenth century drew to a close democracy acquired more supporters.

It was also inevitable that the triumph of party government in the last century would attract the attention of political scientists. The methods of nomination and election of officers, the nature and workings of the party machine, the genesis of platforms, party government in legislatures and committees, and the effect of party government on the several branches of government all demanded very care-ful investigation and analysis. The first successful effort to describe the formal workings of party government was Woodrow Wilson's *Congressional Govern-ment* (1885). James Bryce applied this method more in detail in certain sections of his *American Commonwealth.* The works of the Russian scholar, Moisei Ostrogorsky, on political parties represented the most elaborate development in this field of political writing.

Jurisprudence, or the science of law, passed through the same stages as did political science in the course of its development. We have already analyzed the natural-law theory which played a large part in the political and legal philosophy of the seventeenth and eighteenth centuries, and was revived to some extent late in the nineteenth century, when corporation lawyers and friendly judges appre-hended its great strategic value in defending the rights of private property.

More popular among lawyers today, however, is the so-called analytical juris-prudence which took form in the writings of Hobbes, Bentham, and Austin. This is concerned with the law as the command of a determinate superior, the state. It does not normally deal with such problems as the genesis of the state and law. Nor does it assign any importance to those social forces which create and uphold legal administration. It considers the actual nature of law, and attempts to ascertain its enforcement agents. John Austin (1790-1859) was the chief figure in this school. He attempted to divorce jurisprudence from ethics. Such a theory of law is useful to both judge and lawyer, and furnishes an admirable orientation for the purely legalistic study of constitutions. Among recent distinguished exponents of this doctrine was the well-known jurist T. E. Holland (1835-1926).

The weaknesses of the analytical school in failing to explore legal origins were overcome mainly by the historical and comparative schools. The historical school originated with such writers as Burke and Savigny, and developed in the works of Henry Sumner Maine, F. W. Maitland, Heinrich Brunner, J. C. Carter, and Frederick Pollock. This school looks upon law as the product of a nation's cultural development. Law is the gradually accumulated, selected, and codified wisdom of the nation. In modern times, law may be mainly legislative enactment, but both the legal system as a whole and contemporary legislation are determined primarily by antecedent national history and by existing social institutions.

The so-called comparative school of jurisprudence established by Montesquieu simply expands the historical method. It contends that the "wisdom of a nation" is rarely accumulated by that nation alone. Cultural borrowing is as characteristic of legal as of other institutions. Hence the great legal systems of the world from the code of Hammurabi to the German imperial code of 1900 must be studied by the comparative and historical methods. Comparative anthropologists of the last century like Lubbock, Tylor, Lippert, Post, Letourneau, and Morgan encouraged this view, whose chief exponents were, however, Joseph Kohler and Sir Paul Vinogradoff. No sharp line divides the historical and the comparative jurists; men like Pollock and Maitland wrote monumental works on comparative jurisprudence, and Vinogradoff on historical jurisprudence.

We have already noted how, in the seventeenth and eighteenth centuries, ethics, or the science of conduct, was gradually divorced from religion and became more dependent upon science and art. This trend was greatly accelerated in the nineteenth century. Yet the orthodox coalition of ethics and theology received powerful support to the very end of the century. Immanuel Kant became a bulwark of the orthodox school of ethics. He held that we should postulate a God in order to make moral conduct seem rational. We should be good for the sake of goodness alone and not because we may hope thereby to increase our own happiness or the welfare of society. Kant's doctrines were eagerly embraced by religious groups, particularly by Protestants inclined towards some degree of modernism.

The school of conventional moralists was also supported by capitalist sympathizers. We have already noted that the Puritans laid great stress upon Sunday observance and the suppression of carnal impulses. The new industrialists ruthlessly exploited their laborers by working them long hours in intolerable surroundings and for low wages. In other ways, as well, they showed little regard for human happiness or for the well-being of the masses. They were interested primarily in piling up large fortunes for themselves by any lawful means.

If ethics were to embrace economic morality, they recognized that they would fare very badly. Hence their apologists attempted to restrict morality mainly to sexual behavior, where wealth would be able to protect its possessors from being detected in sin. It is not irrelevant to note that the chief society for the suppression of sexual immorality, founded in the late nineteenth century, was chiefly subsidized by one of the world's greatest bankers.

Economic self-interest played its part in capitalistic ethical theory. The capitalist employers thought their employees should be "good," because they associated morality with industrial efficiency. All that goes by the name of vice demands leisure and consumes emotional and physical resources. Whatever the laborers spend in sensation is lost to industry. The enthusiastic support of prohibition by great industrialists illustrates this attitude, which, in general, was a powerful obstacle to the introduction of secular ethics during the nineteenth century.

The two progressive schools of ethics of the century were the utilitarians and evolutionists. As we have seen, Bentham and Mill, the leading utilitarians, contended that good conduct is what advances the greatest happiness of the greatest number of men here on earth. The evolutionist, Spencer, believed that in order to discover the ultimate good we must examine the nature of man, physically and mentally, in its evolutionary aspects. Those things which contribute to bodily strength and mental growth are virtuous forms of behavior. Whatever operates to the contrary is evil. Thomas Henry Huxley agreed with Spencer, but held that in our day mankind may possibly control the evolutionary process so as to make it less harsh to humanity. The doctrines of the utilitarian and evolutionary schools were combined by Leslie Stephen, who attempted to formulate a naturalistic theory of conduct as rigorous and exacting as any other branch of science. His *Science of Ethics* was the most competent and representative statement of the naturalistic attitude towards conduct which was formulated in the nineteenth century. It was comparable to Hume's achievements in the previous century.

There were, however, other interesting additions to ethical doctrine during the nineteenth century. The aspiration to make beauty and art the basis of moral judgments, suggested by Lord Shaftesbury early in the eighteenth century, was revived with force and eloquence by John Ruskin and William Morris. A sociological theory of morality was suggested by Auguste Comte and Lester F. Ward, who held that moral questions should be directly related to social welfare and human progress, without the consideration of supernatural factors.

We pointed out that in the eighteenth century Montesquieu contended that there is no such thing as absolute right and wrong. Various geographical conditions create special social situations which require compatible types of institutions and conduct. What is right is what best suits a given social condition. Montesquieu thus founded what we know as the comparative school of ethics, whose tenets were elaborately illustrated in the nineteenth century by students of historical and comparative jurisprudence and by anthropologists and anthropogeographers. The most notable book embodying this view of ethics was W. G. Sumner's *Folkways,* which appeared early in the twentieth century.

During most of the nineteenth century the leading historians regarded history as more a branch of literature than a social science. Romanticism stimulated patriotism, and the outstanding historians of the century wrote from an ardently patriotic point of view. While usually more accurate than the earlier Romanticist historians, their patriotic fervor impelled them to write moving and brilliant histories of their lands and heroes. We may now characterize the works of some of the more important of these nationalistic historians.

Wilhelm von Giesebrecht (1814-1889) wrote a glowing account of Germany under the medieval Holy Roman Empire; Johann Gustav Droysen (1804-1884) showered admiration on the Hohenzollerns who founded Prussia; Heinrich von Treitschke (1834-1896) praised Prussian leadership in the nineteenth century; and Heinrich von Sybel (1817-1895) denounced the French Revolution and wrote a eulogy of Bismarck's unification of the second German Empire.

In France, Fustel de Coulanges (1830-1889) tried to combat the idea of Germanic leadership in the Middle Ages and praised Gallic culture; Joseph Michaud (1767-1839) gloried in France's part in the Crusades; François Mignet (1796-1884) lauded the French Revolution; a whole school of historians praised Napoleon; and Victor Duruy (1811-1894) and Henri Martin (1810-1883) told with pride the whole story of French development from Caesar to the French Republic.

In England, John M. Kemble (1807-1857) lauded Anglo-Saxon England; Edward A. Freeman (1823-1892) pointed with pride to medieval England, especially Norman England; Thomas Babington Macaulay (1800-1859) wrote brilliantly on the rise of the Whigs and the "Glorious Revolution" of 1688; Sir John R. Seeley (1834-1895) described the growth of British empire and sea-power; and John Richard Green (1837-1883) produced a deservedly popular history of the English people and their culture.

The United States also had its eminent patriotic historians. George Bancroft (1800-1891) majestically traced the story of American colonization, revolt from Britain, and the foundation of a new government; Francis Parkman (1823-1893) did justice to the rôle of France in America; William H. Prescott (1796-1859) produced literary masterpieces on the Spanish penetration of Mexico and Peru; and John Fiske (1842-1901) wrote of our national development as a phase of Germanic and Anglo-Saxon genius.

Patriotic pride also impelled historians to compile vast collections of national historical source-materials, such as the *Monumenta Germaniae historica;* the French *Documents inédits;* the English *Rolls Series,* and the like.

The increasing interest in history, which patriotism inspired, encouraged the growth of historical scholarship. Led by the great German scholar, Leopold von Ranke (1795-1886), historians sought to write history in exact accordance with the facts. Such historians as Gabriel Monod, Charles Seignobos, C. V. Langlois, and Charles Bémont, in France; Bishop Stubbs, S. R. Gardiner, C. W. C. Oman, T. F. Tout, and F. W. Maitland, in England; Georg Waitz, Wilhelm Oncken, Moritz Ritter, and Erich Marcks, in Germany; and H. B. Adams, H. L. Osgood, G. B. Adams, Edward Channing, W. A. Dunning, G. S. Ford, C. H. Haskins, G. L. Burr, and H. E. Bolton in the United States—all followed the ideals of von Ranke.

These disciples of von Ranke were more reliable than the great patriotic historians, but they were rarely able to write as picturesquely as their nationalistic predecessors. So the patriotic historians continued to remain more popular with the general public, while the scholarly historians gained greater sway over universities and learned circles generally.

Towards the end of the nineteenth century, historians, led by Karl Lamprecht (1856-1910) in Germany, came to regard history as one of the social sciences and held that it should tell the whole story of the growth of human civilization, instead of being content with the history of politics, wars and diplomacy.

SELECTED READINGS

Barnes, H. E., *Society in Transition,* Prentice-Hall, 1952.

Bates, E. S., and Dittemore, J. V., *Mary Baker Eddy,* Knopf, 1932.

Bewer, J. A., *The Literature of the Old Testament,* Columbia University Press, 1933.

Butts, R. F., *A Cultural History of Western Education,* McGraw-Hill, 1955.

Cajori, Florian, *History of Mathematics,* Macmillan.

———*History of Physics,* Dover Publications, Inc., 1962.

Carter, G. S., *A Hundred Years of Evolution,* Macmillan, 1958.

Dorfman, Joseph, *Thorstein Veblen and His America,* Viking, 1934.

Dunning, *History of Political Theories: From Rousseau to Spencer.*

Eby and Arrowood, *The Development of Modern Education,* chaps. xvi-xxii.

Fairchild, H. P., *Profits or Prosperity?,* Harper, 1932.

Gates, P. W., *The Farmer's Age:1850-1860,* Holt, Rinehart and Winston, 1961.

Hayes, C. J. H., *Nationalism: A Religion,* Macmillan, 1960.

Hinsley, F. H., ed., *Material Progress and World-Wide Problems, 1870-1898,* Cambridge, 1962.

Hobhouse, L. T., *Liberalism,* London, 1912.

Hofstadter, Richard, *Social Darwinism in American Thought,* Beacon, 1955.

Kohn, Hans, *The Age of Nationalism,* Harper, 1962.

Laidler, H. W., *Social-Economic Movements,* Crowell, 1944.

Loisy, A. F., *My Duel with the Vatican,* Dutton, 1924.

McGiffert, *The Rise of Modern Religious Ideas.*

Mantoux, P. J., *The Industrial Revolution in the Eighteenth Century,* Harcourt, Brace, 1928.

Mead, G. H., *Movements of Thought in the Nineteenth Century,* Chicago, 1936.

Merz, J. T., *History of European Thought in the Nineteenth Century,* 4 vols.

Monroe, *Textbook in the History of Education,* chaps. xi-xiv.

Murphy, Gardner, *Historical Introduction to Modern Psychology,* Harcourt, Brace.

Perkins, M. L., *The Moral and Political Philosophy of the Abbé de Saint-Pierre,* Geneva, 1959.

Perry, R. B., *The Thought and Character of William James,* Harvard University Press.

Post, Albert, *Popular Free Thought in America, 1825-1850,* Columbia Press, 1943.

Riley, *From Myth to Reason,* Book V.

Rukeyser, Muriel, *Williard Gibbs,* Doubleday, 1942.

Russell, Bertrand, *History of Western Philosophy,* Simon and Schuster, 1945.

Schneider, H. W., *History of American Philosophy,* Columbia University Press, 1946.

Shryock, R. H., *The Development of Modern Medicine,* Knopf, 1947.

Tawney, R. H., *The Acquisitive Society,* Harcourt, Brace, 1946.

Thomas, Franklin, *The Environmental Basis of Society,* Appleton, 1924.

Thompson, *History of Historical Writing,* Vol. II, Book VIII.

Trattner, E. R., *Unravelling the Book of Books,* Scribner, 1929.

Ulich, Robert, *History of Educational Thought,* American Book Company, 1945.

Van Wesep, H. B., *Seven Sages: The Story of American Philosophy,* Longmans, 1961.

Veblen, T. B., *The Theory of Business Enterprise,* New American Library.

———*The Theory of the Leisure Class,* New American Library.

White, E. A., *Science and Religion in American Thought,* Stanford Press, 1952.

Williams, H. S., *The Great Astronomers,* Simon and Schuster, 1930.

XXIV

*Literature and the Arts in the
Nineteenth Century*

I. LITERATURE: ROMANTICISM AND REALISM

The forces of change and counterchange, political, economic, scientific, religious, of the nineteenth century made their mark upon its literature, which on its higher planes sought to grapple with and resolve problems raised by these forces, or even to escape from these problems into "art for art's sake." On lower levels it sought merely to satisfy the demands of a vastly increased reading public. No century has produced so much worthless printed matter, but none has produced work of such variety.

As an earlier chapter has suggested, the romantic movement or romantic revolt which characterized the early years of the century cannot be limited in time or reduced to a descriptive phrase. It is anticipated in much eighteenth-century literature, and its influence persisted, despite later realism and naturalism, through the nineteenth century into our own time. Nor has the word "romantic" one meaning; it suggests rather certain ways of looking at man and the world characteristic of much, but not all, European literature during this period.

As we have seen earlier, the romantics tended to emphasize the importance of the individual, to be .more concerned with his emotions and desires than with critical or moralizing observations upon men in general, to place imagination over reason as a guide to truth. The romantic writer might seek in an unreal past or an ideal future escape from the world as it is. If he thought man naturally good, capable of creating a truly brave new world, political idealism might find a place in his writings. Or he might turn to the supernatural and the marvelous, or find in external nature not only beautiful forms and colors but spiritual impulses to which his own spirit responded.

Fresh themes needed fresh forms—a free rehandling of traditional ones, the creation of new ones, in language either more simple than the formal diction of the last age, or charged with imagery rich in color and suggestion. As was fitting in a literature so filled with the expression of personal feeling, the lyric attained a high position, while satirical and didactic poetry faded into a remoter background.

1. England

In 1798 William Wordsworth (1770-1850) and Samuel Taylor Coleridge (1772-1834) published *Lyrical Ballads,* an unpretentious small volume which later came to be recognized as a highly important landmark in the English romantic movement. For a second edition, in 1800, Wordsworth wrote a preface which is at once a credo and a manifesto, with its attack on eighteenth-century poetic diction, its theory of a simple and natural poetic speech, its emphasis on emotion in poetry.

Wordsworth's insistence that the language of poetry be as closely as possible that really used by men led him sometimes to write lines absurdly flat and prosy, but at its best his work is a perfect fusing of words and mood. This fusing is found in many short lyrics and sonnets, and in *Michael, Tintern Abbey,* the *Ode on Intimations of Immortality,* and his long spiritual autobiography, *The Prelude.* Quiet, smoothly flowing, never brilliantly adorned, his language is perfectly adapted to describing natural objects, reflecting seriously and intensely on man and nature, or mystical communing with nature. As a poet of nature he was not interested primarily in surface beauties, but in the ways by which a knowledge of nature, acquired from childhood through sense-impressions, might bring one in maturity to an awareness of the spirit which, he felt, flows through all living things; to hearing "the still sad music of humanity," and thus to greater love and sympathy for man himself. The restrained but by no means unimpassioned mood of his finest poetry is in these lines from *The Prelude* on a boyhood search for birds' nests:

> Oh! when I have hung
> Above the raven's nest, by knots of grass
> And half-inch fissures in the slippery rock
> But ill sustained, and almost (so it seemed)
> Suspended by the blast that blew amain,
> Shouldering the naked crag, oh, at that time
> While on the perilous ridge I hung alone,
> With what strange utterance did the loud dry wind
> Blow through my ear! the sky seemed not a sky
> Of earth—and with what motion moved the clouds!

As he grew older Wordsworth was increasingly concerned with moral and religious problems, though never losing his love of nature. Other changes affected his work. In early manhood both he and Coleridge had shared the revolutionary spirit of the age, and found high promise in the French Revolution. Their enthusiasm was chilled by the Reign of Terror and the rise of Napoleon, and their politics, together with their religion, increased in orthodoxy. But, despite hostile critics, neither was completely spoiled as a writer by political defection. Coleridge's weaknesses are due rather to temperamental shortcomings.

Tremendously read in many fields of knowledge, from ancient lores to the new German aesthetics and philosophy, a volcanic conversationalist, with a rare combination of intellect and imagination, Coleridge was inhibited by a lack of perseverance, an excessive fluidity of mind, a tendency to wander off into the thickets of metaphysics, to form vast and unattainable projects. Years of addiction to opium complicated these failings, although it is in part to this addiction that we owe the magic word-music of *Kubla Khan*. But his accomplishment was great, nevertheless, and gives him a sure place in English poetry and first place in English criticism. *The Ancient Mariner* succeeds better than any other English poem in giving reality and meaning to a story set among phantoms and specters, in lands of ice or in a windless sea where

> About, about, in reel and rout
> The death-fires danced at night;
> The water, like a witch's oils,
> Burnt green, and blue and white.

Christabel reflects the poet's interest in old legends and his skill as a metrist, while more personal poems contain his thoughts on himself, his family, and his friends. In *Dejection: An Ode* he uttered his grief at the decline of his "shaping spirit of imagination."

But it is as a critic who urged the supreme importance of the imagination that Coleridge has had his greatest influence, both for brilliant generalizations on the creation of poetry and estimates of specific works. His lectures on Shakespeare influenced his century, and still make fruitful reading. *Biographia Literaria,* his best-known prose work, contains, together with much misty speculation, admirable criticism of Wordsworth's theories of poetry.

The novels of Sir Walter Scott (1771-1832) will be mentioned later, but his place in the romantic movement may be indicated here. Unlike many contemporary writers, he was at no time in his life a radical in politics, but as a good Tory accepted the order of things as they were, admired the aristocratic traditions of Britain and the power of wealth and place. His interest as a writer was in the past, especially in the history of Scotland and Scottish legend. An antiquarian, he not only reconstructed this past in his own work, but made a large collection of ancient border ballads. His long narrative poems, like *The Lay of the Last Minstrel* or *Marmion,* are never subtle or intellectual, but, in simple and often galloping rhythms, tell stories of adventure and battle, with glittering trappings and a touch of magic and mystery. Better and more enduring as poetry are certain of his lyrics, in which he recaptures something of the spirit of old Scotch song; such are *Proud Maisie, Jock of Hazeldean, Pibroch of Donald Dhu.*

Scott, with George Gordon, Lord Byron, was the most influential of the English romantics outside England. But it was Byron (1788-1824), both in the legend and scandals which grew up around his life, and in his works, who typified for the age the romantic man. In *Childe Harold, Lara, Manfred,* and other narrative and dramatic poems the Byronic hero stalks, a half-veiled projection of the poet himself, a "pilgrim of eternity," "link reluctant in a fleshly chain," "proud though in desolation," bearing within him secret sin and secret sorrow, identifying his solitary spirit with the great forces of nature, mountains and oceans. This strange figure, so largely pose, fascinated the enthusiastic youth of Europe, as did the poet's attacks on tyranny and his death at Missolonghi during the Greek war of independence.

In such works as those mentioned Byron poured out swift, highly colored passages of description or action, purple patches like that in the third canto of *Childe Harold* picturing Brussels on the night before Waterloo. But he could assume another mood, smile at himself as "a broken dandy lately on my travels," and satirize the follies and pretensions of the world he knew, especially upper-class England. A lover of Pope, scornful of Wordsworth and Coleridge, he turned into such poems as *Beppo* and *Don Juan* (his greatest work) shrewd, amused observation of men and manners. Despite willful carelessness in language and organization, his style has a colloquial ease and concreteness which sets him apart from most of his contemporaries, and part of his charm is his fondness for digressing. He did not live to finish the already long *Don Juan*, with its rambling mixture of passionate escapades and satirical reflections on human behavior, its idyllic sentiment and cool common sense, characteristically juxtaposed in such a stanza as this on young Don Juan:

> He pored upon the leaves, and on the flowers,
>   And heard a voice in all the winds; and then
> He thought of wood-nymphs, and immortal bowers,
>   And how the goddesses came down to men:
> He miss'd the pathway, he forgot the hours,
>   And when he looked upon his watch again,
> He found how much old Time had been the winner—
> He also found that he had lost his dinner.

Percy Bysshe Shelley (1792-1822) and Byron were friends who shared a hatred of the hypocrisies of the ruling class into which both were born; but Shelley was far more passionately opposed to tyranny, to kings and institutions. He was the most intensely political-minded of English romantic poets. Yet his poems are so filled with abstractions, with luminous and intangible images of mist and light and running water, with unworldly idealism, that judgments of his ideas, and his possible future had he not died in his thirtieth year, have been at widest variance. Conventional opinion has long accepted Matthew Arnold's famous picture of him as "an ineffectual angel beating in the void his luminous wings in vain." Browning thought that he would have become a Christian, Karl Marx that he would have been a socialist. In *Adonais,* his noble elegy in memory of Keats, he describes himself as

> A pardlike Spirit beautiful and swift—
> A Love in desolation masked:—a Power
> Girt round with weakness;—it can scarce uplift
> The weight of the superincumbent hour;
> It is a dying lamp, a falling shower,

A breaking billow;—even whilst we speak
Is it not broken? On the withering flower
The killing sun smiles brightly: on a cheek
The life can burn in blood, even while the heart may break.

Shelley passed indeed from the atheism of his youth, for expressing which in print he had been expelled from Oxford, and from his early materialism to an increasing Platonic idealism; he modified his acceptance of the doctrines of the philosophical radical, William Godwin. Yet he did not relinquish the hatred of oppression and the rapturous hopes for the future of man which went into the youthful *Queen Mab,* the final chorus of *Hellas,* and *Prometheus Unbound.* It is in expressing such hopes that Shelley is most characteristic as a political poet, as in his lyrics it is a corresponding urge to get away from the earth into ethereal realms, with the skylark, symbol of joy and freedom, or the west wind, symbol of strength and freedom. But with all this "escapism," with all his sometimes fatal skill in dissolving the solid material of the earth in musically lovely but vaporous images, his doctrines at their core are not all phantasies, and his poetic mind, at its best was not vague, but so passionate, so intense as to dazzle not only his readers, but often himself.

Sympathetic as a man with the liberal ideas of his friends, John Keats (1795-1821) as a poet was not concerned with political or moral problems. "Oh for a life of pure sensation rather than thought," he wrote, and though thought is not lacking, his verse is chiefly remarkable for the skill with which it communicates the poet's own sensuous delight in the beauties of the world, the feel, taste, smell as well as the appearance and sound of things:

candied apple, quince, and plum, and gourd;
With jellies soother than the creamy curd,
And lucent syrops, tinct with cinnamon. . . .

Self-dedicated to poetry despite the difficulties of a life less well provided for socially or financially than that of Byron or of Shelley, he passed from writing marred by lushness and effeminacy to the richly adorned and skillfully organized narrative of *The Eve of Saint Agnes* and *Lamia;* to his great *Odes,* a few of the finest sonnets in English, and the unfinished *Hyperion.* In the *Ode to a Nightingale* he makes the favorite romantic contrast between life's pain and sorrow, the passing of youth and earthly beauty, and the endurance of ideal beauty, here represented in the figure of the nightingale—a contrast more real to Keats than to many poets, since he wrote the poem when he was eaten within by the consumption which would kill him as it had shortly before killed his brother. Toward the end of the poem he described the bird's song as it had been heard in ages past, as

The same that oft-times hath
Charm'd magic casements opening on the foam
Of perilous seas, in faery lands forlorn.

These lines, more perfectly than any others in English, contain the essence of romantic yearning for escape into realms of magic and wonder.

Among the English romantic essayists and critics, besides Coleridge, who attained a lasting distinction were Charles Lamb (1775-1834), William Hazlitt (1778-1830), and Thomas De Quincey (1785-1859). Lamb's essays, informal and rambling in style, dotted with archaisms reflective of his love of seventeenth-century prose, are vehicles for his opinions on old books and writers, human foibles, and the small pleasures of life. Hazlitt was throughout a rationalist and radical who remained faithful to causes which others abandoned. He was, after Coleridge, the most important English romantic critic, and a familiar essayist whose prose is full of the "gusto" which he thought so important in life. De Quincey was a precocious boy, and a strange man, a wanderer, dreamer, and visionary, addicted to laudanum. He wrote on many learned subjects, but is best known for the *Confessions of an English Opium Eater,* an account of his wanderings and dreams related in ornate and balanced prose.

2. *Germany*

Goethe and Schiller have been discussed as the greatest figures in German literature of the late eighteenth and early nineteenth centuries. Toward the beginning of the nineteenth century a group of younger writers rebelled against the literature of the classical period, and shared with the rest of Europe the romantic turning away from classical art and culture, toward a concern with individual emotion, exaltation of the imagination, and a belief that life itself should be enriched with poetry. These writers looked for their themes into the medieval past (developing a corresponding sympathy for Catholicism and Catholic ritual), and to the Orient. Old and new foreign authors influenced German romanticism as translations were made of Dante, Cervantes, Byron, Scott, and above all Shakespeare. Other influences gave the movement in Germany a special cast: the rich national folklore, the bent of the German mind toward criticism and scholarship, the rise of national consciousness during the period of Napoleonic domination. And their self-consciousness led the German romantics to make fun at times of life and their own work; to cultivate a "romantic irony" in which nothing could remain entirely serious.

To a far greater extent than elsewhere the spirit of the age was expressed in Germany by speculative writing and research, by a desire to investigate the past as well as to write poetry about it. Romantic thought was influenced by the philosophers Johann Fichte (1762-1814), with his theory of the all-importance of the ego, the individual mind, and Friedrich Schelling (1775-1854). With both of them the dominant philosopher of the age, Georg Wilhelm Hegel (1770-1831), was early associated. There was a development of archaeology, mythology, philology, and a great interest in aesthetic theory and literary criticism. We owe our familiar *Grimm's Fairy Tales* to the researches in German folklore of two brothers who lived in this period, Jakob Grimm (1785-1863) and Wilhelm Grimm (1786-1859).

Among the early romantics influential as teachers and critics were the Schlegel brothers, August Wilhelm (1767-1845) and Friedrich (1772-1829). Both turned their hands to creative writing, but both were more successful as teachers and critics, the former producing an important translation of Shakespeare. In 1798 (the year of *Lyrical Ballads*) they founded the *Athenäum,* during whose two years of existence critical articles appeared of great effect on the young romantics. The circle which surrounded the Schlegels at Jena included among others Ludwig Tieck (1773-1853), distinguished chiefly as the author of the first great German short stories, and Friedrich von Hardenberg (1772-1801), known better by his pen name, Novalis. The latter's *Hymnen an die Nacht (Hymns to Night),* inspired by the death of his sweetheart, are filled with thoughts of death and mystical faith. His unfinished novel, *Heinrich von Osterdingen,* reflects romantic "escapism" in its medieval setting and strange dreams and phantasies. Friedrich de la Motte Fouqué (1777-1843) is remembered best for the fairy romance *Undine,* which Goethe löved. Joseph von Eichendorff (1788-1867) was a fine lyricist, with a gift for bright, warm little songs on the charms and the lasting beauty of nature.

Heinrich von Kleist (1777-1811) ended by suicide a miserable life, but he managed to write plays which, though romantic in much of their treatment of life, show a classic concern for form and clarity of statement. His handling of character reveals a strength and intelligent insight which many romantics lacked in their desire to be off in the clouds or in fairyland.

Many German poets were moved by the French rule to write of freedom and fatherland, or to compose war poems when war finally came. One of these poets of the liberation, Theodor Körner (1791-1813), was himself killed in battle. In the south-German kingdom of Swabia an important group of poets developed, especially gifted in composing ballads. Chief among them was Ludwig Uhland (1787-1862), a philologist, professor, and politician as well as writer of poems, romances, and dramas.

In the years which followed the defeat of Napoleon there existed under Metternich a period of reaction in Germany and Austria which turned much creative genius into the writing of political journalism or satire, chiefly among the liberal writers known as Young Germany. Important both for his relations to romantic literature and the political concerns of Young Germany, as well as for his own imaginative achievement, was the greatest German poet after Goethe, Heinrich Heine (1797-1856).

Although Heine was an orthodox Jew by birth, and a Christian for expediency's sake by conversion, he himself was contemptuous of Jews and Christians alike as "spirit-obsessed Nazarenes," and his work is marked by Hellenic clarity and a pagan zest for the life of the body. After unenthusiastic ventures in business and law studies, he found his true vocation in poetry and political journalism. Sympathetic with the search for beauty, with the fresh fields of expression opened up by the German romantics, he was antagonistic toward the reactionary politics implied in their fondness for the Middle Ages and Germanic tradition. Though much of his own poetry is romantic, even sentimental in tone, he ridiculed contemporary romantic writers, chiefly A. W. Schlegel, whom he had once known and praised. His ironic spirit saw through the political and religious pretensions of men and the heavy pedantry to which much German scholarship came, and he did not spare them the lash of his poetry or of his clear strong prose. His chief enemies were the "Philistines," complacent burghers, petty officials, callous to beauty and culture, whom he stung with his wit, as he did reactionary politicians and ponderous professors.

Heine went to Paris in 1831, inspired by the July Revolution of 1830 to hope that a new world might be in the making. It was not—but he remained in France for the rest of his life, writing on politics or literature, infuriating his fellow-countrymen with the mockery of such works as *Deutschland, ein Wintermärchen* (*Germany, A Winter's Tale*), and enduring with courage and even wit the boredom and agony of his last eight years, which he spent confined to his bed by a disease of the spinal marrow. In these years he wrote *Romancero,* one of his best volumes of poetry.

His political and critical articles and satires still live through the perfection of their prose and the sharpness of their wit; but Heine is known to most readers by the little volume first published in 1827 called the *Buch der Lieder* (*Book of Songs*). With irony, tenderness, sentimentality, melancholy, and bitterness he exposes his shifting moods, chiefly the joys and sorrows of love. His poems of the sea are among the finest in all literature; his verse recaptures the force and fury of the surging waters. And if he ridiculed Germany and Germans, and cultivated a French grace in his style, he was not entirely without affection for his own country as is shown by the poem *Ich hatte einst ein schönes Vaterland* (*Once I had a lovely fatherland*).

Heine was one of the great spirits of his century; his hatred of tyranny and reaction and of complacent acceptance of these things made him indeed what he hoped he would be remembered for, "a brave soldier in humanity's war of liberation."

3. France and Italy

The romantic movement was longer getting under way in France than in England and Germany; not until the third decade of the century did it reach full expression. But the doctrines of Rousseau and the principles of the Revolution had paved the way for new subjects and fresh means of expression. Pioneers in French romanticism were Madame de Staël (1766-1817) and François René de Chateaubriand (1768-1848). In her novels, criticism, and books of travel the former sought to broaden the interests of the French mind, to show the excellences of German romantic ideas, to stimulate the qualities of passion and enthusiasm lacking in classical tradition. Chateaubriand exerted a strong influence in the romantic turning away from the reason, clarity, and common sense of the eighteenth century. He was an ardent Christian, who found in the Christian religion mystery, poetry, and freedom. In his novel *Atala* he tells of love and passion in exotic settings, among the Indians of North America, and in *René* portrays himself as a romantic hero, touched with melancholy and weary of the world. His religious sentiments, exotic themes, fresh vocabulary, and musical prose contributed to breaking the shackles of tradition.

First important French romantic poet was Alphonse de Lamartine (1790-1869). His early poetry showed him to be a tender lyricist of nature, religion, and melancholy; but the Lamartine of the *Méditations poétiques* (1820) later became a forceful figure in national thought. A diplomat, a statesman, a militant fighter for liberal Catholicism, Lamartine was one of the few internationally-minded French writers of the middle of the nineteenth century. Alfred de Vigny (1797-1863) was a very different sort of poet. Contrary to Lamartine and Victor Hugo, both of whom participated in the life of the times, Vigny advocated "an ivory tower" for the artist, an above-the-battle attitude. A pessimist, he saw weak man the victim of an indifferent fate, and found no hope in religion. To him a stoical resignation was the true way of life, but in his sense of man's loneliness there is no Byronic pretense. His calm and dignified verse achieves at times something of the grand style in such poems as *Moïse* (*Moses*) or *La Maison du berger* (*The Shepherd's House*). His view of life is summed up in the last lines of *La Mort du loup* (*The Death of the Wolf*). The courageous beast seems to speak with his dying eyes:

> Gémir, pleurer, prier, est également lâche.
> Fais énergiquement ta longue et lourde tâche
> Dans la voie où le sort a voulu t'appeler,
> Puis, après, comme moi, souffre et meurs sans parler.

(To groan, to weep, to pray, all are equally cowardly. Do energetically your long and heavy task in the path to which fate has willed to call you; then, at last, like me, suffer and die without speaking.)

"Spoiled child of romanticism" was Alfred de Musset (1810-1857), whose fine lyrics reveal the varying sentiments of an unstable but brilliant mind.

Victor Hugo (1802-1885) was the great voice of French romanticism, a more monumental figure in his own land than any English poet in England. Dramatist, novelist, lyric, narrative, satirical poet, he exploded during the long years of his life in an unending fireworks display of words on a vast range of subjects. He lived well on into the days of anti-romanticism and realism, but they did not intimidate him.

Robust, an extreme egoist, temperamentally well-adjusted, and lacking both the finer sensitiveness and the soul-sickness and self-pity of less "normal" poets, he had neither the clarity of mind nor the powers of discrimination needed in a theorist or critic. But he was a powerful front-fighter in the battle to establish romantic freedom against traditionalist attacks. In the drama especially worship of old forms and restrictions was strong, and these Hugo attacked in 1827 in the preface to *Cromwell,* urging a return to nature and life with their mingling of beautiful and ugly, sublime and grotesque, and greater freedom in form and language. His play *Hernani* caused a ferocious battle of old and new when it was presented in 1830. It enraged those who believed in a limited poetic vocabulary from which all common or vulgar words were barred, and delighted the rebellious younger generation.

Hugo's strong imagination went into lyric utterance of emotion, happy pictures of children, satires (in *Les Châtiments*) on contemporary life and politics, descriptions of natural scenes, the sweeping historical tableaux of *La Légende des siècles.* His extraordinarily rich language gives movement and life to his varied pictures.

Théophile Gautier (1811-1872) expressed with uncommon intensity his hatred of bourgeois morality and money-grubbing, a hatred shared by many literary-minded young men of his day. This contempt for the dominant class, unaccompanied by any drive toward social reform, led him to detest all art which might be utilitarian, and those who supported such art he called "fools" and "goiterous cretins." He thought art more perfect in proportion as it was less useful—the doctrine of art for art's sake. But his own best work escapes the excesses of romantic rhetoric and word-mongering. The title of his best-known volume, *Emaux et camées (Enamels and Cameos)*, indicates the quality of his poems, which have the brilliance, smoothness, and sharpness of outline of enamel-painting or finely-carved cameos. Unlike more typical romantics, he was less interested in giving vent to his emotions than in describing with clarity and precision a perceived object. He was of great influence on poets later in the century who turned from romantic moods and manners.

Italy shared in the romantic period the ideas and feelings fermenting in the rest of Europe, though there was no great Gothic past to attract the attention of poets, and much Italian romanticism was inspired by foreign example, by the introduction of such authors as Shakespeare, Goethe, Scott, Byron. As in Germany, political conditions absorbed the energies of many writers, both during the period of Napoleonic rule when the ideal of a unified Italy first received tangible form, and in the following years when this ideal was fought for by the leaders of the Risorgimento.

Early in the century two writers stood far above all others: Alessandro Manzoni (1785-1873) and Giacomo Leopardi (1798-1837). Like Chateaubriand, Manzoni regarded the Catholic faith with ardent romantic feelings reflected in all his work. He was most influential through *I Promessi sposi (The Betrothed)*, a novel called by Sir Walter Scott the "best ever written." Its scene is seventeenth-century Milan, and although at times its historical detail is a little heavy, it shows a profound knowledge of human life in all classes.

Leopardi, greatest of Italian poets since Ariosto, is one of the first of European poets. Crushed by illness all his life, he lived within himself, achieving distinction not only as a poet, but as a scholar (especially in Greek), and as a writer of prose dialogues equal in perfection of form to his poetry. His mood is one of melancholy and despair, though at times he reflects the spirit of Italian patriotism, and the prevailing tone of his work is intensely sad. But there is no posturing, no disgorging of rhetoric in his pessimism; his verse merges form and emotion with classic grace. This quality may be seen in such poems as *La Sera del Di di Festa (The Evening of the Festival)*, in *A Silvia (To Silvia)*, in his unsurpassed lyric, *L'Infinito (The Infinite)*.

4. Russia

The romantic movement penetrated Russia from the west in German or English form, came into conflict with neo-classical principles acquired from France, was modified in expression by the national temperament. Russian literature really begins in the nineteenth century, and its first name of high importance is that of Alexander Pushkin (1799-1837). But Pushkin, though he knew and was influenced by Western literature, did not become merely a Russian romantic poet; he retained a classic respect for form and a native sense of the real. During his short life, which was ended by a duel, he established Russian as an important literary language, laid the foundations of a national literature, and became a world poet still insufficiently recognized as such because of the difficulties of adequately translating him.

As a boy he wrote promising poems in French and Russian, and his reputation was made in 1820 by *Ruslan and Ludmilla,* a poem on a folk-tale theme, but treated in a sophisticated fashion. Like many young men of the day, he came under the influence of Byron, and his early work shows his attraction to the Byronic hero. But Pushkin came to recognize the weaknesses of Byron as he did the greatness of Shakespeare, and his own best work excels that of the English poet in control of subject, in handling poetic speech.

Pushkin wrote lyrics, narrative poetry, prose, and plays. His themes come from folk and fairy tales, legends, gypsy and Tartar life, history, and his own time. *Boris Godunov,* his best-known drama, is a kind of chronicle play, effective rather by scenes than as a unified work. His most famous work is *Evgeni Oniegin,* a long narrative finished in 1831, and though a poem often called the first Russian novel. It recalls the Byron of *Beppo* and *Don Juan* in its humorous treatment of contemporary life, but in some respects is superior to either; more dramatic in its treatment of character, better organized despite somewhat Byronic digressions, more carefully written in a style colloquial and humorous if need be but with none of Byron's tendency to self-conscious carelessness. The story is that of a young man of the world who realizes too late that he really desires the woman who once offered him her love. This charming and intelligent heroine, Tatiana, is one of the most attractive women in literature. The action of the poem moves in the city among soirées and balls and officials, and in the quiet and beauty of the country. The language is brilliant and precise, close to earth, in a fashion not found in most Western literature of the time.

More truly romantic than Pushkin was Michael Lermontov (1814-1841) who like Pushkin died in a duel, after a violent life in the army. He has put much of himself in the chief character of his novel, *A Hero of Our Days.* Stubbornly individual, of difficult and uncertain temper, Lermontov expressed himself in intensely subjective lyrics, or caught the excitement and color of life in romantic tales of the Caucasus. These tales, exotic and filled with strange visions (*The Demon* and *Mtsyri* are the best known), combine high imagination with a typically Russian simplicity, concreteness, and closeness to common life.

5. The Novel

Despite the huge editions of certain popular poets, the novel was the most popular literary form in the nineteenth century, as it is today. The reading public continued to increase in size and found delight in many novels now fortunately forgotten. But many of lasting value appeared as well, chiefly in England, France, and Russia. Elsewhere in Europe prose fiction was cultivated, and often with distinction, but these three countries were preëminent.

Of all literary forms, the novel may give, through its flexibility and inclusiveness, the completest representation of life, manners, and setting. It is free of the restrictions of drama, though it lacks in general the compression and intensity of great tragedy, and may absorb the methods of drama together with those of other forms. In the nineteenth century in the hands of skilled writers it was used both to portray familiar human experience and to comment upon and criticize, in terms of imagined incident, the forces which were altering the traditional bases of this experience.

The greatest novelist of the romantic period in England was a woman, in whom we meet not those passionate concerns with the world and nature and destiny found in the poets of the time, but an amused and sensible treatment of man's absurd behavior. Jane Austen (1775-1817) lived uneventfully, and wrote of the limited world of upper middle-class country gentry. Her heroes and heroines fall in love, overcome complications, and marry with no tearings of passions, amid no phenomenal settings or events. But in the deft cool prose of *Pride and Prejudice, Emma, Persuasion* and her other novels, she created a lasting picture of the vanities, poses, and eccentricities of men and women, their love of gossip, their neighborhood jealousies, their domestic pleasures and tribulations.

Jane Austen wrote six novels, and compared her work to a two-inch square of ivory. Sir Walter Scott was the most productive English writer of the age, as poet, novelist, translator, editor, biographer. His verse has been mentioned; he owed to his novels the tremendous popularity and influence which extended east to Russia and west across the Atlantic. Like his poems, his most characteristic novels deal with past English and Scottish history, the thirty-two Waverley novels ranging in time from the twelfth century (*The Talisman*) to the late eighteenth (*The Antiquary*). His object was always to entertain, not to display erudition or to moralize, and he leads his heroes and heroines, against a background of historical settings, events, and personages, through surprisingly movie-like plots, full of action and suspense. His settings are often too theatrical, his central figures, especially the women, lifelessly conventional, his stories imperfectly planned. But there is nevertheless strength and life in his work, and humorous and living characters, especially those from the Scottish peasant or working classes.

Across the Channel Alexandre Dumas (1803-1870) wrote historical novels with a color and narrative force comparable to Scott's, who influenced him. The adventures of D'Artagnan and his musketeer companions are as familiar to the English-speaking boy as to the French. Hugo also produced historical novels of conflict and adventure, and in 1862 would attempt in *Les Misérables* a large-scale picture of life combining exciting action with a humanitarian purpose. Georges Sand (her real name Aurore Dupin, 1804-1876) wrote lyrical romances of love, novels of country life, and social novels with a strong liberal bias. But the two chief figures in French fiction during the first half century, although they do not escape romanticism entirely, are best known for pictures of life closer to actuality.

Stendhal (his real name Henri Beyle, 1783-1842), onetime soldier of Napoleon, felt, though without plaintive self-pity, that his own age would not appreciate his work, and addressed one of his novels to "the happy few." Such critics of his own time as Balzac did appreciate him, but fame came slowly. In *La Chartreuse de Parme,* which reflects his knowledge of Italy, and most of all in *Le Rouge et Le Noir* (*The Red and Black*), which recounts the ambitious career and miserable death of young Julien Sorel, he treated life without romantic flights, objectively, and in a simple style, with careful analysis of complex psychological states, and truth of detail. It was Stendhal, among French novelists of the first half of the nineteenth century, who was to be most influential in the twentieth because of the startling modernity of his thinking.

Honoré de Balzac (1799-1850) was one of the most prolific of novelists; Henry James called him the greatest. For more than thirty years he flooded the world with novels, tales, plays, countless articles.

In his most important work, assembled as the *Comédie Humaine,* he aspired to render the whole history of the time in France. Arranged as *Scenes of Provincial Life, Scenes of Parisian Life,* and so on, the novels of the *Comédie* (of which the best known are *Eugénie Grandet* and *Le Père Goriot*) display in a multitude of characters the crude desires, the stupidity, avarice, and baseness of men and women, chiefly in the dominant bourgeoisie. Balzac drew man in his *milieu,* among the myriad circumstances which formed and expressed him, and his novels are loaded with detail, with exhaustive descriptions which sometimes drag, but are essential to an understanding of character as the author saw it. Not subtle, weak in portraying finer or gentler emotions, marred by strains of romantic excess or melodrama despite its realism, his style is clumsy, crude, involved; but through its power and range we have an unparalleled picture of the inner and outer life of an age.

Victorian novelists, like Victorian critics and poets, have suffered from the anti-Victorian reaction, and are still too easily thought of as dull, lumbering, moralistic —a view which ignores the energy, patience, and skill with which they tackled the problems of human life in the conditions of their time. They were giants, and their novels are monuments of fiction, but with all their earnest concern with life, custom and convention prevented their pressing too far into those forbidden realms of experience (conventionally known as "morbid" or "immoral") from which fewer qualms barred their French and Russian contemporaries. And so they were forced at times into evasion and sidestepping.

The names of Dickens and Thackeray are linked with the same careless ease as those of Dryden and Pope, Keats and Shelley, but the two novelists are fundamentally as different as the two poets in each pair. William Makepeace Thackeray (1811-1863), something of a bohemian, a skillful caricaturist as well as writer, cultivated in his life and work a smoothness and grace not sought by Dickens. Anti-sentimental (though not always unsentimental), tolerant, fond (with reservations) of the eighteenth century which he reconstructed in *Henry Esmond,* he turned to account his somewhat eighteenth-century wit in satirizing the pretensions and snobbery of London society, chiefly that of the upper middle-class to which he belonged. In his most famous novel, *Vanity Fair,* he shows the turning to ashes of worldly pretension as he leads the adventuress Becky Sharp through complications and intrigues in Paris and London. Convention prevented his picturing her in the situations to which her actions would seem naturally to be leading her; Balzac would not have been so hesitant, as we may see by comparing Becky with the somewhat similar Madame Marneffe in *La Cousine Bette*. With all his humor, his skill in drawing people, situations, settings, Thackeray is often tiresome: he poses, his digressive essays tend toward smugness, he is too conscious of his own smartness, he remains very much on the surface of things.

Charles Dickens (1812-1870) was the novelist of the lower middle classes as Thackeray was of the upper. Neither subtle nor urbane, he painted with broad humor (in the sturdy English tradition which stems from Ben Jonson) or with excessive pathos a gallery of eccentrics (Mr. Pickwick and Mr. Micawber have not yet worn thin), of cruel fathers and employers, virtuous heroes and heroines. His sentimentalism is tear-jerking, as Little Nell's death, in *The Old Curiosity Shop*, illustrates too well. He leans strongly toward caricatures and grotesques in comic and villainous characters. But withal much of his comedy still amuses, and there is still power in his attacks on social abuses, on corruption and stupidity in law and education, for experience had taught him something of the bitter lot of the poor. The autobiographical *David Copperfield* is Dickens' masterpiece, illustrating at its most mature his art, which began primarily as caricature in *The Pickwick Papers*. His novel about the working class, *Hard Times,* and the melodramatic *Tale of Two Cities,* about the French Revolution, show Dickens' wide range.

Among England's distinguished women writers of the nineteenth century were the Brontë sisters. None of the three Brontës, Charlotte (1816-1855), Emily (1818-1848), Anne (1820-1849), reached middle age. Brought up in the desolate village of Haworth in Yorkshire, in a family stalked by misfortune, sickness, and death; patient and hard-working, Charlotte and Emily saved for their novels, and Emily for her fine poems as well, those passions which they suppressed in their lives. Emily's *Wuthering Heights* was the most unlikely of novels to come from a Victorian young woman; but its author did not fit the type. The story is dominated by no conventional hero and heroine, no sentimentalizing. Its chief figure, Heathcliff, is a monster of hatred and vengeance; its action works out in violence and suffering. There is no break in emotional intensity, and there is throughout a mystic sense of the strange, terrible forces in nature and man.

Charlotte's two best novels are *Jane Eyre* and *Villette,* the latter laid in Brussels, where its author had been a teacher. Her work contains elements of romance and melodrama, but also a fidelity to truth, an honest realism which shocked many readers of *Jane Eyre,* which had for heroine a plain governess who admitted frankly to herself that she was in love. Charlotte Brontë was a pioneer in breaking down complacent myths taken for granted by her age, about the quality of womanliness.

George Eliot (her real name Marian Evans, 1819-1880) was a serious woman of tremendous learning, who began novel-writing after years devoted to study, translation, the writing of articles on ethical, religious, philosophical, and literary questions. Though she was an advanced thinker for her time, independent in judgment, her novels reflect a profound moral sense, a preoccupation with sin and retribution, conscience and self-discipline. Her chief interest was psychological analysis, the exploration of motives for action, of alterations in character. She was one of the first and remains one of the greatest of psychological novelists. Her most readable novels are *Adam Bede* and *The Mill on the Floss,* in which she combines analytical skill, realistic drawing, and humor with an effectiveness lacking (except in *Middlemarch*) in her weightier and more studious fiction.

Anthony Trollope (1815-1882) produced a vast quantity of fiction with a businesslike dispatch and attention to daily output which he describes frankly in his *Autobiography.* Though Trollope wrote on a variety of subjects, he is known chiefly for the Barsetshire novels, a series dealing with imaginary clergymen in an imaginary diocese, of which the most widely read are *The Warden* and *Barchester Towers.* Written with humor and good sense, with plots which hold the interest, these tales of ecclesiastical bickering and intrigue are interesting humanly, as well as for the picture they give of a society in which the affairs of the clergy were of more general concern than they are today. In his political novels, Trollope has created a fictional world that is remarkably vivid and apropos, and the leading character, the Duke of Omnium, is a masterpiece of portraiture. Trollope's reputation has risen steadily in the twentieth century.

George Meredith (1828-1909) was a poet as well as novelist, and carried over into his novels his poetic interest in nature, and in the harmony between man and the physical universe which he thought the reasonable state of existence. But man's ego, his affectations and pretensions often violate this harmony, and in such excesses Meredith found food for comedy. Comedy in his sense might have a tragic outcome, as it does in *Richard Feverel,* where a father's attempt to control his son's destiny by supposed scientific means leads to bitter unhappiness. It is the women in his novels who are most likely to possess common sense, to be lacking in pretense or sentimentality, to approach most nearly to the calm wisdom of nature. His style is at times too lushly poetical, and in his later work especially tended to increasing obscurity, an excessive load of intellectual and epigrammatic language. Although Meredith at his best is a subtle analyst of character, a master of prose, an entertaining commentator on the shortcomings of man, he is now out of favor.

Very different from the Comic Muse of Meredith is the Fate which oversees life in the novels of Thomas Hardy (1840-1928). This last great novelist of the Victorian age (he published no fiction after 1895) yielded neither to the complacent optimism of his time nor its eye-shutting compromise with the unpleasant facts of existence. His is a darker picture than any of his contemporaries dared draw. His people, though not entirely unresponsible for their own destiny, are victims of chance and circumstance, of ironic accidents and coincidences which bring tragic turns of fortune, of nature's indifference, which seems at times almost malevolent. Environment thus plays an important role as his central figures— Tess of the D'Urbervilles, Jude the Obscure, Michael Henchard (in *The Mayor of Casterbridge*)—move to their inescapable downfall. His work, though somber in tone, is not without comedy, earthy and gross, in the figures of peasants and workmen, types which he knew well. Hardy's prose is forceful, though not easy or always well-managed; but his novels show a fine sense of structure, heightened by his training as an architect and his reading in Greek tragedy.

In France the greatest novelist after Balzac was Gustave Flaubert (1821-1880). Romantic in his hatred of the bourgeoisie and of bourgeois morality, an admirer of Hugo, in his work he was the most finished of realists, even when treating, in *Salammbô,* a historical subject. He insisted upon complete impersonality in the handling of character; the author must never intrude his own opinions, take sides, moralize, or sentimentalize. Absolute attainment of this objective is, of course, impossible, and Flaubert's own hatreds explode in his account of the consummate boobies Bouvard and Pécuchet. But his success was large, nevertheless. Driven by an intense artistic conscience, he lavished upon his work untiring patience and labor; polishing and repolishing his style, seeking always the precise word, attentive (to the extent if need be of doing elaborate research) to what may seem the most trifling detail. His non-historical characters are neither heroic nor important, but no one has rendered more clearly than he the drab existence, the futile flashes of passion and aspiration of ordinary and rather stupid people like Frédéric Moreau in *L'Education Sentimentale. Madame Bovary* is his finest novel; its central figure achieves something of dignity lacking in most of his people as she passes to her doom through conflicts raised between her dull life and her sentimental dreams.

"Realism" is a convenient, not too exact term, by which novelists and dramatists, especially since the romantic age, have sought to suggest the picturing of actuality, the creation of an illusion of familiar experience. The realist need not be limited in his moral, religious, or philosophical view of the world. But the naturalist has a narrower view of experience. He examines man (or pretends to examine him) scientifically, as a helpless product of blind natural forces. Nineteenth-century naturalism, the product of scientific thought of the day, was at its worst the crudest of materialisms.

Thomas Hardy represents in some degree the extension of naturalism in the English novel, but the name which is synonymous with naturalism in fiction is that of Émile Zola (1840-1902), who was distinguished in his day also by his heroic defense of Captain Dreyfus. Zola sought to regard action and character in a laboratory manner, to induce laws from given human circumstances. His work is therefore filled with documentation, a display of scientific method. In the Rougon-Macquart series he traces the influence of heredity and environment in the history of a family eaten by vice and crime. Man the animal is his object, and he treats him, individually and in the mass, as a dull or vicious brute, though with sympathy for the working classes, for whose role in future social change he had high hopes. But Zola was not without a strong, at times even romantic, imagination. *Germinal,* a story of miners in the north of France, and *L'Assommoir,* a story of Parisian workers and tavern and tenement life, are his best-known works.

Other realists and naturalists of the time were the Goncourt brothers, Edmond

(1822-1896) and Jules (1830-1870); Alphonse Daudet (1840-1897); and Guy de Maupassant (1850-1893). The last, a friend and disciple of Flaubert, is better known for his short stories than for his novels. He handles in a clear, impersonal fashion the lives of very ordinary people, especially their sexual relationships. The Goncourts, less formidable in their naturalism than Zola, whom they preceded, wrote of morbid or pathological states in an impressionistic style. The naturalistic method affected the work of Daudet, but there is in him more humor and sentiment than in Zola and the Goncourts.

It is through her novels that Russia is best known in the world's literature; in them experience is explored with insight and power surpassed in no other country. Pushkin's *Evgeni Oniegen* opened the way to narrative treatment of contemporary life, and Lermontov's *A Hero of Our Days* was a forerunner of the century's great prose fiction. But it was with Nicolai Gogol (1809-1852) that the golden age of the Russian novel really began. Gogol showed, especially in his early work, a romantic interest in the supernatural and the mysterious, but his strength lay in his knowledge of the people and the Russian soil, in his power of observation, his humor, and his irony. His best work, *Dead Souls,* is a comic novel despite the sound of its title.[1] It relates the wanderings through Russia among all types of people of its hero Chichikov, one of the great comic rogues of literature. Gogol's achievement was not only the writing of a lasting work of comic art, but the opening up to Russian writers of new fields for fiction, among the grosser and more vulgar regions of life.

Best known to western Europe of Russian writers in the nineteenth century was Ivan Turgenev (1818-1883), who spent most of his life abroad, chiefly in France. Lacking the force and deep knowledge of man of Dostoyevsky and Tolstoy and their immediate acquaintance with Russian conditions, Turgenev in his easy and delicate style drew fine pictures of places and characters, especially of women. *Fathers and Sons,* his chief work, contains in Bazarov, the nihilist, one of the strongest characters in Russian fiction.

Alexander Goncharov (1812-1891) created in Ilya Ilyitch Oblomov, the central character of his novel *Oblomov,* a type found with variations in much Russian literature as well as in Russian life: that of the man full of dreams and ideals but spiritually inert, incapable of doing anything about them, of making a decision. Oblomov lies in bed, gets dressed with difficulty, is fearful of infection from the outside world, sinks ever deeper into his lethargy, and the world passes him by—his active and capable friends, the woman who genuinely loves him.

Of all the world's writers who have known through experience the cruelty of life, none has produced more lasting work against greater odds than Feodor Dostoyevsky (1821-1881). Sentenced to death for political activity, he was sent instead to exile in Siberia, of which bitter period there is a record in *The House of the Dead.* His life after his return to Russia was plagued by sorrow, poverty, and sickness. But through all these misfortunes Dostoyevsky retained his Chris-

---

[1] Russian landlords paid poll-taxes on their serfs, of whom a census was made every ten years. They continued in the intervals between censuses to pay even for serfs who died. Gogol's rascally hero sees a chance for gain in getting the titles to these "dead souls" and using them as security for bank-loans.

tian faith, no narrow one, for he had a vast love of man and sympathy for the suffering, the "abnormal" of the world. His sympathy and understanding fill his novels, which are repellent to readers who do not see that the so-called seamy side of life may be treated by a great artist with tragic intensity and profound moral sense.

Thus Dostoyevsky's novels—*The Brothers Karamazov, Crime and Punishment, The Idiot*—have not unjustly been compared with *King Lear,* with its almost unendurable emotional struggle and anguish. A great scene in Dostoyevsky gives a nervous shock similar to that given by the storm scene in *Lear,* or by such lines as

> I am bound
> Upon a wheel of fire, that mine own tears
> Do scald like molten lead.

Count Leo Tolstoy (1828-1910) shares with Dostoyevsky the name of "Russia's greatest novelist." Of noble birth and wealth, he became a critic of society, renounced his career in middle-age to seek a true way of life, opposing himself in his search for a rational religion to all human institutions, religious and political, and damning even such a writer as Shakespeare if he felt that writer lacking in what he thought real moral values. An idealist indeed, but little of a mystic, his observation of human behavior was crystal clear, so that in his fiction no relevant detail escaped him, no corner of the inner man was too obscure for his analysis, no mass too unwieldy for him to handle. In *War and Peace* he reconstructed the Napoleonic years from 1805 to 1812. It is the greatest of historical novels, for it possesses an actuality, an immediate human significance which most works of the type fall far short of. In *Anna Karenina* he treats the contemporary life of both city and country. Although the latter, through the simple and benevolent figure of Levin, has his sympathy, the dramatic force and interest of the work lies in the figures of Anna, Karenin her husband, and her lover Vronsky, and in the tragedy which comes of their passions and weaknesses.

The important names in Russian fiction after the great age are those of Anton Chekhov (1860-1904) and Maxim Gorky (1868-1936). The latter belongs as much to the twentieth century as to the nineteenth, and lived to be honored by the Soviet Union. His work deals with a world of harshness and violent action, of tramps and criminals. Like Gogol he opened new realms for fiction. Chekhov's best work in fiction was in the short story, which he found a perfect medium for representing, with economy of detail, the futile and trivial lives of all manner of people, whom he treats humorously, but also with a sense of their sadness and pathos.

6. *Later Poetry of the Century*

The word "Victorian" has for many years suggested a narrow morality abstracted from the family Bible by solemn men in beards and severely pure women in crinolines. This view has recently begun to undergo a needed revision. The Victorians did indeed have their faults. Middle-class evangelical religion was dominant in an age controlled by middle-class evangelical industrialists and shopkeepers. A sense of moral righteousness and physical well-being made it possible to ignore the unpleasant facts of life—in personal behavior and in the industrial system—by a compromise which assumed that they did not exist. Thus hypocrisy was not unknown. But the age was one of intellectual ferment; science clashed with faith, industrial abuses brought movements for reform, feminists sought to make woman less womanly and more human. There was a literature which accepted, but also one which protested, the conventions of the time.

In poetry the romantic tradition carried on, though subdued, for the great age of revolution and poetic discovery had passed. The lyric continued as the most popular form, and with much saccharine sentimentality, but in poetry as in prose the conflicts of the time were echoed. There was also, eventually, the cultivation of art for art's sake, as delicate young men sought to protect their sensibilities against the vulgarities of life.

Alfred Tennyson (1809-1892), who succeeded Wordsworth as Poet Laureate in 1850 and became Lord Tennyson in 1884, was not only the official poet of England, but to many thousands a moral teacher and a bard. It has been all too easy for a reaction which began in his own time to condemn the effeminate softness of his early verse, his jingoism, the lugubrious moralizing of the *Idylls of the King,* which he planned as his greatest work, a view not held by posterity. For the cloaked and bearded figure whose picture looks down from so many classroom walls was one of the finest of English lyricists, one of the most perfect of English metrists. A careful student and a master of sounds and rhythms, he wrote in *The Lotos-Eaters,* in *Ulysses,* in *Tithonus,* in the songs from *Maud* and *The Princess,* and in other short poems, verse marvelously varied and musical, with often a haunting undertone of sadness which came from deep within. These various qualities are perfectly summed up in the poem on a visit to the country of the Latin poet Catullus:

> Row us out, from Desenzano, to your Sirmione row!
> So they row'd, and there we landed—"O venusta Sirmio!"
> There to me thro' all the groves of olive in the summer glow,
> There beneath the Roman ruin where the purple flowers grow,
> Came that "Ave atque Vale" of the Poet's hopeless woe,
> Tenderest of Roman poets nineteen hundred years ago,
> "Frater Ave atque Vale"—as we wander'd to and fro
> Gazing at the Lydian laughter of the Garda Lake below
> Sweet Catullus's all-but-island, olive-silvery Sirmio!

His noblest poem, *In Memoriam,* was written during several years after the death of his dear friend, Arthur Hallam. Though long, it is a series of lyrics revealing his passionate grief, and reflecting in despair, doubt, and final hope the struggle between old faith and new science which shook so many sensitive men of the age even before Darwin, nine years after *In Memoriam* appeared, published the earthshaking *Origin of Species.*

Robert Browning (1812-1889) achieved fame more slowly but not less solidly than Tennyson. A robust (sometimes too robust) Christian optimist, who felt that the imperfections of this world would be made perfect in the next, he is more convincing as a poet than as a thinker. His great achievement was the dramatic monologue in which a single speaker, among carefully suggested settings, addresses imagined hearers and in so doing reveals the essence of his being—cruelty, joy in life, frustration in love, his whole history. *My Last Duchess, Fra Lippo Lippi, The Bishop Orders His Tomb,* reflect his skill in this form and his delight in the color and violence of life in fifteenth- and sixteenth-century Italy. Although Browning wrote much in conventional forms and rhythms, he was a pathbreaker, creating rugged or broken rhythms suggesting conversational speech, using language strange or colloquial; often obscure to no purpose, grotesque or bumptious; but at his best capable of dramatic compression and intensity. His longest poem, *The Ring and the Book,* is the story of an old Roman murder, in a series of monologues by actors or observers of the drama. There is much long-windedness and display of learning, but there is power and beauty in the monologues of Pompilia, the heroine; Caponsacchi, the priest, her friend; Guido, her villainous husband.

Famous chiefly as a critic, Matthew Arnold (1822-1888) was also the author of many enduring poems. In them there is an elegiac quality, a tone of personal sadness given wider meaning by reflections on man's isolation "in the sea of life enisled," by the impact upon a sensitive mind of the crumbling of creeds, by

this strange disease of modern life,
With its sick hurry, its divided aims. . . .

Arnold's language is calm, reflective, capable of describing the beauties of nature, of a moonlit night or the sea, or of evoking deep feelings of melancholy. He is at his best in *To Marguerite, A Summer Night, Dover Beach,* in the narrative *Sohrab and Rustum,* or the longer reflective and descriptive poems, *The Scholar Gypsy* and *Thyrsis* (an elegy for his friend Arthur Hugh Clough).

In 1850 a group of young painters and poets founded the Pre-Raphaelite Brotherhood, devoting themselves to restoring to painting the simplicity, fidelity to detail, and brightness which they found in Italian painting before Raphael. Leading figure of this group was Dante Gabriel Rossetti (1828-1882), a better poet than painter, who stimulated a new romantic spirit in the literature of the age. His poetry reflects the sometimes synthetic medievalism by which various men of the time sought to escape the pervading evangelicalism, although he was himself not religious by temperament as was his poet sister, Christina. His early poems and ballads are pictorial, clear in color, sensuous, and represent a transference to words of his theories of painting. As he grew older he tended to greater complexity and obscurity of style, to intellectualism. His earlier manner may be seen in *My Sister's Sleep, The Blessed Damozel, Sister Helen;* his later in the sonnets of *The House of Life,* a sequence inspired by his love for his dead wife.

William Morris (1834-1896) was a man of many skills, as will be later indicated, and wrote poetry with the same zest and aliveness with which he tackled other enterprises. His poems are chiefly long narratives on classical, medieval, or Norse themes; the best-known are found in *The Earthly Paradise.* They move swiftly and strongly, but make sometimes rather tiring reading. Like Morris a disciple of Rossetti was Algernon Charles Swinburne (1837-1909), whose smooth verses on passion and luxury have long since failed to disturb the moral sense as they did that of his contemporaries. Skillful in many forms, fond of alliteration and other devices of verbal melody, Swinburne is as often a slick as a good poet, though there is genuine emotion as well as soothing sound in his best poems, in *Ave Atque Vale,* for instance, written in memory of Baudelaire, or in the choruses to *Atalanta in Calydon;* and a welcome hardness in a revolutionary poem like *A Song in Time of Order,* composed before he turned reactionary.

Not frightened off by the new views of man and nature which the science of the age introduced were George Meredith and Thomas Hardy, both better known as novelists. Meredith accepted enthusiastically the theory of evolution, viewing nature not, like Tennyson, as "red in tooth and claw," but rather as a just mother, source of strength and sanity, with whom man's spirit ought harmoniously to be adjusted. Hardy found less joyous tidings in the new theories. His poetry, as in *The Dynasts* and in the poems written after his wife's death, plain, unadorned, sometimes harsh and irregular, is occupied with the ironies of man's life, caught in a whirlpool of natural forces indifferent to his fate and beyond his power to control.

But the sadness of man's lot, the pessimism of the century's end, was perfectly voiced in *The Shropshire Lad* of A. E. Housman (1859-1936), lyrics as simple in speech and form, with the simplicity that defies imitation, as any written in English. Death is their theme, the passing of youth, the cruel frustrations of life.

Other poets of the last decades retreated into a partly real, partly literary Catholicism, and still others into art-for-art's sake, an escape from the turmoils of the age. Gerard Manley Hopkins (1844-1889), a Jesuit priest, was a remarkably original poet whose single volume, *Poems,* was not published until 1918. He is known for a powerful and subtle analysis of nature and religion which links him with the seventeenth-century Metaphysical poets; his intricate rhythms, elliptical phrasing, and compound metaphors have influenced many contemporary American and British poets.

The cult of art-for-art's sake in France was taken up by the Parnassians (from their journal, *Le Parnasse Contemporain*). They sought themes away from the sordid present, in the Greek and Roman past, in the exotic scenery of imagined tropics. The chief members of this group were Leconte de Lisle (1818-1894) and José-Maria de Hérédia (1842-1905), a fine sonneteer. But the greatest French poet of the second half-century, though he shared much of the anti-bourgeois spirit of contemporary poets, belonged to no group. He was Charles Baudelaire (1821-1867).

Baudelaire, unhappy, maladjusted, eccentric, died at a comparatively early age after a life of bitterness and debauchery. His name early became a byword for perverseness and decadence, especially among certain English poets resentful of the rigors of the Victorian moral climate. This too easy picture has happily been corrected, for Baudelaire at his best was far above Swinburnian concern with flesh and perfume and languorous sin.

In his verse he restored something of the classical order, restraint, and respect for form against which the romantics had excessively revolted. Yet he was no Parnassian cultivating beauty for its own sake, in detached realms. Satanism and bourgeois-shocking fleshliness are indeed to be found in his work, but they are not all. He had a profound sense of evil; his disgust, his awareness of corruption, his concern with death came from within, and these were aroused among the people and buildings of Paris, that

> Fourmillante cité, cité pleine de rêves,
> Où le spectre en plein jour raccroche le passant!

(Swarming city, city full of dreams, where at noonday the specter accosts the passer-by!)

Thus his poems come to grips with experience; grimness and terror are not lacking in verses of intense beauty.

After Baudelaire, and influenced by him (he had written of nature as a forest of symbols), the most important development in French poetry was the movement called "Symbolism," a confusing term which indicates a search by the poets of the movement for words and metaphors better fitted than conventional language to suggest the nature of their sensations and emotions. The symbolists reacted against the objectivity and the often metallic perfection of the Parnassians, and against the scientific materialism and naturalism so influential in the literature of their day. Elsewhere in Europe a similar reaction occurred. These poets sought to suggest rather than to describe their feelings, and to do so in language possessed of the indefiniteness and mystery of music, so that frequently it is so obscure as to seem a language known to the writer alone. They carried to an extreme the violation of traditional forms begun by the romantics, writing irregular meters in which no rules were observed.

The name of Paul Verlaine (1844-1896) is associated with symbolism, though his simple and tender lyrics are not especially difficult of comprehension. Stéphane Mallarmé (1842-1898) wrote more obscure poetry, carefully designed, full of musical sound and flow, with an intellectual tendency. Jules Laforgue (1860-1887), witty, ironic, with a gift for startling imagery, has greatly influenced the work of T. S. Eliot and through him modern poetry in English.

Arthur Rimbaud (1854-1891), a precocious genius, was an important forerunner of Symbolism and in some respects of Surrealism. Paul Claudel called him a "mystic in the wild state"; his poem, *The Drunken Boat,* and prose-poem, *A Season in Hell,* describe Rimbaud's youthful, tortured spiritual experiences in a supremely visual style.

7. Critics and Historians

Not all Victorians accepted the assumption that nineteenth-century industrial democracy was the best of all systems. Thomas Carlyle (1795-1881), John Ruskin

(1819-1900), and Matthew Arnold (1822-1888) were far from infallible judges of the social and cultural shortcomings of their time, but they refused to accept the popular compromise and were not afraid to tackle problems which others evaded.

Carlyle abandoned the strict religion of his Scotch peasant forebears, but retained their independence, stubbornness, zest for controversy, and puritan sense of duty. From German literature and philosophy he acquired a transcendentalist belief in the reality of an unseen world, and a Teutonic crabbedness in his prose. His was a prophetic vein; he lashed at the evils of his time with the fire of Elijah, and most that he saw was evil to him: the industrial system, democracy, evangelical Protestantism, Anglo-Catholicism, evolutionary science. From his first book, *Sartor Resartus,* with its comparison of human institutions and manners to clothes, to his last, he did not spare the whip. Much that he said was true and needed saying, but he reacted (despite sympathy for the masses) against democracy toward a conception of government not far removed from Nazi doctrine of rule by a strong man (a "hero" in his sense) and against nineteenth-century industry toward a belief in medieval economy (set forth in *Past and Present* in his picture of Glastonbury Abbey, where Abbot Samson is the strong ruler). Other important works are *The French Revolution,* the anti-democratic pamphlet on Chartism, and the books on Cromwell and Frederick the Great, two of his chief heroes. Carlyle's influence has waned considerably.

Ruskin was much influenced by Carlyle, but differed in his proposal of remedies. Achieving fame as a critic of art, he turned more and more to social and economic problems. But the two interests can never be mutually exclusive, and in Ruskin they were closely related. For to him art was not an isolated phenomenon, existing in a void, but a condition of the society which produced it, and his strong moral sense felt good art the product of a good society, bad art the product of a corrupt society. This belief led him to wrong conclusions (especially in his condemnation of art of the so-called Renaissance), but it led him also to attack those elements in contemporary society which made impossible the production of beauty. He regarded as wrong the Victorian conception of money-wealth, the degradation of the working classes, the inequality between production and wages, for men could not hope in a society so organized to live as men should live. No socialist (he was, like Carlyle, anti-democratic), his concern with the good, the beautiful, and the true led him to propose reforms later urged by socialists, and as a result he was bitterly attacked in his time. His important works in art-criticism are *Modern Painters, The Stones of Venice,* and *Seven Lamps of Architecture;* in economic criticism, *Unto This Last, Munera Pulveris,. A Crown of Wild Olive.*

Matthew Arnold was a poet for part of his life, a critic for the rest. That troubled concern with the ills of the modern world which we find in his poetry became in his criticism a calm and thoughtful examination of those ills, with proposed remedies for their reform. To him as to Ruskin art was not isolated, and his essays are therefore occupied with social and religious as well as literary problems, as in *Culture and Anarchy* and *God and the Bible.* More European-minded than his contemporaries (he attacked the insularity of Victorian England), his prose has a Gallic clarity and ease, together with a certain schoolmasterish care in making a point. He too attacked English concentration on material prosperity, which he thought anarchic, since it had no concern with the ends to which wealth was to be put. To him the landed aristocracy were Barbarians, uninterested in any but animal pleasures, and the working classes a Populace debased and brutal. But his chief object of attack was the Philistines: the middle classes intent on the accumulation of riches, self-satisfied in their evangelical respectability. Arnold's remedy for the world's evils was "culture," the dissemination of the "best that is known and thought in the world," to be found in the great literature of the past. Poetry would supersede dying religion, and through culture would come enlightenment, improvement in society, a raising of the moral and intellectual level of all classes. Arnold was less aware than Ruskin that culture could not be applied, but must depend on fundamental economic reforms.

William Morris was the most alive and active of the great Victorians, turning his energies into poetry, painting, decoration, manufacture, printing, socialism, always with an eye to enriching the life of man, to making life "happy and dignified for all people." He too saw art in its social context, and felt that happiness and dignity for all people could come only when capitalist class-society had been overturned. His socialism was somewhat confused by the medievalism which is so strong in his poetry and his craftsmanship. Besides romances on Icelandic and medieval themes, Morris wrote *The Dream of John Ball* and *News from Nowhere,* the latter set in 2000 A.D. when social reforms had been won.

In contrast, Walter Pater (1839-1894) in a half-dozen volumes of essays and impressionistic sketches, and in his novel, *Marius the Epicurean,* exemplified the deliquescence of English prose; in his works art-for-art's sake reached the ultimate development in its obsession with nuances of sensation and expression.

Among other prose writers of the Victorian era, early and late, who reflected and influenced the various movements of thought of the time, were Thomas Babington Macaulay (1800-1859), John Henry Newman (1801-1890), Charles Kingsley (1819-1875), and Thomas Henry Huxley (1825-1895).

Macaulay, already famous before Victoria became queen, was an essayist, historian, and politician, whose brilliant but metallic prose helped to make popular the study of English history, which he described, though not with blind partisanship, from the viewpoint of Whig and Protestant prejudice. Newman was the leader of the Oxford movement, a reaction against possible liberal church reform and towards a conception of the church as something more than a mere human institution. He became himself a Roman Catholic and a Cardinal. The author of novels and poems, he set forth clearly and fluently his spiritual history in the *Apologia pro Vita Sua,* inspired by a remark of Kingsley's on the Roman clergy's (and Newman's) lack of concern with truth for its own sake. Kingsley, best known as a novelist, also wrote poetry and pamphlets. He was a Christian socialist, interested in industrial reform and opposed to the medievalism and Catholicism of the Oxford movement. Huxley was the chief fighter on the side of science in the battles raised by the theory of evolution, the great apologist of Darwinism.

His exact, clear prose was an admirable weapon in his fight against the "ecclesiastical spirit."

In France the leading writers of critical prose were Charles-Augustin Sainte-Beuve (1804-1869) and Hippolyte Auguste Taine (1828-1893). The former was in early life one of the romantic circle which surrounded Hugo, and the author of novels and poetry. But he moved away from romanticism in his development as a critic towards a detached examination of writers and literary works, an examination which sought to understand its object rather than to make rash personal judgments in the romantic manner, or judgments based on inflexible standards in the neo-classical manner. His study involved a knowledge of a writer's whole experience, its moral, intellectual, and physical conditions. He did much to rehabilitate French poetry of the sixteenth century, and his judgments on writers of the past are in general admirable, though personal prejudice sometimes clouds his opinions of contemporaries. His best work is contained in the *Causeries du Lundi* (*Monday Talks*), a collection of articles contributed over several years to a literary periodical.

Taine represents the ultimate influence in criticism of the century's scientific thought and method. He applied a rigid determinism in his judgments, regarding works of art as the products of forces working in and on the writer: Race (inherited qualities), Milieu (environment), and Moment (the dominant idea of the time). His method is well illustrated in his *History of English Literature*. He was a philosopher and historian as well as a literary critic.

The late century possessed in Ferdinand Brunetière (1849-1906) a conservative and dogmatic critic, a believer in the church, who opposed both the naturalism and symbolism of his time, but in doing so developed an important theory (based on his belief in the importance of the human will) on conflict in drama.

Aside from Taine, whose important historical work was his *Origins of Contemporary France,* the chief French historians of literary importance in the nineteenth century were Jules Michelet (1798-1874) and Ernest Renan (1823-1892). The former's many-volumed *History of France* reflects its author's patriotic and democratic bias, and is valuable less as scholarship than for its imaginative treatment of the past (in which the romantic influence is strong), its language charged with poetic color.

Renan was trained for the priesthood, but lost his faith as a young man, and turned to historical studies in the field of religion. Influenced by science, he ruled out the possible existence of the miraculous and divine, but his treatment of his subjects, though objective, is not unsympathetic; there is tolerance in his skepticism. The beauty of his prose style distinguishes all his work, of which the most famous volume is the *Life of Jesus,* a part of his studies in the origins of Christianity.

8. Nineteenth-Century Drama

Drama in general did not begin to approach the accomplishment of lyric poetry and the novel until well on into the century. But with the subsidence of the early outburst of romanticism, and the turn of literature towards realism and naturalism, plays appeared which followed the novels of the time in a competent handling of familiar experience and in a concern with social questions. By the last decade the theater had revived, and in the Norwegian Henrik Ibsen (1828-1906) a master had appeared whose influence was widely felt.

The lyrical bent of romanticism, its tendency to neglect formal restrictions, to wander away from the earth and the present, made difficult the attainment of the detachment and compactness necessary to successful drama. The English stage was for a good part of the century degraded, with the public taste strong for farce and melodrama, and attempts by the romantic and Victorian poets at serious poetic drama showed ignorance of stage requirements, an inability to avoid loose rhetoric or to secure proper dramatic tension and movement. In Shelley's *Cenci,* the best-known English poetic drama in this century, a few scenes of the struggle between Beatrice Cenci and her tyrannical and lustful father attain a life lacking in most of the play.

The French romantics turned their hands to drama, but even Hugo, whose plays are so important historically, was chiefly successful in occasional effective lyrical or rhetorical passages, in isolated scenes. Of all the drama of that time it is the charming and sparkling comedies of Musset which retain most power to please. Eugène Scribe (1791-1861) wrote plays trifling in content, but through his theory of the "well-made play" influenced European drama in general until a reaction set in against the production of pieces neatly put together but empty of content. Somewhat later, Alexandre Dumas *fils* (1824-1895), illegitimate son of the novelist, created in the "problem play" a type which was to be popular as the drama became increasingly a medium for exploring certain social questions. This type of play very often leaned heavily toward preaching, with the characters obvious mouthpieces for the author's opinions.

In Germany, as we have seen, Heinrich von Kleist to a large degree avoided the faults of romantic drama. The Austrian Franz Grillparzer (1791-1872) combined poetic skill with a true sense of character in his plays on classical themes and Austrian history. A realistic treatment of people and settings is found in the tragedies of Otto Ludwig (1813-1865) and Friedrich Hebbel (1813-1863), whose *Maria Magdalena* effectively pictures the life of a family in the oppressive conditions of a small town. Later Germany produced two of the foremost dramatists of modern times in Hermann Sudermann (1857-1928) and Gerhart Hauptmann (1862-1946). The plays of the former show the influence of naturalism in their attention to detail, and are skillfully constructed. His most famous play, *Heimat* (called *Magda* outside Germany), was acted by Sarah Bernhardt and Eleonora Duse. In Hauptmann both the naturalism and the symbolism of the time made their mark. His subjects range from past history to studies of thieves' life, degeneracy, and infanticide. In *Die Weber* (*The Weavers*) he pictured an uprising of workingmen. *Die versunkene Glocke* (*The Sunken Bell*) is a symbolist play on the conflict between the artist's spirit and worldly temptations. Hauptmann's fine poetic gift and sympathy for men raise him far above cruder naturalists.

The figure of Ibsen dominated the European drama of the second half-century, and in technique, structure, methods of handling dialogue and character, he has profoundly influenced the drama since his time. His method, though realistic in his best-known plays, approached fantasy, symbolism, and mysticism in certain early plays (*Brand* and *Peer Gynt*) and in his last play, *When We Dead Awaken*. But whatever his treatment of subject, he is preoccupied throughout with a criticism of society in relation to the individual, with the individual's attempt or failure to deal with social modes and creeds, to seek his own destiny and happiness. The hero of *Brand* is willing to sacrifice everything to a sense of duty, to the assertion of his own will; to be "free and awake" is his determination.

In the realistic plays of his middle career Ibsen deals with the conditions of middle-class life against which his characters struggle. In *Ghosts* social convention forces Mrs. Alving to maintain a fiction about her marriage to a despicable husband, now dead, and her pretense helps crush her son. The hypocritical business man is treated in *Pillars of Society*. In *An Enemy of the People,* a man is ruined by social hatred in an attempt to help society. He has discovered that the water in the town mineral bath is poisoned by an industry, but the town turns upon him instead of welcoming his help. The position of women in marriage, the fundamental problem of the family, interested Ibsen, and among his finest characters are women placed in positions from which they seek escape, or by which, like Mrs. Alving in *Ghosts,* they are defeated. Nora in *A Doll's House,* Rebecca West in *Rosmersholm,* Hedda Gabler, whose want of an object in life drives her to bring about the destruction of the man she loves—these are memorable women.

The greatest defender and expounder of Ibsen in his own time was the Irishman, Bernard Shaw, whose work will be discussed in another chapter. In him the English drama, after its doldrums, its unactable poetic plays, its well-made plays and problem plays of Henry Arthur Jones (1851-1929) and Arthur Wing Pinero (1855-1934), finally came into its own again.

Oscar Wilde (1856-1900) was the wittiest playwright in the period between Sheridan and Shaw. *The Importance of Being Earnest* is perhaps the best farce in the English language, while *Lady Windermere's Fan* and *A Woman of No Importance,* glittering and superficial, foreshadow the comedies of Noël Coward and his imitators.

In the rest of Europe Chekhov and Tolstoy in Russia, August Strindberg (1849-1912) in Sweden, Benito Galdós (1845-1920), also a fine novelist, in Spain, shared in the wide movement which was bringing new life into the theater, a movement which stimulated the formation in various cities of such organizations as the Théâtre Libre of Paris, devoted to the presentation of important works by the foremost playwrights of the day.

9. American Literature

The chief subjects of colonial literature were religion and travel, colonization, or local history. During the eighteenth century the growing tension between the colonies and England turned writers to politics. Most distinguished of colonial religious authors was Jonathan Edwards (1703-1758) who combined a gift for strict Calvinist logic with a deep, even poetic, mystical strain. The accounts by

Colonel ·William Byrd (1674-1744) of Virginia and North Carolina are among the best of works describing exploration and settlement.

The pamphlet *Common Sense* by the English radical, Thomas Paine (1737-1809), helped considerably in the Revolutionary period to widen the split with the mother country. Philip Freneau (1752-1832), first American poet of genuine importance, was both a political propagandist, bitterly satirical of England, and a fine lyricist.

Two writers of the young republic whose works still bear reading are Hugh Henry Brackenridge (1748-1816) and Charles Brockden Brown (1771-1810). The former in his lengthy *Modern Chivalry* (modeled on *Don Quixote*) satirized the faults of the young democracy. Brown mingled in his novels humanitarian sentiments with the methods of the tale of terror.

With the development during the nineteenth century of a national literature, persisting European, especially English, influences, were modified by contact with the achievements and aspirations of American democracy, by the expanding frontier, and by sectional differences. Despite a settled civilization in the east, life in general tended to be raw and violent, religion to intensify the harsher elements in the Puritan tradition. A feeling of inferiority in the face of more ancient lands produced both a truculent patriotism and a supine "colonial-mindedness," neither of which has disappeared from American life. But out of the conditions which gave birth to faults there came virtues as well: strength and courage, an independence of spirit, too easily ignored by commentators who have emphasized crudeness, hardness, lack of beauty.

From the complex of forces which were making America, certain writers emerged who are at once representative of the national culture and creators of enduring literature. Behind the names of the first rank, to be mentioned here, was an army of lesser men. Great and small, they show in their work the influence of tradition and novelty, of ancient culture and fresh themes; the worst of them sank into genteel echoes of Europe.

Washington Irving (1783-1859) was the first important American man of letters whose life and work alike are contained in the history of the republic. A pleasant periodical essayist, a skillful recreator of European (notably Spanish) as well as native legends, he is best in the Knickerbocker *History of New York,* a humorous mock-history of the Dutch rule, and in such tales of the old communities of the Hudson valley as *Rip Van Winkle* and *The Legend of Sleepy Hollow*. But of all the leading American writers Irving is most faded; he seems too often a sterile copy of Addison and Goldsmith, to have weakened himself as a writer by his regret of the good old days, his escape into the peaceful past.

The first half-century promised more for a national culture than the second half accomplished. Nowhere was this truer than in New England, where for several decades before the Civil War there was a vigorous intellectual life, an eager concern for ideas. We need not set down here the long roster of preachers, lecturers, reformers, teachers, and scholars who shared in this burst of energy. Three men of the day and region rose above the rest: Ralph Waldo Emerson (1803-1882), Henry David Thoreau (1817-1862), and Nathaniel Hawthorne (1804-1864).

Emerson shared the current romantic preoccupation with the individual man and with nature. Influenced by Coleridge, by German philosophy, by Carlyle, he was a transcendentalist, who regarded the physical world as but the visible extension of Deity, of a universal Over-Soul, towards which man must strive, and to some knowledge of which he might attain through intuition. In his early essay *Nature* he set forth his doctrines, revealing in the course of the work not only an intense and sometimes obscure idealism but also a deep love for natural beauties.

To Emerson man was naturally good, and capable of increasing goodness and power—"Who can set bounds to the possibilities of man?" Aspiring to spiritual integrity, the individual must be self-reliant, unafraid of conventional notions or popular opinion. Emerson's optimism was great, yet he was not blind to the elements in American government and life which he thought harmful to the development of the human spirit. But he felt too the possibilities of the sprawling continent, of the unopened West, and urged America to refuse to be limited by too narrow a respect for transatlantic values. "We have listened too long," he wrote in *The American Scholar,* "to the courtly muses of Europe."

Emerson's prose tends often to mistiness as he ascends into ideal realms, but it can be pointed and clear; in his *Journals* especially there is a strong leaven of Yankee common sense. His poetry reaches its highest levels in the mystic *Brahma* and in certain nature lyrics.

Of all the great New Englanders the oddest and in many respects most attractive is Thoreau. Independent-minded, scornful of conventional social and economic values, a transcendentalist, an extreme individualist, he expressed himself freely on life in general, literature, government, and institutions. His best prose is concrete, colorful; in it nature's fresh beauty lives, and the writer's own strong mind. *Walden,* Thoreau's finest work, is an account of a sojourn in the woods where, building his own house and supporting his needs as cheaply as possible, he sought to

> live deliberately, to front only the essential facts of life, and see if I could not learn what it had to teach, and not, when I came to die, discover that I had not lived. . . . I wanted to live deep and suck out all the marrow of life . . . to cut a broad swath and shave close, to drive life into a corner, and reduce it to its lowest terms. . . .

Thoreau's *Journals* are not only highly readable but reflect his odd, memorable personality.

His most famous political statement was the essay on *Civil Disobedience* (1849), an attack on the war with Mexico and on the institution of slavery. Urging refusal to support government which tolerates and protects bad causes, he maintained the supreme importance of the individual. The doctrine of passive resistance suggested in this essay has in modern times greatly influenced the Mahatma Gandhi.

Through ancestry and environment, Hawthorne inherited the Puritan traditions of New England, and most of his short stories and romances deal with the people and manners of the rigorous Puritan times. But in choosing the past for subject he was no mere romantic escapist. Associated with the transcendentalists, though not one of them, for he could not accept their optimistic view of man, Hawthorne was a moral analyst, concerned with exploring the recesses of the human soul and observing the effects upon it of sin and evil, especially those effects which arise from or produce a tragic isolation of the individual from other men. In *The House of Seven Gables, The Marble Faun* (which has an Italian setting), and above all in his masterpiece, *The Scarlet Letter,* he treats at length the problem of sin.

Hawthorne in his probings frequently makes use of symbols to represent moral qualities. They create atmospheres strange and unreal, but often have great effectiveness. His prose is calm, harmonious, and though grave in mood, marked by a rich subdued coloring. Its worst fault is an occasional awkward remoteness from familiar speech, especially in the dialogue.

The early years of the century had produced in James Fenimore Cooper (1789-1851) a novelist far more popular than Hawthorne could ever be. A true understanding of Cooper's place in history involves a knowledge of his novels on social and economic questions and of his opinions on American democracy, but his fame for more than a century, abroad as well as in America, has rested upon his novels of adventure on sea and land. Most famous are those collected as "Leatherstocking Tales" which recount the experiences on a romanticized frontier of the scout Natty Bumpo. However improbable his pictures of life, however great his faults of style, Cooper through his energetic imagination and strength of mind was a valuable force in the growing literature of the nation.

With as great a gift as Cooper's for exciting narrative, but far more deeply concerned than he with getting under the surfaces of life, and master, in addition, of an eloquent surging prose, Herman Melville (1819-1891) stands with his friend Hawthorne at the top of American fiction. A farmer and teacher in early years, he came to acquire a wide knowledge of books, but the most far-reaching fact of his life was a voyage from 1841 to 1844 on a whaling ship in the South Seas. This experience was the basis for his accounts of South Sea life in *Typee* and *Omoo,* and, more important, went into the framework of *Mardi* and *Moby Dick. Mardi* is partly straightforward narrative of seafaring, partly confused fantasy and satire. Melville's storytelling power and his romantic symbolism are successfully fused in *Moby Dick,* which combines thrilling incident with profound searching into the mysteries of nature and man.

The novel is in the first place an account of a whaling-voyage; we feel the roll of the sea, the dangers and joys of the hunt, see the harpoon's flash and smell the trypots. It is also an encyclopedia of whaling-lore and a vehicle for philosophical disquisitions, but loses nothing by being these things, for they add richness to the book. Finally, it represents the struggle of man against the malignant forces of the universe, symbolized in the white whale, Moby Dick, towards whom from first to last the voyage drives. Captain Ahab has lost a leg to him, and with terrible zeal seeks revenge, sparing no one, not himself, nor his mates, nor his strange crew of white men and savages. The three day chase of Moby Dick in the last chapters ends, as it must, in destruction and death.

Both as a prophet and as an artist Edgar Allan Poe (1809-1849) has been honored less in his own country than in France, where he was translated by Baudelaire. Legend has made of him the most mysterious figure in American literature, building a picture of an unstable genius, a drunkard and neurotic. But withal, he was a practicing journalist, much of whose best work as well as his worst was produced under the conditions of his trade. Often a hack-writer of necessity, he was also the first important literary critic in America, a good poet, and a master of the short story. He directed his criticism, though it was frequently wrong in its estimates and extreme in its assertions, towards its object viewed solely as a work of art, towards establishing beauty and not instruction as the standard of judgment. His poems reflect his theories; suggestive, musical, varied in forms and rhythms, they please through sound and not through sense. His short stories catered to the public taste for terror, trappings of mystery and gloom, lush atmosphere. But the best of them create moods not entirely dependent on theatrical settings. Poe had a sure sense of structure, knew how to build a story with unity and economy to achieve the singleness of effect which was his end in view. His skill is shown in such tales as *The Fall of the House of Usher* and *The Cask of Amontillado*. In his tales of ratiocination he was a pioneer of the detective story.

A far cry from Poe's aestheticism is the "barbaric yawp" of Walt Whitman (1819-1892), in whom the American land and people and the democratic ideal found their most exultant voice. He knew and condemned the weaknesses of American society and politics, but he looked with tremendous hope into the future. "Today, ahead, though dimly yet, we see, in vistas, a copious, sane, gigantic offspring," he wrote in *Democratic Vistas*.

Influenced by the teachings of Emerson (who praised *Leaves of Grass* on its first appearance, in 1855). Whitman was a transcendentalist in his spiritual yearnings, his faith in the individual man. And the individual whom he sang chiefly was himself,

> Walt Whitman, a kosmos, of Manhattan the son,
> Turbulent, fleshy, sensual, eating, drinking and breeding.

He found "no sweeter fat than sticks to my own bones." His joy in life, in nature, in his own body (which he celebrated with a frankness shocking to his time)—these are among his major themes. But as he felt that mere individualism was isolation, so he believed in comradeship and love among men, and the individual Walt Whitman is merged with the mass of men; through him speak "many long dumb voices." Across his pages marches an enormous pageant of America—its cities and farms, forests and rivers, from east to west; its animals and birds ("The sharp-hoof'd moose of the north, the cat on the house-sill, the chickadee, the prairie-dog"); its people of all conditions—the common man in whom he put his democratic trust, the soldiers whom he nursed during the Civil War, the western pioneers. In the exquisite lines of *When Lilacs Last in the Door-*

yard Bloomed he mourned the greatest of America's common men and pioneers, Abraham Lincoln.

Whitman's style breaks with all conventional forms of verse: loose, irregular, chanting in rhythm, it makes generous use of slang and colloquial language. It is often awkward, prosy, and monotonous, loaded with interminable catalogues. But at its best its free rhythms beat with a strong music, may express the tenderest emotions and longings, a sense of mystery, the beauties of the

> voluptuous cool-breathed earth!
> Earth of the slumbering and liquid trees!

In the years following the Civil War the literary energy of earlier years subsided, conservatism and gentility were dominant, New England sank into a sterile Brahmanism. A few writers resisted the genteel tone, a few others faced the problems raised by onrushing industrialism. Among the more outstanding were William Dean Howells (1837-1920), a relatively gentle but ardent realist; Hamlin Garland (1860-1940); and Stephen Crane (1871-1900), a pioneer of American naturalism in his slum-tragedy, *Maggie,* and his remarkable Civil War novel, *The Red Badge of Courage.* Frank Norris (1870-1902) pushed naturalism further in *McTeague, The Octopus,* and *The Pit.* Local color was important in the sentimental California tales of Bret Harte (1836-1902); in those of New Orleans by G. W. Cable (1844-1925), and in the fine pictures of Maine places and people by Sarah Orne Jewett (1849-1909).

Mark Twain (Samuel Langhorne Clemens, 1835-1910) inherited a strain of native humor which had grown up on the old southern and southwestern frontier, out of the life and manners of little towns and settlements, of the woods, canebrakes, and rivers. His work reflects its faults—strained exaggeration, an excessive fondness for the grotesque and surprising. It was largely an anecdotal humor, and Mark Twain, strong in anecdotes and single scenes, was weak in handling larger units of structure. But its colloquial excellences are his also, and his genius is his own. With no loving-kindness for the "damned human race," shrewdly aware of the cussedness and meanness as well as of the occasional goodness of men, sharp of eye and keen of ear, he created in his familiar speech a living picture of an America now nearly vanished.

In *Life on the Mississippi* and *Roughing It* he twists fact and fiction carelessly together as he recalls his days as a river-pilot, or the hot excitement of life in silver-mad Nevada. *The Gilded Age,* written in collaboration with Charles Dudley Warner, is an incomparable exposure of corruption after the Civil War. The chief literary value lies in the portrait of Colonel Beriah Sellers, the completest expression in fiction of the American optimist, the boom-time visionary whose tongue drips millions while his stomach goes empty. His creator made him not only a type, but a human being who charms us in spite of his folly. With all the excellences, however, of these and other works, Mark Twain reached his heights in *Huckleberry Finn.* Its characters—Nigger Jim, the King and the Duke, the proud Grangerfords, the simple backwoods people—are enduringly fresh. Its incidents are varied, filled with excitement and entertainment. But it is the great river itself, tying the story together, which gives it strength, beauty, and mystery. The river is no dead thing, and in it lives much of America. Nowhere else are the qualities of Mark Twain so perfectly blended: his knowledge of men, his easy western speech, and his humor.

II. ART FROM THE FRENCH REVOLUTION TO POST IMPRESSIONISM

The period from the French Revolution to the end of the nineteenth century was laden with economic, social, and scientific changes which significantly affected painting, architecture, and sculpture. With the growth of large manufacturing cities in the latter half of the century, a specifically urban art evolved. Swifter means of transportation changed people's (especially artists') way of looking at things. Landscape, for example, no longer appeared static as in the past, but seemed fleeting as one hurried by it. The growing urbanization of life made the city-dweller's day off in the country a socially typical experience, one which became a frequent subject for the Impressionist painters. Other results of the development of a "high powered" approach to life were the application of newer processes in art production, the invention of new methods of reproducing black-and-white illustrations in newspapers, and the use of mechanical means for reproducing sculpture. We may say that by the end of the century the change in tempo developed a looser and more casual style in painting. This is known as Impressionism, one of the real contributions of the age. The change in technique, however, was preceded by a serious change in subject matter.

The conservative academies of art, whose power we have observed in our study of the seventeenth and eighteenth centuries, had by the beginning of the nineteenth become so arrogant that a revolt was certain. The sharp changes in the social and political aspects of civilization inspired a shift from the predominantly religious and aristocratic art of the past to a new form of expression. In architecture the shift was not so marked, for while the new democratic governments fostered such public building as museums, libraries, schools, parliament buildings, hospitals, and asylums, these were executed in styles borrowed from respectable traditions of the past. This is readily understandable when we remember that civic architecture, more than any other art, is official, and therefore slow to progress. (We have only to visit our nation's capital to see recent public buildings in the perhaps handsome but unquestionably abused tradition of ancient Rome!) In painting and sculpture, however, the problems of the nineteenth-century artist were to find proper subjects and techniques for the expression of a new social scene. In both he was hindered by a trite academy and by an ultra conservative public. Every attempt he made to break away from tradition met with opposition and public scorn.

A break thus ensued in the early part of the century between the artist and his public, which has been a most significant cultural problem of the contemporary world. Whereas during earlier periods the artist had been a well-integrated factor in the culture of his particular epoch, in the nineteenth century he moved farther and farther away from his possible patrons. The new industrialized society sprang into being with such terrifying speed that it did not have the time to create its own cultural tradition. The only thing it could do, therefore, was to adhere to those forms of expression which, through long and respectable usage, were considered appropriate and dignified. As we shall see, the history of the art of the first three quarters of the nineteenth century reveals an oscillation among the many historic styles we have encountered in previous chapters.

It is well to observe that the borrowing from past styles also brought with it the borrowing of older subject matter. As the more advanced painter of the last century went to everyday life for his themes, he was being radical only in the eyes of an extremely reactionary society, apparently unsure of its taste; for artists in the past had done the same without causing any great tumult. The Dutch painters of the seventeenth century, for example, had almost exclusively used everyday subject matter and had been both acceptable and popular among their countrymen.

The choice of styles for the nineteenth-century artist was complicated by a number of factors. Archaeological research had brought ideas and forms of the past to the attention of his immediate predecessors, resulting in a revival of ancient styles. Elaborate investigations in philology and comparative literature had awakened an enthusiasm for and interest in foreign cultures. The new facilities for travel now enabled many people to see and derive inspiration from Greece and the Near East. Even the reactionary attitude of the academies, in their adherence to the styles of the Italian sixteenth and seventeenth centuries, helped to keep the past fresh in the minds of the people.

1. Neoclassical Art of the French Revolution: Greek and Roman Revivals

Realism, which had been making progress in the second half of the eighteenth century in the paintings of Chardin and Greuze, was dissipated by the French Revolution. The self-consciousness of the dissatisfied middle classes showed itself in a very dignified reproduction of the style and vocabulary of Roman republican culture which appeared to them the best expression of the democratic ideals for which they were struggling. The familial virtues preached by Greuze were now repeated in an intensified and patriotic manner in the paintings of Jacques David (1748-1825), the most important artistic personality in the French Revolutionary period. He began his Neoclassical (new-classical) works in the decade immediately preceding the Revolution with *Oath of the Horatii,* whose theme, the conflict between love and patriotism, he derived from one of the great classical plays of the seventeenth century. David arranged the figures as though they were a bas-relief, in a long frieze, and posed them in the familiar attitude of the middle-class tragedies of the late eighteenth century. There is little difference between the spirit of Greuze's *Father's Curse* and David's *Oath of the Horatii.* Both show figures with their arms raised in diagonal, powerful gestures, as well as a group of weeping women, who, in David's picture, remind us of Niobe and her children of classical antiquity. In fact, the whole impression is markedly suggestive of a Roman narrative relief which has been emotionally heightened by violent gestures a Roman artist would never have used. The background of the David work is a series of Roman Doric columns, and the total impression of the composition is severely geometrical. In *Brutus Mourning His Son* David preaches that for the welfare of the state the father sacrifices even his child; in *The Death of Socrates,* that the political radical should rightfully sacrifice himself for the good of the state. In all three works David adheres realistically to the archaeological facts— details of costume, architecture, furniture. But this is a romantic sort of realism, interested in facts of the past only so as to use them for contemporary moral purposes. After the emergency of the Revolution was over, when people were more interested in pleasure than they had been, David's art became softer; and instead of borrowing Roman severity he borrowed Hellenistic sensuousness (exemplified in his *Rape of the Sabines*).

Although the Neoclassical spirit emerged shortly after 1750, it finally crystallized during the period of the Revolution and Napoleon. It was unfortunate for the development of art in the nineteenth century that the new classical movement occurred at such a crucial time, for its mode of expression came rapidly to dominate French painting, sculpture, and architecture. In the first two arts it led to a firm favoring of precise methods of drawing and modeling, derived from the classical past or from the Italian sixteenth century.

Architecture in particular was derivative of the classical ideal down to the end of the nineteenth century, even though other historic styles were used. During the period of the Revolution and Napoleon the classical style was unusually fruitful. In Paris the famous arches of triumph were erected in celebration of the emperor's conquests, in the manner of imperial Rome (*l'Arc du Carrousel* and *l'Arc de l'Étoile*). At the same time the church of the Madeleine (Paris) was rebuilt as a temple to glory in the Corinthian style of a Roman temple. Even the stock-exchange was constructed in the same style, another example of adapting classical forms to modern needs. This tendency was not confined to France, but like most art movements of the century was more or less international in scope. There are countless Neoclassical architectural examples in England, Germany, and Italy.

The Neoclassical style naturally extended to sculpture, both to architectural sculpture and the independent form. This began at the end of the eighteenth century with the Italian, Antonio Canova (1757-1822). His relationship to the antique is apparent not only in his subjects (*Napoleon as a Nude Hero, Amor and Psyche, Theseus and the Minotaur*) but in his sometimes Hellenistically graceful figures, with their fine contours and well-organized compositions.

2. *Romanticism: Medieval Revivalism and Exotic Interests*

Neoclassicism as exemplified by David at the time of the French Revolution had a real function in encouraging the middle classes when firmness, singleness of purpose, and courageous patriotism (all Roman virtues) were essential in their struggle for a democratic state. After the Revolution it became merely part of the nineteenth-century tendency toward the revival of past styles. In this sense Neoclassicism was as "romantic" as a revival of any other style, Gothic, Romanesque, "Renaissance," Baroque. Romanticism in painting, therefore, may be defined as a kind of escape to past cultures or strange lands. It was a seeking after new and strange sensations, a reaction away from the everyday realities of an increasingly industrialized civilization. Instead of painting cows and pigs, animals native to their country, artists went to the zoo to find exotic subjects—tigers, crocodiles. Exoticism, however, was only one aspect of Romanticism.

In the post-Napoleonic era there grew up in Europe an interest in the Middle Ages, particularly in the Gothic period. Part of this was undoubtedly the result of the tremendous national self-consciousness fostered in the time of Napoleon. Each country began consciously to delve into its own past literature and art.

Another aspect of this period was the return to religion or to those aspects of it which were emotionally attractive. During the Revolution religion had taken a subordinate position while "reason" reigned. With the full advent to power of the financial and commercial interests, a reaction set in to produce one of the most sentimentally religious periods in modern history. The post-Napoleonic or "Romantic" period in art was a revolt against almost everything the previous epoch had represented, and the emotional outburst took the form of religious and national self-consciousness. These, of course, are broad generalizations to which numerous exceptions can be made, but beyond any question the Romantic era was one of self-expression and of freedom in artistic form as opposed to the regularity and imposed restraint of the Neoclassic period. Where the Neoclassicist preferred the static forms of Roman architecture, the Romantic chose the dynamic, vibrant architecture of the Gothic age. For the sculpturesque quality of Neoclassical painting, the Romantic substituted an art primarily dependent on color. David had emphasized sternness and nobility in the classical subjects and he painted them in a cold, clear light. Eugène Delacroix (1799-1863), the chief exponent of Romanticism, used rich, bright color, mysterious light, and agitated subject matter. His Gothicism is shown in his choice of medieval subject matter and his highly emotional outlook. Many of his themes, among them the *Abduction of Rebecca,* were borrowed from the historical novels of Sir Walter Scott or from medieval subjects in Shakespeare. As can readily be imagined, he made a fine illustrator of Goethe's *Faust,* for which he did a number of splendid lithographs (black-and-white design drawn on stone, then impressed on paper).

What is most significant in Delacroix's work from the Romantic viewpoint is not so much his choice of historical and medieval themes as his emphasis on the suffering of mankind and the right of the individual to freedom. An important element in his subject matter is the conflict between man and the insuperable forces of nature, vividly embodied in his *Christ on the Lake of Gennesaret.* His agitated compositions and his expressively bright and clean colors lend themselves admirably to the tragedy of *The Massacre at Scio,* a story from the current Greek war of independence. To him and other Romantics like Byron, the struggle of Greece against the Turks was of major importance as a human struggle for

freedom. It was only natural that for the expression of his wildly emotional attitude Delacroix leaned heavily on the powerful art of Rubens and on the Baroque
diagonality of composition. We find the influence of Rubens particularly in his
animal paintings. His color reminds us of the Venetians.

Delacroix is further important for having founded a school of historical painting which was to become one of the mainstays of later academic art. Like a
great many other artists, he was also interested in exotic subjects (*Algerian
Women in Their Apartments*). In sculpture Antoine Barye (1795-1875) parallels
the Romantic spirit of Delacroix and his marvelous studies of wild animals repeat
Delacroix's exotic subject matter.

The Spaniard, Francisco Goya (1746-1828), in his many paintings of the Spanish court, expressed his contempt for his pompous and artificial models, and an
exquisite command of the art of painting fabrics. His loose technique, strong
color contrasts, and informally arranged compositions establish him as one of
the ancestors of the Impressionists of the 1870's. His most important work—executed during the first two decades of the nineteenth century, which include the
Napoleonic invasion of Spain—is represented in a series of prints known as *The
Disasters of War*. Here we find a typical romantic preoccupation with the horror
of slain bodies and the intense emotionality coincident with such a portrayal. In
these prints and in his paintings, he achieves his effects by a powerful light-and-
shade technique which molds his figures and by incisive draughtsmanship.

No discussion of the Romantic period can omit consideration of the reactions'
in the other arts. The conscious return to the medieval past evident in the painting
of Delacroix and in the novels and poetry of Victor Hugo had its parallel in
architecture. Public buildings such as the Houses of Parliament (London) were
constructed in the Gothic style. At the same time Wyattville rebuilt Windsor
Castle in late Gothic forms. In France the movement led to an industrious resto-
ration of the medieval buildings, especially Notre Dame Cathedral (Paris). Most
of them had been allowed to fall into disrepair. It might be appropriate at this
point to indicate various styles of medieval revival practiced in architecture during
the last century. The famous church of the Sacré Cœur (Paris) was modeled
after one of the more unusual Romanesque churches of France, the Cathedral of
Périgueux with its Byzantine forms. Pure Romanesque became particularly popular in the United States toward the end of the nineteenth and beginning of the
twentieth century in the designs of Henry Richardson (1838-1886). This style
has been used for university buildings, bank façades, railroad stations, etc. The
most obvious use was, of course, in churches both in Europe and America. (St.
Patrick's in New York is probably derived from Litchfield Cathedral.)

3. *The Academic View: Revival of the Italian Tradition*

Not only were there medieval revivals, but borrowings from the Italian art of
the so-called Renaissance. In architecture we have such a characteristic example as
the Königsbau (Munich) which was adapted from the Pitti Palace in Florence,
a fifteenth-century building. In sculpture the influence is much too diffuse to be
concentrated in any examples. It is in painting that we find a constant reinterpre-

tation of so-called Renaissance style throughout the century. This adaptation was so widespread that we may speak of it as the "Academic View."

Its main exponent in France was J. A. D. Ingres (1780-1867), a contemporary of Delacroix but his direct antithesis in technique. Where the Romantic painter had exploited color and agitated composition, Ingres devoted himself studiously to the most typical device of the early Italian school: draughtsmanship. With him drawing was almost a fetish, color was secondary. Much of his technique was inspired by Raphael, whom he considered the greatest of all artists. In Ingres' large *Odalisque* the head of the beautifully drawn nude is derived from Raphael's *Madonna of the Chair*. Like Raphael, Ingres was interested in the smooth flow of lines across the surface of his paintings. His drawing is tense, alive, and although his works have relatively little vital color, they have life and movement. In the typical eclectic manner of this period, Ingres combined the drawing of Raphael with what he had learned from the study of Greek vase painting. His closest adaptation of the former is found in *The Vow of Louis XIII*, of the latter in his *Oedipus before the Sphinx*. Ingres' most famous work, *La Source,* is a fine combination of the Italian and Greek points of view.

In the work of Hippolyte Flandrin (1809-1864) we find an interesting example of a fairly widespread nineteenth-century movement, which concentrated on the Italian painting prior to Raphael. Flandrin was attracted by fourteenth-century Italian painting and its peculiar religious spirit. In England a group of later painters, the Pre-Raphaelites, spread their doctrine through this art as well as through the poetry of some of their members (Rossetti, in particular). Germany had an analogous group, the Nazarenes.

The Academic style was readily adapted to the pictorial decoration of public buildings. In the work of Puvis de Chavannes (1824-1898) we observe the creation of a monumental decorative style (particularly in the *Life of St. Genevieve* series in the Paris Pantheon), in which the carefully arranged compositions, the precise drawing, and the feeling for decorative effects all point to Italy. Although his painting may not be profound, it was, in its time, eminently acceptable.

4. *Romantic Landscape Painting*

So far we have considered three major aspects of the revivalism in the nineteenth century: Neoclassical, Romantic, Academic. We have made the reservation that all three were essentially Romantic in their attempt to escape from the present into the past or to some faraway land. It is true, however, that the form of Romanticism typified by Delacroix was more personal and emotional than the Neoclassical and Academic and conveyed at all times a sense of struggle or revolt. Delacroix, as a typical Romantic, had been absorbed by the implacable force of nature and its opposition to man, but he made man the chief character in his paintings. This same theme, man's emotional reaction to nature, was treated by a great many painters in the early century who made landscape the chief character.

These Romantic landscape artists in their intense preoccupation with nature may be considered the transition from the Romantic to the realistic attitude of the middle of the century. The transition was stimulated by the English painters Constable, Bonington, Turner. John Constable (1776-1837), most important for pioneering towards realism, was one of the first to realize that sunlight could be represented as an effective part of a landscape; that nature was not brown (as the Academic landscapists had insisted) but green. If we examine a typical Constable landscape we find that natural light can be a dramatizing force; in *Salisbury Cathedral* it is exemplified in the contrast between the shadowy foreground and the brilliantly lighted background. His importance is further seen in such a painting as the *Hay Wain* in which he teaches the nineteenth-century artist a powerful lesson in the application of broken spots of color which reinforce one another as they are placed side by side. More than anyone else at this early stage of contemporary development, Constable was aware of the changing character of light, that this transient quality had to be rendered in terms of flickering color. His influence was immediately apparent in the brightening colors of Delacroix, who saw the *Hay Wain* at the Paris salon of 1824; upon the work of the Barbizon painters and even later movements.

R. P. Bonington (1801-1828) in the short span of his life managed to act in an ambassadorial capacity from the English to the French school of landscape. His sensitive treatment of water seen under conditions of misty light evokes a gentle melancholy. Like his English contemporaries, he was a keen observer of nature, using landscape to express a state of feeling.

The third important member in the English landscape school, J. M. W. Turner (1775-1851), the most overtly Romantic of the group, proved an important influence on the development of the later Impressionist school. He began as an imitator of Claude Lorrain, the seventeenth-century French painter of sea and sunlight, composing his pictures with all of the care of an academician of that age. Soon he turned to more specifically Romantic subject matter which, like that of Delacroix, was frequently influenced by contemporary literature, as in his *Childe Harold's Pilgrimage—Italy* with its reminiscences of the poet Byron and the composer Liszt. This work is redolent of the poetic sentiment of the early nineteenth century expressed in a vague, misty landscape against which the tiny characters move. The most typical aspect of Turner, however, is found in such brilliantly lit paintings as *The Grand Canal, Venice,* and *The Fighting Téméraire* in which he applies his effects of sunlight with a heavily loaded brush that sweeps dizzily across the canvas to indicate sky and clouds. People, when they occur, are shown in small spots of clear, brilliant color, which will later prove an inspiration to the Impressionists.

English directness and realistic interpretation of nature (albeit tempered with Romantic feeling) were far in advance of similar French tendencies. Before we can approach Impressionist painting, we must move through a group of primarily emotional interpreters, known as the Barbizon school, named after the village near Paris where they worked. Their landscape for the most part is comparable to Constable's rather than to Turner's. Such a painter as Théodore Rousseau (1812-1867) shows Constable's emphasis on small details and the flecked effects of sunlight coming through the branches of great oaks; but this very detail tends to make them lose the larger view of nature which most of the Englishmen perceived. The *Sunlit Oak* was Rousseau's most characteristic effort. The tree is enormous in both the physical and psychological senses; it is glorified to such a degree that we lose sight of the fact that it is only one of the many existing aspects of nature. Rousseau, then, may be classified as an epic interpreter of the forces and aspects of nature. Other members of the group expressed themselves differently, but all tended to portray landscape in terms of their own particular emotional response. Jules Dupré (1812-1889) seems to epitomize a tragic reaction while Charles Daubigny (1817-1878), like Bonington, was more interested in its calm, twilight moods.

Most sentimental of the group was Camille Corot (1796-1875). His late works are covered with a silvery haze which bathes his figures in a misty atmosphere. Although he observed nature carefully, the results were more emotional than realistic. His was a gentle emotion, and his misty paintings expressed an idyllic·calm that has been termed classical. Nymphs and shepherds sport about in the theoretically realistic landscape of the Fontainebleau region. Fortunately, these bucolic landscapes are only one side of Corot's art; he is much more significant as a painter of figures and of brightly sunlit landscapes. In his *Belfry at Douai* the details are clearly focused. Here Corot shows himself a keen realist, free from any suggestion of sentimentality.

5. *Romantic Realism*

A sentimental evaluation of man's relationship to nature occurs in the work of a man who has sometimes been associated with the Barbizon group, but who was actually one of the first realists of nineteenth-century France. Jean-François Millet (1814-1875) approached nature as a Romanticist by being most interested in man's struggle against his environment. We are all familiar with Millet's painting *The Man with the Hoe* if only through Edwin Markham's poem, but few of us appreciate its interesting position in the development of subject matter in nineteenth-century art. Like most of the Barbizon group, Millet was cordially disliked by the general public for many years and almost starved to death. *The Man with the Hoe* and *The Sower* impress us today as monumental interpretations of the peasant's struggle against poverty. A certain Michelangelesque grandeur in these figures tends to place them in the Academic category. But for the public and critics of the 1840's and 1850's Millet's work was neither what they wanted nor worthy of approval. There was no quarrel with his particular style but with his themes— the arch conservatism of the academy decreed that a painting should treat a "worthy" and dignified subject, not crude peasants! Millet's chief importance lies in the fact that for the first time since Chardin an artist dared to insist on his own idea of what was worthy of painting, even though he reflected a sentimentalized, Christian vein of human compassion. In some of his landscapes, it is true, his color is dull, but in others (*The Path Through the Wheat*) he shows a more precise interest in intense sunlight than any of his Barbizon colleagues. Millet's glorified peasants will be repeated in the massive sculpture of Constantin Meunier (1831-1904).

Millet marked a transition to a form of realism which became prominent after the turn of the half-century, in the painting of Courbet and Daumier. Gustave Courbet (1819-1877) was even more advanced in his insistence on everyday subject matter. He is important from the contemporary standpoint because he was one of the most self-conscious of artists—self-conscious of what he felt to be the important mission of the artist in society. In his own day he was looked upon as a socialist because of such canvases as *The Stone Breakers* and *The Funeral at Ornans.* Without any of Millet's Christian compassion, Courbet set out to represent things "as he saw them" with as little emotional embellishment as possible. The critics were annoyed because he treated every subject as though it were a piece of still life, ignoring its dramatic or psychological implications. They were further incensed that he chose an extremely large size for his canvases, which automatically assigned them a prominence ordinarily reserved for important historical and allegorical works. Here again he violated the proprieties and brought down on his unbowed head a mess of critical abuse.

The physical aspect of things held the same fascination for Courbet that it had for Chardin. No matter what the subject, the spectator has the feeling that the artist has examined it with thorough, objective eyes, and has attempted to set down in every case the real quality observed. His nudes are a good example of this attitude, which is sometimes overwhelming in its brutality; but there can be no question about his sincerity. He refused to paint what he could not see, and although this is in itself a shallow viewpoint, the fact remains that Courbet was able to make people conscious of the visible world in a manner of which no artist before him had been capable.

A word must be said about his aggressiveness, since it reveals so well his belief in the artist as an important member of society. In *The Greeting* he shows himself greeted by one of his patrons in a most respectful manner; in *My Studio* he places himself in the center of a huge canvas surrounded by various models and friends. To the public such pictures were both amusing and annoying, but to us today they are proof of an intense antagonism between artist and public and of the precarious position of the nonconforming artist at that time. Millet's career proved it and Courbet's stormy course through the 1860's and 1870's reinforced the unpleasant fact. Millet had sinned perhaps in the sense that he brought to people's attention an aspect of society of which they would rather not have been reminded; with Courbet, it was merely his forthright, unsentimental approach to art which incensed them. We cannot conclude this brief résumé of the work of Courbet without pointing out his great achievements in landscape and seascape. We find a strain of Romanticism in such a work as *The Wave,* an amazingly vivid representation of overwhelming natural forces, the reminder of man's ever-present adversary. His whole life was Romantic in its steadfast rebellion against constituted authority.

The name of Honoré Daumier (1808-1879) must be added to this group of Romantic and rebellious Realists, for in his career we are introduced to a much more activated form of social consciousness than had been evident in Millet or Courbet. Daumier devoted his art to sharp protests against the social conditions of his day, particularly as they affected the poor and unfortunate. His satirical representations of dishonest lawyers and judges, whom he heartily detested, fall into this category. In his capacity of caricaturist and social commentator, Daumier spent many years making lithographs for newspapers. They range from relatively innocuous scenes from the everyday life of Paris to some of his pet hates: hypocrisy, courtrooms, politicians, war. The *Rue Transnonain,* an early lithograph, is one of the most dramatic and significant ever produced by any newspaper illustrator. It shows a humble interior, a bedroom, an entire family lying dead on the floor, murdered. Daumier wished to focus attention on the inhuman brutality of the militia. In a time of economic crisis, the militia had been sniped at from windows as they passed through the working-class quarters of Paris. In retaliation, they broke into the suspect's tenement and shot the entire family. Beneath his cartoon Daumier merely recorded the address of the slaughter house and the date. Sometimes with the bitterness of the *Rue Transnonain,* sometimes with the sympathetic good humor of *Les bons bourgeois* series, Daumier satirized the social and political world of his time.

Daumier might possibly be classed as a Romantic in the sense that he was emotionally affected by his environment and painted and drew in a powerful light-and-shade technique what he saw, but his art is in no possible way an escape. Daumier commented on his age with a concern for basic social truths such as no other artist had ever shown. Today his work is still an inspiration to socially conscious artists and writers. His great epic of French life in the last century was comparable only to Balzac's *Comédie humaine.*

With the careers of Millet, Courbet, and Daumier we come to the 1870's, to the beginning of a new movement destined to shake the art world to its foundations. It was the climax of the artistic development of three centuries. The entire evolution of art from the fifteenth century had been involved, one way or another, with the visualization of the world we live in. The fifteenth century had occupied itself for the most part with certain technical factors (perspective, foreshortening) which helped accurately to represent the environment of man. The sixteenth century had concentrated on man himself, on the study of anatomy. In the Baroque period artists began to study the emotional possibilities of light and of composition (diagonality). Landscape as a distinct art was first developed during the seventeenth century, as was everyday subject matter. The eighteenth century had contributed the social consciousness of Hogarth in England and Goya in Spain. In the nineteenth century all of these tendencies were summarized and sharpened. The nature of man and his environment, the conflicts of man with his environment and with society, had been thoroughly exploited and eloquently expressed by the various groups of Romantic painters and the Romantic Realists, Millet, Courbet, and Daumier.

6. *Impressionism*

By the time of the 1870's most possible avenues of realistic interpretation had been investigated by artists. One thing remaining to be achieved was a scientific approximation of the phenomena of nature (since this was an age of scientific development), particularly the effects of light in the open air. Interior light had been intensively studied by the Dutch and the Spanish in the seventeenth century, but the out-of-doors had been only partially seized in the landscapes of Constable and Turner. It remained for the so-called Impressionists of the 1870's, Manet, Monet, Pissarro, to fulfill this final aim and thus to complete the development of realism. Edouard Manet (1832-1883), the great initiator of this movement, believed that one should paint only what one saw; but instead of relying on Courbet's thickness of paint, he regarded light as the most important factor and upon light he concentrated most of his efforts. Naturally he borrowed from the seventeenth-century Velasquez and there are many points of resemblance between the two. Manet, however, used clean and bright colors, which had not been previously mixed upon the palette. This manner of using color influenced the entire modern "out-of-doors" group, although, for the most part, Manet had painted indoors. The public of his day was much incensed by Manet's subject matter, as it had been by Courbet's, but objections to Manet were doubled, for his technique was equally offensive. When the gallery visitors looked at Manet's *Breakfast on the Grass* or his *Olympia* they were shocked by the frank and dispassionate tone assumed by the painter. They resented the casualness with which he set out a group of young men and nude women against a country background—his insistence that the sixteenth-century Giorgione had done the same thing availed him nothing—or the offensive nonchalance with which the nude Olympia looks at the spectator. If these things were irritating, the visitor was even more incensed by the "barbaric" quality of the color which "screamed" at him from the canvases. Manet was once and for all repudiated by society, and so were the Impressionists who were influenced by him.

Today we regard the Impressionist technique as something very fresh and charming, but in the 1870's such an artist as Claude Monet (1840-1926) had a bitter struggle before he won any measure of recognition. What interested such Impressionists as Monet and Pissarro was the momentary appearance of nature under sunlight. They realized that the light on objects changes from moment to moment and that objects reflect light upon each other and undergo further change. Their observation of nature taught them that no pigment in the painter's tubes could be as bright as the colors in nature seen under natural light. Therefore, they would have to find some means of simulating this brilliance.

They were affected by scientific discoveries, particularly in optics and physics. Students in Germany, France, and America had found that ordinary sunlight is composed of a series of colors (the spectrum) into which it can be broken and from which light can be recomposed. Why could not painters do the same thing, reasoned the artists of the time, forgetting that the relatively impure pigments they had at their command were not comparable to the pure quality of the color effects of natural light. But they were on the right track, for by reproducing the relationships between colors which had been promulgated by the scientists they were able to render the most brilliant and convincing impression of sunlight in the out-of-doors up to that date.

One way to achieve brilliant color is to paint in pure, unmixed hues. Blue and yellow, for instance, when physically mixed together become green. The Impressionists found that the pulsating flicker of green in nature, now yellowish, now bluish, can be best approximated by using daubs of blue alternating with daubs of yellow, allowing the eye to mix the two together. They also felt that masses of complementary (opposite) colors—red and green, blue and orange, yellow and violet—when juxtaposed appear at their brightest. All these combinations were worked out directly on the canvas in the presence of nature itself.

Because the effects they tried to reproduce were transitory, the technique of these painters could no longer remain precise but necessarily became loose and casual. The Impressionists hastily applied spots of color without paying much attention to drawing or to three-dimensional form. The result was something vividly pulsating and transitory, which although it seized the momentary quality of light as it struck a particular object, was yet devoid of the solidity of form which is the inherent property of all objects. From the technical side, this is the main criticism we can level at such paintings as Monet's *The Haystacks* and *Rouen Cathedral* and the countless others created during his long life. The vast majority of them lack "form" as we usually think of it, but what is much more serious, they lack content as well, for apart from an almost imperceptible lyric quality, they have no important psychological or emotional message to communicate. "The light was the most important person in the picture." Although as technique these paintings were offensive to the public of their day, for us they are merely extremely clever and lovely pictures.

Many artists worked in this manner, among them Camille Pissarro (1830 - 1903) and Alfred Sisley (1839-1899), and all of them are individually distinguishable in spite of the technical formulas which Impressionism imposes. One of the members of the first Impressionist group was Auguste Renoir (1841-1919) whose art is not primarily concerned with landscape as was Monet's, but who, in his bright colors and informal subject matter, belongs in the group. Renoir used the broken colors of Impressionism to create a beautifully lyrical world of his own where beautiful men and women go through ordinary activities unaware of the fact that there is any such thing as ugliness in the world. In his *Moulin de la Galette,* a pleasant café scene, lovely women and handsome men dance gracefully to an invisible orchestra. Their costumes, attitudes, and emotions fit into the light and tranquil mood. Renoir was very much influenced by the Venetian tradition and the eighteenth-century rococo. His nudes set out-of-doors remind us of Boucher, while the portraits and group paintings of the Paris upper classes, with whom he became very friendly, revive memories of the aristocratic portraiture of Titian and Veronese. No one in the entire Impressionist tradition was as appealing as Renoir and he is, today, still the most popular of the group.

7. Linear Impressionism

Another facet of Impressionism appeared in the work of Degas and Toulouse-Lautrec. These two artists were interested in bright colors and casual subject matter, but their contribution was effective primarily because of lively broken drawing. They were influenced to some extent by the art of Japan and China which became better known at this time through the commercial expansion of Europe toward the East. Both Japanese and Chinese artists had always shown an interest both in genre subjects and the effect of light. This made their art eminently suitable for adaptation by the two nineteenth-century Frenchmen. In Edgar Degas (1834-1917) we find one of the most conservative personalities of the period; most of his work was predicated on one form of borrowing or another. His emphasis on draughtsmanship descended directly from Ingres; his fine portrait effects are reminiscent of Holbein and Clouet in the sixteenth century. Beginning with this distinctly academic affinity, he used a precise technique to express more momentary and impressionistic aspects of the life he saw about him; the cafés, music halls, theaters, and ballets. Although he is known to the general public primarily for his painting of ballet girls, whose attitudes on- and off-stage he reproduced so brilliantly, his work is more significant for depicting in a fine linear technique the transitory aspects in the everyday lives of such types as laundresses, milliners, jockeys. In certain instances (*The Sponge Bath*) he adopted unconventional subjects to show his mastery of the human form. Degas is further noteworthy for reviving the pastel crayon as a medium, which enabled him to draw and color simultaneously, a tremendous advantage to an artist whose primary interest was draughtsmanship.

His contemporary and emulator, Henri de Toulouse-Lautrec (1864-1901), interested in linear quality and in the same subject matter, was much more biting and critical. He portrayed the same milieu in terms of his own bitterness and disappointment (he was physically malformed). Though many paintings were produced by him, his most significant art was done in lithograph and poster, media which he used for recording the nightmarish vice and bestiality of the last two decades of his century. No one can accuse Lautrec of Impressionist lyricism, for he more than any other member of the group was interpreter. He saw what he wanted to see, and if what he saw displeases us (as *At the Moulin Rouge*) it is largely because of our own preconceived notions of acceptable subject matter. We cannot deny the significance of his unusual perspectives, his startling color contrasts, and his ability to sum up the Montmartre of the *mauve décade.*

It has been said that French sculpture of the last century was summed up in the work of Auguste Rodin (1840-1917). In his art there is unquestionably a consciousness of the past, especially in his early works, reminiscent not only of Michelangelo's style but of his monumentality and large emotional expression. But Rodin's work always carries a high degree of Romantic individuality, a preoccupation with purely human problems, as in *The Kiss,* which portrays Paolo and Francesca. Rodin lived a long, full life in the course of which he was bound to reflect most of the currents of the second half of the century. His technical insistence on alternating high and low surfaces which catch the light and create a shimmering, fleshy softness has been compared with the broken surfaces of the out-of-doors Impressionist paintings. But where the painters were solely interested in luminosity, Rodin used light as an emotional and realistic device.

8. Post Impressionism

If we are to summarize the positive contributions of the Impressionists we can point to a more highly developed, colorful treatment of landscape under sunlight and to a wealth of new subjects. The relationship between the technique and subject matter is clear from the work of the landscape painters. Monet, for example, chooses those aspects of nature which lend themselves best to his momentary, broken-color style: ponds strewn with lilies, poplars waving in the breeze, the broken light-and-shade of the lacy pierced stone surface of Rouen Cathedral. The same interdependence of technique and theme is demonstrated by the Linear Impressionists, Degas, Toulouse-Lautrec, who choose such volatile subjects as dancers, singers, jockeys, acrobats, to express through the medium of their nervous line their unusual perspective and unusual manner of posing subjects.

We find that a number of artists of the Impressionist period objected to the formlessness of Monet and his followers. They maintained that Monet and his group used broken colors in a merely inspirational fashion, without a strict understanding and application of the rules of color relationships. These Post Impressionists were led by Seurat and Signac, whose ideas were recorded in *From Delacroix to Neo-Impressionism.* We may take the work of Georges Seurat (1859-1891) as typical of this movement, which is not only a reduction of Impressionism to codified practice but advocates a return to solidity of form—the direct opposite of the practice of the open-air painters. Seurat, in his *A Sunday Afternoon on La Grande Jatte,* reveals his painstaking application of minute dots of color, all of similar shape (which gave to this technique the name "pointillism"), with which he achieved the color gradation to build up his forms. Here the looseness and brokenness of form of Monet gives way to an almost sculpturesque solidity. Seurat maintained that there is a close relationship between the composition chosen and the emotion represented. A gay mood should be indicated by an arrangement diagonally pointed upward; sadness should direct the lines diagonally downward. In his landscapes we are no longer concerned with seizing a momentary aspect of nature, but rather with an evaluation of nature in terms of an almost Egyptian or Byzantine rigidity. No one can look at such Seurat works as *Bathing* and *Woman Powdering Herself* and think in terms of the transient or trivial, even though these themes were introduced by the Impressionists. The serene, reticent quality often found in Renoir is exaggerated in Seurat to such a point that even casual subjects as bathing and powdering the nose take on an almost religious aspect. Indeed, Seurat strove for monumentality in terms of controlled composition and color.

The work of Paul Cézanne (1839-1906) was similarly derived from the Impressionist tradition, but so monumentalized that it must be regarded as a reaction against it. In his own words, he wished to make of Impressionism something as solid and durable as the art of the museums. He modeled his figures very carefully, taking into account all of the gradual transitions of colored light from one side of an object to another, and attempted honestly to put every possible spot of color into it which he felt belonged in his model. In trying to paint solidly in terms of the color of the object as it is changed by the light falling upon it and by the reflections on it from adjacent objects, Cézanne was setting himself an amazing task which could not fail to end in frustration. In many of his works, particularly in his treatment of human beings, there was the obvious difficulty of getting people to sit quiet long enough to be painted in the meticulous, laborious manner demanded by his technique. He was more fortunate with landscape, where we can see immediately the vast difference between an out-of-doors painting by Monet and one by Cézanne. In a Monet work, we remember, a small section of nature was dealt with summarily and transiently, leaving as its final impression a hasty glance at a fragment of landscape under bright light. With Cézanne, we find a carefully composed, deep vista of nature (in the manner of the seventeenth-century Poussin), which although using the bright colors of Impressionism, retains all of the monumentality which exists in nature itself. Many Cézanne landscapes show an insistence on the underlying geometric structure of natural forms which is important for an understanding of his particular approach to the problems of representation. Solidity is the keynote of his art as formlessness was the characteristic of the landscapes, haystacks, and trees of Monet. (The twentieth-century Cubists, will turn to the solidity of Cézanne and his attempt to analyze form as an inspiration for their own efforts.) Cézanne's greatest success was in the still-life, for here he could examine and probe to his heart's content, and with all the time he needed for careful modeling.

If Seurat and Cézanne represent a return to solidity as a reaction against formlessness, Van Gogh and Gauguin are significant for contrasting a high emotional content with the gentleness and lyricism of Monet and Pissarro. Vincent Van Gogh (1853-1890) used the bright, clean colors of the Impressionist palette, but in a quite individual manner—as agitated as Monet's was tranquil. The technical basis of his style is found not in dots of color but in the little worms of broken color which he squeezed out of his paint-tubes. Although to the layman today Van Gogh's career is chiefly interesting as biography, his emotional approach both to life and art exercised important influences on many of the twentieth-century Expressionists. Van Gogh, like his later imitators, threw himself into the spirit of the scene on which he was working, and applied his colors with such haste and in such excitement that his psychological participation in the subject is inevitably conveyed. We have merely to look at his *Landscape with Cypresses* to see the distinct change from the quiet landscapes of Monet. Here everything is alive with an almost frightening energy and although there are no people in the painting the forms themselves induce a powerful excitement. The sky in such a painting has some of the unearthly quality of El Greco's skies but, characteristic of his century, Van Gogh's works are almost always bathed in brilliant sunlight. Similarly, in his treatment of people (*La Berceuse*) and in his still-life (*Sunflowers*), there is the same intensity of feeling.

It is important to observe that psychologically the painting of Van Gogh represents, in many cases, an intensification of the attitude of Millet, many of whose subjects he repeated. Van Gogh's sympathy with the poor and the suffering, evident in his amazing letters to his brother Theo, and in the subject of many of his paintings, places him near Daumier in the nineteenth century and Käthe Kollwitz in the twentieth.

The art of Van Gogh marks not only an emotional intensification of the processes of Impressionism, but a return to an almost primitively personal expression. There is nothing elegant in his work, and it is interesting to note that he paints best when he is under no one's influence, when he is expressing his own peculiar temperament. To some people his art reveals the spiritual decay of the last part of the nineteenth century.

Van Gogh's friend and colleague, Paul Gauguin (1848-1903), keenly felt the decay of this period and openly reverted to what he believed a primitive form of expression. Leaving a prosperous commercial career, he set out to paint. During one period of his life he formed a group of artists who worked in Brittany, one of the most archaic parts of France where native habits had not changed for centuries. Feeling himself out of step with his time, he ultimately left Europe for the Marquesas Islands in the Pacific. There he attempted to absorb the new atmosphere and to record it in his art. It is at this point that the life of Gauguin becomes an interesting symbol of European civilization at the end of the nineteenth century, for not only does he reflect the imperialistic expansion toward the East, but a general attempt on the part of intellectuals to forsake civilization and seek a remedy for their disillusionment in an unspoiled, primitive society. In this Gauguin becomes the predecessor of the primitivist movements of the next century. His pictures are not derived from the art of the people among whom he lived, but he was undoubtedly influenced by the colors of the lush tropical vegetation of these islands. His compositions and drawing are sometimes eclectic in the characteristic fashion of the various "borrowing" schools of the nineteenth century. Since he was aiming for the archaic and the primitive, we find him adapting the drawing and contours of ancient Egyptian painting and bas-reliefs. Although Gauguin remains "European," we are able occasionally to trace a motif from the primitive art of the Pacific. His painting *The Day of God* is as carefully composed as an academic wall decoration by Puvis de Chavannes. The general impression made by the paintings of Gauguin is that of a consciously primitivized but carefully planned decoration of tightly drawn and flatly arranged lines, brightly colored in large, flat, unbroken masses not unlike Egyptian painting, the whole creating an unusual and exotic effect. His startling color contrast may be the result of the fact that he, too, was brought up in the Impressionist tradition, but like most of the members of the group, he used what it had to offer in his own individual way. Gauguin, as much as any artist of the end of the nineteenth century, proclaimed the fact that the realist tradition had reached an end. Would the next step be the primitivism which he advocated, the emotional and expressionistic view of Van Gogh, or the deeply analytical, searching attitude of Cézanne?

III. THE TRIUMPH OF ROMANTIC IDEALS IN MUSIC

The nineteenth century presents an almost bewildering musical panorama. The number of great composers, the diversity of styles, and the presence of many great national schools make it difficult to characterize the epoch. It may be pointed out, however, that musically the nineteenth century paralleled the sixteenth. Just as the music of the sixteenth century was the culmination of the centuries of development of the polyphonic idiom, so was that of the nineteenth century the culmination of the instrumental and harmonic tendencies which had been fostered by the opera at the beginning of the seventeenth century. The outstanding musical phenomena of the epoch were the emancipation of the composer from his former servile status, the infusion of a new subjectivity into music, the triumph of the romantic opera, the rise of national schools. The fact that most of the music played today was composed in the nineteenth century is sufficient evidence of the musical importance of that epoch.

1. *Beethoven*

Ludwig van Beethoven (1770-1827) not only summed up the work of Haydn and Mozart, but by the unique force of his personality so altered the traditional forms which they had bequeathed to him that his works served as a source of inspiration for almost every subsequent composer. The new note of subjectivity which Beethoven infused into his own music fired many other composers to act likewise.

Although born in the Rhine town of Bonn, Germany, Beethoven spent all but the first twenty-two years of his life in Vienna, and it was there that all of his great works were first performed. The servile position of the musician came to a definite end with Beethoven, who never was in anyone's employ. Furthermore, he composed practically no music on commission, and almost all his compositions were the result solely of a tremendous urge for expression. When the list of Beethoven's compositions is compared with Haydn's and Mozart's it is apparent that his output measured by the standards of his day was small—nine symphonies, for example, as compared to Haydn's one hundred and four.

In transforming the sonata and its related forms into adequate media for intense personal expression Beethoven made several important innovations. The minuet, which had served Haydn and Mozart as a third movement, he supplanted with a scherzo, a vigorous, lively, almost explosive movement in a rapid tempo. He integrated the hitherto independent movements of the sonata or symphony into one complete musical unit, either by thematic quotation or actual linking. In enlarging the dimensions of the sonata form Beethoven made another significant contribution. His Seventh Symphony, for example, requires forty minutes to perform, twice as many as the *Surprise* Symphony of Haydn.

Beethoven's expansion of the dimensions of the sonata form, however, was paralleled by an increased economy of thematic material. His works are, therefore, remarkably forceful and compact and contain some of the world's finest examples of long sustained development. The first movement of the Fifth

Symphony with its ceaseless belaboring of a terse four-note motive illustrates this aspect of Beethoven's style.

It was only after long periods of preliminary struggle that Beethoven finally completed his compositions, and the tremendous urge for expression which motivated him is evident in all of them. Yet few bear titles which serve as clues to their emotional content, and even those titles which are used are rather general ones. The most accurately labeled Beethoven work is the Sixth Symphony, the *Pastoral,* but here Beethoven has added the warning phrase, "Mehr Ausdruck der Empfindung als Malerei" (More an expression of feeling than tone-painting).

Beethoven, who was an accomplished pianist, enriched the literature for his instrument with thirty-two sonatas and several fine sets of variations. All of his piano music falls into the category of chamber music, for as we pointed out in Chapter XXII, pianists of this period when making public appearances played only concertos. Two of the better-known sonatas have descriptive titles which did not originate with Beethoven. These are the Sonata in C-sharp minor, Opus 27, No. 2, the so-called *Moonlight Sonata* and the Sonata in F minor, Opus 57, the so-called *Sonata Appassionata.* Beethoven is said to have considered the latter work his greatest sonata.

The evolution of Beethoven as a composer is well demonstrated by his nine symphonies. Best known of all his works, they form an important part of the orchestral repertory today. His First Symphony, completed in 1800, follows many conventions established by Haydn and Mozart. The startling departures begin with the Third Symphony, the *Eroica,* completed in 1804. The gigantic Ninth Symphony (1824), Beethoven's last great orchestral work, was so thoroughly revolutionary in form, in content, and in spirit that it was long regarded as an eccentric work, the aberration of a deaf composer. Not until 1846 when Richard Wagner "revived" the symphony at a concert in Dresden was its true value recognized.

Equally important orchestral works by Beethoven are his great overtures, his most successful efforts in dramatic composition. His solitary opera *Fidelio* (original title: *Leonore*) does not entitle him to be called a great operatic composer, for here his style lacks the impact of his purely instrumental music; and *Fidelio* as an opera does not fulfill the promise made by the masterly *Leonore No. 3* overture with which he prefaced it.

The significant feature of the Beethoven overtures is the singularly effective manner in which they state the basic conflict of a drama, in fact so effective are they that they have outlived the dramas which inspired them. Outstanding examples are Beethoven's overtures to Heinrich von Collin's *Coriolanus* and to Goethe's *Egmont.* Beethoven maintained that he wrote the *Egmont* music "purely out of love for the poet."

For his public appearances in Vienna Beethoven wrote five piano concertos, all of which may be regarded as full-length symphonies with a prominent part for one instrument, rather than as display pieces. The title *Emperor* given to the last of these works, the Piano Concerto in E-flat major, while not inappropriate, did not originate with Beethoven. This work introduced an important change in the formal plan of the concerto: the elimination of the performer's privilege of improvising a cadenza.

Beethoven's works also make up a considerable part of the chamber-music repertory. His most important compositions in this category are the seventeen string quartets and the nine sonatas for violin and piano. The grandeur of conception, mastery of form, and richness of development of these string quartets make them the chamber-music counterparts of the symphonies.

Beethoven has left one monumental choral work, a setting of the Catholic Mass entitled *Missa Solemnis* (*Solemn Mass*). Occasional awkwardness in choral writing combined with Beethoven's characteristic disregard of the limitations of the human voice have not marred its impressive fervor. Beethoven's inscription placed at the head of the work characterizes not only the *Missa Solemnis,* but almost all his compositions. The inscription reads: "Vom Herzen, möge sie zu Herzen gehen" (From the heart, may it go to the heart).

2. *Romanticism in Music*

As we have pointed out in our sections on literature and art, the adjective "romantic" is a broad one and should be treated with a measure of caution. Before discussing the musical implications of the term, it would be profitable to define the musical significance of its conventional antonym, classical. In music, as in the other arts, the adjective classical is usually reserved for works which are objective in their style and restrained in their expression. Classical also implies formal perfection. The almost ideal balance of formal consideration and expressive necessity which exists in the symphonies, sonatas, and string quartets of Haydn, Mozart, and the earlier Beethoven have won for them the designation "classical." Typically baroque products like the cantatas of Bach could hardly be called classical in this sense, and when the term is applied to such music it connotes its universality of acceptance and not its style.

The romantic spirit in all the arts is born of a discontent, of a realization by the artist that what he has to say cannot be communicated through the conventional forms and styles of his day. This discontent is the prime mover in the evolution of many new forms and new styles. The romantic spirit as an essentially innovating spirit, therefore, has been present in all art periods and there is hardly a great creative artist in whose works romantic tendencies may not be observed.

By common acceptance, however, the term "Romantic Movement" in music is reserved for the activity of the composers who were either younger contemporaries of Beethoven, or who came directly after him. The outstanding musical romanticists were Schubert, von Weber, Mendelssohn, Schumann, Chopin, Berlioz, Liszt, and Wagner.

The majority of these composers, while admirers of Beethoven, found the sonata form unsuitable for their purposes. Their temperaments were such as to cause them to create a variety of new forms or styles: the romantic opera, the art-song, the shorter piano pieces, the program symphony, the symphonic poem, and the music drama. Like other romantic artists they laid great emphasis on the expression of subjective states.

An important phenomenon of the period was the greatly increased fraternizing of musicians and writers, and the interest in music displayed by contemporary literary discussions and critical essays. Works of literature inspired a tremendous quantity of music. Goethe's *Faust,* for example, brought forth Berlioz' oratorio *The Damnation of Faust,* Schumann's *Scenes from Faust,* Wagner's *Faust* overture, and Liszt's *Faust Symphony.* Schumann's *Manfred* and Berlioz' *Harold in Italy* were based on works of Byron; Liszt's *Mazeppa* on a work of Victor Hugo; Schumann's *Kreisleriana* on a work of E. T. A. Hoffmann. Like their contemporaries in other arts, composers awoke to the beauties of Shakespeare. Hand in hand with the great Schlegel translations and the Shakespearean performances in Paris went the composition of such works as Mendelssohn's music for *A Midsummer Night's Dream,* Berlioz' *Romeo and Juliet* symphony, and Liszt's symphonic poem *Hamlet.*

All of the works listed above are usually called *program music,* music which has a descriptive purpose. (Music which has no stated descriptive purpose is called *absolute music.*) Program music, as such, did not constitute a distinctly nineteenth-century phenomenon. Nineteenth-century program music differed from previous music of this type in the degree of importance assigned to the program, in the manner in which programmatic considerations—which are extramusical ones—were allowed to dictate the form of a composition, and in the choice of subjects.

The most important musical ensemble of the nineteenth century was the orchestra. Even the history of nineteenth-century opera is given over largely to the account of new orchestral methods. Important in the development of orchestral music were the many improvements made in the mechanism of orchestral instruments. The present-day flute, oboe, and clarinet, for example, owe their ease of action to the mechanism perfected by the German, Theobald Boehm (1794-1881). Thanks to the invention of "valves" (devices for instantaneously changing the lengths of their tubing) the trumpet and the horn came to possess a complete chromatic scale (a scale of half-steps). In this vital improvement an important part was played by the Franco-Belgian instrument-maker Charles Joseph Sax (1791-1865) and his son Adolphe Sax (1814-1894) after whom a family of brass instruments usually used in bands was named *Saxhorns.* Adolphe Sax also gave his name to the saxophone, invented by him in 1840. The modern harp, capable of being played in all keys, was perfected in 1811 by the Frenchman Sebastien Erard (1752-1831).

The piano works of Chopin and Liszt would never have come into existence if the piano had not been materially improved during the early part of the nineteenth century. The introduction of the iron frame permitted an increase in tension of the strings with a resultant increase in brilliancy. Extension of the compass, improvement of the action, introduction of steel strings and improvement of the sounding board resulted in an instrument which was capable of reproducing orchestral sonorities. Improved methods of manufacturing greatly lowered the cost of the instrument and it soon became an indispensable part of the furnishings of the average middle-class household. A growth of popular interest in music was a natural result.

The nature of nineteenth-century orchestral music required a conductor to direct its performance. The nineteenth-century conductor differed from his predecessors by infusing his own personality into the performance and "interpreting" the music, his time-beating function becoming secondary. The pioneer in the art of interpretive conducting was Richard Wagner.

An interesting aspect of nineteenth-century music was the literary activity of musicians in behalf of their art, an indication of the self-consciousness of the romantic movement. Schumann championed musical progressivism in a magazine, von Weber and Liszt wrote numerous essays, Berlioz was for a long time critic of the Paris paper *Le Journal des débats*. Wagner found time to write no less than ten volumes of prose and over six thousand letters.

3. Schubert and the Art Song

The Austrian composer Franz Schubert (1797-1828), a younger Viennese contemporary of Beethoven, managed in the course of his pathetically brief lifetime to write ten symphonies, fifteen string quartets, much piano music, and over 650 songs. Most important are the songs.

The term *art-song* is used to describe a setting of a poem for voice and some accompanying instrument, usually the piano. Schubert, who had been preceded by a great number of German song composers, possessed in addition to a certain dramatic gift apparently inexhaustible melodic fertility.

While Schubert's melodies are eminently tuneful, that is, they could conceivably exist apart from their texts, they are unusually effective illuminations of the poems which brought them forth. The vocal writing of Schubert is not confined to pure melody, however, and recitative-like declamation is frequently employed with excellent effect.

The piano parts of Schubert's songs are not mere accompaniments and the significant role which he assigned to the piano represents one of his great contributions to the technique of song-writing. He used the piano to create moods, to emphasize words, to describe situations or events. The celebrated *Der Erlkönig* (*The Erl-King*) with its realistic portrayal of a wild ride through the night is an excellent example of the pictorial nature of many of these piano accompaniments.[3]

4. Romantic Opera

Romantic opera reached its finest flowering in Germany. The German romantic opera had evolved from an earlier musico-dramatic form known as the *Singspiel*, a folk-like play sung in the vernacular to music which was simple and expressive. The *Singspiel* was converted into an artistic form of great dignity by Carl Maria

---

[3] The following songs will serve as an excellent introduction to Schubert's art: *Heidenröslein* (*Little Hedge Rose*), *Gretchen am Spinnrade* (*Gretchen at the Spinning Wheel*), *Der Erlkönig* (*The Erl-King*), *Die Forelle* (*The Trout*), *Der Doppelgänger* (*The Phantom Double*), *Der Tod und das Mädchen* (*Death and the Maiden*).

von Weber (1786-1826) with his epoch-making romantic opera *Der Freischütz* (1821), meaning "the free-shooter," one who uses magic bullets.

Both text and music of a romantic opera have distinctive attributes. The text resembles a romantic play and may be a rendering of a medieval epic (Wagner's *Tristan und Isolde*); or it may be based on folklore, particularly on legends introducing supernatural manifestations (von Weber's *Der Freischütz*), on historical events (Meyerbeer's *Les Huguenots*), or on exotic subjects distantly removed in time or place (Verdi's *Aïda*). Folk life and folk customs receive realistic treatment (Smetana's *The Bartered Bride*) and patriotic and national sentiments are also frequently emphasized (Rossini's *Guillaume Tell*).

The musical aspects of the romantic opera vary according to country. The most pronounced feature of the German product, as demonstrated in von Weber's operas, is the strikingly original use of the orchestra. It may be observed, to von Weber's credit, that he was one of the first composers fully to avail himself of the dramatic potentialities of the colors extractable from the orchestra. The celebrated overture to *Der Freischütz,* for example, contains a remarkable passage for four horns, which at once creates the forest atmosphere of the opera. Von Weber's innovations in instrumentation exercised an important influence on the orchestral technique of his great admirers, Berlioz and Wagner.

Der Freischütz is von Weber's one great masterpiece. Two subsequent operas, *Euryanthe* and *Oberon,* were unsuccessful. Their brilliant overtures, however, appear frequently on modern orchestral programs. The well-known piano piece, *Invitation to the Dance,* was originally a fragment of an unsuccessful opera. The composition is usually heard today in an orchestration made by Berlioz.

Gioacchino Rossini (1792-1868), the most celebrated Italian opera composer of the early nineteenth century, had won his fame through an *opera buffa, Il Barbiere di Seviglia* (*The Barber of Seville*), composed in 1816. This great comic opera, whose text, like that of Mozart's *Le Nozze di Figaro,* was based on the celebrated comedy of Beaumarchais, is the oldest full-length Italian opera to hold a firm place in the operatic repertory. Its style, however, is predominantly that of the late eighteenth century, and neither in text nor music does it display any well-marked romantic characteristics. Rossini later established himself in Paris and the result of this sojourn will be apparent in our discussion of French opera.

The two typically romantic Italian opera composers were Vincenzo Bellini (1801-1835) and Gaetano Donizetti (1797-1848). In comparing their works with those of their German colleagues, we observe that the romantic features of the Italian works appear predominantly in their texts, and that emphasis on orchestral coloring is almost entirely absent. The thoroughly lyrical style of both of these composers was analogous to that found in the piano music of their time. Chopin, for example, had a strong admiration for Bellini. Bellini's more lasting operas were *La Sonnambula* (*The Somnambulist*) (1831) and *Norma* (1831). Of Donizetti's sixty-six operas the only one regularly given today is *Lucia di Lammermoor* (*Lucy of Lammermoor*) (1835), after Scott's novel *The Bride of Lammermoor.*

The earlier works of Giuseppe Verdi (1813-1901) exhibit stylistic characteristics resembling those found in the works of Bellini and Donizetti. Inasmuch as his most important works are those of his later years, we shall discuss him later.

French romantic opera presents diverging tendencies, thanks to the appearance in France of influential foreign composers, who themselves were not stylistically consistent. The foreign composers, of whom the most important were the Italian Gioacchino Rossini, and the German Jakob Meyerbeer, brought forth a distinctive type of romantic opera known as *grand opéra*. The *grand opéra* differed from the German romantic opera in possessing a text which was factual rather than fictitious. Consisting almost invariably of five acts, and introducing ballet performances in the second and fourth acts, *grand opéra* emphasized large crowd scenes, extravagant spectacles, and the portrayal of intense emotional conflicts. In short, as the name indicates, everything was carried out on a grand scale.

The fashion in *grand opéra* had been set by Rossini with his brilliant *Guillaume Tell*, given in Paris in 1829. The prime mover in *grand opéra*, however, was Jakob Meyerbeer (1791-1864) who, in association with Eugène Scribe, one of the most important French librettists, produced an imposing series of works in this genre. Of these the most important were *Robert le Diable, Les Huguenots, Le Prophète*, and *L'Africaine*. Meyerbeer was an excellent musician with a fine melodic gift and a flair for effective instrumentation. Unfortunately, he was more of a showman than a serious writer of dramatic music, and his works suffer through his attempts to achieve instantaneous effect.

French composers of *grand opéra* were Daniel F. E. Auber (1782-1871), whose now almost forgotten *La Muette de Portici* (*The Dumb Girl of Portici*) (1828), was a celebrated opera in its day; Jacques F. E. Halévy (1799-1862), whose *La Juive* (*The Jewess*) (1835), is still in the repertory; and Hector Berlioz (1803-1869), primarily a composer of symphonic music, who, however, made unsuccessful attempts at operatic composition.

While German and Italian composers were dominant in the field of *grand opéra*, French composers were achieving a measure of success in the field of *opéra comique*. The *opéra comique* had been at one time the French equivalent of the Italian *opera buffa*. Eventually, however, the form lost any characteristics which might have effectively differentiated it from *grand opéra* except the fact that it usually possessed spoken dialogue. In no sense is the name to be taken literally, particularly in its late nineteenth-century usage.

The first genuine *opéra comique, Le Devin du village* (*The Village Sorcerer*) (1752), inspired by Pergolesi's *opera buffa, La serva padrona*, was the work of the many-sided Jean-Jacques Rousseau (1712-1778). Nineteenth-century exponents of *opéra comique* were François Adrien Boildieu (1775-1834), whose most celebrated work was *La Dame blanche* (1825), the previously mentioned Daniel F. E. Auber, best represented by *Fra Diavolo* (1830), and Louis J. F. Hérold (1791-1833), composer of *Zampa* (1831).

5. *Mendelssohn and Schumann*

Not all the romantic composers were cast in the same mold, and the degrees of divergence which characterized their breaking away from past traditions varied. Hence, we may speak of Felix Mendelssohn (1809-1847) and Robert Schumann (1810-1856) as the more conservative romanticists, composers whose works possessed features which, although new, were neither radical nor startling.

Mendelssohn, brought up in Berlin in an atmosphere of culture and refinement, wrote his famous overture to Shakespeare's *A Midsummer Night's Dream* when he was only seventeen years old. When he was twenty he revived and directed Bach's *St. Matthew Passion,* the first performance of this work since the death of its composer in 1750. Mendelssohn's brief but colorful career included appearances as a pianist and organist, the direction of music festivals, the founding and direction of the famous Leipzig Conservatory, extensive travel, and prolific composition. His culture and refinement seem to have acted as retarding forces on the expressiveness of his music, for its fastidious correctness is at once its virtue and its vice.

Although adhering fairly closely to the classical sonata form, Mendelssohn often cloaked movements written in it with descriptive titles. He possessed unusual facility in handling the orchestra, and the colorfulness of his instrumentation has elicited much praise. An excellent example of this aspect of Mendelssohn's art is his beautifully scored concert overture *Fingal's Cave,* inspired by a visit to a grotto in the Hebrides.

Mendelssohn's contributions to modern programs are, in addition to the two overtures mentioned above, the *Italian* Symphony (1833), a fine violin concerto (1844), the incidental music for *A Midsummer Night's Dream* written in 1843 at the request of King Frederick William of Prussia, the oratorio *Elijah* (1846), and much piano and chamber music.

Robert Schumann was one of the most literary of musicians. As editor of and later contributor to the musical journal *Neue Zeitschrift für Musik,* he made important contributions to nineteenth-century musical criticism. He signed his articles with pseudonyms which represented different aspects of his personality. Two of his pseudonyms also characterize his music: *Florestan,* personifying the ardent, fiery, impetuous Schumann, and *Eusebius,* personifying the gentle, calm, meditative side of his character.

Sensational programs and virtuoso display are wholly abjured in Schumann's music. His works, which abound in broad, warm melodies and in vital rhythms, usually possess a rich texture. Fanciful whimsicalities of various sorts are occasionally found in them, as, for example, the celebrated *Carnaval* (1835), a series of descriptive sketches based on four notes, which in the German language represent the musical letters in Schumann's name (A, S, C, H, equivalent to our A, E-flat, C, B).

Schumann was happiest in piano music. His four symphonies, for example, while they contain a wealth of inspired melody, suffer from inept orchestration. His attempts at opera were also failures. It is his many unusually fine piano compositions, all of them creations of his early manhood, that have immortalized his name. In addition to *Carnaval* his piano music includes the brilliant *Symphonic Etudes,* three sonatas, and several sets of typically romantic shorter pieces bearing titles such as *Papillons* (*Butterflies*), *Novelletten* (*Romantic Tales*), *Phantasiestücke* (*Phantasy Pieces*), *Nachtstücke* (*Nocturnes*), *Album für das Jugend* (*Album for the Young*), and *Kinderscenen* (*Scenes from Childhood*). The last-named collection includes the popular *Träumerei* (*Reverie*), a fine example of the warmth of Schumann's melodic style. Schumann is also the composer of an especially fine piano concerto, many songs and some excellent chamber music.

6. The Development of Pianism: Chopin and Liszt

The two most important nineteenth-century contributors to the technique of writing for the piano were the Pole, Frédéric Chopin (1810-1849), and the Hungarian, Franz Liszt (1811-1886). Their personalities, their styles and their contributions, however, were strikingly dissimilar.

Chopin belongs with those composers who have confined themselves almost exclusively to one type of musical expression, for with some unimportant exceptions, all of his music was written for the piano.

Although born in Poland, Chopin spent the greater part of his life in Paris and lived for a long time with the French novelist George Sand. He rarely appeared in public, and usually gave his performances in smaller halls better adapted to his intimate and refined style. Although Chopin's works are now frequently used by concert virtuosi to electrify audiences, the composer himself was a modest individual devoid of flamboyancy.

Chopin's contributions to pianistic technique grew out of a desire to surmount the primary limitation of the instrument—its inability to produce sustained tones. His piano-writing attempted to overcome this by the use of widely spaced chords made doubly effective by the sagacious use of the damper pedal, which when depressed, raises the dampers from all of the strings. The resulting sympathetic vibrations produce a full, rich sonority. Chopin's harmonic idiom was also unusually original, and his extremely subtle use of dissonance imparts a distinctive character to his works.

Like so many of his contemporaries, Chopin achieved his greatest successes as a composer in the shorter forms. We should notice, however, that almost all his works bear only generic titles, and that descriptive titles such as *Raindrop, Butterfly* and so forth, given to some of them, did not originate with him.

Among these shorter forms, almost all of which possess three-part patterns, we may mention the nineteen *Nocturnes,* the four *Impromptus,* the twenty-four *Préludes,* the twenty-four *Études,* and the four *Scherzos.* The four *Ballades* are extensive narrative pieces supposedly inspired by the Polish poet Mickiewicz.

Chopin's music in dance forms represents one of the first products of that growth of nationalistic interest in music which was a feature of the nineteenth century. The two Polish dances immortalized by Chopin are the lively peasant *Mazurka* and the courtly processional *Polonaise.* Chopin's *Waltzes* are interpretations of a German dance form.

Franz Liszt, unlike Chopin, was a figure of international fame, who for many years made triumphant appearances as a piano virtuoso in almost every important city in Europe. It was Liszt who brought the piano recital into being, for under his hands the piano became capable of effectively reproducing all the sonorities and color contrasts of an orchestra and consequently able to furnish a full evening of music in a large hall.

Liszt's technical achievements were prodigious. He was probably the greatest pianist the world has ever known. Prominent features of his style were continual use of as many fingers as possible, simultaneous use of the several registers of the piano requiring great accuracy in leaping; trills, tremolos, brilliant octave passages, elaborate cadenzas.

With the outstanding exception of his great Sonata in B Minor, the greater part of Liszt's original music for the piano is written in the shorter forms, treated, however, with great freedom. Programmatic titles appear in abundance: *Au Bord d'une source* (*At the Spring*), *Feux-follets* (*Will o' the Wisp*), *St. François de Paule marchant sur les flots* (*St. Francis of Paula Walking on the Waves*). The nineteen Hungarian Rhapsodies represent Liszt's later interest in the music of his native Hungary.

Into his lengthy recital programs Liszt introduced a new form, the *transcription,* a free translation of an organ, orchestral, or vocal work by another composer into the idiom of the piano. Of his approximately two hundred transcriptions the most valuable were those of the organ music of Bach and the songs of Schubert. Thanks to these transcriptions, public interest in the work of these heretofore neglected composers was greatly stimulated.

Liszt also wrote nine works for piano and orchestra, of which the Concerto in E-flat major is the most important and the *Todtentanz,* a set of diabolical variations on the *Dies Irae,* the hymn for the dead, the most striking.

Almost every branch of nineteenth-century music felt the impress of Liszt. For thirteen years (1848-1861) he was a conductor at Weimar, producing works of all his fellow composers, notably Wagner. Composers came from far and wide to consult him, play their works for him, and receive his advice. The list of composers so befriended by him is a long one. In addition, Liszt gave a great amount of piano instruction. He restricted his classes, however, to talented pupils, and in a manner which was characteristic of the man, gave them their instruction gratis.

7. *The New Orchestral Music: Berlioz and Liszt*

The chief symphonists to follow in the footsteps of Beethoven were Schubert, Mendelssohn, and Schumann. But as we have already indicated, the symphonies of these particular masters are not their finest works.

The real advances in orchestral music were made by the Frenchman, Hector Berlioz (1803-1869), and by Franz Liszt, and these advances were entirely along programmatic lines. All of their orchestral works bear descriptive titles, and since their day the validity of program music has been universally recognized.

The fiery Berlioz wrote gigantic program symphonies in which he not only attempted to portray such readily recognizable aural images as the sounds of nature, but also the ebb and flow of mental states. In order to achieve this, however, Berlioz frequently sacrificed the all-important consideration of form, and a listener without prior knowledge of the program may find himself confused by the lack of organization of Berlioz' compositions.

The Fantastic Symphony (1830), inspired by the composer's "interminable and inexhaustible passion" for an Irish actress, Henrietta Smithson, is Berlioz' greatest work. The five movements of the symphony are entitled: 1. *Reveries. Passions*, 2. *A Ball*, 3. *Scene in the Fields*, 4. *March to the Scaffold*, 5. *Dream of a Witches' Sabbath*. His two other program symphonies, *Romeo and Juliet* and *Harold in Italy,* are frequently performed today.

Berlioz also ranks as one of the world's greatest masters of orchestration. He made a close study of the instruments of the orchestra and embodied the results of his investigation in a famous manual of instrumentation. It is in this sphere that Berlioz' influence has been most significant.

The orchestral form brought into being and fostered by Liszt was called *symphonic poem*. In no sense is it as rigid a form as, for example, the symphony, and, in general, no two symphonic poems are alike. The symphonic poem, in contrast to the symphony, is a single orchestral movement which, however, may contain many changes in tempo. This single movement constitutes an orchestral representation of some poetic concept which may be either implied by the title or given in detail in a prefatory program. The best known of the Liszt symphonic poems, *Les Préludes,* was published with a quotation from the *Méditations poétiques* of the French poet, Alphonse Lamartine. The music of *Les Préludes,* however, was not inspired by the poem. Liszt merely attached the poem to his score as a sort of poetic guide to its contents.

The symphonic poem has since found universal acceptance as an art form. But the pioneering aspect of Liszt's work is often overlooked.

8. *The Music-Drama: Richard Wagner*

Thomas Mann, the twentieth-century German novelist, called Richard Wagner "the supreme symbol of the nineteenth century." This statement was doubtless inspired by the grandiose nature of Wagner's works, their gigantic dimensions, and their overwhelming power. Wagner (1813-1883) was from about 1855 until his death the most talked-of musician in Europe. His works and his theories struck responsive notes in other arts. The Symbolist school of French poets, for example, was greatly influenced by Wagner's creations.

His whole life marked an unswerving progress towards one goal: the fusion of music and dramatic poetry. And in the attainment of this goal, Wagner not only wrote the texts and the music for ten great operas, but also raised funds for the erection of a theater to be devoted solely to the production of his own operas. This theater, situated in Bayreuth, was opened in 1876 with what constituted the first complete performance of Wagner's *Ring* cycle.

Wagner has often been called a reformer. It is obvious, however, that he was merely following in the footsteps of Gluck and Monteverdi. His first step ahead was in the choice of his texts. As opposed to prevailing trends, they were all of high literary value, and with the exception of one opera, *Die Meistersinger von Nürnberg,* were based on mythology or folk legend. Wagner purposely chose the myth because of its universality. It should not be overlooked that Wagner wrote all the poems for his operas, and that it is only his accomplishments as a composer which have obscured his attainments as a poet-dramatist.

The ten Wagner operas regularly given today may be divided into two groups. These are: (1) the earlier works, the romantic operas, *Der fliegende Holländer* (*The Flying Dutchman*) (1843), *Tannhäuser* (1845), and *Lohengrin* (1848); and (2) the mature works, the music-dramas—the four operas of the *Ring* cycle: *Das Rheingold* (*The Rhinegold*) (1854), *Die Walküre* (*The Valkyrie*) (1856), *Siegfried* (1871), and *Götterdämmerung* (*The Twilight of the Gods*) (1874); *Tristan und Isolde* (1859), *Die Meistersinger von Nürnberg* (*The Mastersingers of Nuremberg*) (1867), and *Parsifal* (1882). We may confine our discussion of Wagner's style to the music-dramas.

Wagner firmly believed that the achievement of a dramatic purpose was the sole aim of opera, and that all of the various arts entering into an operatic performance, poetry, music, painting, and acting, might be fused into what has been called the *Gesamtkunstwerk* (approximate translation: the art work in its totality).

To Wagner the singer was not a vocal exhibitionist but a singing actor, a performer whose lines were declaimed musically in melodious recitative. The sole purpose of this recitative was intensification of the words and the result was a type of musical speech of greatly augmented powers of expression. At certain emotional climaxes, however, the vocal writing might become pure melody.

The orchestra of the Wagnerian music-drama is a huge but extremely flexible instrument possessing under Wagner's hands apparently limitless possibilities of communication. By means of a continuous flow of music which progresses simultaneously with the stage action, the Wagnerian orchestra continually comments on the dramatic action, creates the atmosphere of a situation, recalls past happenings, or foretells future occurrences.

Wagner's orchestral language acquires a certain measure of directness through the use of short musical phrases identified with some personage, thing, or abstract concept of the drama. These phrases, which are called "leading-motives," are continually subjected to a process of variation, and it is through subtle transformations of them that the unfolding of the drama is accentuated.

In its day Wagner's harmonic language—the structure of his chords and the nature of his modulations—was extremely novel, and proved one of the more formidable obstacles to the general appreciation of his work. In his urge for dramatic expression, he broke down earlier concepts of melody and harmony, and in his *Tristan und Isolde* carried the conventional major and minor scales to their absolute limits. He also carried chromaticism (the use of half-steps) to new extremes.

The specifically musical influences of Wagner did not manifest themselves so much in the opera, where it would have been difficult to succeed him, but rather in purely orchestral and purely vocal music. Wagner taught composers a new instrumentation, a new harmony, a new manner of combining the voice with instrumental music, and he greatly raised the standards of operatic composition. He is universally recognized as one of the greatest composers the world has ever known.

9. Italian Opera of the Late Nineteenth Century

Italy's great opera composer Giuseppe Verdi (1813-1901), unlike Wagner, was not a revolutionary. Although following for the most part in the footsteps of Bellini and Donizetti, he adhered faithfully to a dramatic purpose in his work. At the same time, however, he provided his audiences with a wealth of ingratiating melody and his singers with ample opportunity for fine vocalism.

In evaluating Verdi's work we must realize that his style, like that of many other creative artists, underwent changes. The list of his twenty-six operas is usually divided into three parts corresponding to three successive stages in his evolution as a composer. All of the operas of this first period (1839-1850) now have only historical interest. Of the second period (1851-1867) the following are the more popular: *Rigoletto* (1851), *Il Trovatore* (1853), and *La Traviata* (1853). The works of the last period (1871-1892) are Verdi's masterpieces and warrant assigning him a place beside Wagner as an operatic composer. These three great operas are: *Aïda* (1871), *Otello* (1887), and *Falstaff* (1892).

The popularity of the more obvious tunes from Verdi's earlier works has resulted in the undervaluation of Verdi's purpose as a composer of opera. His aim was the same as Wagner's, but his method was different. The texts he chose for musical setting were lacking in complex symbolism or involved philosophy. He relied not on the eloquence of the orchestra but on the invariable effectiveness of vocal melody, simple and yet not obvious, direct and yet not banal. He handled the orchestra with understanding, and in his later works it becomes almost Wagnerian in its activity. But at no time does Verdi's orchestration contest the absolute domination of the voice.

Towards the end of the nineteenth century an emphasis on *verismo* (realism) manifested itself in Italian opera. The preferred operatic text was short, based on events in the life of the common people, highly spiced with emotional situations, and usually brought to a conclusion with a bloody episode. Two products of *verismo* remain in the repertory, and since both are short, they have been grouped together to afford a full evening of music. These Siamese twins are *Cavalleria rusticana (Rustic Chivalry)* (1890) of Pietro Mascagni (1863-1945), and *I Pagliacci (The Clowns)* (1892) of Ruggiero Leoncavallo (1858-1919).

The real successor to Verdi, and in many respects the last of the long and great line of Italian opera composers, was the exceptionally gifted Giacomo Puccini (1858-1924). Possessing an excellent sense of the theater, Puccini wrote tremendously effective operas in a style which was a fusion of the expressive melody of Verdi, the vividness of *verismo* and the orchestral fluency of Wagner. Puccini was especially fortunate in his choice of texts. His chief fault is one common to most Italian opera composers, namely, the overinflation of emotional situations.

His masterworks are *La Bohème* (1896), *Tosca* (1900), *Madama Butterfly* (1904), and the brilliant one-act comic opera *Gianni Schicchi* (1918).

10. *Johannes Brahms*

We must discuss the German composer Johannes Brahms (1833-1897) as an individual, for he was not the spearhead of any movement, and both he and his music constitute a somewhat isolated phenomenon of the late nineteenth century. In an era in which brilliant piano music, program symphonies, symphonic poems and music-dramas were the prevailing forms, Brahms chose to confine himself to the classical forms, that is, the forms of Beethoven's day, the sonata, the symphony, the string quartet, the theme and variations. In the forms which he employed Brahms was a neo-classicist, but in the lyrical character of his subject matter he was a thorough romanticist.

In his habits of composition Brahms recalls 'Beethoven. His works, too, were released to the world only after much painstaking labor upon them. It is said that he wrote and destroyed twenty-six string quartets before publishing his first work in this form. Like Beethoven, Brahms was a master of the art of development, and his works are terse and compact.

Brahms stands apart from most of his contemporaries in his apparent insensitivity to tone-color both in his piano and orchestral music. Stolidity and a rather thick sonority characterize his writing. Brahms's primary interest was in the substance and the form of his works, and tone-color was a secondary concern. With the exception of the opera, Brahms has given important works to every branch of musical composition.

His better-known piano compositions are a fine sonata in F minor, two impressive sets of variations, the *Variations and Fugue on a Theme of Handel* and the *Variations on a Theme of Paganini;* and several shorter pieces of romantic flavor such as the *Capriccios,* the *Intermezzi,* the *Rhapsodies,* and the *Ballades.* The four sets of *Hungarian Dances* were originally written for piano duet, but are now most often played in orchestral transcription.

As a writer of songs Brahms achieved great distinction. Many of his songs possess a melodic simplicity which breathes the spirit of German folk music and it is in them that Brahms's romantic trends stand most fully revealed.

The important contributions of Schubert, Schumann, and Mendelssohn notwithstanding, Brahms is held to be the finest writer of chamber music since Beethoven. He was singularly equipped to write music of this type, for chamber music places a premium on power of development. His chamber music output comprises twenty-four works, including three great string quartets, a celebrated piano quintet, three sonatas for violin and piano, and an unusually romantic clarinet quintet.

Of Brahms's many choral compositions several are regularly given by American choral organizations. The most important is the *Deutsches Requiem (German Requiem).* The Requiem, which is not ritual music, is a setting of seven biblical excerpts chosen by Brahms himself.

Brahms was the greatest German symphonist since Beethoven. Some critics even go so far as to call him the last of the great line of German symphonists. In any case, he is perhaps the last universally accepted German symphonist, for the works of Anton Bruckner and Gustav Mahler, the only other important German symphony composers, have only recently awakened widespread response outside of the German-speaking countries and Holland.

Brahms' four symphonies represent the culmination of his career as a composer. In form they are as classical as the symphonies of Beethoven, their spirit, however, is thoroughly romantic. The four symphonies, while typical of their creator, are, like those of Beethoven, decidedly individual works about which generalization is difficult. At one time considered austere and forbidding, they have within the last two decades become favorites in the symphonic repertory.

Other important orchestral works of Brahms are the two concertos for piano, the concerto for violin, the double concerto for violin and violoncello, the *Variations on a Theme of Haydn,* and the *Tragic* and *Academic Festival* overtures. The last-named work, based on German student songs, was composed by Brahms as a token of appreciation for the honorary degree of Doctor of Music which the University of Breslau had conferred upon him in 1879.

11. *Nationalism in Music*

Up to this point our account of the development of the art of music has concerned itself almost exclusively with the composers of Italy, France, and Germany. From the dying out of Flemish influence about 1600 up to about 1850, these three countries practically dominated the European musical scene. We should not forget that the Pole, Chopin, and the Hungarian, Liszt, migrated early in life to Paris.

Nationalism, in its musical implications, is a term usually reserved for a phenomenon of the nineteenth century: the self-conscious rise of national schools in an attempt to throw off the domination, actual or implied, of foreign musicians and thereby to create a truly indigenous national musical literature. The first great musical nationalist was Carl Maria von Weber who with his romantic operas freed Germany from the yoke of Italian operatic composers. The most important nationalistic schools, however, were those of Bohemia, Norway, and Russia.

Bohemian musical nationalism resulted in a large measure from the Austrian oppression of the Czech minorities. The two great Czech composers Bedrich Smetana (1824-1884) and Antonin Dvořák (1841-1904) were both ardent patriots, the former's activities making him for several years *persona non grata* with the Austrian authorities.

Smetana's deep love for his fatherland and the music of its people found expression in a colorful folk opera, *The Bartered Bride* (1866), and in a cycle of six symphonic poems called *My Country.* Of these poems, the second, *The Moldau,* glorifying the great river of Czechoslovakia, is frequently performed today.

Dvořák, who spent four years of his life as director of the unsuccessful National Conservatory of Music in New York, is best known for his symphony *From the New World,* with its celebrated *Largo.* Several of his nationalistic operas are heard today, but only in Prague.

Norway's most important composers have been Johan Svendsen (1840-1911),

Eduard Grieg (1843-1907), and Christian Sinding (1856-1941), of whom the most famous and also the most typically Norwegian was Grieg. Grieg's works made full use of the rich store of Norwegian folk melody, often treated, however, in a somewhat sentimental manner. His concerto for piano, the incidental music for Ibsen's *Peer Gynt,* and a few songs are his best-known compositions.

Of all the nationalistic schools, the Russian has made the most important contributions and has most successfully built up a national literature of music.

Michael Glinka (1803-1857) was the first Russian composer to upset the German-Italian domination of Russian music. This he did by means of two nationalistic operas, *A Life for the Czar* (1836) and *Ruslan and Ludmilla* (1842). His immediate successor was Alexander Dargomijsky (1813-1869), composer of *The Stone Guest* (completed by Cui and Rimsky-Korsakoff and first performed in 1872).

The nucleus of the Russian school consisted of a group of composers known to history as "The Russian Five." The individuals who made up this group were: Mily Balakireff (1837-1910), César Cui (1835-1918), Nicholas Rimsky-Korsakoff (1844-1908), Alexander Borodin (1834-1887), and Modeste Moussorgsky (1839-1881). Balakireff was the only member initially to possess any extensive musical training; the other four were amateurs who subjected themselves to his tutelage. Only three members of "The Russian Five" figure with any frequency on modern programs: Rimsky-Korsakoff, Borodin, and Moussorgsky.

Rimsky-Korsakoff, who at first planned to be an officer in the Imperial Russian Navy, prepared himself for a career as a composer by a long process of self-instruction. Eventually he became the most technically skilled member of the group, and functioned as the posthumous mentor of Borodin and Moussorgsky, whose works he either orchestrated or revised after the premature deaths of their composers.

Rimsky-Korsakoff was the Russian Berlioz, for he also made a penetrating study of the orchestra and issued a valuable textbook on orchestration. All of his works are scored in a brilliant manner, often Oriental in style. Although Rimsky-Korsakoff was predominantly a composer of operas, he is best known in America by three early orchestral works: the *Spanish Caprice* (1887), the symphonic suite *Scheherazade* (1888), and the overture *The Russian Easter* (1888). Despite this undue emphasis on Rimsky-Korsakoff's orchestral music, two of his operas, *Sadko* (1897) and *Le Coq d'or* (1908), have been given in America with some degree of regularity.

Borodin was a physician and professor of chemistry whose hobby was composition. This hobby had magnificent results: two symphonies, a string quartet, an opera, *Prince Igor,* and several shorter works. He possessed a fluent melodic style and a keen sense of form. His colorful Second Symphony (1876) ranks as the finest purely instrumental work to be written by a member of "The Russian Five."

Moussorgsky, who for the greater part of his life was a clerk in the Russian Civil Service, was the most talented member of the entire group. According to conventional standards he was an untrained musician. So great was his urge for expression, however, that the technical deficiencies, largely inept orchestration, which his works display are of no consequence. Moussorgsky was primarily an operatic composer and he sought to achieve his dramatic purposes in a straightforward fashion. Thus his works lack the complexity of Wagner's music-dramas. His great masterpiece is the opera *Boris Goudonoff* (1874), after Pushkin's historical drama of the same name. Moussorgsky's skill in swift characterization manifests itself in a series of short piano pieces, *Pictures at an Exhibition,* inspired by a showing of water-colors.

Not all Russian composers were as self-consciously nationalistic as the ones we have just mentioned, and some of the Russian contemporaries of "The Five" were even unsympathetic with their efforts. But although the endeavors of these contemporaries may not have been so ardently nationalistic, they also resulted in the emergence of Russia as a first-class musical power.

The most important of these essentially cosmopolitan composers was Peter Ilitch Tchaikovsky (1840-1893), with a long list of compositions to his credit. Tchaikovsky's melodic fluency, colorful orchestration, and predilection for sensational climaxes have earned him widespread popularity. He was thoroughly at home in the larger musical forms, as his excellent symphonies and concertos attest.

Other Russian composers deserving of mention are Anatol Liadow (1855-1914), best known for his symphonic poem *The Enchanted Lake,* Michaël Ippolitoff-Ivanoff (1859-1935) whose colorful *Caucasian Sketches* is about the only work of his heard in America, the important symphonist Alexander Glazounoff (1865-1936), the pianist-composer Sergei Rachmaninoff (1873-1943), and the mystical Alexander Scriabin (1872-1915). Scriabin undertook some bold experiments in harmony, constructing a new chordal system. For his orchestral work *Prometheus,* he demanded a color-organ to project various colors as the music was played, thus initiating another attempt to effect a fusion of the arts.

12. *The Late Nineteenth Century*

Emphasis on symphonic and chamber music and the relative subordination of interest in opera were the most prominent characteristics of French music of the late nineteenth century. All due credit must be given, however, to two essentially eclectic operatic composers, Charles Gounod (1818-1893), whose *Faust* (1859) introduced a note of sentimentality into *grand opéra,* and Ambroise Thomas (1811-1896), whose *Mignon* (1866) is also couched in a sentimental vein. The greatest French opera of the period, if not the greatest French opera of all time, was Georges Bizet's (1838-1875) *Carmen* (1875). The sentimental lyricism of Gounod was perpetuated by Jules Massenet (1842-1912) in works such as *Manon* (1884) and *Thaïs* (1894).

The rebirth of purely instrumental music in France was largely a result of the Franco-Prussian War. After the defeat of France, French composers formed the *Société Nationale de Musique* to aid in the dissemination of French compositions. The resources of the society were limited, resulting in a focusing of attention on instrumental rather than operatic music. In a sense, the formation of the society constituted a nationalistic manifestation, though, to be sure, not as ardent as those which had taken place in Russia or Bohemia. But the members of the society, despite their pro-French leanings, could not escape falling under the influence of the formal innovations of Liszt and the new harmonic language and rich orchestration of Wagner.

The first president of the society was the versatile Camille Saint-Saëns (1835-1921), a composer who has often been called "The French Mendelssohn." Saint-Saëns' writings were strongly influenced by Liszt, as is shown by his four symphonic poems of which the *Danse macabre* is the best known. His biblical opera *Samson et Dalila* was produced in Weimar in 1877 after Liszt had interceded in the composer's behalf.

César Franck (1822-1890), succeeding Saint-Saëns as president of the *Société Nationale de Musique,* practically founded the modern French school. His influence, like that of Liszt, manifested itself as much by his interest in other composers as by his compositons. Franck wrote in a highly personal harmonic idiom which, however, derived from the chromaticism of Wagner. The scheme of organization underlying his larger works was an outcome of Liszt's procedures. The general effect of his composition is one of deep sincerity and earnestness.

Despite his numerous and often wearying duties, Franck composed a rather large amount of music of which only a small fraction merits performance today. The fame which he enjoys is based chiefly on the following compositions, all works of his later years: the *Prelude, Choral and Fugue,* and the *Prelude, Aria and Finale* for piano; the *Symphonic Variations* for piano and orchestra, his sonata for violin and piano, his string quartet, and his symphony. He composed only one work in each of these categories. A fine organist, Franck also enriched the repertory of this instrument.

The faithful band of disciples who surrounded Franck kept alive the traditions he had established. Among the members were: Henri Duparc (1848-1933), composer of some excellent songs, Vincent d'Indy (1851-1932), composer of the symphonic variations *Istar* and Franck's most ardent apostle; Ernest Chausson (1855-1899), composer of a *Poème* for violin and orchestra and a fine symphony.

The following composers, while not actually products of Franck's school, were contemporaneous with it: Emmanuel Chabrier (1841-1894), composer of the brilliant orchestral rhapsody *España,* Paul Dukas (1865-1935), composer of the celebrated symphonic poem *L'Apprenti sorcier* (*The Sorcerer's Apprentice*), and Gabriel Fauré (1845-1924), an essentially conservative composer best represented by his songs and chamber music.

The Wagnerian style was successfully perpetuated in Germany and Austria not so much in opera as in instrumental music. Many operatic composers tried to imitate Wagner but with no success. Only one, Engelbert Humperdinck (1854-1921), succeeded in writing an original work cast in the Wagnerian mold, the delightful children's opera *Hänsel und Gretel* (1893).

Wagner's musical heir was Richard Strauss (1864-1949) who, however, put Wagner's methods to work in the service of an instrumental form, the symphonic poem. Within eleven years (1887-1898) the facile pen of Strauss brought forth a celebrated series of symphonic poems, or tone-poems, as he called them, of which the following have now become repertory pieces: *Don Juan, Tod und*

Verklärung (*Death and Transfiguration*), *Till Eulenspiegels lustige Streiche* (*Till Eulenspiegel's Merry Pranks*), *Also sprach Zarathustra* (*Thus Spake Zarathustra*), *Don Quixote* and *Ein Heldenleben* (*A Hero's Life*).

Strauss possessed almost limitless technical facility. His orchestration, though deriving from Wagner, is bold and daring, and his works have helped considerably to raise standards of orchestral performance. Strauss' polyphonic skill imparted great richness of texture to his works. His melodies possess uncommon strength and are intensified through a complex system of harmonization.

Chronologically the operas of Strauss belong to a discussion of twentieth-century music, but they are primarily projections of a nineteenth-century technique into the succeeding century. The great Strauss operas are *Salomé* (1905), *Elektra* (1909), and *Der Rosenkavalier* (*The Rose Cavalier*) (1911). *Der Rosenkavalier* is one of the world's great comic operas. Strauss' powers later declined. Strauss is an excellent example of an artist whose works became classics during his lifetime.

The huge orchestra, the melodic and harmonic complexity, and the elaborate polyphony of Strauss' works represent the highest stage of technical development of the melodic, harmonic, and instrumental resources of nineteenth-century music. Strauss' compositions constitute the musical borderline between the nineteenth and twentieth centuries.

Two Austrian composers, Anton Bruckner (1824-1896) and Gustav Mahler (1860-1911), transferred the Wagnerian technique to the field of the symphony. Their works, though unusually fervid and earnest, suffer from excesses of length which until recently militated against their becoming popular in America. The German-speaking countries and Holland, however, have always manifested great enthusiasm for the symphonies of these composers.

Hugo Wolf (1860-1903), an Austrian composer, confined himself almost exclusively to the art-song. An ardent worshiper of Wagner, he transplanted Wagner's idiom to the song and enriched it with new standards of declamation and new harmonic procedures. Wolf coupled keen literary insight with an acutely sensitive faculty for producing the proper musical setting for a poem. Many of Wolf's finest songs are amazingly brief and in an age given over to music of grandiose dimensions he stands out as an outstanding musical miniaturist.

The course of music in England during the second half of the nineteenth century was an erratic one. Continental influences and traditions, notably that of Mendelssohn, were particularly strong. We find no predominant composer like Wagner, and no self-consciously active national school as in Russia. Many excellent composers, however, helped to reëstablish the great musical traditions of England. The two most important, from the historical standpoint, were Charles H. H. Parry (1848-1918), composer of much excellent choral music and an able writer on musical subjects, and Charles Villiers Stanford (1852-1924). England's greatest nineteenth-century composer was Edward Elgar (1857-1933), universally known for his stirring *Pomp and Circumstance* march. Elgar was essentially classical in his outlook and chose to express himself in the larger forms. His finest works are a violin concerto, the *Enigma Variations,* a series of character sketches, and the *The Dream of Gerontius,* one of the world's great oratorios.

The most distinctively English contribution of the period, however, was the brilliant series of light operas created by W. S. Gilbert (1836-1911) and Sir Arthur Sullivan (1842-1900). The biting satire and uproarious nonsense of Gilbert's texts coupled with the facile tunes of Sullivan resulted in a convincing demonstration of the possibilities of opera in English. The most successful of the numerous Gilbert and Sullivan operas were: *H.M.S. Pinafore* (1878), *The Pirates of Penzance* (1880), *Iolanthe* (1882), *The Mikado* (1885), and *The Gondoliers* (1889).

Despite the fact that the names of no really great composers are associated with it, music was assiduously cultivated in America, and a lively concert life was to be found in the larger cities. The music performed then as now was predominantly by European composers. The celebrated Handel and Haydn Society of Boston, founded in 1815, was one of the outstanding choral organizations. The New York Philharmonic-Symphony Orchestra, one of the world's oldest symphony orchestras, came into being in 1842.

The significant creative artists of the first half of the century were Stephen Collins Foster (1826-1864), composer of famous songs, and Louis Gottschalk (1829-1869), composer of piano music. In the latter part of the century a number of outstanding talents appeared. The majority were European trained. Their works, while seldom striking a distinctively American note, laid a firm foundation on which twentieth-century American music might build. Significant composers were: John Knowles Paine (1839-1906), George Chadwick (1854-1931), Edward MacDowell (1861-1908), and Horatio Parker (1863-1919).

SELECTED READINGS

Abraham, Gerald, *A Hundred Years of Music,* Macmillan, 1949.
Abrams, M. H., ed., *English Romantic Poets: Modern Essays in Criticism,* Galaxy Books, 1960.
Artz, F. B., *From the Renaissance to Romanticism: Trends in Style in Art, Literature, and Music, 1300-1830,* University of Chicago Press, 1963.
Babbitt, Irving, *Rousseau and Romanticism,* Meridian Books.
Baring, Maurice, *Landmarks in Russian Literature,* Barnes and Noble, 1960.
Barzun, Jacques, *Berlioz and His Century,* Meridian Books.
——— *Darwin, Marx, Wagner,* Anchor Books, 1958.
——— *Romanticism and the Modern Ego,* Little, Brown, 1944.
Bell, A. F. G., *Contemporary Spanish Literature,* Knopf, 1925.
Bernstein, *An Introduction to Music.*
Bertaux, Felix, *A Panorama of German Literature from 1871 to 1931,* McGraw-Hill, 1935.
Bowra, C. M., *The Heritage of Symbolism,* Schocken.
Brandes, Georg, *Main Currents in Nineteenth Century Literature,* 6 vols., Boni & Liveright, 1923.
Brenan, Gerald, *The Literature of the Spanish People,* Meridian Books, 1953.
Brereton, Geoffrey, *An Introduction to the French Poets,* Barnes and Noble.
Brion, Marcel, *Schumann and the Romantic Age,* Collins, 1956.

Brooks, Van Wyck, *The Flowering of New England, 1815-1861,* Random House, 1936.

———— *New England: Indian Summer, 1865-1915,* Dutton, 1940.

Calvocoressi, M. D. , and Abraham, G., *Masters of Russian Music,* Knopf, 1936.

Chase, Gilbert, *America's Music,* McGraw-Hill, 1955.

Cheney, Sheldon, *The Theatre: Three Thousand Years of Drama, Acting and Stage-craft,* Longmans, 1958.

Clark, G. K., *The Making of Victorian England,* Harvard University Press, 1962.

Edel, Leon, *Henry James,* 4 vols., Lippincott, 1953-1963.

Einstein, Alfred, *Music in the Romantic Era,* Norton, 1947.

Elsen, A. E., *Rodin's Gates of Hell,* University of Minnesota Press, 1960.

Elton, Oliver, *Survey of English Literature, 1780 to 1880,* 4 vols., Macmillan, 1920.

Friedlaender, W. F., *David to Delacroix,* Harvard University Press, 1952.

Gassner, John, *Masters of the Drama,* Dover Publications, Inc., 1953.

Geiringer, Karl, *Brahms, His Life and Work,* Anchor Books, 1961.

Grierson, H. J. C., *Lyrical Poetry of the Nineteenth Century,* Harcourt, Brace, 1929.

Grout, *A Short History of Opera.*

———— *A History of Western Music,* Norton, 1960.

Grove, George, *Beethoven and His Nine Symphonies,* Dover Publications, Inc., 1962.

Guthrie, Ramon, *French Literature and Thought since the Revolution,* Harcourt, Brace, 1942.

Hamburger, Michael, ed., *Beethoven: Letters, Journals and Conversations,* Anchor Books, 1962.

Hardy, F. E., *The Life of Thomas Hardy, 1840-1928,* St. Martin's Press, 1962.

Harvey, W. J., *The Art of George Eliot,* Oxford University Press, 1962.

Hitchcock, H. R., *Modern Architecture, Romanticism and Reintegration,* Payson, 1929.

Hoffman, D. G., *Form and Fable in American Fiction,* Oxford University Press, 1961.

Howard, J. T., *Our American Music,* Crowell, 1955.

Kennard, J. S., *A Literary History of the Italian People,* Macmillan, 1941.

Kerman, *Opera as Drama.*

Madariaga, Salvador de, *The Genius of Spain,* Oxford University Press, 1933.

Madsen, S. T., *Sources of Art Nouveau,* Wittenborn, 1955.

Mumford, Lewis, *The Brown Decades,* Dover Publications, Inc., 1955.

Myers, B. S., *Modern Art in the Making,* McGraw-Hill, 1959.

Newman, Ernest, *Wagner as Man and Artist,* Vintage Books.

———— *Life of Richard Wagner,* 4 vols., Knopf, 1933-1946.

Nichol, Allardyce, *World Drama,* Harcourt, Brace.

Nicolson, Harold, *Sainte Beuve,* Doubleday.

Nitze, W. D., and Dargan, E. P., *A History of French Literature,* Holt, 1938.

Parrington, V. L., *Main Currents in American Thought,* 2 vols., Harcourt, Brace.

Peckham, Morse, *Beyond the Tragic Vision: The Quest for Identity in the Nineteenth Century,* Braziller, 1962.

Praz, Mario, *The Romantic Agony,* Meridian Books.

Priestley, J. B., *Literature and Western Man,* Harper, 1960.

Raynal, Maurice, *History of Modern Painting,* 3 vols., Skira, 1949-1950.

Rewald, John, *History of Impressionism,* Museum of Modern Art, 1962.

———— *Post-Impressionism,* Museum of Modern Art, 1958.

Robertson, *A History of German Literature.*

Rolland, Romain, *Essays on Music,* ed. by David Ewen, Dover Publications, Inc., 1959.

Schapiro, Meyer, *Van Gogh,* Abrams, 1950.

Schauffler, R. H., *Florestan: The Life and Work of Robert Schumann,* Dover Publications, Inc., 1963.

Simmons, E. J., *An Outline of Russian Literature,* Cornell University Press, 1943.

———— *Leo Tolstoy,* 2 vols., Vintage Books, 1960.

Sloane, J. C., *French Painting Between the Past and the Present,* Princeton University Press, 1951.

Spencer, Philip, *Flaubert,* Evergreen, 1952.

Thayer, A., *Life of Ludwig van Beethoven,* Southern Illinois University Press, 1960.

Thoreau, Henry D., *The Journals of Henry D. Thoreau,* ed. by Bradford Torrey and F. H. Allen, 2 vols., Dover Publications, Inc., 1963.

Turnell, Martin, *The Novel in France,* Vintage Books, 1958.

Untermeyer, Louis, *Lives of the Poets,* Simon and Schuster, 1959.

Walker, Frank, *The Man Verdi,* Knopf, 1962.

Walker, Hugh, *The Literature of the Victorian Era,* Cambridge University Press, 1931.

Wernaer, R. M., *Romanticism and the Romantic School in Germany,* Appleton, 1910.

Wilson, Edmund, *Patriotic Gore: Studies in the Literature of the American Civil War,* Oxford University Press, 1962.

Wright, C. H. C., *History of French Literature,* Oxford University Press, 1925.

Part Six

CONTEMPORARY CIVILIZATION AND THE FUTURE OF MAN

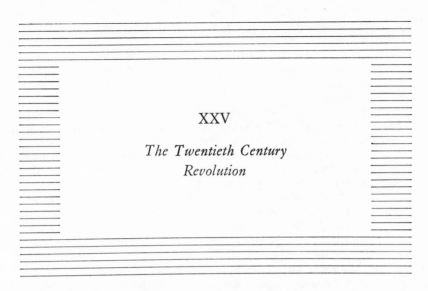

XXV

The Twentieth Century Revolution

I. THE INSTITUTIONAL FRAMEWORK

It is difficult for the historian to view our own age against the panorama of human history. Yet the only important service history can render man is to help him understand how the past created the present and thus illuminate the probable course of future events. We are now living in a great transitional age which differs from any previous epoch of transition in two ways. The first contrast lies in the rapidity with which the change is bound to be carried out. The second contrast lies in the choice facing our age—either utopia or barbarism, if not extinction. We have created a machine age uniquely prepared to serve us or to wreck us. Upon the type of social control imposed on our empire of machines will depend the outcome.

The Five Industrial Revolutions.—This book is not directly concerned with problems of mechanical and industrial development, but at least a brief summary of the mechanical advances which furnish the material background of twentieth-century culture and thought is indispensable.

In an earlier chapter we dealt with what is commonly called *the* Industrial Revolution, namely, the introduction of mechanical manufacturing in the textile and iron and steel industries, the introduction of the steam engine, and its application to manufacturing and transportation. This great change came gradually between the sixteenth and the nineteenth centuries, attaining full momentum around 1800.

Following 1850 came the second industrial revolution, characterized mainly by large-scale industry, better division of labor, the applications of chemistry to the steel and rubber industries, great improvements in railroad and ocean transportation, and such improvements in communication as the telegraph and telephone.

Shortly after 1900, a third industrial revolution brought in the assembly line, mass production, wider use of electric power, and notable advances in transportation and communication, such as the origins of air transport, wireless telegraphy, and the radio.

These trends and innovations moved on so rapidly that they led to a fourth industrial revolution by 1935 which centered around automatic machinery, increasing use of electric power and the growth of electrical controls over transportation, industry, and communications, producing by the mid-century what could accurately be called the "electronic age."

But already, before 1950, it was evident that a fifth and even more momentous industrial revolution was in the making: that which would be developed around the use of nuclear energy, and might involve human travel into outer space.

Contrasts and Conflicts in Twentieth-Century Culture.—The most characteristic aspect of our twentieth-century civilization and that which makes our age inevitably transitional in character is the unprecedented contrast between the material and the non-material factors in our culture. We have a thoroughly up-to-date material culture, complete, diverse, and potentially efficient beyond that of any earlier ages. Today we are in the midst of the fourth and fifth industrial revolutions, characterized by applications of electrical and atomic power—the age of electrification, automatic machinery, electric control over manufacturing processes, air transport, radios, television, and so on. On the other hand, our institutions and the social thinking through which we seek to control and exploit this novel and complex material culture are an antiquated mosaic, compounded mainly of accretions from the StoneAge to the close of the eighteenth century.

The national state was a legalized institution of wide prevalence in 1648. The theories of representative government and democracy were worked out in the seventeenth and eighteenth centuries. Capitalistic ideals and practices were well established long before 1800. The legal theories which dominate us today rest fundamentally upon Roman law, the medieval English common law, and the seventeenth-century doctrines of natural law. Our educational curriculum and much of its subject matter come from ancient, medieval, or early modern times. The prevailing religious system dates from the beginning of the Christian Era and embodies many elements far older than that. Our basic economic theories appeared in Adam Smith's *Wealth of Nations,* published in the same year as our Declaration of Independence. Indeed, Smith was a much more erudite and enlightened expositor of such theories than most of the business leaders, financiers, and lawyers in our own day who hark back to him. Our moral code has developed over a protracted period, stretching from Moses to Augustine, the Puritans, and Immanuel Kant. Nine-tenths of our philosophical speculation is a rehashing and rationalization of mental antiquities, originally suggested by thinkers between the ages of Socrates and Hegel. It is, therefore, fair to say that the dominant institutions and thought of our day derive from the eighteenth century or earlier. Such a discrepancy has never existed before, except among the Attic Greeks and, to a lesser degree, the Romans. In their case institutions and social philosophy were in advance of material culture.

Not only does this vast gulf exist in our age between material culture and social thinking and institutions but we seemingly do everything possible to widen the abyss. We usually reward those who extend our already topheavy material equipment, but the social inventor we make an outcast or deride as a crank. We are restrained from narrowing this gulf because of sharply contrasting psychological attitudes with respect to material and mental antiquities. For example, we demand the most up-to-date models of automobiles, and the average man would be unutterably embarrassed to have to drive along a public thoroughfare in a 1930-model automobile, even though the vehicle were in perfect condition. Yet that same man may worship ideas and institutions dating from the stage-coach era. So long as this state of mind exists there is little hope of closing the gap between material culture and institutions—another way of saying that there is slight hope of preserving civilization—since we cannot go on for long with one foot in an airplane and the other in an oxcart.

Another phase of this paradox lies in our reaction towards expert guidance. When a man wants a bathroom faucet repaired, or a tooth pulled, he deems it necessary to call on an expert. But for the much more difficult problems of social, economic, and political life, he seems completely satisfied to be guided by the all too often ignorant, traditional, and emotional opinions of the man on the street or the appeals and dogmas of politicians seeking to be elected or to retain office.

This striking discrepancy between our machines and our institutions has already exacted a frightful penalty and may exact the supreme penalty—extinction of civilization. It has produced severe depressions and other economic disasters. It has almost destroyed democracy. It has made our legal system inadequate and produced widespread contempt for law in general. It has permitted and encouraged two disastrous world wars which have undermined the economic and political framework of contemporary life. It has bred moral chaos and educational futility. If we go on as we have so far in the twentieth century, the ultimate result will be the collapse of Western civilization from internal weaknesses, with the grave probability that the process will be greatly hastened by a devastating third world war. If society awakens in time and brings our institutions up to date, we may literally "inherit the earth."

Political Developments.—The outstanding political developments during the first half of the twentieth century were the termination of such political autocracy as existed in 1900, the crisis in democratic government, and the rise of dictatorships as the emergency answer to the inadequacy of many democratic governments to meet the postwar problems after 1918.

The chief autocratic government which still remained at the beginning of the twentieth century was that of tsarist Russia. This was brought to a decisive end by the Russian Revolution of 1917. While this was launched by liberal, democratic forces, they were too weak to maintain control for more than a brief period and their regime was followed by the Bolshevik socialist government which seized control in October, 1917, and has remained in power to the present time, gaining in strength over the years, especially as a result of Anglo-American assistance during and after the second World War. It was helped into power by the Anglo-American pressure exerted on the Kerensky government in 1917 to continue the first World War, for which exertions this moderate socialist government was by no means prepared. Revolutionary Russia was solidified by the Anglo-American effort to suppress the Bolshevik government in 1918-1919. This aroused the nationalistic and patriotic sentiments of nearly all Russians, many of whom opposed the Bolshevik system but rallied to resist foreign invasion. The venerable Austro-Hungarian Empire had been extensively democratized before 1914 and was completely dismantled by the "peacemakers" of 1919. The result was to increase the disastrous "Balkanization" of Europe and add to the problems of democratic government in the segmentary countries that grew out of the dismantling process. The power of the Prussian Junkers in Germany was notably reduced under both the Weimar Republic and the National Socialist regimes, and was obliterated after 1945 when East Prussia was handed over to Poland.

Democracy underwent a notable ordeal between the two World Wars, in considerable part as a result of the economic crisis produced by the first World War and the Versailles settlement. A main slogan of the Allies during the war was that it was being fought to make the world safe for democracy. Whereas there had been eighteen national states in 1914, the Versailles Treaty created twelve new ones and all of them were ostensibly set up as democracies. But strains and stresses led most of them to gravitate toward some form of autocracy or dictatorship between the two World Wars.

Democracy made a number of temporary gains following the first World War. One was the establishment of more new democratic states, even though most of them had lapsed into totalitarian or quasi-totalitarian states before 1939. In England, universal male suffrage was achieved in 1918 and female suffrage in 1928. But this was more than offset by the serious weakening of the Liberal party which had been the main bulwark of democracy in England since the Reform Bill of 1832. The Conservative party was not abreast of the times and the Labor party was not prepared or powerful enough competently to assume the direction of the English government. Conservative incompetence and radical warmongering led England into the second World War, which so undermined the British economy that drastic economic measures had to be instituted by both the Conservative and Labor parties. But democracy still remained the formal framework of the governmental system.

The defects in the constitution of the Third French Republic were intensified by the *bloc* system of parliamentary government which led to serious instability. In the mid-1930's France was governed by a Popular Front coalition of radical parties. The lack of sound statecraft on the part of both French moderates and radicals led France into the second World War. The Fourth French Republic inherited the defects of the Third Republic, led to greater instability in the government, and made it inevitable that the outcome would be the establishment of some form of authoritative or autocratic system. Italian democracy was utterly swamped by the chaos created by the first World War and quickly succumbed to fascism. Although the latter was destroyed by the second World War, Communism has menaced Italy ever since the collapse of Mussolini's government in 1943.

Despite even greater handicaps, the Weimar Republic survived in Germany until the National Socialists took over early in 1933. The republic was harassed by such economic burdens as inflation and reparations and by the lack of preparation for a thoroughly democratic system. It would perhaps have been wiser to have continued a more thoroughly democratized Hohenzollern constitutional monarchy. Democracy in Austria and Hungary was severely handicapped by territorial losses which led to fatal economic problems. The attempt to democratize the Spanish government by a revolution in the mid-1930's failed, and a Fascist system was set up by General Franco. Despite the establishment of a Chinese Republic in 1912, democracy made few substantial gains in Asia in the twentieth century, and after the second World War China moved into a Communist dictatorship. Although the British were ousted from India and a formal democracy was set up there under Nehru, the new system was seriously handicapped by a backward economy, poverty, illiteracy, and an appalling increase in population. Japan was temporarily forced into a formal democracy after the second World War under a constitution written by the United States and introduced into practice by General Douglas MacArthur.

In the United States, democracy retained its formal existence. But lack of domestic and international statecraft in the 1920's led to the great depression following 1929. The New Deal administrations of President Roosevelt, which vainly sought to end the depression, brought about a great increase in the power of the executive branch of the government at the expense of the legislative and judicial departments. This trend was enormously extended after the entry of the United States into the second World War, the launching of the Cold War in 1947, and entry into the Korean War in 1950. No important changes occurred when the Republican party took over in 1953, save for the fact that Congress regained some of the power it had lost under Roosevelt.

All in all, one may fairly say that, although the first World War was ostensibly fought to "make the world safe for democracy," the net result was to place democracy in greater jeopardy than it had been in 1900. The second World War, as a result of the new strains and stresses which it imposed, still further undermined the democratic system. Even in the United States, few of the basic assumptions upon which American democracy had been based were vindicated by the facts of history or those set forth by psychological and social science. That democracy endured in the United States was due mainly to the remarkable achievements of its technological and industrial system. But it is dubious as to whether even these can indefinitely survive the burdens imposed by the financial outlays produced by the Cold War, which seems likely to last for years or decades. It is certain that, if democracy is to continue as the dominant political system, it will require international peace and realistic and drastic improvements that do not appear on the horizon in any part of the world. That democracy can "muddle through" in the face of the increasingly complex problems of an atomic age is no less than a fantastic illusion.

Perhaps the greatest weakness of democracy is that it must work through representative government, which requires the political party to operate it. Whatever the abstract theory, the political party has thus far proved fatally deficient as the main agency of democratic government. Partisanship promotes emotional orgies rather than calm deliberation. Parties create political confusion, instability, or even anarchy when broken up into many *blocs*. They encourage both political corruption and autocracy as a result of the inevitable development of party machines. When either the two-party or *bloc* system breaks down, there is a tendency to resort to a one-party system, which is one of the main symptoms and traits of political totalitarianism.

It is frequently asserted that the remedy for democratic defects and failures is "more democracy," meaning such progressive devices as the initiative, referendum, recall, direct primaries, and the like. But where these have been tried they have usually failed through public apathy. It has been observed with some logic that if voters were alert and intelligent enough to operate such methods as are involved in the "more democracy" program they would not need them. The civil service or merit system had actually produced an increase of political honesty and efficiency, but on the whole it has proved quite inadequate, in part because it has not been extended to the legislative and judicial branches of the government. The current need for the merit system is far greater in the legislative department of the government than in the executive.

Aside from the increasingly severe ordeal of democracy, the most notable political development in the twentieth century has been the frank abandonment of democracy in a number of countries and the establishment of totalitarian governments, whether radical, as in Communist Russia, or conservative, as in Fascist Italy, National Socialist Germany, and the Spain of Franco. While it has been popular to regard these totalitarian systems as reversions to the Dark Ages, this is a dangerous illusion. They are strictly novel and twentieth-century reactions to the breakdown of democracy. They are, as Lindsay Rogers correctly designated them, "crisis governments," and there is no doubt that they will be reinstituted wherever and whenever crises comparable to those in Russia in 1917, Italy in 1922, and Germany in 1932 reappear. Such crises are already in the making, especially since the institution of the Cold War in 1947. Spanish fascism survived the second World War, Soviet Russia under communism has become far and away the most powerful state in the Old World, and the temporary obliteration of Italian fascism and German National Socialism provides no guarantee that comparable systems will not reappear in the future if sufficiently serious crises arise to require totalitarian methods to insure public order.

These new totalitarian systems are only the most drastic example of what James Burnham has called "the managerial revolution." This produces a system in which non-elective or fictitiously elective persons take over most of the important functions of government, whatever the formal political system which prevails. The growth of such managerialism within the current governments that still maintain a nominal democratic system is perhaps a greater menace to the future of parliamentary democracy than the older fascist and Nazi totalitarianisms that have been eradicated for the time being. The success of Russian managerialism may well further stimulate managerialism even in countries that ostensibly cling to democracy and at least pretend to abhor the economic system and other features of the regime in Soviet Russia.

The growth of nationalism and the national-state system was one of the more striking political developments following the era of the French Revolution. Most important and dramatic here were the unification of Germany and Italy in 1870, the revolts and independence of the Latin American states, and the expansion and consolidation of the United States. Extreme nationalism played an important role in producing the first World War. Some recognition of this fact led to the determination to curb nationalism through the creation of the League of Nations. But this proved a deplorable failure. The League operated as a league of victors, perpetuating the evils of the postwar treaties and stimulating the nationalism of countries that had been penalized. In addition to this, nationalism was encouraged by the creation of a dozen new national states in 1919. Hence, nationalism was also a main cause of the second World War. The United Nations proved as futile in checking national sentiment as had the League of Nations. The Cold War also strengthened national emotions. In the era after 1945, the chief area of nationalistic upsurgings was no longer Europe or the American continent, but Africa and Asia, where the so-called colored races sought emancipation from the old colonial empires and the domination of the white man. This vast and widely dispersed nationalistic uprising may well prove the greatest challenge to peace in the second half of the twentieth century.

We have just mentioned the fact that the century-old efforts to create international sentiment and world organization, which culminated in the League of Nations in 1919, proved futile. The League was authorized and given a mandate to revise the postwar treaties and promote good-will in Europe and Asia. Instead of this, it perpetuated the unjust settlement of 1919 and the resentment which this created. Hence, it invited the rise of Hitler, with his effort to revise the Versailles Treaty by unilateral methods, and the struggle of Japan to obtain living room on the continent of Asia. The United Nations organization was launched before the end of the second World War, but the failure to work out a just peace after the War led to the Cold War which split the United Nations down the middle and greatly decreased its effectiveness. Its weakness was demonstrated in the Korean War of 1950-1953 and the inconclusive outcome of that conflict. Nationalism still continues to be rampant, and the United Nations will be no safeguard against war until the Cold War is brought to an end and the demands of the rising newer nations are adjusted in some effective fashion. Because of the ever more destructive technology which may be employed in warfare, it may fairly be said that war was a far greater threat to the human race as we entered the second half of the twentieth century than it was in 1900.

Like democracy, civil liberties have had their "ups and downs" since 1900, but there can be little doubt that they were less well established and secure at the mid-century than they were at the outset. The first World War led to the suspension of most liberties during the contest and they never regained their pre-war scope. Soviet Russia had established a totalitarian government before the war was ended. Italian fascism curtailed many liberties after 1922, although not as completely as Soviet Russia. German National Socialism was as ruthless in limiting liberty as Russian communism. The one unique aspect of the Russian situation was that the Soviet rulers did not suppress liberty because the Russians had never enjoyed any. Spanish fascism under Franco was more repressive than Italian fascism under Mussolini. The dictatorships that sprang up in Latin America also curtailed civil liberties. There were many invasions of civil liberties even in democratic countries, although they were not as extreme except during wartime.

The second World War, like the first, brought the suspension of most liberties for the duration, and there was no notable revival after 1945 as there had been after 1919. The Cold War brought with it fears and a drive for secrecy and security which impaired freedom in various ways. The additional fears conjured up by the Russian launching of space satellites in 1957 inevitably increased the tensions and restraints of the Cold War system and placed still further restrictions on the liberty of citizens, especially those of the "free nations." While the United Nations has a unit ostensibly devoted to promoting civil liberties on an international scale, its powers and efforts are trivial compared to the new factors stimulating fear and restraint.

The alleged contrast between the "free nations" and the "slave nations" is largely a propaganda fiction. While it is obvious that the citizens of the United States, Canada, Mexico, England, France, Italy, and West Germany enjoy more civil liberty than those behind the so-called Iron Curtain, it is also true that certainly a majority of the countries included among the so-called free nations are neither democracies nor libertarian. Even fewer of them permit unrestrained free enterprise in the economic field.

We noted in an earlier chapter that whereas the chief inroads upon freedom until the modern age arose chiefly from theological forces, contemporary repressions of liberty are motivated mainly by political, military, and economic factors. At and after the mid-century, the military pressures became more numerous and extreme, mainly due to the impact of the second World War and the Cold War.

Economic Trends.—The most conspicuous trends in the economic field in the twentieth century were: (1) the undermining of industrial capitalism; (2) the rise and decline of finance capitalism, especially in the United States; (3) the growth of state capitalism, manifested in moderate fashion in the state activity of conservative Britain, the Popular Front in France, and the New Deal in the United States, and taking an extreme form in the fascist countries; (4) the growth of both moderate and revolutionary Marxian socialism, and (5) the efforts of the Scandinavian countries to work out a mixed or eclectic economic system which combined private capitalism, state capitalism, and the cooperative system.

In 1900, the capitalistic system was constituted of the older commercial capitalism that had developed following the expansion of Europe, and the industrial capitalism which came on the heels of the Industrial Revolution. In this latter system, the managers of commercial and industrial enterprises owned them and profits were made primarily from the earnings of their operations. In case the owners mismanaged their properties such losses as resulted fell upon themselves. Hence, there was a direct incentive to produce and manage efficiently, even though this did not always take place.

Beginning early in the present century, and most notably in the United States, a new form of capitalism, usually described as finance capitalism, gained headway at the expense of the older industrial capitalism. It was associated with the increasing prevalence of corporations as the means of owning and operating great enterprises of all types and the rise of investment banking to handle the securities of such corporations. Ownership tended to become divorced from management, which fell into the hands of corporate officials and the investment bankers who were almost invariably interlocked. Ownership became widely distributed through the dispersed holding of corporate securities.

It thus became easy for a few well-integrated owners of such securities to take over the management of economic enterprises even though they actually owned only a very small fraction of the securities. It was commonly believed that a controlling group must own at least 51 per cent of the securities, but it was often the case that the managing coterie owned 5 per cent or less of them. Even then, they owned more than any contesting group of owners could muster in opposition. In this way, it came about that these few well-integrated insiders, mainly the corporate officials, found that they could often make greater profits by various forms of speculation and manipulation than through efficient management of their corporations. They obtained all the income from such non-productive operations while they personally had to bear only a slight fraction of any losses incurred. This finance capitalism flourished especially among the many new and rapidly growing public utility (power and light) corporations, but it gradually dominated the whole business picture from 1900 until the depression of 1929.

The central agency or organization in the creation and operation of finance capitalism until 1929 was the investment banking house of J. P. Morgan and Company. Finance capitalists also branched out widely in foreign investment and the sale of foreign bonds, which often brought great losses to American investors. Since actual business prosperity was a secondary issue with the finance capitalists, they failed to keep wages up to a level which guaranteed the mass purchasing power needed to provide the effective demand for goods required to maintain permanent prosperity.

The methods of finance capitalism were first effectively exposed by the able Harvard economist, William Z. Ripley, in a striking article on "From Main Street to Wall Street," in the *Atlantic Monthly,* January, 1926. The most complete treatment was embodied in A. A. Berle and G. C. Means, *The Modern Corporation and Private Property,* published in 1932. Ripley's warnings were not heeded, and finance capitalism not only led to the great depression of 1929 and ensuing years but failed to recover from this great economic shock. It was followed by the state capitalism of the New Deal, the war period, and the Cold War system which ensued. Corporations also tended to free themselves more and more from investment bankers, to draw needed funds more usually from loans made by the great insurance companies or from their own reserves, and to float their own securities. Finance capitalism never developed on any such scale in Europe, although the most dramatic and colorful figure associated with the era and methods of finance capitalism was a Swede, Ivan Krueger.

While private capitalism has continued to dominate capitalistic countries since 1929, it has been buttressed in differing degrees by state capitalism. The latter is devoted to public activities and expenditures that are at least theoretically designed to bolster and perpetuate the capitalistic system. But, to the extent that it has intervened, it has tended to limit the power and control the activities of private capitalism. The problems created by the first World War compelled even the British Conservative party to take notable steps along the path of state capitalism. The most complete and rational statement of a plan of state capitalism in a democratic country was the book, *Full Employment in a Free Society* (1945), written by a respected English economist, Sir William Beveridge. It reflected the ideas of a vastly influential English economist, John Maynard Keynes, who occupied much the same position of intellectual dominion in the opening period of state capitalism as Adam Smith had in the early days of individualistic capitalism.

Another leading effort to promote state capitalism was the more dramatized New Deal of President Franklin D. Roosevelt, deliberately set up to restore prosperity under the capitalistic system that had been temporarily shattered by the depression of 1929. This was also based mainly on the economic philosophy of Keynes. Despite numerous and varied policies and plans, the New Deal was unable to solve the problems created by the depression and insure full employment and general prosperity. The latter was not provided until this country entered the second World War, and during the war military state capitalism completely dominated the economic scene in the United States. The return to a greater degree of private enterprise had by no means been completed when the Cold War was launched during the administration of President Truman. State capitalism was revived and made great advances during the Korean War. While under a Republican administration the Korean War ended in a draw, the Republicans intensified the Cold War, especially after the notable Russian achievements in military aviation, atomic and nuclear warfare, and ballistic rockets had been decisively demonstrated. It is not only fair but essential to point out that since the end of the New Deal and the rise of an armament and war economy after 1939, state capitalism not only in the United States but throughout the world has become military state capitalism. The Cold War fixed it as a permanent pattern of economic life for an unpredictable period. It is likely that military state capitalism will increase its power and position in the American economy until some effective program of co-existence and disarmament is worked out.

The most extreme forms of state capitalism were those set up in the form of the corporative state under Mussolini's fascist system in Italy, and in the National Socialist program in Germany under Hitler. Fascism greatly increased material prosperity in Italy until Mussolini engaged in the expensive Ethiopian War. National Socialism, based in part on Keynes and better planned than the fascist scheme, worked what was almost a miracle in economic recovery, but Hit-

ler's totalitarian government and his racial policies created a hostility in democratic countries that brought war in 1939, and the whole National Socialist
system was doomed by Hitler's ill-advised and ill-fated invasion of Russia in June,
1941. The economic recovery of West Germany since the second World War
has frequently been hailed as a decisive vindication of free enterprise. The latter,
obviously, had greater scope under Adenauer than under Hitler, but there is a
vast amount of state capitalism in the West German Republic, much of it going
back to the Bismarckian era. One can fairly and safely say that such capitalism
as may survive the Cold War will be either preponderantly state capitalism or
private capitalism substantially bolstered by state capitalism. For better or worse,
the days of unimpeded free enterprise now lie definitely and permanently in the
past.

There has been much confusion in regard to state capitalism and state socialism. It is common to brand all state activity as "socialism." Both state capitalism
and state socialism make wide use of state activity in controlling the economy,
although state socialism usually goes much further in this direction. But the aims
of the two systems are diametrically different, so far as capitalism is concerned.
State capitalism is designed to preserve the capitalist system, even though it be
thought necessary to introduce a large amount of public legislation in order to
supplement or guide private enterprise. State socialism has as its goal the actual
termination of capitalism. Legislation is passed for the purpose of destroying
capitalism as well as maintaining prosperity in the era of transition. This basic
fact must be kept in mind in case one wishes to have any firm grasp on economic
ideology in our day.

State socialism has been of two main types in the present era: revolutionary
Marxian socialism, whether the revolution be peaceful or violent, and Fabian or
Revisionist Socialism, which repudiates rapid and revolutionary changes and
seeks to replace capitalism by socialism introduced gradually and by legislative
means. The only instance of any marked success of revolutionary socialism has
been the development of this movement in Soviet Russia since 1917. There it
has created the most powerful state in the Old World, although no small part
of this success has been due to the unwise foreign policy of capitalistic states,
and has involved many deviations from strict Marxian doctrines. There is no prospect that this system will be uprooted in Russia, short of a third world war of
universal extermination. It is quite possible, however, that Communist China
may ultimately supersede Russia as the strongest Communist power. The use of
the term "Communist" is unfortunate and confusing, since what is really meant
is Marxian or revolutionary state socialism. The Marxian doctrine recommends
opportunism in the selection of the best method of revolutionary activity to install
socialism. In mature capitalist and democratic countries, it favors peaceful changes
by means of legislation. In backward and autocratic states, like tsarist Russia, it
advocates the violent overthrow of the old system, and this is the policy which
Lenin and his associates followed in 1917.

Fabian or Revisionist Socialism was formulated in England in the 1880's and
1890's by a group of leading English intellectuals, such as George Bernard

Shaw, Mr. and Mrs. Sidney Webb, H. G. Wells, and others. These so-called Fabians rejected the Marxian position that socialism must be introduced *in toto* and suddenly by revolution, whether of legislation or bloodshed, and that socialists must not cooperate with any capitalist government in remedial programs. They held that socialism could and should be introduced gradually by legislation which would promote well-being for the moment and also undermine capitalism.

These ideas were assimilated by Eduard Bernstein, a German socialist refugee who had fled to England to escape from Bismarck's persecution of German socialists. He gave the name of Revisionist Socialism to English Fabianism, returned to Germany and battled the Marxians. By the time of the first World War, revisionism had won out over Marxism in all important countries except Russia. The revisionist German Social Democratic party was the largest in the German Reichstag in 1914, and the ablest leader of the revisionists was the Frenchman, Jean Jaurès, who was assassinated at the behest of tsarist officials in the Russian embassy in Paris in August, 1914, to prevent him from making any effort to keep France out of war. Revisionist Socialism also dominated the Weimar Republic, and was the main political and economic force in Italy until Mussolini set up fascism in 1922. It once more became powerful in Italy after 1945, but has never recovered its former strength in Germany. The Popular Front government of Léon Blum in France from 1936 to 1938 was a mixture of state capitalists, Revisionist Socialists, and Communists, but the socialists were the most powerful. Fabian Socialism has dominated the ideology of the Labor party in England, which won the election of 1945 and for several years gradually introduced socialistic legislation. The English economic situation has now become so critical that even a Conservative government has to retain many Labor party measures. Indeed, the state capitalist program of Beveridge does not differ greatly, save in ultimate aim, from the Fabianism of the Labor party. In France after the second World War, the Revisionist Socialists held the balance of power in the government, although the Communists outnumbered them. Most of the so-called free nations of Europe in the Cold War are actually in differing degrees permeated by Revisionist Socialism. Both the Marxian and the Revisionist Socialists envision a stateless, cooperative society, once socialism is fully established. That this will actually prove to be the case is doubted by many realistic students of political and economic history.

The remaining outstanding economic program which has developed in the twentieth century is the so-called Middle Way, which has made most headway in the Scandinavian countries and Finland. This seeks to combine in proper measure private capitalism, state capitalism, and the cooperative movement. Where private capitalism works well, it is encouraged and protected; where it fails, it is superseded by state capitalism or cooperative agencies. State capitalism has been limited mainly to the lumber and extractive industries, public utilities and some government monopolies, and cooperation has been applied chiefly to housing and other welfare projects. Many students have contended that this Middle Way program offers the best prospect of combining economic efficiency and prosperity with democratic government and civil liberty. But invariably, outside the Scandinavian countries, the conservative forces have resisted reform until such a moderate program has become inadequate to meet the existing economic crisis or is believed to be such by the exponents of radical reform. The Cold War regime will further frustrate any progress of the Middle Way regime, since the latter is based on a peaceful way of life and is quite unsuited to the tensions and restrictions of a system of permanent war psychology.

Changes in the Social Hierarchy, Social Classes, and the Social Structure.— The twentieth century produced notable changes in the class structure and class influence in society. The old landed aristocracy was rather thoroughly wiped out. The Russian aristocracy either fled or were killed off before they had an opportunity to escape. Such of them as existed in China have met much the same fate since 1948. The Junkers of East Prussia lost some of their power under Hitler and were either killed or expelled when East Prussia was turned over to the Communists. The powerful landlord group in Hungary was dislodged when the Communists took over. Both World Wars, but especially the second, dealt heavy blows to the English landed nobility. Crushing taxes, increased expenses, the difficulty of providing servants, and agrarian reforms led many to sell or otherwise abandon their holdings. Save for southern Italy, where even Mussolini could not oust them, and Spain, the landed aristocracy has already disappeared or is on its way out.

The middle class or bourgeoisie attained the high point of its wealth, power, and prosperity in Europe in the decade prior to the first World War, and in the United States in the decade following that war. The first World War dealt this class a heavy blow in most European countries. In Russia, members of the middle class were exterminated, fled, or in a few instances, went over to the Bolsheviks. Devastating inflation after the first World War deprived most of the middle class of their fortunes in Germany, Austria, and Hungary. Even in France and Italy, members of the middle class had to face an inflation of vastly greater proportions than that which frightened many American businessmen in the 1960's. The English middle class was confronted with taxes such as it had never known before. In Italy, the middle class was demoralized by the first World War and then regimented under fascism. National Socialism in Germany reduced the middle class to useful puppets when they were not Jews. The latter fled or were humiliated and their property expropriated. West Germany became a middle-class state, while East Germany was dominated by Communists.

But the first World War brought to the American middle class a temporary power, prestige, and wealth unprecedented in the history of the country. This was well mirrored in the statement of President Calvin Coolidge that "the real business of government is business." The business class had already become the social aristocracy in the United States. The depression of 1929 and thereafter changed all this. The business class was blamed for the depression, lost heavily in the Wall Street collapse, and suffered severely in prestige. At the outset of the New Deal administration of President Roosevelt many businessmen seemed inclined to clamber aboard the reform bandwagon. The National Industrial Recovery Act was framed mainly by business leaders. But business quickly became alarmed at New Deal measures and tended to oppose the New Deal bitterly. Business regained some influence during the war economy after 1941, but under strict governmental control.

The second World War also dealt heavy blows to the middle class in Europe. Communism greatly extended its territory and power in eastern and central Europe. The air bombardment, land invasion, and brutal postwar policies had a devastating effect on the German middle class that had survived or developed under National Socialism. A new middle class is developing in the Western German Republic, but it is unlikely ever to approach the wealth or power of the German middle class under the Kaiser before 1914. In England, the increasing burden of taxation, the loss of much of the Empire and the lucrative trade which went with it, and the overwhelming problems of economic recovery greatly weakened the middle class there. In France, the Nazi occupation, the destruction accompanying the Allied invasion, and ever-increasing inflation further undermined the middle class, a process aided by the impotence and instability of the government of the Fourth Republic. The Communists have become a powerful political party in France, which does not bode well for the future of the French middle class. The Italian middle class was demoralized by the fall of fascism and the invasion of Italy, and Italy emerged from the second World War with a government dominated by socialists and Communists. The latter were prevented from taking over Italy after 1945 only by lavish financial aid to the anti-Communists provided by the United States. The Spanish middle class was harshly affected by the Spanish Civil War and the resulting fascist system. Nowhere in Europe did the middle class dominate the scene in a major country at mid-century.

It was mentioned above that the middle class in the United States recovered some of its lost power and prestige under governmental supervision in the war economy after 1941; it never, however, regained the status that it enjoyed in the heyday of the 1920's under Harding, Coolidge, Mellon, and Hoover. Heavy income taxes make it impossible to pile up the greater individual fortunes characteristic of pre-war times. The loss of political power and prestige was reflected in early 1958 when business admitted the growing impotence of its lobbies at the national capital. The power once exerted by big business, its legal representatives, and its publicity organizations is being taken over by a new managerial elite, who owe their origin and influence in large part to the system which has grown up out of the war economy and the Cold War. This managerial elite is constituted mainly of the directly military managers in the Pentagon, those who control military technology and industry, the leading scientists and technologists, especially those whose work is most closely related to the new technology of warfare, the leading corporation executives, and those who control communications agencies and advertising. Their make-up, nature and operations are well described in the able work of C. Wright Mills, *The Power Elite*. The lower or salaried middle class is being pinched between the managerial elite and the increasingly powerful and well-unionized wage earners. Their precarious condition has been realistically presented in another work by Professor Mills, *White Collar*.

The proletariat, made up mainly of the industrial wage earners, has fared better than any other class during the present century. Soviet Russia, theoretically a proletarian polity, has become the most powerful country in the Old World. But the notion that Russia is actually run by the mass of workers is largely a fiction. Under even the most favorable interpretation, Soviet Russia is a government for the proletariat rather than one of the proletariat. Perhaps more completely than is the case with any other country in the world, Russia is controlled by a managerial elite, in which special rank is assigned to scientists and technicians. Its pretensions to provide a good life for the working masses were held back at the outset by technological lag, and more recently by the military efforts connected with the second World War and the Cold War. Whether it will ultimately make good on these is something that the future will have to reveal. At least, it can be safely observed that the strivings of the working classes will not be opposed by a landed aristocracy or a business class. The same is true of Communist China, although the masses there are a backward peasantry for the most part rather than industrial workers.

The proletariat have probably gained far more complete control of the British Labor party than of the Soviet Union. The Labor party rather genuinely represents and serves the working classes. The proletariat has also made notable gains in France and Italy since the second World War. In both countries, the socialists and Communists represent a numerical majority and constitute the largest parties in the legislature. In the United States, while there is no formal labor party, the workers are becoming more completely unionized and constitute a powerful pressure group working through both political and economic organizations. For better or worse, the power of labor in the United States is far more potent and better integrated than in 1900.

Surely the most novel and impressive proletarian uprisings of the latter part of the twentieth century will be those of the hitherto repressed colored races of Africa and Asia. While at present, in large part, a backward or semi-barbarous peasantry, their countries are bound to become more thoroughly industrialized and the proletariat will ultimately emerge as industrial wage earners. They are already challenging the dominion of the white man, the traditional social aristocracy, and any retention of Western imperialism. Whatever the outcome for the welfare of humanity at large, these uprisings are destined to be the most dynamic element in the proletarian movements during the last half of the present century, and their achievements will shatter most of the past economic and racial precedents. Whatever their honesty and integrity in motives, Soviet Russia and, especially, Communist China are bound to encourage the non-white revolt against the traditional economic and colonial order.

Two other social trends of the twentieth century relate to the increase of world population and the greater mobility of peoples. It has been a truism with population experts that, when industry and medical science reach any important area, the population increases about fourfold in the course of about two centuries, and then the population tends to level off as the conditions of urban life offer various checks to the previous rapid growth. This was the case with Western Europe, where the population grew from about 140,000,000 to about 550,000,000 between 1750 and 1950. Even in the Western world the prediction that the rate of population growth would fall off markedly by the mid-century has not been borne out by the facts. A notable growth in population set in during and after the second World War and still continues at what seems to many an alarming rate. In the 1930's it was predicted by expert students of population problems that the population of the United States would level off somewhere between 1955 and 1970 at around 135,000,000 to 170,000,000, and would gradually decline thereafter. Actually, the population of the United States had reached 190,000,000 by mid-1963 and was growing rapidly. A population of 250,000,000 has been predicted by 1970. The population of Latin America is growing even more rapidly. The possibilities of population growth in Asia in the decades to come are even more alarming. Communist China had a population of about 675,000,000 in 1963. If it follows the pattern of population growth that prevailed in Western Europe between 1750 and 1950, China might someday have a population nearly equal to that of the entire present-day world. India will follow closely behind. One population expert has predicted a total world population of around 7,000,000,000 in the year 2000, as compared with one of 3,000,000,000 today. By 1963, there were about 50 million new mouths to be fed each year. It is obvious that this problem of spectacular population growth—the so-called "population explosion"—will impose serious strains and stresses on both the economic and political realms and may constitute serious pressures leading to devastating warfare.

Another important social trend in the twentieth century has been the increased migration and mobility of peoples. Some of this has been due to better transportation facilities on land, on sea, and in the air, some due to changed economic conditions which have affected employment possibilities, and a very large amount the result of the forced movement of peoples, mainly associated with the impact of the two world wars.

Immigration to the United States from foreign lands reached its height between 1900 and the first World War. Nearly 14,000,000 foreigners came to this country during this period. Other millions moved about in various portions of the Old World. The first World War temporarily ended mass immigration into the United States, and in 1921 restrictive legislation began. While some millions of persons moved about voluntarily after 1914, the great era of voluntary migrations ended for some decades with the first World War. But there was a revival after 1945, and from 1946 to 1955 some 7.2 million Europeans migrated overseas. Over 2 million came to the United States.

During the twentieth century, down to 1950, nearly twice as many persons were compelled to leave their homes in Europe as came voluntarily to the United States in the whole period from 1820 to 1950. It has been estimated that nearly 70,000,000 persons were forced to leave their homes in Europe from 1900 to 1950, as against some 40,000,000 immigrants to the United States from 1820 to 1950. Between the Balkan Wars of 1912-1913 and the outbreak of the second World War in 1939, about 14,000,000 persons were forced or induced to leave their former homes. During the course of the second World War, from 1939 to

1945, about 26,000,000 were forced or induced to move. After 1945, between 13,000,000 and 15,000,000 Germans were expelled from their homes in eastern Germany and the Sudeten area. Six hundred thousand Balts fled from the Baltic States or were deported to Siberia, about 2,500,000 Russians and 5,000,000 Poles moved into the Baltic provinces and former eastern Germany, and about 2,000,000 Czechs entered the Sudeten area. Unnumbered millions of Russians and German and Italian prisoners of war were shipped by Russia into the slave labor camps of Siberia. The number of persons who voluntarily or under compulsion shifted their residence in Asia and Africa between 1900 and 1950 has not even been estimated because of lack of data, but it surely runs into the tens of millions.

Voluntary movements of peoples within a country in recent years are also impressive. They may be illustrated by the situation in the United States. In 1947 about 13,000,000 Americans were living in a different state from the one in which they lived in 1940. At least 20,000,000 were living in a different county. It is estimated that at least 30,000,000 Americans change their residence in a single year.

These movements of peoples since 1900 have created serious social, economic, ethnic and racial problems which still plague the world and have brought about many severe and unsettled tensions, as well as often producing some advantages to both the migrants and the lands into which they moved. Most of the forced migrations since 1912 were accompanied by great hardships and incredible cruelties, including wholesale massacre of millions. The brutalities and bloodshed far surpassed anything known during the barbarian invasions of the later Roman Empire and raised serious doubts as to whether human civilization, even in Europe, was more than a thin veneer over basic savagery. Germans, Russians, Czechs, and Poles indulged in barbarous behavior which would have brought blushes of shame to the face of Attila the Hun.

The last social trend we may note here is usually passed over with little knowledge or comment but it probably ranks next to war and peace in its bearing upon the future well-being of the human race, especially in urbanized areas. We refer here to the disintegration or disappearance of the primary or face-to-face groups that have disciplined the civilized portions of humanity and given them the traits of character and morality which separate them from wild beasts. Such were the rural family, neighborhood, play groups, school groups, local religious gatherings, and neighborly cooperative groups. Whatever separates the human beings of today from the selfish animals which they are by nature has been due to the shaping and conditioning imposed by such primary groups from birth to death, but especially during youth and adolescence. Various conditions of city life in the great urban areas of an industrial society have undermined or destroyed most of the above groups. Only the family persists in urban areas and that has lost most of its old disciplinary influence. Even in rural areas, the newer methods of transportation, communication, and entertainment have urbanized the behavior and interests of the people.

Social scientists and psychiatrists have worked out in theory, backed by some successful practice, community agencies which can duplicate most of the disciplinary and civilizing functions once executed by the former rural primary groups. But no country has been willing to spend anything like enough money to create and operate an adequate number of such agencies. Unless this need and challenge are met, anarchy and crime may well swamp humanity, even if a war of nuclear extermination is avoided. That this is no alarmist fantasy is already demonstrated by the menacing growth of social pathology and crime, especially juvenile crime, in recent decades. The human race is not automatically civilized and disciplined.

II. THE IMPACT OF TWENTIETH-CENTURY SCIENCE UPON CONTEMPORARY THOUGHT

1. *Causation in the Light of the New Physics*

If the changing institutional framework caused severe adjustments in man's thought during the twentieth century, no developments called for more overwhelming adjustments than the revolutionary changes in modern science. In the scientific revival of the seventeenth century the achievements in mathematics and astronomy had been the most remarkable of all. In eighteenth-century science, mathematics and chemistry took the lead. In the nineteenth century the outstanding discoveries were made in biology and physics. In the twentieth century, however, many of the most notable developments took place in astrophysics and electromechanics. In these fields a veritable scientific upheaval was achieved, upsetting what appeared to be some of the most assured results of Newtonian astronomy and nineteenth-century physics. The twentieth century thus witnessed a revival of the priority of the mathematical and physical sciences, which had been temporarily forced into a subordinate position in popular interest as a result of the remarkable progress in the biological sciences in the nineteenth century.

The combination of mathematics and the new physics produced a revolution in scientific notions unparalleled for novelty and disconcerting implications since the age from Copernicus to Newton. Applied to the investigation of the mysteries, vast expanses, and myriad stellar bodies of the heavens, this new mathematical and physical science, the developments of which will be shown in more detail in the next chapter, has made necessary a transformation in human perspective even more striking than that involved in the evolutionary biology of the previous century.

Increased knowledge of the physical universe or cosmos has involved amazing discoveries concerning the incredible extent of the universe and the vast number and size of the so-called "heavenly" bodies. Better instruments, such as larger telescopes, the improved spectroscope, spectrograph, spectro-comparator, the interferometer, and celestial cameras have "taken chemistry into the skies" and enabled scientists to discover the chemical constitution of the heavenly bodies, to measure the speed of light, to locate and compute the size of incredibly distant heavenly bodies, and to detect the existence of stars hitherto invisible to the human eye through the most powerful telescopes. In these achievements we owe much to Fraunhofer, Bunsen, Albert A. Michelson, Harlow Shapley, and recent relativistic and nuclear studies by physicists and astronomers. The as yet extremely incomplete revelation· of the vast extent and complex organization of the cosmos is perhaps the most striking intellectual achievement of the twentieth century. It dwarfs the discovery and confirmation of the doctrine of evolution in the last century, and its implications are much more disconcerting to traditional dogmas and human presumptuousness than the theory of evolution.

New and impressive theories of the origins of the universe have been provided, the latest being those based in part on the application of quantum and nuclear physics to astronomy. Among these one might mention the theories of G.E. Lemaître, George Gamow, and Fred Hoyle.

Lemaître and Gamow believe that the present universe (cosmos) originated in a brief and colossal atomic explosion of a giant cosmic atom or concentrated mass of nuclear fluid which resulted in rapidly expanding atomic gas. Due to the force of gravity the homogeneous gas broke up into gigantic clouds which were later condensed into galaxies and a multitude of stars. Smaller masses of gaseous material were attracted by the stars and contracted into planetary systems. Gamow's striking conclusion is that "it took less than an hour to make an atom, a few hundred million years to make the stars and planets, and three billion years to make man."

Fred Hoyle of Cambridge University, Harry Gold of Cornell University, and others suggest in another ingenious theory that space is filled with widely separated atoms of hydrogen. In the far distant past, masses of hydrogen were attracted to each other by gravity and formed the stars. As the stars moved through the rarefied interstellar gas at terrific speed, they attracted the nearby hydrogen atoms, leaving a tunnel-like path from which most of the hydrogen atoms were removed. In some unexplained way new hydrogen atoms are continually formed so that, despite the hydrogen that is picked up by the speeding stars, the total amount of rarefied hydrogen between the stars ultimately remains about the same. As stars reach the end of the nearby supply of hydrogen, they become relatively dead "red giants." These eventually contract so violently that they blow up in atomic explosions. The gaseous detritus from the explosion of a companion star to the sun furnished the material from which our planets were formed.

Some of these nuclear theorists, such as Lemaître and Gamow, contend that between five and ten billion years ago there was nothing in the visible universe except "a concentrated mass of nuclear fluid of enormous density and temperature." Then came a gigantic explosion which, in less than an hour, created all the known elements. Clouds of gas condensed and formed dust out of which the galaxies, stars, and planets have evolved. This process has continued to the present time. As we have noted, Hoyle and his associates reject this theory. The fact is, that despite the impressive nature and extent of the discoveries already made as to the vast extent and complexity of the cosmos, the most highly trained astronomers and astrophysicists readily admit that we remain in the infancy of the task of observing, describing, and explaining the origins, nature, extent, and destiny of the physical universe. This task constitutes the outstanding challenge to the human intellect and our scientific technological equipment.

In astrophysics Albert Einstein by his doctrine of relativity modified the Newtonian conception of gravitation, of the course of light, and of the paths of the heavenly bodies. As a corollary of Einstein's discoveries came the demonstration of the equivalence of mass and energy, the atomic bomb itself a convincing demonstration of the truth of Einstein's basic principle. Increased knowledge of the physical universe or cosmos meanwhile involved amazing discoveries concerning the incredible extent of the universe and the vast size of the heavenly bodies. The 200-inch telescope, for example, made at the Corning (N.Y.) glass works and installed in the observatory at Mount Palomar in California extended astronomical vision as far as three billion light-years from the earth. Electronic telescopes are rapidly and amazingly extending the nature and extent and this penetration of cosmic distances and previous mysteries. Man's universe thus expanded at an unparalleled rate, and his concepts of it also underwent comparable changes. A generation ago the background for an appraisal of evolution and of the story of man's rise in the physical world could be sought in geology and historical biology. Now it is recognized that we must go one step back of this and acquire a truly cosmic perspective. Harlow Shapley has developed this important consideration in eloquent and authoritative fashion in his book, *Man and the Stars* (1958).

These facts and considerations reveal the so-called contemporary "space race" to reach the moon as the fanciful travesty which it actually is. Many prominent scientists, expert in the field involved, have expressed much doubt as to whether an astronaut can actually be landed safely on the moon. If, however, this should prove possible, the first astronaut who did arrive safely would qualify as a conqueror of space in cosmic terms about as much as a man who had walked around his block in a suburban town would qualify as an experienced world traveler. In the light of cosmic space, the moon is not far different from a garbage pail placed rather close to the back porch of a house. To be sure, attempts to reach the moon will reveal many important new physical and astrophysical facts, but more could be learned about cosmic space by an expert astronomer spending one night at the Mount Palomar Observatory than will be learned over any imaginable period of time by the lunar, or any planetary, space race. Moreover, the costs of our space race are well-nigh criminally wasteful and exorbitant when compared to what could be done to improve human welfare by the use of such a sum of money. Perhaps the only thing about the space race that is astronomical is the expense.

The older interpretations of the universe rested upon the assumption of the primary importance of the earth in the cosmos. Hence man, as the dominant element on our planet, could regard himself as veritably "the lord of all creation." Taking these premises for granted, it did not appear unreasonable that man might be the product of God's direct and unique creative endeavor. In the last half-century, however, these conventional assumptions have been completely shattered. Astrophysics has given us a new and devastating perspective on any reasonable attitude towards man's place in the universe, his physical nature, and the manner in which he has reached his present position on the earth.

It is well-nigh impossible for us to envisage or to describe in mundane terms the extent of that small portion of the cosmos known to man, which is only a small fraction of the total. Even the most remote reaches of the cosmos revealed by the Mount Palomar telescope, some three billion light-years away, are crowded with giant galaxies far more numerous than those around our galactic system or even the center of the known cosmos. They are actually massed together and are moving out into hitherto unrevealed space at incredible speed. No other physical fact known to mankind is as impressive and spectacular as this. In even so incomplete a cosmic perspective as we have today, our earth immediately shrinks from the position of the largest and most important unit in the cosmos to a relatively insignificant and recent planet—a celestial juvenile and cosmic dwarf. It is, in time and space, certainly most inconsequential. Man likewise tends to shrink in the new cosmic outlook. Far from being "the lord of all creation," existing from the beginning of things, he now appears to be but a highly temporary biochemical episode on a tiny planet. In Harlow Shapley's conspectus of the cosmos, man appears low in the cosmic scale, as a colloidal aggregate, subclass *beta*. Astronomically speaking, man is almost totally negligible, while in biological antiquity he is far outdistanced by the lowly cockroach, which appears to have existed substantially unchanged for more than fifty million years. These facts regarding the insignificance of the earth and man in the face of our modern views of the cosmos were well stated some years ago by Shapley:

> The thing that appalls me is not the bigness of the universe, but the smallness of us. We are in all ways small—little in foresight, shriveled in spirit, minute in material content, microscopic in the vastness of measured space, evanescent in the sweep of time—inconsequential in every respect, except, perhaps, in the chemical complexities of our mental reactions. In that alone our advance may surpass that of other terrestrial organisms.
>
> But the sanctity of all protoplasm has practically disappeared in this, the heroic age of the physical sciences, when knowledge of the material universe, its content, structure, and dimensions, has so completely overthrown egocentrism. It should sufficiently deflate the organism, you would think, to find that his fountain of energy, the sun, is a dwarf star among thousands of millions of stars; to find that the star around which his little parasitic earth will-lessly plods is so far from the center of the known stellar universe that sunlight, with its incomprehensibly high velocity, cannot reach that center in a thousand generations of vain men.
>
> The deflation, however, is not stopped at that point. We now reach much deeper into space than a few years ago, find millions of stars mightier than our sun, find greater velocities, larger masses, higher temperatures, longer durations than we have previously known. Even more illuminating, in this orientation of organisms in the physical universe, is the revelation that the earth, whose surface we infest, is not a parcel of grand antiquity. Rather recently, as astronomers now measure time, a singular incident happened in the life-history of the sun. Before that time the earth was not, nor were the animals of the earth. Nevertheless, for trillions of years, in the absence of the "Lords of all Creation," the stars had poured out their radiant energy, the celestial bodies had rolled on, law had governed the universe. Before that event, you and I, the material of our bodies, were electrons and atoms

in the solar atmosphere. Since then we have been associated with the inorganic and organic evolution of a smaller concern.

The earth, as I have intimated, appeared only a few thousand million years ago. Our sun, it seems, had already passed its prime of radiance when in its wanderings through celestial space it met up with another star—a stellar romance—a marriage made in the heavens. From that affair—realistic astronomers call it an encounter—the planets of the sun were born. The passing star, ruffling up the exterior of the sun, detached some relatively small fragments of the solar atmosphere. Now we strut on one of the surviving fragments and wonder and speculate and discuss: "How can we *better* the world?" Crown of absurdities:—*we* repairing the world! That cast-off fragment, the ancestor from which and on which we descend, was composed wholly of gas! An emblem for us, that ancestral hot vapor.

The gaseous planet quickly liquefied as out in cold space it began its tireless revolutions around the parent sun. Soon after a crust formed, and, we may thank our lucky stars, the distance from the sun was right, the atmospheric and crustal chemistry was right, and other adjustments of the physical environment happened to be suitable for an elaboration of chemical reactions. The energy of the everflowing sunlight aided in complexifying this protoplasmic chemistry, a green mold formed in spots on the planet, and here we are—parasites on the energy of the sun that cast us forth.[1]

Some of our concepts, as we shall see in the next chapter, have been extended since Professor Shapley made this statement, but few can deny the essential revolution in man's point of view that it describes.

Another subject of recent astrophysical investigation which equally challenges anthropomorphic pride or arrogance, makes the cosmos a more interesting subject of study and contemplation, and upsets most of the orthodox religious conceptions and interpretations of nature is the possibility that in the total cosmos there may be millions, if not billions, of planets on which conditions exist which would permit the development of life similar to that of the vegetable, animal, and human life on our earth. Harlow Shapley estimates that there are 100 million even in that portion of the total cosmos already known to astronomers. Some might even support types of life superior to that which we know on our planet. There seems no probability, however, that life like that on our planet can exist on any other planet in our solar system. There is no doubt that the intellectual implications of the scientific advances made during the twentieth century have been more sweeping and unsettling than any which mankind has faced since the days of Galileo and Newton, and they are far more spectacular.

Nineteenth-century science, for one thing, however much it might disturb and upset older notions, was always able to fall back upon one fundamental and reassuring conception—that a definite cause-and-effect relationship exists in all the operations of physical nature. But the researches in mathematical physics and electromechanics in the twentieth century by Planck, Heisenberg, Einstein, and others, have undermined this very cornerstone of scientific thought. A generation ago, scientists believed that while the theologians and metaphysicians might be engaged in elaborate self-deception, the scientists were sure of their own ground.

[1] Harlow Shapley, "Man and His Young World," *Nation*, May 7, 1924, pp. 529-30.

Today, the most candid scientists quite frankly confess that science cannot discover any ultimates, even in its own realm. This admission was admirably stated by Professor P. W. Bridgman in the following paragraphs:

> The thesis of this article is that the age of Newton is now coming to a close, and that recent scientific discoveries have in store an ever greater revolution in our entire outlook than the revolution effected by the discovery of universal gravitation by Newton. The revolution that now confronts us arises from the recent discovery of new facts, the only interpretation of which is that our conviction that nature is understandable and subject to law arose from the narrowness of our horizons, and that if we sufficiently extend our range we shall find that nature is intrinsically and in its elements neither understandable nor subject to law. . . .
>
> The same situation confronts the physicist everywhere; whenever he penetrates to the atomic or electronic level in his analysis, he finds things acting in a way for which he can assign no cause, for which he can never assign a cause, and for which the concept of cause has no meaning, if Heisenberg's principle is right. This means nothing more nor less than that the law of cause and effect must be given up. The precise reason that the law of cause and effect fails can be paradoxically stated; it is not that the future is not determined in terms of a complete description of the present, but that in the nature of things the present cannot be completely described. . . .
>
> The physicist thus finds himself in a world from which the bottom has dropped clean out; as he penetrates deeper and deeper it eludes him and fades away by the highly unsportsmanlike device of just becoming meaningless. No refinement of measurement will avail to carry him beyond the portals of this shadowy domain which he cannot even mention without logical inconsistency. A bound is thus forever set to the curiosity of the physicist. What is more, the mere existence of this bound means that he must give up his most cherished convictions and faith. The world is not a world of reason, understandable by the intellect of man, but as we penetrate ever deeper, the very law of cause and effect, which we had thought to be a formula to which we could force God Himself to subscribe, ceases to have a meaning. The world is not intrinsically reasonable or understandable; it acquires these properties in ever-increasing degree as we ascend from the realm of the very little to the realm of everyday things; here we may eventually hope for an understanding sufficiently good for all practical purposes, but no more.[2]

Paradoxically enough, it thus seems that, when we get down to those "ultimates" involved in the realm of the atom, the only certainty in science today is the certainty of uncertainty. For all practical purposes, we may still follow most of the scientific laws and formulations worked out in the nineteenth century. Superficially and practically, they seem to describe the behavior of most physical phenomena as well as ever. Particularly is this true with respect to the exploitation of older scientific conceptions in the various fields of technology. But when we get down to fundamentals we have to take over a new set of concepts. As C. W. Gray puts it: "Uncertainty reigns, and whether the universe is a world of fortuitous atoms or a world of freewill, it cannot be described in its fundamental physical aspects today as a world of causality."

2 Bridgman, "The New Vision of Science," *Harper's Magazine*, March, 1929, pp. 444, 448, 450.

2. The Age of Uncertainty

A general air of assurance and finality pervaded the learned classes in previous generations. They felt convinced that they possessed precise and extended knowledge concerning God, the world, human destiny, the purpose and meaning of life, and all the other basic problems that confront man.

Now all this is changed. We do have, to be sure, much more exact knowledge about the material universe and the biological nature of man, and we are coming to know more about the types of behavior most likely to insure human happiness. But the meaning of the whole human drama and its setting in the cosmic scheme has become ever more baffling. The dualistic philosophy, which originated with the Persians and found the ultimate meaning of the cosmos in an all-inclusive struggle between good and evil, scarcely seems plausible in the light of modern knowledge. We are beginning to have impressive confirmation of Descartes' intuition that if there is a "divine" purpose in the universe it exists on a divine level, obviously beyond the comprehension of man. Indeed, the whole teleological conception, which insists that there is a purpose in everything, understandable in human terms, is, indeed, nothing but a circumscribed human way of looking at things—a survival of primitive animism and anthropomorphism.

The older idea that there is a definite time limit set to the existence of the earth and man, which will be terminated by a day of judgment, is now seen to possess no substantial foundation. It would seem that most creatures on the earth may look forward to a future as extensive as their past has been, terminated only by natural processes at a time so far distant as to be almost incalculable, although an annihilating cosmic accident or nuclear war of extermination are not outside the range of possibility.

Not only do we have to give up the sense of certainty and security based upon the older anthropomorphic and geocentric theology, but, as Charles Sanders Peirce suggested and recent physicists have demonstrated, the very conception of uniform, invariable, and universal scientific laws may also have to be abandoned.

The old symmetrical unity and completeness of knowledge, which seemed possible in an age of limited information and circumscribed outlook, was embodied in such works as those of Aristotle, the *Summa* of Thomas Aquinas, and the *Encyclopedia* of the eighteenth-century *philosophes*. It was also reflected in the curriculum of the old "liberal college" of half a century ago, based on the classics and Christian evidences. Today, such inclusive unity of knowledge and experience is all but impossible. Montaigne's intuitive vision of the implications of pluralism has been confirmed in detail by Peirce, James, Dewey, Kallen, and others, who have endeavored to state the bearing of modern scientific discoveries on the reconstruction of philosophy. The futile anguish of even cultured intellects with a retrospective yearning was illustrated by the following lamentation of Nicholas Murray Butler in one of his annual reports as President of Columbia University:

> No small part of the social and political diseases and disorders that are now so generally discussed may be traced to the destruction through unsound educational methods of that common body of knowledge and intellectual and moral experience

which held men together through a community of understanding and of appreciation. A steadily growing unity has been displaced for a chaotic multiplicity. Pluralism, the non-religious form of polytheism, is practically what William James, who was greatly enamored of it, described it to be, "a turbid, muddled, gothic sort of effort, without a sweeping outline and with little pictorial nobility." In all its forms, philosophical and other, it is a flat denial of all that is most worth while in human experience and an open surrender of any hope either to understand or to improve the universe. Moreover, it is self-contradictory, for if there is no One there cannot possibly be a Many. It might have been supposed that Socrates had made this postulate plain once for all, but perhaps it is no longer fashionable for philosophers to know either Greek or history.[3]

This attitude towards contemporary learning and our current perplexities was presented at much greater length by Robert Maynard Hutchins, formerly president of the University of Chicago, in his *The Higher Learning in America* (1936), written under the influence of Professor Mortimer J. Adler, then of the same institution. He reverted to Plato, Aristotle and Thomas Aquinas for guidance of the human intellect in the twentieth century.[4] This theory was also applied at St. John's College, Maryland, under the presidency of Stringfellow Barr.

Indeed, science and technology may have created too complicated a situation for man to wrestle with and may have spread before him a cosmic panorama too vast for him to comprehend or digest. His failure to grapple successfully with the issues of the present age may mark the last stages of the "divine experiment" when applied to man. Professor Lynn Thorndike, towards the close of his *Short History of Civilization,* has stated with much wisdom this uncertainty as to the outcome of the perplexities of contemporary civilization:

> Furthermore, not only with the mass of contemporary writing is it difficult to keep track of the past masters in many lands, or *vice versa,* but science and learning have so ramified, so specialized, so progressed, that knowledge and theory have perhaps grown even faster than population or popular education. No one man, however learned and characterized by breadth of interest, can even fully appreciate to say nothing of mastering, the achievements in all the different fields, while the ordinary man has no conception of the present state of knowledge. If the system of public education were more truly disciplinary, if the newpapers largely replaced crime, sensation, and sentimental matter by straightforward statement of political, social, and economic happenings, and the progress of knowledge, if the magazines minimized love stories, adventure, and personality in favor of matters of more moment to civilization, if advertisements gave sound advice as to good manners in public thoroughfares and conveyances, or sensible medical, legal, and financial counsel, if the moving pictures were employed more for purposes of instruction— perhaps the average man could keep up better with the onward march of civilization. Can science shepherd the herd? That is the question. Has scientific specialization proved fatal to the humanism which enabled many leaders of thought in previous generations to publish their views in an acceptable, graceful, and forceful form? Can we have only a caste of intellectuals, as in China and India? Will the

3 Columbia University, *Annual Report of the President and Treasurer for the Year Ending June 30, 1921,* Columbia University Press, 1922, pp. 30-31.
    4 See John Dewey's comments in *The Social Frontier,* January, 1937, pp. 103-4, and March, 1937, pp. 167-69.

popular demand, vulgar taste, and utilitarian attitude lower everything to its own level and swamp civilization? Or is civilization now unfolding in more varied flower than ever before with more individuals of high rank in each field and with an ever increasing public following which is able to appreciate their work?[5]

Whatever the difficulties that lie ahead for mankind, science has certainly eliminated a number of bogeys and produced several epochal advances. Professor J. Arthur Thomson suggested some of these: First, science has destroyed "the old fear of forces leagued against man, and of evil spirits waiting eagerly for his destruction." Today, we need only meet the foes that we can recognize and battle with. Second, we can abandon "the old sense of bewildering confusion, for almost everywhere there is order. A phantasmagoria has given place to a cosmos." Third, "gone is the old bogey of the capricious.... Given a reasonable acquaintance with the facts, it is far safer to predict the return of a comet than to tell how a cat will jump; yet there are laws of cat-jumping, and the Mendelian counts and describes his chickens before they are hatched." Fourth, "another of the dispiriting phobias which we are warranted in leaving behind is the picture of an eternal world-eddy —nothing new but has already been, and nothing new under the sun." Evolution and change are real, whatever our new problems and difficulties. Finally, "gone too is the inhibiting belief that there are certain evils which cannot be got rid of." Many things that are so regarded might be eliminated immediately if we were to apply our present knowledge, and many problems that today seem insoluble may be easily wiped out with the further advance of human knowledge.

3. *A New Challenge to the Doctrine of Progress*

The twentieth century has witnessed a marked change in our attitude towards the doctrine of progress. In the nineteenth century the theory of progress was very generally accepted by the great majority of alert minds. The optimism that produced the theories of progress in the late seventeenth and eighteenth centuries was adopted by nineteenth-century thinkers and seemingly vindicated through the theory of evolution. The dogma of progress appeared to be founded upon the basic laws of nature.

Only the more optimistic thinkers of the twentieth century have been able to subscribe unqualifiedly to any assured concept of inevitable human progress. Vast and unprecedented progress can be demonstrated in science and technology. Of the impressive material progress since 1850 there can be no doubt whatsoever. But this material advance does not involve human progress unless man shows himself capable of controlling these material gains in the interests of social well-being.

The two World Wars taught us a shocking lesson in this respect. Stupendous advances in science and technology were used to expedite a type of group insanity and mass slaughter that came dangerously near to destroying Western civilization. The deep and prolonged economic depression following 1929 demonstrated that unparalleled capacity to produce goods does not necessarily mean general

5 Thorndike, *op. cit.*, pp. 548-49.

prosperity or mass welfare. Democratic government and majority rule also seem not to be able to produce political rulers competent to deal with the ever increasing complexity of human problems and the assurance of peace. It is quite possible, therefore, that these very scientific and technological advances which have seemed to be the best proof of progress, may turn out to be the chief cause of the downfall of civilization as a whole.

For this reason, in the place of the dogma of progress, discriminating writers have tended to substitute the conception of social change. We can demonstrate the reality of change, but the notion of progress remains a product of wishful thinking. It will probably require another century or more before we can pass any reliable judgment upon its validity. If we are able to socialize the advantages produced by science and technology and end warfare, we may attain a degree of social well-being that will decisively substantiate the theory of progress. So far, however, there is no such positive assurance at hand. The eminent sociologist, William F. Ogburn, stated the situation clearly in his classic work, *Social Change*, over forty years ago.

Some contemporary writers have allowed their emotions to carry them to the opposite extreme from the concept of progress. Foremost here in the 1920's was the German philosopher and historian, Oswald Spengler, whose voluminous work, *The Decline of the West,* became a bible of contemporary social pessimists. Spengler repudiated the theory of progress and revived the older notion of cycles of change. He held that Western civilization has already passed its apex and is on its way towards general decline. This point of view was energetically attacked by an eminent German philosopher, Ludwig Stein, in his *Evolution and Optimism,* which was specifically intended as a refutation of Spenglerism. The attitudes and arguments of both Spengler and Stein may, however, be regarded as the outgrowth of wishful thinking rather than scientific evidence.

Far more impressive and influential was the enormous and learned twelve-volume work of the English historian and theologian, Arnold J. Toynbee, *The Study of History,* which appeared in installments between 1933 and 1961. Its popularity was made possible by widely read epitomes of the larger work. Working out a formula for the rise, maturity, and decline of civilizations based on his thorough knowledge of classical history, Toynbee applied this formula in rather arbitrary and mystical fashion to what he regarded as the twenty-one main civilizations that have thus far existed. All historians and social scientists stand in awe of Toynbee's learning and industry, but few take seriously his general theory of the historical experience of mankind. His work will be considered in greater detail in a later chapter.

The most formidable statement of the contemporary historical pessimism in the United States was embodied in the four-volume work on *Social and Cultural Dynamics* (1937-1941) by Pitirim A. Sorokin, an erudite Russian scholar who had fled from Russia after the revolution of 1917. He portrayed human experience in terms of fluctuating cycles—an unending recurrence of alternating doomsdays and golden ages.

The most sweeping philosophical attack upon the theory of progress, especially as based upon the doctrine of evolution, was that embodied in *The Idea of Progress* (1920) by the Anglican philosopher, William Ralph (Dean) Inge. This work is an expression of a philosophy which stands at the opposite extreme from Herbert Spencer's notion of inevitable cosmic and cultural evolution. The Dean opposes to this an even more flagrant type of wishful thinking, namely, a mystical absolutism and a dogmatic theism which few can accept in this day and age.

4. Obscurantist Revivals in the Contemporary Age

During the eighteenth and nineteenth centuries there was a definite hangover of that honest obscurantism which rested upon a sincere acceptance of orthodox religious concepts and traditions. This position frankly opposed the scientific method and rejected all scientific discoveries that in any way conflicted with the scriptural record. The most systematic statement of this older obscurantism was set forth in Paley's *Natural Theology* and in the *Syllabus of Errors* of Pope Pius IX (1864). In somewhat more sophisticated form the attitude of Pius IX was perpetuated in the writings of Gilbert Chesterton, Hilaire Belloc, and J. J. Walsh.

Without in any way accepting either the premises or the contentions of this school of thought, one must respect the courage and logic underlying it, once we understand the premises and comprehend the historical background out of which it has developed.

Scarcely as much can be said for another group of writers who protest that they are thoroughly conversant with contemporary scientific methods and achievements and are in sympathy with intellectual progress and enlightenment. For, at the same time, they take a decidedly antagonistic attitude toward science, once it is brought out of the laboratory and given some application to an evaluation of life and experience. It is undoubtedly a salutary thing, as John Langdon-Davies indicated in his *The New Age of Faith,* to rebuke naïve and unrestrained advocates of the omniscience of contemporary science, but the "new obscurantism" has gone far beyond this.

Because the more original scientists, with a gift for cosmic perspective and a robust humanitarian motivation, have attempted to set forth a scientific interpretation of man and the world, these "highbrow obscurantists" have accused the scientists of developing a new cult, a new theology, or even a new mythology. When there are scientists brave and logical enough to contrast the scientific perspective and concepts with the archaic supernatural interpretation offered by orthodox religion, our contemporary obscurantists have rushed forward with the assertion that science is merely offering a new religion in place of the older and scarcely less tenable variety. When scientists are modestly willing to admit differences of opinion, conflicting hypotheses, or incomplete knowledge, this new group has hastily assumed such limitations to mean the general impotence of science.

A conspicuous phase of this recent obscurantism was known as the "New Humanism," which must be differentiated from both the classical humanism of the

"Renaissance" and the secular humanism which proposes to establish a reformist cult divorced from belief in God. This new humanism was most popular in the decade from 1920 to 1930. Its leaders were Professors Irving Babbitt of Harvard and Paul Elmer More of Princeton—Babbitt an expert on French literature and More an able conservative literary critic. It was warmly supported in England by T. S. Eliot, an expatriate American poet and critic. It has some affinity with the Neo-Thomism led by Jacques Maritain in France.

A number of elements combined to produce the new humanism. In part, the movement was a reaction against a progressive social interpretation of literature. It represented the leisure-class determination to keep literature free from the disturbing and unpleasant considerations involved in political, economic, and social reform. Then, there was a decided aristocratic strain in the movement. It constituted a sort of literary feudalism, calculated to maintain literature and thought as an esoteric cult out of contact with the masses. Another formative influence was the defensive reaction against the upsetting revelations of modern science. In the moral field, the new humanism constituted an attack upon Rousseauism, or the cult of the natural and spontaneous.

The humanists adopted a Puritanical solemnity in moral matters and demanded an ascetic intellectual discipline over moral conduct. In its intellectual perspective this new humanism was a repudiation of the leadership of natural or social science and of the dictates of "naturalism" as a guide to life. It reverted to the supposedly stern guidance of Aristotle and scholasticism, though Aristotle himself actually favored many of the ideas that the humanists abhorred. Their knowledge of philology and literary criticism was extensive, but their mastery of the history of thought was mostly confined to the few figures and limited periods congenial to their particular tastes. An educational offshoot of this school was the neo-scholasticism of R. M. Hutchins and Mortimer Adler of the University of Chicago. The intellectual reaction to the second World War and the Cold War encouraged a comprehensive and diversified conservative trend in thought and literature. In some ways it has resembled what Gilbert Murray described as the "failure of nerve" during the intellectual breakdown of the Roman Empire in the West.

The reaction against science of a few such leaders, however, should not blind us to the many who never lost faith with the new scientific developments, who felt that with the increasing scientific exploration of the universe it became, as one astronomer has put it, a "larger and more interesting universe" than we had ever seen before. For a record of these accomplishments and an account of corresponding new development in education, the social sciences, philosophy, religion, and other areas, we shall turn to accounts of various authorities in the following chapter. A competent and restrained statement of the scientific approach to human and social problems, such as George A. Lundberg's *Can Science Save Us?*, remains the best guide to the human future.

SELECTED READINGS

Aiken, H. D., *Reason and Conduct, New Bearings in Moral Philosophy,* Knopf, 1963.

Aiken, H. D., and Barrett, William, eds., *Philosophy in the Twentieth Century,* 4 vols., Random House, 1962.

Ashton, E. B., *The Fascist: His State and His Mind,* Morrow, 1937.

Asimov, Isaac, *The Intelligent Man's Guide to Science,* 2 vols., Basic Books, 1961.

Ayres, C. E., *Towards a Reasonable Society,* University of Texas Press, 1963.

Barnes, H. E., *The Twilight of Christianity,* Vanguard, 1929.

———— *Economic History of the Western World,* Harcourt, Brace, 1937, Part IV.

Barnett, Lincoln, *The Universe and Dr. Einstein,* Sloane, 1957.

Beard, Miriam, *A History of the Business Man,* Macmillan, 1938.

Beck, W. A., *Modern Science and the Nature of Life,* Harcourt, Brace, 1957.

Binkley, R. C., *Rationalism and Nationalism, 1852-1871,* Harper, 1935.

Bowden, Witt, *Industrial Society in England,* Macmillan, 1925.

Brinton, Crane, ed., *The Fate of Man,* Braziller, 1961.

Bromberg, Walter, *The Mind of Man,* Harper, 1959.

Campbell, Angus; Converse, P. E.; Miller, W. E.; and Stokes, D. E., *The American Voter,* Wiley, 1960.

Carter, G. S., *A Hundred Years of Evolution,* Macmillan, 1958.

Childs, M. W., *Sweden: The Middle Way,* Yale University Press, 1936.

Clendening, Logan, *The Human Body,* Knopf, 1945.

Colton, Ethan, *Four Patterns of Revolution,* Association Press, 1935.

Commager, H. S., *The American Mind,* Yale University Press, 1959.

Daugherty, Carroll, *Labor Problems in American Industry,* Houghton Mifflin, 1941.

Davis, Forrest, *What Price Wall Street?,* Godwin, 1932.

Davis, Jerome, *Capitalism and Its Culture,* Farrar and Rinehart, 1935.

Davis, Watson, ed., *The Advance of Science,* Doubleday, 1934.

Dewey, John, *et al., Living Philosophies,* Simon and Schuster, 1931.

Dingle, Herbert, *Modern Astrophysics,* Macmillan, 1924.

Dorfman, Joseph, *Thorstein Veblen and His America,* Viking Press, 1934.

Eltzbacher, Paul, *Anarchism,* Libertarian Book Club, 1960.

Faul, Henry, ed., *Nuclear Geology,* Wiley, 1954.

Fermi, Laura, *Atoms for the World,* University of Chicago Press, 1957.

Fisher, H. A. L., *The Republican Tradition in Europe,* Putnam, 1911.

Ford, H. J., *Representative Government,* Holt, 1924.

Gamow, George, *Biography of the Earth,* Viking, 1959.

———— *Birth and Death of the Sun,* New American Library.

———— *The Creation of the Universe,* Viking, 1961.

Gist, N. P., and Halpert, L. A., *Urban Society,* Crowell, 1948.

Gosnell, H. F., *Democracy,* Ronald Press, 1948.

Guillebaud, C. W., *The Social Policy of Nazi Germany,* Cambridge University Press, 1941.

Hacker, L. M., *The Triumph of American Capitalism,* Simon and Schuster, 1940.

Hallgarten, G. W. F., *Why Dictators?,* Macmillan, 1954.

Hammond, J. L., and Barbara, *The Rise of Modern Industry,* Harcourt, Brace, 1926.

———— *The Town Labourer,* Longmans, 1925.

Hawkins, G. S., *Splendor in the Sky,* Harper, 1961.

Hayes, C. J. H., *A Generation of Materialism, 1871-1900,* Harper, 1941.

———— *The Historical Evolution of Modern Nationalism,* R. R. Smith, 1931.

Heisenberg, Werner, *Nuclear Physics,* Philosophical Library, 1957.

Holmes, H. N., *Out of the Test Tube,* Emerson Books, 1956.

Horowitz, I. L., ed., *Power, Politics, and People: The Collected Essays of C. Wright Mills,* Ballantine Books, 1963.

Hubble, E. P., *The Observational Approach to Cosmology,* Clarendon Press, 1937.

Hughes, D. J., *On Nuclear Energy,* Harvard University Press, 1957.

Hyman, S. E., *The Tangled Bank,* Atheneum, 1962.

Jones, W. T., ed., *Library of Contemporary Thought,* 8 vols., Knopf, 1926 *et seq.*

Josephson, Matthew, *The Robber Barons,* Harcourt, Brace, 1935.

Key, C. E., *The Story of Twentieth-Century Exploration,* Knopf, 1938.

Kirchwey, Freda, ed., *Our Changing Morality,* Boni, 1934.

Kirkland, E. C., *Industry Comes of Age: 1860-1897,* Holt, Rinehart and Winston, 1961.

Kirkpatrick, Clifford, *Religion in Human Affairs,* Wiley, 1929.

Kneller, G. F., *The Educational Philosophy of National Socialism,* Yale University Press, 1941.

Langer, Suzanne, *Philosophy in a New Key,* Harvard University Press, 1957.

Leighton, J. A., *Social Philosophies in Conflict,* Appleton-Century, 1937.

Lemon, H. B., *From Galileo to the Nuclear Age,* University of Chicago Press, 1946.

Levy, Hyman, *The Universe of Science,* Century, 1933.

Lichtenberger, Henri, *The Third Reich,* Greystone Press, 1937.

Lyttleton, R. A., *The Modern Universe,* Harper, 1957.

McIlwain, C. H., *Constitutionalism, Ancient and Modern,* Cornell University Press, 1940.

Merriam, C. E., *The American Party System,* Macmillan, 1940.

Mitchell, W. C., *The American Polity,* Free Press, 1963.

Moon, P. T., *Imperialism and World Politics,* Macmillan, 1926.

Morley, Felix, *The Society of Nations,* Brookings Institution, 1932.

Newman, J. R., *Science and Sensibility,* 2 vols., Simon and Schuster, 1962.

Palm, F. C., *The Middle Classes Then and Now,* Macmillan, 1939.

Parshley, H. M., *Science and Good Behavior,* Bobbs-Merrill, 1928.

Perry, R. B., *Philosophy of the Recent Past,* Scribner, 1926.

Piel, Gerard, *Science in the Cause of Man,* Knopf, 1962.

Platt, J. R., *The Excitement of Science,* Houghton Mifflin, 1962.

Planck, Max, *The Universe in the Light of Modern Physics,* Norton, 1931.

Roberts, Stephen, *The House That Hitler Built,* Harper, 1939.

Robinson, John A. T., *Honest to God,* Westminster, 1963.

Rossiter, C. I., *Constitutional Dictatorship,* Princeton University Press, 1948.

Schneider, H. W., *The Fascist Government of Italy,* Van Nostrand, 1936.

Schrödinger, Erwin, *Science Theory and Man,* Dover Publications, Inc., 1957.

Shapley, Harlow, *Flights from Chaos,* McGraw-Hill, 1930.

———— *Galaxies,* Harvard University Press.

———— *The Inner Metagalaxy,* Yale University Press, 1957.

Shipley, Maynard, *The War on Modern Science,* Knopf, 1927.

Struve, Otto, and Zebergs, Velta, *Astronomy of the Twentieth Century,* Macmillan, 1963.

Swisher, C. B., *American Constitutional Development,* Houghton Mifflin, 1943.

Taft, D. R., *Human Migration,* Ronald Press, 1936.

Thompson, George, *The Inspiration of Science,* Oxford University Press, 1962.
Thompson, W. S., *Population Problems,* McGraw-Hill, 1935.
Vahanian, Gabriel, *The Death of God,* Braziller, 1961.
Washburne, Carleton, *Remakers of Mankind,* John Day, 1932.
Wormuth, F. D., *The Origins of Modern Constitutionalism,* Harper, 1949.

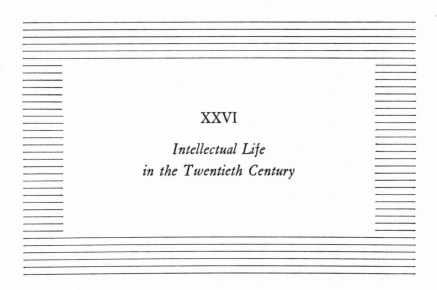

XXVI

Intellectual Life
in the Twentieth Century

I. THE QUANTUM REVOLUTION[1]

By Banesh Hoffmann

Professor of Mathematics, Queens College of the City University of New York

Hardly had the twentieth century opened when the science of the nineteenth century was shaken to its foundations; and shaken not once but twice—by two revolutionary theories so unlike in nature and scope that they remain yet unreconciled. In all its long history, science has seen no epoch to compare with the early years of the twentieth century, which brought, almost simultaneously, the quantum revolution and the relativity revolution. Either one alone would have marked a major turning point in man's understanding of nature. Together they made a golden age whose like will not be seen for many a year.

Of the two, the quantum revolution was the more radical, for it attacked the philosophical foundations of nineteenth-century science and forced the scientist to change his idea of the very nature of his calling.

The revolution began hesitantly, and unspectacularly, in the year 1899, when Max Planck pieced together an empirical formula for the radiation from glowing bodies. Having found that his formula agreed excellently with the experimental facts, he sought to justify it theoretically. But he could do so only if he did violence to all his scientific preconceptions by assuming that energy is given off not smoothly, as scientists had believed, but in small bundles, which he called quanta, the energy of a quantum being proportional to its frequency. The factor of proportionality, which he denoted by h, is now called Planck's constant, and no sci-

---

1 A bibliography for each of the sections of Chapter XXVI will be found at the close of the chapter.

entist could ask for a more enduring monument, for h is at once the cornerstone and the hallmark of modern atomic science.

Yet so fantastic did Planck's idea seem that even Planck himself lacked faith in it. In 1905, however, Einstein, young and unknown, in the same year in which he propounded his theory of relativity, showed that the quantum must be taken seriously: that it would explain hitherto incomprehensible features of the photo-electric effect, and that light itself must consist of quanta. These corpuscles of light are now called photons.

Newton had believed that light is corpuscular, but the evidence that light consists of waves, culminating in Maxwell's electromagnetic theory of light, had long been regarded as conclusive. When Einstein demonstrated that light must nevertheless somehow consist of particles, the old wave-particle controversy was reborn, to perplex scientists for two decades.

A. H. Becquerel's discovery of radioactivity in 1896, the first hint of unsuspected sources of energy within the atom, had been quickly followed by the discovery of the highly radioactive elements polonium and radium by Marie and Pierre Curie. In the early years of the new century Ernest Rutherford and Frederick Soddy proved experimentally that radioactivity is a symptom of something that chemists, scornful of their forebears, the alchemists, had long regarded as a chimera—the transmutation of elements.

In 1911 Rutherford discovered that the atom consists of a positively charged nucleus surrounded by electrons, the nucleus containing almost all of the atom's mass. But according to Maxwell's electromagnetic theory, this structure would be impossibly unstable.

It was here that Niels Bohr, in 1913, made his epoch-making contribution by applying the quantum to the theory of the atom. In defiance of classical concepts, he postulated that the electrons could move around the nucleus only in very special orbits, that when so moving they would not radiate, and that they could jump from one allowed orbit to another, emitting or absorbing a quantum of light in the process. This brilliantly iconoclastic theory, which yielded the frequencies of the hydrogen spectrum with spectacular numerical precision and quickly became the guiding light of atomic physicists, was propounded at a time that Einstein, in his autobiography, describes as follows: "All my attempts to adapt the theoretical foundation of physics to this [new quantum] knowledge failed completely. It was as if the ground had been pulled out from under one, with no firm foundation to be seen anywhere upon which one could have built. That this insecure and contradictory foundation was sufficient to enable a man of Bohr's unique instinct and perceptivity to discover the major laws of the spectral lines and of the electron shells of the atoms together with their significance for chemistry appeared to me like a miracle—and appears to me as a miracle even today. This is the highest form of musicality in the sphere of thought."[2]

In 1915 Arnold Sommerfeld, applying Einstein's theory of relativity to Bohr's theory of the atom, accounted in detail for the intricate fine structure of the

_____

[2] Author's translation of pp. 44, 46 of *Albert Einstein: Philosopher, Scientist*, ed. Paul Arthur Schilpp, Tudor, 1951.

spectral lines of hydrogen. Yet, by the early 1920's, for all its successes, the limitations of the Bohr theory were becoming all too plain. While there was no doubt that a fundamentally new concept was needed, there was no hint of its nature, nor of its imminence. Then suddenly it came—strangely, and in two guises, from two quite different quarters.

In 1922 and 1923, Louis de Broglie propounded, and developed in mathematical detail, the idea that matter consists of particles accompanied by guiding waves, an idea that led Erwin Schrödinger, in 1926, to propose a new type of mechanics, "wave mechanics," in which matter is regarded as consisting wholly of waves—in a fictitious space. His theory yielded, in an unforced way, not only the basic concept of Planck in improved form but also the frequencies of the hydrogen spectrum.

Meanwhile, in 1925 Werner Heisenberg had found a clue in Bohr's theory that led him to develop an apparently even more bizarre theory—a different type of mechanics, called "matrix mechanics," in which quantities p, q, representing momentum and position respectively, were found to be such that $p \times q$ was not equal to $q \times p$, their difference being Planck's constant, h, divided by 2π times $\sqrt{-1}$. This extraordinary relation between p and q, when appropriately grafted onto classical mechanics, converted it into the new matrix mechanics, which was found to yield the same happy results as Schrödinger's wave mechanics.

Here, suddenly, was an embarrassment of riches—and a woeful lack of understanding. But in 1926 P. A. M. Dirac, and, independently, Pascual Jordan, showed that wave mechanics and matrix mechanics were but different aspects of a general theory, now called quantum mechanics. In the same year, Max Born, abandoning the interpretations given by de Broglie and Schrödinger, showed that their waves should be regarded as waves of *probability,* the probability of finding the atomic particles at particular places—an idea which, for all its seeming unlikeliness, was a crucial step forward. And a year later Heisenberg brought major enlightenment with his famous *principle of indeterminacy.* Suppose we shine light on an electron, or other particle, in order to observe its position. Then, as Heisenberg demonstrated mathematically, the light quanta will give the particle a jolt that cannot be precisely determined: the very act of observation disturbs what is observed—and does so in an unpredictable way. In accurately determining the position of a particle we jolt the particle in such a way as to prevent our also determining its momentum accurately, and vice versa. This fact is related to the lack of equality of $p \times q$ and $q \times p$, and it has profound consequences. For if we cannot at the same time know the particle's precise position and motion, we cannot predict where it will be later on, and this plays havoc with classical notions of predictability and causality. Indeed, it forces us to give up the idea that we can picture the electron, or any other atomic particle, as a particle in the old-fashioned sense. Bohr, in his *principle of complementarity,* carried Heisenberg's idea further. He emphasized that we cannot picture the world of the atom in familiar classical terms. We have to learn to live with the idea that an atomic "particle" is an unpicturable entity that exhibits the characteristics of a particle when we make experiments of one type, but the seemingly contradictory characteristics of a wave when we make experiments of a different type. Bohr demonstrated in detail that no actual contradiction resides in this since the disturbance caused by our observing a "particle"—say, an electron —as a particle automatically prevents our observing *that same* electron as a wave, and vice versa.

Thus at last was the wave-particle puzzle resolved, but at a cruel price. For scientists had to give up the nineteenth-century luxuries of simple visualization and predictability. Neither the wave picture nor the particle picture is adequate alone to represent an atomic "particle." In the world of the atom, quantum laws hold sway, and they defeat our efforts to picture that world in comfortable, old-fashioned terms. We can neither predict nor wholly control the motion of an individual atomic particle. And yet, even so, an enigmatic ghost of predictability survives, for the *probabilities* associated with the unpredictable motion flow like waves and obey strictly causal laws. And it is this baffling ghost that endows our macroscopic world with a high degree of predictability, for in that world we deal with billions of billions of particles at a time, and when such numbers are involved, probabilities merge into virtual certainties.

Though most physicists now accept these concepts, some find them most disquieting. Einstein, despite his crucial contributions to the quantum theory, refused to accept these interpretations as final, believing, for powerful reasons, that quantum mechanics is an incomplete theory.

While the theorists were elaborating their theories and learning to understand how revolutionary were the concepts these theories implied, the experimenters were far from idle. In 1919 Rutherford made the crucial discovery of what, for want of a better word, was called "artificial" transmutation. He showed that high-speed particles, emitted by radioactive substances, on striking a nitrogen atom could knock from its nucleus a proton—which is the nucleus of a hydrogen atom. Soon other artificial nuclear transmutations were observed, and with the development of giant accelerators, notably the cyclotron invented by E. O. Lawrence, such transmutations became a commonplace. In 1932 J. Chadwick discovered the neutron, an electrically neutral particle of about the same mass as the proton, and almost immediately Heisenberg realized that all nuclei are made up of protons and neutrons. But theory said such nuclei should fly apart.

The proton has a mass almost 2000 times that of the electron. In 1935 Hideki Yukawa predicted the existence of a new particle, the meson, of intermediate mass, that would act as an adhesive holding protons and neutrons together in a nucleus. Shortly thereafter, a meson was discovered by the cosmic ray experimenters, but it turned out to be different from the meson predicted by Yukawa, which was not discovered till 1947.

Meanwhile Dirac, applying relativity to the new theory, had accounted anew for the fine structure of the hydrogen spectrum. And as a by-product, he had predicted the existence of the positron—the positively charged electron—which C. D. Anderson later discovered. Dirac correctly predicted, too, that a positron and electron coming together could annihilate each other, their masses being converted into energy of radiation—photons—in accordance with Einstein's formula,

$E = mc^2$, and that two photons could merge to create a positron and electron. Moreover it soon became clear that not just the electron and positron but every type of fundamental particle must have its opposite type—its anti-particle—capable of annihilating it, a prediction that led to the discovery, among others, of the negative proton—the anti-particle of the positive proton.

The story of the development of the atomic bomb is well known. If it can be said to have a starting point, that point might well be taken to be the discovery of the neutron, for Enrico Fermi, realizing that this neutral particle would not be repelled by the positive charge of the nucleus, used it to bombard the heaviest known atom, uranium. He thought he was forming new elements heavier than uranium. But in 1939 Otto Hahn and Fritz Strassmann discovered that barium—an atom of medium mass—was being produced, and this implied that the neutrons were causing the uranium nuclei to split into approximately equal halves. When it was found that neutrons were given off that would sustain a chain reaction, mankind entered a desperate age.

Space allows no more than a brief mention of the discovery, in the last decade, of more and more types of fundamental particles that for a while overwhelmed the nuclear theorists but are now beginning to reveal a tantalizing pattern of ill-understood symmetries among the building blocks of the material universe. And there is no room for even a bare listing of the manifold triumphs of the quantum theory.

Had the quantum theory met with only moderate success, scientists might be more hesitant to accept its strange implications. But its successes have been dazzling. The twentieth century has seen many wonders: television, the atomic bomb, the H-bomb, manned orbital flight—the list is a long one. But for all their staggering impact on our lives and our hopes for the future, they pertain more to technology than to basic science. In the physical sciences, the major fundamental achievements of the twentieth century are the theory of relativity and the quantum theory. The latter has corroded the concepts of basic predictability and simple visualization which, over the centuries, had been the mainstay of the imposing edifice of physical theory. Is it a sign that science has come of age? Or is it, as Einstein believed, a transient upheaval of puberty? Only time can tell—and we must hope that mankind will not deprive itself of that time.

II. GENERALIZED RELATIVITY AND THE COSMOLOGICAL REVOLUTION

By Jagjit Singh

Einstein's generalized theory of relativity, together with its interesting offshoot, the unified field theory, is the culmination of one of the two grand themes prominent in the history of science since antiquity. There are at bottom only two, because matter, according to an ancient, well-understood distinction, can exist in two forms—the continuous, such as water in a stream, or the discrete, such as the pebbles on its banks. Because of the polar antithesis of these two forms, it is natural that science should attempt to explain visual discrete objects in terms of an invisible continuum, or conversely, the visible continua in terms of indivisible discrete objects. Xenophanes's "All is one," Aristotle's all-pervasive "substance," Cartesian plenum, nineteenth-century ether are cases in point of the former tendency, while Democritus's atoms in the void and present-day nuclear particles illustrate the latter. Generalized relativity and unified field theory follow the former tradition in that they seek to explain all material activity against a single background—that of a continuous unified field.

Surprising as it may seem, the generalized theory of relativity took as its springboard the theory of discrete masses, or rather the gravitational forces between them already known to Kepler and others in the sixteenth century. Newton discovered their mathematical form, the famous inverse square law of attracting masses, which, grafted onto his own laws of motion, enabled him to explain the motion of planets in the sky as well as that of apples in orchards.

Despite the enormous success of Newton's grand synthesis of planetary and terrestrial motions, his synthesis suffered from two serious handicaps. First, it did nothing to abolish or even mitigate the discrete *vs.* continuum duality. For it had to accommodate both—discrete masses like the sun, earth, planets, and the "fixed" stars, voyaging through a featureless continuum, the void of space, against the background of another continuous but equally featureless flux, the flow of time. Secondly, it was greatly embarrassed by the apparent necessity of admitting a mystical action-at-a-distance, which propagated itself instantaneously in some unknown way across the gulf of space. Newton himself was quite puzzled by it and refused to commit himself with his famous dictum: *Hypotheses non fingo* ("I make no hypotheses"). Consequently, during the following two centuries, there began to grow a movement tentatively developing the idea that the properties of continuous space hitherto believed to be a featureless container, one chunk of whose hollow was as good as another, may somehow be determined by its material content of sun, stars, and galaxies. Gauss, Riemann, Ricci, and others devised the basic mathematical tools which enabled Einstein to make the next major advance since Newton, whereby the local properties of both space and time were shown to be the direct consequence of the existence of surrounding matter, which properties in turn determined the motions of that matter. He thus showed that the law of universal gravitation, albeit in a slightly modified form, was a consequence of the very structure of space-time in which the gravitating masses were embedded.

Einstein formulated this theory in two main stages. First, he amended the principle of Newtonian relativity to make it cohere with the new empirical evidence that had begun to pile up since Newton's day. Newton's relativity principle merely affirmed the truism that it is impossible to determine the absolute motion of any moving body. All that can be done is to measure its velocity *relative* to another. Thus we may be able to determine the velocity of the earth relative to the sun, that of the sun relative to another star, but never their "absolute" velocity. For to do so, we need to have a reference body absolutely at rest, and as

Newton wrote: "It is possible that in the remote regions of the fixed stars or perhaps far beyond them, there may be some body absolutely at rest, but impossible to know, from the position of bodies to one another in our regions, whether any of these do keep the same position to that remote body. It follows that absolute rest cannot be determined from the position of bodies in our regions." But with the subsequent progress of ideas it seemed that one did not have to go to Newton's "remote regions of the fixed stars or perhaps beyond them" to find a standard of absolute rest. It was found to lie at our doorstep— the all-pervading universal medium called ether which was conjured to replace the mysterious action-at-a-distance of one body on another by the more intelligible action-at-contact through the stress and strain of a medium intervening between the two. By the close of the nineteenth century it was almost universally believed that light and all other electromagnetic phenomena were evidence of actions taking place in the ether. For example, the light from distant stars by means of which we see them was supposed to be transmitted to us in the form of wave motions in a cosmic ocean of ether, like water waves in a sea. Without the mediation of the ether between the stars and ourselves we could never see them. It was argued that this ubiquitous ether pervading all space including our laboratories could provide the desired standard of absolute rest, because the observed phenomenon of astronomical aberration and other facts of nature required that the ether should not be dragged by ponderable bodies but remain fixed all the time. However, although really at rest, it would appear to be rushing past us owing to the earth's motion, exactly as the trees alongside a railway track seem to be rushing past a traveler in a train. To determine the absolute velocity of the earth we had therefore merely to measure the velocity of the ether current flowing past us. The actual measurement, however, presents a difficulty in that, unlike the trees flitting past the traveler, the drifting ether is imperceptible. Fortunately, the difficulty is not insurmountable because a light beam can be used to mark the ether drift somewhat as a blown straw indicates the flow of air. The reason is that, light being the outcome of wave motion in the stationary ether ocean, a ray of light is really the track plowed by it therein. It therefore follows that the absolute velocity of the earth could be determined by measuring the velocity of light in two ways—first by sending a ray in the direction of earth's motion through the ether and secondly by sending one in the contrary direction. For if c is the velocity of light in the ether and u that of the earth with respect to the ether, the ray will appear to us to move with velocity $(c - u)$ when sent in the direction of earth's motion through the ether and $(c + u)$ when sent in the opposite direction (see Fig. 1). By taking half their difference we obtain the absolute velocity (u) of the earth, for $\dfrac{(c + u) - (c - u)}{2} = u$.

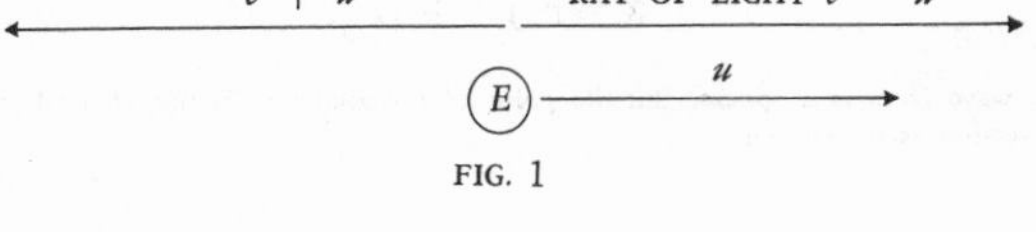

FIG. 1

Unfortunately, the theory did not work in practice. When Michelson and Morley contrived an ingenious experiment sensitive enough to test the theory, it was found that the light ray seemed to move in all directions with the *same* velocity c. In fact, its repeated trials conclusively showed that no matter how an observer moved with respect to others, he would find the velocity of light to be the same as any other. It was a paradoxical finding impossible to reconcile with our usual common-sense notions of space and time. For suppose an observer B moves with uniform velocity u with respect to another stationary observer A along OX. Suppose further that both are coincident at O at the initial epoch $t = 0$. If a ray of light is sent from O at the instant of their coincidence at O, A will observe the wave front of the light signal spread out before him in the form of a circle.[2a] At any later instant t the wave front reaches the points P, Q, R, etc., of the circle of radius ct. The arrival of the light signal at these points will be deemed to be simultaneous by A. Now, since B is moving with uniform velocity u with respect to A, he would be at O' at time t where $O\,O' = ut$. Naturally the circular wave front PQR of A cannot appear circular to the moving observer B, who has by then moved to O', no longer the center of the circle PQR. But if the velocity of light as measured by B is also to remain c (as experimental evidence requires), the wave front as seen by B will also be a circle with himself now at O' as its center. In other words, the points of the circle PQR where the light signal is at time t according to A's reckoning, shall also appear to lie on a circle with center at O' according to B's reckoning. Einstein showed that the paradox that both observers should consider themselves permanently at the center of their *own* wave-front circle arising from one and the same pulse of light could be resolved only by a thoroughgoing revision of our everyday ideas of space and time. The revision he suggested is the heart of his relativity theory.

If the two observers A and B use numbers to denote their observations, they would record them as follows: At any time t, A will find that the ray has proceeded a distance ct from O. Let P be any point of the expanding wave-front circle PQR so that $OP = ct$. If (x, y) are the coordinates of P with respect to two rectangular axes OXY, then an application of Pythagoras's theorem to the triangle OPM (see Fig. 2) clearly yields

$$x^2 + y^2 = ct^2. \tag{1}$$

But the second observer B could do likewise, that is, fix a frame of reference moving with himself, which for the sake of simplicity may be taken as parallel to that already selected by A. He too could denote the coordinates of the corresponding point on *his own* expanding wave-front circle, which we may denote by the accented letters x', y', t' to distinguish them from those used by the first. If B's observation is also to show that light travels with respect to him with the same velocity c, then clearly

$$x'^2 + y'^2 = ct'^2. \tag{2}$$

[2a] Actually the wave front is a sphere. But the point of the argument is not affected if we consider only its two-dimensional version as in the text.

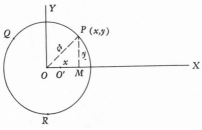

FIG. 2

But according to our common-sense notions of space and time, the relation between the coordinates (x, y, t) and (x', y', t') adopted by the two observers for the corresponding points where the light signal is observed by A and B at synchronous instants t, t' would obviously be (see Fig. 3):

$$\left.\begin{array}{l} x' = x - ut \\ y' = y \\ t' = t. \end{array}\right\} \tag{3}$$

Unfortunately, this leads to a contradiction. For if we substitute for x, y, t in equation (1) their values in terms of x', y', t', it leads to

$$(x' + ut')^2 + y'^2 = c^2 t'^2.$$

This is obviously inconsistent with equation (2) except in the trival case of $u = 0$, in which case both the observers are at rest with respect to each other.

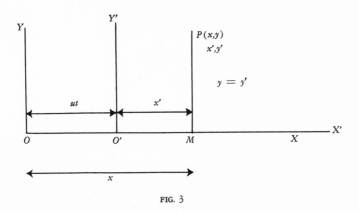

FIG. 3

Einstein showed that the only way out of the dilemma was abandonment of our ordinary notions of space and time which lead us to expect equations (3) connecting the coordinates used by the two observers. By a profound analysis of the basis of our space and time reckonings he showed that if equation (1) is to lead to equation (2), as the new experimental evidence demands, the system of equations (3) must be replaced by

$$x' = \frac{x - ut}{\sqrt{1 - \dfrac{u^2}{c^2}}} ,$$

$$y' = y ,$$

$$t' = \frac{t - \dfrac{ux}{c^2}}{\sqrt{1 - \dfrac{u^2}{c^2}}} .$$

(4)

These equations embody Einstein's new philosophy of space and time, which differs from the old in many ways. We may mention here only three. First, according to our ordinary notions a rod retains the same length whether it is stationary or moving with respect to us. But on the basis of equations (4) it can be proved that the length of a rod placed along OX' and moving with B would appear to A different from that measured by B, who would naturally consider it stationary with respect to himself. If l is its length as measured by A and l' that by B, then it can be shown that

$$l = l' (1 - \frac{u^2}{c^2})^{\frac{1}{2}}$$

(5)

It follows that the length l adjudged by an observer (A) with respect to which it is in motion is always less than that (l') measured by another (B) with respect to which it is stationary. In other words, if a rod begins to move with respect to an observer, it appears to him to contract in the direction of its motion because it changes from l' to l.

Secondly, according to our usual notions a time interval recorded by any clock remains the same whether it is stationary or in motion. But again it can be proved from equations (4) that if a clock moving with B along OX' records an interval of time T' between two events, it will appear to A as recording between the same two events an interval T, where

$$T = T' (1 - \frac{u^2}{c^2})^{\frac{1}{2}}$$

(6)

Consequently T is always less than T' so that a moving clock always operates more slowly than a stationary one. For instance, B's clock, moving with himself, may indicate an interval of, say, one year, which may be reckoned by A as only half as much. As a result, B would appear to A to have been in motion for a much shorter duration than he himself would think. It is this retardation effect which explains the favorite paradox of science-fiction writers, viz., that a space traveler after high-speed voyaging in interstellar space would return to earth younger than his stay-at-home contemporaries. Lest this consequence appear too strange to be credible, it may be mentioned that there is fairly direct evidence of the slowing of clocks in moving systems. During the last few years physicists have been experimenting with elementary particles—mesons—which move very fast with velocities comparable to that of light and act as their own clocks by marking off the instants of their birth and their extinction, thus indicating their span of life. In one of the earliest experiments Rossi and Hall found that the mean life of fast and slow μ-mesons differed by a factor of three. The difference is naturally to be expected if the retardation of the "meson's clock" is taken into account in accordance with equation (6). For by doing so, all μ-mesons can be shown to have the *same* life span regardless of their speeds.

Thirdly, equations (4) also show that the relative velocity of two bodies moving in the same straight line is not obtained in the normal high-school fashion, by adding or subtracting their speeds, but in a somewhat more complicated manner. Thus, if a rocket moves along OX in A's frame of reference with speed v, its velocity as observed by B will not be $v - u$ but larger. In particular, a light ray moving with speed c relative to A will not appear to B to move with speed $(c - u)$ but with speed c, as actually we find to be the case. Indeed, equations (4) were expressly designed to secure just this constancy of the speed of light with respect to all moving systems. It is a consequence of the revised law of compounding the velocity of light with respect to another moving body, that two events such as the emergence of a nova and a lunar eclipse may appear simultaneous to one observer and yet be non-synchronous with respect to another moving with respect to the first. This lack of synchrony between the temporal reckonings of moving observers has necessitated the abandonment of the common-sense idea of time adopted by Newton according to which there is a unique universally valid temporal order in which all observers can place the events they observe.

Having thus established equations (4), which abolished the notion of an absolute, evenly flowing time universally valid for all observers in relative motion as also that of an absolute container-type space, Einstein suggested that every such observer has to have his own system of locating events in space and dating them in time. While the different systems of measuring the spatial and temporal aspects of events varied from one moving observer to another in accordance with equations (4), there was a way of merging both aspects to evolve a higher complex or "unity" which remained the same for all observers. The fusion of space and time to evolve an invariant "unity" did not mean that Einstein contemplated the construction of some new equivalent of a philosopher's stone for turning a foot-rule into a clock or vice versa. What he had in mind was something quite different. Since both locations and dates of physical events can be denoted by numbers,[3] he envisaged the possibility of a *formal* procedure whereby these numbers could be combined to form a new number which would remain the same for all moving observers, no matter what their system of spatial and temporal reckoning. Such a higher "unity" is the famous space-time continuum of Minkowski.

With the space-time continuum as his basis, Einstein proceeded to the second stage of his theory by developing its geometry in accordance with the two funda-

---

3 For instance, the Lisbon earthquake of the eighteenth century may be denoted by three numbers ($4°$ West Longitude, $45°$ North Latitude, in 1755 A.D.).

mental principles he had already enunciated. First was his principle of relativity embodied in equations (4), to which all the phenomena of light and electromagnetism appeared to conform. Second was the principle of equivalence, which asserts the impossibility of distinguishing between a gravitational field and acceleration. Thanks to the progress of aviation and space travel, this impossibility is nothing very strange nowadays. It shows itself daily in such reports as that the "pilot weighs half a ton as he pulls his plane out of a power dive," or that "Gagarin remained in a state of weightlessness as he hurtled around the earth for twenty-five hours." Einstein's sophistication of this equivalence of gravity and acceleration is the heart of his generalized relativity theory, whereby he sought to abolish all "gravitational fields of force" and replace them by acceleration, that is, mere change in velocity and/or its direction. The acceleration of a gravitating body such as a falling apple or an orbiting satellite that shows itself as gravitation "really" arises because of a particular feature called "curvature" of the space-time in which it is embedded.

Einstein's geometry of space-time, based on the twin principles of relativity and equivalence of gravitation and acceleration, was accepted in spite of the complicated mathematical garb it wore, because it predicted three crucial astrophysical phenomena that were later experimentally verified. This success spurred Einstein and his followers to take the next step forward by trying to include electromagnetic phenomena also within the ambit of its sweep, exactly as he had absorbed gravitational fields into space-time in his generalized theory of relativity. In a brilliant paper Hermann Weyl broke new ground when he showed that Einstein's geometry of space-time is far from being the most general geometry which is consistent with the general principle of relativity, and that certain at least of the forces of electromagnetism could be explained very naturally by adding an extra degree of complexity to the geometry of the continuum. In the continuum as imagined by Einstein the length of a measuring rod might change as it was moved about in a gravitational field but its length at any instant would depend solely on its position in space. In Weyl's geometry this concept of length is abandoned and the lengths of standard gauges are assumed to vary depending on how they are carried to their positions in space. Thus, the result of a measurement at any place, say, New Delhi, at any time, say, March 1 by means of the standard platinum-iridium meter bar housed in the underground vault at the Paris international bureau may well depend on the time it is brought to New Delhi. Measurements made by it may not be the same if it is brought, say, on January 1 as when brought on March 1. They may even vary if it is brought to New Delhi by different routes. This may seem to wreck the very basis of our measurement scheme, for gauge invariance is its bedrock. But Weyl managed to salvage it partially at any rate by admitting the concept of length in a modified form. He assumed that when by an arbitrary act of choice we have fixed the meaning of the word "length" at a point P, we can derive a definite meaning for the word "length" at a neighboring point P' provided a certain vector function of position is given. By identifying this vector function with the electromagnetic potential vector, Weyl did succeed in unifying gravitation and electromagnetism.

In 1921, Eddington extended Weyl's geometry into a still more general system of geometry by resorting to two main innovations. In the first place, even lengths at the same points were *not* assumed to be directly comparable. Secondly, by identifying Weyl's vector function not with the electromagnetic potential vector but with $\sqrt{-1}$ times this quantity, he rid Weyl's theory of some of its awkward consequences by banishing them to the imaginary realm where they remain innocuous. He was thus able to build up a more consistent theory of electromagnetic field.

Many other versions of unified field theory, including Einstein's own, formulated in 1953 two years before his death, have been teased out of the pure mathematics underlying the differential geometry of the space-time continuum during the past forty years. But none of them has found much favor with the leading physicists because of their inability to specify any crucial experimental test of their validity, such as the three that proved Einstein's generalized relativity theory. At best they, like those of Weyl and Eddington, do no more than predict precisely the same phenomena as Maxwell's classical equations of electromagnetism. On the other hand, recent discoveries in nuclear physics have revealed a new kind of force —the so-called exchange force between electrons and protons on the one hand and atomic nuclei on the other. It is from this force that all other forces, whether gravitational, electromagnetic, or chemical, seem to stem. The pendulum has thus now swung rapidly from the "field" or continuum pole to the discrete.

Although the "unified field theory" offshoot of Einstein's generalized relativity has so far remained merely a beautifully sophisticated exercise in pure mathematics, its other consequence, the emergence of cosmology as a systematic and scientific study of the structure and evolution of our universe as a whole, has been of much greater significance. For the experimental success of Einstein's space-time geometry underlying his generalized relativity, when applied to the confines of our own solar system, encouraged him to extend its scope to the limits of the entire universe. But if we take the universe as a whole, or even some large slice of it such as modern telescopes reveal, we find therein almost countless concentrations of matter, the galaxies. To compute the motions of these discrete masses separated by vast empty spaces under their mutual interactions is a problem bristling with difficulties—difficulties which have still not been resolved. Einstein tried to mitigate them in an ingenious manner. He thought of softening the hard tenacity of these galactic agglomerations of matter by dissolving[4] them altogether and distributing all their material content evenly throughout the intergalactic void as a tenuous gas. This is no doubt an extreme idealization, but it did yield him what can be regarded as a first approximation to the actual problem. It happens that to describe fully the material features of such a smoothed-out universe, as, for instance, the density, momentum, stress, and energy of the thin medium pervading it everywhere, we require a set of ten numbers, one such set being coupled with each point of the continuum. Thus one member of this set of ten numbers associated with any point may specify the density of material there, another may specify momentum or stress in a particular direction, and

4 In imagination, of course.

so on. For this reason such a set of numbers is called the stress-energy-momentum tensor. But if we treat the space-time continuum geometrically, we find that its particular feature called "curvature" that determines the acceleration of gravitating masses embedded therein in accordance with Einstein's two principles of relativity and equivalence, is also denoted by a set of ten numbers for each "point" of the continuum. Einstein derived his famous field equations of gravitation by equating each of the ten components of the space-time "curvature" with one of the ten components of the stress-energy-momentum tensor.

What is the warrant for postulating the equivalence of the components of curvature and those of the stress-energy-momentum tensor? To understand the reason for this identification, it is necessary to remark that any continuous medium, such as a flowing stream or the material fog pervading our smoothed-out universe postulated in the preceding paragraph, is in a state of perpetual flux. But beneath this ceaseless flux there is an underlying essential continuity, because any element of fluid stream conserves its mass no matter how it is carried away by the stream flow. That is why all fluid-flows treated in hydrodynamics are subject to a condition of continuity which ensures this conservation or permanence of its material content. Its mathematical formulation is the well-known equation of continuity in hydrodynamical theory. Now, if we consider our space-time manifold with its ever-changing geometrical features, we can prove mathematically that an analogue of the hydrodynamical condition of continuity exists also for the components of space-time "curvature." This is a way of saying that although the numbers which define the components of the "curvature" are in a state of flux, that is, vary from point to point of the space-time manifold, yet they do satisfy a condition which is the exact counterpart of the hydrodynamical condition of continuity or permanence of the *material* that flows. It therefore follows that in spite of all the shifts of our number nets whereby we try to trap the geometrical attributes of our space-time, there is an element of *inherent permanence* in the geometrical construct we have created in the "curvature" components. Now it happens that the components of the stress-energy-momentum tensor which, as we mentioned earlier, describe the material characteristics of our smoothed-out universe, also possess the same element of inherent permanence. That is, they too satisfy the counterpart of the hydrodynamical condition of continuity. Since components of space-time "curvature" behave in exactly the same way as those of the stress-energy-momentum tensor, it would seem plausible to identify the two. This identification yields the famous field equations of generalized relativity.

By coupling the geometrical properties of space-time manifold with the corporeal characteristics of the material content of this space-time framework, Einstein's field equations become merely an abstruse way of saying that the "curvature" of the space-time continuum in which material events happen is simply related to the distribution of matter therein. This is why it is possible in principle to discover a purely geometrical feature of our universe such as its spatial curvature by observing its material content. For if (as the relativity theory assumes) the geometrical structure of the universe is conditioned by matter and the distribution of matter on a sufficiently large scale is considered to be uniform so as to obtain a uniform geometrical structure, then our three-dimensional astronomical space must be homogeneous with the same spatial curvature everywhere. A natural corollary of these assumptions is that the number N of galaxies within a sphere of radius r must be proportional to the volume V of the enclosing sphere. We have then only to examine the dependence of the number N, as observed in a sufficiently powerful telescope, on the distance r to determine the dependence of V on r. If N (and therefore V) varies directly as r^3, it means that the volume V of a sphere of radius r is proportional to r^3 as in ordinary high-school (Euclidean) geometry. Our space is then Euclidean with zero curvature. But there are also two other possibilities in theory. N may increase faster or slower than r^3. In either of these two cases the volume V of the sphere of radius r is no longer proportional to r^3. The measurement of the deviation of the increase in V from the Euclidean value, namely, that of strict proportionality to r^3, enables us to compute the curvature. In other words, space curvature leaves its fingerprint on the pattern of galactic distribution in depth over the sky. To identify it we have merely to count the number N of galaxies brighter than a specified limit m of brightness or rather faintness. Since the limiting dimness m is also a measure of the distance r up to which the faintest galaxy included in the count has been seen, we have all the elements required for empirically determining the volume V of a sphere in our actual space as a function of its radius r. Now we can calculate by pure theory the volume V of a sphere in terms of its radius in each of the three kinds of uniform spaces that are theoretically possible. A comparison of the empirical dependence of V on r with its theoretical counterpart therefore enables us to find both the magnitude and sign of spatial curvature.

In actual practice, it is no simple affair to determine curvature in this way, as its effect on the distribution of galaxies gets entangled with a variety of other effects. But it would take us too far away from our present theme to unravel the tangle here. This practical difficulty of empirically determining the curvature of the universe, however, did not deter Einstein from attempting a theoretical solution of the problem on the basis of his field equations applied to a smoothed-out universe. Unfortunately, he found that his field equations would yield no solution permitting a static cosmos that remains in one and the same condition forever. He tried to wriggle out of the impasse by assuming ad hoc that a new kind of force of cosmic repulsion was at work among the galaxies. With this amendment, it proved possible to deduce two static and homogeneous models to which the universe could conform—the Einstein model and the de Sitter[5] model, named after their inventors. The introduction of cosmic repulsion, however, gave rise to other insurmountable difficulties so that Einstein himself later acknowledged it to be the "worst blunder" of his life. For this reason both the Einstein and de Sitter models had to be abandoned. It is now believed that if at all

---

5 At one time these two models were considered to represent the opposite poles of a possible evolutionary tendency in the universe. For in the former the universe contains as much matter as it possibly can without bursting the relativity equations, while in the latter it is completely empty, permitting neither matter nor radiation.

it is possible to condense cosmic history into a capsule (model), it would have to be of the evolving or non-static type. The universe refuses to let itself be strait-jacketed in any static model.

If therefore we make the more realistic assumption that the universe, though uniform all over, is *not* static but has a history, we find that Einstein's original field equations without the ad hoc interpolation of cosmic repulsion suffice for the extraction of solutions. The Russian mathematician Friedmann deduced from Einstein's original equations two non-static models to which our actual universe could correspond. In both the models the universe starts from an initial state of hyperdense concentration in which all its material content is squeezed within the eye of a needle. Originating from such a state of zero or quasi-zero radius, it begins to expand and can follow one or the other of two courses. In one case it continues to expand forever. This is the expanding model. In the other the expansion comes to a halt when its radius reaches a maximum, at which time the direction of motion reverses and the universe begins to contract. The contraction thus initiated continues until expansion begins again on reaching the initial state, and so on ad infinitum. This is the oscillating model. Now an oscillating or expanding universe originating from a hyperdense state of zero radius containing all the matter at present diffused over all the stars and galaxies presents such conceptual difficulties that these conclusions of the theory could never have been even entertained without some corroborative observational evidence. Fortunately for the theory, such evidence was being collected independently by the American astronomer Hubble almost at the same time that Friedmann was carving out his two models.

Hubble showed that the spectral lines emanating from all the distant galaxies are shifted towards the red end of the spectrum by an amount proportional to their distance from us. But a red-end shift of spectral lines of a celestial object means that it is receding from us at a speed proportional to the magnitude of the shift. Hubble's observation therefore shows that all the distant galaxies are receding from us at velocities increasing directly with their distance. If this law of galactic recession holds at all distances, it is easily shown that all the extant galaxies must have been coincident some ten[5a] to twenty billion years ago. In other words, they would be precisely in that peculiar condition of hyperdense concentration that the Friedmann models envisaged—a primeval giant atom whose explosion started the universe on its course of expansion. It is true that such a big-bang origin of the cosmos is a great mystery. That is why some cosmologists do not hesitate to invoke God as the Author of this miracle making

[5a] The first estimate following Hubble's discovery of galactic recession was much shorter, only about 2 billion years. Baade in 1953 showed that it was based on a faulty yardstick of galactic distances. His new assessment of these distances trebled the estimate; but it is well-known that it is by no means final. It has already been revised to 10 to 25 billion years and further revisions are very likely as the estimate of the "age" of the universe based on Hubble's law is in conflict with others derived from the theory of stellar evolution, hydrogen gas depletion in galaxies, solar radioactivity, uranium decay, etc. For instance, according to one such theory globular clusters of old stars in our galaxy are estimated to be 25 billion years old in a universe whose putative age is only 10 to 20 billion years! It is possible that there is an error of a factor 2-3 in the computed ages of old stars. While so large an error seems unlikely, the calculations are difficult and bedeviled by so many pitfalls that the resulting estimates do not inspire great confidence. At the present stage all one can say is that the discrepancies are large and have not yet been resolved.

Him the "asylum" of our ignorance. But the fact of the matter is that relativity equations that underwrite cosmic history encounter a "singularity" at a particular instant of time in the past. That is, they become inapplicable from that instant backwards. It is possible, indeed likely, that under the conditions the universe found itself in then, some new equations or laws would be applicable. But if so, it would not be easy to discover them. This is why cosmologists usually adopt one of two courses. Either they consider the problem of cosmic origins as one grand irrationality of an otherwise rational God that is too deep for science to probe, as Milne and Lemaître did—or they, like Hoyle, amend the relevant equations to ward off the "singularity" by requiring continuous mass generation in direct violation of the energy-momentum conservation laws as they appear in general relativity. While the former attitude is paralogical, the latter exchanges the mystery of a single creation with that of continuous creation. Nevertheless, despite the puzzle of the singular state of the relativity-inspired models, it is worthwhile examining the possibilities of these models.

As mentioned before, relativity models of the universe are of two main types, expanding and oscillating. It is easily shown that the latter can only occur in Riemannian space of positive curvature wherein the number N of galaxies increases at a rate slower than strict proportionality to r^3 obtaining in Euclidean space. If, on the other hand, space is Euclidean or hyperbolic, that is, if the galaxy count N increases at a rate equal to or faster than strict proportionality to r^3, the universe must expand. If therefore we can decide by observation whether our actual universe is expanding or oscillating, we automatically infer the character of our actual space. Now a decision between expansion and oscillation depends on whether or not the law of proportional increase of recessional velocity with increasing distance continues to hold indefinitely or at any rate to the very threshold of our barely visible horizon. But here, as Hubble has justly remarked, our "knowledge fades" and we are obliged "to search among the ghostly errors of observation for landmarks that are scarcely more substantial." Despite the difficulties Humason, Hubble's collaborator in this field, has measured the recessional velocity of remote clusters about 1000 million light-years away, though the results are not certain yet. To measure the recessional velocities of still remoter and therefore faster-retreating galaxies, we need an altogether new technique, because galaxies retreating faster than a certain speed cannot be observed by any possible refinement of the photographic technique of Hubble and Humason. It is here that radio astronomy is likely to stand cosmology in good stead by offering the possibility of detecting the radar equivalent of red shift and thus enabling us to probe farther than ever into the innermost recesses of the expanding universe. Already Lilley and Maclain have detected the first radio red shift of the colliding galaxies in Cygnus, 260 million light years away. They find that the Cygnus source is moving away from us at about 10,500 miles a second, a finding which is fully in accord with the optical calculations of Baade and Minkowski in California. It is all but certain that before long, with more powerful radio telescopes coming into operation, we should be able to study galaxies receding with nine-tenths the speed of light or even more.

While, therefore, we must await the completion of more powerful radio telescopes now under way before we can peer into the edge of the expanding universe, all that we now have is Humason's provisional finding that remote clusters about 1000 million light-years away are moving *faster* than in direct proportion to their apparent distance. This means that 1000 million years ago the universe was expanding faster than now. In other words, the expansion is slowing down. In that case our universe might well conform to the oscillating model and our actual space to a closed Riemannian space of positive curvature. Humason is trying to measure the recessional velocities of two faint clusters whose predicted velocity is more than 62,500 miles per second. Although so far his efforts have not yielded any reliable results, the present observational evidence has been ably summarized by Allan Sandage in Figure 4.

Figure 4 shows the recessional velocity of eighteen known clusters of galaxies plotted against their respective distances. If the velocity increase continues to follow Hubble's law, the velocities of these clusters should lie on the line *C*. If, on the other hand, velocity line follows the curve between *C* and *B*, our universe is expanding and space is hyperbolic, that is, curved, open and infinite. Curve *B*

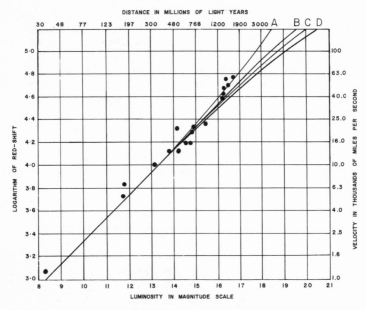

FIG. 4. Recessional velocity of galaxies (from Allan Sandage, "The Red Shift," *Scientific American*, September, 1956).

would arise in the case of flat Euclidean space. If it lies to the left of *B*, it is oscillating and our space is curved, closed and finite, the radius of curvature decreasing as we move to the left. As mentioned before, according to present observations (still crude and inconclusive), our universe is oscillating with closed curved space, for line A is the trend followed by the six faintest clusters.

Another line of evidence that has lent a measure of qualified support to the expanding (oscillating) universe theory is modern nuclear research. This research has shown that elements can be built up only in conditions of extremely high density and temperature such as prevail in the hot interiors of the stars. While such environments can synthesize the nuclei of atoms of carbon, lithium, calcium, silicon, iron, etc., the build-up of still heavier elements like uranium, thorium, etc., requires far more Draconian conditions than the stellar interiors provide. Gamow therefore suggests that the point-source models of relativity theory offer a possibility of a place and time at which such extreme conditions could have occurred.

According to Gamow, in the beginning the entire universe itself was a cosmic furnace whose initial temperature was high enough to forge all the heavier elements we find in it today. Taking his cue from Lemaître, he suggests that the zero state of our universe was a giant primeval atom which exploded a few billion years ago. In this state of ultra compression, the universe was a blaze of radiation, a veritable noontide of light and luster at the very dawn of its creation. But such a cosmic flood of fire soon spent itself. Taking its temperature as a measure of its fury, calculation shows that it dwindled rapidly with the passage of time. It tumbled from about 500 billion degrees a microsecond after its existence to a mere billion degrees five minutes later. Within a day it further dropped to 40 million degrees but took 300,000 years to fall to 6000 degrees and 10 million years to cool down to room temperature. It would thus appear that for the first few moments of its existence after the explosion the entire universe was at a temperature sufficiently high to spark nuclear reactions. At such high temperatures the little matter that it contained could only subsist disintegrated into the most primitive particles, primarily neutrons. For under its state of unimaginably dense condensation, electrons would all be buried deep inside the protons, thus producing neutrons.

As the primeval atom began to expand after the initial explosion, however, some of the buried electrons were released, the neutrons thus decaying into protons. Each proton promptly captured a neutron, the pair forming a deuteron, a species of hydrogen. Some deuterons then captured another neutron and became what is called hydrogen 3. This nucleus soon decays by emitting a negative electron and is thus transmuted into helium 3. In this way, by a rapid succession of neutron captures and electron decays all the elements were built up in the first burst of the universe's expansion. Gamow calculates that the whole process lasted barely thirty minutes, for by that time the temperature of the expanding universe must have dropped below the threshold of the thermonuclear reactions among the light elements.

While cosmic matter was thus forged within the first few minutes of the creation's existence, it remained a prisoner at the mercy of its baptismal bath of fire, like dead leaves driven by the wild west wind. The supremacy of fire (radiation) lasted for about 250 million years, when matter came into its own to blow its gravitational clarion over the wintry wastes of cosmic space and thus kindle anew those living flames, the stars and galaxies that we see in the sky. Although Gamow's theoretical derivation of the evolution of our cosmos agrees in some respects reasonably well with observation, it has not been able to overcome one serious difficulty. This is the absence of any stable nucleus of atomic weight 5, which makes it improbable that the heavier elements could have been produced in the first half hour in abundances now observed. Gamow is therefore obliged to agree that the lion's share of the heavy elements may well have been baked later in the only other alternative manner suggested so far, namely, during the course of supernova explosions.

However, there is a deeper criticism that has been raised against Gamow's explanation and indeed against all relativity-inspired cosmological models. For all of them invoke what is deemed to be a hair-raising extrapolation of the relativity theory to the limits of our cosmos. There is really no warrant for assuming its applicability to the universe as a whole even though it may hold for one of its tiny corners that we have so far surveyed. To guard against this danger, attempts have been made during the past thirty years to *deduce* cosmological models from some plausible world axiom or cosmological principle assumed to be true a priori. Historically, the first deductive cosmology to emerge on an a priori basis was that of Milne, who adopted what has since been called the "narrow" cosmological principle. It stipulates that, minor small-scale irregularities apart, the universe by and large presents the same aspect to all observers from every space location. By grafting it onto Hubble's observation of galactic recession, Milne derived the fundamental features of his model universe, formulating a new theory of dynamical, gravitational, and electromagnetic phenomena. We cannot go into the details of his deductive system here. Suffice it to enumerate some of the main features of Milne's model. First, every galaxy, or rather the observer located at its nucleus, considers himself the center of the entire system. Secondly, he sees every other galaxy as receding with a velocity proportional to its distance from himself while regarding himself as in a permanent state of rest. Thirdly, all the galaxies were crowded together at one point at the epoch of the "creation" of the universe after which they started receding from one another with velocities they are now observed to have. Fourthly, the number of galaxies is actually infinite but the entire system appears to every observer in his own private Euclidean space to occupy a finite volume, namely, that enclosed within a sphere of radius ct, where c as before is the velocity of light and t the epoch of reckoning after the initial creation. As a consequence, space appears to him infinitely overcrowded near the expanding edge of the universe where galaxies move with the velocity of light, just as to an observer at sea all the oceanic waters seem to be concentrated at the edge of his horizon. But this is only an apparent effect, for to another local observer at or near the horizon of the former everything seems normal—the concentration of oceanic waters now receding to his *own* horizon. Fifthly, this singularity or infinite density at the apparent horizon, though in principle observable by and certainly occurring within the experience of the observer remaining at the origin, is forever inaccessible to experience. For since the boundary or the observer's horizon is receding with the velocity of light, it can never be overtaken by an observer setting out from the origin with any speed not exceeding that of light. Sixthly, the outward recession leads to a steady dilution of galaxies, for as time passes, every observer is bound to disappear from the ken of every other so that we are eventually doomed to the prospect of an eternal Cimmerian night when we shall cease to see any other galaxy save our own. Seventhly, at any fixed epoch the density increases outwards till it becomes infinite at the boundary of the system, where the galaxies begin to recede with the velocity of light. Such is Milne's model universe.

But if we are to deduce a cosmology from the "narrow" cosmological principle, why not widen it before proceeding with the deduction? Why, one may inquire, must we limit its scope only to spatial homogeneity as Milne does? The identity of aspect that it postulates for observers scanning the universe at the *same* or equivalent times may well be extended to *all* times. If we extend Milne's cosmological principle to take in its stride temporal homogeneity as well, we obtain the so-called *perfect* cosmological principle. This postulates that, "minor small-scale irregularities apart, the universe by and large presents the same aspect from every space location at *any* time." In other words, the universe does *not evolve* in time but remains in the same steady state forever. Not that there is no change: the galaxies are born and die like human beings, but the aspect of the heavens that their totality presents to any observer stays the same just as the aspect of a steady stream remains unchanged from generation to generation in spite of the perpetual flow of its waters.

But, if the universe is to remain in the same steady state, how reconcile it with the eventual disappearance of the receding galaxies from our ken? For if the universe of galaxies is receding according to Hubble's law, it is doomed to dwindle out in the long run for the same reason as in Milne's model already described.

The only way to reconcile an expanding universe with the perfect cosmological principle is to postulate continual creation of matter to counteract the continual dilution of its material by the ceaseless drift to infinity of the receding galaxies. Accordingly, adherents of the perfect cosmological principle or the steady-state theory are obliged to assume that matter is being continually created in the universe from nothing and appears everywhere from nowhere to provide materials from which to rear new galaxies to replace those which disappear. Since the rate at which galaxies disappear is known from their recessional velocities, the balancing rate at which new matter ought to appear to keep the universe in the same steady state can be calculated. Spread through the whole of space, it turns out to be on the average *one* atom of hydrogen per liter of volume per billion years. Granting continuous creation of new matter at this rate, the general picture of the universe according to the steady-state theory is as follows:

There is no beginning nor end. The universe remains in the same steady state it has always been in and will continue to remain so forever. Consequently, the theory is not concerned with the formation of galaxies from the explosion of a hyperdense primeval atom as in creationist theories such as that of Gamow but only with that of new galaxies in a universe already full of old ones. In other words, it does not have to account for the origin of Adam galaxies but only for that of their successors. It does so by identifying the birth process of new galaxies with the gravitational perturbation by the old preexisting galaxies of the continuously created intergalactic matter. The reason is that this perturbation of intergalactic matter results in a systematic concentration of density in certain regions thereof in such a way as to lead to the formation of new galaxies both singly and in clusters. It is thus possible to deduce the statistical age pattern of old and new galaxies in a typical cluster. This is one way in which a crucial test of its validity may be devised, but it is difficult to apply in practice. However, in recent years two others—one by Stebbins and Whitford and the second by Ryle and Scheuer—have been applied. Although the results (as usual with cosmological tests) are tentative, both have tended to disprove the steady-state theory. In fact, a more recent review by Sandage seems to show that the predictions of the steady-state theory are inconsistent with the red shift of distant galaxies as observed at present.

Such an experimental refutation or at least lack of support has not yet put the hypothesis of continuous creation of matter completely *hors de combat*. Adherents of the hypothesis such as Hoyle have tried to explain the observations by appealing to other factors. After all, the universe is very large and not enough is known about it. Given sufficient ingenuity, almost anything can be explained or explained away. On the other hand, it has been suggested that the creation hypothesis is too restrictive and needs to be widened to include continuous extinction as well. For if matter can be assumed to appear continually out of nowhere, it may also be supposed to disappear in a like manner into the limbo of oblivion. Kapp has enumerated all possible hypotheses about the origin and extinction of matter that can be put forward. They comprise a combination of one of the three in the *A* list with one of the three in the *B* list shown below:

A	*B*
Hypotheses about the Duration of Matter and Energy in the Past	*Hypotheses about the Duration of Matter and Energy in the Future*
*A*1. All matter and energy have existed for all time.	*B*1. All matter and energy will continue to exist for all time.
*A*2. All matter and energy have existed for approximately the same length of time, i.e., from the date of the Creation. According to this hypothesis, no particle has existed for a longer time than has elapsed since the Creation began, nor for a shorter time than has elapsed since the process of Creation was completed.	*B*2. All matter and energy will continue to exist for approximately the same length of time, which is the time that will elapse until the end of the world. According to this hypothesis, no particle will last for a shorter time than will elapse up to the beginning of the end of the world, nor for a longer time than will elapse until the process of destruction is completed.

A3. Any particle of matter or quantum of energy may have existed for any length of time. That is, matter and energy may originate without cause, continuously, at random, and not as a result of anything in the existing state of affairs.

B3. Any particle of matter or quantum of energy may cease to exist at any time. That is, matter and energy may disappear without cause, continuously and by extinction, at random, and not as a result of anything in the existing state of affairs.

There are thus in all nine possible combinations of which only three, viz., (A1, B1), (A2, B2), (A3, B3), are symmetrical in the sense that the hypotheses concerning creation and extinction of matter are alike. After a critical examination of all nine possibilities Kapp chooses the combination (A3, B3) which he calls the hypothesis of symmetrical impermanence of matter, because it seems to involve a minimum of assumptions. By combining it with the relativistic concept of curved space he has recently formulated a new cosmology which includes a new theory of gravitation.

According to Kapp, a particle does not carry its gravitational field around with it, as has been hitherto supposed. The field originates as a momentary pulse only as a consequence of the extinction of a particle in the gravitating mass. Gravitation thus is, to use his own graphic expression, "the swan song of matter and not, as supposed by tradition, its signature tune." It is a novel idea which has yet to suggest some new crucial experimental tests to prove its validity.

The foregoing survey of cosmological principles is by no means complete. They are not the only general principles on which a cosmology may be reared. Dirac, for example, proposed a radically different principle, viz., that "all very large cosmological dimensionless numbers which can be constructed from important constants of cosmology and atomic theory such as the force constant (the ratio of electrical and gravitational forces between an electron and proton), are simple powers of the age of the universe." This is a way of saying that the constants of nature, like the constant of gravitation, are not true constants but vary with time. The principle leads, however, to the awkward result that 200 to 300 million years ago, when the constant of gravitation was 10 per cent higher, the sunshine must have been much fiercer. Calculation shows that at the then prevailing rate of solar radiation the oceans would have been boiling and the earth unfit for habitation in any form. But 200 to 300 million years ago the earth corresponded to what geologists call the Paleozoic period, when life had already appeared. It is true that the assumed changes in gravitational constant may be compensated by corresponding (assumed) changes in other factors such as the opacity of the sun by changing chemical composition. But such multiplication of factors merely to save a principle are quite unwarranted. It is therefore possible that Dirac's principle is merely the first crude intimation of a cosmological message that atomic physics is beginning to write for us in a language that we have yet to understand.

Dirac's take-off into cosmology on the wings of dimensionless numbers of atomic physics, however, is not the only possible approach. Earlier, Eddington too had developed a cosmology of his own by proceeding with three such dimensionless numbers to which he added a fourth, the cosmical number N, representing the total number of elementary particles in the universe. These four numbers, in his view, furnish a "natural and complete specification for constructing a universe." For, according to him, their values are not what they are "by the whim of Nature." They are the inevitable consequence of certain basic assumptions underlying the very mode of our measurement. But his theory of measurement from which he attempted to deduce their values has not been able to ward off the suspicion of being at best merely a post facto rationalization of facts already known empirically. The reason is that it gave no premonition of the amendments to some of these facts which subsequent observations required. Thus his theoretical deduction of the value of Hubble's constant gave no intimation of the large correction necessitated by the subsequent revisions of a grossly faulty scale of galactic distances current at the time Hubble made his discovery. Nor did it yield any indication of the great proliferation of elementary particles that the advance of nuclear research has since discovered.

The foregoing selection of some current cosmological theories is by no means complete. For the cosmological garden is at present in its hundred-flower phase even though many of these buds are doomed to wilt and wither under the scorching light of fast-accumulating new knowledge of the universe around us. However, whatever the ultimate fate of the contending cosmologies, all of them have to face at some stage or other the problem of the evolution of stars and galaxies after its "birth" either in an explosion of a primeval giant atom or otherwise. This is why their underlying ideas have to be interwoven with those of the subsequent evolution of stars and galaxies from gas clouds. To do so, most theories assume that before the emergence of galaxies but after "creation," if any, the universe was a formless, featureless near void. That is, it consisted of an extremely tenuous gas of hydrogen atoms[5b] spread throughout space of density of approximately sixty atoms per million cubic centimeters. As a density this is merely a figure of speech, for a cosmic cloud of this density and of the size of our sun would weigh less than a teaspoon of water. But even such a state of extreme tenuity spread over distances of the order of billions of light-years would suffice to provide enough material for all the extant galaxies we see in the sky. How such an extreme tenuity of matter evolved into the universe we know is a riddle that will take long to divine fully. But ignoring certain sophistications due to the effects of turbulence and magnetohydrodynamics, both of which we have barely begun to understand, we can show that a uniformly homogeneous gaseous cloud, extended over vast distances ranging over billions of light-years, is gravitationally unstable. This is a way of saying that it cannot stay put for long in its initial state of uniform tenuity. During the course of eons it will begin to condense into a series of distinct accretions around separate nuclei. These separate accretions, the

---

[5b] Except that in creationist cosmologies the hydrogen cloud is supposed to contain already a small proportion of heavier elements synthesized during the first half hour of its existence as mentioned before. But as it is unlikely that the heavier elements could have been thus produced in their present abundances, they too have to rely on other processes connected with stellar evolution to account for the observed composition of cosmic matter.

denser first-generation subclouds of the original parent cloud, in turn fragment into a series of second-generation subclouds and so on. Thus each successive generation of subclouds of gas shrinks *as a whole* until it is dense enough to cease further shrinkage. It is then ripe to begin fragmenting into a number of next-generation subclouds. One may imagine this process of condensation and fragmentation to continue indefinitely. But a stage ultimately arrives when new factors emerge to halt the process of fragmentation and the system condenses into a galaxy of stars. It is thus that gravity, aided by turbulence and magnetohydrodynamics, conjures the star-spangled heavens out of the Cimmerian darkness of the deep. But here again there are many variations of the aforementioned basic theme depending on the emphasis laid on the gravitational, turbulent, and magneto-hydrodynamical aspects of the cloud behavior. We cannot go into them here except to remark that the great debate between the rival theories of how the galaxies evolve is still on and as undecided as that on the origins of the cosmos.

If the foregoing survey of the current cosmological controversy reads like the well-known story of blind men wrangling about the elephant, it is because the cosmos is really much too elephantine and our glimpse of it much too small to be readily taken in our conceptual stride. The immense gaps in the observational knowledge of the universe which will take perhaps millennia, if ever, to close allow too many rival cosmologies between which observation is unable to decide. This is why cosmology will remain for long full of controversy and conflict. But no matter what its doubts and uncertainties, it will continue to fascinate us with its faltering, and at times contradictory, answers to the riddle of the universe. Though the wand of cosmology be frail and fragile, the spell it casts is powerful and profound.

III. MATHEMATICS TODAY

By Jagjit Singh

The non-mathematician is likely to regard mathematics as a sort of exercise in manipulating one of three things—numbers (arithmetic), symbols (algebra), or figures (geometry)—though some may also have heard of calculus as a mathematician's mystique for handling variables, that is, quantities in continual flux such as the speed of satellites or the growth of populations. What he may not know is that each of these four branches has diversified during the past 100 years into numerous others. This immense ramification is both a consequence and a cause of the great upsurge of modern science and technology, for no major field within the ambit of their sweep—from space travel and genetics to neurology and economics—is now impervious to the influence of mathematics.

The reason mathematics has been able to penetrate every branch of science and technology to such an astonishing extent is that all its ideas are purely abstract and abstraction is the chief motive power of science and technology.

Whenever we treat some problem mathematically, whether in physics, astronomy, engineering, biology, or the social sciences, there is only one way in which we can proceed. We must first simplify it by having recourse to some abstract model or replica representing only those features of reality considered most essential for the problem in question. Take, for instance, Eddington's famous elephant problem wherein an elephant weighing two tons slides down a grassy hillside of 60° slope. How long did he take to slide down? If we strip the problem of its "poetry" (Eddington's word), that is, if we make an abstract mathematical model embodying its essential features, all that we have is a "particle" sliding down an "inclined plane." Here "particle" is a mathematical abstraction which retains only that essential property of material bodies we call "ponderosity" or "inertia." Similarly "inclined plane" is a geometrical abstraction of hillsides embodying their essential feature "steepness." Abstract mathematical models of this kind not only simplify the real problem by retaining the bare essentials and discarding those encumbrances, the irrelevant details, but also apply to a much wider class of problems than the original. Thus mechanics scored its first resounding success only when it departed from its earlier practice of discovering the separate specific behavior pattern of falling apples, swinging pendulums, ascending gases, and wandering planets, and began to abstract their common features and embody them in the now well-known laws of motion and gravitation equally applicable to them all. The great generalizing power of the right kind of abstraction such as that of the laws of motion to subsume a wide variety of phenomena within its fold explains the paradoxical statement sometimes made, that the more modern mathematics departs from reality (that is, grows abstract), the closer it comes to it. For no matter how abstract it may appear, it is in the ultimate analysis an embodiment of certain essential features abstracted from some sphere of reality.

It is the pursuit of greater and greater abstraction that has enabled each of the aforementioned four branches to sprout into ever wider generalizations. To begin with, consider arithmetic, the manipulation of numbers. Starting with whole numbers, 1, 2, 3 . . ., which were devised for counting discrete collections of concrete objects like flocks of sheep and quivers of arrows, mathematicians soon turned such numbers into abstract symbols denoting the one common quality of all kinds of discrete collectives, viz., the degree of their plurality. From whole numbers to rational numbers (ratios of two whole numbers) and irrational numbers (limits of convergent sequences of such ratios) for measuring continuous magnitudes such as milk yields and field lengths, and thence to complex numbers and vectors for handling more sophisticated entities such as forces, torques, electric currents, and fluid flows, or to transfinite numbers to encompass unencompassable infinity as a sheer intellectual joy ride—all these were but further giant strides in abstraction. This trend towards abstraction reached its culmination with the invention of hypercomplex numbers such as Hamilton's quaternions and Grassmann numbers during the second half of the nineteenth century. Any kind of number which was required to count a crowd, measure a magnitude, or fix any of the more recondite entities of physics and engineering could be shown to be a particular case of some hypercomplex number.

With the closing of the field of making increasingly complex numbers mathematicians returned to the whole number from which they had started in order now to discover its "essence." In endeavoring to do so they created a new subject—mathematical logic. Mathematical logicians like Russell and his followers believed that while all types of numbers such as fractions, complex numbers, vectors, etc., could be successively generated out of integers, the integers in their turn could not be further analyzed in mathematical terms. They could be defined only in terms of the logical concept of a class, that is, an ensemble consisting of all individuals having a certain property, the property of belonging to a logical class.

Although the attempt to derive the concept of whole numbers from the logical concept of class did not quite succeed, it did let loose a deluge of discussion as to how to construct a paradox-free or consistent logic capable of yielding all of mathematics. One of the fundamental problems of mathematics all along has been the reform of mathematical reasoning so as to avoid paradox or contradiction, for mathematical reasoning has been haunted by the fear of paradox since the days of Pythagoras and Zeno. As is well known, Pythagoras found to his dismay that the diagonal of a unit square cannot be expressed as a ratio of two integers, and Zeno astounded Athens by apparently proving that Achilles could never overtake the tortoise. Paradoxes similar to these have been discovered from time to time and as recently as the close of the nineteenth century a whole series of them were uncovered by Burali-Forti, Russell, Richards, König, Berry, and others. The logicalists claim that if mathematical reasoning is to avoid paradox and contradiction not only here and now but "forever," then it must be reduced to logic. To do so extensive use was made of a mathematical symbolism devised to mathematize logic. Such a mathematized logic, or symbolic logic, has no doubt furthered the logical analysis of mathematics itself by providing a logistic "foundation" for mathematics. While this fusion of mathematical logic with the logical analysis of mathematics has greatly illumined the nature of mathematical deduction and proof, it has not been able to fulfill the main object for which it was designed.

The failure of the logicalists to set up a paradox-free mathematics led to the formalist's endeavor to reduce mathematics to a game of manipulating symbols, mere marks on paper like $+$, $-$, $\sim$, $=$, $\times$, etc., in accordance with certain formal rules. The logic of handling these symbols, namely, metamathematics, thus becomes an absolute, a sort of supertheory designed to "justify" mathematical reasoning by showing that it does not lead to any inconsistency or contradiction. But such efforts of the formalists received a shattering blow when Kurt Gödel in 1931 showed that if the game of mathematics is actually consistent, the fact of this consistency cannot be proved within the rules of the game itself.

Since the logicalists' and formalists' analysis of number and mathematical proof raised such a storm of difficulties, the intuitionists sought to cut the Gordian knot by asserting outright that the whole numbers are given us immediately in intuition and that it is vain to try to get behind them. At most, we may consider them as generated by successive additions of unity to other numbers already formed. Thus, starting with unity, we generate the number 2 by the addition of unity to itself, the number 3 by that of unity to 2, and so on indefinitely. The most important element in this construction of whole numbers is, therefore, the concept of unity, a concept given us by our immediate intuition. Once the series of whole numbers is constructed by successive acts of addition of unity in the manner described above, it is quite possible to base mathematics entirely on the notion of integers by a sound analysis of the constructions and processes of mathematics, described in ordinary language and ordinary mathematical symbols, plus a few logical symbols, as has been done by Paul Dienes. But the intuitionist solution of the foundation problem raises the question of the validity of a fundamental law of classical logic, the law of excluded middle, which merely assumes that either a proposition is true or it is not. At first sight it may seem astounding that anyone should challenge this assumption. Nevertheless, a deeper examination shows that its unqualified acceptance does give rise to difficulties. By rejecting it, Brouwer, the leader of the intuitionist school, disposed of the antinomies which harassed the subject, though only by cutting the ground under much of classical mathematics.

One useful outcome of the controversies concerning the "foundations" of mathematics has been the use made of these ideas by electronic engineers to produce new types of ultrarapid automatic calculating machines employing all manner of electrical apparatus. The reason why mathematical logic is applicable to the design of calculating machines is that a calculating machine is, in fact, a logical machine. It is merely a device which, with an initial input of data, turns out the final answer with as little human interference as possible until the very end. This means that after the initial insertion of the numerical data the machine must not only be able to perform the computation but also be able to decide among the various contingencies that may arise during the course of the calculation in the light of instructions also inserted into it along with the numerical data at the beginning. In other words, a calculating machine must also be a logical machine capable of making a choice between "yes" and "no," the choice of adopting one or the other of two alternative courses open to it at each contingency during the course of the computation. It happens that the rules of the logical and arithmetic calculi (in the binary notation)[6] are identical. This is why the apparatus designed to mechanize calculation is also able to mechanize processes of thought.

If the search for the "essence" of integers, the basis of arithmetic, yielded the ethereal abstractions of symbolic logic and metamathematics, those of modern algebra were even more tenuous. As is well known, in elementary algebra we use the mystery symbol x to denote a quantity which we do not happen to know. Although the quantity is unknown, we are ultimately able to find its value

---

[6] That is, a notation in which numbers 0, 1, 2, 3, 4, . . . , in the decimal notation are written as 0, 1, 10, 11, 100, etc.

because by subjecting it to such operations of arithmetic as addition, multiplication, subtraction, division, squaring, cubing, etc., we obtain a known result. But modern algebra no longer restricts the symbols of its discourse to representing numbers, nor even the operations to which the symbols are subjected to those of ordinary arithmetic. It uses them to denote "indefinables." That is to say, x may as well be a symbol concerning which nothing is assumed except that it obeys certain fundamental laws which again may be very different from those of ordinary arithmetic and algebra. "Indefinable" in this context is not the "ineffable" of the mystics, a mysterious something that is too deep for words and cannot be defined. It is simply the *undefined* that is not pinned down to anything concrete in order to create an instrument of analysis that may be as widely applicable as possible. In other words, we leave the mystery symbol x deliberately undefined in order to secure the widest possible generality in our theory and thus reach the summit of abstraction.

To fix ideas, let us start with a set of "indefinables" denoted by the symbol x. If we want to distinguish among the various elements of this set, we may represent them by x_1, x_2, x_3.... For example, x_1, x_2, ... x_6 may represent the set of six different ways of shuffling three cards such as the ace, two, and three of spades. Since there are six and only six *distinct* ways in which three cards can be permuted, any two shuffles successively applied will inevitably yield some one of the six shuffles of the set itself. By combining any two or more of the six shuffles we cannot generate any new shuffle not already included in the original six of the set. In other words, the set of six shuffles is closed. Such a set[7] or collection of "indefinables" as the set of six shuffles of three cards whose elements combine in such a way that any two or more of them in unison are equivalent to some single item of the set is known as a *group*. The essential point is that the elements of the group can be combined according to some law and that any combination of them produces an element belonging to the set itself. It is, therefore, completely self-contained or closed.

More precisely, a group is a system of a finite or infinite number of objects within which an operation is defined which generates from any two elements a, b another object ab also belonging to the system, subject only to two conditions:

(i) The operation according to which the elements of the system are combined obeys the associative law $a(bc) = (ab)c$.

(ii) If a, b are any two elements of the system, there also exist two elements x, y of the system such that $ax = b$ and $ya = b$.

It often happens that the elements of the original group may be divided into two or more distinct sub-sets in such a way that the elements included in each sub-set satisfy the two properties mentioned above separately. In such a case each sub-set possessing the group property in its own right is known as the sub-group of the original group. Thus in the case of the six shuffles of three cards cited earlier, the six shuffles can be so divided into two sub-groups of three

7 Such a set is really a *permutation* group as it is the result of permuting three cards.

shuffles each that each of them possesses the group property in its own right.

It is really a wonder that from the aforementioned two insignificant-looking assumptions underlying the group concept there springs an abundance of profound relations tying up in the single framework of a deductive system an astounding variety of seemingly unrelated branches of mathematics. This is why group theory provides an important tool for the study of many problems in calculus, geometry, and even quantum mechanics.

If algebra soared to ever dizzier heights of abstraction by liberating the symbols of its discourse from their attachment even to numbers, geometry, not to be outdone, went one better. It liberated itself in three major ways to reach the high-water mark of abstraction that it has attained today. First, it wrenched itself free from the slavery of diagrams. Before Descartes's invention of algebraic geometry that proved to be its magna carta there was no way of developing a geometric argument except by drawing a figure. Descartes showed that instead of denoting points by dots and crosses as in a geometrical diagram, we could designate them by their coordinates, that is, distances from a set of mutually perpendicular reference lines. The way is then clear to carry on the argument by manipulation of numbers (coordinates) instead of diagrams. Descartes's innovation in due course paved the way for the second liberation of geometry, this time from its complete domination by Euclid. For over 2000 years Euclid had dominated geometry so absolutely that even philosophers like Kant thought they could "prove" that geometric relations in space could not be other than those laid down by Euclid. The application of Cartesian methodology and calculus to geometry, however, led to the profound investigations of Gauss, Lobachevsky, Bolyai, and Riemann into the foundations of geometry which finally undermined Euclid's domination of it. They showed that Euclidean geometry was only one of many geometries that could be deduced equally logically from postulates differing from those of Euclid—especially his parallel postulate. Furthermore, all this abundance of Euclidean and non-Euclidean geometries could be applied to abstract spaces of still higher dimensions than the three which perceptual space around us seems to possess. Indeed, there was no limit to the dimensions that such abstract spaces could conceivably have. Mathematicians even conjured spaces of infinitely many dimensions such as Hilbert space with its applications to quantum mechanics.

These new geometries were in turn unified by the group concept that had already proved so powerful in extending the horizons of modern algebra. It first invaded projective geometry, a new branch that began to be developed as a self-contained body of doctrine about the beginning of the nineteenth century. The idea underlying such a geometry is precisely that of photography. When we photograph a landscape, the picture no doubt distorts the angles, distances, and shapes observed. Thus a circular pond may appear in the photograph as elliptical and the parallel edges of a track may seem to converge. Despite these distortions, the photograph retains intact enough of the geometric properties of the landscape to remain a recognizably faithful replica of the actual scene. The properties that are preserved in the photograph, that is, the properties that remain "invariant" under the photographic transformation, are the properties studied by projective geometry. This is because if we analyze the mechanism of the photographic transformation, we find that it is exactly what the mathematicians call a projective transformation. The latter is engineered in the following way: Let there be any plane geometric figure (landscape) and let O (the converging center within the camera of the rays of light from the landscape) be any point not in the plane of the figure. Draw straight lines (rays

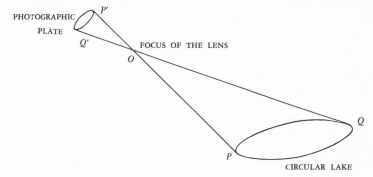

FIG. 1. PROJECTIVE TRANSFORMATION

of light) from O to every point of the plane figure (see Fig. 1). Let this set of lines be cut by any plane (the photographic plate) not passing through O. This plane section of the lines through O gives a new figure (photograph) in the cutting plane which is said to have been obtained from the original by projection and section or a projective transformation. It is obvious that to every point P in the original figure there corresponds one and only one point in the projection so that to every straight line such as PQ in the original there corresponds one and only one straight line $P'Q'$ in the projection yielded by the points P' and Q' corresponding respectively to P and Q of the original figure.

A projective transformation thus transforms points into points and lines into lines and preserves the incidence of points and lines even though it does not preserve distances and angles. Now the set of *all* projective transformations forms a *group* because any two such transformations applied in succession yield a third also belonging to the set. Projective geometry is thus the study of properties of figures which are "invariant" or remain intact under the group of all projective transformations. In exactly the same way the group idea is also applicable to ordinary Euclidean geometry because the set of all rigid motions in space also forms a group. This is a way of saying that any two shifts of a rigid body applied in succession yield a third which too belongs to the set. It therefore follows that ordinary Euclidean geometry is the study of those properties of figures that remain invariant under the group of all such motions. This again is only a particular case of a fundamental principle first enunciated by Felix Klein, to the effect that, corresponding to every group of transformations in space, there is a geometry consisting of those properties of space which are invariant under the given group. Klein's principle is thus a sort of Ariadne's thread running through the whole gamut of modern geometries and providing a systematic method of procedure in studying geometry as a whole by the investigation of all possible groups of transformations. For instance, the group of rigid motions is a sub-group of the general projective groups when the point O of projection recedes to infinity. Likewise there are other sub-groups which are equivalent to the non-Euclidean displacements. It therefore results that all geometries, whether Euclidean or not, are implicitly contained in projective geometry from which they are obtained by specialization. No wonder that Cayley was tempted to exclaim, somewhat prematurely, that "projective geometry is all geometry"!

Cayley's remark was premature because he could not foresee that by the beginning of the twentieth century mathematicians would be able to invent a still more fundamental geometry—topology—by venturing to consider the invariant properties of groups of transformations much more general than those of projection and section utilized in projective geometry. Thus, for instance, if we stretch a circular rubber band, we may turn it into an ellipse, triangle, or any other closed curve. Whatever we do, all the curves into which the band is distorted have one common property, that of connectivity. This merely means that no matter how unlike all of them may look, they are all alike in that the curve remains all of one piece so that one could proceed from one location on the curve to any other without encountering a gap anywhere. More precisely, such curves have two properties:

(i) The omission of a single point leaves them each connected.
(ii) The omission of two points will in each case disconnect the figure.

In this new geometry of distortion or topology, all such figures—circles, ellipses, triangles, polygons, etc.—are on a par and are designated by the same term, a "simple closed curve." Similarly, a sphere, spheroid, ellipsoid, or a cube are topologically equivalent but differ from the surface of an anchor ring (torus) in the following manner: If S is the surface of a sphere or cube, then the omission of a simple closed curve in S disconnects, but a simple closed curve on a torus may or may not disconnect, depending on the particular simple closed curve chosen. Such properties of curves and surfaces as those exemplified here are topological properties. In accordance with Klein's fundamental principle mentioned earlier, topology may be defined as the study of invariant properties under the group of all possible continuous transformations such as twistings, bendings, stretchings, or contractions without anything being torn apart.

If topology is the most cultivated branch of mathematics today, it is because it bids fair to add a new dimension to mathematical thought. Its central concept is neither number nor quantity but what we may call structure, wherein attention is focused not on quantitative but on qualitative differences. This is why many consider that it may well be the mathematics of the future.

Nor is this extension of geometry to topology yet the last word in abstract generalization. For geometry need not be a study of properties of spaces, that is, sets or manifolds of an *infinite* number of points. In recent years there has sprung up a class of finite geometries wherein we study a *finite* number of un-defined elements which we may for suggestiveness call "points" but which may be any objects of thought whatever, subject to a few very general conditions or postulates. To name only two out of the five postulates required to develop one such system of finite geometry, the set S of finite elements or "points" is such that it contains one or more sub-sets called "lines," each containing at least three "points." Secondly, the set S is such that if A and B are two distinct "points" there is one and only one "line" that contains both A and B—the line AB and so on. On such a system of definitions and postulates one can rear logically a body of propositions analogous to that of the usual projective geom-etry except for the one requirement that the number of "points" considered is finite. This is the justification for using the name geometry for the configurations here defined. Many of the propositions of projective geometry can be developed from postulates such as those specified above without saying whether the num-ber of "points" is finite or infinite. In fact, this procedure is so illuminating that the finite geometries justify themselves in the light which they throw on ordi-nary projective geometry. But they also have other uses, particularly in the de-velopment of the theory of permutation groups such as the group of six shuffles mentioned earlier. In fact, finite geometries may be treated as a chapter in group theory and conversely.

Because of the fusion of finite geometries and group algebra, the theory has been extensively applied by mathematical statisticians to evolve the so-called "confounded" as well as balanced block designs, which are only rationalized ways of arranging agricultural experiments for testing varieties of seeds and manures. Thanks to the highly abstract nature of the underlying ideas of finite geometries and group theory, it has been possible to reduce the whole range of statistical problems from balanced designs to error-correcting codes to a geometrical problem of astonishing sweep, versatility, and power. Such a prob-lem has been called by R. C. Bose the "packing" problem because all the problems which it subsumes amount to packing, or finding the maximum num-ber of distinct points, in a finite abstract space so that no pre-assigned number, say, n, of them are "dependent." For example, if n is three, no three of them should be on the same straight line as otherwise only two of them would de-termine the line on which the third also lies and they would not be independent of one another. If n is four, no four of them should lie on a plane to ensure their independence, and so on.

Finally, the calculus too, not to be left behind, began to wear a new look with its flight into the ethereal realms of abstraction, as for example in the new theories of "measure." Till about the close of the nineteenth century it was mainly concerned with rates of growth of entities in *continuous* flux. But entities in real life change continuously as well as abruptly. While the linear continuum—a set of points on a straight line—is a replica of continuous change, a straight line segment punctured with an infinity of gaps embodies the essential attribute of entities subject to abrupt or discontinuous changes. Theories of "measure" came to the fore in order to solve the problem of measuring the magnitude of such absolutely discontinuous infinite point sets as a line segment with infinite gaps. If we have a finite set of discrete objects such as a bunch of bananas, we can define its "magnitude" by merely counting the number of objects belonging to it. But in the case of infinite point sets this method does not work. We have, therefore, to devise some other way of measuring the magnitude of such sets. If the infinite point set is a continuous straight line segment PQ (see Fig. 2) consisting of points whose distance from the origin O lies between

FIG. 2

two real numbers, say, $\frac{1}{3}$ and $\frac{3}{4}$, the length $\frac{3}{4}-\frac{1}{3}=\frac{5}{12}$ of the segment can be taken as the "magnitude" of the set of points on the line segment PQ. But it is not clear how we should define an analogue of length when the point set is not a continuous segment but an absolutely discontinuous set such as the line segment OA, with all the intermediate points whose distance is a rational proper fraction like $\frac{1}{2}$, $\frac{2}{3}$, etc., removed. We shall refer to it in the sequel as the point set S. The length of the full segment OA, namely, 1, cannot a priori be taken as a measure of its "magnitude," as this length also includes an infinity of rational points like $\frac{1}{2}$, $\frac{2}{3}$, ... expressly excluded from the segment.

The first to suggest a method for assessing the magnitude or "measure" of absolutely discontinuous infinite point sets like such an infinitely perforated line segment as the set S was the German mathematician, Hankel. He was followed by Harnack, Stolz, and Cantor, who further developed his idea during the 1880's. It was presently superseded by that of the celebrated French mathematician, Émile Borel. In 1902 Henri Lebesgue, a pupil of Borel, extended his master's theory and showed a way of measuring the magnitude or length analogue of absolutely discontinuous infinite point sets like S. Lebesgue's discovery came none too soon, for already discontinuity had begun to invade physics. Planck, during the preceding year, had discovered that a black body radiates energy in such a way that the associated action varies discontinuously, that is, always in whole numbers of action packets or "quanta," but never in fractions of a quantum. Hitherto it was tacitly assumed that most physical quantities varied continuously. Calculus was therefore almost exclusively preoccupied with continuous variables or functions of such variables, which had no more than a few isolated discontinuities at the most. Now that it began to be realized that the structure of electricity, matter, and action in energy was granular, so that measures of these quantities varied in jumps or discontinuously, studies of point sets, which could serve as replicas of absolute discontinuity, became socially important. Nevertheless, for a time the pure theory of point sets plowed its lonely furrow without any thought of possible applications. For, once Lebesgue had shown the way, more and more abstract theories of measuring the "magnitude" of point sets were created so as to include all the phenomena of continuity, discontinuity, limit, integrability, differentiability, etc., within the orbit of their sweep.

By the late 1920's it seemed as though the "magnitude" or "measure" theory, as it is generally called, had gone too far in advance of its applications. Fortunately the balance between theory and practice was redressed in the 1930's, when Kolmogorov first applied the measure theory of point sets to give a new definition of mathematical probability—now beginning to dominate quantum physics. Since then the measure theory of point sets has been extensively applied in mathematical statistics, electronics, telephone theory, cybernetics, econometrics, theory of games and economic behavior, theory of insurance risks, stochastic or random processes such as the growth of biological populations and the fluctuation problem of cosmic ray showers, and so on.

In all these problems the mathematical abstract model embodying their essential feature is concerned with certain states of affairs denoted by a number of magnitudes. Any such state of affairs can be represented by a "point" in some imaginary space, exactly as a salesman may represent the state of his business by graphing his annual turnovers against his corresponding costs. Here graph paper is the space in which points representing the annual states of his business are located. But when a state of affairs has to be represented by sets of three, four, . . . n, . . . numbers, "graphing" has to be resorted to in imaginary (abstract) spaces of correspondingly higher dimensions. A succession of such states of affairs is then represented by a set of "points" in some such multidimensional space. These problems thus boil down to a consideration of point sets in imaginary spaces of several dimensions. In many cases the point sets obtained are not continuous sets. To give mathematics a foothold in such cases, it is necessary to devise a way of assigning to the point sets some magnitude or measure which plays the same role with respect to them as length does in the case of continuous straight lines. That is why many of these problems cannot be solved without resort to Lebesgue's theory of measure, which attempts to define an analogue of length when the point set is *not* a continuous interval but a complicated set like the infinitely punctured set S already mentioned.

With the invention of Lebesgue's measure theory it became possible to generalize the fundamental problem of the calculus to apply to discontinuous sets as well. For one of the fundamental problems the calculus was designed to solve was that of summing or integrating a function over a continuous interval, area, or space—a problem which crops up over and over again in the most varied fields of science. For instance, to calculate the distance traveled by a moving body like a satellite during any interval of time, we have to integrate the speed function over the time interval. In the design of irrigation dams, it is necessary to integrate the pressure function over the entire area of the dam surface to derive the whole pressure that the dam face has to endure. In many electrical problems we have to integrate the electric force function over a region of space. In all these problems the value of a function is defined at every point of a continuous interval, area, or region of space, and we have to sum these values corresponding to all the points of the interval, area, or region in question.

In more complex problems, the function is not defined over a continuous interval, area, or region but only over a non-continuous set of points lying in such intervals, areas, or regions. The solution of these problems requires the summation of such functions over non-continuous sets of points. For example, consider the fundamental problem of mathematical statistics. Here we wish to infer the unknown characteristic of a given population by observing samples of some fixed size drawn from it in a suitable manner.

For the sake of simplicity let the sample size be such that a single item drawn from our population constitutes the sample. The sample is therefore defined by a single magnitude measuring the particular attribute under study of the selected item. If we take on a straight line a point whose distance from a fixed origin is the single magnitude pertaining to the observed sample, we may represent this single-unit sample by such a point. If the entire population consists of a finite number of members, say 10,000, it is obvious that the number of samples that can be drawn from it is also finite. In fact, in this case the number of single-unit samples that can be drawn is the same, namely, 10,000. Consequently the totality of all possible samples that we can draw may be represented by a set s consisting of 10,000 points on a straight line, each point representing some possible sample. A sub-class of samples out of this totality of all possible samples, such as, for example, those whose sample magnitudes lie between any two arbitrarily given values, will naturally be denoted by some sub-set s' of the main set s.

Now each sample has a probability of its occurrence depending on the method of drawing the sample and the constitution of the population. Hence to each sample point of the set s of the aggregate of all possible sample points there corresponds its probability of selection. In other words, the probability function of the sample is defined only for the non-continuous set s of sample points and no others. But the solution of the sampling problem requires the calculation of the probability that the sample selected belongs to the sub-set s' of some particular sub-class of samples. This means that the probability function has to be summed over the non-continuous set s'. When the population considered is infinite, the corresponding sets s and s' of sample points become infinite point sets which moreover are non-continuous in many cases. This is why it is necessary to generalize the notion of integration so as to permit integration of functions over non-continuous sets. Such a generalization was provided by Lebesgue's theory of measure and integration. Theories of integration thus revolutionized by Lebesgue's concept of measure carried the calculus as far beyond Cauchy and Riemann as those of the latter had carried it beyond Newton and Leibnitz.

The foregoing account of the numerous ramifications of the four traditional branches of mathematics—arithmetic, algebra, geometry, and calculus—by abstraction, generalization, and cross-fertilization of one branch by the ideas of others has inevitably been too selective to be really representative. It has aimed at merely sampling a few of the highlights of this immense creation of human thought during the past 100 years or so, because an adequate communication of something of the diversity, utility, and beauty of mathematics would require several volumes. For such is the versatility and sweep of its methodology that it can handle problems as varied as those of space and motion, chance and probability, statistics and social sciences, art and literature, logic and philosophy, ethics and warfare, music and architecture, value and demand, war and foreign politics, food and population, Röntgen rays and crystals, heredity and inheritance, as well as those of human thinking itself and of electronic brains.

IV. TWENTIETH-CENTURY CHEMISTRY

By O. Theodor Benfey

Earlham College

By the turn of the century eighty-three of the chemical elements had been discovered. In the previous decades the periodic law[8] provided a means of organizing the elements as they were discovered and of predicting the properties of presumably missing ones. Some of these were quickly found and their properties gave remarkable support to the predictive power of the periodic law.

Once chemists had accepted atoms as the conceptual building blocks out of which they would construct their universe, they needed an explanation as to why atoms often cling together (that is, why solid materials exist at all) and more importantly, why a given element associates with some elements and not with others. Further, it had been established that there was a definite limit to the number of atoms with which a given atom can associate. Thus chemical affinity is quite different from gravitational or electrical interaction, for the former is universal and the latter non-specific with regard to the material constituents of charged substances. Chemical interaction seemed to be specific and limited; a saturation combining capacity or "valence" could be assigned to each element.

Organic chemistry, or the chemistry of carbon compounds, had developed a deceptively simple sign language, the language of structural formulas, for depicting the molecules of its thousands of compounds. It was based on a number of "valence" or bonding rules: (1) carbon had four links by which it could attach itself to other atoms, while nitrogen had three, oxygen two, and hydrogen and chlorine one each; (2) for a stable compound all valence links had to be used up, that is, they had all to be involved in linking with other atoms; and (3) carbon atoms have a seemingly unlimited capacity to form carbon chains or rings. The following were some of the formulas which resulted:

8 See page 971.

$$
\begin{array}{cccc}
& & & \text{H H H H H H} \\
& & & \text{| | | | | |} \\
& & \text{H H} & \text{H-C-C-C-C-C-C=O} \\
& & \text{| |} & \text{| | | | |} \\
\text{H-O} & \text{H-N-H} & \text{H-C-C-O-H} & \text{O O O O O} \\
\text{|} & \text{|} & \text{| |} & \text{| | | | |} \\
\text{H} & \text{H} & \text{H H} & \text{H H H H H} \\
\text{water} & \text{ammonia} & \text{ethyl alcohol} & \text{glucose}
\end{array}
$$

In 1874 J. H. van't Hoff (Holland, 1852-1911) and J. A. Le Bel (France, 1847-1930) independently proposed that the valences of carbon must be directed towards the four corners of a regular triangular pyramid (a tetrahedron). The atoms were therefore being endowed both with specific, limited linking powers and with quite definite directional characteristics. Yet the atom was supposed to be the ultimate unit, uncuttable and hence presumably without substructure.

The nature of the valence forces operating in organic compounds was a total mystery at the turn of the century. In salt-like substances, on the other hand, an electrochemical doctrine dating back to J. J. Berzelius (Sweden, 1779-1848) in the 1820's explained compound formation as due to electrical interaction. Table salt (sodium chloride) was written Na^+ Cl^-. Metals and hydrogen were considered electropositive, nonmetals in general electronegative, but the reason for these charges was equally unknown. In 1893 Alfred Werner (Switzerland, 1866-1919) brought the same type of order into one other class of compounds, the complex compounds formed by many metals and known as the coordination compounds. An example is the cobaltammine chloride, $Co(NH_3)_6Cl_3$, in which, according to Werner, six primary valences hold the ammonia molecules (NH_3) close to the cobalt atom while salt-like forces attract the three chlorine atoms to the cobalt-ammonia complex. The six ammonias were postulated to occupy the corners of a regular octahedron. The number six and the directions of the bonds were necessary consequences of experimental facts but no theory was in sight to explain or predict them.

The stage was thus set for scientists of the twentieth century to delve below the established patterns of behavior in order to explain by some model or a set of postulates the necessity of the rules and patterns observed.

The explanation had to await the disintegration of the atom, the cutting of the uncuttable, the recognition of a substructure to account for the specificity of atomic properties.

As early as 1816, William Prout (Great Britain, 1785-1850) had noticed that the atomic weights of many elements seemed to be remarkably close to whole number multiples of the atomic weight of hydrogen. He therefore proposed, within eight years of the enunciation of Dalton's atomic hypothesis, that far from being ultimate, all atoms were probably composed of hydrogen atoms. The proposal met with serious objections but now turns out to have been a remarkably accurate intuition of the later trend of thought concerning atomic structure.

During the latter part of the nineteenth century evidence was beginning to accumulate for the existence of constituents of atoms—particularly for the presence in atoms of the unit of electricity, the electron. In 1898, A. H. Becquerel (France, 1852-1908) asked his student Marie Sklodowska Curie (Poland-France, 1867-1934) to study the strange rays emitted by uranium ores. The radiation was traced to a number of elements, uranium itself, polonium (named in honor of Madame Curie's mother country), and radium. It was found that metallic radium atoms spontaneously emitted a small particle which turned out to be the negatively charged electron, a heavy particle which proved to be a positively charged helium atom, and very high energy x-rays. By losing a helium particle, radium was transformed into the inert gas radon which by a series of disintegrations ended up as the element lead. Electrons were being discovered in all elements, a fact which led to J. J. Thomson's (Great Britain, 1856-1940) "raisin pudding" model of the atom, a mass of positive electricity in which the electrons were embedded (1904). The picture had to be severely and most unexpectedly modified (1911) when Ernest Rutherford (New Zealand–Great Britain, 1871-1937) and his students, bombarding thin metal foils with the charged helium particles, found some of these bouncing back while others passed through almost undeflected. If the atom were composed as Thomson had suggested, the particles should be deflected over a broad range of angles with none suffering complete reversal. The new facts were only explainable if most of the mass of the atom was concentrated in an extremely small portion of the atom's volume. The smeared-out Thomson atom gave way to one that was almost wholly empty space, a heavy but minute positive nucleus in the center with almost weightless negative electrons outside. To keep the electrons from being pulled into the nucleus, they were made to move in orbits, the analogy with planetary motion being irresistible. But the classic electromagnetic theory of Maxwell, unlike gravitational theory governing the motion of planets, demands that a rotating electron must give off light and therefore lose energy. It should accordingly spiral slowly into the nucleus. Niels Bohr (Denmark, 1885-1963), whose courage was strong enough to overcome his philosophical hesitations, saved the day by postulating that the electrons do *not* lose energy while rotating in a planetary orbit. With such an assumption, quantitative conclusions could be reached that agreed accurately with experimental data. The proposal, though eminently successful, brought with it the threat of a permanent split between the laws of everyday experience and those holding on the atomic level. The gulf was bridged in the 1920's by demonstrating that Newton's and Maxwell's laws were the consequences of atomic laws when enormous numbers of atoms are involved.

A link between atomic structure and the periodic table of the elements was established largely through the pioneering work of H. G-J. Moseley (Great Britain, 1887-1915) on x-rays emitted by the elements when bombarded by electrons. The "atomic number," that is, the number assigned to an element when all the elements were placed in the order of increasing atomic weight, corresponded in practically every case to the positive charge on the nucleus and was equal to the number of electrons around the nucleus. Hydrogen, the lightest element, has one electron; if the electronic charge is taken as -1, then the hydrogen nucleus has a charge of $+1$. The next heavier element, helium, has a nuclear charge of $+2$ and two electrons, lithium a charge of $+3$ and three electrons, up to uranium with 92 electrons around a nuclear charge of $+92$.

This information was precisely what was needed to devise valence theories and to account for the periodicity in the properties of the elements. If the third, the eleventh, and the nineteenth element (in order of increasing atomic weight) had similar chemical properties, then this similarity should be describable in terms of some common structural feature of their atoms. The electrons were accordingly grouped in "shells" or "energy levels" and the plausible assumption was made that similar elements contained the same number of electrons in their *outermost* shells. Detailed proposals as to the grouping of electrons were made in 1916 by W. Kossel (Germany, 1888-   ) and G. N. Lewis (U.S.A., 1875-1946), in 1919 by I. Langmuir (U.S.A., 1881-1957), and in 1921 by C. R. Bury (Great Britain) and Bohr. During the subsequent decades these shells have been further divided into subshells and sub-subshells to account for finer details. With their atomic models, Kossel and Lewis in 1916 proposed valence theories for the formation of compounds. In view of the fact that a certain series of elements, the "inert gases," helium, neon, argon, krypton, and xenon, were believed to be completely unreactive (the first "inert" gas compounds were prepared in 1962), the suggestion was made that other atoms and molecules reacted in such a manner as to rearrange electron groups into those of the inert gases by gain or loss or sharing of electrons. Since the reason for the stability of the inert gas electron groupings themselves demanded an explanation, an even deeper level of concepts was sought. It was found through wave mechanics, the application of the mathematics of waves to atomic processes.

Wave mechanics had its origin on the one hand in the quantum hypothesis of Planck and Einstein, the proposal that light was emitted and transmitted in "packets" or quanta, and on the other in the suggestion of Louis de Broglie (France, 1892-   ), based on symmetry considerations, that if light had both wave and particle characteristics, so should material particles. E. Schrödinger (Germany, 1887-1961) accordingly introduced de Broglie's computed wave length for an electron into the standard mathematical equations for wave motion and originated a completely novel and powerful tool for the handling of atomic phenomena. P. A. M. Dirac (Great Britain, 1902-   ) has claimed that through wave mechanics most of physics and all of chemistry can "in principle" be known. The difficulty seems to reside in the complexity of the needed mathematics. Most chemical problems are so complex that they require severe and rather arbitrary simplifications of wave mechanical principles in order to be solved at all. The simplifying assumptions can be justified only by the pragmatic test of agreement with experimental results.

That electrons in fact have wave properties was demonstrated independently in 1927 by C. J. Davisson (U.S.A., 1881-1958) and L. H. Germer (U.S.A., 1896-   ), and by G. P. Thomson (Great Britain, 1892-   ; son of J. J. Thomson). The characteristic behavior of light waves was duplicated by electrons of suitable energy. Electron diffraction techniques have taken their place with x-ray methods as two of the most powerful experimental tools for studying phenomena at the atomic level. The principle of the microscope has been modified to permit the use of electrons in place of light waves. The resulting "electron microscope" has found wide use in "photographing" systems, particularly of biochemical interest such as single protein molecules, viruses (which are also proteins), and biological cell constituents which are too small to be observed with ordinary microscopes.

The newer valence theories were quickly applied to organic chemistry. The valence link of the 1860's was seen to be a pair of electrons, which later became a "charge cloud" or was described in terms of a "probability distribution." Electronic theories were devised, at first almost exclusively in organic chemistry, notably by R. Robinson (Great Britain, 1886-   ) and C. K. Ingold (Great Britain, 1893-   ) to explain why a reagent attacked a molecule at a particular carbon atom rather than another, and why one reagent acted much faster than another, even though their structure was only slightly different. These theories were largely built on information obtained from the study of speeds or rates of reaction. Enormous developments were in turn made in the theoretical and practical understanding of reaction rates and the factors determining their magnitudes, a field now known as reaction kinetics. This field of study together with thermodynamics, or the study of energy and its transformations, largely built on the pioneering work of J. W. Gibbs (U.S.A., 1839-1903), have become the two major approaches to the conceptual mastery of chemical behavior. In the hands of Robinson and Ingold, the line formulas of the nineteenth century became cluttered with straight and curved arrows, intended to show the movement or potential movement of electrons. A parallel approach closer to the procedures of wave mechanics was anticipated by F. G. Arndt (Germany, 1885-   ) and developed by L. Pauling (U.S.A., 1901-   ). It has become known as the theory of resonance. Both approaches have been carried over into the realm of inorganic chemistry and have proved of enormous value. In time these theories and the new techniques developed in conjunction with them made possible the design of syntheses planned in the greatest detail, to create molecules not only with the correct numbers and kinds of atoms linked in the proper order but also with each valence link oriented in a predetermined direction. Such "stereospecific" syntheses are of the utmost importance in biochemistry where the simple change in orientation of one link may turn a life-saving drug into a poison. R. B. Woodward (U.S.A., 1917-   ) has spoken of the new theoretical and experimental tools as having brought about a second revolution in organic chemistry, resulting in the syntheses of extremely complex compounds of biochemical interest and the elucidation of the structure of others. Woodward and W. E. Doering (U.S.A., 1917-   ) in 1944 synthesized the antimalarial drug quinine, and Woodward more recently has made reserpine, the tranquilizing drug found in a Himalayan plant. The syntheses of morphine (M. D. Gates, U.S.A., 1915-), of cortisone, and of penicillin have been reported in recent years representing achievements enormously more complex than those of the sulfa drugs in the 1930's that opened up the era of chemotherapy. Pauling has proposed a detailed helix or spiral structure for proteins, and in the last few years the detailed order in which the approximately twenty different amino acids are organized in a number of proteins, including insulin, has been unraveled. The detailed structure of some nucleic acids, constituents of the cell nucleus and responsible for the transmission of genetic information, has also been worked out.

Parallel to the analysis of proteins and other giant molecules of nature, chemists attempted to make giant molecules of their own. The polymer and plastics industry resulted, creating materials of almost any desired combination of properties from plexiglass to the protein-like nylon (W. H. Carothers, U.S.A., 1896-1937) to "silly putty," and of use industrially as building materials, wearing apparel, kitchen utensils, and toys. A new field, molecular engineering, has emerged, permitting the design on the molecular level of materials needed by architects for particular construction purposes. The economic effect on some established industries has been disastrous, but in others competition has led to extensive chemical research to make the earlier product, such as cotton or wood, more useful.

Biochemists have done more than analyze the structures of their compounds. All the major metabolic pathways have been traced and considerable progress is being made in understanding the action of enzymes, those protein materials in the organism that permit reactions to occur at body temperature in the cell which chemists can only simulate under extreme conditions if at all. Viruses have been crystallized, a property thought characteristic of non-living materials, and yet have been shown to be capable of duplicating again after crystallization. They have also been cut into non-duplicating fragments and reunited. The border between the living and the non-living seems to be bridgeable in the laboratory, though it is hard to define unambiguously at the molecular level what the terms "living" and "non-living" mean. The newer experiments certainly attest to the continuity of evolution at the period of the emergence of "life."

In the inorganic realm, or the realm of compounds not containing carbon, three major factors led to a resurgence of activity. The success of the techniques and new theoretical approaches of organic chemistry led to their application in inorganic systems, with gratifying results. The new tools of x-ray and electron diffraction were permitting the elucidation of the internal structure of molecules and crystals while new spectroscopic techniques permitted the study of their internal motions. And the experiments with high-energy particles begun by Rutherford, led first to the realization of the dream of the alchemists, the transmutation of the elements, the conversion, though only on a minute scale, of base metals into gold, and in 1938 to the demonstration of uranium fission by O. Hahn (Germany, 1879-) and F. Strassmann (Germany, 1902-), and the possibility of utilizing nuclear energy for peace and war. For the practical utilization of that discovery numerous problems in the chemistry of relatively unfamiliar elements had to be solved. As a by-product of the nuclear energy industry, radioactive "tracers" became available for the study of reaction mechanisms and for following biological pathways in plants, animals, and man. G. T. Seaborg (U.S.A., 1912-   ) and co-workers became the creators of new "transuranic" elements, that is, elements whose atoms were heavier than those of uranium. The periodic table currently contains one hundred and three elements, when the limit before the second World War was thought to be ninety-two. A further by-product was the development of the radiocarbon dating technique (W. F. Libby, U.S.A., 1908-   ), of enormous importance to archaeologists and geologists, which deduces the age of materials from the amount of radioactive carbon still measurable in carbon-containing rocks, fossils, or man-made products. Great interest has focused recently on Werner's coordination compounds, and a new "Ligand Field Theory" combining classical ideas of electrical attraction and repulsion with insights from wave mechanics has proved highly successful both in explaining the nature and direction of the valence linkages and in stimulating new research. Developments are also rapid in the understanding of solids and their reactions at normal and elevated temperatures.

One other important fact needs to be mentioned in order to understand modern chemistry—the emergence in this century of a whole series of complex measuring instruments, the "black boxes": mass spectroscopes, spectrophotometers, electron diffraction apparatus, and many others, which turn out information at an unprecedented rate. It has been estimated that published chemical information has been and is doubling every thirteen years. At this rate, as much chemical information will be published in the next thirteen years as all the information ever published in chemistry. Such a rate of increase makes it impossible for anyone to "keep up" with a major field and poses an almost insoluble problem for the scientific journals and abstracting services in their present form.

The expansion of chemical information during the twentieth century has run parallel to an ever greater theoretical mastery of the subject matter. While chemistry in the second half of the nineteenth century had been largely an empirical science, its subject matter has become more and more organized by the two disciplines of thermodynamics and kinetics, and both of these have been enormously enriched and refined by the insights and techniques of wave mechanics. The central conceptual directions of modern chemistry may be said to be the interest in energy changes, in structure, and in the *process* or mechanism of change. These are not interests confined to chemistry, but are broad viewpoints applicable to and pursued in many areas of the biological, physical, and even social sciences. The boundaries between the sciences are becoming blurred and particularly the one between chemistry and physics is fast disappearing. The physicist's current preoccupation with the antics of very short-lived particles seems like a typically chemical activity. One is tempted to suggest that whereas chemistry is becoming a more unified, deductive science, physics since the turn of the century has become more empirical. In any event their activities are becoming remarkably alike and may soon be recognized as a single discipline.

V. TWENTIETH-CENTURY BIOLOGY AND PHYSIOLOGY

By Howard A. Schneider

Rockefeller Institute

Nineteenth-century biology was massively molded by Charles Darwin and the theory of natural selection. The closing years of the century, however, had seen the mists of doubt arise. These doubts arose mainly from the demands which the theory of natural selection made on ideas of heredity, and these latter seemed incapable of giving a clear and corroborative support to the Darwinian synthesis. Darwin himself had recognized the difficulty and had struggled unsuccessfully to solve it. For like tended to beget like, and it was easy to see how natural selection, as conservator, would preserve the fit progeny of fit parents. But Darwin had argued that natural selection was an innovating process as well, that fitter parents and their fitter progeny would be favored, and that there would be a parade of change and progress through the eons. But, precisely, where did these selectable, and "fitter," differences come from? How were they transmitted? Natural selection demanded this transmission. But how was it assured? And with what precision?

The answers to these questions, all now part of the twentieth-century science of genetics, have blown away the mists of doubt, and Neo-Darwinism, or Darwin-Mendelism, must now be regarded as virtually unchallenged. These genetic discoveries began to be supplied before the twentieth century was a year old, and came about through the rediscovery of Mendel's laws, which were the cornerstones of genetics and which had remained unremarked for almost forty years in the volumes of a local natural history society in Brünn, Austria. Simultaneously, in 1900, deVries in Amsterdam, Correns at Tübingen, and Tschermak in Vienna, arrived at Mendel's conclusions on the laws of hybridization. The bewildering ebb and flow of biologic characteristics with the generations were simply explained on the supposition of discrete determinants (genes) in the germ cells of the parents. These were united, as pairs, in the fertilized egg. Alternative aspects of contrasted characters, as, say, dwarfness and tallness in Mendel's famous peas, were under the control of alternative genes (alleles), but one of these (for tallness) was "dominant" while the second (for dwarfism) was "recessive," and so a plant containing both would be tall. Both genes for the recessive dwarfism had to be present for a dwarf plant to result. Biology had, by this outlook, found its atomism, and determinants of biological characters were reduced to indivisible units. The progeny of sexual systems reflected the probabilistic mathematical laws of the statistical "shuffling of the genes." By this analysis biology received the same impetus which was injected into physics at earlier period when the molecular theory of gases, and the quantum theory of energy considered as particle, made intelligible on a statistical basis the predictable behavior of vast numbers in terms of distributions at the same time that a single unit remained shrouded in a cloud of uncertainty.

The materialistic basis for the Mendelian mechanism was soon supplied by studies on the behavior of certain cellular elements, the chromosomes, which were found to be halved (meiosis) in a random fashion at the time of formation of the germinal cells (sperm and ova) and then recombined again to the full chromosomal number at fertilization (zygote formation). In all of the cellular divisions which followed, from the fertilized egg to the adult, this chromosomal structure was found to be faithfully replicated in all of the body cells. Man, for example, has 23 pairs of chromosomes, or 46. A departure from 46, by some mischance, to 47 results in an abnormal individual, such as is found in "Mongolian" idiocy.

T. H. Morgan in America and Bateson in England were early pioneers in the construction of modern genetics. DeVries in Holland directed attention to mutations, the sudden and still-unexplained change in a particular gene, and H. J. Muller showed how radiant energy, such as x-rays, could increase the mutation rate. A link between the gene and its immediate chemical effects was presented by Beadle and Tatum who showed, in the mold Neurospora, that specific reactions, with specific chemical products, were under the direct control, in a 1:1 correspondence, of specific genes. A bridge was thus connected between genetics and the chemistry of living cells. The chemical nature of these genetic determinants was illuminated by the microbiological studies of Avery, McLeod, and McCarty. They succeeded in transforming one heritable type of pneumococcus into another heritable type by material extracted from the latter. The material thus responsible was shown to be a desoxy-ribose nucleic acid, or DNA. Here, in a sense, was a naked dispersible gene. In turn, the DNA macromolecule has been found to have a physical structure represented by a double helix (Watson, Crick), and one DNA varies from another by some "code" by which genetic "information" is conveyed by the spatial and sequential arrangements, in the molecule, of four nitrogenous bases, two purines and two pyrimidines. It is obvious that the solution of this problem will have far-reaching effects.

The use of microorganisms in genetic studies, microbial genetics, brought to the science greatly enhanced powers of resolution of the finer details of the gene, a resolution made possible by the ease of dealing with organisms by the millions. For Tatum and Lederberg in 1947 made the astonishing discovery that some bacteria had sex. Various mating types of the humble colon bacillus, *E. coli,* are now recognized, and theoretical genetics has been enriched by their use. The science of genetics, reborn in the opening year of the twentieth century, has penetrated, in its insights, into most of biology and must now be regarded as central in modern biology. The reason for this is not hard to find if one but recalls the simple fact that it is heredity—that like tends to beget like, that forms tend to persist, even as they change—that conserves life in the face of the vicissitudes of the environment.

But it would be false to convey the idea that the genetic framework is rigid and all-determining. For some characters the rigidity is real enough, as Landsteiner's work on the distribution of the human blood types showed. Here the determinism is such that, for example, the serological identification of blood type for an individual is admissible in courts of law and becomes part of forensic medicine. But modern physiological genetics, founded by Goldschmidt, is replete with examples of how the genetic potential for some characteristics can be achieved, or not achieved, depending on the environment. Thus the older "either-or" alternative—either genetics or environment—as a single available choice between mutually exclusive determinant systems behind biological characters, has lost its force. The modern viewpoint recognizes the biological characteristic as the realization, partial or complete, of a genotype in a particular and, sometimes, a necessarily precisely defined environment.

One can hardly continue at this point without giving account of another facet of twentieth-century biology, the rapidly expanding science of biochemistry. That there was indeed a chemistry of life had been recognized in the nineteenth-century. But this view had been preoccupied with the dominant goal of organic chemists, that of the chemical composition of animals and plants. The opening years of the present century saw a redefinition of the aim, i.e., the chemical definition of the functions and transformations in the organism. The continuous breakdown (catabolism) and rebuilding (anabolism) of living material became foremost as a goal for understanding. Another important aspect in the change in outlook sprang from the revolt against taxonomic preoccupations in biology, a revolt led by Jacques Loeb and Otto Warburg, who directed attention away from the differences between organisms and felt strongly that the proper subject matter for biochemistry was those discernible similarities in the life processes, which were assumed to be common to all living things. The study of whole organisms was replaced by investigation of cells, such as blood corpuscles, yeasts, and sea urchin eggs. On this historic choice lie the reasons for the horizontal, across-the-species, development of modern biochemistry.

Now, the chemical reactions of living cells are carried forward at the relatively modest temperature ranges compatible with life on this globe as we know it. Many of these reactions are duplicated in the laboratory only under severe conditions of heat, acidity, pressure, and the like. How did the living cell achieve this? Biochemistry provided the answer with the elucidation of the bio-catalysts, the enzymes. The enzymes proved to be protein macromolecules, as Sumner (1936), Northrop, and Kunitz showed. Some of these enzymes needed the assisting participation of smaller, dialyzable and heat-stable molecules, which are the co-enzymes. All were caught up in a web of complicated reactions in which, step by step, catalyzed enzyme by enzyme, the organic constituents of cells were broken down to yield the unceasing flow of energy by which the living cell maintains its thermodynamically improbable existence. Some of these reaction systems are of the most ingenious kinds. Krebs, for example, showed that urea was formed in the livers of animals in the constant turning of a cyclic series of reactions, constantly accepting source materials and just as constantly turning out the reaction product for excretion in the urine.

Dynamic biochemistry, since 1936, following George Hevesy, has made great use of radioactive isotopes as "tracers," especially phosphorus 32 and carbon 14, which reveal most impressively the speed by which all the body constituents are kept in constant flux of catabolism and anabolism. The technique has proved especially valuable in detecting intermediate compounds of very short duration in some of the complicated reactions in living cells, as was capitalized by Calvin in studies on photosynthesis.

Time and again, however, the biochemist is brought back to the enzymes and the problem of protein structures they pose. The past decades saw the verifications of the peptide chain theory of protein structure. The study of bits and pieces of these chains and the final units, the amino acids, was advanced by the introduction of chromatography on paper (Martin and Synge) and on columns of adsorbents or ion-exchange resins (Tswett, Moore, and Stein). Such analytical studies reached a climax when Sanger mapped the amino acid chain in a crystalline protein, insulin.

Animal biochemistry had an interest, too, in the growing evidence that the life of the animal had a dependence for some special organic items which were present in minute amounts in natural foodstuffs. Two streams of interest coalesced around 1915 to give rise to a newer knowledge of nutrition and saw the rise of the vitamins (Funk, 1912). One stream was the study of the deficiency diseases—rickets, scurvy, beriberi, and pellagra. The other stream sprang from the attempts to provide diets suitable for animal life composed entirely of chemically purified ingredients (Hopkins, McCollum). The 1930's and 1940's saw the climax of these efforts in the determination of structure and synthesis of fifteen such vitamins.

A striking instance of the deep-seated unity of the biochemical outlook of the period was the finding (Lohmann and Schuster, 1937) that a co-enzyme, cocarboxylase, which is necessary in the metabolism of carbohydrates, was none other than the phosphorylated form of a vitamin, thiamine (vitamin B_1). Several other such connections between vitamins and the biochemical processes of metabolism have been recognized, and we can leave off our brief survey with the view that a clear link exists between the inner world of cellular biochemical events and an outer world of nurture, including the micro-nutrients.

This increasing preoccupation with the world of smaller and smaller dimensions has become a characteristic of modern biology, and any consideration of it will bring into focus the advances in microbiology concerned with the filter-passing viruses, disease-producing agents 10 to 100 times smaller than the bacteria. The viruses are incapable of a continuing and multiplying existence apart from their host cells, and this fact posed great hurdles for their study. The last two decades have seen tremendous advances, however. The introduction of the electron microscope in the 1940's with its greater powers of resolution (400-fold over the light microscope) at last permitted the biologist to "see" the submicroscopic particles about which, however, considerable had been learned by experiment and inference. In 1910 Rous proved that fowl sarcoma could be produced by a filterable virus. In 1935 Stanley isolated the virus of tobacco mosaic disease and showed it to be a nucleoprotein, and in 1936 Max Theiler produced a living vaccine for yellow fever by "adapting" the virus by passage first to mouse brain and then through tissue cultures of chick embryo cells. The valuable technique of growing tissues outside of the organism in nutrient solution was an achievement of Ross Harrison in 1907. Improved techniques resulted, in the 1950's, in a renewed interest in the field, which was capped by Enders in the successful cultivation of poliomyelitis virus and the production of a vaccine administered to millions (Salk).

Even a cursory view of microbiology such as this would be incomplete without the inclusion of the use of chemotherapy of infectious disease. Sulfanilamide in the 1930's (Domagk) broke the air of pessimism which had accumulated that a chemical agent would ever be devised which would neatly deliver a death blow to microbial disease without harming the host. The demands of the second World War revived, at the hands of Florey and Chain, examination of an earlier discovery by Fleming of an antimicrobial agent of fungal origin, penicillin. Fleming's discovery was made part of a more systematic search of the whole globe for such antibiotics, as they came to be called, with a rich return in a whole spectrum of useful anti-infectious agents.

We must return to the beginning of the century to pick up another thread in the fabric of modern biology. The problem of coordination of function in higher forms has its solution in the consideration of two broad mechanisms, the hormones and the nervous system. The beginnings of the first are traceable to the physiologists Bayliss and Starling, who, in 1902, showed that pancreatic secretion is induced by a chemical agent formed in the intestine and transported humorally to the pancreas. These internal secretions, and the list was soon extended, are elaborated at one anatomical locus, transported by the blood to some distant second site, the target organ, and thereby affect its function. Hardy named these agents "hormones." Banting and Best in 1922 discovered the hormone insulin, which controls carbohydrate metabolism and which, in cases of insufficiency, presents features clinically recognized as diabetes. The organs elaborating such materials of interior secretion are now named endocrine glands, and their study has given rise to a whole subject in itself, labeled endocrinology. Thus, the endocrine gland, the thyroid, secretes the hormone thyroxin which controls the rate of metabolism. Thyroid insufficiency in children results in a kind of idiocy known as cretinism. The list of hormones now includes adrenalin, from the adrenal medulla, and a whole family of hormones from the adrenal cortex of which the best known, perhaps, are cortisone, anti-inflammatory in its action, and corticosterone, insufficient in Addison's disease. Male and female sex hormones are known and are chemically characterized, as are those mentioned above. One of the most interesting developments of this period has been the recognition of the anterior pituitary gland at the brain's base as a "master gland" which, by secretion of its proteinaceous hormones, controls the secretion of the other endocrines.

The nervous system, too, has a coordinating role in the higher animals. From 1906 on, the pioneer work was done by Sir Charles Sherrington. An "integration action" was shown by him to be explicable from a study of the simple reflexes and their interactions. Thus an incoming message from the peripheral nerves leading from the sense organs arrives in the central nervous system, and an appropriate signal is sent out to muscle or gland. Sherrington showed the duality possible in the effect of the incoming message on other nerve impulses, either excitation or inhibition. Time relations become of importance, for the discharging neuron has a subsequent refractory period. Modern electronics has done much to facilitate studies on the nervous system, providing inertialess means of measuring in minuscule time relations the very small currents involved (A. V. Hill, Gasser, Erlanger).

Once again we find ourselves entering the world of the very small. For example, in 1904 Thunberg showed that nervous tissue respires just as does other tissue, and in 1913 Tashiro showed that the gaseous exchange is increased on excitation. An increase in heat in the nerve following its activity would seem to be logically predicted. A. V. Hill and Gerard went to some pains to show that the heat changes involved were of the order of one-millionth of a degree centigrade per nervous impulse, with one ten-millionth of a degree attributable to the initial heat of excitation and the rest to the heat of recuperation.

Similarly, time dimensions have proved to be relatively small in the phenomena of nervous activity. When excitation is applied, there is a latency period of about one-thousandth of a second. Excitation is itself followed by a refractory phase, and Adrian (1912) showed that after this period of inexcitability there appeared a period of supernormal excitability followed by the normal state. Lucas in 1912 and Lillie in 1922 related these to metabolic changes in the nerve. Adrian's supernormal excitability phase was related to the anabolic reaction which followed the preceding catabolism.

The transmission of the nerve impulse has thus been found capable of explication in terms of electrical, metabolic, and finally biochemical factors. In these affairs one other event proved capable of analysis, i.e., the transmission of the nerve impulse to the effector cell. Otto Loewi (1931) showed that it was a relatively simple chemical, acetyl choline, which had been known since 1867, which bridged this last gap in the instance of the parasympathetic nervous system. Like many of the most important substances in biological chemistry, acetyl choline has a very short life in tissues, a fact which is due to the presence of a specific hydrolizing enzyme. The symmetry of this story of a chemical transmitter of the nervous impulses of the parasympathetic system was preserved when, for the antagonistic sympathetic nervous system, a parallel chemical transmitter, adrenalin or noradrenalin, was found by Cannon.

That consideration of the higher nervous functions could be given without the introduction of psychological ideas involving consciousness was advanced by Pavlov in 1910. The unconditioned reflexes of the simpler functions, Pavlov argued, passed into more complex reflexes conditioned by other factors, as in the well-known instance of Pavlov's salivating dogs conditioned to respond to the ringing of a dinner bell. Consciousness was thus abstracted out of the Pavlovian focus, and led to the formation of a school of psychology called behaviorism (J. B. Watson, 1914, et seq.). The behaviorists, from mechanical presuppositions, thus came to regard man as a machine, and the proper subject matter of psychology became the study of a nest of stimuli and responses.

Another approach to psychology sprang from a powerful and individual thinker, Sigmund Freud, who, in addressing himself to psychopathology, illuminated the "normal." Freud was led to a different set of assumptions, that the maturation of the individual was accompanied by the rise and maturation of powerful instinctual drives which, if thwarted unduly, or distorted into patterns not congruent with those of one's fellows, led to mental ill-health. In recent years, Freud's own long-term goal of setting forth these matters on a neurochemical basis, has received new interest, and some partially effective pharmacological agents have come to hand.

As for man himself, a unique animal still, the twentieth-century endeavors of anthropologists have cleared some of the mists from man's origins. It now seems clear that man's ancestors first trod the earth in an erect posture, not in Asia, but in Africa, about a million or more years ago. And the view has grown that it was the use of tools, crude to be sure, which led on the path to the development of the brain, from about 600 cc. to the approximate 1350 cc. of man today.

To sum up, the nineteenth-century heritage in biology, dominated by the Darwinian synthesis, began the process of redirecting the life sciences into the mainstream of scientific thought. This process began to erase a compartmentalization which had tended to set biology apart from the development of the other natural sciences, since that study seemed to be addressed to a different subject matter, animate life. But, as Copernicus forced an abandonment of a geocentricism as a fruitful way of looking at our universe, so Darwin displaced an earlier anthropocentrism when man looked at life. Living was a process we shared, and were caught up in, and the student of the process was also part of the subject to be studied. The necessity for objectivity in biology emerged with greater clarity. The twentieth century became bolder, and, as we have seen, the presuppositions of chemistry and physics were found to be of an ever-increasing usefulness. This trend is still going on, but this is not to say that it necessarily follows that *all* of life will be explicable in present-day physico-chemical terms. Chemistry and physics are changing, too, and it seems fruitless—and folly—to attempt to envisage the nature of a final total synthesis. However, the twentieth-century development of biology may be viewed from a more general viewpoint, that of its participation in some of the features which characterize the scientific endeavor as a whole. A common denominator in the advance of each of the special fields of biology, so cursorily surveyed here, is a feature which can simply be described as an ever-increasing preoccupation with the problem of resolution, the capacity to make finer and finer distinctions. As such distinctions are made, they are tested for their congruence with the theoretical construct. When this comparison is intelligible and successful, theory is bolstered. But when the new detail, the new distinction, has no logical antecedent in theory, then a crisis arises which is only resolvable in the reconstruction of theory. Historically *this*, naïvely stated, is what happened in physics when the events of the micro-world of radioactivity forced a complete overhaul of physics, and a new synthesis; and Newton's world was swallowed in a gulp.

Twentieth-century biology, genetics, biochemistry, endocrinology, nerve physiology, and the rest have entered on this revolution in resolution. The finer and finer distinctions yet to be made may well result in—indeed demand—some grand new synthesis.

VI. DEVELOPMENTS IN PSYCHOLOGY SINCE 1900

By Richard D. Walk

George Washington University

The two most outstanding figures of twentieth-century psychology undoubtedly are Ivan P. Pavlov (1849-1936) and Sigmund Freud (1856-1939). Freud, the better known of the two to the layman, perfected a technique for the treatment of emotional problems and coupled with it a profoundly influential theory of psychological defenses, the structure of the mind, psychological development, and even of society, based on sexual motivating forces. Pavlov, the discoverer of conditioned reflexes, influenced the psychology of learning and the field of medicine by providing tools adaptable to many types of research. Pavlov's and his associates' research on conditioned reflexes became the basis for psychology in the Soviet Union. While his own theories were not very influential outside Russia, conditioning was an important influence on behaviorism and on theory in all the social sciences.

But the development of a scientific discipline is only incidentally told in the story of its giants. Rather, it is a continuous interaction of techniques of investigation with the important problems of the field, of small and large researches persistently illuminating the problem areas, uncovering new problems, rephrasing old questions, becoming momentarily stagnant or even sidetracked by attractive side issues, but, withal, slowly expanding the scope of knowledge and revealing new undreamed-of abysses of ignorance. Some of the important problems of psychology concern the nature of learning (acquisition, maintenance, extinction, forgetting, transfer, insight, problem solving, etc.); the nature of reward and of punishment; the nature of perception (its stimulus, the definition of a stimulus, its relation to the sense organs, its organization, the nature of space perception, etc.); an understanding of the sense organs themselves; the problem of nature or nurture (of learning or of innate factors); the problem of intelligence (its definition and testing) and other aptitudes and skills that lead to differences among individuals; the problem of motivation (the driving forces of behavior); the nature of development (of the child and animals); the nature of social relations among men; the understanding of abnormal behavior and of normal behavior; the treatment or cure of behavior problems; and many more, each problem area overlapping with the others.

By approximately 1900 (and in the next decade or two) psychology came of age. It had become an experimental "science" in 1879 with the founding of the first experimental psychology laboratory at Leipzig by Wilhelm Wundt.

The first experimental emphasis was on the structure of the normal adult human mind, but, by the turn of the century and soon after, child psychology, comparative psychology, mental testing, abnormal psychology, and social psychology became firmly established as somewhat independent scientific disciplines. While academic psychology, as represented at least by Titchener, sought to limit psychology to the investigations of the normal adult mind, these boundaries were ignored by investigators eager to investigate the myriad of psychological problems.

The Würzburg school flourished between approximately 1901 and 1909 and helped administer, unwillingly and inadvertently, the coup de grace to structural psychology. Experimental investigation of thought revealed thought without images, "imageless thought" (i.e., the structure of thought could not be analyzed by introspection). Determining tendencies (*Einstellung, Aufgabe*) and attitudes (*Bewusstseinslage*) discovered by the school helped show the importance of set and motivation for psychology, but the immediate result was the rise of gestalt psychology and behaviorism and a general expansion of the legitimate areas of investigation of psychology.

Wertheimer's paper on seen movement, the phi-phenomenon, in 1912, is the beginning of gestalt psychology. The protest of gestalt psychology against structural (Titchenerian, Wundtian) psychology was against the analysis of consciousness into elements. Gestalt psychology stressed the importance of perceptual organization, of that which is given rather than that which is acquired, of wholes as more than the sum of the parts, of fields as part of dynamic wholes, and of relationships. The chief figures of gestalt psychology were Max Wertheimer (1880-1943), best known, in addition to the work on apparent movement, for research on the principles of perceptual organization and for a book on productive thinking; Wolfgang Köhler (1887-   ) known for research emphasizing insight and the perception of relationships in apes and chickens and for research on figural aftereffects; Kurt Koffka (1886-1941) known for books on gestalt psychology, particularly *Principles of Gestalt Psychology* (1935). Gestalt psychology has influenced the whole of psychology, especially perception, but also the pychology of learning and clinical and social psychology. By 1940, however, it was no longer a separate "school."

Other representative contributors to perception are Brunswik, Gibson, Stevens, Hebb, and Michotte. E. Brunswik (1903-1955) stressed the probabilistic nature of perception, pointing out that in distance perception, for example, there are many cues and some are more useful as predictors than others. He conducted distinguished research on the constancies and was also very influential on probability learning. James J. Gibson (1904-   ) has emphasized the importance of movement (motion parallax) for space perception and of gradients of texture in the environment as cues to distance. He has given great impetus to the study of motion and the study of the stimulus for perception. S. S. Stevens (1906-   ), who has been the chief twentieth-century member of the Fechnerian tradition, the study of psychophysics, proposed in 1957 that Fechner's law, which holds that the intensity of a sensation increases as the logarithm of the intensity of the stimulus, is erroneous. Rather, Stevens proposed that sensation grows as a power function of stimulus intensity with possibly different exponents for each type of stimulus. Donald O. Hebb (1904-   ) has stimulated the study of the effect of environment on cognitive processes and of the relationship between physiological and psychological processes. A. Michotte (1881-   ) has shown that, under proper conditions, a moving dot touching another will be seen as "causing" the other to move, a series of investigations reported in his *La Perception de la Causalité* (1946). Other workers have stressed the relationship between perception and personality processes. This has stimulated research on clinical correlates of perception.

John B. Watson (1878-1958) published *Psychology as the Behaviorist Views It* in 1913 and founded behaviorism. Watson protested against an analysis of consciousness and stressed that behavior was important in itself and that consciousness should be ignored. Pavlov's work on conditioning became incorporated into behaviorism, and behaviorism was particularly influential on the psychology of learning.

Thorndike's experiments with cats escaping from puzzle boxes led him to propose the law of effect in 1908, the notion that reward gradually "stamped in" correct responses and that punishment eliminated undesirable ones. He conceived of learning as being gradual and made up of specific elements or bonds that became attached, through reward, to the new situation. Connectionism, as it was called, was the first modern learning theory, one that had tremendous influence on American education because his doctrines were issued from Teachers College, Columbia University. Pavlov's law of reinforcement also emphasized the role of reward. Gestalt theory, on the other hand, emphasized the role of insight, relationships, and the perceptual structure of the situation. In his *Mentality of Apes* (1917), Köhler both criticized Thorndike's learning situation as an artificial one and presented certain experiments with apes to demonstrate insight. Disagreements on the nature of learning culminated in the presentation of several theories of learning. These theories, based on simple experiments with dogs and rats as well as college sophomores, showed that complex learned phenomena could be derived from simple principles; and the theories were applied to clinical psychology, child psychology, social psychology, sociology, social anthropology, and political science. The years 1930 to 1950 were the main ones for learning theory *qua* learning theory, and the main theoretical contenders were theories by Guthrie, Hull, Skinner, and Tolman. Edwin R. Guthrie (1886-1959) charmingly advanced contiguity of stimulus and response as necessary and sufficient for learning, demoting reward to a correlated but unnecessary role. Edward C. Tolman (1886-1959) in his *Purposive Behavior in Animals and Men* (1932) made reward unnecessary but instead advanced the importance of "sign learning"; the white rat may learn the location of the goal by traversing the path to the goal even though never *rewarded* at the goal. Certain experiments in this type of "latent learning" supported his position. Clark L. Hull (1884-1952) was by far the most influential theorist of this period. His theory emphasized the role of reward based on the reduction of a primary drive, such as hunger, as the basis for learning, all other learning being secondary, acquired originally in situations in conjunction with drive reduction. More importantly, his theory stressed the hypothetico-deductive method, the notion that all complex learning could be deduced from basic posulates that would yield theorems which could be proved wrong. The whole theory thus could be (and was) revised continuously in the light of experimentation. B. F. Skinner (1904-   ) eschewed the role of a theorist, but rather adopted the position of carrying out experimentation on the modification of behavior. His basic principle is that of the "empirical law of effect," that certain known rewards are important in modifying behavior. His *Behavior of Organisms* (1938) reported a series of experiments using an apparatus (now known as a Skinner box) in which a rat obtained food by pressing a lever. The tendency of the animal to press the bar was related to the frequency with which bar presses were rewarded (the schedules of reinforcement), with motivation, punishment, and as influenced by drugs. Skinner's program of research has continued for many years and was in 1963 being used, for example, to evaluate the effect of tranquilizing drugs, to train primates that orbit the earth, and to investigate the behavior of mental patients. Skinner has written a novel, *Walden Two* (1948), describing a utopia that utilizes his learning principles. The principles of immediate reward and the "shaping" of behavior through gradual modification have been applied to "teaching machines" where a machine presents instructional material to a pupil and the pupil is rewarded with immediate knowledge of results. Teaching machines may have a wide influence on American education.

While more encompassing learning theories declined in importance between 1950 and 1955, their place has been partially filled by mathematical learning theories. The aims of mathematical learning theories are more modest: they are confined to predictions in rather definite situations. Other types of models, not necessarily mathematical, also tended to be more modest in scope after 1955. A representative example of a more modest theory is Neal E. Miller's (1909-   ) analysis of conflict behavior based on stimulus-response principles. Postulates about goal-directed behavior in approach-avoidance situations are used to derive a number of deductions that are tested in experiments. Harry F. Harlow's (1905-   ) analysis of errors in the discrimination learning of monkeys, learning set and error factor theory, is another example. Harlow also represents another trend, that of primatology. Largely because of the impetus from his own years of research in primates, work on primates has become a large, increasing segment of the field, necessarily dependent on large-scale financial support from the government and private foundations.

In physiological psychology, Shepherd I. Franz (1874-1933) showed that destruction of both frontal lobes of cats and monkeys led to loss of recent habits, not old ones, and that the recent habits may be reacquired, an example both of research questioning localization of function and of research that shows how complex brain function is. Karl S. Lashley (1890-1958) was the most distinguished physiological psychologist of the first half of the twentieth century. He investigated the relationship between excision of brain tissue and "intelligence" as measured by maze learning in rats. Like Franz, he found no localization of function but a relation between amount of tissue excised and learning: the more tissue removed, the greater the impairment. "Equipotentiality" and "mass action" were terms he used to describe the effects. Recent work in physiological psychology makes use of psychological techniques, such as complex mazes, delayed reaction tasks, choice discrimination tasks, the "Skinner box," and also the wide variety of neurophysiological techniques for extirpation, coagulation, precise local electrical stimulation (J. Olds and P. Milner discovered "pleasure centers" in the brain in 1954), and electronic recording. G. von Bekesy's investigations of the inner ear received the Nobel Prize for Medicine in 1961.

Prior to the twentieth century, Sigmund Freud had collaborated with Josef Breuer (1842-1925) on neurological therapy during the period 1882 to 1895. They treated hysterical patients with hypnoses and, under hypnosis, had the patients discuss the emotional cause of their trouble. They discovered that abreaction, a complete emotional living through of the experience, was an important factor in cures. Breuer fell out with Freud in 1895 over the problem of transference, the tendency of the patient to "fall in love with" the doctor, and over the importance of sexual factors in therapy. Freud pushed on, abandoned hypnosis for free association, began to analyze dreams, and published *The Interpretation of Dreams* in 1900. This book showed many psychological defense mechanisms and demonstrated sexual symbolism in dreams. After 1900 Freud developed psychoanalysis in association with disciples and associates. Some of the most influential features of his work are the following: (1) The development of psychotherapy, a process in which the patient by free association uncovers and "talks out" the roots of his problem; psychoanalysis is thus rooted in a method of modifying behavior to alleviate misery. (2) An analysis of human motivation in terms of underlying drives, particularly sexual motives. (3) An analysis of psychological defense mechanisms whereby the self protects itself from reality; some of these are repression, projection (imputing one's own motives to others), reaction formation (according to which the opposite impulse is prominent, as with a mother who hates her child but becomes oversolicitous and protective), regression, and fixation. (4) A system of stages of development in the first few years of life—the oral, anal, and phallic—showing that the mouth, the eliminative functions, and sex organs are important in childhood and that the stages may influence adulthood. (5) A motion of the mind as structured of id, ego, and superego; the id is the primitive, selfish, hedonistic, most powerful part; the superego or conscience can cause much neurotic misery; the ego or self is the weakest portion of the triumvirate. Freud applied his ideas beyond psychotherapy, first to all human motivation and later to an analysis of societies. His ideas profoundly influenced not only psychology, where his theories must be considered in any discussion of motivation, but also all Western civilization through literature, drama, and popularization.

Soon after psychoanalysis was founded, in 1911, Alfred Adler (1870-1937) broke away to found a new school called "individual psychology" that substituted the need for superiority and power for motivation based on sexual energy. Carl G. Jung (1875-1961) also disassociated himself from psychoanalysis and in 1913 founded "analytical psychology," a complex system that stresses underlying racial origins of personality including that of a "collective unconscious" in which ideas from man's ancestry are stored. In popular thinking Adler is associated with the "inferiority complex" and Jung with introversion and extroversion.

Other theorists that break with Freud's emphasis on instinctual genetic sexual forces are those of the sociological or cultural school: Karen Horney (1885-1952), Harry Stack Sullivan (1892-1949), and Erich Fromm (1900-   ). For all of these, interpersonal relations, between man and society and man and other individuals, are the focus of the basis for neurotic conflict.

Projective techniques to aid in the clinical diagnosis of personality have been developed for use with all types of behavior disorders among adults and children. Jung helped develop a free-association test around 1910 and Kent and Rosanoff published norms for large numbers of normal persons and psychotics on a similar test in the same year. While many tests are available to the clinician, the most widely used ones are the Rorschach test and the Thematic Apperception Test (TAT). Hermann Rorschach (1885-1922) published his *Psychodiagnostiks* in 1921, a monograph on the use of ink blots for personality diagnosis. With standardized scoring and a skilled examiner, the Rorschach test has been used to diagnose anxiety, neurosis, sexual problems, types of psychosis, mental deficiency, and creativity. The Thematic Apperception Test was introduced by Henry A. Murray (1893-   ) in 1935. The subject is shown a series of pictures and is asked to make up a story about each one of them. The test is used with normal persons and mental patients and is most useful in diagnosing emotional conflicts.

Freud's method of psychotherapy, a free-association "talking out" method, has remained little changed, although there are many minor variations on it. Carl Rogers's (1902-   ) client-centered therapy or "non-directive" therapy is a major departure in that the therapist assumes a much less active role than does the psychoanalyst. Group therapy is used with groups of people, such as prisoners or alcoholics, that have similar problems. Therapies based on "conditioning" principles have achieved a great deal of success with the phobias; the therapist assumes an active role in making the patient overcome the difficulty itself rather than in uncovering its "roots in the unconscious." While psychotherapy is difficult to assess on scientific grounds and the difficulties of proper scientific evaluation are enormous, the psychotherapeutic process is the focus of an increasing amount of research.

Alfred Binet (1857-1911) introduced methods of testing intelligence that were to have tremendous influence on education. Between 1896 and 1903 the tests on school children were perfected and the first intelligence scale for children issued (in collaboration with T. Simon) in 1905. Intellectual capacity in school children was rated according to the norm for that age of child (the mental age); the notion of IQ (intelligence quotient) as mental age divided by chronological age (MA/CA) was soon to follow. The Stanford-Binet, based on norms from a large number of American school children, was issued in 1916. The first World War gave an impetus to intelligence and aptitude testing; over two million men took the group-administered Army Alpha, a measure of intelligence. The results of the tests given to army recruits well established their validity. The more professional occupations were shown to have much higher IQ's than lower-skilled occupations. The army results also contributed to the social emancipation of the American Negro. Large overlap in Negro-White IQ scores was shown, and Southern Whites were found to have lower average intelligence scores than the Northern Negroes, a finding very difficult to explain away by those who tried to justify subservience of the Negro on the grounds of innate inferiority.

The Stanford-Binet was revised in 1937 and again in 1960. Individual intelligence tests constructed by David Wechsler (1896-   ) for adults and children yield a percentile score or ranking in relation to one's contemporaries rather than an IQ score. They are widely used as are many other individual tests and group tests. Factor analysis, a technique of factoring out the basic dimensions of a test, was introduced in the 1930's and has become very influential not only on group intelligence tests but in all types of test construction.

Social psychology has been defined by G. W. Allport (1897-   ) as "the attempt to understand and explain how the thought, feeling and behavior of individuals are influenced by the actual, imagined or implied presence of other human beings." Herbert Spencer's use of Darwin's theory of evolution to explain the development of society, Gustave Le Bon's discussion of crowd mentality, and Gabriel Tarde's laws of imitation are representative nineteenth-century philosophical antecedents of social psychology. But the first experiments of the influence of the group in individual performance were Tripplet's in 1897.

In 1908, William McDougall's (1871-1938) *Introduction to Social Psychology* was published in the same year as a text by sociologist E. A. Ross and may be said to represent the beginning of social psychology as a separate psychological discipline. McDougall's social psychology emphasized the biological basis of human behavior and described the instincts, to each instinct of which there corresponded an emotion, on which behavior is based. While his views were popular, the textbook going through many revisions, instincts as explanations lost favor soon after the first World War (the instincts were not defined independently enough; each textbook writer had a different list; and to explain fighting, for example, as an instinct for pugnacity is no explanation at all) and gave ground to behaviorism. F. H. Allport's *Social Psychology* (1924) reflected this new trend. He rejected the easy enumeration of instincts and preferred an explanation in terms of habits for most complex motivation. The book also reports a series of experiments, similar to Moede's, on the influence of the group on individual performance. This type of experimentation was later to culminate in the study of group dynamics.

Attitudes and their measurement are one of the foundations, and in the opinion of some, the foundation, of social psychology. The most important early example of attitude measurement is the Bogardus social distance scale (1925) where nationalities and races were rated in their degree of acceptability on a scale from acceptability (close kinship by marriage) to rejection (exclusion from one's country). A more general method of measuring attitudes was the method of equal-appearing intervals developed by Thurstone (1927) which was used not only to measure attitudes toward, for example, the church, but also the change of attitudes as when, for example, school children were shown the motion picture *Birth of a Nation* and afterwards were found to have less favorable attitudes toward the Negro. Gallup demonstrated the superiority of the stratified random sample in 1936 to predict the victory of Roosevelt over Landon while a mail ballot failed because it was based on telephone ownership and, therefore, biased in favor of upper socio-economic classes. Public-opinion polling has since 1936 been an important segment of social psychology. Public-opinion polling was used by Cantril, for example, to assess shift in attitudes of the American public toward giving aid to the Allies prior to the entry of the United States into the second World War and it helped form governmental policy.

Moreno founded sociometry in 1934, a technique whereby individuals in groups choose one another on the basis of criteria such as friendship or leadership. The method has been used to show changes in patterns of friendship as school children enter higher grades and for many other purposes such as predicting the "line of communication" (who talks to whom) within a group or even to predict the morale of a group. High morale groups choose one another as friends while low morale groups look outside the group for friendship and reject their own leaders.

After the second World War, *The American Soldier,* a four-volume series, plotted the attitudes of soldiers in wartime and made many contributions to more precise attitude measurement. *The Authoritarian Personality* (1950) by T. W. Adorno and others put forth the hypothesis of the coexistence of attitudes of racial prejudice and fascism or authoritarianism in individuals tested in the United States. Attitude scales designed to measure prejudice (the E-scale) and fascism (the F-scale) were developed in the course of this study. These scales were very influential in promoting other investigations of attitudes.

While there were many early investigations of groups, Kurt Lewin (1890-1947) was the founder of both field theory and group dynamics. While the basic tenets of field theory are much influenced by gestalt theory, the precise points of influence are only partial. Lewin was an extremely ingenious experimenter. Representative experiments were on the topic of autocratic, democratic, or laissez-faire leadership, on the changing of attitudes through group concensus, and on regression in children's mental age as a function of frustration. Research on group dynamics is a large and important part of social psychology.

Two outstanding figures in child psychology are Arnold Gesell (1880-1961) and Jean Piaget (1896-   ). Gesell is best known for his research on motor and behavioral developmental sequences in children from birth through age

10. Jean Piaget has used many ingenious situations and techniques to study the development of the child's processes of thinking.

An important influence on any scientific field is the outstanding books and handbooks that collect together the current status of the discipline. E. G. Boring's *A History of Experimental Psychology* (1929, 1950) is an example. The dean of experimental psychology, R. S. Woodworth, published *Experimental Psychology* in 1938 and revised it (with H. Schlosberg) in 1954. Handbooks of social and general experimental psychology and also autobiographies of psychologists were published under the general editorship of C. Murchison in the 1930's.[9] A series of volumes titled *Psychology: A Study of a Science* covering the "conceptual and systematic" and the "empirical substructure" of psychology under the general editorship of S. Koch began publication in 1959 and six of seven projected volumes were published by 1962. *The Annual Review of Psychology* (Annual Reviews, Inc., Palo Alto, Calif.) began publication in 1950 with annual reviews of major fields and occasional reviews of special fields of psychology.

Psychology has benefited from many advances in other fields. Advances in statistics have developed small sample statistics, non-parametric statistics, simple and complex analysis of variance models, and many procedures for special uses. Mathematical models have been applied to all areas of psychology, but particularly to learning theory and decision processes. High-speed computers are used to process data and even to simulate perceptual and cognitive processes. Electronic techniques are used for precise programming of human and animal experiments. Medical electronic instrumentation makes possible precise physiological implantation and recording.

Since 1900, psychology has grown from a small academic discipline to one that touches the life of every citizen. Intelligence tests help determine whether a child is ready for school. The child's learning tasks are partially determined by psychological research. Further tests control admittance to college and to many jobs. Human engineering tests the adaptability of man to machine. Tests help diagnose emotional disorders and psychotherapeutic techniques may cure them. These are but a few examples of the expanding scope of the field.

The break-throughs have come from application of new techniques to important problems. Freud's technique of psychotherapy, Pavlov's method of producing conditioned reflexes, Binet's method of assessing intelligence are important examples. Technology is not science, but science depends on technology. New techniques are constantly being invented, from new apparatus to better methodology, and used to investigate the old problems or new problems that are a by-product of research success. The problems are paramount, but their solution awaits better techniques of thinking.

---

9 See the bibliography at the end of this chapter for other recent influential handbooks.

VII. MEDICINE IN THE TWENTIETH CENTURY

By Thomas E. Keys

Librarian, Mayo Clinic, Rochester, Minnesota;
Associate Professor of History of Medicine, Mayo Foundation,
Graduate School, University of Minnesota

In the Western world, medicine has advanced more in the last 60 years than in all previous centuries. One has only to look at the life-expectancy rates to be made aware of this progress. Whereas life expectancy in the United States was 47.3 years[10] in 1900, it was 69.7[11] in 1959 and it continues to rise. The countries of Europe, too, have an increased life expectancy.

Factors that have contributed to this spectacular achievement include: (1) application of the medical discoveries of the nineteenth century, (2) improvements in medical education, (3) development of diagnostic tools, (4) advances in surgery, (5) refinements in medical therapeutics, (6) progress in mental health, and (7) introduction and growth of group practice.

Application of Nineteenth-Century Discoveries.—Even though anesthesia was introduced in 1846 and made modern surgical techniques possible, high mortality rates still continued and surgery was not extensively practiced. Pasteur's discovery that heat sterilization destroyed microorganisms led Lister to prevent the development of them in wounds. This eliminated the septic conditions under which surgery had been practiced, and reduced surgical mortality rates. But these advances in knowledge lay dormant until the beginning of the twentieth century. Similarly, Röntgen's discovery of rays that bear his name and other diagnostic devices awaited the twentieth century for their exploitation.

Improvements in Medical Education.—While in the latter part of the nineteenth century medical education in the United States was at its lowest ebb, it was at its zenith in Europe, especially in France and later in Germany. The improvement in American medicine was brought about by the growing concern of the American Medical Association, the American Academy of Medicine, the Association of American Medical Colleges, and state licensing boards over the poor quality of American medicine. The Council on Medical Education of the American Medical Association was founded in 1904, and through its efforts medical education in the United States began to improve. A further stimulus was provided by the impartial survey of American medical schools in 1908 by Abraham Flexner and N. P. Colwell. The results were published in 1910.[12]

Another factor that was to improve standards in medicine in the United States was the creation of the examining boards in the specialties. The first, the American Board of Ophthalmology,[13] originated in 1915. It was established to certify competence in a specialty and also to advise and guide aspirants for

10 U.S. Bureau of the Census, *Statistical Abstract of the United States, 1958,* United States Government Printing Office, 1958, p. 60.
11 *World Almanac, 1961,* New York World-Telegram, 1961, p. 449.
12 Flexner, Abraham, *Medical Education in the United States and Canada: A Report to the Carnegie Foundation for the Advancement of Teaching,* New York, Privately printed, 1910, 346 pp.
13 Keys, T. E., "Historical Aspects of Graduate Medical Education," *Journal of Medical Education,* May, 1955, XXX, 256-64.

certification concerning the planning of their training programs. After the first World War the specialty-board movement spread rapidly and now covers practically every field relating to medicine.

Development of Diagnostic Tools.—Medicine has kept pace with scientific growth. Of great significance are the many diagnostic aids developed or improved upon in the twentieth century. Electrocardiography (the study of the electrical changes that accompany the heartbeat) has been improved by the recent advent of radioelectrocardiography, which permits the recording of electrocardiograms during exercise without wire connection. Intracardiac catheterization (the insertion of a tube into the heart by way of a blood vessel) is used mainly to obtain samples of heart blood in the diagnosis and evaluation of congenital and rheumatic lesions of the heart. Radiology (the application of Röntgen rays and radium) has been of great importance. It now includes the use of radioisotopes, especially in the measurement of thyroidal function and in the localization of tumors.

Electron microscopy (the visualization of exceedingly minute structures) has given physicians a better understanding of disease processes and allowed the correlation of biochemical processes and cellular morphology. Clinical laboratory tests (study of urine, blood, feces and so forth) have been most useful in establishing diagnoses. Electroencephalography (the graphic recording of the electrical activity of the brain) is useful in the localization of lesions within the brain, such as brain tumors, and in distinguishing between diffuse and focal lesions of the brain in epilepsy. The determination of certain chemical constituents of the body, as in blood or spinal fluid, and the determination of certain physiologic processes at the bedside are further diagnostic aids of great value.

The mathematical approach to diagnosis is now being developed; for instance, the computer is being used in psychologic testing and in other medical fields. Developments in storage and retrieval of the medical literature by means of the computer are significant now, and future possibilities are unlimited. Another important development has been that of medical biometry, especially aided by the use of punch cards which are sorted automatically for the recording and study of diseases. Recently, equations of conditional probability have been derived to express the logical process used by clinicians in making diagnosis from clinical data.

Recent Advances in Surgery.—After the development of surgical anesthesia and the general use of aseptic measures in the operating room, with the spectacular drop in operative mortality, surgery forged ahead. Besides the extensive growth in abdominal surgery, there has been growth in the fields of plastic surgery, especially in the treatment of burns with electrolytes followed by early homografting. Transplantation of whole organs, especially kidneys in identical twins, and the grafting of blood vessels, hitherto impossible, are now successful. Neurologic surgery has made rapid strides, including the removal or fusion of disks between vertebrae, prefrontal lobotomy (incision into the front part of the brain) for psychiatric and other conditions, and cranioplasty (correction of defects of the skull), just to mention a few advances. Chest surgery has progressed.

Complete removal of the lung for cancer and partial removal for certain tumors of the lung have been successful. Surgical treatment of diaphragmatic hernias have been successful by either thoracic or abdominal approaches.

Injuries of the heart and great vessels have become amenable to treatment during our time, and congenital heart lesions are now repaired by "open heart" operation with the aid of general hypothermia, perfusion and cardiopulmonary bypass (temporary interference with blood flow through the heart and lungs). Orthopedic surgery, too, has taken rapid strides, attributable especially to the shocking increase of automobile accidents. Arthroplasty (the making of an artificial joint for the hip) and new technics of bone cutting for surgical purposes such as bone implantation have contributed to the crippled patient's welfare. A recently invented stapling machine sutures surgical wounds rapidly and with comparative ease and freedom from infection attributed to the use of tantalum wire.

The heartbeat in patients presumed dead of cardiac arrest has been restored by mouth-to-mouth breathing (artificial respiration), by insertion of a tube into the trachea for rapid and direct administration of oxygen, by direct massage and by rhythmic compression of the heart. Another epoch-making operation was the grafting of an entire extremity after complete severance. In disorders of the blood supply to the brain, vascular surgery has achieved remarkable results by bypassing or reopening the narrowed or occluded arteries. Recent advances in energy-amplification technics have brought about a new light source, the laser. This unusually intense monochromatic beam is used in place of regular diathermy in eye surgery and may find wide application in the biomedical field.

Refinements in Medical Therapeutics.—With increase in our understanding of disease and disease processes came successful measures for their cure. For instance, Schaudinn in 1905 discovered the germ of syphilis, Spirochaeta pallida, and Ehrlich in 1910 introduced an arsenic compound, Salvarsan, which proved to be a specific against the disease. The cause of diabetes mellitus was determined (1889-1893) by Joseph von Mering, and the remedy for diabetes, insulin, was discovered by Banting and Best in 1922. Since that time, enormous strides have been made in therapeutics.[14] New drugs include the chemotherapeutic agents, especially the sulfonamides; the antibiotics (penicillin and later streptomycin, chloramphenicol, the tetracyclines, and so forth); the hormones, especially the steroid hormones (testosterone, adrenosterone, corticosterone, 17-hydroxy-11-dehydrocorticosterone, and so forth); the protein and protein-derivative hormones (prolactin, adrenotropic hormone, parathyroid hormone, insulin, and so forth); the anticholinergics; antihistamines; hypotensive drugs; analgesics; morphine antagonists; potentiators; sedatives; tranquilizers; and stimulants. Having this huge number of medicines available is not without its pitfalls —many are powerful and many are dangerous, but under the skillful use of physicians they have contributed greatly to the general health of the people.

Recently heart block (interference with rate of heartbeat) has been corrected by the use of an electric pacemaker implanted in the body. The treatment of vari-

14 Cullinan, E. R., "Trends in Medicine, 1939-1958," Presidential address, *Tr. M. Soc. London,* October 13, 1958, LXXV, 1-14.

ous forms of cancer with radioactive cobalt has proved to have great advantage in addition to conventional x-ray treatment. Radioisotopes have been successful in the treatment of cancer of the thyroid gland. Radium still continues to be useful in the treatment of many forms of cancer. The artificial kidney (an apparatus through which the blood is circulated outside the body), is useful in removing excretory products in certain cases of severe renal insufficiency, especially in anuria.

Aviation and Space Medicine.—With the development of pressurized cabins it was found that problems in aviation medicine were mostly those of civilian medical practice. The problems in space medicine will be much more complicated. A new journal, *Aerospace Medicine,* is devoted entirely to these two subjects.

Progress in Mental Health.—The strides made in the problems of the diagnosis and treatment of the mentally ill must be mentioned. Among these has been the necessity, now recognized by the public, of the acceptance of the difference attached to mental illness, and the fact that mentally ill persons are sick, the same as if they were physically sick, and should be viewed no differently from other sick persons.[15] Freud's postulate in this regard made the unreasonable reasonable. It brought about an orderliness that is now emerging in the acceptance of psychiatry as a scientific discipline. As far as therapeutic measures[16] are concerned, these include the introduction of new methods of treatment with drugs, the application of psychoanalytical methods to treatment of the psychoses, an increased emphasis on treatment of other members of the family in addition to the patient, and great improvement in institutional care.

Introduction and Growth of Group Practice.—The idea of large-scale medical group practice can no doubt be traced to the Mayo brothers. About 1900, the surgical practice of Drs. W. J. and C. H. Mayo was growing and it became necessary to enlarge the staff then and from time to time thereafter; the enlargement extended into all the fields of medicine so that the various health needs of the individual patient could be served competently and conveniently. The idea of group practice has subsequently caught on very well in the United States and in Canada. In the annual report of the executive director of the American Association of Medical Clinics for 1961, Jordan[17] states that the membership is composed of 135 full-member clinics and 16 associate members.

The advantages of group practice are those of teamwork and of making the various special skills in medicine immediately available in the care of the patient. Dr. W. J. Mayo[18] expressed it this way: "The internist, the surgeon, and the specialist must join with the physiologist, the pathologist and the laboratory workers to form the clinical group, which must also include men learned in the abstract sciences, since physics and biochemistry are leading medicine to greater heights. A union of all these forces will lengthen by many years the span of human life."

15 Joint Commission on Mental Illness and Health, *Action for Mental Health, Final Report of the Joint Commission on Mental Illness and Health, 1961,* Basic Books, XXXVIII, 338 pp.
16 Ewalt, J. R., and Havens, L. L., "Advances in Psychological Medicine," *Practitioner,* October, 1959, CLXXXIII, 442-47.
17 Jordan, E. P., "Report of Executive Director," *Group Practice,* November, 1961, X, 851-57.
18 Quoted in Clapesattle, Helen E., *The Doctors Mayo,* University of Minnesota Press, 1941, p. 706.

Conclusion.—With our progress in the understanding of medical problems we can look forward to an ever-increasing span of human life. The twentieth century has been characterized as the era of preventive medicine. During the century so far, maternal and infant mortality have been greatly reduced, many of the so-called communicable diseases have been brought under control, and vaccines have proved most useful in the eradication of a number of such diseases. It is probable that by the end of the century, medicine's fight against the leading causes of death—heart disease, cancer, vascular lesions, and accidents—will also prove to have been successful.

VIII. DEVELOPMENTS IN GEOLOGY AND GEOGRAPHY

By Carroll Lane Fenton

Before 1900, much geologic thought was based on the Laplacian concept of a progressively cooling earth whose thin crust covered a still-molten core. During the first three decades of the twentieth century this idea was rejected and in large measure was replaced by the planetesimal hypothesis of T. C. Chamberlin and F. R. Moulton and the gaseous-tidal hypotheses of James Jeans and Harold Jeffreys. Both explanations said that the planets evolved from streamers of matter that had been drawn from the sun by a passing star. This material collected in rotating balls which were either solid from their beginning (Chamberlin and Moulton) or were gaseous and then fluid (Jeans and Jeffreys), but hardened just before the beginning of geologic time.

More recent studies by C. F. von Weizsächer, A. Eucken, Gerard Kuiper, and others suggest that the earth began as a rotating mass of gas and interstellar dust that separated from a flattened nebula. According to Kuiper, heavy elements spiraled to the center of the mass while light ones moved outward and were lost. When the material that remained became a molten ball, its elements were sorted by gravity, and the outer part of the ball began to harden. This took place about 4,600 million years ago.

Kuiper's hypothesis seems to explain the earth's structure, which was determined by study of earthquake waves, chiefly after 1906. These waves show that our planet contains a solid inner core, an apparently viscous outer core, a solid mantle, and a hard crust whose thickness ranges from 6 to 22 miles. Both mantle and crust are strong, but the cores seem to consist of iron, nickel, and perhaps silica.

Estimates derived from salt in the sea, sedimentary formations, and a supposedly cooling globe had given the earth's age at figures ranging from 20 to more than 600 million years. Beginning about 1904, physicists began to study the rates at which radioactive substances disintegrated. Geologists then used these rates to determine the ages of rocks in which those elements could be found. This method, greatly improved and expanded since 1945, has given figures as great as 2,700 and (less reliably) 3,300 million years. They are consistent with astronomic computations which set the earth's total age at about 5,000 million years.

Also since 1945, measurement of Carbon 14 in plant and animal material has provided a means of determining ages of 50,000 years or less. Carbon-14 dating is most important in studies of the latest, or Pleistocene, ice age and in archaeology.

As estimates of the earth's age increased, so did those of the antiquity of fossils. Late Pre-Cambrian animals have been found in South Australia and in the American West; limy sea plants some 1,200 million years old are widespread, and plantlike cells from northern Michigan are at least 1,600 million years old.

Though Pre-Cambrian fossils are very old, they lived long after earth's mantle hardened and its first crust developed. Many geologists have sought that original crust, but J. T. Wilson maintains that it is covered by 6 to 22 miles of later deposits which form the crust we know today. Wilson traces the rocks in this crust to vulcanism, though many of them have been reworked into sediments or remade by heat, pressure, and other agents of change, or metamorphism.

Both irregularities and movements of the crust are now attributed to isostasy. This principle, formulated by C. E. Dutton before 1890, has been widely applied since 1910. It holds that continental masses are both thicker and less dense than ocean basins. Both "float" upon the mantle, which is rigid yet yields under pressure, pushing continents upward as they are reduced by erosion. Ocean basins, however, remain stable or sink. With uplift go breaking, arching, and folding, which produce both high plateaus and mountain systems.

Continents rise because they are light, but other factors make them grow larger. Wilson concludes that each continent began as an island of once-molten rock. Erosion of this rock produced sediment that settled in surrounding oceans, chiefly near shore. As the weight of this deposit increased, it produced curved fractures along which lavas and hot gases ascended, and changed sediments themselves were forced upward. The result was curved chains of new, mountainous islands which roughly paralleled the original shore and sent sediment into the shallow sea that lay between them and the continent.

When this sea was filled, the continent grew. At the same time, rivers carried sediment to the surrounding ocean, causing the cycle to be repeated. Repetitions have brought continents to their present size, and cycles now in progress give assurance of future growth.

Besides making continents grow, sediments indicate their sources, the agents that produced them, and the conditions under which they accumulated. Many geologists (especially the late Charles Schuchert, of Yale) have used sedimentary deposits to reconstruct the geography of ancient seas, oceans, and continents. Though paleogeographic maps require endless improvement, they seem to give a generally reliable picture of the earth's surface during past ages. Study of sediments themselves provides more detailed information about the production, transportation, and deposition of rock materials, and of changes that have taken place since they settled.

Ancient climates can be inferred from fossils, for some plants and animals need warm surroundings, though others thrive in temperate or cold ones. This method, which requires careful comparison with living groups whose requirements can be examined, has been refined and elaborated, especially in studies of Tertiary and later epochs. Between 1946 and 1950, however, H. C. Urey and his associates discovered that ancient temperatures are revealed by the ratio of "heavy" Oxygen-18 to common Oxygen-16 in calcareous, or limy, fossils. This method has been used to trace climatic fluctuations during the past 300,000 years, as well as to determine the temperature of seas that existed as much as 135 million years ago. Results are accurate within one degree Centigrade.

Fossils, sediments, and oxygen ratios agree that climates have varied greatly during the geologic past. Most geologists hold that major climatic changes have been world-wide, but this opinion has been opposed by Alfred Wegener and his followers in their theory of continental drift. In its extreme form, this theory holds that continents float upon a layer of very hot viscous rock. As a result, they have moved from warm regions to cold and back again, repeatedly and at various times. Continental drift received much attention during the late 1920's and early 1930's, but many geologists reject the theory.

Less spectacular is the theory of polar wandering. S. K. Runcorn and others have found that magnetized mineral grains, which should point toward the north or south magnetic pole, are variously oriented in rocks of varied ages. This is taken as evidence that the earth's axis has shifted, causing both its magnetic and its geographic poles to "wander." Subtropical fossils in northern Greenland, for example, supposedly lived when the earth turned so far that regions which now are frigid lay near what then was the equator. Similarly, glacial deposits in India are said to reflect another shift that put southern Asia into the subarctic North. There was no general, world-wide cooling, just as no world-wide warming was needed to make Greenland subtropical.

Whether the poles have shifted or not, ancient organisms were adjusted to their environments and to each other. These adjustments, as well as the associations which they produced, form the subject matter of paleoecology. Up to 1962, most paleoecologic studies emphasized physical factors in the environment and distribution of fossils, but the associations in some ancient faunas and floras have been analyzed.

One of the outstanding features of twentieth-century geology is its attention to economic resources. They have been described, mapped, and estimated; their origins have been investigated; both lands and shallow seas have been searched for additional deposits. New techniques, such as seismic mapping of underground structures and air surveys using magnetometers, have proved successful. Many studies of water supplies have been made, since ever-increasing amounts of water are needed by agriculture, by industry, and by growing cities and suburbs.

In the field of geography, the twentieth century has seen the discovery of both North and South Poles and ascents of the earth's highest mountains, including Mount Everest. Both Arctic and Antarctic regions have been explored by means of surface vehicles, airplanes, and (in the Antarctic) submarines traveling under sea ice. Much of this work was done during the International Geophysical Year, a cooperative program of research and exploration that actually began in 1956 but officially extended from July 1, 1957, to December 31, 1958.

Submarines have proved especially suitable for gravity measurements and studies of ocean depths, and have been adapted to the observation of marine life. Ocean basins have also been explored by means of dredges, echo sounders, the bathyscaphe, and submarine photography. Instead of being an almost featureless plain, the ocean bottom has proved to be more rugged than continents, with mountains as much as 33,000 feet high and trenches 35,840 feet deep. Its greatest feature, however, is a system of volcano-studded ridges 40,000 miles long, which usually rise at least 10,000 feet above the surrounding sea floor. Other major features are five great scarps that run eastward and westward across the floor of the Pacific, reach heights of two miles, and are marked by lines of volcanic peaks. In other places, muddy currents sometimes rush down the sides of continents, wearing deep canyons and flowing far across ocean floors.

The combination of military needs and increasing population pressures has led to detailed studies of Arctic lands and of deserts, especially in Africa and Asia. Dealing with such factors as soil, water, mineral resources, and plant and animal associations, these studies show what can and cannot be done to increase the productivity of arid lands. Reservoirs impounded for water power and irrigation have become important geographic factors in many regions. Besides modifying or remaking local industry and agriculture, they require extensive adjustments on the part of plant, animal, and human populations.

Less spectacular, but of great significance, are new determinations of the earth's shape and of distances on its surface. Its diameter at the equator is 26.7 miles greater than that from pole to pole, and its bulge south of the equator is a little greater than that to the north. With man-made satellites, distances as great as that from New York to London have been measured with a probable error no greater than 300 feet.

IX. PROGRESS IN THE SOCIAL SCIENCES[19]

By Harry Elmer Barnes

Advances in the social sciences in the twentieth century have been extremely significant. For a time, these studies became less dominated by preconceived philosophical dogmas, and the historical and scientific methods were extensively applied to them. More refined statistical investigation and analysis were introduced. There was somewhat less interest in working out a pseudo-scientific defense of the existing order, and a somewhat more realistic determination to discover the actual facts, wherever they might lead. In the task of introducing the scien-

19 Economics and anthropology are not included in this brief review since they are discussed elsewhere in this book. For economics, see p.1189. Many recent developments in anthropology are noted in Volume I, chaps. i, ii.

tific method into the social sciences, perhaps the most widely discussed twentieth-century figure was the Italian economist and statistician, Vilfredo Pareto (1848-1923), whose work, summed up in his four-volume *The Mind and Society: A Treatise on General Sociology*,[20] was variously appraised. Some authorities regard Pareto as the sociological Newton. Others rate him as a pompous pretender. The truth probably lies somewhere between these two extremes.

Definitions, descriptions, classifications, and methodological disputes in the social sciences have increasingly given way to analysis of social functions and processes. To some extent, petty departmental jealousies have been put aside in order to arrive at a more unified and comprehensive conception of modern society. In the United States a determined movement was launched to emphasize the teaching of the social sciences in schools and colleges. A great *Encyclopaedia of the Social Sciences* was inspired by Alexander Goldenweiser and Howard B. Woolston, launched by E. R. A. Seligman, and edited by Alvin Johnson. It has come to be pretty generally recognized that the preservation and progress of modern civilization through the application of intelligence to public problems will depend primarily upon the improvement and exploitation of social science.

In historiography there has been a definite trend away from the exclusive concern with the annals of politics, diplomacy, and war. Historians have shown much more regard for the evolution of civilization, and have become interested in tracing the growth of human institutions and describing the manner in which our twentieth-century civilization has evolved from earlier cultural periods. In Germany, Karl Lamprecht outlined the history of civilization in the light of the changing mental attitudes that have characterized the successive stages of human development. In France, Henri Berr edited a vast history of civilization revealing in detail the evolution of human culture, and Georges Renard edited a comprehensive history of the evolution of economic institutions. In the United States, James Harvey Robinson took the lead in developing an interest in the history of human thought and culture, a field in which he has been followed by such disciples as Carl L. Becker, Preserved Smith, Lynn Thorndike, and Howard Robinson. James T. Shotwell did pioneer work in stimulating interest in the history of civilization and social institutions, subjects cultivated more zealously by historical-minded economists, such as Sombart, the Webbs, Tawney, and the Hammonds, than by professional historians. Frederick J. Turner, Charles A. Beard, Harold Faulkner, E. C. Kirkland, and L. M. Hacker analyzed the data of economic and institutional history in order to give us a better understanding of the development of the United States. An extensive history of civilization to run to nearly two hundred volumes was launched under the editorship of C. K. Ogden and the present writer. An ambitious six-volume history of the world, designed to indoctrinate vigorous internationalism, has been sponsored by UNESCO under the editorship of Julian S. Huxley and Ralph E. Turner. H. G. Wells and Will Durant popularized the newer aspects of historical interpretation.

---

20 Vilfredo Pareto, *The Mind and Society: A Treatise on General Sociology*, 4 vols. bound as 2 vols., Dover Publications, Inc., 1963.

Sociology has advanced from controversies over definitions and classifications to a realistic analysis of social processes and institutions. Gustav Ratzenhofer, Albion W. Small, and Arthur F. Bentley analyzed the relationship between social interests and the growth of social institutions. Émile Durkheim paid special attention to the domination of the group mind over the individual mind, and made the most extensive sociological analysis of the division of labor. Franklin H. Giddings sketched the evolution of civilization and worked out a systematic theory of social causation. Edward A. Ross described with force and ingenuity the operation of psychological factors in social control. Charles H. Cooley and G. H. Mead dealt with group life, democracy, and the nature of the social process. Edward C. Hayes, Robert E. Park, and Ernest W. Burgess contributed important studies of the social process. Social institutions have been dealt with by Joyce O. Hertzler, Constantine Panunzio, and Harry E. Barnes. William I. Thomas and Charles A. Ellwood first introduced a competent application of modern psychological facts into systematic sociology. Leonard T. Hobhouse developed a system of sociology which drew heavily upon philosophy and anthropology, and aimed fundamentally at rationally guided social reform. Leopold von Wiese produced an impressive systematization of sociological principles, based on the theory that sociology is a rigorous schematic exposition of the facts of human behavior and social relationships. Alfred Vierkandt, W. I. Thomas, and William F. Ogburn emphasized the broad cultural approach to society and its problems. Robert E. Chaddock, W. F. Ogburn, George A. Lundberg, Stuart A. Rice, Samuel A. Stoufer, Stuart C. Dodd, and J. L. Moreno stressed the importance of quantitative methods in sociology. Talcott Parsons took the lead in attempting to formulate a theoretical synthesis of the newer attitudes and methods in sociology.

Trained specialists in social science have shown the bearing of historical, biological, psychological, and geographical factors upon group life. Notable here were the writings of Harry E. Barnes, Howard Becker, Frank H. Hankins, E. B. Reuter, Ellsworth Faris, Kimball Young, and Franklin Thomas. Howard W. Odum combined these approaches and produced the most important work in what is know as the field of regional studies. Special attention has been given in recent years to the study of social classes and social stratification, and their bearing on the important problem of status-seeking, by August B. Hollingshead, Melvin M. Tumin, P. K. Hatt, Ralph H. Turner, Joel B. Montague, Kingsley Davis, Wilbert E. Moore, Richard M. Stephenson, and others.

In political science, the older penchant for definitions of governmental forms and the description of party strife, has been supplanted by a penetrating analysis of the influence exerted by institutional forces upon political life and of the social functions executed by our political institutions. Franz Oppenheimer, C. A. Beard, and H. J. Laski showed the influence of economic factors upon political activity and institutions. Graham Wallas, Scipio Sighele, Gustave Le Bon, Robert Michels, Émile Durkheim, Walter Lippmann, and others analyzed the psychological basis of political behavior. Edward Jenks followed the teachings of Gumplowicz in tracing the effect of warfare and social struggles upon the evolution of political institutions. J. N. Figgis and H. J. Laski extended the studies of Gierke and

Maitland on the relation between social groups and political organization. Laski and other "pluralists" have compelled a reconsideration of the whole conception of political sovereignty in the light of its social foundations. Ratzenhofer, Small, A. F. Bentley, E. P. Herring, and H. L. Childs have investigated the significance of interest-groups in political life. Charles A. Beard, C. E. Merriam, and A. N. Holcombe have emphasized the bearing of the social sciences upon the reconstruction of political science. The historical and comparative approach to politics, initiated by men like Montesquieu, appears in its best contemporary manifestation in such books as Edward Jenks's *The State and the Nation* and W. Christie MacLeod's *The Origin and History of Politics.* Far the best study of political institutions has been produced by Edward M. Sait. The legislative process, so important in democracies, has been studied in detail by Joseph P. Chamberlain and others.

Under the influence of such students as Eugen Ehrlich, Leon Duguit, Roscoe Pound, Justice Benjamin Cardozo, John A. Wigmore, and Justice Hugo M. Black, the conceptions of law and jurisprudence have been socialized, and law is now looked upon by many as a technique for guiding social change.

Ethics, so long the exclusive province of religion and metaphysics, has been placed upon a scientific basis by such men as Bertrand Russell, C. E. M. Joad, Max Otto, James H. Tufts, R. C. Givler, A. K. Rogers, and Durant Drake. According to these recent students of ethical problems, guidance for our conduct must be derived from a study of the nature of man and his social surroundings. The aim of ethics must be to provide standards and knowledge which will lead to a complete and happy life here on earth. The whole Augustinian orientation is abandoned. The objective of life is portrayed as the provision of a secure, comfortable, and enlightened existence here and now. And this secular goal must be reached by equally secular guidance. Secular and aesthetic theories of conduct have been elaborated by Havelock Ellis, George Santayana, and others.

One of the most important phases of the growing interest in the social sciences is the larger place made for them in education. But the situation at the present time is still unsatisfactory. The subject matter presented is, for the most part, traditional, and it tends to uphold the present social order rather than to suggest intelligent modes of change to a better social system. The social studies in most institutions of learning today definitely incline towards conservatism. At best, they merely describe in realistic fashion the present state of society. Those who write progressive books in the field find it difficult to get them used, and teachers who present realistic material place their tenure in jeopardy.

The stupendous changes wrought by critical thought, science, and technology in our material civilization have produced problems that can be solved only by a corresponding development of the various social sciences. We can no longer receive adequate guidance in these matters solely from the theologian, metaphysician, or politician. Instead, we must bring the social sciences up to something like the same level of development and objectivity that has already been attained by natural and applied sciences. Not only must we develop accuracy and comprehensiveness in the social sciences, but we must also provide for intelligent cooperation between them. As modern society is a unity of diverse processes and institutions, so the social sciences must be a cooperative enterprise, enriched by contributions of investigators in many realms of endeavor.

An excellent statement of the contrast between the progress of natural and social science in the last century, as well as an eloquent appeal for the development of social sciences in the years to come, is embodied in the following quotation from the stimulating address delivered by Walter Dill Scott, then president of Northwestern University, on "The Discovery of Truth in Universities":

> The universities justly claim first place as agencies for training men in effective methods of research and for formulating and teaching the principles that form the basis for later discoveries and applications. A survey of the progress of the agencies which promote human welfare reveals the fact that universities through the accomplishments of their teaching and research staffs have formulated principles and made discoveries and applications which have rendered the world a service much greater than is generally known.
>
> Specific illustrations can be drawn most readily from such experimental sciences as physics, chemistry, and geology and their application to engineering; or from such observational sciences as zoology, botany, and bacteriology and their application to agriculture and to medicine....
>
> Advance in the physical and the biological sciences during future decades will certainly prove as helpful as at any previous time. But the most fruitful researches during the twentieth century will probably be conducted not in the natural sciences, but in the social sciences. We are at last coming to see that the proper study of mankind is man. We are beginning to direct our researches to the whole life of mankind—to the nature of man as a social and political being and to the achievements of man recorded in languages, literature, and institutions. There is recognized a need for a thorough rewriting of all our texts on history, economics, politics, sociology, psychology, esthetics, pedagogy, ethics, and religion. The social sciences are fostering a progress that may be measured not in mere billions of dollars or in millions of human lives, but rather in the finer, though less tangible, terms of appreciation, service, and sacrifice.
>
> Research in the natural sciences has been effective in aiding the race to adjust itself to its physical environments. No such discovery of truth in the social sciences has been made in aiding the race to adjust itself to its human environments. Men are not now working together happily and effectively. There is said to be a lack of control in the home, restlessness in the school, apathy in the church, shirking in the shops, dishonesty in the counting houses, grafting in politics, crime in the city, and Bolshevism threatening all our institutions....
>
> All our human relations will be improved as rapidly as we make progress in the social sciences, and I am convinced that our universities will make as great a contribution in the social sciences during the twentieth century as they did by the discovery of truth in the natural sciences during the nineteenth century.
>
> We may expect the most helpful contributions to the betterment of human relations from universities possessing certain favorable characteristics.
>
> First, the university must be untrammeled by traditions or superstitions, by politics or cults; but must be animated by a love for truth, and the members of the teaching and research staff must be zealous in their pursuits of truth in their respective fields....

Second, the university must sustain a graduate school and a group of professional schools, all in intimate contact with city life. [Only in such an atmosphere and in such an environment is the seeker after truth in touch with the most progressive thought and with the most persistent presentation of the problem of human relations.][21]

These are noble sentiments, but it is not without significance that President Scott seemed to have had little success in applying his ideals at Northwestern University, nor has any other great university taken his challenge seriously. Indeed, it would be quite impossible, under the present university set-up, to do so. It is obvious enough that competent and fearless research in the social sciences would produce results that would dismay prospective benefactors of these institutions, which must exist by virtue of private endowments. Even ostensible organizations for research in social science can make little effort to come to grips with the social realities of our age. At the very moment in which Yale University was boasting of a formidable Institute of Human Relations, it was releasing Jerome Davis because he took too realistic an interest in the improvement of human relations.

Unfortunately, the trends in the social sciences during the wartime and postwar decades have not made for much confidence in their ability to lead society into a more secure and prosperous era. Until these trends are reversed, it would avail little to introduce the social sciences more extensively into either secondary or higher education. Social scientists seem to be affected by wartime emotions about as much as the man-in-the-street. They had an opportunity to recover after the first World War, and the social sciences attained unprecedented popularity, excellence of content, and educational influence. But warlike emotions once more gained ground long before the outbreak of war in 1939, not only in Fascist but also in democratic countries. Bellicose emotions engulfed the social sciences in the second World War, and this time no opportunity was offered for recovery. Before the troops had been all recalled from the European battlefields, the Cold War was in the making and was proclaimed in March, 1947. Most social scientists transferred their hostile reactions from fascism to communism. Even those who recovered some objectivity were affected by fear of persecution for, in the intellectual temper of the Cold War, even progressivism was almost equated with communism and was subject to official scrutiny. McCarthyism in the United States represented the high point in the security and persecution mania. There was, of course, no freedom of thought for social scientists in Communist lands. Their ideology had to be the specific brand or distortion of Marxism prevalent at the moment.

All this came to conform rather closely to the operations of what George Orwell, in his penetrating work *Nineteen Eighty-Four,* called "The Ministry of Truth," or public propaganda attitudes and methods. Many social scientists entered directly into the Ministry of Truth through accepting government service. Others adopted similar protective attitudes voluntarily in academic and community service.

21 Scott, *op. cit., Century,* August, 1924, pp. 556, 559, 560. Bracketed sentence not published in the magazine article, but given in the original address, which was delivered at the inauguration of Chancellor C. W. Flint of Syracuse University, October, 1921.

Allied with this trend was an effort to introduce into social science an extreme imitation of the methods of natural science, especially statistical measurement. In reasonable degree, this was commendable, but it went to ludicrous extremes. It was deemed necessary to restate even the commonplace truisms of social science in terms of higher mathematics, thus producing a literal quantitative mysticism. The subjects which could be directly measured in a statistical manner were necessarily limited, and often descended to mere triviality. Related to such measurement was a tendency to develop and state general theory in the social sciences in tortuous metaphysical obfuscation.

In due time, these two trends came to fuse when it was discovered that obscurity, whether achieved through calculus and higher differential equations or involved and confused verbiage, was not only "scientific" but also protective. There appeared to be an ever greater fear and aversion to taking positive stands on major problems or to state any conclusions in clear and straightforward language. One leading social scientist frankly stated his belief that the essential service of a good social-science textbook was to confuse rather than enlighten students.

Perhaps the most disastrous result of these esoteric and protective trends and the almost frantic drive to appear "scientific" in social science has been the virtual suppression of value judgments and the depreciation and denigration of the ameliorative function of social science. The latter, by quantitative measurements of a complex nature, establishes certain facts, often of a trivial or obvious nature. To interpret and utilize these for the betterment of society involves a real risk of forfeiting one's claim to honorable standing as a social scientist. To some, this prevalent attitude appears to relegate social science to pompous futility.

Such tendencies were especially deplorable and dangerous when the very destiny of civilization depended upon the ability to eliminate the ever increasing and more dangerous cultural lag between pure and applied science and our social institutions, and when the Cold War was exerting a powerful influence to speed up education and achievements in the already overdeveloped fields of natural science and technology.

X. TWENTIETH-CENTURY DEVELOPMENTS IN ECONOMICS

By John Fred Bell

University of Illinois

At the beginning of the twentieth century the doctrines of Alfred Marshall (1842-1924) were beginning to be widely accepted. His *Principles of Economics* (first edition, 1890) presented a forceful, logical, and realistic analysis. It avoided the extremes of classical economics, with its emphasis on cost of production or the supply side, and of marginalism, which emphasized the subjective or demand side of price analysis. Marshall presented an explanation which made demand and supply coordinate—a new or neo-classical approach.

The *Principles* went through eight editions, the last one being in 1920. Even though the first World War interrupted scholarly pursuits, the 1920's saw a great resurgence of neo-classical, or Marshallian economics. Textbooks were written for college use along the Marshallian pattern but in somewhat less difficult terms. The assumptions on which the analysis rested (never completely true or entirely false) were those of free, even pure, competition and the automatic functioning and equilibrium of the market price economy.

These basic assumptions were severely challenged in the early 1930's by the American Edward H. Chamberlin, in *The Theory of Monopolistic Competition* (1933), and in England by Mrs. Joan Robinson, in *The Theory of Imperfect Competition* (1933). These two volumes forced a reevaluation of the neo-classical equilibrium concepts by showing that competition was seldom free. A new rash of economic terms followed: imperfect competition, monopolistic competition, product differentiation; monopsony, which means control of a market situation by the buyer, had a counterpart in monopoly, or control by the producer or seller. Few buyers (oligopsony) had a counterpart in oligopoly (a few sellers). Scholars proved empirically that competition had declined and that many prices were often "fixed" by non-market forces. This brand of analysis led to more accurate market and price studies and even to legislation.

The early 1930's also saw most nations in the throes of one of the greatest of depressions. The postwar boom had nearly run its course by 1930 when the economy faltered and the depression set in. Falling prices, bank and business failures, unemployment, political unrest, were but a few of the many characteristics of the period.

Efforts to find a way out met only limited success. Business cycle studies were largely empirical and not designed to tell how to bring about relief measures and final recovery. Economic gloom prevailed as a result of beliefs in some quarters that we had reached a state of mature economy in which dynamic incentives were lacking. The end of the capitalistic system was forecast, and state activities designed to reverse the downward trend took on new dimensions.

The economic disorders were not confined to any one nation. The devastating effects of total war affected every country at all levels of economic and political life. Remedial measures were taken by national governments, designed to restore former or to improve prevailing conditions. Despite heroic attempts, mainly in the form of heavy governmental expenditures, the general level of economic conditions and economic activity was not significantly restored until the outbreak of the second World War late in 1939.

The most important change, which bordered on a revolution, in the economic thinking of fifty years came when John Maynard Keynes (1883-1946), the English public servant and economist, wrote the *General Theory of Employment, Interest and Money* in 1936. He broke with his neo-classical training and pointed out that the economy, if left to its own ends, could not and would not restore the levels of employment and income necessary to maintain a healthy economy. He introduced new dimensions in the analysis by pointing out that a macro or aggregate analysis rather than a micro or money-price approach should be employed. He also felt the state must assume economic functions never before associated with a free economy.

Of Keynes's suggestions the aggregate-income approach is of greatest importance. Government officials, business and labor leaders, individual and institutional investors, and informed citizens are deeply concerned with the levels of aggregate income. The aggregate-income levels reflect in large measure the condition of the national economy. This in turn reveals the strength and weakness of the national system, the standard of living of the people, their growth potential, and their general economic welfare. This approach was new and far removed from price analysis.

The so-called Keynesian analysis was depression-born; its avowed objective was to bring recovery without sacrificing capitalism to the extremes of communism. Most nations adopted measures that led to heavy expenditures, deficit finance, and rigid fiscal policies in an attempt to reverse the trend of falling prices and halt the depression. The outbreak of war in 1939, with heavy expenditures for war material, reversed the downward trends. The full import of Keynesian policies as recovery measures may never be known; however, his economic analysis as applied to peacetime procedures is well known. There can be no doubt that John Maynard Keynes was the most influential economist produced in the first half of the twentieth century. He exerted pronounced influence in both economic theory and in national economic policy.

In this period there were numerous developments in economics which attained some significance. The leading one was institutional economics, which dates from the late 1920's. The roots of institutionalism are found in the German historical school of the last half of the nineteenth century (roughly 1843-1883). The emphasis of this school was on the historical setting of peoples as determining factors in their economic and political growth. There was little or no reliance placed on theoretical, deductive analysis of earlier schools, notably classical economics; rather it was held that each nation should examine its own institutions, which would be found to reflect the characteristics of the people.

The movement was strongly aided by the views of the American Thorstein Veblen (1857-1929), who emphasized the pecuniary motives of society. The motives and the institutional behavior of peoples were further emphasized by John R. Commons (1862-1945) and others. Among the worthwhile results of institutionalism were some excellent studies of segments of the economy, notably corporation and business practices, the profit motive, labor unions, and especially the behavior of the business cycle. Penetrating analyses of business statistics were made by Wesley C. Mitchell (1874-1948) and Joseph A. Schumpeter (1883-1950). Largely as a result of the emphasis on institutional analysis, we know more about the functioning of the economy than known heretofore.

The most significant economic development which came as a by-product of the war years is quantitative economics. This in turn is made possible by machines —computers and data-processing equipment which process data at rates almost beyond comprehension. Mathematical analysis is now applied in practically every economic process—in linear programming, input and output analysis, decision theory in production management and in marketing of goods. Mathematical symbols and formulae permit short-cut analysis and the use of many variables in the analysis. Model simulation permits analysis of every dimension, from a small firm to national economics.

It has been found that quantification of data permits new dimensions in nearly every phase of human relations. It has opened new vistas in social sciences and logistics as well as in economic data. It has demanded new operational as well as analytical skills in educational background and training. The movement is more than in mere techniques; economic literature is tending more toward quantitative and away from institutional exposition; quantitative economics bids fair to move the whole of economic analysis more closely to an exact science than ever before visualized.

It is noteworthy that economics in the sense used here is not the product of any one nation. The vast increase of scientific journals in the field, the common language denominators, the interchange of professional people, and international conferences have had marked unifying influence. As a result of the many grants-in-aid and fellowships endowed mainly by foundations and by governments, there has been an interchange of students far exceeding the number who found their way to German and Austrian seminars when marginalism was at its peak in the last thirty years of the nineteenth century. Translations of many economic volumes, especially textbooks, have provided a common core of economic knowledge to nearly every linguistic group.

Concurrent with the basic economic fundamentals associated with capitalism, there has grown a brand of economics socialistically oriented. Many shades of emphasis appear, which range from mild socialism or Fabianism to extremes usually associated with communistic states. Policies and practices range from liberalism to totalitarianism, and along with this one finds the supporting literature. This, in turn, ranges from apologetics to basic philosophical explanation. Questions may be raised relative to freedom of investigation and analysis versus the party-line policy; however, there can be little doubt that much of the published material is effective. One must not lose sight of the objectives in any evaluation of the work done in this area.

Economics has also taken a strong turn in the general direction of applied economics. Many professional bureaus and research institutes may be found which carry on investigations in virtually every area of economic analysis. Professional economists play important roles in practically every phase of decision making in industry and business. The governments of most nations continue to be the largest single employers of trained economists next to academic institutions. The economists deal not only with current economic conditions and policy but with projections in areas of growth and development and impacts which may result from economic change.

The goal of economics remains unchanged over the years. The purpose of all economic inquiry is twofold in character: (1) the acquisition of knowledge which aids in the understanding of the economic world we live in; and (2) the control of our environment, the ability to solve economic problems. In order to control our economic environment we must be able to predict the result of a given policy or event; quantitative prediction is the ultimate test of science. The task is a difficult one, yet it must be attempted. Nations have learned that economic interdependence is vital to their existence and that economic assistance demands a careful, scientific appraisal of many factors.

In view of the complexities associated with national economic existence in the twentieth century, economists are challenged to develop their analysis to ever higher levels of scientific perfection.

XI. PHILOSOPHY IN THE TWENTIETH CENTURY

By George Dennis O'Brien

Assistant Professor of Philosophy, Princeton University

Diversity of philosophic opinion has been a scandal since ancient times. The apparent inability of the philosophers to agree on almost any issue has led many sober minds to judge that the enterprise was mere folly and to turn to more hopeful pursuits. In the twentieth century the continuing, and even worsening, condition of philosophic dispute stands in sharp contrast to the ability of the natural sciences to secure unanimity even across the most divergent of political and cultural borders. Ever since the rise of science in the late Renaissance, philosophers have sought to remedy the sad state of their discipline by modeling it on the procedures of the sciences. Descartes, the traditional founder of modern philosophy, had hoped that all doubts could be cured by adopting the methods of the geometers to philosophy. Once a scientific philosophy had been established, it would then be possible to sort out the true and the false once for all. But unfortunately the proposal to reform philosophy on a scientific basis turned out to be unclear, since the nature of science itself was unclear. Descartes' scientific reform was based on mathematics, but other philosophers using the same slogan saw in some other science—physics, biology, or psychology—the proper tool for the needed reform. Was the essence of science found in its use of mathematical technique or in its experimentalism? Should philosophy become more formal, or should it try to base itself more closely on experience? Various proposals were made from the time of Descartes down to our own day, and as the philosopher chooses his position, so he will find the writings of those who chose otherwise wrongheaded and false. In writing an account of twentieth-century philosophy one can choose some philosophic position and then show how various twentieth-century thinkers are either mistaken or anticipate in some fashion the insights correctly developed in pragmatism, positivism, phenomenology, existentialism, and so forth; but in a short history this catalogue of error is not likely to impress the reader with the soundness of the discipline. The claim, furthermore, that in the favored philosophy truth is at last to be found is not likely to be convincing when the reader considers how many times that claim has been made since Thales triumphantly declared that all things were water. Instead, let us set forth the character of modern philosophy as a series of answers to the challenge of science. Some philosophers have tried to ally philosophy to science; some have seen philosophy as a "higher science," a metaphysics; some have tried to establish philosophy as something altogether different from science; but in their varying attitudes to the single problem posed by science a pattern may be detected in diversity.

Two of the great reformers of twentieth-century philosophy, Bertrand Russell and Edmund Husserl, were proclaiming in the period just prior to the first World War that philosophy should be made, in Husserl's words, "a strict science." Both Husserl and Russell were notable mathematicians, and each was to become the spiritual father of a predominant mode of philosophy in the 1960's— the Anglo-Saxon school of analysis and the European existentialists—two schools which not only were unable to communicate with one another but generally rejected the programs of their spiritual progenitors. When these two philosophers proclaimed in their separate ways that philosophy must become a science in order to remain respectable, it should be noted that the claim was really no different from that made by the nineteenth-century philosophers. From the time of Hegel philosophers had assumed that philosophy was a science and had proceeded to demonstrate to their own satisfaction various truths which philosophy alone was capable of revealing. To Russell and Husserl, however, it appeared that the methods of the nineteenth-century thinkers were not really scientific. We shall examine each philosopher separately to see what he found unacceptable in the nineteenth-century's mode of philosophizing.

Russell's monumental contribution to philosophy was the *Principia Mathematica,* written in collaboration with Alfred North Whitehead and published in 1910. The two authors worked out in this book a powerful and elegant logical apparatus by which it was proposed to show that the principles of mathematics could be deduced from pure logic. This claim remains a matter of dispute, but the reform of the logical apparatus has, with some stylistic variations, been among the major achievements of twentieth-century philosophy. Instead of the older Aristotelian logic which used words of ordinary language like "some," "all," or "and," Russell and Whitehead, following the lead of the brilliant nineteenth-century logician and mathematician, Gottlob Frege, substituted a complete algebraic notation. The old logical example, "All men are mortal," now looked like this $(x) (Fx \supset Gx)$, which was to be read, "If any x is an F (man), then x is a G (mortal)." The new notation was perspicuous and as such allowed a great simplifying and clarifying of logical techniques. However, as with all logics from the time of Aristotle, it turned out to be based on certain metaphysical assumptions which were to appear in different forms in the subsequent careers of Whitehead and Russell.

Russell's proposed reform of philosophy was to proceed in two directions. Philosophers in the past had become confused and had populated the world with unnecessary entities because of the faultiness of the logic of ordinary language. With Russell's new logical notation it was possible to display clearly the logic of any sentence and thus dismiss claims to existence which were based on misunderstanding. The classic example was Russell's reduction of the statement, "The present king of France is bald." The difficulty with the statement as it stands is that it is impossible to be sure what is asserted if we declare the statement to be false. Do we mean to say that the king is not bald, or that there is no king at all and hence that his baldness is beside the point? And if there is no king at all, in what sense can the sentence be meaningful, since it would seem that one cannot make any statements about non-existent entities? Russell proposed that the statement be rewritten in proper logical notation and that it would then be quite clear that it was actually a compound assertion which said in effect, "There is an *x* which is the present king of France *and x* is bald, *and* for any *y* if *y* is the present king of France, *x* and *y* are identical." Spelled out in the appropriate way, it was clear that the compound statement is unequivocally false, since there is no item having the properties of being the present king of France.

The logic of everyday discourse having been reformed, Russell's other reform was to be directed toward what would be the appropriate predicates to be filled in for the *F*'s and *G*'s in the logical notation. Not only had past philosophers peopled the world with entities created out of logical confusion, but they had also introduced predicates which could not be given an empirical base. The second line of reform, then, was to reduce all complex predicates like "apple" to their sense equivalents, e.g., "red, shiny, round, sweet to taste." Any predicate which could not be reduced would be declared "senseless." Philosophy was to become scientific in two ways: (1) its basic tool, logic, was to be reformed along mathematical lines, and (2) the content of its concepts was to be established as in the empirical sciences by direct observation. The nineteenth-century idealist philosopher's claim to be scientific was rejected because he had tried to secure material content, real truths about the world, from a priori reflection; but Russell hoped to show that a priori reflection could be used only to obtain the formal results of mathematical logic and that material content could be derived only from sense experience.

Russell's program was given many names—"logical atomism," "logical positivism," "philosophical analysis," and "phenomenalism." "Phenomenalism" is not to be confused with "phenomenology," the school of philosophy founded by Edmund Husserl, to whom we can now turn.

Husserl's program for reform in philosophy does not at first glance seem to be very different from Russell's. Both purport to break from the nineteenth century by turning directly to "things as we experience them." Russell thought that this meant the immediate sensations of color, shape, weight, and so forth, but Husserl would have argued that this was precisely not how we *immediately* perceive things. Russell's sense data are not *immediate* data; rather they are highly refined data such as only a philosopher would be likely to encounter. No, what we immediately perceive are the objects of our ordinary world such as apples and men. Phenomenology takes as its task a discriminating report on these objects of our immediate world as we experience them in our life. The search for the meaning of our language does not proceed in the direction of reduction of our everyday vocabulary to simple sense predicates, but rather to a search for essences. The essence is the stable structure of our everyday experience that we grasp through a distinctive act of cognition which Husserl calls "the intentional act." The mind is not a blank slate on which sense impressions are recorded; rather it is an active agent which formulates and seeks out an object through its "intentions." Russell's reform of philosophy on a scientific base looks for its models in reductive analyses like chemistry, where the "real" nature of the compound is to be discovered by breaking the complex into its atomic parts (thus the names for his philosophy, "logical *atomism,*" "philosophical *analysis*"). Husserl's model would have to be found in a science which was descriptive and did not try to reconstitute the everyday world out of atomic parts. Russell's philosophy from the standpoint of phenomenology was not a sufficient break from the nineteenth century. F. H. Bradley, Russell's teacher from whom he professed to differ sharply, had written a major idealist study called *Appearance and Reality,* in which he attempted to show that the common-sense world was unstable appearance and that only in the Absolute could reality be located. Russell differed from Bradley only in his location of reality in the sense data, but the basic structure of an everyday world of appearance and an underlying reality remained. Russell was countering Bradley's idealistic metaphysics with an empiricist metaphysics, but the phenomenologist wanted to do away with metaphysical speculation about reality versus appearance. Reality *is* what appears, the phenomena. As the name "phenomenology" indicates, the *logos,* science, was to be a science of the appearances themselves, not a science arrived at by re-constructing appearances from the "real" data.

In 1919 the American philosopher, John Dewey, delivered a series of lectures entitled *Reconstruction in Philosophy* at the Imperial University in Tokyo in which he summed up in a popular manner much of the work that he had done in the first twenty years of the century, and prepared a sort of preface for al-most thirty more years of extraordinary interesting work ranging over meta-physics, theory of knowledge, aesthetics, and philosophy of logic. Dewey, like Russell and Husserl, had been brought up under the heavy influence of the German idealist school. Early in his career, however, he came under the influence of the pragmatists James and Peirce, and turned decisively away from idealism. Using the insights of Peirce—a philosopher regarded by the twentieth century as a truly major figure, quite outstripping the more elegant William James— Dewey had already marked his separation from nineteenth-century thought by an early work, *Essays in Experimental Logic,* which was a careful analysis of defects in the logic of Lotze. Where Whitehead and Russell had sought to reform logic on a mathematical model, Dewey sought to reform logic by adapting it to the techniques of the experimental procedures developed by scientific research. "Logic" was only a further refinement of the techniques of inquiry which man displays in rudimentary form in every practical adaptation to his biological and cultural environment. Philosophy must reconstruct itself by becoming more scientific in the sense that it must change its method from the a priori reflections of the idealists to the method of experience. Russell's reform was incorrect in two counts. First, his logic was an a priori logic allied to mathematics which was not the logic of actual scientific practice; secondly, his material content, sense data, was not at all what we experience. Dewey, like Husserl, would find the content of experience closer to the data of common sense. "Experience" is not a passive undergoing, but is the product of the practical interaction of the organism with the environment. The world is always the lived world in which objects are the tools singled out by the organism to foster its practical life. Russell's reform of philosophy was in the direction of a pure theory, but Dewey, as a pragmatist, found the divorce between theory and practical life the besetting sin of almost all past philosophy. Husserl's phenomenology shared Dewey's respect for the everyday world, but still envisioned a pure theory of phenomena and did not realize that the world of experience was a world generated by practical interests.

Dewey's philosophy was a major influence in American philosophy until recent times, when the conviction has grown upon many philosophers that philosophy is not at all like science and that perhaps all the reforms proposed by the early giants of twentieth-century philosophy were ill-conceived at the very start. Let us turn then to the roots of this anti-scientific philosophy among the contemporaries of Russell, Husserl, and Dewey.

It was said of G. E. Moore, comparing him to Russell, "Mr. Bertrand Russell produces a new philosophy every ten years, and Mr. G. E. Moore none at all." Moore, almost Russell's age, his onetime teacher and lifelong friend, developed a mode of philosophical discourse that has virtually captured the field in Anglo-Saxon philosophy at mid-century. Russell remains, for all his gestures of revolt, a philosopher in the traditional pattern—a system builder who is proposing a metaphysical interpretation of the world. Moore, for many years the editor of the influential British journal *Mind,* published mostly short pieces treating in minute detail very limited problems. His attempt was not to decide what really existed—although he did not deny that that was possible—but simply to understand what was being claimed by certain philosophical theses. One of his most famous essays "Refutation of Idealism," was a straightforward defense of common sense against claims made by philosophers like Bradley that the world was unreal. Moore said that surely no one could mean that I could doubt that this is my hand, or that I am sitting in a chair typing. And if the idealists did not mean to cast doubt on these statements of common sense, then what was the point of their claims? The charge brought against the idealist was not that his doctrine was false because he needed a special empirical metaphysics, but that it was confusing since he simply could not mean to impute the obvious validity of our everyday judgments. Moore's philosophy was a fragmentary philosophy in which particular problems were analyzed for their claims. This type of philosophical analysis contrasts sharply with Russell's. Russell's analyses were metaphysical and reductive—offensive entities were to be reduced to their empirical parts—but Moore's analyses were not in the interest of any preferred metaphysics, but sought to make plain ordinary sense out of the puzzling utterances of philosophers. Analysis was not a science but an art. Moore's rejection of scientific method in philosophy is best brought out in his very influential ethical writings in which he developed a theory of intuitionism. He claimed that "good" was a non-natural predicate which could be apprehended by a special moral sense. In the final analysis one had simply to see that the action or character to be judged was good.

In 1922 Russell wrote the introduction to a book by one of his former pupils, Ludwig Wittgenstein. The book was entitled *Tractatus Logico-Philosophicus,* and is one of the most remarkable books in the whole history of philosophy. Written in the form of short numbered aphorisms, it had first appeared in the original German as an article and was later presented to the English public in a parallel translation—a precedent to be followed in most of Wittgenstein's subsequent published material. In a short compass Wittgenstein developed a comprehensive philosophy, touching all the classical issues of philosophy in a manner so paradoxical and compressed that the doctrine has been subsequently claimed by schools ranging from logical positivism to Zen Buddhism. Russell hailed the book but evidently had some trouble comprehending it, though he obviously thought it supported his own views. One part he did understand and found very disturbing. In the book Wittgenstein made a sharp distinction between what can be known, the facts of the world, and what can only be *shown* or intuited in what he chooses to call "the mystical." Unfortunately for Russell, almost all of his philosophy turned out to be in the area of the mystical. Russell had hoped to establish a scientifically based logic and theory of meaning, and now Wittgenstein claimed to show that logical structure can only be shown, not demonstrated, and that theory of meaning was a contradiction in terms.

Wittgenstein's central thesis can be stated very simply—it is a form of strict empiricism. The meaning of any statement is determined by the relation it has to some possible fact. Only statements sketching out some possible fact can be said to have a meaning. This meaning relation between the statement and the world of possible facts is not itself a further fact. Therefore, any statement *about* a meaning cannot be a meaningful statement in the sense of sketching out a possible fact. To pretend to have a theory of meaning is a misuse of the notion of "theory." Theories are based on fact statements, but meaning is not a fact at all, and hence there can be no statements true or false about meaning. The meaning relation can be shown, but it cannot be factually established. If we had to establish factually that such and such was the meaning of a statement, then "whether a proposition had sense would depend on whether another proposition was true." The question that a worried Russell raised to Wittgenstein was: How, if what he claimed was the case, had he managed to write a book in which so many things were obviously said about the mystical? Wittgenstein's answer was contained in the famous final propositions of the *Tractatus:*

6.54 My propositions serve as elucidations in the following way: anyone who understands me eventually recognizes them as nonsensical, when he has used them—as steps—to climb up beyond them. (He must, so to speak, throw away the ladder after he has climbed up it.)

He must transcend these propositions, and then he will see the world aright.
7 What we cannot speak about we must consign to silence.[22]

22 Ludwig Wittgenstein, *Tractatus Logico-Philosophicus,* trans. D. F. Pears and B. F. McGuinness, Humanities Press, 1961.

The past history of philosophy, including the philosophy of Russell, had been a series of attempts to say what could only be shown and was therefore, in a precise sense, "nonsense." The task of philosophy, Wittgenstein averred, was simply to elucidate propositions pointing out, to those tempted to say what can only be shown, that they have in fact said nothing. Russell's attempt to be scientific was a misunderstanding of the function of philosophy as pure elucidation of "the mystical."

Wittgenstein had written his book while a prisoner of war at Monte Cassino during the first World War; persuaded, after the war, that he had indeed found what he had claimed in the preface, "the final solution of the problems," he retired to teach school in a remote village in Austria. He was a strange and difficult man with many of the eccentricities of genius who sought a life of isolation. Nevertheless, his book was read eagerly by several philosophers in Vienna, and a few unsatisfactory contacts were made. The Vienna group were stimulated by the strict empiricism of the *Tractatus* but continued to be unhappy about the mystical conclusions. Developing a suggestion of Russell's in the introduction to the *Tractatus*—that meaning might be talked about in a "meta-language"—this group under the guidance of Rudolph Carnap hoped to reconstitute a scientific philosophy in which a strict theory of meaning and logic could be developed. They became known as the Vienna Circle and were formally the founders of "logical positivism." Prominent in the group were Carnap, Moritz Schlick, Otto Neurath, and Herbert Feigl. Schlick was killed by a crazed Nazi student, and the others fled to the United States to escape the oppression of the Hitler regime. Logical positivism continues to flourish widely in the United States although it is somewhat tempered. In America it turned away from its more extreme claims to establish philosophy as a rigorous science; nevertheless it comes as close as any currently vigorous school to supporting the hopes of Russell. The positivists continued an interest in formal logic which has been fostered in the twentieth century by a brilliant series of logicians among whom David Hilbert, Kurt Gödel, Alonzo Church, and W. V. O. Quine must be mentioned. The continued espousal of some form of the verification theory of meaning or its ancestors (i.e., the meaning of a statement is given by designating the method of its verification) has kept the school decidedly anti-metaphysical, and restricted its scope in the area of value theory.

Carnap's metalinguistic "solution" to the mystical paradox of the *Tractatus* was rejected with some heat by Wittgenstein, who returned to the scholarly world in 1929 at Cambridge. From that time until his death in 1951 Wittgenstein was the most influential philosopher in Britain. Although he published only one brief unsatisfactory paper in that entire period, his "lectures" at Cambridge were attended by many of the major philosophers of the United States and England. Moore, to whose chair Wittgenstein succeeded in 1939, was a frequent attendant at the sessions, which were mostly agonized dialogues that left the lecturer exhausted and his listeners bewildered. Since Wittgenstein would not publish, surreptitious transcripts of some of the sessions were distributed in mimeographed form. Only after Wittgenstein's death was the book he had been preparing, *Philosophical Investigations,* published; subsequently his literary executors have published further notes.

By Wittgenstein's own admission a striking reorientation of his thought occurred in 1933, but the exact nature of the change is by no means clear. In one important particular his thought remained the same—his rejection of a "scientific philosophy." He abandoned the aphorisms of the *Tractatus* for books which are no more than "series of sketches," to emphasize in a new way that the philosophical task was a matter of winning through to insight rather than of gaining new facts about the world. Gathering the meaning of a sign is not a matter of grasping a new fact but is like seeing a line drawing *as* a human face. When a person "sees something *as* such and such," he sees not a new fact but a new order in the facts that he had seen perfectly well before. Philosophy was to be concerned with analysis of meaning but not in the reductive sense of the Russellians or the positivists; rather philosophy was to be "purely descriptive," assembling cases in which words can be *seen* functioning in an environment. Philosophy was not a theory but an activity, and its point was to reorient words to their use. Metaphysicians "take language on a holiday" when they utter words which do not have any use. The popular scientist who tells his listeners that the desks they write on are not solid because each desk is composed of electrons is not *using* the notion of "solid." The listener thinks of "unsolid" as designating certain qualities in contrast to others—rickety, not firm; dangerous, not safe and so forth. A word has a "use" when it directs one way and not another. Unfortunately, the popular scientists's word "unsolid" is like a directional sign that points in two directions at the same time because as he applies the word it fails utterly to contrast rickety and firm desks, since they are all "unsolid" in so far as they are composed of electrons. What appears at first blush to be an interesting factual generalization turns out on inspection to be a disguised linguistic decision.

Wittgenstein's methods were appropriated by many philosophers, and the notion of analysis was revived as "linguistic analysis" or "ordinary language philosophy." Prominent among the practitioners of this new school, the slogan of which was "Don't ask for the meaning, ask for the use," were John Wisdom, Gilbert Ryle, and John Austin. Some philosophers showed an almost apostolic zeal in promulgating what they took to be the oracles of Wittgenstein, while others branched off on lines which were independent of his thought but generally fell under the label of "ordinary language philosophy." The main divisions could be found about the notion of "use." Wittgenstein's contrastive notion of "use" and "ordinary language" appears to be a special notion. Others have interpreted "use" more pragmatically, and some even hoped to return to a scientific philosophy by grounding the notion of what *is* used on the results of descriptive linguistics. Russell's puzzles about "the present king of France" can be solved not by elaborate formal transformations, but simply by noting that in actual contexts of use, the meaning of the phrase would be obvious or else the question of truth or falsity simply would not arise.

Wittgenstein's philosophy was suited to the state of native English philosophy since it had roots in Russell and appeared in its last phase a continuation of the work of G. E. Moore. We have already detailed some of the sharp divergences from Russell's notion of analysis; Wittgenstein, however, also broke with Moore. Moore was interested in preserving the *truth* of common sense by showing that the attacks of the metaphysicians were incomprehensible if they meant to deny the obvious facts. Wittgenstein applauded ordinary language not because it embodied truths, but because its method of imparting meaning to words was the only legitimate method.

British philosophy at mid-century appears to have turned decisively away from metaphysics or philosophy as a science toward a conception of philosophy as an activity of linguistic analysis. Let us now retrace our steps in European philosophy to see what factors present at the time of Husserl's attempts at a new scientific grounding of philosophy conspired to produce a similar reversal in Continental thought.

While tending the wounded during the first World War, the Frenchman, Gabriel Marcel, was moved to write out a series of largely unconnected and unfinished meditations on various philosophical themes. These sketches in their unpolished state were later published in the form of a "metaphysical diary." Marcel was attempting throughout the course of his speculations to free himself from the idealism of the nineteenth century, particularly as expressed in the American philosopher Josiah Royce. It is interesting to note that at the very time that Wittgenstein was writing the *Tractatus* as a series of unconnected aphorisms in order to escape the scientism and metaphysics of Russell, Marcel was trying by a similar device to escape a metaphysical view which identified philosophy with a special kind of knowledge. What is so startling about the initial similarity is the complete and utter divergence between the existentialism which Marcel helped to foster and the Anglo-Saxon method of analysis that grew out of Wittgenstein's work.

Marcel's efforts were closely allied with the thought of Henri Bergson, who proposed by a special intuition of temporal flow to escape the static world view which science and technique had created for the purpose of practical control. The necessity of a special kind of attitude toward reality which could not be enclosed in the methods of rational detachment had its roots in Schopenhauer, and was much favored by various schools prominent in the first quarter of the twentieth century. Under titles such as *"Lebensphilosophie"* and "the philosophy of the spirit," philosophers like Max Scheler and Louis Lavelle attempted to elucidate the world not as known but as lived and experienced.

One could say either that this philosophy was a kind of "higher science" yielding "knowledge" of areas which the abstractive methods of the ordinary sciences failed to comprehend, or that philosophy was really no science but a shared experience analogous to poetry.

If one chose the first option, then metaphysics was a possible "science," but by and large the influential European philosophers avoided metaphysics. The one major figure who did opt for a "higher science" growing out of an intuition of the flux of things was Russell's collaborator Alfred North Whitehead. Whitehead turned in old age from mathematics to speculative philosophy in the grand manner and for some twenty years as University Professor at Harvard developed a "process metaphysics" which paralleled much in Bergson and the more speculative pragmatists like George Herbert Mead.

The logic of *Principia* suggested this view to Whitehead. *Principia* logic dissolved the old Aristotelian substances such as "man" into *X*'s in which a property such as humanity was present. Whitehead gave a metaphysical interpretation of this logic, which viewed the world as the "ingression" of eternal patterns into the flux of existence. Through intuition of structures in process, one could reach true reality and avoid the partiality of the physical sciences. He labeled the mistakes of an abstractive science the fallacies of "simple location" and "misplaced concreteness" in order to emphasize his view that true reality was dynamic process grasped by participation in reality rather than by observation from a distance. Even God was involved in change and becoming while at the same time acting as a principle for stability within process. Whitehead's metaphysical views enjoyed a considerable vogue in theological and philosophical circles because, despite the radical nature of many of his conceptions, they ran counter to the restricted analytic and anti-metaphysical aims of the positivists. Whitehead's philosophy is one of the few clear cases of a new metaphysical system produced in the twentieth century. Other philosophers have either eschewed the title of metaphysician or tended, if they continued in that tradition, to be new versions of older modes, such as the idealist Benedetto Croce or the numerous Neo-Thomist philosophers.

Despite some commonality of thematic material, Whitehead's philosophy is distinguished from contemporary Continental philosophy by the consciously anti-scientific, anti-systematic nature of the predominant European school, that of "existentialism." The existentialists all make use of notions similar to participation, and see participation as the key to a penetration of reality, but they deny that what they are doing is "metaphysics." Philosophical speculation is not capable of giving a "higher knowledge"; rather it is closer to an elucidation of faith. "Knowledge" is to be restricted to what is appropriated by the neutral observer, *das Mann,* as the German existentialist Martin Heidegger referred to him. The philosopher moves in the area of "mystery," which Gabriel Marcel defined as "a problem that encroaches on its own data." The philosopher does not stand outside the material he is investigating, eavesdropping on a world that is not his; rather he participates in the world, and his investigations help to shape the very data he wishes to examine. The most widely known existentialist, Jean-Paul Sartre, presents at great length a typical *philosophical* problem in his discussion of the phenomenon of "self-deception." In attempting, he says, to investigate what sort of person I am, it is obvious that I cannot stand outside the data. The whole method and manner of the investigation, and consequently the answers I am likely to produce, are affected by the kind of person that I am. Self-deception is almost inevitable since I alter the data in the very process of appropriating it.

The name "existentialism" is eschewed by all the major figures except Sartre. The meaning of the label must be understood at least minimally as a rejection of a doctrine which would have to be called "essentialism." "Essence" denotes some conceptual pattern or standard which defines a thing to be just such and such. A plant which fails to achieve its natural growth would fail to realize its essence. In its sharpest formulation in Sartre, existentialism denies, at least in the case of man, that there is any essence. For man there is no essence which says what he ought to be. The "essence" of man is just that he has no essence; he is the creature who defines himself in his existential career, his history. Man is completely free—what he is is what he makes himself by his actions, so that one cannot say that a man is (define him) until he is dead, until his history is complete. The only guide to right action is the preservation of that freedom. An anti-Semite (using Sartre's example) is "immoral" not because he violates in some way the nature of manhood, but because he barters away his freedom, adopting toward other men the hard, impenetrable character of stone—a being which indeed *is* its fixed essential character, having no history, no freedom. In terror of history, freedom, and change, men adopt some essence which closes them off from others.

Other so-called "existentialists" also point to the centrality of history, existence, and freedom and reject the static categories of "essentialism," but they differ from Sartre in rejecting the radical dualism between existence (freedom) and essence (nature) which makes life a complete absurdity for Sartre. The necessity to "essentialize" human existence is pervasive in Sartre but it falls upon man like a plague without any possibility of understanding or salvation. Heidegger rightly styles himself an ontologist and Gabriel Marcel has meditated long on what he calls "the ontological mystery." Without doing away with the centrality of history and existence, these men try to discern from a reflection on how man lives and makes history what permanent structures underlie his struggles as goals. Essentialism was wrong in thinking that one could understand life a priori by first deducing essences to which existence can be seen to conform. Instead of seeking for essence we search for Being, which is the goal pointed at and understood in terms of our existential experience. Insight into Being provides a point of conjunction between the world of human existence and the world of nature— the tendencies toward freedom and the necessity to fixate that freedom. Marcel does not hesitate to identify the Being which he discovers by this process with the Christian God, the Lord of Nature and History. Freedom need not be only in protean revolution, it can "fixate" itself in love and genuine communication. Love is the paradoxical solution of man's dilemma whereby he gives away his freedom only to receive it back enriched and fulfilled.

Although the major existentialist philosophers differ sharply about many issues (Marcel is a Roman Catholic, Sartre is an atheist), yet there is a common approach which it is useful to emphasize in a brief account. Since they all believe that reality is participated in but not observed, they have had to adopt radical methods for communicating their views. Marcel accordingly pleads in his Gifford lectures, *The Mystery of Being,* for an audience of "connoisseurs." The philosopher and the audience participate in a common reality and they must both share a common experience of this reality. Reality is not to be talked *about,* it is to be grasped immediately. It is for this reason that the existentialists have turned so often to the production of plays or novels. Marcel and Sartre are playwrights, Albert Camus was a novelist, Martin Heidegger has done some of his most significant work in the form of commentaries on the poetry of Rilke and Hölderlin. The play can *present* a view of the world which the audience shares, while the ordinary philosophical lecture only talks *about* reality and by adopting this neutral stance is bound essentially to distort the subject matter. When the existentialists do turn to philosophy directly, it is more likely to be in the form of the metaphysical sketchbook, or a meditation on some pregnant philosophical epigram.

Existentialism, for all its radicalness in terminology, has ancient roots. Forebears have been found in Kierkegaard, Pascal, Augustine, and even Plato. In all these philosophers the person of the philosopher is as important as, or sometimes more important than, the "doctrines" he may expound. Philosophy is not a study which one might choose, such as engineering or chemistry; it is a reflective adjustment to the fact of life itself. In Socrates' words, it is "learning how to die." Philosophy is a human reaction to deep and fundamental problems which all men have in virtue of their existential status. Since existentialism does focus on philosophy as a basic human activity, it legitimately turns its attention to emotions like fear, anxiety, and desire for love and community which produce the activity of philosophy. We can understand reality by noting its effects directly on the life of the person. Existentialist philosophers and psychoanalytic theorists share a common field because both are concerned with the efficient causes in reality which lead to various practical and theoretical adjustments. The nature of existential philosophy can be expressed not by asking for a philosopher's doctrine, but by asking what is it in the nature of things that makes him perform philosophic activity.

Philosophy at mid-century has split into two non-communicating camps—the analysts and the existentialists. Both schools are alike in rejecting metaphysics and all attempts to make philosophy a science yielding new data about the world. Analysts, broadly defined to cover positivistic analysts, see philosophy as a purely formal investigation either in technical logic, or in the adjudication of category confusions by attention to the use of words. Philosophy, according to this group, does not give us any material knowledge. The existentialists see philosophy as an activity of life which does not yield knowledge but rather illuminates from within the conditions of human existence. As a reaction to existential pressures, philosophy is not properly a theory but a "practical" activity. Despite their separate claims to having achieved the final revolution in philosophy, a reader with a glance at history may still entertain a reasonable doubt.

XII. NEW TRENDS IN RELIGION

By George Dennis O'Brien

Assistant Professor of Philosophy, Princeton University

Special problems arise in writing a history of religion in the twentieth century. We are no longer confident that we can locate the religious phenomenon in the traditional churches. People speak of political movements such as fascism or communism as "religions." Studies in psychology have led many to doubt whether there is any peculiarly *religious* phenomenon. But most striking of all is the guidance of twentieth-century theologians in this matter. One noted theologian has said that the greatest Protestant thinkers of the nineteenth century were Marx, Freud, and Nietzsche, none of whom will be found in the previous sections on nineteenth-century religion. Indeed, the nineteenth-century theologian and philosopher most influential on twentieth-century theology, Sören Kierkegaard, was barely mentioned in books published during the 1920's and 1930's. A history of twentieth-century religion, if it is to be written in the thought patterns of the twentieth century, must give some attention to the nature of the subject matter to be discussed.

Paul Tillich, one of the most influential contemporary theologians, locates religion in the phenomenon of "ultimate concern." Where a man's ultimate concern is, there is his religion. This definition of religion cuts across traditional lines and permits the designation of communism as a religion since it does form the locus of ultimate concern for many people. Nominally religious institutions may lack ultimate concern—in the multiple concerns connected with keeping his institution solvent, a clergyman may let slip the drive of ultimate concern and the church will become another worldly institution. "Ultimate concern" alone gives merely a subjective determination of religion. A religious *attitude* is present wherever there is ultimate concern, but the theologian makes a separation of true and false religion in terms of the object of this attitude. If the ultimate concern is turned to some object which is not itself ultimate, then the religious attitude is perverted. Common speech takes note of this when we say of someone (disapprovingly), "He makes his hobby (work, sports, etc.) his religion." True religion would be the turning of ultimate concern toward some object which is ultimate.

Even such a brief sketch of the meaning of religion puts us in a better position to speak of the place of religion in the twentieth century. It is quite easy to point to statistics showing the enormous drop in church attendance on a world-wide scale in the period since the first World War and say that this is indeed a non-religious age. It has even been called in recent years, "the post-Christian era." But if we wish to get at a more fundamental non-religiousness in modern society, we would look at the erosion of the sense of ultimate concern among Christian peoples. Urbanization, a continuously rising standard of living, and the mass media of entertainment have led many people to seek security as an end in itself, to replace ultimate concerns with the proximate concerns of day-to-day living. In

Christian terms, there has been a great triumph of the world over the spirit. It is no longer possible to build a bridge from the pressing physical concern for "our daily bread" to the concern for spiritual sustenance in a day of widespread plenty. Basic needs are being met, and where matters of ultimate concern remain, such as death, convenient fictions may serve to mask their reality. With the increase in secularization one can surely say that the twentieth century has been less religious than previous ages.

At the same time, many of the forces operative in eliminating basic needs have produced tensions in modern society that have led to the revolt of the spirit— sometimes in demonic forms. Technical progress has made it possible to feed and clothe vast populations, but the impersonal pressures of the machine and the great urban centers that have grown up to tend the tools of material production have produced deep anxieties in many who feel the loss of their human importance in the face of the great industrial complex of the modern state and economy. Religious concerns have expressed themselves wherever men have sought to personalize the threats of their world. In the United States the economic depression of the 1930's revived the Ku Klux Klan, which registered in anti-Jewish, anti-Catholic, anti-Negro campaigns the protests of the rural middle class against the threatening tide of industrialism. In the 1960's in America, there has been a burgeoning of Christian anti-Communist crusades presenting in the devil theory of history a type of religious heresy which is comforting to those who find the pressure of international tensions insupportable. The culmination of demonic religion in the twentieth century was in fascism, particularly as expressed in Nazi Germany under Hitler. There, in the figure of the infallible leader who expressed in his person the will of the *Volk,* leading the nation to an eternal destiny, casting out devils from their midst, we have all themes of religion perverted to the most degraded ends. One could seek to recover a sense of person within the Nazi party because the attachment was not to an impersonal standard or cause but to the *Fuehrer* who summed up in himself the cause and the nation.

In order then to escape the depersonalizing pressures of the modern age, men have sought in ways both tragic and comic to repersonalize their existence. Whether it is through a life vicariously lived in the doings of some wayward star of the entertainment world, or the dedication to the cult of personality surrounding some dictator, men have not ceased to be "religious" in the sense of seeking an interpretation of existence which pushes through abstract causes and discovers persons as the ultimate actors in history. Man, finding his dignity threatened in an ultimate way by a battle with impersonal forces, will seek an enemy to combat, a hero to assist him. He retains an ultimate concern with himself as *person,* and in seeking to interpret the world in personalistic terms he will be making the genuinely religious move. In this sense we can say that the twentieth century *because* of its secularization has been a great age of religion—though from a Christian point of view it has all too frequently been demonic religion.

The threat to persons offered by the technical age has been expressed most clearly in the World Wars which were carried on in a manner and on a scale befitting a vast industrial complex. Not only were more people destroyed on a wider area of the globe than at any previous time in history, but more significantly, the manner of killing became gradually more impersonal until we had progressed from the naked heroism of the trench warfare of 1914 to the quite remote "push-button war" projected for the future.

The World Wars made plain to the theologians that the liberal gospel of the nineteenth century as put forward by Ritschl and Rauschenbusch was inadequate to the forces at work in this century, and new theological beginnings were made during and following the first World War. Karl Barth, who had been trained in the Ritschlian school at Marburg, found himself pastor of a small mountain church in Switzerland during the war. His attempt to preach the liberal gospel of moral progress while the big guns boomed from across the border in Alsace led him into profound inner conflict. How could one speak of rational cooperation for the betterment of mankind when it was so manifest that there was a madness in man which made this gospel idealistic in the worst sense?

The theology which Barth inherited was the product of a predominant strain in nineteenth-century religious thought. Taking their cue from Hegel, successive theologians interpreted God's action as immanent in history. Higher criticism of the Biblical texts seemed to make supernaturalistic interpretation of the New Testament impossible, and the great triumphs of science, particularly the theory of evolution, seemed to bring the Bible into direct conflict with reason. The liberal gospel tended to de-emphasize the supernatural aspects of the Christian tradition and to emphasize the role of Christianity as a moral force in Western civilization. Jesus became the great ethical teacher and model, and the point of the Christian church was not sacramental and supernatural but to act as a moral leaven for the world. Christian forces in the form of the church were at work *in* history. Christ's "victory over the world" was, according to the Ritschlians, an assurance of the eventual triumph of men of good will in history.

There was one major nineteenth-century theologian who dissented violently from the prevailing idealistic cast which Hegel's philosophy had lent to Christian theology; this was Sören Kierkegaard. Kierkegaard was born in Denmark in 1813 and died in 1855. Partly because he wrote in Danish and partly because his thought was so uncongenial to the prevailing temper of his century, Kierkegaard lived out a life of passionate protest which yielded him nothing but contempt and scorn from his contemporaries and almost total lack of recognition after his death. Only in the first World War, when his works were translated into German and when the times were more congenial to his anguished view of human existence, could he be acclaimed as one of the great Christian thinkers of all time. In a vast outpouring of works marked by a superb literary gift and great aesthetic sensitivity, Kierkegaard attacked again and again the idealistic "system" of history. To call attention to his break from the ordered marshaling of the facts of existence to which the Hegelians pretended, Kierkegaard gave his books such titles as *Philosophical Fragments* and *Concluding Unscientific Postscript*. If the Hegelians and their followers emphasized God's immanence in history, Kierkegaard pointed to God's utter transcendence over history. Instead of finding the evidence for faith in God in the existence of rational morality in man, Kierkegaard, in

Fear and Trembling, nominated Abraham as the "father of faith" because he was willing to suspend the ethical and to perform what was to all appearances an absurd act, the sacrifice of his only son, Isaac, at the command of God. Since God was utterly transcendent, there was no way that we could come to *know* him by pointing to this or that fact in history—even the facts of the supposed moral progress which showed God's will in the world. When God does appear in history in the person of Jesus Christ he is as much hidden as revealed. In a striking story in the *Philosophical Fragments,* Kierkegaard compares the coming of God in Christ to the coming of a great king to his beloved who is a poor peasant girl. The king cannot come in splendor and power, since then he will not know whether his beloved loves him or is awed by his power. So he comes in the form of the servant, a humble one. Now she can love him for what he is. But he is not simply the humble one, he is also the king; for that he was born and for that he came into this world. He must therefore convince her *as the humble one* that he is king. If the maiden believes, it is because of faith, not because of rational evidence. Faith does not build on rational evidence in history; it is the acceptance of the paradox that in Jesus Christ the God who is wholly other becomes what is most immediate, human.

Barth was moved by the reading of Kierkegaard, and in 1918 he published a commentary on the Epistle to the Romans which established his own theology. It was called *crisis* theology, not as one might suppose because it was produced by a personal and world crisis, but in the ancient sense of *krisis,* which refers to judgment. Barth's theology was a *judgmental* theology in that he interpreted God as standing over against man's history as judge, not acting within it as reformer. Not the least of the human institutions against which God directs his judgment is the Christian church. Barth's *Epistle to the Romans* heaps scorn on religion and the church. In particular he excoriates liberal theology which did not see that "one can *not* speak of God simply by speaking of man in a loud voice." The church, like all men, must work out its salvation with fear and trembling. Barth's forthright attack on the churches in his early book seemed to make him an unlikely candidate for the position which he accepted at Göttingen in dogmatic theology. There he began writing one of the monumental theological works of the whole Christian era—a work which he first entitled *Christian Dogmatics* but later retitled, in an apparent reversal of his previous attacks on the church, *Church Dogmatics.*

Revolutions in dogmatic theology seldom turn on the material to be studied. The Christian theologian is committed in some sense to the classic documents of the Christian church. Barth's revolution, like most theological revolutions of the past, stemmed from a new method applied to the old material. The nineteenth century had read the Gospel through the eyes of the historian and grammarian. Attempts were made to discover the "historical Jesus" and the meaning of terms and phrases of the New Testament for the contemporaries of Jesus. But Kierkegaard had taught Barth that the "contemporary disciple"—he who has seen Jesus in his historical context—is no better able to appropriate the content of a paradoxical revelation than the man of today. The philological, historical approach to the Gospel necessarily compromised its universality by confining it to the trappings of first-century Palestine. On the other hand, in seeking universality, the liberal theologians had simply by-passed the historical Jesus to seek a moral teacher who preached in parable Kant's categorical imperative. Barth's theology was not to be the theology of the scholar or the moral reformer but the theology of the preacher. Our interest in the Gospel is not in terms of what Christ's Palestinian audiences would have understood in his Aramaic tongue, but in how the Word of God speaks to us in our contemporary world. The Word of God is always what is preached and witnessed to in the body of those who have faith in Jesus Christ. The church does not speak with the reserve and diffidence of the scholar *about* the Word of God, rather the church is a continuous witnessing to the reality of Jesus as himself the Word of God to men. Barth's own inability to speak with scholarly reserve has in fact scandalized the academic community, as in, for example, his bitter invective directed at a long-time colleague, Emil Brunner. The scholar weighing evidence is professionally committed to personal indifference about the result of his research, but the believer, if he believes that Christ is his personal Saviour, cannot pretend to detachment about whether this is in fact the case or not. Indeed, if he were to take up the attitude of the detached inquirer, he could not from that base reconstitute the relation of faith and trust. Faith then is more than the assent to the truth of propositions *about* Jesus, e.g., that he is God, that he is the Messiah; rather it is living in a world transformed by the reality of these truths. It is fitting, then, for Barth to turn to *Church Dogmatics,* for the church is not the body of those who assent to the truth of propositions about Jesus as much as it is the body of those who live in and through their Lord. From this life *in* Christ the preacher speaks and bears witness to the reality of his faith. One could say, with some oversimplification, that preaching is a piece of faith behavior as a cry is a piece of pain behavior. The cry is not information about the pain, it is part and parcel of the pain; so preaching is not words about faith, about Jesus, it is the unique activity of faith, the activity of living in Christ.

Barth's career has been long and his influence world-wide. Protestants of fundamentalist or liberal tendencies have differed sharply with his preacher's theology. Roman Catholics, on the other hand, have found much to their liking in his work, and Hans Küng has claimed, much to Barth's amazement, that he and the Roman church are one on the crucial Reformation issue of justification. Barth directly influenced the work of most twentieth-century Continental theologians, particularly Emil Brunner, a fellow Swiss, and the German theologian Friederich Gogarten. Barth's impact on the churches was equally great. He was one of the guiding spirits behind the Confessing church in Germany. Under the direction of men like Martin Niemöller, the Confessing church, following Barth's early lead, was steadfast in its resistance to the Nazi regime. Barth broke theologically with Brunner and Gogarten at the beginning of the Nazi era because he felt that their attempt to compromise the utter transcendence of God by the doctrine of "orders," or analogy, would undermine the protest of the church against the demonic Hitler regime which sought to identify its destiny in history with divine destiny.

The Hitler regime's racist and religious intolerance caused a great internationalization of scholarship, since many distinguished philosophers, scientists, and theologians were forced to flee to other lands. Barth himself returned to Switzerland. Paul Tillich came to the United States and through his teaching at Union Theological Seminary in New York City and later at Harvard had a great impact on American theological writing. Just as Barth found himself in an atmosphere formed by the liberal gospel of Ritschl, so a theologian in America would find himself dealing with the tradition of the "social gospel" taught by men like Walter Rauschenbusch. The "social gospel," as its name may indicate, was a theology for moral reform. Just as Barth had struggled with the inconsistency between the horror of the first World War and the veiled optimism of Ritschl, so the American theologian, Reinhold Niebuhr, had struggled during the 1920's in a parish in industrial Detroit with the contradiction between the optimism of a "gospel of love" and the seeming need for power and violence to overcome the injustices of the modern age. Partly through Kierkegaard, partly through Karl Marx, Niebuhr came to reject the idealism of the social gospel while keeping its concern with the need for action. History was a field of "irony" and "ambiguity" in which no cause could be blessed. As Barth had pointed out, God stands in judgment on the world, but for all that, we must act and decide even though we can never escape the burden of sin. Niebuhr's theology and its political consequences have been labeled "realistic" in contrast to the "idealism" of those who sought to alleviate the suffering of the masses through moving the hearts of the powerful. Marx's savage attack on sentimental liberalism convinced Niebuhr that justice will be effected by power, and he found in the classic Christian notion of sin a theological interpretation for that "hardness of heart" which requires force to effect the good. Niebuhr's unsentimental approach to the problems of domestic and world strife have caused him to be labeled as "immoral" (by Irving Babbitt, a neo-humanist) and un-Christian by many liberals and fundamentalists, but he has earned the respect of many statesmen and political theorists.

Tillich's theological writings are not as politically or socially oriented as Niebuhr's, but the two men complemented one another during the period that they were on the faculty of Union Theological Seminary. Although "un-Christian" is a common epithet in theological polemic, Tillich has been accused of outright atheism. Playing upon the common twentieth-century theme of the utter transcendence of God, Tillich has tried to isolate what he calls "the Protestant Principle." The Protestant Principle is simply a manifestation of the transcendence of God over all possible earthly confinements. Tillich finds in the prophetic witness against idolatry the heart of Protestantism, and he goes so far as to assert that in the end theism itself cannot contain God. Theism must be transcended because, as Tillich says in a striking phrase, "the content of absolute faith is 'the God above God.'" God can be caught, as it were, in the prophetic movement away from and against the concretion of God in a person, place, nation, or religion. God is found in "the *dynamics* of faith," to use the title of one of his many books. Granted this notion of faith, Tillich is quite correct in locating true awareness of the Protestant Principle in men like Nietzsche and Marx who witnessed prophetically against the confinement of God to the bourgeois culture of the nineteenth century. Tillich's theology does have a place in the Christian tradition, and we would look for his antecedents not only among the reformers but among the whole school of "negative theologians" who emphasized that all we could say about God was that he was not this, not that. In the fourteenth-century mystic, Meister Eckhart, there is the direct analogue to "the God above God" when Eckhart characterizes the divine reality as "the wilderness beyond God." Nevertheless, negative theology has always been somewhat under suspicion from the churches—perhaps because it invariably attacks the organization of God in the church—and while Tillich's doctrine of the radical transcendence of God obviously does have Christian roots, there is a suspicion among many theologians that there may be as much Socrates as there is Christ in the almost demonic no-saying to any historical manifestation of the divine.

If we end our brief survey of three major Protestant thinkers with the suspicion of Platonism, we have no trouble detecting Aristotelianism in Roman Catholic theology of the twentieth century. Leo XIII had commended Thomas Aquinas, the great synthesizer of Aristotle and Christ, to Catholic theologians as a model and standard in the late nineteenth century, and the majority of twentieth-century Catholic theologians professed some brand of Thomism. Prominent among the stricter Thomists was the French Dominican priest, Reginald Garrigou-Lagrange. The school nourished by Garrigou-Lagrange put forward the claim in its influential journal *Revue Thomiste,* that the thought of St. Thomas represented "the scientific state of Christian thought" and that theological progress would only be an addition to the original synthesis. It is said that it was Garrigou-Lagrange's influence which prevailed in the papal encyclical *Humani Generis,* in which Pius XII condemned certain trends in Catholic theology centering in existentialism and in a revival of patristic studies which challenged the preeminence of St. Thomas.

More prominent on the world scene were two French laymen, Jacques Maritain and Étienne Gilson. Maritain was greatly influenced by the philosophy of Bergson and the personality of the half-mad, poverty-stricken thunderer against the French establishment, Leon Bloy. Maritain has written extensively on a wide variety of topics ranging from theology to aesthetics and from logic to politics. He came to the United States in the early 1940's and greatly influenced Roman Catholic thought there. He was a professor of philosophy at Princeton University, and an institute for the study of his thought was established at Notre Dame. Despite a professed Aristotelianism, Maritain's thought still shows strong signs of the Bergsonian influence. He has aimed his sharpest attacks at the rationalist tradition, which he sees epitomized in Descartes, whom he accuses of the sin of "angelism." To counter extreme rationalism Maritain frequently utilizes something like Bergsonian "intuition" as an organ of cognition which puts man in contact with fundamental reality. For all the appearance of scientific rigor borrowed from Aristotle, Maritain seems at his best when he employs his sensitivities on a concrete problem in the arts or politics. Without the accents of prophetism utilized by Barth, Maritain has nevertheless taken powerful and controversial stands on many political issues, as, for example, his early condemnation of Franco Spain.

Etienne Gilson is surely the most prominent historian of medieval philosophy in our time. Through lectureships at Harvard and Yale, as well as by his teaching at the Pontifical Institute of Medieval Studies in Toronto, his work is well known to North American audiences. By means of brilliant historical scholarship, Gilson has attempted to show how St. Thomas speaks to the perennial problems of philosophy and theology. Roman Catholic theology, as presented in Gilson's revival of St. Thomas, comes into sharp conflict with the theology of Barth and his followers over the central issue of the relation between God and the world. Gilson quotes with approval, and some astonishment, St. Thomas's statement: "The natures of creatures point out the fact that none of them shall be reduced into nothingness." The Roman Catholic theologian suspects that the Protestant theologian, with his emphasis on God as the wholly other, with the Calvinistic strain of "All Glory to God Alone," is in danger of reducing the creation to nothingness for the greater glory of the transcendent God who is not contained within nature. Gilson insists, through the words of Thomas, on a decent respect for the creation, which is, after all, God's work. The creation attains a certain independence and value in Roman Catholic thought. The implications of this view are easy to trace. Instead of God utterly transcendent over all things of the world, judging them, we return to an immanence of God in things. Thus, while the church does stand under the judgment of God, in virtue of the new creation in Christ it has a certain "independent" value that it cannot lose, no matter how short it falls of expressing the fullness of the divine. To the extent that Protestant theology has Platonic tendencies, it is likely to find the historical, the world of becoming, inherently infected with ambiguity, sin, and unreality. To the extent that Roman Catholic thought hearkens back to Aristotle, it is likely to find the world real and, in its own order, good. If the Protestant accuses the Catholic of idolatry for locating his God in a worldly thing, the Catholic is likely to accuse the Protestant of blaspheming against the creation and God's covenant with man. It may not stand to reason that God can be confined in the temporal, but the promise of the creation, and particularly the fact of Jesus as the manifestation of God in history, leads Catholic thinkers to accept an immanence of God in the church.

Catholic immanentism has been carried forward more explicitly in the work of two distinguished French patristic scholars, Jean Danielou, S.J., and Henri de Lubac, S.J. They have led a theological movement which calls for a reworking of theology from its sources in the Fathers. While temporarily checked by the strictures of *Humani Generis,* their influence continues to grow. Their interests have turned toward the more speculative and mystical of the Eastern Fathers, rather than to the more legalistic Fathers of the Roman West. The work of another French Jesuit, Pierre Teilhard de Chardin, an eminent paleontologist, goes so far to erase the line between God and nature and history, that it is in constant danger of becoming a Gnostic pantheism.

Before leaving the theological discussions which have marked the twentieth century, we must make mention of two prominent and influential thinkers whose religious allegiance is neither Protestant nor Catholic—Martin Buber, a Jew, and Nikolai Berdyaev, a member of the Russian Orthodox church.

Buber's influence has spread far beyond the confines of his ancestral faith. Indeed, in some ways one could say that his influence has been greater on Christians than on the Jews. Although Buber holds a position at the Hebrew University in Jerusalem, his firm rejection of rabbinic Judaism of the Talmudic period has not endeared him to his orthodox brethren. Buber finds the roots of his thought in Hasidism, an eighteenth-century Jewish revival movement centering in Poland and Russia. Buber himself edited and retold the legends of the Hasidim, and they present to the twentieth-century reader a strange combination of magic, mystical longing, and joyous religiosity. In the midst of fierce persecution, the Hasidim were urged by their rabbis to "seize the quality of eagerness with might." At the very moment when their thoughts might naturally have turned toward hopes in another world, the Hasidim were urged to hallow the everyday in song and act.

Buber's permanent contribution to theological vocabulary has been the distinction between "I-thou" and "I-it" relations. In his book, *I and Thou,* as much a poem as a work in theology, Buber distinguishes between the objective, diffident attitude that we take toward things and objects, the I-it relation, and the open, permeable revelation of a "thou" in love and faith. God is the absolute Thou, since he can never be regarded as an object who stands indifferently under anyone's cognitive scrutiny. The idolatry which Tillich and Barth bring under the judgment of a transcendent God, Buber would avoid by pointing to God as the absolute Thou who can never be regarded as objectified. God escapes objectification not so much to protect his otherness and glory, but as a manifestation of his being wholly a Beloved. Human loves of human things always verge on the brink of objectifying the beloved, reducing I-thou to I-it. God can only be seen as person, as Thou; thus we appropriate him only in the relation of loving. It is not the *otherness* of God that makes him beyond human limitation, it is the intimacy and nearness of God that prevents our putting him outside us as an It to be known. The intimacy with God expressed in the mystical life of the Hasidic communities is the figure of God's relation to men.

Nikolai Berdyaev, who died an exile from his native Russia in Paris in 1948, brought into Western theological circles, long confined to the aging polemics of the Reformation, the fascinating speculations of the Orthodox East. Separated by centuries of schism, political isolation, and linguistic difference, the Orthodox church had had little impact on the thought of the West until this century, when political emigration and the movement for church reunion forced communication. Through the work of the Catholic patristic scholars, through Buber's introduction of Hasidism and through Berdyaev and his fellow emigrés, religious thought in the West has been infused with religious forces much less legalistic and dogmatic. Orthodoxy and orthodox Judaism are in fact more rigid than the speculations of Berdyaev or Buber would suggest, but it is the capitalization by these theologians on the mystical strains in the Eastern traditions that caught the imagination of the West. Berdyaev's thought is an amalgam of a native Russian messianism with an unrestricted allegiance to the freedom of man which he discovered in the Russian novelist Dostoyevsky. God's revelation to man must be such that it does not in any way compromise the freedom of either. In the parable of the Grand Inquisitor in *The Brothers Karamazov*, Dostoyevsky presented what was to be the core of much of Berdyaev's theology. There Christ is seen confronting the old inquisitor, who says that the burden of freedom is too much for man to bear, and that he, representing the church, has acted the part of the true anti-Christ in removing this great burden from man. But this temporizing with the necessity for bread and miracles which the church effects, rules out the very possibility of the messianic revolution, the complete transformation of the world into the kingdom of perfect freedom.

Despite the obvious dangers involved in trying to find a common thread in the varied presentations of twentieth-century theologians, there is a certain commonality that cannot be overlooked. In the nineteenth century the religious world view was under attack from both the scientific and historical disciplines. Theologians attempted to answer these attacks on the grounds proposed by the attackers; it was hoped that better historical method would reveal the facts in the Bible, closer attention to scientific fact might produce a proof for the existence of God from the order of nature. In the twentieth century the most influential theologians have insisted on the radical uniqueness of the theological method and thus attempted to bypass the conflicts with the sciences. In one way or another all the theologians we have discussed reject the possibility of a cognitive awareness of God which is in any way commensurate with the cognitive awareness we might have of the facts of history or science. This turning away from scientific method has brought down the accusation of "irrationalism" against much twentieth-century theology, but this supposed irrationalism can also be seen as a revival of the sense of the supernatural which the theologians of the nineteenth century, working with naturalistic methods, had to reject. When the modern theologian picks up the language of Kierkegaard and says that when man is in contact with God he is in the realm of the "absurd," the theologian does not mean that man has gone mad, but simply that the dimensions of the spirit are incommensurate with the world of natural fact. God is indeed supra-natural and he is to be appropriated only in a mode of awareness that goes beyond the objective stance of the scientist.

The most vivid and controversial example of a change in attitude toward the Bible can be found in the work of the theologian and Biblical scholar, Rudolph Bultmann. Bultmann proposed a program of what he called "demythologizing" the Gospel, which at first glance appears to be little different from the liberal attempt to delete embarrassing supernatural material. In fact, capitalizing on the insights of Kierkegaard and Heidegger, Bultmann is reemphasizing the fact that the mere historical veracity of the texts will not serve as a foundation for faith. Faith moves in the area beyond the detached acceptance of any facts, even the fact of the empty tomb on Easter. Religious faith does not mean accepting impossible scientific world views as true, but it is putting trust in the person of the Lord. If we recall Kierkegaard's parable of the king who takes on the role of the servant, we will see that trust cannot be generated by direct evidence. Unfortunately, Bultmann does not make clear what bearing, if any, the usual factual picture of the New Testament would have on faith. The facts are not a sufficient condition for trust, but they may be a necessary condition. Seeing the empty tomb may not produce faith, but in what sense could one believe in Resurrection if the tomb were not empty?

The state of religion in the twentieth century cannot be confined to the discussions of the theologians. We must turn, however briefly, to some of the mass movements that have characterized religious life in this era. The twentieth century has not seen any major new sect preaching a millenarian social reform to the masses as did the Anabaptists or Levellers of earlier ages. Christian social effort has been directed into the establishment of political parties in Europe such as the Christian Democratic Union in Germany, which has held power since the end of the second World War. Numerous movements were initiated throughout Europe in the 1920's organizing workers, students, professional men, employers under various Christian auspices. The absence of sects preaching social apocalypse is due in part to the improved standard of living and the wide appeal of the secular apocalypse presented in the Communist vision of the classless society. New sects which have gained prominence such as the Seventh Day Adventists, the Pentecostals, and the Oxford Group (later Moral Rearmament) organized by Frank Buchman, have concentrated on personal moral reform. Whether advanced by the fervid preaching of the Pentecostals to the lower classes or the more sedate "house parties" of the Oxford Group, the new sects did not look for communal revolution in society, but at best a reform of the world through the moral example of the individual. Perhaps only in Zionism was there the blend of social upheaval and religious concern that had marked earlier sectarian movements. In America in the mid-1960's most of the major denominations strongly backed the Negro struggle for legal equality. The dominance of the Rev. Martin Luther King in the Negro community gave to the movement the accents of his own personal blend of Ghandian non-violence and Christianity. Since the American churches had long been split along racial lines in Northern and Southern jurisdictions it is not surprising that the only religious schism that has grown out of this social struggle is the Black Muslims with their total rejection of Christianity.

Religion enjoyed a considerable intellectual revival after the first World War. Not only were theologians writing material in a new and persuasive vein, but writers like T. S. Eliot and François Mauriac were castigating modern society in religious terms. Although there has been a general world-wide trend away from the formal observances of religion in all denominations, there were periods after the World Wars in which a "religious revival" was proclaimed among the general populace. "Billy" Graham, the American evangelist, experienced great success in his campaigns of preaching in the major cities of the world. Books and films on religious themes had a wide circulation. The opposition of the Communists to the Christian churches convinced many that going to church was an act of patriotism. This popular revival of religion, however, was viewed with suspicion by the theologians. Reinhold Niebuhr attacked the "shallowness" of Billy Graham's evangelical message; Karl Barth found a spiritual sickness in the West's moral self-satisfaction as the opponent of "godless communism."

Two major movements, one in the Roman Catholic, one in the Protestant world, were of great significance. The "Liturgical Movement" in the Roman Catholic church had its roots in a late nineteenth-century aestheticism. The ceremonies and trappings of the Catholic service had great appeal to sensitive minds revolted by the ugliness of the industrial cities. Continued study of the liturgy, particularly in Germany and France, resulted in a complete reversal of attitude, however. Rather than a place of retreat from the pressures of life, it was discovered that the liturgy was originally conceived as growing out of the intimate everyday life of the people. Attempts were made to revive the liturgy as a living experience for the congregation. Prayers were put into the vernacular, congregational responses and congregational singing were fostered, new churches were built after the destruction of the second World War which emphasized architecturally the participation of the laity in the religious act. Led by scholars like Msgr. Romano Guardini of Germany, the Liturgical Movement began to work out a whole new theology for the church in which the "priesthood of all believers" became not simply a Protestant aberration, but an approximation to the share of all in the life of the church. The Liturgical Movement with its Christological emphasis came into sharp conflict with many popular pieties such as the veneration of Mary. Despite checks from the Popes themselves, the movement has continued to spread a quite radical reorientation of Catholic spirituality—one which was much applauded by Protestants, many of whom were also finding their own liturgical roots. So widespread were the forces of the Liturgical Movement that by the 1960's even Cardinals of the Church were proclaiming the twentieth century to be "the century of the laity."

The Ecumenical Movement, which culminated in the establishment of the World Council of Churches at Amsterdam in 1948, embraces in a loose organization most of the major bodies of Christendom except the Roman Catholics. During the first World War, Nathan Söderblom, Archbishop of Uppsala in neutral Sweden, had attempted to foster Christian contact above the conflict of nations. He saw that the division of the churches made them increasingly ineffective in moments of great crisis. After the war he sponsored the Universal Conference on Life and Work, which met in Stockholm in 1925 and at which some of the Orthodox and many of the Protestant denominations were represented. Later he was a sponsor of the broadly representative World Conference on Faith and Order. These conferences paved the way for the Amsterdam conference and subsequent meetings at Evanston, Ill., and New Delhi. The Ecumenical Movement began simply as a gesture of fellowship among separated

Christians; it was infused with practical concerns by common challenges from secularism and communism and the need to establish a unified missionary effort. In its most recent phase, the movement has begun the arduous task of straightening out theological and dogmatic diversity. So far, the World Council has no real administrative function but is largely a visible sign that the churches want to communicate on a regular basis. The Liturgical Movement, with its concern for a broad participation of the laity, and the Ecumenical Movement, with its drive for order among the churches, have brought about the greatest growing together of the Christian communions since the Reformation.

The Ecumenical Council of the Roman Catholic church called by Pope John XXIII was by the very fact of its summoning a shock to the more conservative curial officials. The strong position of the so-called "liberal" wing of the council led by the bishops of northern Europe did little to allay their fears. The official Protestant observers were generally heartened by what they saw and heard during the first session. The death of John XXIII and the accession of Paul VI (formerly Cardinal Montini of Milan) raised some concern about the progress of further sessions.

Finally, in our account of twentieth-century religion we can turn briefly to the institutional churches. The Roman Catholic church entered the twentieth century in a conservative mood. The long pontificate of Pius IX had climaxed in the definition of papal infallibility, a move which outraged liberal opinion within and without the church. The twentieth century had opened with controversy about a new liberal wave, Modernism, which in the figures of Loisy, Duchesne, and Tyrrel attempted to accommodate traditional teaching to the new sciences. The Bible was to be interpreted metaphorically, and a reworking of Christian doctrine was to be effected in line with this new approach. Pius X condemned the Modernists in the strongly worded encyclical *Pascendi Gregis* (1907). The Biblical Commission, in line with the edicts of the Popes, took an official position on the Bible that is best exemplified by its firm adherence to the Mosaic authorship of the Pentateuch, one of the points most firmly contradicted by the "higher criticism."

New seeds, however, were stirring. Pius X began to encourage broader participation in the sacramental life of the church through frequent reception of the sacrament, and he championed traditional church music which could be sung by the congregation. These moves encouraged the budding Liturgical Movement which was to have a profound effect on the whole life of the Roman church. By the 1960's the Catholic church's attitude to the Bible had changed radically to accommodate higher criticism, partly because of increased awareness of the nature of the Gospel brought about by the Liturgical Movement.

As a united body the Protestant world has expressed itself most clearly in building the Ecumenical Movement to its present dimensions. Complete constitutional reunion of some denominations has already occurred. The Lutheran church especially has expressed a liturgical renewal which points up its resemblances to Roman Catholicism. Individual churchmen have stood out within their own communions and in the world picture. The Anglican church, though plagued by a severe drop in attendance and a great shortage of clergy, had in Randall Davidson, Cosmo Gordon Lang, and William Temple, Archbishops of Canterbury from the first World War through the second World War, men of remarkable stature and vision. Davidson refused in the first World War to pray directly for victory. Temple, in the second World War, spoke out vigorously against reprisal bombing of civilian populations and was diligent in protecting the rights of conscientious objectors. Pastor Martin Niemöller of the Confessing church in Germany was imprisoned by the Nazis for his outspoken resistance. The theologian Dietrich Bonhoeffer was imprisoned for his resistance and later shot. Lutheran Bishop Eivind Berggrav as Bishop of Oslo denounced the Quisling regime and was first placed in a concentration camp, later kept under house arrest. Bishop Otto Dibelius, a leader of the resistance in the Confessing churches against Hitler, found himself, as Bishop of Berlin, engaged in a prolonged struggle to assert the rights of the church in the face of the opposition of the Communist government of East Germany.

Despite the new theology, the mass movements for renewal and reunion, the guidance by far-sighted churchmen in the spiritual crises of our time, and the individual witness of religious heroes and martyrs, it nevertheless appears that the future of the churches is perilous. In the nineteenth century material progress and advancing science seemed to assure man that the future would be bright—knowledge and technique would erase the dark areas of mystery which had been the field for religious life. But in the twentieth century science and technology inadvertently conspired to reveal in the World Wars depths of human existence that appeared incommensurate with rational comprehension and control. The nineteenth-century gospel of progress, victory over the multiple evils of the world by rational means, seemed incapable of standing up to the demonic evil of the concentration camp or obliteration bombing. The twentieth century, if it is less godly than other centuries, is more convinced of the reality of sin than its predecessor. The traditional churches have barely shaken off their identification with the rational moralisms of the nineteenth-century establishment, and so the search for salvation has been carried on outside the churches in revolutionary parties, radical movements in the arts, and the various ecstasies of drugs, sex, and Zen Buddhism. Whether the churches will be able to speak again of a meaningful salvation to this century is surely problematic, but the revelation of something in men, even demonic evil, which is beyond mere rational comprehension, has at least reopened the field of the Spirit.

XIII. EDUCATIONAL NOVELTIES AND CONFLICTS

By Harry Elmer Barnes

In the twentieth century free, universal, and compulsory education triumphed in all the more civilized countries of the Western World. In Russia, the Soviet government set up a thorough system of free public education in what had been the most illiterate of the major countries of Europe. Education was further removed from the control of the church and almost completely secularized, notwithstanding the continuation of church schools, especially Catholic schools. Consequently, enormously increased numbers of children flocked to the schools. There were about 34,000,000 pupils in American kindergartens and elementary schools in 1960-61. This made necessary the extension of the methods of mass production to pedagogy.

These mass-production methods were first introduced into education by Andrew Bell and Joseph Lancaster at the opening of the nineteenth century, in an effort to provide more economical instruction, first in orphan asylums and later in schools. There was little general need for such procedure, however, until education became free and universal. In order to promote administrative convenience and financial economy, the administration of our public schools then became rather decisively mechanized. Discipline and instruction were adapted to mass situations. This development greatly facilitated education on a large scale but also greatly reduced personal or individualized instruction. One of our major educational problems is to work out a successful compromise between mass production and proper attention to the special needs of the individual student.

Though mechanized mass education may be an obstacle to the effective education of the individual, it will probably remain dominant for a long time to come, in spite of a strong current reaction against it. This is obvious because of the unprecedentedly rapid growth of the population since the second World War. Therefore, while mass education prevails, it creates an administrative problem of unprecedented complexity and extent. Many specialists in educational administration, of whom George D. Strayer of Teachers College, Columbia University, was one of the outstanding experts, have attempted its solution.

In spite of the tendency towards overmechanization in public education, much headway has been made in studying the mind of the individual child, and in adapting educational ideas and methods to his needs. This had, of course, been the basic conception of Froebel, but Froebel possessed little valid psychological knowledge with which to interpret the real nature of children. Truly scientific child study was brought into being by G. Stanley Hall, whose work in linking psychology and education with evolution was referred to in earlier chapters. Hall's genetic psychology first placed child study upon a reasonably scientific plane.

Froebel's emphasis upon cultivating and directing the spontaneous tendencies of the child was given a fresh impetus by the Italian physician and educator, Maria Montessori (1870-1952). Her educational doctrine grew, in part, out of her work with feeble-minded children. She believed that the same methods which had proved so successful with them might be applied to normal children. Her first experiments with normal children took place in 1906. T. L. Smith thus describes her work:

> The fundamental principles which distinguish Dr. Montessori's method are the complete liberty of the child in its spontaneous manifestations and the utilization of every atom of its natural energy.
>
> True discipline can be founded only on liberty, and must necessarily be active and not passive. A child who has been reduced to silence and immobility, who does only what he is told to do, is a paralyzed, not a disciplined child.... The liberty of the child must have as its limit only the collective interest. He must then be hindered from any acts offensive or harmful to others. All else that he does must not only be permitted but observed by the teacher, and the teacher must have not only the capacity, but the interest to observe this natural development. She must avoid rigorously the repression of spontaneous acts and the imposition of work at the will of another. To interfere with this spontaneity is, in Dr. Montessori's view, perhaps to repress the very essential of life itself. The aim of discipline is to train to activity, to work, for the welfare of self and others. To this end the development of independence in the child is necessary.
>
> In Dr. Montessori's system rewards and punishments are banished. Reward comes in the child's own sense of mastery. Failure is a mere negation, to be taken as a sign that the child is not yet ready for that particular exercise. The teaching is almost entirely individual and the three fundamental rules for lessons are that they shall be brief, simple, and objective.[23]

Signora Montessori's ideals had a wide influence on twentieth-century education. Linked with those of Froebel and of psychologists and educators like E. L. Thorndike and John Dewey, they have shaped the development of the kindergarten and elementary education in our generation.

The most important theoretical contribution to education in the twentieth century has been the effort to fuse pedagogy with sound contemporary psychology. The great classic educators, from Comenius to Froebel, possessed little technical knowledge of psychology, since there was little in existence for them to master. They had to rely chiefly on intuitions which were always in danger of running wild and going contrary to the facts of child psychology.

In the last half century a resolute effort has been made to associate the learning process with established psychological principles. The first notable example in this field was the famous study of the psychology of memory, published in 1885 by Hermann Ebbinghaus (1850-1909).[23a] The foremost contributor to the psychology of learning has been Edward Lee Thorndike of Teachers College, a competent student of comparative psychology and mental measurements. He has laid great stress on trial-and-error as the basic technique of learning. He brought together many of his doctrines in his *Psychology of Learning* (1914). John Dewey collected the conclusions of a common-sense functional psychology regarding the

23 *The Montessori System in Theory and Practice,* Harper, 1912, pp. 6-8.
23a Ebbinghaus, Hermann, *Memory,* Dover Publications, Inc., 1964.

technique of learning in an immensely influential little book, *How We Think* (1909). The latest contribution to the psychology of learning has been made by the Gestalt psychologists, especially by Kurt Koffka. This school has sharply attacked the validity of Thorndike's trial-and-error formula and assigns a much larger role to insight.

Another important contribution to this more natural type of education was the creation of experimental and laboratory schools where the educational process might be studied and controlled. The first of these was founded by Francis W. Parker at Quincy, Massachusetts, between 1875 and 1880. In 1896 John Dewey and his wife linked the experimental school with formal education by establishing a laboratory school at the University of Chicago. Here educators were perfectly free to direct education and observe its results without interference from formal administrators. Out of this laboratory school and other studies grew Dewey's educational theories, which have had a profound influence upon twentieth-century education in the United States. They have also widely affected education in Europe and the Far East, particularly in Russia and China.

The development of a more natural and scientific educational method ultimately led to a revolt against the mechanized procedure of the traditional public schools, and produced the movement known as Progressive Education. The need for it has been stated by Professor A. Gordon Melvin:

> Public school systems in many places today are bound in a net of tradition and established ways of doing things. The teacher finds herself caught in a web of timetables and systematic groupings, of statistical reports of administrators who don't use them, of supervision, of regulations, and of academic prejudice. The new teacher longs for freedom. She is anxious to teach well, she is able to teach well, but her wings are caught and damaged in the web of an antiquated system of school administration.[24]

Conventional educational methods are just as disastrous to the mental life of the pupils as to the enthusiasm of teachers. Education is all too often an irksome compulsion rather than a spontaneous interest or pleasure. Probably few pupils would attend the public schools if not compelled to do so by parents and the law. Progressive education aims to make education so attractive to the pupils that they will cooperate spontaneously and enthusiastically. Education is designed to be an exciting adventure to teachers and pupils alike. Self-expression is encouraged, and the educational process is associated, so far as possible, with real life situations. The expression and the gratification of curiosity are encouraged. Education is not sharply divided into formal subjects. History and geography or literature and drama may be intermingled. The old type of repressive discipline is absent. While disorderliness is discouraged, discipline is corrective and positive, rather than punitive. This type of education requires many more teachers per student than mechanized and mass procedure. The public has never been willing to spend enough on our schools to supply the number and quality of teachers required

24 A. G. Melvin, *The Technique of Progressive Teaching,* Day, 1932, p. 4.

for successful progressive education. Its introduction without proper support and equipment may only invite educational anarchy.

One progressive educational movement represents the extreme reaction against the prescribed curriculum of the conventional school system. This is the so-called Dalton system, first introduced in Dalton, Massachusetts. According to the Dalton plan, the pupil studies such subjects as he wishes, when he wishes to do so. Instruction is offered in all conventional subjects, but the pupil passes from one to another solely as his interests move him to do so.

Biological, psychological, and medical science have been applied to education in various ways. A rational school hygiene, designed to conserve the health and stimulate the energy of students, has been provided for in school construction and discipline. Professor W. H. Burnham, a disciple of G. Stanley Hall, took the lead in this movement. Physical training and mental hygiene have been introduced on a wide scale, with the aim: "a sound mind in a sound body." Mental testing has been used extensively to ascertain the innate mental endowment of students and to adapt instruction to different levels of intelligence. This has enabled the teacher to handle exceptional pupils, as well as retarded types, more intelligently. It has been found that ordinary academic education is rather futile for children with too low an intelligence level. Manual training and other simple and direct subjects of instruction have been introduced as the best methods of training more deficient types. Indispensable as it may be to realistic education, many educators have emphasized the danger of overzealous use of mental testing and have charged that it contributes to further mechanization of education. Burnham has especially cautioned against identifying true mental defect with pseudo-feeble-mindedness, since the latter can be remedied by proper education or medical treatment. Vocational and aptitude tests have been widely employed in order that students may be guided into types of study and activity best adapted to their individual talents and abilities.

Democratic ideals have continued to influence education. The belief that education will eliminate inequalities has persisted in many circles, in spite of vigorous criticism by eugenicists, mental testers, and others. More important, however, has been John Dewey's insistence that in order to achieve a successful democracy children must be educated in such a fashion as to adjust them to democratic realities. Schools and curricula must be organized so as to visualize and reproduce the fundamental processes of rational community life. Effective education cannot be a matter merely of instruction in isolated departments of knowledge, but must be a well-integrated preparation of the individual to live as a member of society and a citizen of the state.

With the growth of fascism in the twentieth century, democratic ideals were repudiated in fascist states, and an educational system was created which aimed to produce unquestioning loyalty to the state. In communistic Russia, while the ultimate aspiration is to create a classless and democratic society, the educational system today promotes fanatical devotion to communism and the state, and leaves as small a place for democratic freedom as did fascist education. Since the revolution of 1917 Russia has, however, carried through the most amazing campaign against illiteracy in the history of education. In 1917, some 65 per cent of all Russians were illiterate. By 1958, this had been reduced to 5 per cent, a situation on a par with that in the United States or any other Western country. There were 30 million pupils in Russian elementary and secondary schools, and over 400,000 attending 33 universities and 732 technical institutions. These students attending institutions of higher learning were specially picked, of high intelligence, and given aid and encouragement by the government. Heavy emphasis was placed on scientific and technical education. About 150,000 scientists and engineers are turned out each year in Russia, compared to about 70,000 in the United States. The Russian launching of space satellites in late 1957 illustrated the efficiency of Russian scientific and technical education.

The twentieth century witnessed a continuance of the curriculum changes which set in at the close of the nineteenth. Somewhat less stress was placed upon mathematics and the ancient languages. More attention was paid to natural and social science, technology, modern literature, and art. Most of this progress in breaking away from the older type of studies was achieved in the United States, postwar Germany, and Russia. In most English schools, and in Continental schools outside Germany and Russia, the curriculum still closely resembles that which existed at the opening of the nineteenth century. With the growth of quantum physics and nuclear studies in the 1930's and thereafter, which required an impressive mathematical background, more stress was laid upon instruction in higher mathematics, but this had little impact in the schools and colleges until after the launching of the Russian satellites in 1957.

The educational reforms in the German schools were a product of the revolution of 1918 and the demand for a type of education adapted to preparing one for life as it is lived today. The Educational Reform bill, largely the work of Professor Hans Rickert, was finished in 1924. It was put into operation at Easter, 1925. All children who had passed through elementary schools were compelled to attend the grade school for the next four years. Then the more capable students entered the gymnasium. The gymnasia were divided into four types—one that studied ancient languages and literature; one that specialized in European history and civilization; one devoted mainly to mathematical and natural sciences; and one primarily concerned with German history and culture. Students could elect the type they preferred to enter. Those who did not attend the gymnasium were compelled to attend a public school for four more years and an evening vocational school for three years thereafter. Autocracy, paternalism, snobbery, and exclusive attention to an archaic classical curriculum were abolished in German schools. New German universities were established at Frankfort and Hamburg, and an effort was made to encourage better teaching in the universities. Much of this praiseworthy progress was upset by the Hitler regime, which cut educational budgets, destroyed freedom of teaching, banished academic liberty from the German universities, drove out some of the ablest professors, and laid great stress upon an ultra-patriotic study of German history and culture and nordic racism. With the ousting of the National Socialists, following their defeat in 1945, the Western German Republic restored much of the educational system introduced under the Weimar Republic. The system in East Germany is a mixture of the Weimar program, some hangovers from the National Socialist ideals, and considerable introduction of Russian educational dogmas and practices.

In French secondary education there has been retrogression rather than progress since the first World War. The amount of instruction given in modern languages and natural science has been diminished as a result of a "reform" measure of 1923. Little social science is taught. Attention is more than ever centered upon Greek, Latin, and French. Humanism thus still maintains its paralyzing grip on French secondary education. Italian education clearly reflected the ardent nationalism of the fascist regime, but has been liberalized since 1945.

As a result of the English Education act of 1918 and other improvements, not only was a true public school system finally established, but an effort was made to break down the class character of English education, to provide better technical and scientific instruction, and to stimulate British patriotism. But the curriculum of the exclusive private schools (called public schools) remains preponderantly classical, and there has been little modification of traditional education in the universities with the exception of the University of London and one or two of the newer universities.

In some continental European universities there has been a break with tradition. Natural science has received a larger place and more attention has been allotted to scientific studies in general. The social sciences have not as yet become thoroughly respectable in conventional European centers of learning, although they are more widely taught today than in the last quarter of the nineteenth century.

In the last thirty-five years, a considerable movement has been under way to promote the social sciences in the United States, especially in the secondary schools, where they had made less headway than in higher education. Where the social sciences have been extensively added to the curriculum, they have usually tended to be mainly formal and descriptive. At best, they describe the existing social system but fail to provide a scientific attitude or program designed to create an improved social order.

Another interesting curriculum change is the introduction of more practical subjects, such as domestic science, manual training, graphic arts, and commercial studies. The devotees of traditional education have, however, vigorously resisted the suggestion that such subjects can be truly educational, and most instruction along these lines has been conducted in specialized schools.

With the passage of laws limiting child labor, greater numbers of children have been provided with a high-school education. There were some 11,500,000 students in high schools in the United States in 1962. The secondary schools should give ample opportunity for the training of intelligent citizens of the modern world. But excessive attention is still devoted to archaic and irrelevant subjects having no relation whatever to the problems of modern life. Moreover, it is often very difficult in the United States for even progressive educators to make much headway in our high schools because of the tyranny exerted in many localities by college entrance examinations. These are strongly conservative in prescribed subject matter and make it necessary for high-school students to devote most of their time to traditional subjects if they expect to enter institutions of higher learning. Since an increasing number of high-school students wish to go to college, undue stress is given to antiquated materials in high-school instruction. High schools should, for the most part, serve other needs. The situation in Europe outside of Russia and Germany from 1925 to 1933, is even more thoroughly characterized by the ascendancy of outworn ideals in secondary education.

By all means the most promising movement in secondary education has been the above-mentioned attempt to stimulate an increasing interest in the social sciences. W. H. Kilpatrick, Harold Rugg, George S. Counts, Leon C. Marshall, R. M. Tryon, C. H. Judd, C. A. Beard, and others have taken the lead in this important drive for a more realistic and modernized curriculum. There is a possibility, however, that this desirable trend will be submerged in a tidal wave of emphasis on increased attention to the natural sciences, stimulated greatly by the revelation of the remarkable advances in this field in Soviet Russia. If so, this will be highly unfortunate since scientific education and achievements have already far outrun the development of social science and any planning to use intelligently the science and technology we already possess.

Apart from a growing interest in the natural sciences and a slightly greater tolerance of the social sciences, European colleges and universities outside of Russia remain about as they were in 1890. There has been no such mass movement towards college education in Europe as there has been in our country. Higher education in Europe, outside of Germany and Russia, is still, for the most part, the privilege of a select few. Buildings devoted to higher education are rather few and simple, some of them having been occupied by the same institution for centuries.

The most striking development in American higher education has been an overwhelming mass movement to colleges and universities since 1900. At the close of the nineteenth century a large college or university in the United States rarely had more than a thousand students. The typical college had fewer than 500 students. Today, there are several American universities which boast over 35,000 students (of all classifications) annually, and ten universities have over 25,000 full-time students. Women's colleges have also become larger and more popular. Some of the important women's colleges of the country have more than two thousand students. The total enrollment in the 2,043 colleges and universities in 1962 was over 4,200,000, an increase of 55 per cent since 1950. College students constitute, then, about 30 per cent of all American youth of college age. About 420,000 are graduated annually. The plant investment in institutions of higher learning amounts to over $3,000,000,000.

A result of this increased enrollment has been the construction of more commodious and pretentious buildings. A third-rate American college frequently has a more impressive architectural equipment than many of the most distinguished European universities. Some of the richer American universities have student residential buildings of an elegance matched only by the homes of wealthy private

citizens or European royalty. These sumptuous surroundings create serious problems of psychic and economic readjustment when students leave college life and
attempt to make their way in the world, since they often have to live for years in
straitened circumstances.

These large plants are costly to operate. Except for the state universities, the
money to run such institutions has to be raised largely from contributions made
by generous private benefactors. Hence the university president must not only
be an educator, but also a business man and a money-raiser. Dependence upon
gifts from the wealthy almost makes caution mandatory in university instruction,
especially in matters pertaining to economics, politics, morals, and religion.

There has been a definite trend towards classification and differentiation in
higher education. Junior colleges have been established to give two years of
collegiate work for those who cannot pursue instruction for four years. There
has been a tendency to separate the undergraduate college from the postgraduate
university. A generation ago, most college professors gave both graduate and undergraduate instruction. Today, in our larger universities, graduate instruction is
often given by men who pay little or no attention to undergraduate work. Our
more important professional schools have tended to become graduate schools requiring the bachelor's degree as a prerequisite.

While normal schools for the training of teachers are still numerous and popular, we have now developed professional teachers' colleges that not only instruct
in formal pedagogy but also give teachers some idea of the relationship between
education and modern life. Indeed, it has been maintained with some justice that
Teachers College at Columbia University, raised to a position of independence
and repute by James E. Russell, provided a more thorough and realistic introduction to the problems of modern society than any general college or university in
the United States.

Although most American higher education remains rather strictly conventional
and traditional, there have been a number of notable efforts to make higher education more productive of intellectual curiosity and social realism. At Rollins College in Florida, formal classes were largely dispensed with in favor of directed
reading and informal and voluntary conferences with instructors. The Benning-
ton (Vermont) College for women took more moderate steps in this direction.
At the University of Wisconsin, Dean Alexander Meiklejohn experimented with
a radical alteration of the curriculum. This was divided between a study of
Greek civilization and that of modern industrial civilization since 1750, the idea
being to acquaint the student with the two outstanding types of civilization that
have thus far appeared. The opposition of the traditionalists forced the abandonment of this praiseworthy innovation. At Antioch College in Ohio, Arthur E.
Morgan introduced an interesting combination of educational and practical
work. Each student devotes equal alternating periods of his time in college to
(1) practical industry or professional work anywhere he chooses, and (2) regular study at college. This plan is designed to give greater realism to education.
The University of Chicago waived the strict time requirement for the bachelor's
degree and permitted achievement, as ascertained by a comprehensive ex-

amination, to determine the length of residence required. An effort has also been made to extend the advantages of higher education to those unable to enter universities as regular students. Extension evening courses are numerous, and elaborate summer-school curricula are offered by most leading universities and colleges.

After Russia launched the first successful space satellites in the autumn of 1957 and Americans came to realize the impressive progress that had been made in natural science and technology in Soviet Russia, there arose an almost frantic effort to stimulate and subsidize more scientific education in the United States. Discerning social scientists and educators regarded this as not only an unfortunate but even an alarming trend, since it would increase the cultural lag between science and technology, on the one hand, and institutions, on the other. Already this cultural lag was threatening the integrity and security of modern civilization in all literate areas.

One of the most astonishing developments in American higher education has been the increased popularity and commercialization of intercollegiate athletics, especially college football. Athletic activities in institutions of higher learning are theoretically designed to promote the physical health of the whole student body, and most institutions do provide adequate gymnastic facilities for all their students. University football has, however, become highly commercialized. Great stadiums have been constructed, with a larger seating capacity than the Colosseum of Rome, receipts from football games have totaled over $750,000 for a single institution in one season, football coaches have been paid higher salaries than university deans, and an otherwise entirely inconspicuous college or university has often been raised to a position of national prestige solely because of a successful football team. Other branches of intercollegiate athletics, especially basketball, have been commercialized, but to nothing like so marked a degree. It has been alleged on good evidence by certain critics that intercollegiate athletics of this commercialized type have been a serious distraction from the fundamental purposes of education.

The thorough industrialization of modern life has reacted upon education in many ways. Industrial education of a technical type, which began in the nineteenth century, has gained in popularity and extent. Colleges and universities have established schools of business administration and schools of commerce. Some of these have been made graduate professional schools. Such schools have, however, rarely taken an inquiring attitude towards modern economic life but give the student technical training in business according to the theory of business enterprise and finance capitalism. Hence, their graduates have done little or nothing to check disastrous trends in American economic life and put it on a sounder basis.

Some employers have established courses for their employees. Progressive labor leaders have seen the necessity of training workers if labor is to compete with the better-educated class of employers. More than a century ago, Robert Owen in England and Thomas Skidmore in the United States urged the importance of educating the masses. In the middle of the nineteenth century both Karl Marx and Friedrich Engels did their best to promote the education of workers. The

English Fabian Society, headed by leading English intellectuals, was especially sympathetic towards labor education. University extension facilities have been extended to workers by institutions of higher learning which have taken a kindly attitude towards labor education. This has been particularly true in England. Labor colleges have been established; among the most notable are Ruskin College, Oxford, established in 1899 by English and American liberals, and Brookwood Labor College at Katonah, New York, founded through the collaboration of academic radicals and American trade-unions. In Germany after the first World War a number of important labor schools were set up, the most famous being the Berlin Trade Union School, opened in 1919, and the Academy of Labor at Frankfort, established in 1920. The Rand School of Social Science, opened in New York City in 1906, and intended to promote socialistic education of workers and others, has had an important influence on the labor movement in the United States.

In spite of these promising beginnings in labor education, only the surface has yet been scratched. Little has been accomplished beyond very inadequate provision for training labor leaders. The facilities are so extremely limited that there has been little opportunity to educate the mass of workers in either the realities of modern life or the technique of labor-union strategy. Education is still overwhelmingly in the control of the employing class and devoted to inculcating its point of view. In Russia, of course, the opposite is true, and education is controlled solely by the proletariat and propagates a purely proletarian attitude.

Rapid changes in culture and the growing popularity of higher education have stimulated an important movement known as adult education. Many who did not have the opportunity in youth to secure higher education, later acquire enough money but cannot leave their business or professional work to matriculate in a formal institution of learning. They must remedy their educational deficiencies by part-time study. Moreover, those who did have a college education a generation ago find themselves notoriously out of touch with present-day knowledge. Some of these persons endeavor to bring themselves intellectually up-to-date.

These two needs have led to a marked development of adult education. Millions of Americans are enrolled in such classes. University-extension courses endeavor to reach these groups. Such courses have been given not only in university cities but also in outlying urban centers able to engage teachers from a university. Indeed, even university instruction by mail has developed to considerable proportions, and radio and television have been invoked in behalf of adult education. There have been notable special institutions designed primarily to provide adult education. Cooper Union in New York City, long administered by Everett Dean Martin, has offered a diversified program for adults. But the foremost experiment in adult education to date has been the New School for Social Research, founded in 1919 by James Harvey Robinson, Charles A. Beard, Thorstein Veblen, Wesley C. Mitchell, and others. This has provided adult education in which instruction is given in a great many fields by distinguished European and American scholars. The Labor Temple in New York City, presided over in turn by Will Durant, Edmund B. Chaffee, and A. J. Muste, has done much to bring adult education to the working classes.

The importance of adult education has lately been brought into high relief through the growing recognition of its urgency. The social crisis has become so acute that an intelligent solution of our current dilemmas will probably have to be reached before many of the children now in school have attained adulthood. Hence, it is of the utmost importance to enlighten the present generation before it is too late. This thought led the government of the United States to undertake an extensive, though very inadequate, program of adult education under the direction of Dr. J. W. Studebaker, when he was United States Commissioner of Education. Its termination was a national disaster.

Questions of academic freedom still persist. This problem has been surveyed in great detail in the courageous book by Professor Howard K. Beale, *Are American Teachers Free?*[25] Indeed, with the increasingly critical state of the capitalistic system, we have witnessed extensive repression of independent thought upon the part of university professors. Especially notable has been the recent movement to compel teachers to take oaths to uphold existing institutions and, by implication, to refrain from taking a critical view of current problems. A majority of the states have adopted teachers' oath laws. In Fascist countries, such as Italy and Germany, academic freedom completely disappeared in all subjects which in any way related to economics, politics, or other current issues. Russia, engaged in a life-and-death struggle to challenge capitalism, has likewise obliterated academic freedom. Even in those countries which still formally maintain both capitalism and democracy, to express realistic views on economic, political, ethical, and religious topics is becoming increasingly difficult. A subtler method than the old, crude procedure of summarily dismissing progressive teachers is employed by conservative university trustees and executives. Today a more usual technique is to take every precaution to see to it that no realistic or "dangerous" men are added to the faculties, whatever their scholarly achievements or special capacity for efficient instruction. Thereupon, much ado is made about the complete freedom extended to this select and cautious teaching staff. This device is known as "the Lowell formula," since it was introduced by President A. Lawrence Lowell of Harvard University.

The result is a great decline in the freshness, originality, vitality, and realism of instruction in institutions of higher learning. As in the Middle Ages, there is less intolerance of ideas propagated in the classroom than of those expressed for popular consumption. Great educational endowments—"foundations"—have cooperated in the effort to promote academic docility. Under the guise of ultra-scientific rigor, their directors both extol the spirit of research and then condemn as unscholarly those professors who venture critical opinions on current economic, political, or social matters. They assume that research, however devastating the facts uncovered, will never prove dangerous if the results are not clearly divulged to the public. Vast resources are squandered in many cases to investigate and document the obvious. Where startling facts are uncovered, it is not

25 Scribner, 1936.

uncommon to obscure them by conclusions so cautious as to border on misinformation. The fact that the lavish grants of foundations go chiefly to professors and other scholars with a reputation for a delicate sense of discretion is another strong incentive to academic caution.

In the United States an effort has been made to defend progressive college teachers through the organization of the American Association of University Professors, in which John Dewey and A. O. Lovejoy were most active in promoting academic freedom. But this group can do little beyond giving publicity to the more outrageous examples of the abridgment of academic freedom, thus all too often preventing the victims from securing another post. They have usually compiled eloquent academic obituaries. American teachers are not likely to assure for themselves complete academic liberty unless they are strongly organized in some guild or union of teachers.

In democratic countries the foes of academic freedom are motivated chiefly by economic factors, with no little aid from nationalistic or patriotic forces. In fascist states the pressure was primarily nationalistic, although this fierce nationalism was generated by a social system created to defend capitalism. The study of patriotic education in Europe before the first World War by J. F. Scott, *Patriots in Making,* presented a dolorous spectacle, but his account of postwar education in his *Menace of Nationalism in Education,* is far more alarming. Although the second World War produced a United Nations organization, world trends since 1945 have stimulated nationalistic sentiments far more than international sympathy and unity.

XIV. SOVIET CULTURE

By Donald W. Treadgold

Professor of Russian History, University of Washington

The culture of the Union of Soviet Socialist Republics is regarded by the Soviet leaders as a natural product of the Bolshevik Revolution which established the Soviet regime and of the socialist mode of production which it introduced. From 1917 to 1936 this was taken to mean that a new proletarian culture was being created by the social class that, in the form of the Communist party, had seized power. After 1936, when "socialism" was said to have been fully built and class antagonisms eliminated in the USSR, Soviet culture was said to be that of the "new Soviet man," of the peoples of the USSR as a whole, with no further emphasis given to the notion of "proletarian" culture. Ever since 1917 it was assumed that the changed economic foundation of life was naturally tending to produce new cultural forms and phenomena, but that it would be the function of the Soviet state to organize, plan, and direct the course of this cultural development. Lenin, Stalin, and Khrushchev all contrasted "consciousness" with "spontaneity" in a manner that expressed their reliance on the former and their deep distrust and fear of the latter. Thus complete state ownership and management have come to the cultural life of the USSR as to all other branches of activity—political, economic, and social.

"Union of Soviet Socialist Republics" is the name given in 1922 to the state known as the Russian Soviet Federated Socialist Republic, proclaimed after the Revolution of November 7, 1917, by which the Bolsheviks (renamed Communists in March, 1918) seized power. The Soviet state, headed by Vladimir Lenin (1870-1924), overthrew a democratic Provisional Government of the Russian Republic; this government had supplanted the government of the Russian Empire, which perished with the abdication of the last Romanov, Nicholas II, in the face of the Revolution of March 12, 1917, a revolution which occurred in the midst of the first World War and was partly the result of the failures of the Imperial government in the face of the strains and demands of the war.

Especially in the half-century preceding the outbreak of the war, Russian culture had earned widespread admiration throughout Europe and the world. The old religious (Eastern Orthodox Christian) culture of the Russians before Peter the Great (1682-1725) had during the two centuries of the Empire which he founded been gradually displaced by the secularizing and scientifically oriented culture of Western Europe, first in the court circles and nobility and among the urban population, though to a much lesser extent among the peasantry, which constituted the overwhelming mass of the people. In the eighteenth century a small group of Russian artists and writers confined themselves mostly to imitating the West, though such a man as Michael Lomonosov (1711-1765) by his versatile and indefatigable achievements in both literary and scientific arts could earn himself the apt sobriquet of "Russia's Benjamin Franklin."

In the nineteenth century the leaders of Russian culture went on to reach heights of attainment unsurpassed anywhere else by using a sophisticated knowledge of Western techniques and forms in writing, painting, and music in giving expression to the values and aspirations of the Russian nation and of themselves. In literature Alexander Pushkin (1799-1837), Nikolai Gogol (1809-1852), Ivan Turgenev (1818-1883), Leo Tolstoy (1828-1910), and Fedor Dostoyevsky (1821-1881) wrote some of the greatest modern poetry and novels. In music Peter Tchaikovsky (1840-1893) and Modest Moussorgsky (1839-1881) contributed to the permanent symphonic and orchestral repertoire of the world. In painting men of first-rate ability were fewer, but the output was large and interesting. The Eastern Orthodox church emphasized the place of the ikon in worship, and a great tradition in painting thus existed for artists to build on or rebel against. There was no use in the church for sculpture, which may partly explain the feeble development of sculpture in Russia; however, there was an ancient and rich tradition in the design of churches, though modern Russian architecture seemed to benefit relatively little from it. This so-called Golden Age of Russian culture was followed and in part accompanied by a growing preoccupation of intellectuals with political and social questions, which resulted in the so-called "social command" (*sotsial'nyi zakaz*) or widespread critical insistence that the only justification of art could be the extent to which it dealt with such questions—or, more precisely, to which it furthered the cause of revolution. The 1880's and 1890's saw a decline of artistic standards, partly because of the revolutionary monomania of the critics, partly because of the fact that several of the greatest figures died about the same time, in the early 1880's.

In the reign of Nicholas II, however, a new flowering of the arts occurred that has been called the Silver Age. It was not an age of giants, but it was an era in which the number of competent or better writers and painters and musicians was higher than ever before, an era in which the popular demand for and appreciation of the arts became widespread in the cities as public education grew and literacy levels rose, and one in which the artistic interchange between Russia and the West became more intimate and frequent than ever before or since. It was also an age of unprecedented diversity. Poetry was revived by the new Symbolist school, whose greatest exponent was Alexander Blok (1880-1921), and by the quite different Acmeist, Futurist, and other groups. The novel and short story were used in new ways by the naturalist and politically minded Leonid Andreyev (1871-1919) and Maxim Gorky (1868-1936). The drama was reshaped by Anton Chekhov (1860-1904), whose Western admirers became legion. Experimentation was the key to the efforts of new musicians, such as Igor Stravinsky (1882-   ), and new painters, such as Alexander Benois (1870-1960). The *World of Art* society attempted to bring all the fine arts closer to one another in their studies and publications, in which they drew on the inspiration of both the old Russian ikons and the new Western developments of the day. The Russian ballet, in the Ballet Russe company founded in 1909, combined the innovations in painting (of scenery) and music with a new choreography; the results dazzled the West, and the Soviets have not disdained to continue without substantial change this, one of the finest products of prerevolutionary Russian culture, for the sake of popularity and profits at home and abroad.

The makers of the Bolshevik Revolution found few of the leaders of the culture of the so-called Silver Age ready to come to terms. The majority, probably the large majority, promptly emigrated to the West, though a few later returned. Some writers who remained, including the Symbolist Blok, placed their own non-Marxian interpretation on the Revolution (see Blok's superb poem, *The Twelve*), regarding it as a harbinger of salvation for Russia; but their coexistence with the Soviet regime was usually brief and unhappy, and in several cases ended in despair or even suicide. The chief Futurist poet, Vladimir Mayakovsky (1894-1930), tried his best to sing the praises of the Revolution in a thoroughly Bolshevik spirit, but he too finally killed himself.

The Civil War (1917-1921), in which the Bolsheviks were victorious after the narrowest of escapes from destruction by their enemies of all shades, was a period of suffering for most Russians, including the artists. Nevertheless a group of ardent Bolshevik theorists in the group that published the magazine *Proletarian Culture* were already trying to arrogate to themselves the right to determine the future course of cultural development, and another (the "Smithy-Cosmist") circle of uncompromising young writers planned to tear up prerevolutionary culture as completely as the social system had been ripped to shreds. The retort to this kind of talk was given by Eugene Zamiatin (1884-1937) in the novel *We,* in which he foresaw the transformation of modern society into a dehumanized social order with all the lineaments of what would decades later be called "totalitarianism." The publication of this novel, like that of *Doctor Zhivago,* has never been permitted in Russia.

Premature efforts at building communism straightaway, known as "War Communism," were after the end of the Civil War followed by a period of deliberate, temporary compromise with the dissatisfied masses known as the New Economic Policy (1921-1927), and the compromise was extended to include the artists. Leon Trotsky (1879-1940), then one of the chief Soviet leaders, accepted them as "fellow-travelers" (a word which later acquired a different meaning abroad) as long as they did not oppose the regime. A group of writers calling themselves the "Serapion Brothers" (the reference was to an enigmatic story by the German E. T. A. Hoffmann), refusing participation in the ideological struggle one way or the other, exemplified the response of the artists.

Despite official restraint, a group of young radicals (the "Left Front of Literature," or LEF) representing both literature and the theater, including the enthusiastically Bolshevik producer Vsevolod Meyerhold (1874-1942), attacked the fellow-travelers, only themselves to fall under attack as insufficiently revolutionary from the militants around the magazine *On Guard.* In 1925 another party leader, Nicholas Bukharin (1888-1938), had to come to the defense of the fellow-travelers, but in the next three years a period of definite artistic recovery and apparent normalization of cultural relations with the West accompanied the economic recovery that resulted from the NEP. Its results in the arts included novels of quality by Isaac Babel (1894- ?) and Leonid Leonov (1899-   ); lively satire by Valentine Katayev (1897-   ) and the team of Ilia Ilf (1897-1937) and Katayev's brother, "Eugene Petrov" (1903-1942); great films by Sergei Eisenstein (1898-1948), beginning with *Potemkin;* daring music by young Dmitri Shostakovitch (1906-   ), and much else. There seemed to be a modest revival of the Silver Age in the diversity and relative freedom of the culture of the 1920's. Even organized religious bodies, from the Orthodox church of the Russians and Ukrainians to the Islamic hierarchy of the Turkic peoples of Central Asia and the Buddhist clergy of the Buriat Mongols, experienced a breathing spell in the Soviet regime's campaign to undermine religion by a combination of atheist propaganda and efforts by pro-Communist clergy to foster dissidence within the churches.

In 1928, however, the NEP was abruptly ended. Lenin, after a struggle with Trotsky and other major Bolshevik figures, had been succeeded as dictator by Joseph Stalin (1879-1953). Stalin declared that the Communists were now prepared to resume the offensive postponed in 1921, and proclaimed a gigantic program of social and economic reconstruction under the rubric of the First Five-Year Plan. The fellow-traveling writers and artists were relegated to the dustheap, along with their defenders, Trotsky and Bukharin; now "shock workers" in "artistic brigades" of the Russian Association of Proletarian Writers (RAPP) undertook to do for culture what Communist activists were trying to do for the economy—namely, to wipe out the old and create the new overnight, if possible. Novels about tractor drivers, steel workers, and collective-farm chairmen began to flow from the presses; Soviet painting descended to the level of calendar art where it has ever since remained; music purported to reproduce the sounds of the factory. A single readable novel depicted the chaos and misery that attended the mass forced collectivization of agriculture—Michael Sholokhov's 1905-   ) *Virgin Soil Upturned;* and the latter's *The Quiet Don,* the most popular Soviet novel, though it dealt with the Civil War, was mostly written during the First Five-Year Plan.

However, the victors were not the enthusiastic theorists of RAPP, but the party, which now intervened directly in the artistic debates. All writers were in effect nationalized, being forced into one Union of Soviet Writers; and similar organizations embraced composers, painters, and other sorts of artists. Thenceforth the cultural dictatorship has been direct and effective. Sometimes the regime has chosen to tighten the controls over Soviet cultural life; sometimes it has been willing to loosen them. But the controls have remained in existence.

The object of the full cultural dictatorship was to enforce the ideological line of "socialist realism." This phrase, credited to Stalin himself, was explained by Karl Radek (1885-1939) as meaning "not only knowing reality as it is, but knowing whither it is moving." That is to say, mere "realism" that depicted all that was sordid along with what was bright was not to be confused with "socialist realism," which sought to depict how things ought to be and were, it was hoped, rapidly coming to be under the guidance of the Communist party. The artists were now to become, as Stalin put it, "engineers of human souls"; they were to mold the thoughts of the Soviet people, especially the youth, as the regime required.

In the early 1930's the pressure of Stalin's regime on the artists was gradually intensified. In 1932 the Union of Soviet Writers was created. In 1934 Stalin's personal attack on the late Michael Pokrovsky (1868-1932), dean of Soviet historians for fifteen years, warned artists against veiled attacks on the existing dictatorship through injudicious criticism of dead Russian rulers. Alexis Tolstoy (1883-1945), one of the abler writers, depicted Ivan the Terrible and Peter the Great in glowing terms suggesting Stalin's presumed virtues, and many other writers followed suit in submitting to the dictator's whims in return for official favor and high incomes.

Nevertheless, no matter how complete the artist's submission, he remained in danger. In 1936 official denunciations of artists and musicians mounted, and in 1937-1938 a number perished in the Great Purges. Paradoxically, Soviet artists and intellectuals generally were suffering more cruelly than in any period since the Revolution when, in the enthusiasm of the "Popular Front" policy of Communist attempts at cooperation with liberals abroad, many foreign intellectuals were increasingly expressing admiration for the tormentor regime.

When Hitler invaded the Soviet Union in 1941, however, Stalin abruptly loosened the cultural controls through which he had terrorized the entire artistic community. The expression of any feelings—including Russian nationalism, religion, and romantic love—that might lead the peoples of the Soviet Union to fight in defense of the regime, as they seemed in the summer of 1941 reluctant to do, was countenanced. However, the interlude of relative freedom was brief.

Once victory had been won, Stalin undertook to punish those who had wavered or renounced their loyalty to the Communist regime, and to reimpose discipline more rigorously than ever before, though there was no blood-bath of a magnitude comparable to that of the 1930's. In 1946 Stalin's most trusted assistant, Andrei Zhdanov (1896-1948), opened a full-scale attack on those who showed a willingness to "bow before bourgeois culture." He singled out a gentle, introspective poetess, Anna Akhmatova (1888-   ), and a popular humorist, Michael Zoshchenko (1894-1958), for violent personal abuse, and soon the denunciations were extended to include musicians, film-makers, scholars in the humanities and social sciences, and even circus managers. Zhdanov finally invaded the natural sciences, supporting a charlatan in genetics named Trofim Lysenko (1898-   ), who contended that acquired characteristics could be inherited. After Zhdanov abruptly died, Stalin carried on the campaign of re-ideologizing Soviet culture by attacking physiologists and linguists, and stepping up an anti-Semitic policy which resulted in great suffering for most Soviet intellectuals of Jewish origin.

Stalin's death in 1953 inaugurated a new period for Soviet culture, in which once again the cultural dictatorship has to date fluctuated between a sometimes surprising degree of permissiveness and a threatening and punitive attitude. For two or three years an atmosphere of hope prevailed, symbolized by the novel *The Thaw* by Ilya Ehrenburg (1891-   ), one of the few Jewish intellectuals to escape repression in Stalin's last years, and heightened by official repudiation of the doctrinal monopoly of Lysenko's genetics. Since Nikita Khrushchev (1894-   ) has attained the position of the single most important Soviet leader, there have been several contradictory tendencies at work. On the one hand cultural exchange with non-Communist foreigners has been resumed (especially since 1956) on a sizable scale; Dostoyevsky's works have circulated again in the USSR; and jazz, long banned, has been permitted. On the other, the great novel of Boris Pasternak (1890-1960), *Doctor Zhivago,* was not allowed to be printed in the USSR; Pasternak was forced to refuse the Nobel Prize for literature; and his close friend, Olga Ivinskaia, was arrested after his death. In a speech to Soviet writers made in the aftermath of the Hungarian Revolution of 1956, Khrushchev declared that if any in his audience should ever behave as the Hungarian intellectuals had done, "my hand will not tremble." Khrushchev has repeatedly made it clear that the literary men and artists are still to be, as he has quoted Stalin approvingly in saying, "engineers of human souls"—and engineers on behalf of a "correct Marxist-Leninist outlook." What that is likely to mean in practice during the next few years is difficult to say.

Soviet education is still fully and directly controlled by a regime that demands of all pupils first and foremost unquestioning loyalty to the Communist party and its leadership, and to the Soviet fatherland which, it is claimed, in turn embodies the hopes of "all progressive mankind" and the path that the latter desires and is historically destined to take. By his attention to educational changes

Khrushchev has made clear his belief that the Soviet school must play a crucial role in preparing the citizenry for the "transition to communism" as the final and ideal form of society and the coming of the rule of the Communist party to the two-thirds of the world still remaining outside it—objectives he apparently believes lie within the scope of the next few decades.

The publication in November, 1958, of forty-eight Theses on education by the Central Committee of the Soviet Communist party signaled extensive revision of the standard practices of Soviet schools. There was a call for greater attention to physical labor in the training of all children, for the expansion of a system of boarding schools for selected pupils, in which the child would be entirely deprived of the influence of his family, and above all for the more effective inculcation of the principles of "Communist morality"—that is, inflexible loyalty to the party and regime. It has been suggested that these changes constitute a synthesis, in the Hegelian-Marxian sense, of features of the two main periods in the history of Soviet education.

During the first period, from the early 1920's to the early 1930's, the Marxist notion of "socially useful labor" was stressed, in keeping with the labor theory of value in economics and the high valuation placed on the role of the industrial proletariat in world history, in particular in the Soviet scene. The "unified labor school" of the 1920's endeavored to promote the performance of useful work by the children in their communities, but also and fundamentally to destroy the old pre-revolutionary school system in which the teacher's authority was paramount and in which high standards of performance in definite curricular areas were exacted. The school of the 1920's was one in which the children themselves were encouraged to decide what they wished to study or when they wished to adjourn school to perform some extracurricular project, as well as to report to party officials any suspicions of teachers who seemed guilty of ideological deviation. The school of the 1920's achieved its objective of undermining the authority of teachers who had been trained in pre-revolutionary times in the belief that learning had its own proper criteria not to be overriden by any imposed by the state. However, it did not succeed in doing more than extending a degree of rather rudimentary literacy to any large segment of the population.

In the early 1930's Stalin inaugurated a new educational era in which the emphasis was laid on the "mastery of knowledge," and the authority of the newer, Communist-trained teachers was firmly established. A severely academic curriculum with high standards of performance was introduced into the new ten-year primary and secondary school. To be sure, the Communist teacher was not allowed to apply exclusively or even primarily academic criteria in judging the pupil's performance; and the curriculum, although its divisions resembled those of the West European or the pre-"progressive" American school, actually reflected an attempt to apply Marxist-Leninist ideas wherever possible and to use the traditional subjects as vehicles for indoctrination in Communist principles of thought and action. Thus the ten-year school of the 1930's was no more akin to the American "traditional" school than the unified labor school of the 1920's was to the American "progressive" school, despite the superficial similarities that attracted wide attention. In both periods of Soviet educational history, the Communist party, as official interpreter of Marxism-Leninism, determined everything from the choice of literary selections in readers to the kind of arithmetical exercises prescribed. The objective has been not to prepare the ordinary student to take the initiative in political action, since he is in adult life given no opportunity at all to make significant political choices, but rather to condition him to accept each new decision of the party leadership, no matter how much it may conflict with previous party decisions, notions of traditional morality, or his own conscience.

Soviet culture has thus, both in the field of the arts and in the field of education, long ago come to mean something quite different from what many Bolsheviks and non-Bolsheviks expected in 1917, when it seemed the result would be art for the people, a culture in which the whole population freely and spontaneously created and consumed, aided by generous assistance to artists and the provision of ample facilities for artistic performance and exhibition. The leaders of the Communist party decide what Soviet culture is to be like, what is to be encouraged and praised, what is to be merely tolerated, and what is to be prohibited altogether. In the words of a *Pravda* editorial of 1956, for the USSR "the Communist party has been, is, and will be the sole master of the minds, the voice of the thoughts and hopes, the leader and the organizer of the people in their entire struggle for Communism." The object of art, according to the Soviet cultural dictatorship, is to advance that struggle; the object of education is to inculcate unfailing submission to the dictates of the party that leads that struggle, but to induce enthusiastic response to such dictates in performing whatever kind of mental or physical toil is required of the given person at the given moment to secure victory in that struggle.

There is no doubt that the Soviet regime is aware of the extent to which art and education have fallen short, judged by those criteria, but there seems to be no evidence that Khrushchev's reaction to shortcomings in the realm of culture, any more than in the economic or political realms, is to conclude that the criteria themselves are defective. That would be to admit weakness in the foundations of the system itself. The success of the Soviet space program, the rise in output of Soviet heavy industry, the expansion of the Communist system to a point where it rules one-third of the globe and affects all sorts of developments within the other two-thirds daily and intimately—these and other phenomena are invoked to prove to the citizens of the USSR and the world that the goal of a worldwide Communist society is very much nearer today than it was in 1917. A few disgruntled artists and writers and even a larger number of inadequately indoctrinated school pupils are evidently regarded by the party leaders as annoying but merely temporary by-products of the immense enterprise of creating what Jules Monnerot calls an *imperium mundi*.

SELECTED READINGS[26]
QUANTUM PHYSICS

Asimov, Isaac, *Intelligent Man's Guide to Science*, 2 vols., Basic Books, 1960.
Bohm, David, *Quantum Theory*, Prentice-Hall, 1951.
Broglie, Louis de, *Matter and Light: The New Physics*, Dover Publications, Inc., 1955.
D'Abro, A., *The Rise of the New Physics*, 2 vols., Dover Publications, Inc., 1951.
Dogigli, Johannes, *The Magic of Rays*, Knopf, 1960.
Einstein, Albert, and Infeld, Leopold, *Evolution of Physics*, Simon and Schuster, 1938.
Gamow, George, *One Two Three—Infinity*, New American Library, 1954.
——— *Biography of Physics*, Harper, 1961.
———*Tompkins Explores the Atom*, Cambridge University Press, 1945.
Heisenberg, Werner, *Nuclear Physics*, Philosophical Library, 1957.
Hoffmann, Banesh, *The Strange Story of the Quantum*, 2nd rev. ed., Dover Publications, Inc., 1959.
Hughes, D. J., *On Nuclear Energy*, Harvard University Press, 1957.
Lansdell, Norman, *The Atom and the Energy Revolution*, Philosophical Library, 1959.
Planck, Max, *The Universe in the Light of Modern Physics*, Norton, 1931.
Schilpp, P. A., ed., *Albert Einstein: Philosopher-Scientist*, Tudor, 1951.
Schrödinger, Erwin, *Science Theory and Man*, Dover Publications, Inc., 1957.
Yang, C. N., *Elementary Particles*, Princeton University Press, 1961.

RELATIVITY AND COSMOLOGY

Barnett, Lincoln, *The Universe and Dr. Einstein*, Sloane, 1957.
Bondi, Hermann, *Cosmology*, 2nd ed., Cambridge University Press, 1961.
Bondi, Hermann, *et al.*, *Rival Theories of Cosmology*, Oxford University Press, 1960.
Born, Max, *Einstein's Theory of Relativity*, rev. ed., Dover Publications, Inc., 1962.
Couderc, Paul, *The Wider Universe*, Harper, 1960.
Eddington, A. S., *The Expanding Universe*, Ann Arbor Books, 1958.
Edgeworth, K. E., ed., *The Earth, Planets, and the Stars*, Macmillan, 1962.
Einstein, Albert, *Relativity: The Special and General Theory*, Crown.
Einstein, Albert, *et al.*, *Principle of Relativity*, Dover Publications, Inc., 1951.
Gamow, George, *The Creation of the Universe*, New American Library.
——— *Birth and Death of the Sun*, New American Library.
Hoyle, Fred, *The Nature of the Universe*, New American Library.
Hubble, E. P., *The Observational Approach to Cosmology*, Clarendon Press, 1937.
Kapp, R. O., *Towards a Unified Cosmology*, Basic Books, 1961.
Landau, L. D., and Rumer, G. B., *What Is Relativity?*, Basic Books, 1961.
Lemon, H. B., *From Galileo to the Nuclear Age*, University of Chicago Press, 1946.
Lyttleton, R. A., *The Modern Universe*, Harper, 1957.
Moore, Patrick, and Jackson, Francis, *Life in the Universe*, Norton, 1963.
Munitz, M. K., *Space, Time and Creation*, Collier Books.
Shapley, Harlow, *Flights from Chaos*, McGraw-Hill, 1930.
——— *Galaxies*, Harvard University Press.
——— *The Inner Metagalaxy*, Yale University Press, 1957.
——— *Of Stars and Men*, Beacon Press, 1958.
Singh, Jagjit, *Great Ideas and Theories of Modern Cosmology*, Dover Publications, Inc., 1961.

[26] For selected readings in anthropology, see bibliographies for chaps. i, ii, Volume I.

Tolman, R. C., *Relativity, Thermodynamics and Cosmology,* Oxford University Press, 1934.
Toulmin, Stephen, and Goodfield, June, *The Fabric of the Heavens,* Harper, 1962.
Weyl, Hermann, *Space, Time, Matter,* Dover Publications, Inc., 1952.
Whitrow, G. J., *The Structure and Evolution of the Universe,* Harper Torchbooks, 1959.

MATHEMATICS

Bell, E. T., *Development of Mathematics,* 2nd ed., McGraw-Hill, 1945.
Birkhoff, Garrett, and MacLane, Saunders, *Brief Survey of Modern Algebra,* Macmillan, 1953.
Bourbaki, Par N., *Éléments de Mathématique.*
Carmichael, R. D., *Introduction to the Theory of Groups of Finite Order,* Dover Publications, 1956.
Courant, Richard, and Robbins, Herbert, *What Is Mathematics?,* Oxford University Press, 1941.
Dantzig, Tobias, *Number, the Language of Science,* rev. ed., Anchor Books, 1956.
Hardy, G. H., *Pure Mathematics,* Cambridge University Press, 1959.
Hilbert, David, *The Foundations of Geometry,* Open Court.
Hodge, W. V. D., and Pedoe, D., *Methods of Algebraic Geometry,* 3 vols., Cambridge University Press, 1947-1954.
Kasner, Edward, and Newman, J. R., *Mathematics and the Imagination,* Simon and Schuster, 1940.
Kattsoff, L. O., *Philosophy of Mathematics,* Iowa State College Press, 1948.
Kline, Morris, *Mathematics in Western Culture,* Oxford University Press, 1953.
Newman, J. R., ed., *The World of Mathematics,* 4 vols., Simon and Schuster, 1962.
Reid, Constance, *Introduction to Higher Mathematics,* Crowell, 1960.
Sawyer, W. W., *Mathematician's Delight,* Penguin Books, 1943.
———— *Prelude to Mathematics,* Penguin Books, 1955.
Singh, Jagjit, *Great Ideas of Modern Mathematics,* Dover Publications, Inc., 1959.
Veblen, Oswald, *Analysis Situs.*
Veblen, Oswald, and Young, J. W. A., *Projective Geometry,* 2 vols., Ginn, 1938-1946.
Weyl, Hermann, *Philosophy of Mathematics and Natural Science,* Princeton University Press.
Wilder, R. L., *Introduction to Foundations of Mathematics,* Wiley, 1952.
Young, J. W. A., ed., *Monographs on Topics of Modern Mathematics,* Dover Publications, Inc., 1955.

CHEMISTRY

Baldwin, Ernest, *Dynamic Aspects of Biochemistry,* 3rd ed., Cambridge University Press, 1957.
Cartmell, E., and Fowles, G. W. A., *Valency and Molecular Structure,* 2nd ed., Academic Press, 1961.
Clements, Richard, *Modern Chemical Discoveries,* Dutton, 1954.
Coulson, C. A., *Valence,* 2nd ed., Oxford University Press, 1961.
Farber, E., *The Evolution of Chemistry,* Ronald Press, 1952.
Glasstone, Samuel, *Sourcebook on Atomic Energy,* 2nd ed., Van Nostrand, 1958.

Ingold, C. K., *Structure and Mechanism in Organic Chemistry,* Cornell University Press, 1953.
Jaffe, Bernard, *Chemistry Creates a New World,* Crowell, 1957.
Lapp, R. E., *New Force: A Story of Atoms and People in Peace and War,* Harper, 1953.
Pauling, Linus, *Nature of the Chemical Bond and the Structure of Molecules and Crystals,* 3rd ed., Cornell University Press, 1960.
Scientific American, Editors of, *New Chemistry,* Simon and Schuster, 1957.
Slosson, E. E., *Creative Chemistry,* Century, 1930.

BIOLOGY AND PHYSIOLOGY

Carson, H. L., *Heredity and Human Life,* Columbia University Press, 1963.
Clendening, Logan, *The Human Body,* Knopf, 1945.
Dampier, W. C., *A Shorter History of Science,* Meridian Books, 1957.
Gates, R. R., *Human Genetics,* 2 vols., Macmillan, 1946.
Goldschmidt, R. B., *Understanding Heredity,* Wiley, 1952.
—— *Theoretical Genetics,* University of California Press, 1955.
Holmes, H. N., *Out of the Test Tube,* Emerson Books, 1956.
Huxley, Julian, *Man in the Modern World,* New American Library, 1948.
Moore, Ruth, *The Coil of Life,* Knopf, 1960.
Nordenskiöld, Erik, *The History of Biology,* Tudor, 1960.
Pi Suñer, Augusto, *Classics of Biology,* Philosophical Library, 1955.
Singer, Charles, *History of Biology,* Abelard-Schuman, 1959.

PSYCHOLOGY

Allport, G. W., *Pattern and Growth in Personality,* Holt, Rinehart and Winston, 1961.
Ansbacher, H. L., and Ansbacher, R. R., eds., *The Individual Psychology of Alfred Adler,* Basic Books, 1956.
Attneave, Fred, *Applications of Information Theory to Psychology,* Holt, Rinehart and Winston, 1959.
Bartlett, F. C., *Remembering: A Study in Experimental and Social Psychology,* Cambridge University Press, 1932.
Beck, S. J., *Rorschach's Test,* 3 vols., Grune and Stratton, 1945-1952.
Boring, E. G., *History of Experimental Psychology,* Appleton-Century-Crofts.
Brett, G. S., *History of Psychology,* ed. R. S. Peters, Macmillan, 1953.
Bromberg, Walter, *The Mind of Man,* Harper, 1959.
Bruner, J. S., *The Process of Education,* Harvard University Press, 1962.
Buros, O. K., ed., *Mental Measurements Yearbook,* Gryphon, 1938-1959; 5th ed., 1959.
Carmichael, Leonard, ed., *Manual of Child Psychology,* Wiley, 1946, 1954.
Cronbach, L. J., *Essentials of Psychological Testing,* 2nd ed., Harper, 1960.
Eysenck, H. J., ed., *Handbook of Abnormal Psychology,* Basic Books, 1961.
Freud, Sigmund, *The Standard Edition of the Complete Psychological Works,* ed. J. Strachey, Hogarth Press, 1953 *et seq.*
Fryer, D. H., and Henry, E. R., *Handbook of Applied Psychology,* 2 vols., Rinehart, 1950.
Gibson, J. J., *The Perception of the Visual World,* Houghton Mifflin, 1950.

Goodenough, F. L., and Tyler, L. E., *Developmental Psychology,* 3rd ed., Appleton-Century-Crofts, 1959.

Guilford, J. P., *Psychometric Methods,* 2nd ed., McGraw-Hill, 1954.

Hall, C. S., and Lindzey, G., *Theories of Personality,* Wiley, 1957.

Hebb, D. O., *The Organization of Behavior,* Science Editions, 1961.

Hilgard, E. R., *Theories of Learning,* 2nd ed., Appleton-Century-Crofts, 1956.

Hilgard, E. R., and Marquis, D. G., *Conditioning and Learning,* rev. by G. A. Kimble, Appleton-Century-Crofts, 1960.

James, William, *Principles of Psychology,* 2 vols., Dover Publications, Inc., 1950.

Jones, Ernest, *Sigmund Freud: Life and Work,* 3 vols., Basic Books, 1953-1957.

Jung, C. G., *Collected Works,* ed. Herbert Read *et al.,* Pantheon Press, 1953-1960.

Klopfer, Bruno, *et al., Developments in the Rorschach Technique,* 2 vols., Harcourt, Brace and World, 1954-1956.

Koffka, Kurt, *Principles of Gestalt Psychology,* Harcourt, Brace, 1935.

Lashley, K. S., *The Neuropsychology of Lashley,* ed. F. A. Beach *et al.,* McGraw-Hill, 1960.

Lewin, Kurt, *A Dynamic Theory of Personality,* McGraw-Hill, 1945.

Lindzey, G. E., ed., *Handbook of Social Psychology,* 2 vols., Addison-Wesley, 1954.

Maccoby, E. E., *et al.,* eds., *Readings in Social Psychology,* Holt, Rinehart and Winston, 1958.

Masserman, J. H., *Principles of Dynamic Psychiatry,* 2nd ed., Saunders, 1961.

Menninger, K. A., *The Human Mind,* Knopf, 1945.

Miller, G. A., *Language and Communication,* McGraw-Hill, 1951.

Morgan, C. T., and Stellar, Eliot, *Physiological Psychology,* 2nd ed., McGraw-Hill, 1950.

Munn, N. L., *Psychology,* 4th ed., Houghton Mifflin, 1961.

Munroe, R. L., *Schools of Psychoanalytic Thought,* Holt, Rinehart and Winston, 1955.

Murphy, Gardner, *Historical Introduction to Modern Psychology,* rev. ed., Harcourt, Brace, 1949.

Mussen, P. H., ed., *Handbook of Research Methods in Child Development,* Wiley, 1960.

Pavlov, I. P., *Conditioned Reflexes,* Dover Publications, Inc., 1960.

Piaget, Jean, *The Language and Thought of the Child,* Meridian Books, 1955.

Rogers, C. R., *Client-Centered Therapy,* Houghton Mifflin, 1959.

Shaffer, L. F., and Shoben, E. A., *Psychology of Adjustment,* 2nd ed., Houghton Mifflin, 1956.

Skinner, B. F., *The Behavior of Organisms: An Experimental Analysis,* Appleton-Century-Crofts, 1938.

Stevens, S. S., ed., *Handbook of Experimental Psychology,* Wiley, 1951.

Thibaut, J. W., and Kelley, H. H., *The Social Psychology of Groups,* Wiley, 1959.

Thompson, Clara, *Psychoanalysis: Its Evolution and Development,* Nelson, 1950.

Thompson, G. G., *et al., Educational Psychology,* Appleton-Century-Crofts, 1959.

Thorndike, R. L., *Personnel Selection,* Wiley, 1949.

Tiffin, Joseph, and McCormick, E. J., *Industrial Psychology,* 4th ed., Prentice-Hall, 1958.

Wechsler, David, *The Measurement and Appraisal of Adult Intelligence,* 4th ed., Williams and Wilkins, 1958.

White, R. W., *The Abnormal Personality,* 2nd ed., Ronald Press, 1956.

Woodworth, R. S., *Contemporary Schools of Psychology,* Ronald Press, 1948.

MEDICINE

Advances in Cancer Research, 7 vols., Academic Press, 1953 *et seq.*

Advances in Clinical Chemistry, 5 vols., Academic Press, 1958 *et seq.*

Advances in Internal Medicine, Interscience Publications, 1942 *et seq.*

American Foundation, *Medical Research: A Midcentury Survey,* 2 vols., Little, Brown, 1952.

Annual Review of Biochemistry, Palo Alto, Calif., Annual Reviews, 1932 *et seq.*

Annual Review of Medicine, Annual Reviews, 1950 *et seq.*

Annual Review of Microbiology, Annual Reviews, 1947 *et seq.*

Annual Review of Physiology, Annual Reviews, 1939 *et seq.*

Antimicrobiol Agents and Chemotherapy, Detroit, American Society for Microbiology, 1961 *et seq.*

Garrison, *Introduction to the History of Medicine,* chap. xii.

Medical Clinics of North America, Saunders, 1917 *et seq.* (Monthly publication).

Methods in Medical Research, 9 vols., Year Book Medical Publishers, 1948 *et seq.*

Nicole, J. E., *Psychopathology,* Williams and Wilkins, 1946.

Noyes, A. P., and Kolb, L. C., *Modern Clinical Psychiatry,* 5th ed., Saunders, 1958.

Progress in Neurology and Psychiatry: An Annual Review, 17 vols., Grune and Stratton, 1944 *et seq.*

Progress in Surgery, 3 vols., Hafner, 1961 *et seq.*

Sanders, M. K., ed., *The Crisis in American Medicine,* Harper, 1961.

Surgical Clinics of North America, Saunders, 1921 *et seq.* (Monthly publication).

Year Book of General Surgery, Year Book Medical Publishers, 1933 *et seq.*

Year Book of Medicine, Year Book Medical Publishers, 1933 *et seq.*

GEOLOGY AND GEOGRAPHY

Barghoorn, E. S., "Origin of Life," in *Treatise on Marine Ecology and Paleoecology,* ed. H. S. Ladd, 1957.

Bates, D. R., ed., *The Earth and Its Atmosphere,* Basic Books, 1957.

Dyson, J. L., *The World of Ice,* Knopf, 1962.

Emiliani, Cesare, "Ancient Temperatures," *Scientific American, 198:* 54–63 (1958).

Ewing, Maurice, and Donn, W. L., "A Theory of Ice Ages," *Science, 113:* 1061–1066 (1956); *117:* 1159–1162 (1958).

Faul, Henry, ed., *Nuclear Geology,* Wiley, 1954.

Fenton, C. L., and Fenton, Mildred A., *Giants of Geology,* Doubleday, 1952.

Gamow, George, *Biography of The Earth,* Viking, 1959.

Glaessner, M. F., "Pre-Cambrian Animals," *Scientific American, 204:* 72–78 (1961).

Hurley, P. M., *How Old Is the Earth?,* Anchor Books, 1959.

Key, C. E., *The Story of Twentieth-Century Exploration,* Knopf, 1938.

Libby, W. F., *Radiocarbon Dating,* 2nd ed., University of Chicago Press, 1955.

Mason, Brian, *Principles of Geochemistry,* 2nd ed., Wiley, 1958.

Moore, Ruth, *The Earth We Live On,* Knopf, 1956.

Runcorn, S. K., "The Earth's Magnetism," *Scientific American, 193:* 152–162 (1955).

Sullivan, W. L., *Assault on the Unknown: The International Geophysical Year,* McGraw-Hill, 1961.

Wilson, J. T., "Geophysics and Continental Growth," *American Scientist, 47:* 1–24 (1959).

SOCIAL SCIENCES AND EDUCATION

Babbidge, H. D., and Rosenzweig, R. M., *The Federal Interest in Higher Education,* McGraw-Hill, 1962.

Barnes, H. E., ed., *History and Prospects of the Social Sciences,* Knopf, 1925.

———— *Economic History of the Western World,* Part V.

———— *A History of Historical Writing,* chaps. xiv-xv.

———— *The New History and the Social Studies,* Century, 1925.

Barnes, H. E., and Becker, Howard, *Social Thought from Lore to Science,* 3 vols., Dover Publications, Inc., 1961.

———— *Contemporary Social Theory,* Appleton-Century, 1940.

Bromberg, Walter, *The Mind of Man,* Harper, 1959.

Caplow, Theodore, and McGee, R. J., *The Academic Marketplace,* Basic Books, 1959.

Commager, H. S., *The American Mind,* Yale University Press, 1959.

Cremin, L. A., *The Transformation of the School: Progressivism in American Education, 1876-1957,* Knopf, 1962.

Curti, M. E., *The Social Ideas of American Educators,* Pageant.

Dewey, John, *Democracy and Education,* Macmillan.

Dewey, John, et al., *Living Philosophies,* Simon and Schuster, 1931.

Dorfman, Joseph, *Thorstein Veblen and His America,* Viking Press, 1934.

Eby and Arrowood, *The Development of Modern Education,* chaps. xxii-xxiii.

Hayes, E. C., ed., *Recent Developments in the Social Sciences,* Lippincott, 1927.

Hewett, Dorothy, and Mather, K. F., *Adult Education,* Appleton-Century-Crofts, 1937.

Hofstadter, Richard, and Smith, Wilson, eds., *American Higher Education: A Documentary History,* University of Chicago Press, 1962.

Kandel, I. L., *American Education in the Twentieth Century,* Harvard University Press, 1957.

Kilpatrick, W. H., ed., *The Educational Frontier,* Century, 1933.

Kimball, S. T., and McClellan, J. E., *Education and the New America,* Random House, 1963.

Lazarsfeld, P. F., and Thielens, Wagner, *The Academic Mind,* Free Press, 1959.

Mayer, Martin, *The Schools,* Harper, 1961.

Nelson, Jack and Roberts, Gene, *The Censors and the Schools,* Little, Brown, 1963.

Pareto, Vilfredo, *The Mind and Society: A Treatise on General Sociology,* 2 vols., Dover Publication, Inc., 1963.

Rudolph, Frederick, *The American College and University: A History,* Knopf, 1962.

Sanford, R. N., *The American College,* Wiley, 1962.

Schmidt, G. P., *The Liberal Arts College,* Rutgers University Press, 1957.

Schramm, Wilbur, ed., *The Impact of Educational Television,* University of Illinois Press, 1961.

Stoke, H. W., *The American College President,* Harper, 1959.

Tugwell, R. G., and Keyserling, L. H., *Redirecting Education,* 2 vols., Columbia University Press, 1934.

Washburne, Carleton, *A Living Philosophy of Education,* John Day, 1940.

———— *Remakers of Mankind.*

Weidner, E. W., *The World Role of Universities,* McGraw-Hill, 1962.

Welter, Rush, *Popular Education and Democratic Thought in America,* Columbia University Press, 1963.

ECONOMICS

Bell, J. F., *A History of Economic Thought,* Ronald Press, 1953.
Dorfman, Joseph, *The Economic Mind in American Civilization,* 5 vols., Viking Press, 1946–1959.
———— *Thorstein Veblen and His America,* Viking, 1934.
Gray, Alexander, *Development of Economic Doctrine,* Wiley, 1931.
Haney, L. H., *History of Economic Thought,* Macmillan, 1949.
Heilbroner, R. L., *The Worldly Philosophers,* Simon and Schuster, 1961.
Hutchison, T. W., *A Review of Economic Doctrines, 1870-1929,* Oxford University Press, 1953.
McCracken, H. L., *Keynesian Economics in the Stream of Economic Thought,* University of Louisiana Press, 1962.
Rogin, L., *The Meaning and Validity of Economic Theory,* Harper, 1956.
Schumpeter, J. A., *History of Economic Analysis,* Oxford University Press, 1954.
Scott, W. A., *The Development of Economics,* Appleton, 1933.
Seligman, B. B., *Main Currents in Modern Economics,* Free Press, 1962.
Spiegel, H. W., ed., *The Development of Economic Thought,* Wiley, 1952.
Taylor, O. H., *A History of Economic Thought,* McGraw-Hill, 1960.

PHILOSOPHY AND RELIGION

Ayer, A. J., *Language, Truth and Logic,* Dover Publications, Inc., 1953.
Ayer, A. J., et al., *The Revolution in Philosophy,* Macmillan, 1957.
Barth, Karl, *Dogmatics in Outline,* Harper Torchbooks, 1959.
Berdyaev, Nicholas, *The End of Our Time,* Sheed and Ward, 1933.
Buber, Martin, *I and Thou,* Scribner, 1958.
Bultmann, Rudolf, *Jesus Christ and Mythology,* Scribner, 1958.
Collins, James, *The Existentialists,* Regnery, 1952.
Desan, Wilfred, *The Tragic Finale: An Essay on the Philosophy of Jean-Paul Sartre,* Harper Torchbooks, 1960.
Dewey, John, *Experience and Nature,* Dover Publications, Inc., 1958.
Gilson, Étienne, *Unity of Philosophical Experience,* Scribner, 1937.
Latourette, K. S., *Christianity in a Revolutionary Age,* Harper, 1961, Vol. VI.
Lubac, Henri de, *Catholicism,* Sheed and Ward, 1958.
Maritain, Jacques, *Degrees of Knowledge,* Scribner, 1959.
Niebuhr, Reinhold, *Nature and Destiny of Man,* Scribner, 1949.
Russell, Bertrand, *The Problems of Philosophy,* Oxford Galaxy Books, 1959.
Spiegelberg, H., *History of the Phenomenological Movement.*
Tillich, Paul, *The Dynamics of Faith,* Harper Torchbooks, 1958.
Urmson, J. O., *Philosophical Analysis: Its Development Between the Two World Wars,* Oxford University Press, 1956.
Whitehead, A. N., *Science and the Modern World,* New American Library, 1948.

SOVIET CULTURE

Bunt, C. G. E., *Russian Art from Scyths to Soviets,* Studio-Crowell, 1946.
Calvocoressi, M. D., *A Survey of Russian Music,* Penguin Books, 1944.
Counts, G. S., *The Challenge of Soviet Education,* McGraw-Hill, 1957.

————— *Khrushchev and the Central Committee Speak on Education,* University of Pittsburgh Press, 1960.

Counts, G. S., and Lodge, Nucia, *The Country of the Blind,* Houghton Mifflin, 1949.

Curtiss, J. S., *The Russian Church and the Soviet State, 1917–1950,* Little, Brown, 1953.

Eastman, Max, *Artists in Uniform: A Study of Literature and Bureaucracy,* Knopf, 1934.

Johnson, W. H. E., *Russia's Educational Heritage,* Carnegie Press, 1950.

London, Kurt, *The Seven Soviet Arts,* Yale University Press, 1938.

Menhert, Klaus, *Soviet and the World,* Praeger, 1962.

Miliukov, Paul, *Outlines of Russian Culture,* 3 vols., A. S. Barnes.

Mirsky, D. S., *A History of Russian Literature,* ed. F. J. Whitfield, Vintage Books.

Rice, Tamara T., *Russian Art,* Pelican Books, 1949.

Slonim, Marc, *Modern Russian Literature: From Chekhov to the Present,* Oxford University Press, 1953.

Struve, Gleb, *Soviet Russian Literature, 1917–1950,* University of Oklahoma Press, 1951.

Trotsky, Leon, *Literature and Revolution,* Ann Arbor Books, 1960.

Voyce, Arthur, *Russian Architecture,* Philosophical Library, 1948.

Washburne, Carleton, *Remakers of Mankind,* Day, 1932.

————— *A Living Philosophy of Education,* John Day, 1940.

Weidlé, Wladimir, *Russia: Absent and Present,* Vintage Books.

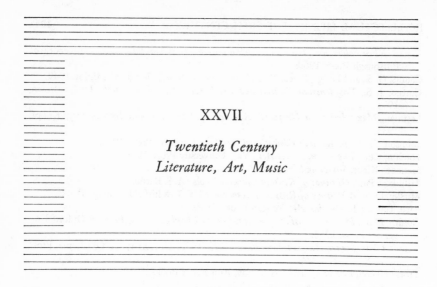

XXVII

Twentieth Century Literature, Art, Music

I. LITERATURE: "WITH VOICES AND APPLAUSE OF EVERY SORT"

By Anthony Netboy

Portland State College

1. *Drama*

Time winnows the chaff from the wheat in literary production. Every year hundreds of dramas are produced in the Western world; many are printed, admired for a time, and then, for the most part, forgotten. A small portion of this mass of theatrical work is remembered because it comprises supreme literary masterpieces, like the comedies of Richard Brinsley Sheridan or Oscar Wilde; expresses viable truth, like the dramas of Ibsen; or presents immortal characters, like the plays of Chekhov. The rest pass into limbo, from which few are ever rescued.

The literature of the nineteenth century has been subjected to the selective process of the years, and we can find a way through it with less confusion than through twentieth-century literature. The final test is time, but time has even less consideration for us than for books, and we cannot wait to hear what it has to say. Without any hope of finality, and realizing that we cannot mention all the major writers who ought to be discussed, we must survey the twentieth-century theater and choose a few of the most impressive playwrights for consideration. Viewing the drama of the Western world from this perspective, it is impossible not to observe that the twentieth century is one of the greatest periods of dramatic prosperity, and that within this period there is an imperfectly defined but observable trend: the rise of the realistic social drama, a subsequent dissatisfaction with realism, and an orgy of experimentalism exemplified in the current popularity of existentialist drama and the theater of the absurd.

As we have seen earlier, modern drama begins with its most distinguished writer, Ibsen (1828-1906), whose important work extends from *Brand* (1866) to *When We Dead Awaken* (1899). The vital impulse he gave to the theater was realistic in the best sense of the word. By realism we usually mean the method by which a writer presents an illusion consistent with our own impressions of reality; we look at his work and say, "That's right. That's the way things are." Ibsen's work includes realism of this sort, and goes beyond it. He desired not only to have his plays accord with our impressions of reality, but to present characters of dignity and worth in situations which intelligent men must face, to avoid the staginess and cheap theatricality of contemporary plays, and to make his dramas embodiments of vital truth. The power which animates the hero of his poetic play, *Brand,* is the desire to find "a place on the whole earth's circuit, whereon to be wholly himself." And this problem is at the heart of all Ibsen's plays. *Brand* and *Peer Gynt* are a kind of poetic drama which Ibsen later discarded in order to present his characters in terms of more immediate experience; but the problem persists. It is the driving power of the later plays, where it is expressed in terms of man's relation to society. Because Ibsen saw clearly and was a writer of consummate skill, some of his works—*Ghosts* (1881), *The Wild Duck* (1884), and *An Enemy of the People* (1882), for instance—are masterpieces of playwriting.

There were other dramatists in the late nineteenth century who devoted their works to the expression of truth as they saw it, notably the Russian Anton Chekhov (1860-1904). In *The Seagull* (1896), *The Three Sisters* (1901), and *The Cherry Orchard* (1904), which established the glory of the Moscow Art Theater, Chekhov created a relatively new type of drama in which naturalism dominates both dramaturgy and character creation; there are no plots in these poetically realistic works, little action, merely conversation. An aura of sadness hangs over Chekhov's world, generally induced by contemplation of life's failures; yet his real power comes from quiet laughter and compassion for the gentle people who fill his stage. While not a crusader, Chekhov felt that he was limning the end of an era and heralding the advent of a new and more fruitful epoch in which the bourgeoisie, symbolized by Lopakhin in *The Cherry Orchard,* would triumph over the futile aristocracy and lead Russia into the modern world.

In France the naturalist, Henri Becque (1832-1899), wrote *The Vultures* (1882) and *The Woman of Paris* (1885) with a hard and searching irony and minute fidelity of detail, but his work, lacking the humanity which animates Ibsen, is arid. On the other hand, Edmond Rostand (1868-1918) turned his back upon the contemporary scene in *Cyrano de Bergerac,* produced in 1897. This is a superior example of the kind of poetic drama Ibsen wanted to avoid. Emotional and vividly romantic, it has, through its brilliant verses, given millions of spectators a vicarious romantic experience for which, in gratitude, they willingly suspend a large portion of their critical powers, failing to recognize the absurd situation on which the story rests. The play is prevented from ending happily only through Cyrano's unquestioned conformity to a code of honor which forces him to keep a promise to a dying friend. Sentimental to the core, it is utterly remote from human experience, not because it is romantic or sentimental, but because it presents a morality which could exist only in books. It is quite outside the main current of modern drama.

Literary naturalism, as in Becque, was the product of an interpretation of nineteenth-century science. Maurice Maeterlinck (1862-1949), a Belgian scientist of modest achievements, reacted to science in another way. Dissatisfied with scientific materialism, he portrayed in his plays the mystery that lies beyond science. His works have little action and his characters are symbols rather than people; he portrays, as it were, disembodied spirits in an immaterial world. A mystic and symbolist, he presents the horror of the ghost story without the ghost, the terror of death without a knowledge of the dying man. His best-known play, *Pelléas et Mélisande* (1892), was made into an opera by Debussy and owes some of its reputation to his exquisite music. Neither Maeterlinck nor Rostand was searching for a place on "earth's circuit," and Becque, firmly upon earth, did not create a world in which a man can be "wholly himself." In contrast, Eugène Brieux (1858-1932) in such plays as *Damaged Goods* (1902) launched the drama of ideas which was to flower in the works of George Bernard Shaw.

Unquestionably the greatest figure in the modern English theater is the Irishman, George Bernard Shaw (1856-1950). A novelist, pamphleteer, dramatic and music critic before he abandoned journalism for the theater, Shaw became the self-appointed champion of Ibsen when *Ghosts* and *A Doll's House* were first presented before hostile English audiences. He devoted many of his weekly articles in *The Saturday Review* to a defense of the new social drama and to attacks upon everything that stood in its way. Weary of the endless revivals of older plays, the inanities and pallid sensuality of the London theater, Shaw as a playwright endeavored to create an intellectually respectable drama which would discuss honestly the social forces of the modern world.

To Shaw, human institutions are made for man, not man for human institutions. As institutions become atrophied, man finds it impossible to derive satisfaction from them; this resistance of the will to the institution is the basis of dramatic conflict in many of Shaw's dramas. Social evil is at the root of many of his works—slum landlordism in *Widower's Houses,* his first play (1892), prostitution in *Mrs. Warren's Profession* (1898), warmongers and munitions profiteers in *Major Barbara* (1905), medical quackery in *The Doctor's Dilemma* (1906), muscular and meek Christianity in *Androcles and the Lion* (1913). Shaw's heroes and heroines are usually dominated by the life force which finds expression in their strength of will; they are lucid, voluble, endowed with "Shavian" wit, and at the same time quite credible as dramatic personages. Joan of Arc in *St. Joan* (1923), perhaps his most effective play, is a classic example of the Shavian heroine, as Sir Andrew Undershaft in *Major Barbara* is the archetype of the Shavian hero.

Shaw's dramaturgy is sometimes amorphous, the drama being lost in the conversation and preachments, and it is customary to observe that he sacrificed dramatic conflict to propaganda. This tendency is most notable in the plays of his last period, beginning with *The Apple Cart* (1929) and ending with *In Good King Charles's Golden Days* (1939). Apart from the ebullient, intellectual tours de force of which perhaps *Caesar and Cleopatra* (1899) and *Pygmalion* (1913) (converted into the successful musical *My Fair Lady*) are the best examples, Shaw was capable of writing conventional "comedies of fun" in which the conflict is not between the individual and the social institution but between man and woman. *Candida* (1895) and *The Devil's Disciple* (1897) fall into this category.

Shaw was a prolific dramatist. He adapted the problem play of Ibsen to the English theater, giving it his own socialistic interpretation; he added a modicum of Brieux, salted it with Irish wit and gallimaufry, and produced a body of dramatic work that exasperated, shocked, and provoked theatergoers for almost half a century. In the process he expounded innumerable social and political ideas, exploded many fetishes, and while adding to the gaiety of nations also provoked intellectual ferment. How much of his work will endure only time will tell, since the topicality of his themes often subdued his real gift for creating vivid and believable characters.

The social criticism of John Galsworthy (1867-1933) is clearer than Shaw's but not as searching. *Justice* (1910), a grim tragedy of a weak character caught in the wheels of the law, is directed not against a social system but one of its manifestations, an unjust law. This is characteristic of Galsworthy. Although intensely sympathetic to the downtrodden classes, he accepted the point of view of the English upper classes. To him, social discord arises from an absence of human understanding. This being a matter for pity rather than scorn or wit, the mood of his plays is tender. Sober and gray, they are saved from drabness by their brilliant structure. Galsworthy was one of the most popular English dramatists of his time, and we must not underestimate him because he is out of public favor now. A distinguished novelist, though not a completely satisfactory playwright, he fails where most realists fail: his work does not embrace enough of life. Sir James Barrie (1860-1937) is best known for his humor and fantasy, but his plays are fundamentally more grim than Galsworthy's. His most famous character, Peter Pan, is the boy who would not grow up. Barrie's adult characters, more often than not, are objects of satire, presented with whimsy and tempered with pity; it is not in themselves, but in their stars, that the characters are underlings. Perhaps Maggie in *What Every Woman Knows* (1908) is his most admirable creation.

One of the most exciting aspects of the renaissance of the British drama was the emergence of a distinctly Irish drama centering around the Abbey Theatre in Dublin which was inspired, and directed in its early years, by the poet William Butler Yeats. A coterie of gifted writers, including Yeats, John Millington Synge, Lord Dunsany, Lady Gregory, and Sean O'Casey, poured out for a brief period dramatic works based on Celtic and Irish materials which pushed the lyrical drama to heights that had not been attained since the days of the Elizabethans. For example, Sean O'Casey (1884-   ) set his *Juno and the Paycock* (1924) and *The Plough and the Stars* (1926) in Dublin against a background of the Irish struggle for independence, writing in a prose style which is often more poetic than the poetry of his later work, *Within the Gates* (1932). When this prose, especially the passages of vituperation, was spoken by the Abbey Players, it was not only a sheer delight to the ear, but stirred the sympathies of playgoers with the lowly and downtrodden people he depicted. Equally moving are Synge's *Playboy of the Western World* (1907) and the short *Riders to the Sea* (1904), which evokes an atmosphere close to the true spirit of tragedy. Synge's poetic dramas, written in prose, capture the rhythms of the language spoken by the Irish peasantry, enriched by borrowings from the native Erse.

Coming somewhat later than the Irish dramatic renaissance, American playwrights also ventured into the realm of poetry. Maxwell Anderson (1888-1959) wrote over a score of plays, ranging from light comedy to poetic drama. *Winterset* (1935), *Elizabeth the Queen* (1930), *Mary of Scotland* (1935), and *High Tor* (1936) contain stirring scenes and poetic flights that are more than pale echoes of Shakespeare, but in an age of unbelief and absence of values the true tragic sense escapes them. As Allardyce Nicoll tersely says, "the conditions of the world in which we live well-nigh deny the playwright to reach, as Anderson would fain have reached, the exhilarating terror and the agonized serenity of the true tragic concept."

The most lauded American playwright of the twentieth century was Eugene O'Neill (1885-1953), whose early plays were produced during the first World War and whose last appeared posthumously. In these intervening years O'Neill dazzled audiences with ambitious dramaturgical displays, experimented with many technical devices, and moved rapidly from one form to another—realism, expressionism, and impressionism. A decade after his death, we are better able to assess his achievements than was possible when he was alive. It now seems clear that O'Neill fell short of greatness. Although he had an exalted conception of the drama and a nobly tragic sense of man's struggle with the complex forces of twentieth-century American life, he lacked the sheer power of language that is needed to produce imperishable works of art: the words which should carry the full emotion to the audience are all too often singularly absent. The powerful scenes do not have the magnificent speeches one expects, the inspired language which lifts the audience to the poet's imaginative level. This is especially evident in O'Neill's most ambitious works, such as *Strange Interlude* (1928) and *Mourning Becomes Electra* (1931). In these plays the splendid acting partially compensated for the weakness of the script. Nevertheless, O'Neill's experiments, as in the expressionistic *Hairy Ape* (1922), *The Great God Brown* (1926) in which he introduced Greek masks, and *Strange Interlude* in which much of the dramatic effect is conveyed through asides, helped to free the theater from a slavish imitation of the surfaces of everyday life. The appearance in 1956 of O'Neill's lengthy autobiographical play, *Long Day's Journey into Night,* has raised the possibility, as Joseph Wood Krutch says, of an "upward reassessment" of his contribution to the contemporary theater. In this searching analysis of his own early life as it was intermeshed with that of his unhappy and doomed family, O'Neill discusses in a powerful and convincing manner the question of human responsibility for what is often attributed to fate—a question which obsessed the ancient Greek writers of tragedy. This posthumous work may well be O'Neill's greatest achievement.

O'Neill was too individualistic a writer to inspire imitators, but the "tragic" muse was taken up by two talented younger dramatists, Arthur Miller (1915-   ) and Tennessee Williams (1914-   ). Miller's *Death of a Salesman* (1949), dealing with the final dismal years of a traveling salesman, is labelled by the author as a tragedy. It is, however, more like a conventional study in naturalism, showing the inability of an undistinguished character to extricate himself from the web created by his futile striving for material success; Willy Loman's death is neither heroic nor moving. Williams chose the decayed Southern aristocracy for his milieu in *The Glass Menagerie* (1944) and *A Streetcar Named Desire* (1947). He depicted with considerable insight and sensitivity the tragedy of two women, one a shabby genteel widow and the other a nymphomaniac Southern belle, torn between their ideals and the inexorable realities of the modern world. The pathetic Blanche DuBois in *A Streetcar Named Desire* and the sad Laura Wingfield in *The Glass Menagerie* are relics of a romantic age living in a hard, vulgar world that crushes them. Neither Miller's nor Williams's later works received the literary accolades that greeted their early plays; Williams has been a prolific writer but his recent dramas tend to be melodramatic, filled with repulsive, abnormal characters dear to the heart of Hollywood.

The poetic dramas of the distinguished British-American poet, T. S. Eliot (1888-   ), are written on a lofty intellectual plane. *Murder in the Cathedral* (1935) is a study of the martyr, Thomas à Becket, the archbishop who dared to oppose King Henry II; *The Family Reunion* (1939) is based on the ancient legend of Orestes which has fascinated many modern playwrights. *The Cocktail Party* (1949) has a contemporary setting. *Murder in the Cathedral* is a deeply moving tragedy raised to a philosophical level by the use of the Greek chorus. *The Family Reunion* and *The Cocktail Party* proved to be successful theater but lack poetic grandeur. Less redolent of ancient tragedy but stamped with genius are the poetic dramas of Federico García Lorca (1899-1936), the Spanish poet murdered by the Falangists during the civil war. Among Lorca's dramas, *Blood Wedding* (1933) has been successfully transplanted to the English-speaking world. In this work the unhappy marriage of two young people is delineated against the background of a family blood feud with an extraordinary economy of language and in a stark dramatic style.

If the twentieth century is, on the whole, not an age suitable for the writing of high tragedy, although many playwrights essayed this medium, it is preeminently an age of comedy. Noël Coward (1899-   ) has for almost forty years enlivened the British and American stages with deft and witty plays that delineate the brilliant surfaces of modern society. Lacking the seriousness of his graver contemporaries, he is always entertaining; this is no small virtue, since the theater must entertain before it can do anything else. Coward came into favor after the first World War, when the theater was afraid to trust emotion; he owes his success partly to alternating wit and sentimentality in rapid succession, so that his audiences, enjoying the luxury of sentiment, are made to laugh before they realize they have been sentimental. When his plays are serious, they arouse the accepted emotions—patriotism, for instance, in *Cavalcade* (1931). Coward has a facile style, and since he deals mainly with sophisticated people, it is rich in persiflage, well exemplified in the tautly written *Private Lives* (1930) and in the fantasy, *Blithe Spirit* (1941), a minor comic masterpiece.

The plays of the Hungarian, Ferenc Molnár (1878-1952), like those of Noël Coward, are essentially comedies of manners, but they are often steeped in a kind of fantasy, as in *Liliom* (1909), which raises them above the sphere of realism. Molnár's vein of sophisticated comedy is brilliantly displayed in *The Guardsman* (1910) where the jealous husband disguises himself as an officer to test his wife's love, and in *The Play's the Thing* (1925) with its play within the play. The wit of Budapest proved to be captivating to audiences in New York (and elsewhere), especially in the hands of such excellent performers as Alfred Lunt and Lynn Fontanne in *The Guardsman* and Holbrook Blinn in *The Play's the Thing*. Molnár was not only a master of the comic scene, he created credible characters in incredible situations, thus permitting audiences the willing suspension of disbelief.

S. N. Behrman (1893-   ) is not a blithe spirit like Coward or Molnár, for his wit is spiced with intellectual substance, and his achievement is perhaps greater: he established an American comedy of manners in four successful plays, *The Second Man* (1927), *Meteor* (1929), *Biography* (1932), and *No Time for Comedy* (1939). There is a great deal of philosophical and social discussion in these plays as the author reflects on the follies and evils of men. Where many contemporary dramatists have handled such topics in a serious and often mordant (and Freudian) fashion, Behrman treats them as matters of pure comedy, thus blending the tradition of Sheridan and Wilde with that of Bernard Shaw.

The Spanish theater displayed a remarkable fecundity in the twentieth century, at least before the triumph of General Francisco Franco and the institution of a totalitarian regime in 1939 that dampened the Spanish literary renaissance by dispersing many of its greatest figures and instituting a censorship which, while not as prescriptive as that of Soviet Russia, tended to discourage the full freedom of expression vital to literary creation. The reader who first approaches Spanish literature through its dramas of the present century will be unaware both of the tradition of vigor and action which has dominated the Spanish theater until recent times and of the long accumulating social forces which brought about the Spanish revolution. In its quiet urbanity, this theater resembles that of Chekhov, although it lacks his sharp strength.

The plays of the incredibly prolific Jacinto Benavente (1866-1954), of Gregorio Martínez Sierra (1881-1947), and of the Quintero brothers, Serafín (1871-1938) and Joaquín (1873-1944), do not constitute a popular drama. They are polished, reflective, gay or tender, witty, sometimes ironic, but never approach the vitality of Lope de Vega, and are usually unaware of the dominant social and intellectual forces in contemporary Spain. Benavente's social point of view, for instance, is outmoded nineteenth-century liberalism. His themes are likely to be the struggle of the individual for expression, or, as in *The Princess Bebe* (1904), feminism. Sierra is best known in America for his *Cradle Song* (1911) and *The Kingdom of God.* The former is a simple drama of life in a convent. In the first act a foundling is left to the care of the sisters. In the second act, the foundling, now grown to young womanhood, leaves the convent to be married. There could hardly be a play with less action, yet through its precise details it tells eloquently of the love and satisfaction the sisters have found in caring for the child, and of their grief at her departure. Not by any means the best of modern Spanish plays, it is representative of their purpose and method.

Until the twentieth century Italy did not have a thriving national theater as did England, Spain, and France. This was doubtless due to a lack of cultural unity. What pleased an audience in Rome was not likely to please an audience in another city, and the audience is part of the play. A healthy theater is a popular theater. So it happens that the most famous of Italian playwrights, Luigi Pirandello (1867-1936), was not a dramatist of the people and did not, except in a superficial way, reflect Italian culture. In 1916, near the age of fifty, he began his period of greatest success with *Right You Are If You Think You Are,* whose theme is that truth is unknowable to man. It concerns Madame Ponza, whose mother thinks she is one person, and whose husband thinks she is another; she herself says that she is no one, that she is whoever you believe her to be. As stated here, the story seems preposterous, yet Pirandello makes it a strong play. His most original and powerful drama, *Six Characters in Search of an Author* (1921), develops the same theme in a manner which defies description. This theme is at once the source of Pirandello's strength and weakness. An audience cannot long be satisfied with the assurance that it does not know anything, that, indeed, there is nothing to know.

The 1930's was a decade of depression which exploded into the second World War. In nearly every country there were playwrights who expressed the mood of revolt against a capitalistic system that had suddenly stopped producing enough goods and services, that had thrown millions of persons out of work, generated bread lines and doles, and seemed paralyzed with fear. This mood usually took the form of proletarian drama, best represented in America by Clifford Odets (1906-1963). His first play, *Waiting for Lefty* (1935), is the work of a literary artist who seeks to arouse political action; this short drama is probably the best of the Marxist plays produced in the United States. In *Awake and Sing!* (1935) Odets still flaunts his anger at an economic system which destroys the dreams of gentle people but his delineation of the Berger family is thoroughly realistic with a kind of poetic realism borrowed from Chekhov. Odets' later plays show a diminishing realism and a tendency to take refuge in melodrama; although they usually retain their theatrical effectiveness, they seem to be permeated with the tinselry of the cinema.

The 1940's and 1950's brought forth a new school of dramatists, notably in France, who seem to reflect the helplessness, despair, and strangling fear which first the war and then the threat of nuclear annihilation has imposed on Western man. As in other literary forms, dramatists have tended to experiment with theatrical conventions with brazen audacity, and even when they expound serious philosophical or social ideas they often seem to be more interested in unconventional techniques than in character portrayal or plot. The realistic drama of Ibsen has thus come full circle: impressionism and expressionism have given way to bizarre experiments that have little relation, at least in structure, to the dramas of Ibsen or Strindberg or even Chekhov.

The new school of French dramatists—Giraudoux, Anouilh, Sartre, Camus, Ionesco, and Beckett—have not only revitalized the French theater but reinvigorated (sometimes in watered-down translations) the postwar theaters of England and the United States. The wonderful fecundity of the American theater seems to have come to a halt with the death of Eugene O'Neill, while recent British drama has been marked by superficial cleverness rather than profound insights or analysis of human life. A brief study of the new French playwrights will therefore give us an opportunity to observe the postwar theater in its most expressive and impressive forms.

Jean Giraudoux (1882-1944) died during the second World War, but his unmistakable dramatic genius, recognized during the 1930's, left a deep impression on many postwar dramatists. Like other French playwrights, Giraudoux was also an eminent novelist, but it was in the theater that his literary gifts were most advantageously revealed. Giraudoux showed a preference for the symbolist drama. The French critic, Louis Cazamian, has well summarized his dramatic work: "Most of the characters are mere sketches, and develop hardly at all; while the plot itself is reduced to an unsubstantial outline, and genuine dialogue is sacrificed to long speeches. Yet these fanciful plays act well, and can keep a responsive audience spellbound. They shift us bodily onto a poetical sphere, where truth and reality have wings, and golden sense, mixed with paradox, transfigures into intoxicating surprises the commonplaces of life, history or ethics. Audacious views are expressed, which only the exceptional talent of a wizard can make acceptable and accepted, and at the end we recognize that beneath its wit and artifice Giraudoux's work is packed with significance."[1] The best known of Giraudoux's plays are *Amphitryon 38* (1929), *Electra* (1937), *Song of Songs* (1939), *Ondine* (1939), *Sodom and Gomorrha* (1943), and the posthumous *Madwoman of Chaillot* which had a resounding success in the United States.

The most impressive and influential trend in the contemporary European theater is probably existentialist drama. Jean-Paul Sartre (1905-   ), the French philosopher, novelist, and dramatist, is the most eloquent spokesman for existentialism. Stripped of its technical terminology, existentialism, in brief, assumes "the existence in man of powers entirely outside the range of reason, but at the same time it does not propose to concentrate all its attention upon such powers. Rather, the existentialist declares that as man applies himself rationally to the consideration of any aspect of life he is constantly being confronted, to his dismay, by concepts which, so far from merely being outside the range of reason, are utterly opposed to it. In human life, therefore, there is an ever-present irony and para-

1 Louis Cazamian, *A History of French Literature*, Clarendon Press, 1955, p. 425.

dox. It is precisely this paradoxical irony that the existentialists claim should be the subject matter of art."

Reduced to dramatic terms, "man makes the social world in which he lives, and yet each individual finds himself in a situation over which he has no control, and there he is forced to act (if he would live), not necessarily doing things he would have liked to do, but, instead, doing things which seem to offer the best alternatives."[2]

This conception of man and his fate is the subject matter of Sartre's plays, such as *The Flies* (1943), *No Exit* (1944), *Unburied Dead* (1946), *The Respectful Prostitute* (1946), and *Dirty Hands* (1948). Sartre's dramatic method and interpretation of human life are exemplified in *The Flies,* a retelling of the classical Orestes story which is here converted into a political drama of tyranny and belief in freedom. The Greek Furies have become flies that plague the city of Argos and bring putrefaction in their midst. Orestes is not the heroic protagonist of Aeschylus but a rational, mild, lonely, and detached man who has never met any test before. Inspired by his sister Electra to kill his mother Clytemnestra and her lover Aegisthus in order to avenge the murder of his father Agamemnon, he liberates his native city from the plague; but, having drawn the Furies away from the city and released the people from their penitence, he refuses the throne and goes into exile with his sister. The character of Orestes is powerfully drawn. As Eric Bentley says, he "turns from sophisticated aloofness to passionate participation."

In *Unburied Dead* Sartre piles horror upon horror, including the torture of a member of the French Resistance by the Vichy police. *The Respectful Prostitute* is the story of a lynching in a Southern American town. *No Exit* concerns three oddly assorted people, the cruel Garcin, the Lesbian Inez, and the child murderer Estelle, condemned to spend eternity together in a Second Empire drawing room; the drama centers around the corrosive interaction of their botched characters. While dramatizing the existentialist philosophy, Sartre manages to create a tragic situation, fraught with irony, that makes clear his interpretation of free will. Orestes avenges his father's death because of a "commitment" (*engagé*), a social responsibility which he assumes almost unwillingly. He kills in the name of freedom, having first freed himself from within, without remorse. He scorns divine help, although the gods play a part in the drama. "I am doomed to have no other law but mine," he says. Orestes' parting message is, "Human life begins on the other side of despair." As in his other plays, Sartre in *The Flies* projects the image of the individual as alone in the world, free and unfree, committed to make choices but without any real belief in his destiny. A man is his life, there is nothing else—that is the existentialist's credo. Essentially, Sartre sees little more in human life than brutality and ugliness, rarely the beauty and compassion that inspired Shakespeare, Sophocles, and Aeschylus.

Albert Camus (1913-1960), a successful novelist as well as dramatist (he was awarded the Nobel Prize in 1957), belongs by definition to the existentialist school. His plays *Cross Purposes* (1944), *Caligula* (1945), and *The Possessed,*

2 Allardyce Nicoll, *World Drama,* Harcourt, Brace, n.d., p. 906.

a dramatization of Dostoyevsky's novel, elaborate on the basic theme that life is absurd but that this does not necessarily rule out nobility, courage, valor; man creates his own values out of rebellion; however, there are no absolute values, and the individual chooses to act out of indifference, with no real motives behind him. *Cross Purposes* is the brutal drama of an elderly woman and her daughter who run a boarding house and kill several travellers for their goods; their last unwitting victim is their son and brother. *Caligula* is the powerful study of a man granted power of life and death over the civilized world. Caligula is a lunatic, seeking to possess the moon and thereby showing the absurdity of living. Camus did not win the great success in the theater awarded to Sartre. He was more at home in the novel.

Jean Anouilh (1910-   ) is regarded by many critics as the most original and versatile dramatist of the contemporary French theater. He has been a prolific playwright for over a quarter of a century and has drawn large audiences in theaters all over the world. Anouilh divides his work into four main classifications: Dark Plays, Rosy Plays, Grating Plays, and Glittering Plays, and he moves from comedy to serious drama with consistent facility. Infected with the pessimism of his generation, his dark plays are concerned with the influence of the evil world and evil people on "pure souls." This is the theme of *Eurydice* (1941), a play about a modern Orpheus (a violinist in a saloon) and Eurydice (a third-rate actress). Perhaps Anouilh's essential vision is best revealed in *Antigone* (1944) where the heroine goes to bury her brother Polyneices not because she feels it is her moral duty but out of antagonism to the crass and meaningless society around her. Even when she is offered mercy by Creon, she refuses it. The contrast with Sophocles' drama is startling: neither Creon nor Antigone is heroic and the drama drags on through long speeches of self-justification. Antigone goes to her death in the belief that the most precious things can only be found in whatever there may be beyond earthly existence. Anouilh's rosy plays, such as *Thieves' Carnival* (1932) and *Waltz of the Toreadors* (1951), with their brittle wit and lively comic sense, have been more palatable to American audiences.

Futility and despair permeate the plays of the two most popular avant-garde playwrights of the 1950's, Eugène Ionesco (1912-   ) and Samuel Beckett (1906-   ). Their works belong to what has been called "the theater of the absurd." Ionesco is half-Rumanian and half-French; Beckett was born in Dublin, settled in France in the late 1920's, and writes novels and dramas in English and French. Ionesco says that his plays take root not from an idea or a character but from one of two moods, "light" or "dark." In the light mood, his feeling is that "the world is dream-like, the walls are no longer solid, we seem to be able to see through everything into a spaceless universe made up of pure light and color." In the dark mood, "what is light grows heavy, the transparent becomes dense, the universe is crushing me." It is readily understandable that to Ionesco "comic and tragic are two aspects of the same situation," that "there are no alternatives: if man is not tragic, he is ridiculous and painful, 'comic,' in fact, and that by revealing his absurdity one can achieve a sort of tragedy." In Ionesco's short "anti-plays" or farces such as *The Bald Soprano* (1949) there is no movement, the world is upside down and non-sense reigns. Ionesco's first full-length drama, *The Killer* (1950), concerns Bérenger, a city planner, who has built a City of Light, but one in which nobody wants to live because there is a killer abroad. The Administration can do nothing about it. Bérenger finally meets the killer, and although he is taller and more powerful, he tries to persuade him by exhortation to reform but in the end collapses from futility and is about to be stabbed. The moral of this highly effective play, lightened with comic interludes, would seem to be that it is utterly futile for the human race to go on living. Ionesco's second full-length drama, *Rhinoceros* (1960), depicts the human race as turning into rhinoceroses, despite all that the savior, Bérenger, can do; in the end Bérenger is left alone, the last to maintain human identity, and even he weakens and desires for a moment to become a rhinoceros.

Beckett's talent as a dramatist went unrecognized until *Waiting for Godot* was produced in Paris in 1953; *Endgame* and *Happy Days* came later. *Godot* presents two hoboes, Estragon and Vladimir, who seem to be two sides of a split personality. Nothing whatever happens in this play; time has stopped. They remain tied to an enigma which holds them in common servitude—waiting for Godot, who is never identified. In *Endgame* two of the characters are confined to a single room and the other two to ash cans. In *The Unnameable* the hero is not even sure of his own name, or whether he is alive or dead. Thus Beckett's characters are in a more advanced state of dissolution than Ionesco's. They are unable to cope with the external world and even unaware of a world outside themselves; their only concrete sin is that they exist at all. The European drama, reeling from the tensions of the Cold War which threatens every day to result in thermonuclear annihilation of a large part of the human race, can hardly become more pessimistic. The wonder is that with such attitudes playwrights can create highly actable and often amusing plays.

2. Poetry

The first half of the twentieth century was marked by a revolution in poetic taste. In England it was comparable to the change from neoclassicism to romanticism that occurred at the end of the eighteenth and beginning of the nineteenth century. The result was the abandonment of the Victorian tradition with its genteel romanticism in favor of more intellectual, formless, and imagistic verse as exemplified by the school of T. S. Eliot on the one hand and the more earthy poetry of Rudyard Kipling and John Masefield on the other. Kipling's *Departmental Ditties,* published in 1886, violated all the Victorian canons of verse. It was slangy and profane; it dealt with the lives of soldiers and sailors and ordinary men throughout the Empire. Masefield's *Salt Water Ballads* (1902) exalted the sailors as Kipling did Tommy Atkins. The fact that Masefield's collected poems sold 100,000 copies in a decade showed that readers were tired of the romantic idealism of Tennyson and Browning and the exoticism of Swinburne and eager for poetry dealing with ordinary people and familiar things.

In England poets were soon writing about the life of the people they knew best and in a new and simpler language. Rupert Brooke (1887-1915), whose career was ended by the first World War, spoke for youth. W. W. Gibson (1878-   ) dramatized stonecutters, carpenters, berry pickers, farmers and ferrymen, people who earned their bread by their muscle and sweat. D. H. Lawrence (1885-1930) in his early poems wrote about the inarticulate colliers and townspeople of his native Nottinghamshire and dealt frankly with sex, a subject that was taboo in Victorian literature. Other members of this group of "Georgian poets" were Lascelles Abercrombie, Walter de la Mare, Harold Monro, Siegfried Sassoon, James Stephens, and W. J. Turner. The Georgians issued five biennial anthologies, and then the first World War scattered them. Some died in battle, others returned to write sentimentally about the pastoral scene, and still others ceased to produce any poetry at all.

In America there was a similar reaction against the sterile genteel tradition of nineteenth-century poetry which was so impressive it gained the undescriptive but complimentary title of "New Poetry." It was new in many ways: poets usually forsook traditional rhymes and meters for *vers libre* (free verse); found materials in regional cultures (New England, the industrial Midwest, the prairie small towns, the Far West, polyglot, fast-paced New York); and tried to express the spirit of a vigorous, industrializing America that eventually was to become a world power. *Poetry,* a magazine founded by Harriet Monroe in Chicago in 1912, gave the movement an organ and inspiration. Scores of poets arose to limn the strident vigor and brashness of our country, to delineate its folk heroes and its humbler men, to give us a body of work which, stemming from Walt Whitman, spoke in an original voice and with an original technique. As the century wore on, both the manner and matter of poetry lost its novelty; some of the greater writers died or declined into old age, but its early accomplishments have never died, and they represent a major contribution to the literature of the Western world.

Representative of the new poets are Robert Frost (1875-1963), Carl Sandburg (1878-   ), Edgar Lee Masters (1869-1950), Edwin Arlington Robinson (1869-1935), Vachel Lindsay (1879-1931), and Hart Crane (1899-1932). Frost has interpreted rural New England in a speech which we recognize as authentic; he has given voice to the reticent farmer and the stony soil he plows, to the hired man and the cow in apple time, and to many a fleeting aspect of that remote land, in a style that is simple, bare, yet stamped with his own rough, granitic strength. Carl Sandburg created poetry from the smoke and fog of Chicago,

> Hog Butcher for the World,
> Tool Maker, Stacker of Wheat,
> Player with Railroads and the Nation's Freight Handler;
> Stormy, husky, brawling,
> City of the Big Shoulders.

Edgar Lee Masters in his shocking *Spoon River Anthology* (1915), modeled on the *Greek Anthology,* a series of imaginary epitaphs in a country churchyard, stripped the hypocrisies from Midwest puritanism as Sherwood Anderson did in his short stories, *Winesburg, Ohio* (1919). Vachel Lindsay in his treks around the South and West found beauty in the songs sung at revival meetings, in college yells, and in the "hants" and religious ecstasies of the Negroes, but he also wrote feelingly of Altgeld, an Illinois hero, John Brown, General Booth, and wrote a magnificent, stirring chant about the Congo in rhythms borrowed from Negro revivals.

Edwin Arlington Robinson was less of an innovator, but his best poems are about the people of his native Maine, their dreams and frustrations, like Miniver Cheevy who

> ... loved the days of old
> When swords were bright and steeds were prancing,

and Richard Cory,

> ... A gentleman from sole to crown
> Clean favored, and imperially slim,[2a]

and contrastingly about Tristram and Ben Jonson and Shakespeare. Hart Crane, a tortured, neurotic soul, drunk with genius, who committed suicide at thirty-two, made a valiant effort and succeeded in *The Bridge* (1930) in creating a poetic synthesis of onrushing American life and history, catching the very rhythms and pulsings of New York and the great America beyond, in a style that is memorable for its graphic images and language that ripples with American speech. These men are but a sample of the multitude of poets who touched American life in its numerous currents and eddies and succeeded in delineating the new civilization, hard, materialistic, dynamic, sentimental, and world-conquering.

From another quarter and in a very different form came another attack on the dying romantic poetry of the last century. Inspired partly by the French experimenters in free verse, a group of English and American poets calling themselves Imagists sought to create a hard, clear poetry which would summon up in the reader whatever emotion the poet desired to call forth by precise images. There must be no description or comment, no imposed moral, and the poet must be free to choose any rhythmic pattern which would fit his subject. The English Imagists found an organ in *The Egoist,* which published the verses of Ezra Pound (1885-   ) and T. S. Eliot, both expatriate Americans, Richard Aldington, D. H. Lawrence, F. S. Flint, J. G. Fletcher, and others. The American captain, Amy Lowell (1874-1925), who possessed a genius for organization, "sold" free verse and Imagism to the American critics and public in a well-conducted publicity campaign.

When the first World War ended, many of the poets who survived found relief from the disillusionment which followed the shattering of their idealism in bitter, satiric verses that concealed their utter despair. No one voiced this postwar

[2a] Edwin Arlington Robinson, *Complete Poems,* Macmillan.

agony so well as Eliot, now a naturalized British subject. His first book, *Prufrock and Other Observations* (1917), already revealed his great talent, but *The Waste Land* (1922) became a classic of the new poetry both in form and content. A difficult and often obscure poem, filled with mythical, anthropological, Christian and Oriental imagery, it professed to describe the dilemma of the postwar intellectual who found himself in a spiritually barren and frustrating world. *The Waste Land* was to provide the model for an entire generation of poets and propel Eliot to the forefront of avant-garde poetry. His wide reading in the classics, philosophy, Elizabethan drama, and the French symbolists, from whom he drew his seemingly obscure imagery, together with the strangeness of his themes, made Eliot at first a difficult poet and fixed upon him the reputation of willful inaccessibility. His subsequent career shows that he has come more in tune with his age. Actually Eliot is a poet with a strong religious faith whose earlier hypersensitive disgust with the licentious, money-mad 1920's is supplementary to the ardor with which he has sought by means of religion to find a secure place in the bewildering flux of our times. In later poems, such as *Ash Wednesday* (1930) and *The Four Quartets* (1943), he turned increasingly to the traditional Christian symbols and in his allusive way—his poetry has never ceased to be packed with difficult images—tried to find meaning in the Christian experience, somewhat in the manner of John Donne. As David Daiches says of *The Four Quartets,* "This is the tone of mystical peace, of brooding over the still centre, of moving through history not, as in *The Waste Land* and other early poems, to provide ironical contrasts between past and present, but in order to find a way out of the temporal process altogether, an escape from time in the fleeting visionary glimpse of eternity."[3] This is the refrain of the *Quartets*:

> Time present and time past
> Are both perhaps present in time future,
> And time future contained in time past.
> If all time is eternally present
> All time is unredeemable.[3a]

Although Eliot's influence has been immense in criticism as well as in poetry, it is not altogether beneficent, since his style has become a mannerism in those who do not possess either his talent or his faith.

Standing apart from the Georgians, the Imagists, and the Eliot school was William Butler Yeats (1865-1939), who used Irish materials to fashion a body of verse which some critics regard as the major accomplishment in twentieth-century British poetry. Yeats began as a dreamy romantic, seeking in poetry compensation for the drabness of a world which science had robbed of its traditional values:

3 David Daiches, *The Present Age in British Literature,* Indiana University Press, 1958, p. 40.
3a T. S. Eliot, *Complete Poems and Plays,* Harcourt, Brace & World, 1952.

The woods of Arcady are dead,
And over is their antique joy;
Of old the world on dreaming fed;
Grey Truth is now her painted toy.[3b]

In his later years Yeats engaged in an earnest search for mystical experience which might replace the faith he had lost, as described in his book, *A Vision*. Various movements of his time touched him deeply; he reacted sympathetically to the struggle for Irish independence and served the Free State as a Senator, helped found the Abbey Theatre and wrote plays for it, and continued to produce original poetry and rewrite his published verses almost to the end of his life. In Yeats's work the struggles and ambitions, dreams and disillusionments of a long and active life are described with courage and verve, in a style that is neither conventional nor esoteric, harking back to the nineteenth century yet implicit with the new melodies of the twentieth. In contrast to Eliot's feeling of assurance, Yeats believed that there may be a heaven or a reincarnation after death, or that there may be nothing.

A host of lesser poets enriched British and American literature in the first half of the twentieth century. Archibald MacLeish (1892-   ), William Carlos Williams (1883-1963), Wallace Stevens (1879-1955), E. E. Cummings (1894-1962), and Marianne Moore (1887-   ) are among the older and Richard Eberhart, Theodore Roethke, and Robert Lowell among the younger poets who find representation in anthologies of modern American poetry; their achievements are diverse, their range is wide. In England, W. H. Auden (1907-   ), Stephen Spender (1909-   ), Louis MacNeice (1907-1963), and Cecil Day Lewis (1898-   ) emerged in the 1930's as poets of considerable ability. They have been associated with liberal movements—Spender actually joined the Communist party, fought for the Loyalists in Spain, and finally, resenting regimentation, repudiated it. Dylan Thomas (1914-1953), a Welshman who died of alcoholism at the age of forty, flamed like a meteor across the literary sky. His tempestuous verses, as J. B. Priestley says, seems to have been composed "in some bardic frenzy. Marvelous lines, satisfying and moving at once, came and went among passages of the densest obscurity, although even these, unlike so much of the earlier and determinedly 'difficult' verse approved by Valéry or Pound, were charged with passion."[4]

Four French poets of the last century exercised a tremendous influence over the style of their younger disciples—Baudelaire, Verlaine, Rimbaud, and Mallarmé. In 1917, on the fiftieth anniversary of Baudelaire's death, the homage offered his name showed that he was without doubt the progenitor of the modern style. Although the literary groups have quarreled and divided and subdivided since the words "Parnassian" and "Symbolist" were rallying cries of two camps, poets of diverse natures united to honor him. The younger symbolists praised Mallarmé as the "inventor of a system of poetics founded on the fusion of sensations, on the connection between the mind and the senses, between the visible

[3b] William Butler Yeats, *Collected Poems*, Macmillan.
[4] J. B. Priestley, *Literature and Western Man*, Harper, 1960, p. 409.

and invisible world."[5] The analytical realists like Paul Bourget (1852-1935) and Maurice Barrès (1862-1923) admired his knowledge of psychology; the religious poets such as Paul Claudel (1868-1955) revered him as they did Verlaine; the admirers of classical form and discipline like Jean Moréas (1856-1910) and Charles Maurras (1868-1952) respected his use of the traditional Alexandrine verse and his affinity to Racine.

Symbolism survived as a direct and active force, especially in the poetry of Henri de Regnier (1864-1936), Paul Fort (1872-   ), and Emile Verhaeren (1855-1916), a Belgian. Paul Claudel, who began his career as an admirer of Baudelaire and a frequenter of Mallarmé's famous Tuesday soirées, passed beyond the symbolism of his masters to religious poetry. He reverenced Rimbaud as a true seer but a "wild mystic" (*mystique à l'état sauvage*); Mallarmé was for him also a *voyant* but one without hope. In Claudel's plays, like *L'Annonce faite à Marie (The Annunciation)*, Claudel found his way back to the tradition of the Christian symbolists from Dante to the present. The great facts of the Catholic religion, the doctrine of revelation and grace, are the burden of his poetry.

As one looks back, the most important fact about French poetry since 1900 is the great number of short-lived movements which have followed each other in bewildering succession, leaving behind in each instance a brave manifesto, a magazine which ran through a half-dozen issues, and possibly a reputation or two. In 1899 the first and second books of Jean Moréas' *Stances (Stanzas)* were published in the *Bibliothèque Artistique et Littéraire*. Six books in all were published by 1906. They are the foundation of a humanistic revival, of an "École Romaine" in which Charles Maurras joined. The influence of these two men checked the excessive symbolism and the crude naturalism popular at the moment and taught the need of measure, balance, and harmony. The idols of the school were Lamartine and Baudelaire; their particular devil was Victor Hugo.

The other important movement was an outgrowth of symbolism: the war over *vers libre*. French poetry has always been more rigidly rule-bound than English. The French poet must be careful to regulate the *enjambement* (running over of one line into the next), the caesura (mid-line pause), the alternation of feminine and masculine rhymes. The advocates of *vers libre* fought for emancipation from rhyme and the tyranny of the Alexandrine (the twelve-syllable line traditional in French poetry) and for the poet's right to use any rhythm suited to his purpose. The leaders in this revolt were de Regnier, Paul Fort, and Jules Laforgue, who also introduced all sorts of bizarre effects of language into his verse.

Of the multitudinous poetic revolutions which lasted long enough to find themselves a name the following should be mentioned: impulsionism, founded by Florian-Parmentier in 1904; neo-romanticism, founded in 1905 by Joussan; unanimism, which proposes that poetry shall speak only of groups and not the individual, founded by Romains in 1908; and futurism, founded by Marinetti. The list could be extended almost indefinitely, but a few more designations will give some idea of this spectacle of disintegration: primitivism, subjectivism, sincerism, intensism, druidism, dramatism, simultaneism, paroxysm (sic), dadaism. Finally comes surrealism. Two important poets emerged from the smoke of these literary battles: Guillaume Apollinaire (1880-1918) and Jean Cocteau (1892-1963).

Possibly the most distinguished French poet of the twentieth century is Paul Valéry (1871-1945), one of the most fascinating intellects among the writers of our time. After a brief career as a symbolist, Valéry in the late 1890's practically renounced the world. Like Yeats, he pondered the significance of modern science and the strange loss of faith which the modern world was experiencing. Brought back from his voluntary exile by his friend André Gide, he began again to publish poetry in 1917. His verse is intellectual. He scorns the inspiration and enthusiasm of the romantic poet, believing that poetry is a "contrivance of words, sounds and rhythm and syntax, and thoughts and emotions concern him only in so far as they can fit in with his instruments."[6]

The movement which has had the greatest influence on French poetry since the death of Valéry has been surrealism. It has been called the third great revolution in French poetry since the decline of neoclassicism: the first was the romantic, the second the symbolist. Surrealism has gone much further, however, than its predecessors in liberating poetry by aiming to give a fuller and freer expression to the human psyche and therefore has practically abandoned any semblance of form, since a concern with form implies conscious preoccupation with the means of expression and a curb on spontaneity. It is not surprising that the surrealists do not even distinguish between prose and verse in their writings, since the artist is obliged to treat his material in whatever medium best fits his temperament. Prominent practitioners of surrealism are Paul Eluard (1895-1952), Louis Aragon (1897-   ), René Char (1907-   ), and Raymond Queneau (1903-   ). An accomplished poet who stands outside the movement is the diplomat Aléxis Leger (who writes under the name of Saint-John Perse), whose volumes *Anabase* (1924), *Exil* (1942), and *Vents* (1947), are highly cherished by a small circle of connoisseurs.

The philosophy of Nietzsche pervaded most German poetry before the second World War. His Zarathustra speaks most clearly through the Rhinelander, Stefan George (1868-1933), whose poetry is significant both for its own sake and for the subsequent course of German verse. Many influences played upon him, although they do not readily show up in his work, which is highly individualistic. Finding a model of artistic discipline in the conscientious Mallarmé, he sought to perfect his knowledge of the mother tongue by learning several languages. George also achieved a practical familiarity with verse and verse forms by translating, accomplishing in this respect an incomparable rendering of Shakespeare's sonnets, not to mention much of the poetry of Baudelaire, Verlaine, Dante, Rossetti, and Swinburne. He was convinced that the verse form is an intrinsic part of the poetic experience, which he considered a dynamic process transforming reality into a static work of art. Considering form the fundamental attribute of poetry, he would have nothing to do with free verse and his work throughout shows an exacting and disciplined workmanship.

6 Regis Michaud, *Modern Thought and Literature in France*, Funk & Wagnalls, 1934, pp. 204-5.

Perhaps the best verse written during the first period of his poetic creation is the aptly titled *Jahr der Seele* (*The Year of the Soul*). However, all the poetry composed during the period of the *Blätter für die Kunst* (a periodical dealing with art) is earnest rather than deliberate, individualistic without being egocentric. If not actively, he is intensely concerned with the condition and fate of humanity, as, for example, in the *Teppich des Lebens* (*The Tapestry of Life*), the last product of this period, which appeared in 1900.

Soon after this, George underwent much the same experience as Dante when he met Beatrice. He found the embodied realization of his ideal in the German youth "who made the thousands possible" and who appears to us in his poetry under the name Maximin. In his later work, George stands like a prophet before his people, exposing the evils of materialism and heralding the advent of the *Neue Reich* (*The New State*, 1928), which would be based on reality but also imbued with high ideals. Long accused of isolating himself in an ivory tower and of writing for a select group of overeducated friends, George was never a popular poet. However, critics have gradually disposed of that conception and reveal him as a poet who wished to be rooted in his age but who would not act simply as a mirror, or to use his own words, as both "Herrscher" and "Diener" (Master and Slave).

Rainer Maria Rilke (1875-1926) likewise begins with a "Sprachkunst" (an art ensuing primarily from the skillful use of words). It is in the *Stundenbuch* (*The Book of Hours*) that his verse first becomes poetry. Here we find Rilke eagerly pursuing the secret of creation and existence. He finds God everywhere, *in everything;* if only one will project himself into it. His philosophy, however, is not based upon a blind, optimistic faith; it is not the benevolent "pathetic fallacy" of the Romantics. He is convinced that God is there, but also that one must actively and consciously humble himself before this presence can be recognized. Since God is also in him, Rilke's religion is not a passive submission, but rather an active overpowering of God. The free verse of the *Sonette an Orpheus* (*Sonnets to Orpheus*, 1923) and of the *Duineser Elegien* (*Duinesian Elegies,* 1923) marks the end of realism, while their metaphysical content anticipates their author's death three years later.

Among the group of young writers surrounding Stefan George, one was destined to proceed in his own way and attain a very personal kind of artistic greatness. Expressed in drama, the genius of Hugo von Hofmannsthal (1874-1929) is essentially lyrical. He typifies the decadent culture which was the outgrowth of the symbolist and neo-romantic movements. A rococo delicacy and charming weariness are the keynotes both of his lyrics and lyric dramas, which are exceptionally subjective. Claudio, the passive, miniature Faust of the *Tor und Tod* (*The Fool and Death*), provides perhaps the most obvious illustration of the introspective quality characteristic of the poet himself. Hofmannsthal's frequent use of soliloquies invariably reminds one of Browning's dramatic monologues, while the organic use of landscapes, especially in the *Tod des Tizian* (*The Death of Titian*), harks back to the symbolists, particularly to Verlaine.

A reaction to the sensuous quality of the impressionists and symbolists appeared in the so-called expressionistic poetry. Actually this movement was one more phase of the modern search for religion, for a scale of values. German expressionistic poetry is characterized chiefly by its tearful, admonitory, self-exposing outbursts and by an ecstatic longing for an ethical world. Its style suffers from excessive repetition and an unwieldy expression which tends to become monotonous. The leader as well as the extreme German expressionist was Franz Werfel (1890-1945).

A later development in German poetry was the *Neue Sachlichkeit* (New Realism), a reaction against the pathos and ecstasy of the expressionists which attempted to reach the essential truth of life through an objective portrayal of reality.

The collapse of Hitler's empire and dismemberment of Germany put an end to German literary movements. Many of the great poets and novelists died in exile.

Russia after the Bolshevik Revolution ceased to produce literary figures of international repute, since literature under Marxist ideology became an arm of the propaganda machine. The works of relatively few Communist writers are known outside the Iron Curtain. In poetry the name of Boris Pasternak (1890-1960) became familiar when he was awarded the Nobel Prize (but not allowed to accept it) in 1958. Pasternak is an extreme subjectivist, obscure and almost meaningless to the ordinary reader (in translations which probably do him less than justice), producing his effects through novel, sharp images. Nature, love, and revolution are his principal themes. Entwined with nature is love, sometimes strange, incomprehensible and willful, but always elemental. Pasternak's novel *Dr. Zhivago* (1958), which achieved world-wide fame except in Russia (where it was banned), showed that the author's views about the Revolution had changed considerably; where once he had portrayed it as a liberating and ennobling force, he now saw it as an ugly distortion of human ideals, steeped in blood.

Summing up the modernistic movements in poetry, we may quote Louis Untermeyer's conclusion to his book, *Lives of the Poets,* published in 1959:

> It is a sense of turmoil which, in the widest possible varieties of expression, has been sounded by the poets of our time. We can see how they have interpreted the fevered temper of the age in their very choice of complex and often chaotic subject matter. Some express directly or in parable their personal dilemma and the plight of mankind—distrust of the past, despair of the present, and fear of the future. Many of them cast their concepts in contemporary molds, shaping odd forms, disrupting syntax, playing with typographical arrangements, and attempting to synchronize their rhythms with the rhythms of a mechanically driven, atom-powered era. Intensive competition increased the pressures in the sphere of culture as well as in the spheres of commerce and politics, and many poets, in a deliberate effort to achieve individuality, distorted language, invented techniques, and carried experimentation beyond comprehensibility.[7]

7 Louis Untermeyer, *Lives of the Poets,* Simon and Schuster, 1959, p. 721.

3. The Novel

Like the drama and poetry, modern fiction has no simple history. It has grown out of a world becoming increasingly complex and confused; it has reacted to the enormous growth of capitalistic industry, the unceasing explorations of science, the shifting of moral standards, the shock of two world wars and their economic, social, and emotional consequences. The novel has been deeply affected by Freudian psychology, by various schools of economic theory. It has expressed man's defeat, frustration, and despair in its projections of a bewildered society, an unbalanced economic order, and a disintegrating culture. Or it has retreated from actuality into realms of fantasy or madness, into cynicism, into the dark world of force and violence. As a literary type the novel has in general retained the hegemony it enjoyed during the nineteenth century; its vitality has been undiminished. Serious novelists have endeavored to present life in a realistic fashion, although methods have varied widely, from the more or less conventional manner of earlier writers to experimentation with new and sometimes bizarre techniques that sought to probe into the deepest crannies of man's conscious and subconscious life.

In England the new century brought forth a group of novelists, influenced by the French realists, especially Flaubert and Zola, who threw off some of the Victorian conventions and taboos and produced impressive and well-documented social commentaries. In the forefront were H. G. Wells (1866-1946), Arnold Bennett (1877-1931), Joseph Conrad (1857-1924), George Moore (1852-1933), and John Galsworthy. Moore, an Irishman, impressed as a young man in Paris by the freshness and freedom of French art and literature, turned in his novels (*Esther Waters,* 1894; *Evelyn Innes,* 1898; and *Sister Teresa,* 1901) and autobiography to an attack on conventional British morality, to the treatment of themes disapproved by that morality, in a carefully cultivated, musical prose. Galsworthy, dispassionately balancing good and evil, wrote of economic and social conflicts. In *The Forsyte Saga,* a series of novels written over a long period, he traces the workings of the acquisitive instinct in a family's history, the struggles it arouses between wives and husbands, children and parents. Bennett, a brilliant journeyman, described in his *Old Wives' Tale* (1908) and the "Clayhanger" novels the lives of plain people in the drab pottery towns of the North Midlands, and through his objective method, his eye for meaningful detail, succeeds in communicating a sense of pathos as well as the drama in very ordinary existence. Wells's many novels include scientific fantasies, humorous studies of character, and examinations of social problems. Informative, often amusing, interesting frequently as sociology, his work generally reveals no great imagination, no genuine power of conceiving character.

Joseph Conrad was a master of the tale of action. A Pole by birth, a sailor by trade, he became a naturalized Englishman and acquired a control over the English language which few writers born to it have attained. Conrad knew the sea in its infinite moods, and the men who go to sea, and he combined with this knowledge a sense of wonder and mystery, felt in storms, in tropic sunlights, in steaming jungles. *Lord Jim* (1900), *Victory* (1915), the shorter *Heart of Darkness* and *Youth* show his command over subject and language at its best.

In the United States the new generation of novelists reacted sharply against the effete nineteenth-century traditions exemplified by Henry James (1843-1916), a Bostonian who lived in Britain most of his life and became a British citizen. James spent his career probing the relations between the old world and the new, portraying Americans, usually upper middle class, in *Daisy Miller, Portrait of a Lady,* and *The American,* as crude and lacking in the elegance and sophistication of Europeans. He produced novels which are masterpieces of character analysis but written in a style that bogs down in syntactical mazes and convoluted sentences. James's popularity declined as the realistic school led by Frank Norris (1870-1902) and Theodore Dreiser (1871-1945) opened new vistas into the American character and American civilization, although there was a surprising revival of interest in his work in the 1930's and 1940's. Using the naturalistic methods of Zola, Norris and Dreiser applied the surgeon's scalpel to the social fabric. Dreiser's first novel, *Sister Carrie* (1900), was banned in the United States and had to be published in England; his next, *Jennie Gerhardt* (1911), found a more receptive audience; and by the time *The Financier* (1912) and its sequel *The Titan* (1914) appeared, his reputation was established, at least with such critics as H. L. Mencken, who extolled the revolution which the naturalistic novel had effected in the United States. Dreiser's masterpiece is *An American Tragedy* (1925), a book banned in Boston. In retrospect, as literary reputations fluctuate, Dreiser remains a giant in American literature. Although he lacked humor and his prose was plain and often crude, Dreiser evinced a remarkable talent for reportage, combined with an almost Tolstoyan skill in character dissection and a profound insight into social, economic, and political processes. Perhaps he was carried away by the determinist philosophy of Zola, but his novels delineate American life far more realistically than those of Henry James or his follower Edith Wharton—the surging industrial age with its swarming cities, the alliance between corrupt politicians and greedy industrialists—in sum, the brutal strength of America on the make. Dominated by qualities of temperament and circumstances they cannot control, Dreiser's characters seem to move in a world without purpose or meaning, devoid of any values except self-indulgence and self-aggrandizement. But Dreiser has a sort of brooding pity for these people—whether it be the financier Frank Cowperwood or the young factory worker, Clyde Griffiths of *An American Tragedy*—whose dreams end in frustration and ruin. Dreiser's novels hold the reader by an inescapable cumulative force because they deal with identifiable persons and are based on painstaking observations of the American scene.

The works of Willa Cather (1876-1947), perhaps the greatest of America's women novelists, broke no new paths either in style or technique, but they have become hallmarks of distinguished fiction. She wrote mainly about the people she knew best, the prairie pioneers of her native Nebraska, as in *O Pioneers!* (1913), *My Ántonia* (1918), and *One of Ours* (1922), with intense sympathy for the sod-breakers and the hardships they endured. She had a penchant for writing about musical people, as in *The Song of the Lark* (1915), which depicts the career of a great opera singer from her childhood in a Western village to her triumphs in Europe and New York. Towards the end of her career she turned to pioneers of another kind, the builders of civilization: in the Southwest, as in the starkly created *Death Comes for the Archbishop* (1927), and in old Quebec, in *Shadows on the Rock* (1931). In these books she was writing about men of heroic will power and simple faith trying to plant a Catholic empire on virgin soil.

In France near the turn of the century and after, Anatole France (1844-1924) turned out polished fiction on ancient and modern themes. His irony, dilettantism, and skepticism are all worn somewhat thin with the passing of time. Of greater significance are André Gide (1869-1951) and Marcel Proust (1871-1922). Gide's novels range from the poetic and rather lushly Oriental type through analyses of moral decay like *The Immoralist* (1902) to the grim farce of *The Vatican Swindle* (1914), in which a foolish bourgeois, in Italy to rescue the Pope from an imagined plot, is pushed cold-bloodedly to his death from a speeding train. Gide's most important novel probably is *The Counterfeiters* (1925), a brilliant study of the artist's temperament and of crime, perversion, and youthful malice.

Along with James Joyce, Proust is the most widely discussed novelist of modern times. The French critic Henri Peyre says, "There can be little question . . . that his place is secure among the French novelists, indeed, that he must rank with the four or five greatest among them."[8] In the eight parts (sixteen volumes) of his *À la recherche du temps perdu* (*Remembrance of Things Past*, 1913-1928) Proust summed up the Third Republic's decadent upper-class society in the decades before the first World War shattered and transformed it. The story, told in the first person, mingles introspection—a minute examination of the narrator's own shifting desires and jealousies—with exhaustive description and narration. But these are not set down in the manner of the conventional realist or naturalist. The narrator's memory, stimulated by certain associations— a familiar strain of music, the odor of a certain flower—ranges over times past, summoning up the people and places he has known. All the snobbery, pretense, degeneracy, unsatisfied love, and fruitless aspirations of the world enter into Proust's stupendous picture, and also the effects upon it of time's changes—most completely realized in the final volume, *The Past Recaptured*. No novelist has been more acutely observant or possessed a more absorbing curiosity or appetite for detail than Proust. Long years of illness, of confinement with asthma, only increased his sensitivity to impressions. And so it is that in his novel no one merely acts or speaks, no place is simply painted or piece of music described, but each action, each phrase, each room or building, emerging into his consciousness from his unconscious mind, is broken up for analysis, blends with auras of association, so that a single moment may swell into pages, an afternoon party may fill a volume, a discussion of place names may expand into thousands of

8 Henri Peyre, *The Contemporary Novel*, Oxford University Press, 1955, p. 67.

words. This is the method of the *pointillistes,* like Seurat, who painted their pictures not with broad brush strokes but with an infinite number of dots. Proust, of course, runs into intolerable excesses (notably in the hundreds of pages devoted to exploring the narrator's feelings towards his perverse mistress, Albertine), but through them we penetrate deeply into the heart of his fictional world. With all his independence and originality, Proust owed a great deal to earlier psychological novelists and especially to the contemporary philosopher Henri Bergson, who conceived of time as a continuous flow or duration in which the past and present are inseparable to consciousness and memory.

In the forefront of experimental novelists is James Joyce (1882-1941), whose major works have become classics of modern literature. Joyce rebelled against his Irish Catholic ancestry and Dublin background, and moved to Paris in 1912 where he eked out a scanty living as a teacher and clerical worker. His major novel, *Ulysses,* was banned in England and the United States until the 1930's. For much of his life Joyce suffered from partial blindness; he was a lonely figure, out of touch with his native land, widely misunderstood, or regarded as obscene and unintelligible, but adulated by younger writers who flocked to Paris in the 1920's. The beautifully modulated prose of *Dubliners* (1914) and *Portrait of the Artist as a Young Man* (1916) shows Joyce's concern with language and his passion for handling words as though they were tangible objects. In his masterpiece, *Ulysses* (1922), this interest has resulted in the creation, for all practical purposes, of a new language. The *Portrait* revealed Joyce's search for freedom, his hostility to familiar moral values, and his rebellion against Irish Catholicism. Its hero, Stephen Dedalus, reappears in *Ulysses,* the story of a group of people during one day in Dublin. As the title indicates, the novel is a parallel, carefully (though far from obviously) wrought out, of Homer's *Odyssey.* As the Greek poet described the wanderings of Ulysses among the Aegean islands, so Joyce traces the wanderings of the Jew Leopold Bloom in Dublin; Penelope is Bloom's erotic and faithless wife, Molly. We follow the fortunes of Bloom (and Stephen Dedalus) at home, in Dublin streets and pubs, at a funeral, during a walk on the beach, during a visit to a maternity hospital, among the brothels of Nighttown. The book closes with a lengthy unpunctuated revery of the sex-obsessed Molly. Obscene at times, blasphemous, grotesque, the novel teems with life, with the energy of its author's wide-sweeping knowledge and imagination. Joyce writes in a variety of styles, indulges in parody (of the Catholic Mass, various sorts of prose), mingles reality with dreams, as in the scene among the brothels suggestive of Goethe's *Walpurgisnacht* in *Faust.* Most striking of his technical devices is the use of the stream-of-consciousness method of representing thoughts and feelings from within a character, approximating the broken, discontinuous nature of ordinary thought processes. Seen by this means, the world is a very different place from the orderly universe of conventional description: "Everything is significant in human life, he seems to be saying, and by the same token nothing is significant—it all depends on how you look at it. And if you can cultivate a sufficiently multiple vision, and find a way of presenting that vision, you can conceive a wholly new kind of comedy, a comedy of multiple identity."[9]

Joyce has influenced many British and American writers by his method, his style, vocabulary, and experimentation with language. Like Joyce, Virginia Woolf (1882-1941) was skilled in getting inside a character and in reproducing the flow of mind, most notably in such novels as *Mrs. Dalloway* (1925), *The Waves* (1913), and *The Years* (1937). Mrs. Woolf was a highly cultured, sensitive person, daughter of the critic and biographer, Sir Leslie Stephen, and a leading member of the Bloomsbury group of postwar writers which included her husband, Leonard Woolf, Lytton Strachey, and others. She wrote about the upper classes she knew best and of the inseparable relationship of time and experience, and was an especially perceptive creator of female characters. Although her lovely prose, lacking inner strength and fiber, tends to dissolve into thin air, she has a gift of evoking memorable personages and vivid scenes, floating on the stream of time and subconscious memory. D. H. Lawrence, son of a coal miner, belongs to quite a different school than the aristocratic and aesthetic Bloomsbury group. A prolific writer of poetry, fiction, criticism, and travel books, Lawrence made his deepest impression with highly subjective and sex-obsessed novels that breathe the spirit of revolt against middle-class and especially puritanic values. *Sons and Lovers* (1913), one of his first novels and regarded as his masterpiece, foreshadows much of his later work: the hero tries through relationships with women, usually on the physical level, to attain to some kind of harmony with the universe, to capture the meaning of life and its values. This search, which usually ends in frustration or tragedy, becomes a monotonous theme of Lawrence's novels, and was to a large extent the basis of his own wanderlust and exploration of many primitive cultures. *Lady Chatterley's Lover* (1928), which could not be published in its entirety in the United States until 1959, exhibits Lawrence's sex obsession at its height. Lawrence wrote in a vigorous, nervous style and brought a new kind of poetic imagination to English fiction without tampering, like Joyce or Aldous Huxley, with the structure and form of the novel.

Aldous Huxley (1894-1963) in a series of novels, *Crome Yellow* (1921), *Antic Hay* (1923), and *Point Counter Point* (1928), turned a witty, informed and entirely cynical intelligence upon upper-class postwar English society, pinning down like bugs his soiled specimens of humanity. With *Brave New World* (1932) and *Eyeless in Gaza* (1936) he evinced a growing social consciousness and a tendency to ignore the basis of fiction, which is character creation and the relationship of individuals to each other, for extensive moralizing and sermonizing on a wide variety of topics. Huxley's novels, essays, and biographies cover almost the entire range of man's knowledge. His early novels remain the best; written in a crisp, brilliant style, and although suffering perhaps from too much glitter, too lavish a display of encyclopedic reading, they remain, like *Point Counter Point,* readable and entertaining commentaries on decadent postwar society. A more widely popular novelist than Huxley, whose best work (ignored by

9 David Daiches, *op. cit.*, p. 93.

the academic critics) reaches a high literary level, is W. Somerset Maugham (1874-   ), best known for *Of Human Bondage* (1915), *The Moon and Sixpence* (1919), and numerous short stories dealing with the impact of the tropical Orient on white people.

The vitality of the contemporary British novel is well exemplified in the works of Evelyn Waugh (1903-   ), Graham Greene (1904-   ), E. M. Forster (1879-   ), George Orwell (1903-1950), and C. P. Snow. Waugh made his reputation in the 1920's with biting satiric studies of the aesthetes and society people of London, as in *Decline and Fall* (1929); his later novels are generally more sympathetic and probe more deeply into his characters, as in *Brideshead Revisited* (1945) and the books based on his war experiences (*Men at Arms,* 1952, and *Officers and Gentlemen,* 1955). Graham Greene is a master of the action novel depicting peculiarities of sinister psychology, as in *The Power and the Glory* (1940). The most conscious craftsman of this group is E. M. Forster, whose *Passage to India* (1924), dealing in a quietly ironic style with the British middle class in the empire they once ruled, is regarded as a masterpiece. C. P. Snow is one of the most widely read novelists of the post-World War II generation; his numerous works deal mainly with Cambridge dons, the new breed of scientists, and the intellectuals of contemporary England. Undistinguished as a stylist, Snow has risen to the forefront by dint of taut psychological analysis and by depicting characters who seem to be not only credible but interesting as personages. His range is narrow, but within his limited scope Snow reveals considerable talent, and, what is more important, contemporaneity.

George Orwell's reputation as one of the most thought-provoking political novelists of the century rests upon his *Animal Farm* (1945) and *Nineteen Eighty-Four* (1949). The first is a satirical fable designed to ridicule with wit and humor the policies and methods of a totalitarian society, a work unexcelled of its kind. Less amusing but far more significant was *Nineteen Eighty-Four*, which portrayed the astute planned tyranny of a rigorous totalitarian regime. This system Orwell felt to be impending and he described it with remarkable prophetic insight. No other novel of the mid-century stirred as much public attention or presented such cogent warning of the combined threat of totalitarianism and the ruthless exploitation of cold-war propaganda. As a novelist, Orwell wrote in a direct and forceful manner with a marked economy of verbiage, and as an essayist he possessed an easy and graceful style.

Perhaps the most accomplished and original American novelist of the postwar generation was Sinclair Lewis (1885-1951), the first American to win the Nobel Prize. Lewis laid bare the provincialism and dullness of small-town life in *Main Street* (1920); the "Babbittry" of the American business man in *Babbitt* (1922); the crass materialism of the medical profession in *Arrowsmith* (1925); and the shams of religious evangelicism in *Elmer Gantry* (1927). With this quartet, Lewis's fire was largely burnt out; his many succeeding novels range from mediocre to poor, but in nearly every one the flash of his mordant genius occasionally comes through, particularly in *Dodsworth* (1929), a sort of sequel to *Babbitt,* and *It Can't Happen Here* (1935), where he effectively visualizes a possible fascist revolution in the United States. More than any other novelist perhaps, Lewis exposes the narrowness, flashiness, and cheap optimism of middle-class America; *Babbitt* gave a lasting name to a familiar type of American businessman. Lewis's humor sometimes smacks of the obvious fun of the hundred-percenter, and there is a touch of plain American sentimentality on many of his pages. His gusty manner is sometimes overdone because of the compulsion of an admirable indignation, but his best work has staying power.

The clipped, hardboiled prose of Ernest Hemingway (1898-1961) does not always entirely conceal a soft streak in his novels and stories—as in *The Sun Also Rises* (1926) and *A Farewell to Arms* (1929)—but it has had a valuable influence on the style of modern American fiction, which in general possesses a toughness and directness lacking in English fiction. *For Whom the Bell Tolls* (1940), a story of love and war in the Spanish Revolution, is one of the best examples of fictional realism in modern American literature. Hemingway became the idol of many novelists during his lifetime and hatched a school of fiction which glorifies tough and brutal characters, and thus, like the work of Faulkner, exaggerates the violence and evil in our society. Since Hemingway's death, his place in American literature remains obscure; his works need the test of time for evaluation. It may be that he was greatly overrated, although his stylistic manner has probably left a permanent impression on American prose.

The novels of F. Scott Fitzgerald (1896-1940) touched off the revolt of the "jazz age." *This Side of Paradise,* which appeared in the same year as *Main Street,* dramatized the search of sophisticated young people after the first World War for hedonistic sensations through romance, bootleg liquor, and forgetfulness. Prewar moral codes were destroyed forever, and as the title of a musical comedy of the period said, "anything goes." Fitzgerald's subsequent novels are written in the same sharp prose as *This Side of Paradise* and deal with the same types, but only one, *The Great Gatsby* (1925), is a tightly knit artistic work. Like one of his heroes, Fitzgerald moved from one frantic experience to another, wound up in Hollywood, and both his talent and body sputtered out at an early age. Thus he became a kind of martyr to the jazz age itself.

In John Dos Passos (1896-   ) the disordered, pointlessly rapid life of postwar and boom-time America has had its most effective interpreter. In his trilogy *U.S.A.,* consisting of *The 42nd Parallel* (1930), *1919* (1932), and *The Big Money* (1936), Dos Passos embraces almost the entire range of contemporary civilization, focusing the action on the lives of a few characters as set against the factual background of their times. Thus he has developed an effective technique for reproducing the stress and frenzy of the period: a discontinuous, nervous narrative style highlighted by the "Newsreel" which uses newspaper headlines to report the social scene and the "Camera Eye" which reflects the author's reactions by a stream-of-consciousness method. In contrast, Thomas Wolfe (1900-1938) tried to delineate the central conflicts of modern life through the introspective method: the protagonist of his massive novels, *Look Homeward, Angel* (1929) and its sequel, *Of Time and the River* (1935), is the author himself, trying to capture, with a Proustian sense of detail, the expression and meaning of American civilization as it touches the artist's consciousness. A realistic treatment of contemporary social problems is found in the early novels of John Steinbeck (1902-   ), such as *In Dubious Battle* (1936), which concerns the plight of migratory workers in the California orchards, and *The Grapes of Wrath* (1939), an unequaled portrayal of the plight of the Dust Bowl victims and their trek to California.

The South has received full and unflattering treatment in the works of William Faulkner (1897-1962), one of the most controversial American writers of our time. A regionalist like Thomas Hardy, Faulkner used as the setting of many of his novels the imaginary Yoknapatawpha County in his native Mississippi. This environment gives him an endless opportunity for dredging up unsavory characters from the mixed black-and-white world, creating in their totality what Professor Don M. Wolfe calls "the concept of inherent evil in man without an accompanying assumption of inherent benevolence." Faulkner's best novels, *The Sound and the Fury* (1929), *As I Lay Dying* (1930), *Sanctuary* (1931), and *Light in August* (1932), belong to his early period. Although written with considerable power, the prose at times strains intolerably after effect, is perversely thick with parentheses, even with parentheses within parentheses. It is ironic that not only should Faulkner have been awarded the Nobel Prize, which was set up as a reward for achievement in "idealistic literature," but that he should express in his acceptance speech the belief "that man . . . is immortal, not because he alone among creatures has an inexhaustible voice, but because he has a soul, a spirit capable of compassion and sacrifice and endurance," a belief which seems significantly absent from his work.

In the United States, as in England and France, much of the literary activity of the later twentieth century has gone into the production of literary criticism; literary journals, each with its relatively small circle of devoted readers, have been spawned with prodigality: e.g., the *Partisan Review, Kenyon Review, Sewanee Review,* and *Hudson Review.* Critics abound; books of criticism pour from the presses; old and new authors are dissected with the energy and fervor usually devoted to the scientific laboratory. Despite the confusion which seems to reign among the various schools of criticism, America has produced in the twentieth century many critics of distinction. Van Wyck Brooks (1885-1963) has brilliantly illuminated the lives and works of nineteenth-century New England writers, among others; Edmund Wilson (1895-   ) has ranged far and wide among the literatures of the world, with the catholicity of a Sainte-Beuve. The New Criticism, which appeared in the 1940's, probably owed its impetus to I. A. Richards, but was forged into a coherent school by Kenneth Burke, John Crowe Ransom, Yvor Winters, Cleanth Brooks, R. P. Blackmur, and Allen Tate. These men have subjected literature, especially poetry, to intensely subtle analysis, often writing in a style that is excessively *outré* and precious; while there may be some justification for their method and explications, they have often succeeded, as William Barrett, himself an editor of *Partisan Review,* said, in creating "a kind of separation of literature from life," and using "an elaborate apparatus to reach a point which I find usually trivial, even banal." The New Criticism has invaded many of the universities and has not only influenced the teaching of literature but stimulated the writing of numerous treatises and monographs, many of which reveal valuable insights into the literary process.

In addition to Gide and Proust, twentieth-century France has had many novelists of distinction, among them Valéry Larbaud (1881-   ), Jean Cocteau, Jean Giraudoux, the Catholic François Mauriac (1885-   ), and André Malraux (1895-   ). Mauriac, author of *Genitrix* (1923), *Desert of Love* (1925), *Thérèse Desqueyroux* (1927), and *Triangle of Vipers* (1932), is regarded by some critics as ranking next to Proust among modern French novelists. He does not depart from traditional techniques, sets his stories of vice and passion in his native southwest with its stretches of moor and pine, and as a good Catholic specializes in the psychology of sin. Malraux has fused his adventurous life and art into striking novels; he explored the Orient, followed the Communists in China, served with the Loyalists in Spain, and with the underground in France during the war. *Man's Fate* (1933), a novel about the Chinese Revolution, *Days of Wrath* (1935), set against a background of concentration camps in Nazi Germany, and *Man's Hope* (1937), dealing with the Spanish Civil War, reveal a feeling for the movements of man in the mass and at the same time sympathy and understanding of the individuals who are at once separated from and impelled by these movements. No more horrible or hopeless vision of modern life has appeared than *Journey to the End of Night* (1934) by Louis-Ferdinand Destouches (pen name Céline, 1894-1961). Savagery, hatred, disease stalk its pages; in its harsh language of the street it is as far removed as any work is likely to be from the traditional ease and clarity of French prose. It is unequaled as a singular kind of picture of the prewar world.

Proust may be said to have introduced into French literature the *roman fleuve*, which tells the story of a group of characters in a series of interwoven volumes and has more consistent unity than such precursors as Zola's Rougon-Macquart novels or the recurring characters in Balzac's *Human Comedy*. The best known of *romans fleuves* are *Men of Good Will*, begun in 1931, of Jules Romains (1885-   ), and *The World of the Thibaults*, completed in 1941, of Roger Martin du Gard (1881-   ). These novels attempt to portray not only the individual and the family but an entire society; like Galsworthy's *Forsyte Saga*, they are sociological documents. Romains' *Men of Good Will* grew like a fungus. Interested in the totality of society, Romains has made all Paris his hero, developing his novel through a multitude of characters, tracing each in his activities, working in and out among them, accumulating many effective scenes. *Verdun*, for example, is a moving panorama of the first World War and its impact on Frenchmen of all ranks who took part in it; *Aftermath* shows the disorganizing, demoralizing effects of the first year of peace. *The World of the Thibaults* won for its author the Nobel Prize. Its theme is the impact of twentieth-century problems and the outbreak of war in 1914 on the persistent characteristics of French family life and bourgeois traditions.

The most talented and provocative French novelists who became popular in the late 1930's and 1940's are Jean-Paul Sartre and Albert Camus. Sartre's

Nausea (1938), regarded as one of the century's masterpieces, is a typical existentialist study of an odd character, the young scholar Roquentin, who in the end discovers the meaninglessness of being, and "blessed with such an inverted 'mystical' ecstasy . . . returns to the world of man as if he were alienated from him, like a crab or some crawling beast."[10] The three volumes of Sartre's *The Roads to Freedom,* published in the 1940's, are regarded by percipient French critics as towering above most French fiction of the last two decades. Camus' novels are *The Stranger* (1942), *The Plague* (1947), and *The Fall* (1956). While Camus displays considerable fictional talent, his pessimistic outlook, his drab characters, and his prepossession with the muck and slime of human life tend to repel American readers. Like Sartre, Camus seems to say that human life has no meaning, Christianity is irrelevant; yet Camus regarded himself as a "humanist," and affirmed that "if we consent to do without God and hope, we are not so easily resigned to do without man."[11]

The dominant figure in the modern German novel is Thomas Mann (1875-1955). In his North German blood there was a Latin strain which brought into his work a southern warmth and brightness. His prose, though not simple, suffers from no Teutonic heaviness. In his brilliant short works, *Tonio Kröger* and *Death in Venice,* Mann treats a favorite theme, the position of the artist in society. In his early novel *Buddenbrooks* (1901), Mann traces the emergence of an artist out of the ruin of a declining patrician family of Lübeck (Mann himself was a member of an old Lübeck family). His most important work, *The Magic Mountain* (1924), is set in a Swiss sanatorium. Through the minds of the tubercular patients, variously affected by disease, Mann presents an elaborate discussion of modern life—of philosophy, love, religion, science, death. In *Doctor Faustus* (1947) Mann returned to the theme of the artist's position in society, this time depicting the tragedy of the musician Leverkuhn, who lives a solitary, ascetic life, withdrawing from the normal activities of his acquaintances and forgoing happiness and love; through his hero and his musical compositions, Mann formulates his criticism, which is really an indictment, of bourgeois society in the twentieth century. In the *Joseph* tetralogy, completed in 1942, "Joseph the dreamer is the narcissistic artist, who comes in perilous conflict with the society into which he is born, but who ultimately is reconciled with the community by changing himself and it."[12] This is the theme of *The Magic Mountain,* placed in a mystical-historical setting and expressed in religious, psychological, and moral terms.

One of the strangest (and by many critics most admired) of modern German-language novelists is Franz Kafka (1883-1924), whose *The Trial* (1924) and *The Castle* (1927) are weirdly symbolic, mystical accounts of an unfinished search for truth, written with considerable dramatic power.

---

10 Henri Peyre, *op. cit.,* p. 226.
11 Quoted by Peyre, *ibid.,* p. 251.
12 Roy Pascal, *The German Novel,* Manchester University Press, 1956, p. 270.

II. DIRECTIONS IN TWENTIETH-CENTURY ART

By John C. Galloway

Professor of Art, Oakland University

It is more difficult for us to analyze the qualities of the art of our own time than to evaluate the major characteristics of past styles. The variety of individual interpretations of older themes, the advent of abstract or non-objective painting and sculpture, and the daring exploitation by architects of traditional building materials have been met since about 1900 by controversial responses on the part of public and artists alike. Yet despite the partisanship of many creative groups and individuals and the occasional bewilderment of society at large, many deeply impressive purposes and achievements of twentieth-century art are now clearly manifest. It is even possible to refer to "old masters of modern art." At least a half-dozen styles of painting, sculpture, and architecture have already outlasted, in terms of time alone, the length of the periods dominated by certain traditional modes.

In any case, no earlier epoch of the history of art has witnessed such a widespread interest in the visual arts of its time as does the present one. Public programs of instruction sponsored by museums and galleries, perfection of reproduction techniques which enable millions of persons to see contemporary works in popular magazines, and the increasing importance of art as an academic discipline in universities have all contributed to an unparalleled appreciation.

No ready-mixed formula can provide the instant understanding of all recent kinds of art. Some individuals and groups insist upon "social purpose" while others demand "pure form." As many controversies exist among artists and architects themselves as among persons untrained in art. But several outstanding movements, especially those which were developed before the end of the second World War, have become an established expression of the general culture of our time. It is to our advantage to consider modern architecture, industrial design, painting, and sculpture individually.

1. *Architecture*

The style of most contemporary industrial buildings and group-dwelling projects gives the appearance of being more clearly based upon cubic, angular geometry than were older structures. There is also a more candid evidence of the physical materials which go to make up both exterior and interior images of buildings.

While concrete, glass, iron, and even the "modern" cantilever principle were all known to ancient Mediterranean architects, they were usually concealed within the greater usage of masonry construction and the post-and-lintel or vaulted system of support. The first genuinely modern, large-scale employment of glass-and-iron building occurred in Sir Joseph Paxton's Crystal Palace of 1851 at the London International Exposition. Supplanting heavy masses of stone or brick, this surprisingly advanced enclosure anticipated the towering glass-screened, steel-skeletoned buildings of our own time.

The development of reinforced concrete (cement strengthened by rods of iron or steel placed inside it) by Hennebique and Coignet of France marked another advance, around 1890, of modern exploitation of traditional materials.

The concentration of industrial activity in American and European cities during the late nineteenth century and the attendant need for monumental office buildings, factories, and collective housing led to new demands upon architects. The modern skyscraper is more easily explained stylistically and historically than logically. The gradual perfection of the mechanical elevator during the late nineteenth century helped make possible, but did not account for, the powerfully vertical modern building. Moreover, the skyscraper, which we think of in connection with the soaring towers in New York City, actually originated in the American Midwest where ground space was relatively abundant. L. S. Buffington (1847-1931) designed the first "cloudscraper," as it was called, but did not construct it. William Jenney's Home Life Insurance Building in Chicago, 1885, was probably the first skyscraper to be built. Many office buildings and churches alike in this period reflected the aesthetic of H. H. Richardson (1838-1886), who, following visits to France, had developed an "American Romanesque."

Louis Sullivan (1856-1925) pioneered modern industrial architecture in the United States. His stratagem, "form follows function," was misinterpreted by a majority of his several followers to mean a discarding of beauty in favor of emphasis upon sheer physical materials. His pupil Frank Lloyd Wright, one of the most distinguished architects of all time and the greatest of modern builders, fortunately resolved Sullivan's formula and combined a personal feeling for artistry with profound knowledge of engineering. Wright's work will be discussed below.

Cass Gilbert's Woolworth Building of 1913 in New York was for years the world's tallest structure. Its height of 800 feet was reinforced by Gothic detail which emphasized the vertical character of its great tower.

The Chicago Tribune Building of 1928, also Gothic in its ornament, continued the skyscraper tradition in America. Its designer, Raymond Hood (1881-1934), was later to help build Rockefeller Center in New York, one of the outstanding complexes of metropolitan architecture of our time. The second-place award in the competition for the Chicago Tribune project went to the Finnish-born Eliel Saarinen (1873-1950). The Saarinen design, free of definitive influences such as the Gothic, has probably stimulated more younger American architects than has Hood's winning entry.

The development of the structural steel cage, walled by concrete or stone slabs and glass, eliminated the need for heavy masses of vertical masonry of the traditional kind. The weight of each story of modern skyscrapers is relieved at its own level, not fully thrusting down upon the footings at the ground area. An even greater employment of glass window spaces has resulted from full application of the cantilever principle, as in the Philadelphia Savings Fund Society Building of 1932 by George Howe (1886-1955) and William Lescaze (1896-

). Articulation of the horizontal stories of offices is attractively resolved with the upward sweep of the exterior.

Rockefeller Center in New York, built from 1931 through the late 1940's, demonstrates an imaginative use of the modern office building within the very heart of an overcrowded city. Located on four square blocks, fifteen buildings combine varying heights and widths so that each unit sustains individuality. Exterior space and light flow about each of the geometrical structures. Among the architects represented there are Raymond Hood and J. A. Fouilhoux, W. K. Harrison, L. A. Reinhard, H. W. Corbett, Henry Hofmeister, and W. H. MacMurray.

The skyscraper has continued since the second World War to challenge the imagination of modern architects. The lightly glass-screened metallic skeleton and constantly improving adaptations of reinforced concrete and plastic materials have enabled the building of scores of imposing office structures and factories since the 1940's. The United Nations Secretariat Building of 1950 (New York), designed by an international group of architects, is characteristic of recent emphasis upon the tall, rectangular slab. Generally related in style is Lever House, the main offices of the Lever Soap Company. Not one of the tallest of New York buildings of its purpose, Lever House sacrificed invaluable commercial space to the aesthetic principle of fuller visibility from ground level, and at the same time opened up the first story to thoroughfare by pedestrian traffic. The cantilevered tower begins at the third story above the street. Gordon Bunschaft of the firm of Skidmore, Owings, and Merrill was the designer of this 1952 structure.

At the close of the nineteenth century in Europe, the architecture of a number of countries had become influenced by the decorative style known as *Art Nouveau* in France and Belgium and as *Jugendstil* in Germany and Austria. Strongly curvilinear, undulating designs based upon the forms of vine tendrils and coming in part from the paintings of such Post-Impressionists as Paul Gauguin and the Norwegian, Edvard Munch, were adapted to both exterior and interior ornamentation of residences and public buildings. A similar aesthetic was apparent in England at the same time.

Soon after 1900, however, the European pioneers of the so-called International Style, partly out of reaction against such surface decoration and partly in response to the early works of Frank Lloyd Wright in America, began simplifying their designs and more clearly emphasizing the organic nature of modern building materials. The Austrian Adolf Loos (1870-1933) pointed out the dangers of concealing poor basic design with excessive surface ornament. The Turbine Factory of the German General Electrical Company of 1909 by Peter Behrens in Berlin bespeaks the new awareness of the "form and function" principle. Wright's contribution to the development of the International Style was made partly through the lectures of the Dutch architect H. P. Berlage (1856-1934), who had visited the United States.

Outstanding among the recent European designers are Walter Gropius (1883-   ) and his student Marcel Breuer (1902-   ) of Germany, both of whom have resided in America since the 1930's and whose material-conscious formulae have stimulated many younger architects; Erich Mendelssohn (1887-1953), also German; Le Corbusier (Charles-Édouard Jeanneret; Swiss-French, 1887-   ); and J. J. P. Oud, Dutch (1890-1963). The movement known as the International Style was not precisely a collectively planned one, although its originators were conversant with one another's styles in most parts of Europe and America. Not only recent developments in architecture but the painting and sculptural movements, Cubism, Suprematism, and *De Stijl*, were known to this group. Several of the architects were also painters, for example, Le Corbusier.

One of the earliest works by Gropius which disclosed the candid, practical interpretation of modern materials was his factory in Altfeld of 1910. His *Bauhaus* workshop and related buildings of 1926 at Dessau, designed for the school of which he was director, are a more advanced statement. The cantilever and the glass screen supported by thin metallic mullions are effectively used.

Mies van der Rohe (1886-   ), also German, is closer to the extremely geometrical aesthetic of the Dutch *De Stijl* group. Stress upon the supposed beauty of contemporary structural metals and glass typifies his approach. An early residence, the Tugendhat House at Brno, Czechoslovakia, of 1931 testifies to Mies' understanding of the need of uniting exterior and interior space. Immense glass windows may be retracted into the basement level, and living and dining spaces are thoughtfully fluid. His commercial projects dating from the time of his arrival in the United States have, however, sometimes been referred to as "monolithic." The apartment building at 860 Lake Shore Drive, Chicago (1951), embodies Mies' aesthetic for stark, slab-like glass enclosures visually relieved by continuous vertical strips of steel. Curiously, the final accents of such buildings sometimes depend upon relatively impermanent substances such as the black paint covering the steel verticals of the Lake Shore apartments, and the uniform, gray window blinds of the same façade.

Few European exponents of the so-called International Style have equaled the influence of Le Corbusier. City planning and the integration of single, modern structures within older complexes have long intrigued him. His Dormitory and Lounge for Swiss students at the Cité Universitaire in Paris combines the cube-conscious aesthetic of his self-styled "machines-for-living" houses of the 1920's with curved surfaces and a refreshing open ground story. Thinnish supports of concrete support a rectangular slab containing the dormitory itself, and a floating effect results. Le Corbusier's sculpturally conceived Church of Notre Dame du Haut at Ronchamp of 1955 represents an imaginative counterpoint of powerful curves and sudden angles. Its imaginative play of contrasting materials and shapes exceeds in lyricism the often blunt cubes and flat forms of the International Style.

While many distinguished European and American architects of the twentieth century have created office buildings, factories, or large private residences, few have devoted their best talents to low-cost group housing. An exception is J. J. P. Oud of Holland, who was appointed official architect of Amsterdam in 1918 because of his concern over that problem and his capacity to deal with it. Usually with a strongly limited budget, Oud developed a number of dwelling projects of which the Hook of Holland Workers' Houses of 1926 are character-istic. Recognizing that shelter and plumbing alone are inadequate for human comfort, Oud made important use of plazas and courts within the over-all con-ception. A number of similar projects have been carried out in both Europe and America during recent years, but almost no contemporary architects are best known for their efforts to solve mass housing problems, especially when limited budgets are involved. Unfortunately, the insensitivity of many municipal, state, and Federal agencies in the United States has been of little encouragement to de-signers of outstanding talent. A study of most suburban communities in America with their almost regimented types of houses and crowding of ground space is hardly less depressing than the sight of metropolitan slum tenements which re-main with us decade after decade. Far more imaginative projects have been un-dertaken in the bombed-out sections of London and West Berlin.

The most resourceful architect of the twentieth century and one of the great designers of all time was Frank Lloyd Wright (1869-1960). One of the few followers of Louis Sullivan who sensitively interpreted the latter's "form follows function" credo, Wright was always too much the artist to depend upon the bare bones of structure and materials alone. Often called a romantic because of his outspoken opposition to the sparse forms of technology, Wright was a highly expert engineer whose knowledge of structural techniques as such was brilliant. He declined to apply the same formula to a factory which he had developed for a rural house.

Wright's early works such as Unity Church in Chicago (1906) and Robie House of 1909, also in Chicago, were far in advance of any modern European structures in expressing both the function of material and the attendant aesthetic adjustment to technique. His Imperial Hotel in Tokyo, designed somewhat later, is a masterpiece of engineering.

Wright's Laboratory Tower of the Johnson Wax Company buildings at Ra-cine, Wisconsin, exemplifies his total awareness of contemporary structural de-vices and the needs of occupants of a given shelter. A central core containing the mechanical organs of the building is articulated by the vertical mushrooming of alternately squarish and circular, cantilevered bands defining the office levels. The effect, especially when studied under night illumination, is dramatic and convincing.

Begun like the Johnson Company buildings in the late 1930's is Wright's Kaufmann House at Bear Run, Pennsylvania, a masterpiece of the resolution of the cantilevered block to a lyrical, romantic natural setting. The flow of exterior-to-interior space, so frequently clumsily handled by lesser architects who simply lay bare the activities of occupants by glassing any available wall, respects pri-vacy and the distinction between nature and dwelling.

Wright's last major design to be completed during his lifetime is the Guggen-heim Museum in New York (1951-1957). This spiral-shaped building was based no more upon the curvilinear forms of nature, such as that of the snail, than upon the great tradition of spiraled stairways known to the Baroque epoch. Although the Guggenheim Museum by Wright was strongly challenged by many thoughtful critics because of its competitiveness with the paintings it housed, it is a triumphant example of ·contemporary architectural design.

R. Buckminster Fuller (1895-   ), Canadian-born American designer, has repopularized as a modern form the dome, developed by the Romans and later adapted in Renaissance and Baroque times. The principles of geodesic mathematics have been so ingeniously applied by Fuller that his domical buildings may be constructed from prefabricated units of polyhedronal, flat plastics or plywood, the whole ceiling strung upon a mesh of hollow metallic tubing strung together by powerful wiring. Theoretically, such domed structures may be built to any given size, and the exterior forces of nature, including winds of hurricane force, serve merely to shrink and strengthen the basic form. Rapidity of construction is another asset.

The importance of industrial art in daily life has increased steadily since the 1920's. The problems of factory production of textiles, electrical appliances, commodity packages, furniture, ceramics, hand tools, tableware, office machinery, and other utilitarian objects have been conditioned by an almost universal desire for attractiveness along with efficiency. Many of the most appealing of functional objects have been designed by artist-craftsmen who ordinarily create individual, handmade works and who adapt their styles to factory methods. Professional industrial designers, many of whom have been trained recently in the fine arts as well as in engineering design, have also contributed.

Late nineteenth-century pioneering in modern industrial art included the efforts of William Morris (1834-1896) of England and the Arts and Crafts Movement in the British Isles; the influential work of the *Art Nouveau* leaders in France and Belgium; and the *Jugendstil* of Germany and Austria.

The first twentieth-century movement dedicated to the improvement of utilitarian design was the German *Werkbund* of 1907. Its leader, Hermann Muthesius (1861-1927), had been strongly influenced by the British crafts program. *Werkbunds* were organized in other European nations between 1910 and 1915, with Sweden becoming an active affiliate. In recent decades the several Scandinavian design groups have been among the leaders in this field, especially in the area of interior furnishings.

The machine and the technological or engineering aesthetic conditioned the production of the *Werkbund;* but it was not until after the first World War that a formally established, state-recognized German institution of modern design appeared. The *Bauhaus* at Weimar and later at Dessau was led by Walter Gropius. A distinguished faculty of engineers, artists, and theorists, several of whom were to leave for America when the Nazi régime closed the *Bauhaus,* taught the values of industrial design as these relate to daily human experience. Influential advances in poster style, typography, and various other practical arts were made.

Meanwhile the famous Armory Show of 1913 in New York, which had assembled hundreds of avant-garde European and American paintings and sculptures, had an indirect but important influence on modern designers in the United

States. Although a certain amount of superficial "streamlining" and the sometimes garish use of color resulted, the effects were at least revitalizing and brought to a mass public the boldness, however clumsily translated, of contemporaneous developments in art.

Italy, a nation which came late to the industrial field, has recently produced some of the most strikingly handsome of modern functional objects. Sewing machines, typewriters, and related forms of Italian design are outstanding.

In general, the automotive industries in both Europe and the United States have lagged in the competition for resolving utility with beauty. The exceptions to this principle are numerous, of course. American automobiles disclose the weakness of their engineers for attempting to substitute size of product for integrity of basic form, although a healthy trend toward "compacts"—smaller versions of the bloated, uselessly big "regular"-sized vehicles—appeared in the late 1950's. The influence of the popular and sensible Volkswagen of Germany and the sports cars of England, France, and Italy has made at least a slight inroad upon the bulk-based aesthetic of American automotive engineers.

2. Painting

The principal styles of early twentieth century painting followed two modes which had been formulated in Europe during the late nineteenth century. A remarkably fresh style, characterized by its spontaneity of brushwork and brilliancy of color, emerged in the early canvases of the French *Fauves* in about 1904. Fauvist painting derived largely from the emotional, potently colored works of Vincent van Gogh and the broad, exotically conceived works of Paul Gauguin. A technically related style also formed about 1904 was German Expressionism, which owed much to the intensely personal paintings of the Norwegian Edvard Munch (1863-1944), James Ensor of Belgium (1860-1949), and Ferdinand Hodler (Swiss, 1853-1918). Stimulating to both Fauvists and Expressionists were the so-called primitive sculptures of both West Africa and the South Pacific.

The second major tendency in modern painting emerged in the style known as Cubism in 1907-1908. More analytical and at first less vehement in approach than Fauvism or Expressionism, Cubism is derived from the measured aesthetic of Paul Cézanne and Georges Seurat. It is to be noted that the broken, patchy brushwork of Cézanne and the looser application by Paul Signac of the *pointillist* technique of his colleague Seurat were also of influence upon the *Fauves;* but it was the ordered, architectonic quality of Cézanne and Seurat which guided the Cubists.

The *Fauves,* or "beasts of nature"—a term applied at first scornfully by a critic at the first formal exhibition of the group in Paris in 1905—were first led by Henri Matisse (1869-1954). Matisse, like many of his fellow Fauvists, had been trained originally in conservative, naturalistic techniques, but had felt the necessity to incorporate in his style the lessons of late nineteenth-century individualism of color and composition. Other members of the group included André

Derain (1880-1954), Maurice de Vlaminck (1876-1961), Georges Rouault (1871-1958), Othon Friesz (1879-1949), Raoul Dufy (1877-1953) and Georges Braque (1882-1963). The style of the *Fauves* was almost a collective one between 1905 and about 1908, the characteristics being randomness of touch, brilliant colors, and inventive composition, the latter sometimes altered as the artist progressed with the individual painting. The effect of Fauvist style was one of liberation and spontaneity. Except in the case of Rouault, Fauvist themes involved few moral or religious overtones. Landscape and the human figure were dominant. Matisse's pagan *Joie de Vivre* of 1907 and his *Young Sailor* of 1905 typify the outgoing, refreshing modernity of color and brushwork common to the movement. Flat planes and extremely shallow space were sometimes devised by the *Fauves* as in Matisse's series of works on the theme of *The Dance* and Derain's *Figures in a Meadow* of this early, vital period.

Rouault was consistent in his development and is best known for his religious canvases. His heavy black outlines defining areas of smoldering color and the over-all gravity of his expression are present in his *Christ Mocked by Soldiers* of 1932. His earlier, socially conscious paintings of prostitutes and corrupt judges are no less typical.

After about 1910, most of the various Fauvists developed in different individual directions. While Rouault clung to his favored subjects and techniques, Matisse became increasingly decorative in expression. Vlaminck's landscapes of the 1920's and later bespoke a more or less set formula as did the works of Dufy. Most of these men, derided at the outset of the twentieth century as "wild beasts," grew tame and popular among the enlightened followers of modern art.

Contemporaneously with Fauvism in France appeared the German Expressionist movement known as *Die Brücke* ("The Bridge"). The German painters shared the French attitude toward technical spontaneity and brilliant coloring, but their choice of subject matter related more closely to either collective or individual sociological interests of the early twentieth century. There was an intense awareness of the gradual displacement of the artist and poet, long honored in Germany, by the technologist of the decade preceding the first World War.

The "Bridge" group was formed in Dresden in 1904 by E. L. Kirchner (1880-1938), Emil Nolde (1867-1956), and Karl Schmidt-Rotluff (1884-   ), who were joined later by Otto Mueller (1874-1930), Max Pechstein (1881-1955), Erich Heckel (1883-   ), and others. The name, *Die Brücke,* was adopted with the idea of espousing a linkage between early twentieth century aesthetic and that of sympathetic expressions of the past such as German medieval art, primitive art, and the unconscious mind. More emotional in fabric than French Fauvism, the paintings of *Die Brücke* represent an exploration of the inner psychological feelings of subjects. Powerful, even harsh delineations and colors were rapidly stated upon the canvas. The angularity of Oceanic primitive art as well as its curved decoration, known to German artists not only through the great ethnographical collections in their country but because of their visits to the South Seas, reinforced this strident approach. Mueller's *Women on the Beach* and Schmidt-Rotluff's *Evening on the Sea* reveal affinities with primitive art. The

"Bridge" exposition of religious subject matter is exemplified by Nolde's *Christ and the Children* and his *Pentecost* of 1909. An almost frenzied intensity of interpretation is disclosed.

Oskar Kokoschka (1886-   ), Austrian-born painter who was later resident in London, is closely linked with the spirit of *Die Brücke* and was first recognized in Berlin. His early portraits such as those of *Dr. and Mrs. Hans Tietze* and *Herwath Walden* are incisively analytical of the inner lives of the subjects and have been likened to Freudian psychological studies. Kokoschka's "portraits of cities," landscapes of such renowned European capitals as London and Naples, are intensely personal in conception.

Other painters whose styles may be related to German Expressionism but who are essentially independent in development are Chaim Soutine, Lithuanian-born French resident (1894-1943), and Marc Chagall (Russian-French, 1889-   ).

A movement in Germany known as *Die Neue Sachlichkeit* ("New Directness") emerged during the early 1920's, partly in reaction to the romanticism of certain phases of Expressionism and partly because of the growing consciousness of Germany's then disturbed political and economic situation following the first World War. George Grosz (1893-1959) and Otto Dix (1891-   ) were instrumental in shaping a clearly sociological art. Grosz, whose drawings and paintings had gotten him in trouble with German governments as early as the 1910's, came to the United States after the advent of the Nazi régime.

Max Beckmann (1884-1950) was another Germanic artist who left Europe to take up residence in America during the late 1930's. His painting style is related to both the vehemence of "The Bridge" and the objectivity of *Die Neue Sachlichkeit*. His triptych *The Departure* of 1935 and *The Falling Man,* painted shortly before his death, are almost medieval in depth of symbolism and strength of linear approach. Another German artist known for the sociological potency of her works, especially her drawings and lithographs, was Käthe Kollwitz (1867-1945).

The ideas which had led to the formation of *Die Brücke* helped shape a second modern movement in Germany known as "The Blue Rider" (*Der Blaue Reiter*). This group was more specifically interested in the formal aspects of composition and relationships of color than were the "Bridge" painters. Established in 1910, "The Blue Rider" included Franz Marc (1880-1916), who was killed in the first World War, Paul Klee (Swiss-German, 1879-1940), August Macke (1887-1914), Heinrich Campendonck (1889-   ), Gabriel Münter (1877-   ), once resident in America, and Wassily Kandinsky (Russian-born, 1866-1944). The intellectual disposition of most of the Blue Rider artists, typified by the almost Cubist compositions of animal subjects by Franz Marc and the landscapes of the American-born affiliate, Lyonel Feininger (1871-1956), led ultimately to Kandinsky's totally non-figural or abstract pictures of 1910 and later years. The Swiss-born Paul Klee also painted non-objective works. Both Kandinsky and Klee were members of the *Bauhaus* faculty. While Klee managed to retain his poetic, highly personal semi-abstract style, Kandinsky fell victim to the technological aesthetic of the *Bauhaus*. Nevertheless, his early abstractions in painting were a turning point in twentieth-century art. His influence has been momentous.

Meanwhile, the development of the Cubist style had occurred in Paris under the guidance of Pablo Picasso (Spanish, 1881-   ) and Georges Braque, originally a Fauvist. Picasso, the outstanding master of twentieth-century painting, had rejected in 1906 the looseness of both Fauvist and early Expressionist approach. Partly under the stimulus of African primitive sculpture, his *Demoiselles of Avignon* (1907), with its geometrically shaped interpretations of the female nude figure, was the initial document of Cubist art. As in subsequent examples of this style until about 1913, color was subordinated to the analysis of third-dimensional form placed in shallow space.

After 1914, Cubist painting became more daring in both color and texture. Both Picasso and Braque had already introduced into their works sand mixed with paints and such materials as corrugated pasteboard. *Papiers collés,* or paper-mounted pictures, were also created by the Cubists.

Juan Gris (1887-1927), like Picasso a Spaniard, and Fernand Léger (1881-1955), Robert Delaunay (1885-1941), and Roger de la Fresnaye (1885-1925) were also instrumental in the development of Cubist painting. Movements known in France as Orphism and in America as Synchromism, likewise developed during the 1910's, closely linked to Cubism but more nearly abstract in total impression.

Aesthetic rather than sociological in conception, Cubism was nevertheless to lead to one of the masterpieces of our time which condemns warlike forces. Picasso's *Guernica* of 1937, a mural painted on a movable background, was a telling response to the aerial bombing of a small Spanish town by Fascist planes. This work, executed in blacks, grays, and whites, is saturated with highly personal symbolism; but it amounts to an indictment of all aggressive, inhuman hostilities of its day.

In Italy a movement called Futurism resulted partly from the same artistic influences which had led to Cubism in France and additionally from a self-conscious awareness among painters and poets of Italy's backwardness in modern technological achievement. At once making use of French-Spanish Cubism and disavowing its influence, such Futurist artists as Marinetti, Balla, Severini, Carra, and Boccioni proclaimed in 1910 their rejection of Italy's classical past in favor of the dynamism of the machine. Russolo's *Dynamism of an Automobile* of 1912, the *Armored Train in Action* by Severini of 1915, and Balla's *Street Light* of 1909 testify to a style which interpreted contemporaneous mechanical forms as vibrant and mobile in space. One of the great documents most clearly bespeaking the Futurist concern for fragmented motion was created, however, by a Frenchman, not an Italian. Marcel Duchamp (1887-   ), later to be identified with the international "Dada" movement, painted one of the most controversial of early twentieth-century works in his *Nude Descending a Staircase* of 1912.

The Cubist and Futurist movements, roughly contemporaneous in development, both reveal the search by modern artists for an analytical approach to the unseen but real substance of material objects and their rhythms.

The paintings of a number of American artists, some of whom lived in Europe during the 1910's, were related in conception to either Cubist, Futurist, Expressionist, or abstract art. John Marin (1870-1953), Joseph Stella (Italy-U.S., 1877-1946), Stanton MacDonald-Wright (1890-   ), Morgan Russell (1886-1953), and Marsden Hartley (1877-1943) were pioneers of modernism in the United States. Arthur G. Dove (1880-1946) was another pathfinder.

Following the momentous invention of abstract or non-objective painting by Wassily Kandinsky in 1910, several individuals or groups developed independent styles of so-called subjectless art. The Suprematist movement in Russia headed by Kasimir Malevich (1878-1935) and El Lissitzky (1890-1941) espoused a rigid, geometrical aesthetic which lacked Kandinsky's poetry of form. The art of Alexander Rodchenko (1891-   ), as much interested in architecture as in painting, also derived from the confined notions of geometry. An outgrowth of Suprematism, influenced by both Cubism and the Dutch *De Stijl* aesthetic, was Constructivism. The openwork sculptures in plastics and metals of the brothers Naum Gabo (1890-   ) and Antoine Pevsner (1886-1962) are related more closely to the painting of the 1910's than to the sculpture of that period.

De Stijl was developed in Holland by Piet Mondrian (1872-1944), Theo van Doesburg (1883-1931), and Bart van der Leck(1876-1958). A search for "pure" form, *De Stijl* painting was closely related to the sculpture of Vantongerloo (1886-   ) and the architecture of Oud and others associated with the group. Mondrian's *Composition in Blue and White* of 1935 and his *Composition in White, Black and Red* of 1936 typify the purely flat, rectangular shapes and simple colors of the *De Stijl* painting aesthetic. The ideas of this group were influential upon the industrial-design concepts of the German *Bauhaus*. The Swiss-born Fritz Glarner (1899-   ), long a resident of the United States, has remained an adherent of *De Stijl*.

Two additional modern movements which were founded before the second World War were Dada and Surrealism. The former name was taken at random by its founders from a book in 1916 in Switzerland. At first a literary movement headed by Tristan Tzara, Hugo Ball, and Richard Huelsenbeck, Dada was soon joined by a number of gifted painters such as Marcel Duchamp, Francis Picabia (Spanish, 1878-1953), Man Ray (American, 1890-   ), and the Germans Kurt Schwitters (1887-1948) and Max Ernst (1891-   ). A disillusionment with the militarism of the first World War and the pragmatism of many aspects of society led to an ironical attitude among the Dadaists. "Junk paintings" composed of rubbish mounted on canvas, drawings created solely from the subconscious, and "ready-made" sculptures composed of, for example, intimate plumbing fixtures were exhibited in a derisive fashion. Nonsensical poems and paradoxical public behavior—for example, organized applause in theaters when the villain was outdoing the hero—were also part of the Dada aesthetic.

Surrealism, like Dada upon which it was largely founded, was primarily a literary movement and depended significantly upon the exploration of the unconscious. Appearing in 1924, Surrealism was often likened by its practitioners to the dream imagery of Freudian psychology, usually very imprecisely (only one of its spokesmen, André Breton, was seriously trained in that science). Many "orthodox" Surrealists, among them Salvador Dali (1904-   ), Yves Tanguy (French, 1900-1955) and the Belgians Paul Delvaux (1897-   ) and René Magritte (1898-   ) created images of a dreamlike subject content meticulously painted in a precise, sometimes overworked realistic technique. Dali's *Invisible Man* and *Paranoiac Face* exemplify the style. Extremely deep perspectives were employed. More nearly abstract than realistic in approach was the art of André Masson (1896-   ) and Joan Miró (1893-   ). Certain phases of the art of Paul Klee and even Picasso have been imputed to the Surrealist idiom, though neither was a member of the movement; nor was Giorgio de Chirico (1888-   ), an Italian "metaphysical" painter whose finest canvases dated during the 1910's and anticipated the intense loneliness of Surrealist deep space and lighting. Surrealism reached its apogee during the 1930's Its combination of an almost literally realistic technique and pseudo-paranoiac, dreamlike themes found wide popular reception in both Europe and America.

Few of the modern styles we have thus far considered were understood, at least when they first appeared, by the public. But in both the United States and Mexico vigorous schools of sociologically oriented mural and easel painting of basically realistic style flourished during the 1930's. In Mexico this art was officially sponsored as an instrument of social reform. Diego Rivera (1886-1957), David A. Siqueiros (1898-   ), and José Clemente Orozco (1883-1949) were outstanding as muralists, and their works appear in grand scale in any number of public buildings in Mexico City. Rivera's and Orozco's styles may also be studied in the United States at, respectively, the Detroit Institute of Arts and Dartmouth College in New Hampshire. The social-conscious art of the 1930's in the United States was less intensely nationalistic in theme than that of the Mexicans although many officially sponsored murals in public buildings depicted Federal construction, famous court decisions of the time and similar topical subjects. Thomas Benton (1889-   ), George Biddle (1885-   ), and Henry Varnum Poor were among the more imaginative practitioners.

In certain respects linked with the themes of state or Federally sponsored art were the works of hundreds of American artists, admittedly of uneven talent, known as "The American Scene." The national government of the United States began in the 1930's to recognize the resources of its own painters for the first time, at least in terms of large-scale encouragement. Not the least of the achievements of New Deal support of the fine arts was the sponsorship of several young men who were later to be numbered among the country's outstanding abstract artists.

Abstract or non-objective painting had enjoyed a continuing practice in the United States since the time of the Armory Show of 1913, and its development paralleled that of European abstract art during the 1920's and 1930's. It was not until after the second World War, however, that the United States became the leader in this particular field of expression. Pioneers such as MacDonald-Wright,

Dove, and Hartley had already shown the way in America very shortly after the initial non-representational works of Kandinsky had appeared in Europe in 1910. The post-World War II movement in America, and especially in New York, became known as "Action Painting" or "abstract-expressionism." Hans Hofmann (1880-   ), German-born, was a leader in this school. Willem de Kooning (1904-   ), Jackson Pollock (1912-1956), Franz Kline (1910-1962), and Robert Motherwell (1915-   ) are among the best-known exponents of the "Action" style of the 1950's. Other internationally known Americans are Arshile Gorky (1904-1948), Mark Rothko (1903-   ), and Clyfford Still (1904-   ). On the West Coast, Mark Tobey (1890-   ) was a forerunner of abstract-expressionism with his "white-writing" canvases which relate no less to the highly imaginative ornament of early medieval European manuscripts than to Oriental calligraphy.

Abstract-expressionist painting may or may not, depending upon the artist in point, project images of the human figure; more often its aesthetic depends upon the forcefulness of the formal components of pictures, namely, color, shape, line, texture, rhythm. De Kooning, whose early pencil portraits are almost classically naturalistic in style, proceeded to semi-abstract, haunting interpretations of the seated female figure in the 1950's, then to a totally abstract handling of form and color. Jackson Pollock, one of the most original artists of the middle twentieth century, is closer to Kandinsky's founding inventions in abstraction but arrives at an even more complex idea of the dissolution of forms and colors within the picture-space.

Stuart Davis (1894-1964) has remained an "old master" of abstract painting in America. His style, developed during the 1920's and reminiscent of decorative Cubism in some ways, is gayer, intentionally less disturbing than are the efforts of the Action group.

No European movement of the post-World War II period has matched the vigor and imaginativeness of recent American art, although many gifted young painters throughout Europe who work along abstract-expressionist lines are contributing importantly to this essentially international style.

More or less periodically the opponents of any but the most unimaginative realistic styles predict a "return" to naturalism. Undoubtedly there will be significant changes in later twentieth-century painting; but returns to older modes of expression have seldom occurred in the history of art, and any such reversions of the future will be achieved only after the full assimilation of the disciplines of Cubism, Expressionism, abstract-expressionism, and other modern styles.

3. Sculpture

The development of twentieth-century sculpture is related closely to the history and aesthetics of modern painting. There are also certain parallels between recent sculpture and architecture. Each of these branches of the fine arts has strong affiliations with the styles of the past, yet extraordinary changes have taken place in all of them, sculpture by all means included. Like the architects of our century, modern sculptors have made ingenious use of new, exciting materials including plastics and metals. They have at the same time continued the ancient traditions of bronze-casting, direct carving in stone, and fired clay. Like the painters of this century they have reinterpreted the human figure geometrically or with emphasis on its emotional capacities, and they have shared in the creation of non-figural or abstract forms. Since the second World War especially, sculpture has enjoyed, as have both painting and architecture, a vigorous and abundant expression carried out by many gifted, original personalities.

Modern influences in sculpture, like those in painting and architecture, originated in the late nineteenth century. The powerful, basically naturalistic style of Auguste Rodin (1840-1917) of France carried Expressionist overtones in its mature phases. Rodin's imaginative, broken handling of bronze surfaces, usually likened by critics to late nineteenth-century Impressionism in painting, is actually closer to much later sculptural techniques of our time. His *Gates of Hell,* begun in 1880 and still not quite finished at the time of his death, is a summation of his remarkable development. Its scores of allegorical bronze figures, many of which are derived from earlier individual works by Rodin, are notable for their extremes of physical movement or its reverse. Rodin, like Michelangelo (whom he revered), used the human figure as the vehicle of inner tortures or ecstasies. Rodin's style and techniques were to be of immense influence, whether affirmatively or negatively, upon a generation of young twentieth-century artists.

Another important source of modern style in sculpture is the art of Aristide Maillol (1861-1944), also of France. A painter by training, Maillol did not become a sculptor until the turn of the present century. His characteristic works involve the female nude interpreted with a simplified aesthetic based upon classical norms, healthy and fully formed. Maillol's art lacks the emotional complexity of Rodin's, concentrating rather upon the harmony to be found in the human figure in repose or in gentle stages of movement. His *Mediterranean* of 1901 or his *Night,* both studies of the female nude, are characteristic of the quiet sensuousness of his style.

Another pioneer of modern sculpture whose aesthetic was formed during the late nineteenth century was the Italian Medardo Rosso (1858-1928). Although the Impressionist painters Degas and Renoir both practiced sculpture in bronze, Rosso's broken, highly textural surfaces are closer to the touch-conscious technique of Impressionism. His *Sick Man at the Hospital* of 1889 reveals the spontaneous modeling and light-shade contrasts so typical of his work.

The sculptures of Henri Matisse, the *Fauve* universally known as a painter, were also important to the development of early twentieth-century art. As in his paintings, Matisse used the figure as a liberating force for his ideas of form and texture. His standing bronze *Slave* of 1903 discloses rapidity of modeling and startling departures from normative proportions of the human figure. The *Head of Jeannette, Fifth Stage,* and *Reclining Nude* of 1911-1912 go even further in revealing the bodily shapes as the carriers of artistic thought and emotion.

An independent, remarkably gifted sculptor whose work is related in some ways to Cubism was the Rumanian Constantin Brancusi (1876-1957), whose style developed in Paris following his arrival there in 1904. Like most masters of early twentieth-century art, Brancusi proceeded from an originally naturalistic mode of expression to a personally disciplined, more imaginative one. His *The Kiss* of 1908, a cube-like, semi-abstract form, allows linear incisions to define the gesture between two persons which leads to the title of the work. His *Bird in Space* of 1919 is a powerfully reduced synthesis rather than a conventional representation of the vertical flight of a bird. This work, like so many of Brancusi's sculptures, is carried out in highly polished metal. Brancusi's early inclination toward abstraction has been of profound influence, directly or indirectly, upon most younger modern sculptors.

The Russian-born Alexander Archipenko (1887-1964), who first practiced in Paris, later settled in the United States and has for decades been of guidance to the more imaginative of American sculptors. His *Woman Combing Her Hair* of 1915, a smallish bronze work of Cubist inspiration, comprises a series of turned planes and concavities defining limbs and torso, while the head, the section of the human body about which we feel most sensitively, is formed as a void space. It is a gesture almost Dadaist in its paradox.

It was the painter Picasso, however, who created the first truly Cubist sculpture. His *Woman's Head* of 1909 exploits in three dimensions the identical concepts which Picasso had recently applied to his painted works. The forms of the back of the head are bent about, plane-like, toward cheeks and temples. In theory at least, a fourth-dimensional effect results. The general impact of this important bronze study suggests a sympathy on Picasso's part with specific types of wooden tribal masks of the Dan group in West Africa. Picasso also anticipated the "constructions" of certain Russian artists by building upon flat surfaces with such materials as wood, folded pasteboard, and chair caning. Although generally abstract in appearance, Picasso's constructions usually derived from the objects so familiar to Cubist painting—musical instruments, for example. While Picasso's welded iron and steel compositions of the early 1930's approached abstraction of form, his strongest sculptural statement occurred in the *Man Holding a Lamb* of 1944, an over-life-sized monument derived, as are most of this master's great works, from the human figure in movement.

Other contributors to the Cubist movement in sculpture were Henri Laurens (1885-1954) and Raymond Duchamp-Villon (1876-1918) of France. The latter is best-known for *The Horse,* 1914, a thoroughly Cubist interpretation of animal forms in movement. The Lithuanian-born Jacques Lipchitz (1891-   ), long resident in the United States and France, worked in a generally Cubist style during the 1910's and 1920's. One of the highly gifted sculptors of our time, Lipchitz grew away from the Cubist discipline, as evidenced by his *Man with a Guitar* of 1915, to an abstract-expressionist approach apparent in, for example, the bronze *Prayer* of 1943.

While Cubism and Italian Futurism shared many ideas about painting, only one major sculptor was produced by the Futurist movement. Umberto Boccioni (1882-1916), a significant painter, created in 1912 *Development of a Bottle in Space*, a bronze which is close to Cubist time-space relationships. His better-known *Unique Forms of Continuity in Space,* also in bronze, is one of the signal monuments of Futurist style, concerned as it is with the vibrancy of third-dimensional action.

Meanwhile, the tradition of the human figure as the medium of inner emotion was being given new exaltation by the outstanding German sculptor of the twentieth century, Wilhelm Lehmbruck (1881-1919). Influenced at first by Maillol, Lehmbruck was actually closer to Rodin in expression. The "heroic" poses of Rodin were softened and made more introverted in total impact. A distinctively German medieval quality, especially attenuation of form, is present in Lehmbruck's *Kneeling Woman* and *Standing Youth* of 1911-1913. The gesture of the head in Lehmbruck's figures is always poetic; a brooding impression almost always results. The son of a German miner and acutely aware of the militaristic and other social evils of his day, Lehmbruck designed a memorial known as *The Fallen One* in 1916 which was later condemned by the Nazi regime for its implied pessimism.

While no modern German sculptor explicated fully the aesthetic of Expressionism as it was practiced by painters, the outgoing movement of the works of Ernst Barlach (1870-1938) is closely related. His favorite medium was woodcarving (many of his works in this form have been bronze-cast). As opposed to Lehmbruck's quiet, extremely lean images, Barlach's figures were fully-formed and often aggressive in movement. His *Man Drawing a Sword* of 1911 is characteristic. The Germans Georg Kolbe (1877-1947) and Gerhard Marcks (1889-   ) likewise used the human figure in substantially naturalistic, though simplified, form subordinated to the qualities of action or repose.

German sculpture following the second World War has, with notable exceptions, reflected the interference with all modern creative expression imposed by the Nazi government of the 1930's and 1940's. Karl Hartung (1908-   ), Hans Uhlmann (1900-   ), and Bernard Heiliger (1915-   ) are influential in restoring a more imaginative aesthetic in modern Germany than was allowed in the period bracketing the second World War.

As has been the case in recent painting, a number of artists have appeared whose sculpture is difficult to identify with that of the major movements of the twentieth century. These include Gaston Lachaise (1882-1935) and Elie Nadelman (1882-1946), both trained in France and later resident in the United States. The female nudes of Lachaise, typified by his *Standing Woman* of 1932, have striking physical attributes—huge breasts and hips magnified by tiny waists and ankles. Nadelman's figures, on the other hand, are smoothly lined and almost devoid of the monumental sexuality of Lachaise's bronzes. But each man sustained in his own way the long tradition of the human figure in Western sculpture in the face of a burgeoning movement toward the abstract.

The non-representational styles of modern sculpture had grown apace during the first three decades following 1900. Semi-abstract creations by several Cubist artists and by Amadeo Modigliani (1884-1920, Italian) plus the styles of the several sculptors discussed above had acted as a liberating as well as a disciplining force. The Russians Alexander Rodchenko (1890-   ), Naum Gabo

(1890-   ), and Antoine Pevsner practiced abstract sculpture in their native country before the advent of the Soviet regime. After 1920 this government became hostile to non-representational art, and Gabo and Pevsner, as well as the pioneer of abstraction, Kandinsky, removed permanently to other parts of the world. Constructivism, a style announced by Gabo and Pevsner around 1920, was conditioned by both engineering techniques and the more mechanistic geometry of Cubism, Suprematism, and *De Stijl* as well as by a preoccupation on the part of its creators with newer European plastic and metallic materials. The constructions of both men, which have influenced many industrial designers as well as a few creative sculptors in both Western Europe and the United States, have remained basically technological in conception, though expert in their adaptation of modern materials to abstract techniques.

A more poetic, less substance-bound contributor to abstract sculpture of the 1920's was Hans (Jean) Arp, an Alsatian born in 1887. Identified as a co-founder of the Dada movement, Arp created purely non-figural sculptures as early as 1926. His plaster *Human Concretion* of 1935, in its organic, smoothly flowing simple shapes, is typical of his mature expression. Arp's materials, whether wood, marble or plaster, serve to articulate his highly personal aesthetic rather than to dominate it.

Alberto Giacometti (1901-   ), a Swiss-born artist, is outstanding among sculptors who have undergone Dadaist and Surrealist conditioning. His *Palace at Four A.M.* of 1948 bespeaks the solitude and strangeness of the styles of such nonconformist Surrealists as de Chirico and Miró rather than, for example, Dali. But the most characteristic of Giacometti's works are the remarkably attenuated figural shapes in scored, pitted metal, which are akin to archaic Etruscan style. These are among the most impressive of recent, semi-abstract European sculptures.

The British sculptor Henry Moore (1898-   ) was closer to abstraction in the 1920's than in more recent years. Using the human figure as the ultimate source of his aesthetic, Moore has reflected the influences of primitive art as well as European medieval figure style. Most often his works are semi-abstract in feeling. His *Reclining Figure* of 1938 and his series of *Seated Figures* dating from the same period are smoothly finished in surface but monumental in conception. Moore has exerted an abiding influence upon scores of younger twentieth-century sculptors by opening up the figure with perforations through the chest so that space not only flows around the silhouette but actually participates in the form.

The welded and brazed metallic techniques favored by most younger sculptors since the second World War were actually advanced well beforehand by several European and American artists. The Spaniard Julio Gonzales (1876-1942) was a pioneer in the joining and forging of metals in modern sculpture and even instructed Picasso in such techniques. Alexander Calder (American, 1898-   ), whose completely non-figural, flat-cut free shapes of sheet iron or aluminum are arranged upon skeletons of steel rods to form mobile abstractions, was one of the first United States artists to become widely recognized in Europe.

England has been strongly represented in recent, non-figural or semi-abstract sculpture by the art of Reg Butler (1913-   ), Lynn Chadwick (1914-   ), Robert Adams (1917-   ), and Eduardo Paolozzi (1924-   ). Their most characteristic works reveal an awareness of abstraction and of the welded metallic techniques referred to above.

In Italy, where the lengthy tradition of figural sculpture is at its strongest, a number of post-World War II artists have worked in both ancient media and recently developed ones. Representation of the human figure still prevails. Marino Marini (1901-   ), whose theme of horse and rider is one of the best-known in recent semi-abstract art, combines modern formalization with synthetically introduced antiquity of surface. Luciano Minguzzi (1911-   ) and Giacomo Manzu (1908-   ) likewise express the contemporary Italian tradition through subjective, but by no means anti-traditional, interpretation of the human figure. Fantastic or semi-abstract forms, which are not without precedent in ancient Mediterranean art, are more typical of the style of Mirko (Basaldella), born in 1910.

The most imaginative of modern French sculptors identified with the post-World War II period is Germaine Richier (1904-1959). Like many British, American, and Italian artists, she has employed the human figure as the carrier of emotional forces which far exceed its mere appearance.

Since the second World War the United States has taken the lead in sculpture which it has enjoyed in painting. The presence of Marcel Duchamp and Alexander Archipenko of Europe, to mention only two artists who have long stayed in America, has undeniably exerted an influence which has been at once liberating and of useful discipline. The Armory Show of 1913 had earlier provided a challenging impetus to American painters and sculptors alike. But, until the 1930's, sculpture in the United States had not revealed the modernity of attitude to be witnessed in painting. The stone sculptures of William Zorach (1887-   ) and John Flannagan (1908-1942) are notable for their great economy of form, and the mobiles of Calder are even more advanced in terms of the time in which they were executed.

The abstract-expressionist movement in American sculpture since the second World War has paralleled roughly the development of painting. Among its most gifted exponents are David Smith (1906-   ), Theodore Roszak (1907-   ), Seymour Lipton (1903-   ), Herbert Ferber (1906-   ), Ibram Lassaw (1913-   ), David Hare (1917-   ), Richard Lippold (1915-   ), and a score of even younger men, all of whom are aware of the great traditions of the past as well as the spirit of the recent twentieth century.

It is often said that the more abstract styles of twentieth-century art fail to divulge the pressures of reality in our time. Quite to the contrary, the bestialities and tensions of the later twentieth century are so immense that they defy either verbal accounts in literature or naturalistic representation in art. Since man has had repeated occasions in our time to fear for his very survival, it is not at all surprising that artists, who are instantly sensitive to the threats of society within itself, have developed heretofore unknown means of expression. If the painting, sculpture, and architecture of the near future should undergo significant changes, as indeed they may, these shifts must necessarily take into account the potency of present forms.

III. THE NEW SYNTAX AND THE NEW SOUND

By Saul Novack

Associate Professor of Music, Queens College of the City University of New York

From the earliest beginnings of polyphony in the ninth century until the twentieth century the music of Western civilization slowly unfolded, developed, and expanded a system of tonal relationships characterized by what is known as *triadic tonality*. The structure of a composition was conditioned by a tonal centrality termed *key*, out of and towards which all events in the composition moved. The major and minor scales evolved as the principal abstractions of the tones chosen to represent tonality, given further meaning by the simultaneous sound of three specific tones in consonance with each other: the *triad*. This sound-syntax, the mainstream of Western art and folk music, became more and more complex during the course of its growth through the centuries, until in the nineteenth-century chromaticism of Wagner, Strauss, and their followers the outer limits were reached. The retention of a sense of tonality became increasingly more difficult because of the intensity of chromatic motion. Dissonance, a constantly expressive device in the music of the Romantics, further tended to remove the syntax from its triadic source. Tonality based upon the triad had evolved to the point where it was ready to burst its seams. The twentieth century witnessed the next logical stage in the gradual evolution of tonal interrelationships. New paths were set to find new "systems" for achieving tonal unity within a composition.

To the layman, the most characteristic and obvious feature of these new relationships manifested in the music of our time is the high degree of dissonance. This phenomenon is present in traditional counterpoint and harmony. But in the music of the past, dissonance, always an important expressive device, is subservient to consonance out of which it arises or towards which it flows. Dissonantal tensions are succeeded by points of consonantal repose. In its evolution the vertical aspect of music, i.e., the chord, contained more and more dissonance until in the twentieth century, having lost its function in relationship to consonance, the dissonant chord, sometimes of a very complex nature, became the basis of a new musical vocabulary. The breakaway from triadic tonality and the "emancipation" from consonance resulted in the use of dissonance as a norm, the composer choosing his combinations on the basis of his a priori set of determinants derived from his own "rules" of musical syntax.

Transition.—The expressive dissonances of the Wagnerian aesthetic were pushed to the outer limits of the tonal world of tradition by Richard Strauss,

Bruckner, Mahler and Reger. Arnold Schönberg followed in their footsteps, as shown by his youthful *Verklärte Nacht* (Transfigured Night, 1899). During the next decade he continued to move into the dissonantal area until he had gone beyond the pale of tonality. Thus did Schönberg discover the world of *atonality*, or, as he preferred to call it, *pantonality*. During the succeeding years Schönberg sought to attain a new means of musical organization that would endow his world of dissonance and non-tonality with coherence and structural unity. This resulted eventually in the *twelve-tone system.*

The change from the old to the new is nowhere seen with greater clarity than in the monumental ballet scores of Igor Stravinsky: *L' Oiseau de Feu* (The Fire-bird, 1910), *Petrouchka* (1911), and *Le Sacre du Printemps* (The Rite of Spring, 1913). The first of these three scores, brilliantly orchestrated, full of pulsating and exciting rhythms and abounding in the most exotic colors, reveals Stravinsky's indebtedness to his immediate nineteenth-century background, particularly his teacher, Rimsky-Korsakov. The traditional aspects of tonality, both in melodic and harmonic constructions, are crystal-clear. The second ballet score still leans heavily on traditional elements, but contains more dissonance, creating shimmering vertical sonorities that sometimes distend the tonal language and occasionally touch on polytonality through the superimposition of triads. The last ballet completes the bridge to a non-triadic sonority in which dissonances are combined and projected in a percussive manner that overwhelmed the ears of its first audience. Since then Stravinsky has moved through a number of different styles, even embracing in his latest phase the techniques of serialism and the twelve-tone system.

Béla Bartók likewise reveals his solid roots in tradition out of which his new style emerged. His early works, most noteworthy of which are the *First String Quartet* (1908) and the one-act opera, *Duke Bluebeard's Castle* (1911), are cast on the one hand in the chromatic post-romantic style, while in the latter work taking on some impressionistic qualities. Many of his earlier works are involved in the cultivation of his native Hungarian folk music in a direct popular style. In the *Allegro barbaro* for piano (1911) he already demonstrates the primitivistic, percussive language that was to constitute a primary value in his later music. By the *Second String Quartet* (1917) the influences of romanticism and impressionism had been completely absorbed into his new style. The tonal center was still apparent but no longer based on the traditional scheme. Most characteristic was the absorption of Hungarian folk elements, the rich variety of which were known intimately to Bartók. During the next ten years he pursued a consistent path into areas of greater dissonance, tonal ambiguity, and for a while, non-tonality.

While the transitional aspects of the three outstanding composers of the twentieth century are outlined above, by no means does this summarize the tendencies and changes in musical syntax that have taken place. Experiments with new orders of sounds have not necessarily been developed by composers into complete systems. Thus many have made use of the concept *polytonality,* the simultaneous existence of two or more keys. Stravinsky's *Petrouchka* already reveals the use of this device. Darius Milhaud, the French composer, has employed it extensively. Two or more concurrent key structures, however, result in dissonance in which the independence of the individual keys no longer appears valid to the ear.

The abandonment of the major-minor orders has led at various times to new orders without negating tonality. Composers have worked with various *modes* which were in existence in polyphonic music before the seventeenth century and which characterize the folk music of many lands. There are many examples, such as the uses of English background made by Vaughan Williams, or the neo-Judaic, non-Western expressions of the Swiss-American, Ernest Bloch (e.g., *Schelomo,* for 'cello and orchestra). The unusual melodic formations in much of Bartók's music spring from the ethnic sources of Hungarian, Rumanian, and Bulgarian song.

The attempts to find new sounds have resulted in a number of experimental tendencies that have not become part of the mainstream of musical change. In the realistic tendencies of the third decade of the century, an urbane, machine expression resulted in such works as Honegger's *Pacific 231* (1924), which is a musical abstraction of the journey of a locomotive, Mossolov's *Iron Foundry* (1927), and George Antheil's *Ballet Mécanique* (1927). New sounds are conceived in completely non-traditional terms. Percussive sonorities of new dimensions are intertwined with the sounds of orchestral instruments. Alois Hába (1893-   ), the Slovakian composer, first wrote extensive pieces (as early as 1919) using the quarter-tone, thus dividing into two equal parts each step in the twelve steps of the chromatic scale, thus doubling the number of available tones within the octave. Others followed in this path that attempts to parallel the musical sounds of the Far East, even reaching into the smaller divisions of the individual steps. These mutations, however, have failed to find a continuous line of development.

Edgar Varèse (1885-   ), one of the most original creative minds of our time, rejected tradition completely and concentrated purely on sonority and rhythm. These unfold in a series of cell-like projections, the geometric nature of which has suggested to some a comparison to cubist painting. Emphasis is placed on unusual combinations of instruments, especially involving the percussion. His best-known work, *Ionization* (1931), is scored for thirty-five different instruments of percussion and friction.

Varèse's experiments with sound anticipated by many years the advent of *electronic music* which, beginning around 1950, has made rapid strides in Europe and the United States. Essentially, electronic music involves techniques of conceiving and producing sounds electronically. It offers the composer the freedom of selection of all pitch levels through the control of frequency, the absolute control of dynamics, and an infinite variety of rhythmic patterns no longer conditioned by the severe limitations of conventional musical notation. By producing sounds first on electronic tape and then varying the speeds of the same tape, sounds can be won that are completely new to the human ear. Further, multiple sound tracks can be made through the superimposition of any number of sound tracks. The experiments in France (Pierre Boulez, Pierre Schaeffer, and Olivier Messiaen) and Germany (Herbert Eimert and Karlheinz Stockhausen) were paralleled and extended in America, principally centered at Columbia and Princeton Universities' jointly operated Electronic Music Center. Here such composers as Milton Babbitt, Otto Luening, and Vladimir Ussachevsky have made further explorations through the use of the complex RCA Synthesizer. The possibilities in the use of electronic tape are limitless. The expressive objectivity is convincing, for the composer, in eliminating the performer, is able to communicate to the listener the exact nature of his musical ideas. The avant-garde composers consider electronic music the music of the future.

1. The New Aesthetics

The romantic outlook of the nineteenth century could not survive under the impetus of the changing society of the twentieth century and the new aesthetic outlooks that developed as its expression. True, it survived for a while in the post-Wagnerian symphonic epics of Mahler and in the operatic pathos of Richard Strauss, posing the outer limits to which this style could move. Composers reacted violently against the romantic attitudes which were characterized in part by excessive outward emotionalism, redundancy, and extreme length. The French particularly took a dim view of the state of affairs posed by this Austro-Germanic nineteenth-century style. Out of this reaction was born *Impressionism.*

Impressionism.—The new viewpoints in the paintings of Claude Monet and his followers, paralleled in poetry by the symbolists, Mallarmé, Verlaine, and Rimbaud, found their counterpart in music principally in the compositions of Claude Debussy (1862-1918). The term *impressionism* originates in painting but is validly applied to the aesthetic principles in Debussy's works in that they emphasize sonorous color, have a sensuous quality that seeks to entertain the ear (rather than the eye) with considerable plasticity of formal elements and with an abundance of constantly changing harmonic, rhythmic, and melodic color. The programmatic allusions given through the titles of his compositions are suggestive and atmospheric, rather than an expression of personal inner feeling or realistic representation, e.g., his best-known orchestral work, *Prélude à L'Après-midi d'un Faune* (Prelude to the Afternoon of a Faun, 1894), based on Mallarmé's poem. The delicacy of his orchestral palette, in which splashes of sound replace those of color, is further demonstrated by his three major works for orchestra: *Nocturnes* (1899), *La Mer* (The Sea, 1905) and *Images* (1909). Debussy's piano pieces are monuments in keyboard literature and establish him in a position analogous to that of Chopin in the nineteenth century. The two books of *Préludes* (1910-1913), twelve in each, and the *Études* (1915), dedicated to the memory of Chopin, are models of the exquisite mastery of a style in which the resources of the keyboard are exploited in a new and unique manner. Sonorities of the extreme ranges are blended, and a true pianistic style engulfs the impressionistic sound-world, the evocation of which is aided by such suggestive titles as *Voiles* (Veils), *La Fille aux Cheveux de Lin* (The Girl with the Flaxen Hair), *Des Pas sur la Neige* (Footprints in the Snow). The opera, *Pelléas et Mélisande* (1902), based on the symbolist Maeterlinck's play, is a long excursion of mood and atmosphere in which the traditional elements of opera are discarded to create a lyric drama with muted orchestral sounds providing the framework for the unfolding of a freely, almost continuously moving recitative.

In all of his works Debussy adheres faithfully to the established principles of tonality. He imbued them, however, with a new richness of harmonic, vertical color through the subtle extension of the combination of dissonances and consonances. The color of the chord became an end in itself. Debussy realized the limitations of his style, and near the end of his life turned towards abstract forms, achieving superb results in his three chamber sonatas. Likewise, while many tried to imitate Debussy, the aesthetic viewpoint has managed to survive only in works of minor importance or commercial orientation, and has become the stock stylistic requirement in background music for films. Mention should be made, nevertheless, of the English composer, Frederick Delius(1862-1934), the Italian Ottorino Respighi (1879-1936), and the American Charles Griffes (1884-1920).

Maurice Ravel (1875-1937), the leading disciple of Debussy, developed a style that is more reserved, artificial, and polished. In his orchestral compositions, such as the early impressionistic *Daphnis et Chloé* ballet (1912), he reveals a dazzling virtuosity in orchestration; in his piano pieces he demonstrates a Lisztian brilliance, as in *Gaspard de la Nuit* (1908). The chamber music and piano concerti are models of classical outlook cast within a clear sense of tonality expanded within the framework of impressionistic harmonic technique.

Primitivism.—The refined facets of impressionistic style resulted in a counter-reaction manifested directly and overwhelmingly through the use of percussive rhythm, particularly of massed dissonantal chords. Much use was made of ostinato rhythms and constantly changing assymmetrical rhythmic formations, frequently supporting elemental folk material that did not spring from the central European tradition. The monumental examples of this powerful and sometimes relentless expression are the already mentioned Bartók's *Allegro barbaro* (1911) and Stravinsky's *Le Sacre du Printemps* (1913). The latter work is aided in this task by the relegation of the entire string section of the orchestra to a purely percussive function. Primitivism was another important step in the emancipation of rhythm from its metrically regular and periodic organization. The bar-line, once the symbol of regular accent, now frequently served only as a convenient aid to the eye of the performer.

Expressionism.—Expressionism was the German counterpart to French Impressionism. In post-Wagnerian ultra-chromaticism Arnold Schönberg (1874-1951) found the means of intensity necessary to express the deepest inner feelings. Thus he pursued in music the same drives found in the paintings of Wassily Kandinsky and Paul Klee, and the poetry of Richard Dehmel and Stefan George. The subconscious, the center of attention in the new psychoanalytic concepts of his Viennese contemporary, Sigmund Freud, became the springboard for fantasy and distortional representation on the canvas and in words. Beauty became synonymous with inner intensity. Expressionism may be viewed as a reaction against Romanticism by its conscious movement away from the *outer* manifestation of feeling to the search for inner meaning. *Atonality,* i.e., the non-existence of a tonal center, became Schönberg's musical rhetoric for this expression. The transitional period from the Wagnerian influences was already preoccupied with this point of view, especially in the settings of Stefan George texts: *Das Buch der hängenden Gärten* (The Book of Hanging Gardens, 1908) and *Pierrot Lunaire* (Pierrot of the Moon, 1912). These and other texts of the period concern themselves with intensely emotional, symbolic, and sometimes bizarre subject matter, musically projected by extreme dissonance, free rhythms, and melodic lines that are severely angular. In *Pierrot Lunaire* he employs a type of declamation that lies between speech and song. Alban Berg (1885-1935) continued the expressionism of his teacher, Schönberg, in his two monumental operas, *Wozzeck* (1925) and *Lulu* (1935). Since then expressionistic tendencies have been found among many composers just as they are prevalent in literature and art.

Neo-Classicism.—The cultivation of a point of view that was diametrically opposed to the excesses of form, structural looseness, and sentimentality of late romantic music resulted in the reformulation of the principles of order. In directing their attention to the classical ideal composers once more sought to recapture the Apollonian ethos of order and structure such as was achieved by Haydn, Mozart, and Beethoven. Since the first World War many composers have been won over by this point of view that knows no one school or country. Interestingly, the first significant paths towards it were the result of a reaction against the impressionistic style of Debussy by his colleague, Eric Satie (1866-1925). He rejected the sonorous opulence of the Debussyan aesthetic and turned instead to simplicity, unpretentiousness, and directness that was unhampered by any sentimentality. His sparse orchestrations with finely wrought melodic lines absorbed some of the Parisian music-hall characteristics, revealing works of urbane wit and sophistication. In the decade before the war he wrote pieces with such peculiar titles as *Trois Pièces en Forme de Poire* (Three Pieces in the Form of a Pear, 1903), or *Embryons Desséchés* (Dried-Up Embryos, 1913), which, in their economy and highly controlled discipline, foreshadowed subsequent currents more than twenty-five years later. Satie was the inspiration of a group of French composers known as *Les Six,* the most important of whom were Darius Milhaud (1892-   ), Arthur Honegger (1892-1955), and Francois Poulenc (1899-1963). They, too, eschewed emotionalism and cultivated a bright, sophisticated language reflecting Gallic wit. The prolixity of Milhaud is enormous and represents no single direction. Although the earlier works such as *La Création du Monde* (The Creation of the World, 1922) reflect the preoccupation with music-hall and jazz elements, many of his later works are concerned with more formal problems. Honegger, of Swiss-German background, turned directly toward symphony and chamber music, finding in these genres the purest molds for the objective language of the classicist. His five symphonies, particularly the *Fifth* (1951), are an important landmark in the history of French symponic writing. While Poulenc was France's outstanding lyricist, master of the art song, and successful composer of opera, he is to be considered essentially a composer of elegance and charm.

Igor Stravinsky (1882-   ) is the consummate classicist of our time. His three great ballets were followed by a series of compositions in which he rejected the large symphonic apparatus that had characterized the grandiose late romantic manner. *L'Histoire du Soldat* (The Soldier's Tale, 1918) is scored for seven instruments only. Other works of this period use small groups and chamber orchestras, the reduction in forces constituting his first step towards the new classical principle. In the ballet *Pulcinella* (1919), for which Picasso provided the scenery, he modeled his material on themes drawn from music ascribed to the early eighteenth-century composer, Giovanni Pergolesi. At times the music sounds as though it belongs to the past. Now and then Stravinsky cleverly departs from traditional sound, creating a new dimension that belongs to his own time. Traditional tonality based on the triad is fused with new dissonances and rhythmic innovations. This is a very specific neo-classical attitude— the blending of the old and the new. The Russian composer, Sergei Prokofiev, brilliantly achieved a tour de force in the *Classical Symphony* (1917) which mirrors the spirit of Haydn. Ernest Bloch reconstitutes the Baroque spirit in twentieth-century garb in his *Concerto Grosso* (1925). Stravinsky continued on this path, invoking Tchaikowsky in the ballet *Le Baiser de la Fée* (The Fairy's Kiss, 1922), Weber and Mendelssohn in *Capriccio* (1929). *Symphony in C* (1940) and the ballet, *Orpheus* (1948), spring from eighteenth-century sources. This technique of allusion to past styles was paralleled by a more vital acknowledgment of traditional values: the quest for abstract principles of structure and order. Stravinsky's major compositions exemplifying this aesthetic attitude are the *Octet for Wind Instruments* (1923), the opera-oratorio *Oedipus Rex* (1927), the *Symphony of Psalms* (1930) for chorus and orchestra, and the *Symphony in Three Movements* (1945). Since 1952, as we shall see later, he has pursued a new musical means to attain the same goals.

The German composer, Paul Hindemith (1895-1963), is another leading exponent of neo-classical principles. Imbued with a strong feeling for the historic past and its innermost values, much as was his forebear, Johannes Brahms, he turned to the contrapuntal, linear styles of J. S. Bach and his precursors as the springboard for his own compositions. In a vast output of music for many genres, chamber music emerges in primary position. His works are based on a clear-cut conception of tonality in which the triad retains a structural role, being achieved as points of repose after continuous linear motion in which the dissonantal combinations of varying tension are the by-products of horizontal activity. The collection of preludes and fugues for the piano entitled *Ludus Tonalis* (Tonal Play, 1943) embodies in purest form his mature style. The theoretical backgrounds of his systematically disciplined technique are set forth in his book *The Craft of Musical Composition* (1937). The serious, devoted student who pursues all the exercises with care will find himself writing in the style of Hindemith! His compositions, nevertheless, are not without expressive power, particularly those written for the lyric stage. Best known through the orchestral suite derived from it is the opera *Mathis der Maler* (Matthias the Painter, 1934), based on the life of the fifteenth-century painter, Matthias Grünewald.

Since Neo-classicism is essentially an attitude rather than a style, its spirit is almost universal, its advocates and practitioners many, while the various techniques and the resultant styles may be quite different. It is also not to be assumed that the sparse and carefully chiseled style of Stravinsky's middle years is *the* ideal. The expression of feeling can be a concomitant to the primary demands for order and musical structure. The intensification of emotional qualities does not lead necessarily to a romantic utterance. Thus many of the large symphonic compositions and the chamber music of such composers as the Russians Prokofiev and Shostakovitch, or the Americans Aaron Copland, Roger Sessions, Walter Piston, and Elliott Carter are classical in outlook.

2. *National and Ethnic Musical Expression*

The desire of composers to identify themselves with the roots of their native soil has played an important role in twentieth-century music. Differentiation must be made between the conscious employment of national subject matter or folk music in quotation or paraphrase and the more artistically sophisticated utilization of folk ingredients as the source from which musical expression springs.

Béla Bartók (1881-1945) was without question the most accomplished composer of our time in the use of ethnic material. In his early days he toured the hinterlands of his native Hungary, as well as those of neighboring countries, recording and examining a vast variety of folk songs. His subsequent studies and publications of his work are regarded as classics in the field of ethno-musicology. It is from this rich harvest that his music springs, not in quotation or imitation but rather through the absorption of unusual non-major and non-minor formations, rich melodic patterns and rhythmic nuances foreign to Western art music. The obvious nature of these characteristics is metamorphosed in his compositions. His works are powerful, intense, and sometimes austere. Dissonances are frequently used with savagery. Tonality, as in his folk sources, is almost always present, although the complexity of his style often makes its perception most difficult. He is a master of his craft, and each composition fulfills the requirements of order and coherence in its own unique way. The six volumes of the piano collection, *Mikrokosmos* (1926-1937), proceed systematically from the simplest style to the very complex. In it are the essential principles of his musical language. The six string quartets (1910-1939) reveal different stages in his development and stand as monuments in the history of that genre. The *Music for Strings, Percussion, and Celesta* (1936) reveals the masterliness of his craftsmanship (the first movement is an ingeniously constructed fugue), the beautiful control of unusual sonorities, and the constant employment of melodic activity that is derived from its ethnic source. In his last works written in America Bartók moved away from complexity, thereby making his works much more accessible, particularly so in the *Concerto for Orchestra* (1943) and the *Third Piano Concerto* (1945).

England has enjoyed a renascence in major musical composition after having endured a dry spell for almost two hundred years. In the forefront of this revival was Ralph Vaughan Williams (1872-1958), whose great interest in folk song as reflected by his compositions established him as virtually *the* national composer. He caught the spirit of the English folk tradition not only in its non-chromatic melodic lines but also in its modal settings. In his symphonies he is a landscape painter; in his songs and operas he draws on English folklore and background. Benjamin Britten (1913-   ), England's leading composer today, shows his great interest in English subject matter particularly in the selection of locale of most of his operas (e.g., *Peter Grimes*, 1945), projecting vivid canvases of English life.

Ernest Bloch (1880-1959) successfully assimilated the melodic inflections of Judaic cantillation and traditional song without reconstructing it. *Schelomo* (Solomon, 1916), for 'cello and orchestra, is one of the most widely known of his many works in this vein. Manuel de Falla (1876-1946) expressed Spanish nationalism at its best, though his style was more obvious in the imitation of melodies and formulae and the use of characteristic Spanish rhythms.

Russian music has its problems. The ideology of the Soviet Union dictates artistic creativity within the framework of *socialist realism.* The work of the Soviet artist must be intended for the masses. Formalism and esoteric structures, such as are frequently involved in twelve-tone music, belong to decadent Western bourgeois culture. Thus Igor Stravinsky, an expatriate since the Revolution, has never been accepted in Russia *except* for the three great early ballets which are Russian in character. Sergei Prokofiev (1891-1953), who voluntarily returned to the Soviet Union in 1934 after an absence of sixteen years, scored his greatest success in film music (from which suites have been derived) and programmatic music. Noteworthy are *Lieutenant Kije* (1934), *Peter and the Wolf* (1936), and *Alexander Nevsky* (1938). Many of his works are neo-classical in nature, and his penchant for "pure" music earned him the condemnation of the Central Committee of the Communist Party in 1948. Dmitri Shostakovitch (1906-   ) has had similar difficulties. Much composition in the Soviet Union is devoted to the setting of texts that are nationalistic. During the past decade much interest and investigation has centered on the rich folk materials of the more remote and varied ethnic groups that constitute the vast USSR. Ultimately they may have a considerable effect on serious art music as has already been demonstrated in the case of Aram Khatchaturian (1903-   ), the Georgian composer.

In the United States the development of jazz as an indigenous musical expression occupies an important place. It has received serious attention and study as a social and artistic phenomenon. It pervaded the serious art forms and influenced European composers such as Stravinsky, Milhaud, and Prokofiev, among many others. The first successful bridge from the popular to the art forms was accomplished by a composer whose career began in jazz, George Gershwin

(1898-1937). The American folk-opera, *Porgy and Bess* (1935), is his greatest work. The United States continued to win its independence from the domination of central Europe through the creation of fresh scores that captured the American spirit. The New Englander, Charles Ives (1874-1954), whose energies were devoted to building a most successful insurance agency during the day and to musical composition during the night, is a good case in point. In the first decade of the century he foreshadowed some of the harmonic and rhythmic complexities of the second decade. In his highly original music he called upon the traditions and values of his native New England, capturing the transcendental qualities of his literary forebears, Hawthorne, Emerson, and Thoreau. Hymn tunes and popular songs provide the occasional anchor. The orchestral *Three Pieces in New England* (1911) and the piano composition *Sonata No. 2, Concord, Mass., 1840-1860* (1915) reflect characteristically this spirit.

Aaron Copland (1900-), sometimes referred to as the "Dean of American Composers," has richly explored the American landscape in many ways and in a number of compositions, particularly in his ballet music, *Billy the Kid* (1938), *Rodeo* (1942), and *Appalachian Spring* (1944). In his abstract chamber music and symphonies he retains the same vitality and exuberance. Except for those of his earlier years and some of his more recent output, Copland's compositions, though abounding in dissonance and unique harmonic combinations, are clear in their tonal organization, thus affording ease in communicating with the wide audiences to which much of this music has been addressed and from which he has won enthusiastic response. The uniformity of his style is noteworthy; many aspects prevail in his abstract compositions as well.

Latin America has provided fertile soil for its own nationalistic music, particularly through the use of indigenous melodic and rhythmic patterns that were untouched and unexplored until recent years. Outstanding among the many are the Mexican Carlos Chavez (1899-), the Brazilian Heitor Villa-Lobos (1887-1959), and the Argentinian Alberto Ginestra (1916-).

3. Dodecaphony

Dodecaphony (*Dodeka*, 12), or twelve-tone music, first formulated by Arnold Schönberg, has had a host of followers and has established itself as the most unified form of musical syntax since the departure from the major-minor tonality of tradition. Arnold Schönberg did not consciously "invent" it. Rather, he came upon it empirically through his consistently directed expansion of the post-Wagnerian chromatic impulse which nurtured his earliest years of creativity. By 1923 he had achieved a type of music in which the twelve different tones that comprise the chromatic scale take on a new type of relationship representing the ultimate in constant variation. A *specific* order or series of the twelve tones, selected by the composer, subdivided into groups or *sets,* becomes the basis for the coherence and structural unity of the entire composition. The traditional considerations of melody and harmony in terms of functional relationships to a single tone do not apply. The complexity of the structure is furthered by the use of the chosen series of tones and its subdivisional sets in various ways: inversion, retrograde, retrograde of the inversion, and transposition on different levels. The innovations of Schönberg were subsequently further developed by him and were brought to a high degree of invention, as in the *Violin Concerto* (1936) and the *Fourth String Quartet* (1937).

Schönberg's great disciples were Alban Berg (1885-1935) and Anton Webern (1883-1945), both of them intimately associated with the master during the important years of artistic struggle in Vienna. Berg brought to the Schönbergian doctrine a personal warmth of expression which he was able to communicate with consummate skill and great success, particularly in the quartet, the *Lyric Suite* (1926), and in his two masterpieces of opera, *Wozzeck* and *Lulu*, the latter remaining unfinished at the time of his death. *Wozzeck*, already mentioned as a great example of expressionistic composition, is a model of order. The composer is always conscious of structure and form, each scene being constructed in a traditional form such as fugue, sonata-allegro, or theme and variations. While this opera, as is also the case with *Lulu*, does not adhere to the *strict* procedures of the twelve-tone system, it is ordered on the same principles, even extending them to sections that are tonal.

Webern's music is radically different in style. He compressed the twelve-tone system into its most compact and economical utterances. Not one of the *Five Pieces for Orchestra* (1913), an early atonal pre-twelve-tone composition, lasts for more than one minute! This concise, terse expressive style prevails in his later works as well. There are no thematic repetitions. Each tone assumes a preciousness in function. He used instrumental color as an intimate protagonist of his style so that the succession of melodic activity, moving rapidly from one color or instrument to another creates a unique effect that has been described by a term borrowed from painting: "pointillism." The economy of his ideas, as well as the strict and severe discipline of his procedure explains the fact that his complete works have been recorded on four long-playing records. It was not until after his death that Webern emerged as the purest of the dodecaphonic composers, with the result that his music has had in recent years considerable influence on musical thought and expression.

The most illustrious follower of the dodecaphonic "school" is Igor Stravinsky, who, after he had attained the age of seventy, increasingly cultivated the procedures of Schönberg and Webern, enriching them with his consistent style of melodic and rhythmic invention. Those who see in the twelve-tone system a convincing means for the projection of the formal abstraction of musical expression point out that this latest phase of Stravinsky's creative life is the logical consequence of his pursuit of the classical ideal. Notable among recent compositions are the ballet *Agon* (1957) and *Threni-id est Lamentationes Jeremiae Prophetae* (Threnodies-Lamentations of the Prophet Jeremiah, 1958). Of the many composers working in this system mention must be made of Luigi Dallapiccola (1904-   ), whose Italianate sensitivity has effected a reconciliation of his native land's tradition of vocal lyricism with the formal constructivism of twelve-tone music. His instrumental and vocal compositions, especially his operas, express eloquently the lyrical passion that is possible within this system.

Many composers have followed the path of twelve-tone music without adhering to the system. Rather it is the *serial* procedure that is their underlying principle, and from which Schönberg evolved his system. The implications of the Schönbergian doctrine extend considerably beyond his devoted followers and provide a large common denominator for much of the art music of our time. Nevertheless, adherence to its principles does not guarantee good composition, just as music of all qualities was produced within the major-minor system. Furthermore, completely different styles within this system have emerged, even to the extent of being able to operate within tonality, e.g., Berg's *Violin Concerto* (1935). The possibilities of melodic, rhythmic, and chordal invention are infinite. Within its orbit distinctive paths may continue to emerge and develop.

4. *Music and Social Values*

The Theater.—Since the abstract nature of music precludes the expression of non-musical ideas, composers must rely upon its relationship to other media such as the word and the stage for such representation. Twentieth-century opera has been in the forefront of this aspect of communication, and has developed its own unique means of attempting to achieve this goal. Opera, nevertheless, has retained traditional values more than any other genre for, in the relationship of voice and orchestra, the composer has been faced with the same problems; the solutions are different. Never before has the composer been more conscious of *drama per musica*—drama *through* music.

The contemporary social scene and its problems have been projected at times with power and conviction. *Mahagonny* (Kurt Weill, 1927) satirizes American life; the *Three-Penny Opera* (Kurt Weill, 1928), based on John Gay's *Beggar's Opera* of the early eighteenth century, penetratingly portrays the evils of postwar Berlin. Both operas, with original German libretti by the playwright Berthold Brecht, employ the jazz idiom. The same composer's first venture in America was the brilliant anti-war semi-opera, *Johnny Johnson* (1935). Opera assumes the functions of social propaganda in some of the works of the American, Marc Blitzstein (1905-1964). *The Cradle Will Rock* (1936), a product of the depression era, expresses the protest of the working class against the iniquities of capitalism. In his most elaborate work, *Regina* (1949), based on Lillian Hellman's *The Little Foxes,* Blitzstein succeeded in portraying personal evils symbolic of social immorality. Both Weill and Blitzstein have brought about a reconciliation of popular musical styles with serious opera.

The human condition has been the favorite object of operatic representation. The contemporary composer has sought to express the innermost emotions, frequently exploring the psychological nature of man. Berg's *Wozzeck* is the great model of the representation of man's helplessness, anguish, and torture at the hand of his fellow man. His other masterpiece, *Lulu,* is a penetrating psychological study of the forces of sex in conflict with the structure of society. The twelve-tone technique also provided the Italian lyricist, Luigi Dallapiccola, with the musical modus operandi for the depiction of suffering in *Il Prigionere* (The Prisoner, 1948) and in the biblical drama, *Job* (1950). Britten's *The Turn of the Screw* (1954) and Douglas Moore's *Wings of the Dove* (1961) are based on the imaginative works of Henry James. The Italo-American composer, Gian-Carlo Menotti (1911-   ), gaining much popularity through his adherence to Italian operatic traditions and conventions and an accessible tonal style, likewise has dealt with such subjects as spiritualism (*The Medium,* 1946), human suffering in totalitarian society and the inhumanity of bureaucracy (*The Consul,* 1950), and religious mysticism (*The Saint of Bleecker Street,* 1954). Menotti is a master craftsman whose keen sense of what is theatrically effective is manifested in his fusion of the musical, textual, and dramatic functions as composer, librettist, and director.

National background and color are important settings, especially for the English and Americans. Mention already has been made of Britten and Gershwin, the latter's *Porgy and Bess* capturing with striking poignancy and artistic truth the atmosphere and emotions of a Southern Negro locale. Douglas Moore (1893-   ) writes of the historical past of New England (*The Devil and Daniel Webster,* 1938) and of the silver mines of the Far West (*The Ballad of Baby Doe,* 1956).

Certainly there has been strong involvement with the principles of the theater in its highest sense, and composers have sought libretti derived from dramas of high quality and meaning by important literary figures such as Tolstoy (Prokofiev), Wedekind (Berg), Strindberg, Yeats, and Pirandello (the American, Hugo Weisgall), and Arthur Miller (the American, Robert Ward). The great variety of subject matter enables the composer to choose the type of libretto that satisfies his aesthetic point of view, that permits him to express his non-musical ideas, and that is conducive to his musical style. Never before has there been such richness, diversity, and freedom from stereotyped form and procedure in operatic expression.

Communications Media.—The technical developments of radio, phonograph, and television transmission have extended the communication of the composer beyond the concert hall. Film music has enjoyed a new and forceful role. From its beginnings as an art medium in Germany in the 1920's (the film scores of Karol Rathaus) to the most recent productions in Hollywood, many of the leading composers have participated. Most films, however, have been infused with nineteenth-century romantic excesses or impressionistic background of poor quality rather than artistic inventiveness. The introduction of the long-playing record has led to the expansion of recorded literature that richly extends from the Middle Ages to the present day. Musicological research of the past decades has resulted in the rebirth of the music of the historical past. The role of the contemporary composer is placed within the framework of total historical development. He must overcome the forces of tradition without impairing its validity. The task is a difficult one.

The composer is severely handicapped by the great distance between him and his audience as he struggles to find performances for his music. European government-operated radio stations and orchestras and municipally supported opera houses encourage these performances. In the United States the commercial emphasis on communications media has limited the promotion of art music of all eras, let alone the music of our own time. In recent years special private funds and foundations have encouraged creative activity and provided performances for new works.

5. Conclusion

Europe no longer is the center of musical art. In the 1920's music in the United States began to develop its own independence and stature in such composers as Copland, Sessions, and Thomson. The rise of Hitler resulted in a movement of Europe's leading composers to the United States, including Bartók, Hindemith, Milhaud, Schönberg, and Stravinsky. The development of musical education and the acceptance of music as a humanistic discipline in the university strengthened the strong creative activity which has made the United States the new center of musical culture. Although its society has not as yet reconciled successfully its aesthetic and materialistic values, the future is a bright one.

The composer is conscious of his role as an intellect in modern society. He teaches in universities; he lectures extensively; he writes for journals of opinion, newspapers, and scholarly periodicals; he writes books which explore the nature and meaning of music and the role of the composer. The writings of Copland, Hindemith, Sessions, Schönberg, and Stravinsky have received wide circulation. There are many others as well whose works reflect serious attention to the problems of music, both past and present.

The universality of Stravinsky, the genius and artistic integrity of Bartók, the intellectual originality of Schönberg—these are the most important mainstreams in the music of our time. There are many tributaries, confluences, and independent currents. There are many composers of great gifts whose names were not mentioned in this brief survey. Surely some of them will take their places of importance in the future developments of musical art in our ever-changing society.

SELECTED READINGS

Abraham, Gerald, *This Modern Music,* Norton, 1952.
Aldridge, J. W., *After the Lost Generation,* Noonday Press, 1958.
Barr, A. H., *Masters of Modern Art,* Museum of Modern Art, 1954.
Baur, J. I. H., *New Art in America,* New York Graphic Society–Praeger, 1957.
Beach, J. W., *The Twentieth Century Novel,* Century, 1933.
Bentley, Eric, *The Playwright as Thinker,* Meridian Books, 1960.
Bermel, Albert, ed., *The Genius of the French Theater,* New American Library, 1961.
Brée, Germaine, and Guiton, Margaret, *An Age of Fiction: The French Novel from Gide to Camus,* Rutgers University Press, 1957.
Brenan, Gerald, *The Literature of the Spanish People,* Meridian Books, 1957.

Brereton, Geoffrey, *An Introduction to the French Poets, Villon to the Present Day*, Essential Books, 1957.

Cazamian, Louis, *A History of French Literature*, Clarendon Press, 1955.

Chase, Gilbert, *America's Music from the Pilgrims to the Present*, McGraw-Hill, 1955.

"Contemporary American Poetry," *The American Scholar*, Summer, 1959.

Copland, Aaron, *Music and Imagination*, Harvard University Press, 1952.

——— *Our New Music*, Whittlesey House, 1941.

Cowley, Malcolm, *The Literary Situation*, Compass Books, 1958.

Daiches, David, *The Present Age in British Literature*, Indiana University Press, 1958.

Debussy, Claude; Busoni, Ferrucio; and Ives, Charles, *Three Classics in the Aesthetic of Music*, Dover Publications, Inc., 1962.

Deutsch, Babette, and Yarmolinsky, Avram, eds. and trans., *Russian Poetry*, International, 1927.

Giedion, Siegfried, *Space, Time and Architecture*, Harvard University Press, 1954.

Giedion-Welcker, Carola, *Contemporary Sculpture*, Wittenborn, 1961.

Goldwater, R. J., *Primitivism in Modern Painting*, Harper, 1938.

Hamlin, T. F., *Forms and Functions in Twentieth Century Architecture*, 4 vols., Columbia University Press, 1952.

Hindemith, Paul, *A Composer's World*, Harvard University Press, 1952.

Howarth, Herbert, *The Irish Writers, 1880-1940*, Hill and Wang, 1958.

Hunter, Sam, *Modern French Painting*, Dell, 1956.

Jones, D. E., *The Plays of T. S. Eliot*, Routledge and Kegan Paul, 1961.

Karl, F. R., and Magalaner, Marvin, *A Reader's Guide to Great Twentieth-Century English Novels*, Noonday Press, 1959.

Kazin, Alfred, *The Inmost Leaf*, Harcourt, Brace, 1955.

Krutch, J. W., *American Drama Since 1918*, Braziller, 1957.

Machlis, Joseph, *Introduction to Contemporary Music*, Norton, 1961.

McCollom, W. G., *Tragedy*, Macmillan, 1957.

Motherwell, Robert, ed., *Documents of Modern Art*, Wittenborn-Schultz, 1944 *et seq.*

Motherwell, Robert, and Reinhardt, Ad, *Modern Artists in America*, Wittenborn-Schultz, 1951.

Myers, B. S., *Mexican Painting in Our Time*, Oxford, 1956.

——— *The German Expressionists*, Praeger, 1957.

Nicholl, Allardyce, *World Drama*, Harcourt, Brace.

Pascal, Roy, *The German Novel*, Manchester University Press, 1956.

Perle, George, *Serial Composition and Atonality*, University of California Press, 1962.

Peters, H. F., *Rainer Maria Rilke*, University of Washington Press, 1961.

Peyre, Henri, *The Contemporary French Novel*, Oxford, 1955.

Priestley, J. B., *Literature and Western Man*, Harper, 1960.

Raynal, Maurice, *Modern Painting*, Skira, 1956.

Read, Herbert, *Form in Modern Poetry*, Sheed and Ward, 1932.

Reti, Rudolf, *Tonality, Atonality, Pantonality*, Macmillan, 1958.

Richards, J. M., *An Introduction to Modern Architecture*, Penguin, 1953.

Ritchie, A. C., *Sculpture of the Twentieth Century*, Museum of Modern Art, 1952.

Rosenblum, Robert, *Cubism and Twentieth-Century Art*, Abrams, 1961.

Salazar, Adolfo, *Music in Our Time*, Norton, 1946.

Schönberg, Arnold, *Style and Idea*, Philosophical Library, 1950.

Schorer, Mark, *Sinclair Lewis: An American Life,* McGraw-Hill, 1961.

Selz, P. H., *German Expressionist Painting,* University of California Press, 1957.

Sessions, Roger, *The Musical Experience of Composer, Performer, Listener,* Princeton University Press, 1958.

Seuphor, Michel, *The Sculpture of This Century,* Braziller, 1961.

Shaw, G. B., *The Quintessence of Ibsenism,* Brentano, 1917.

Stansbury, M. H., *French Novelists of Today,* University of Pennsylvania Press, 1935.

Stravinsky, Igor, *Poetics of Music,* Harvard University Press, 1950.

Stravinsky, Igor, and Craft, Robert, *Conversations with Igor Stravinsky,* Doubleday, 1959.

—————— *Expositions and Developments,* Doubleday, 1962.

—————— *Memoirs and Commentaries,* Doubleday, 1960.

Struve, Gleb, *Soviet Russian Literature, 1917-1950,* University of Oklahoma Press, 1951.

Sweeney, J. J., *Plastic Redirections in Twentieth Century Painting,* University of Chicago Press, 1934.

Thorp, Willard, *American Writing in the Twentieth Century,* Harvard University Press, 1960.

Untermeyer, Louis, *Lives of the Poets,* Simon and Schuster, 1959.

Whittick, Arnold, *European Architecture in the Twentieth Century,* 3 vols., Lockwood, 1950 *et seq.*

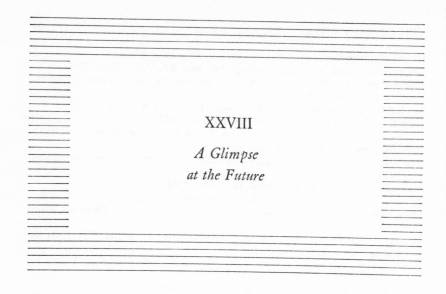

XXVIII

A Glimpse at the Future

I. ON ORIGINS AND DESTINIES

The Reverend Dr. Harold C. Phillips of Cleveland, speaking in Riverside Church, in New York City, declared that the present age is "strong on the origins and weak on the destinies of things."

Dr. Phillips is right. Uncertainty about the future is one of the penalties we have paid for getting enlightenment. Only a century ago we were very certain about both origins and destinies. The physical universe, the earth, and all forms of life thereon had been created some 4,000 years before Christ. Our primitive parents lived for a time in Paradise, then were expelled. Cain and Abel started the agricultural and pastoral industries, and Tubal-cain invented metal-making. At the Tower of Babel man acquired the power of speaking in different tongues and the various languages of the world arose. The sons of Noah founded the existing races of mankind.

The destiny of the race was almost as precise and clear-cut in the mental picture of olden days. At no distant date—perhaps A.D. 4000—witnesses of the end, Enoch and Elijah, would appear. These would be slain by the Antichrist. Whereupon, the devil would be cast into hell and chained for a thousand years. At the end of this millennium the devil would be loosed and would gather all the powers of evil to do battle against the hosts of the blessed. In this great final conflict—Armageddon—the devil and the wicked ones would be worsted. Then would come the awful day of judgment, the wicked would be cast into the lake of fire and brimstone and the saved would pass on to eternal bliss. The old earth and heavens would give way before the New Jerusalem in all its matchless splendor and permanence.

This old picture of the drama of man crumbled with the rise of modern science.

1310

Astrophysics, geology, biology, anthropology, and biblical criticism wiped away the old views of an earth-centered universe, a special creation, and biblical legends. Biblical scholarship and cultural history indicated the way in which early and unlettered peoples had gradually contrived the traditional notions of the soul, immortality, heaven, and hell—notions which had sifted down through India and Persia to the later Jews and to the Christians. Likewise, modern physiological chemistry and psychology have undermined the old belief in the soul and a literal immortality.

The results of modern scholarship have admittedly taught us more about origins than about destinies. The evolution of life has been explained. We know that man appeared more than a million years ago and gradually built his culture through the long Stone ages to the beginnings of civilization. Scientific historical writing has given us a reliable account of man's dramatic experiences since that time. There is no longer any reason why an ambitious man cannot inform himself as to "how we got this way."

It must be admitted, however, that we are by no means as clear about "where we go from here." We may rejoice that we no longer have to face the prospect of the old heaven and hell. But just where and how the race will end, no one can say.

The historian is, of course, primarily concerned with the past, but we have made it clear already that a knowledge of the past is of little consequence unless it explains the present. Further, a clear knowledge of the genesis of the present will avail little unless it enables us to peer with some assurance into at least the immediate future. If an informed historian cannot render a better than average intelligent verdict with respect to the proximate destiny of man, it may be reasonably said that he has made very unintelligent use of the facts at his command.

There is another consideration—a very important one. History can free us from the paralyzing influence of the "dead hand," as Herbert Spencer used to call the customs and superstitions of the past. We could boldly plan our own future. The sciences of life, man, and society now enable us, if we will, to build a human utopia on this earth. Where we go from here need no longer be a myth or legend. It is a challenge to human imagination and to social engineering. And it cannot be ignored. If we drift without planning, then indeed the human future will be a brief and tragic voyage on a stormy and uncharted sea.

II. CAN MAN BE CIVILIZED?

"Civilization," the dictionaries tell us, is "the state of being civilized." The definition is undoubtedly accurate but hardly enlightening. Even when we are further told that to be "civilized" is to be "in a state of civilization," our knowledge does not seem to be substantially increased. If we know that such a pathetic resort to semantic verbalism is itself a characteristic of the pre-civilized stage, we may infer that the makers of dictionaries are not civilized, but even this does not help us far along our road.

Nor do we gain much aid from older writers on the subject. What was formerly the accepted view was expressed over a century ago by François Guizot in his *His-*

tory of Civilization in Europe when he wrote, "Civilization . . . is an improved condition of man resulting from the establishment of social order in place of the individual independence and lawlessness of the savage or barbarous life." Anthropology has now proved that primitive society is not characterized by "lawlessness" but by rigid customs, and that the "individual independence" of the savage never existed outside of modern romantic dreams. As Robert Briffault says, "The human mind is from the first essentially a social product."

The old and sharp distinctions of savagery, barbarism, and civilization have broken down. Humanity has all along been busy at the same job, that of obtaining greater control over its environment and over itself. Tragically enough, the two parts of this task have rarely been mastered at the same time; the outer conquest may be accompanied by an inner defeat; and, as a matter of fact, most of our present-day difficulties arise from this situation. Nevertheless, the two aspects are clearly phases of a single problem. Man labors to control external nature in order to satisfy his own desires, but these desires, and the ways of gratifying them, are in turn modified by the new environment which he creates.

Civilization is simply the social ideal toward which men have always striven. It might be called the study of perfection, but this phrase would really be much too lofty, since the desired perfection is always relative to human needs and its outline changes from generation to generation. Certain elements, however, have remained the same. Men have always desired power over nature, many of them have always desired knowledge, and some of them have always desired that state of harmony with one's self and one's neighbor which we call goodness. Of the three, knowledge is evidently primary, not in the sense that it is the first to be desired but as the necessary foundation of the other two. There can be no steady mastery of nature and no effective goodness without a knowledge of the habits of both nature and man.

Thus the question, "can man be civilized?" resolves itself into two questions: Do we, or can we ever, know enough about nature and ourselves to ensure the preservation and progress of the human species? Can the available knowledge ever be so widely distributed that men, as a group, will guide their actions by it?

These questions concern society, not the individual. The individual's power over nature will always remain very limited, unless reinforced by that of his fellows, and, at the most, it can never, so far as we can see, secure his survival beyond a brief span of years. As individuals, we may live down a score of diseases and avoid all accidents, yet the worms get us in the end. Aside from the doubtful promises held out by certain religions, our only hope of survival—and this, at least, we are sure of—is through our influence upon our fellows. Hence those who feel a deep interest in immortality would do well to direct their thinking to this more generous end.

With the group, however, it is otherwise. Barring cosmic accidents which we have no reason to anticipate, man, among the puniest of animals physically, would seem to have secured by his mental ability an indefinite tenure of life upon this planet—so far, at least, as any threats of external nature are concerned. It is conceivable, of course, that some invasion of insects or bacteria will sweep us away, but, again, we have little reason to anticipate such a catastrophe. If man perishes, it will be because mankind has committed suicide through social incompetence, such as permitting a nuclear war of extermination to break out or carrying on such rash nuclear experiments as may blow up our planet. Such a result, or a relapse into a lower state comparable to it, is, if not exactly probable, still not entirely impossible. Should it occur, it will be not so much because of the failure of knowledge as because of the failure to apply the knowledge which we have. But that, too, looked at more subtly, might be considered a failure of knowledge —only, this time, a failure of knowledge, not of nature, but of ourselves.

III. THEORIES OF WHY CIVILIZATIONS PERISH

The number of so-called civilizations that have perished in the past is disquietingly large. In his much discussed work, *The Study of History*, Arnold J. Toynbee lists some twenty-one main human civilizations which have existed in the course of history. Fourteen of them have perished entirely, and six more are in their terminal period. Only Western civilization has a fighting chance to survive. Leaving out of account those nomadic tribes which subsisted by hunting and are usually considered pre-civilized, we have a long succession of vanished peoples each of which had a highly developed agriculture and commerce, a settled polity, an established social organization, peoples enduring for centuries, sometimes even for millenniums. They, too, had "conquered nature," if not as spectacularly as we, yet sufficiently for their purposes. The fundamental demands of food, clothing, and shelter had all been met. Adequate means of transportation had been found. The arts flourished. Why did these civilizations perish?

It may be, as Henry Adams suggested and Oswald Spengler maintained, that there is a limited amount of vital energy in every culture, so that each is destined by its own nature to pass into old age and death, but such analogies between the individual organism and the social group are unverifiable and exceedingly dangerous. Suggestive if taken for poetic fancies, they are misleading if accepted as established, or even establishable, facts.

Almost equally dubious is the popular view that civilized nations inevitably become "effete" through luxury and decline as a result of their own vices. Luxury, it is true, unfits men for living on a simpler scale. Thus during the crises on the stock exchange in 1929-1930 there were instances of millionaires who committed suicide when their assets were reduced to a paltry hundred thousand dollars. But luxury has never been widely enough distributed to corrupt an entire community.

More to the point is the view which sees in militarism the direct or indirect cause of the destruction of past civilizations. When a single nation, like Assyria or Persia or Rome, succeeds in dominating the scene, it is tempted by its military success to expand over a greater extent of territory than it can govern; when a group of nations, like the Greek states, develop at one time, its members are tempted into mutually destructive fratricidal wars. And always in militaristic civilizations—and all civilizations hitherto have been militaristic—there is a slow or sudden draining of the nation's best blood in warfare. When it is the strongest who perish, the weakest who survive, the decline of civilization is inevitable.

Warfare is the most striking instance of the failure of intelligence to master the problem of human relationships. The general causes of war are well known: economic rivalries, national jealousies, religious hatreds, the pressure of over-population, the influence of a military class, the influence of profiteers. Every one of these causes is preventable. War, the supreme, the tragic folly of mankind, is made possible by many minor follies.

Unfortunately, there seems to be little prospect of throwing off the military folly. At the close of the great "war to end war" (1914-1918), a peace treaty was made which rendered inevitable a second and more devastating world war. At its close, public intelligence was at an even lower ebb than in 1918-1919, and not even a bad general peace treaty could be negotiated. Less than two years after V-J Day, the world entered a "Cold War" of infinite duration, which was more costly financially than any previous "hot" war and also risked or invited a hot third world war which was likely to obliterate civilization, if it did not actually exterminate the human race.

There are other instances, almost equally striking, of the failure of social intelligence. One is the persistence of crime, which is, essentially, warfare among the members of a given community. Another is the persistence of poverty, utterly inexcusable today when machinery has made possible sufficient production to satisfy the needs of all. Another is the unnecessary amount of sexual misery and domestic maladjustment which persists only because of the continuance of unscientific and antiquated customs.[1]

The two most widely read and discussed accounts of the rise and fall of civilizations produced in this generation have been those presented by the German philosopher Oswald Spengler, in his *The Decline of the West* (1917, 1921), and by Arnold J. Toynbee in his massive twelve-volume work, *The Study of History* (1933-1961).[2] Spengler's work combined the cyclical theory of historical development, the organismic theory of society and social evolution, and the Romanticist idea of a culture-soul which dominates the traits and activities of any people. He held that each great historic culture passes through the inevitable life-stages of any organism: birth, youth, maturity, and old age. There have been six great historic cultures: the Egyptian, the Old Chinese, the Classical, the Indian (Hindu), the Arabian, and the Western. All except the last have now passed away, and even Western culture is in its terminal stage—that of "civilization"—and probably making way for the revival of a new culture in the Far East. Many informed and realistic critics regard Spengler's work as more of a contribution to historical poetry than to substantial social and institutional history.

Toynbee's work, which was not completed until 1961, is still widely read and debated. Not even the most severe critic has questioned the vast learning of the author, but his frame of reference and methodology are open to serious criticism.

1 H. E. Barnes, *Society in Transition*, Prentice-Hall, 1952

2 For a brief survey of the ideas of Spengler and Toynbee, see H. E. Barnes, *Historical Sociology*, pp. 103-12. For an appreciation of Toynbee, see Hans Kohn, in *Christian Register*, April, 1955, pp. 9-12. For critical evaluations, see Pieter Geyl, "Toynbee's System of Civilization," in *Journal of the History of Ideas*, 1948; in *Christian Register,* April, 1955, pp. 13-19; and *From Ranke to Toynbee*, Smith College Historical Studies, 1952; and H. E. Barnes *et al.*, *Introduction to the History of Sociology*, chap. xxxvii.

Toynbee holds that civilization arises as a result of the challenge of the physical environment to human effort. This environment must not be so austere as to discourage effort or so rich as not to require any extensive activity to survive. The rise of civilization is directed by a creative minority of leaders who command the respect and loyalty of the peoples. But, when civilization is established, the once creative minority loses its dynamic and unselfish nature and becomes a relatively lethargic and exploitative minority. Incompetent rule leads to internal tensions and civil wars and to disastrous foreign wars. To curb the latter, a world state is established but it proves ineffective. An external proletariat, made up of foreigners or "barbarians at the gate," force their way into the country and create added problems of race mixture and cultural confusion. These "times of troubles" produce ever-recurring periods of crisis and recovery, but as time goes on the crises become more serious and frequent and the recoveries more brief and temporary. Finally, the civilization collapses. Out of some twenty-one historic civilizations, Toynbee holds that only seven—the Orthodox Christian, the Orthodox Russian, the Islamic, the Hindu, the Chinese, the Korean-Japanese, and the Western—still survive. All except the Western are now in a hopeless terminal stage. Western civilization has a possible chance of survival if it can produce a great religious revival under Anglican auspices in time to check the powerful forces of decay.

Most students of the history of civilization do not take too seriously Toynbee's theory of the destiny of mankind, for it is obviously derived from his study of the rise and fall of the civilizations of Greece and Rome, about which Toynbee was professionally well informed. He then sought to impose this pattern upon all the civilizations which he studied. The actual evidence has not seemed to vindicate his contentions in this respect. Moreover, the book is as much a contribution to theology as to history. Joseph Hergesheimer brilliantly epitomized the outcome and significance of the work when he wrote that "Toynbee buries the universe in an Anglican churchyard."

IV. THE HUMAN QUEST FOR MASTERY

Man has all but conquered nature. Can he ever conquer himself? That is the question on which the preservation of civilization depends. Have we any reason to believe that we are today in a better position to give an affirmative answer to this question than were those peoples of the past whose failure to answer it meant their disappearance?

There is a popular misinterpretation of evolution which assumes that man's mental powers have greatly developed during the brief course of his history—brief, if estimated in terms of total biological time. The ordinary white man, if told that he is not mentally superior to an African head-hunter, would look upon the remark as something very like an insult. We are fond of imagining that even if brought up from infancy among head-hunters we would assert our mental endowments and live in a more Christian manner than other members of the tribe. As a matter of fact, there is little ground for such an assumption.

It would seem that man's neuro-psychic equipment has been much the same during the last fifty thousand years or more. In this period, his intrinsic powers of cerebration have probably hardly increased at all. The differences in thinking since the Aurignacian period of the Stone Age result not from an increase of innate capacity for thought but from the social inheritance and exploitation of knowledge, in other words, from advances in culture.

Every other animal but man begins, aside from occasional sports, exactly where his parents began. Man, primarily by means of language, and secondarily by his material creations, hands on some of his experience to his descendants. The son inherits his father's fields, but they would be of little use to him were he not taught what his father and others had learned concerning the means of cultivating them. Being so taught, and adding in turn the fruits of his own individual experience, even if he is intrinsically no better farmer than his father, he will yet have a more prosperous farm.

Primitive man's thinking is inadequate because it has so small an amount of social experience behind it. The number of facts open to his observation is very limited, and he has no scientific means of checking the observations that he makes; hence his generalizations are often utterly wild. He notes the strength of certain wild animals; he observes that when they lose their blood if wounded their strength departs; hence he reasons that the strength resides in the blood and that if he drinks it, or is even sprinkled with it, he will grow strong. Or, on a higher level, he assumes that the forces of nature on which he is dependent are personal beings like himself, to be swayed by favors and flattery. The assumption happens to be incorrect; but it is not intrinsically irrational. Often the events seem to confirm it. There is a drought; the appropriate incantations are made; and rain follows. Therefore, the incantation was the cause of the rain. Can we say that a Nebraska farmer would reason differently if the prayers for rain still offered in the churches should happen to meet with success? Why are the prayers still offered unless there is some faint lingering of the ancient hope?

Religion was man's first attempt to control his environment. The creation of imaginary supernatural beings behind natural phenomena was not, as might appear at first thought, a vain duplication of these phenomena: it reduced them to a system and seemed to make them indirectly amenable to human control. A vast amount of native shrewdness, as well as some higher qualities, went into man's traffic with the gods. Magic influenced primitive science, ritual was primitive art, mythology primitive philosophy. As much intellectual energy was spent in producing these systems as, later on, in the discoveries of modern science. But, being built on assumptions contrary to facts, they could have no effect in modifying the facts. For the latter, that is, for the conduct of his daily life, man more and more resorted to common sense which took natural objects for the mere natural objects that they seem to be. But the use of common sense, which seemed a lowly and vulgar thing, was left mainly to those too stupid to be able to follow the fine flights of religious fancy. Life and nature were supposed to be governed in principle by religion; common sense could manage the details.

Thus at the outset there was introduced into human thought a fatal dualism that has not yet been overcome. Human development, however, has brought with it a steady restriction of the realm of the supernatural. The gods have retreated as men advanced. This was inevitable, because the very function of the gods was to afford man an indirect control where otherwise he would have been entirely powerless. In proportion as he obtained secular power the gods became less essential. We may still pray for rain, because we have no control over the weather, but we do not pray as formerly for guidance in the planting of our crops, because we have no need for supernatural assistance in that field. Man's first grandiose attempt to control his environment through religion was a failure. Such control as he actually gained was won through the exercise of the despised quality of common sense. But it has taken him many centuries to realize this fact.

A second attempt to take the realm of knowledge by storm, closely connected with the first, was through an exaggerated reliance upon the efficacy of words. Considering the actual importance of language and the power over human affairs conferred by a mastery of it, there was a natural tendency to press its use further than it would go. Man always runs the risk of being enslaved by his own creations, as we see today in the case of machines. The first instance of this on a large scale was the widespread acceptance of the linguistic fallacy, that is, the confusion between words and the things or events which the words merely symbolize. It was supposed that the course of events could be altered by the repetition of magic formulae. So long as the religious hypothesis held sway this was not an unreasonable supposition. Men are notoriously influenced by verbal reiteration; repeat any fantastic story often enough and it will be believed. If the gods were like men, they could be moved in the same manner.

Furthermore, irrespective of the gods, reiteration has its human uses. By its means, the narrator not only convinces his audience; he often convinces himself of matters which he desires to believe. The role of verbal repetition in the phenomena of hypnotism and autosuggestion is proverbial. Its importance in religious liturgy and in poetry is equally evident. The solemn invocations of the litany and the most exquisite refrains of lyric poetry are alike descendants from the formulae of primitive magic.

The tendency to substitute words for things persists even when its religious background is removed. Words are simple and easily handled; the entities for which they stand are often enormously complex and difficult to comprehend. Thus we read in the papers some years ago, "Germany Invades Russia." The sentence was as simple as could be desired, but the real meaning of the two nouns was anything but simple. Was the German land invading the Russian land, or the German army invading the Russian army, or the German government invading the Russian government, or the German people invading the Russian people? The fact which the sentence meant to state was simply that the German army was invading Russian territory, but back of this the further connotation of the words seemed to involve the entire German people in the violation of the pact with Russia. The popular myths of the conscienceless Germans and the heroic Russians developed from just such verbal ambiguities. So today such vague and ill-understood words as "Communism," "Bolshevism," "Fascism," or

"Democracy" arouse the most violent emotions of hatred or affection among those who might feel very differently toward the realities involved. Words tend to break loose from their moorings in fact and sail off on piratical cruises of their own, leaving destruction in their wake.

Perhaps the most striking example of the continued power of sheer verbalism is seen in the development of Christian Science. Here we have a large group of people still addicted to the use of magic formulae, such as, "God is all. God is love. There is no sickness or death." By the repetition of such phrases they are enabled to deny, both to others and to themselves, two of the most obvious facts in all human experience. Both characteristics of primitive thinking are present: the substitution of words for reality, and the practice of "vain repetitions such as the heathen use." Evidently, savages have no copyright on the linguistic fallacy.

The resources of verbalism were analyzed and reduced to a pseudo-science by the Greeks, under the name of rhetoric. This formed the basis for an art of emotional persuasion, irrespective of truth, against which Plato vainly warred. Its aid to legal and political trickery was too great to be abandoned. It became a part of traditional education and is still taught in our schools and colleges. With appropriate modifications to suit contemporary conditions, it is perpetuated, with even greater potency than among the Greeks and Romans, in the contemporary arts of propaganda, advertising, and salesmanship.

But the close study of language made by the Greeks also had more beneficial consequences. It revealed to profounder minds the connection between language and thought and led to an analysis of thinking. The genuine sciences of logic and mathematics resulted. By means of rigorous logical definition, one is enabled to clarify his own meanings; through knowledge of the syllogism one may guard against inconsistent and irrelevant ideas. But neither logic nor mathematics is, in itself, an organ of discovery. Taken together, they provide a guide for disciplined and accurate thinking, but for the acquisition of new knowledge long and painstaking observation of facts is necessary. For fruitful thought, it is not enough that one should have something to think about. This the leisure-loving and speculative Greeks tended to forget. They were temperamentally averse to the tedious labor of studying mere facts.

Had the more practical-minded Romans been more interested in knowledge, they might have turned the abstract sciences of the Greeks to good results. But they were concerned almost solely with problems of political and military power. They produced an external civilization of peace and plenty, with a shrewd legal system, but they were rather deficient in intellectual curiosity or pleasure in experiment.

The ancient civilizations had made little headway toward understanding man's real place in nature. The primitive dualism had been "rationalized" but not superseded, and it was paralleled by the dualism in social organization between the patricians who monopolized both wealth and culture and the plebeians who were more and more deprived of both. The mass of the people, excluded from the benefits of civilization, found the world a drearier place than it had ever been before. Hence when Christianity came with its doctrine of the infinite importance of every individual soul, its promise of personal immortality, and its conception of a more intimately human deity (Jesus) than any of the ancient religions had possessed, it met with the favorable response that might have been expected. Christianity was revolutionary in its social code, but in its theology it stressed more heavily than ever the traditional dualism between mind and matter, definitely fastening it upon the world until well within modern times. Its social teaching, which was admirable, declined. Its theology, which was deplorable, remained unchallenged for many centuries.

The medieval period, up to a certain point, repeated the course of ancient civilizations. Its culmination in the scholasticism of the thirteenth and fourteenth centuries recovered the substance of classical learning, including the sciences of logic and mathematics. But the so-called Renaissance, which followed, was no reproduction of Roman imperialism. The men of the Renaissance, reacting against the restraints of scholasticism and devoting themselves with enthusiasm to the delights of concrete living, had the spirit of discoverers and explorers. The result for a time was confusion, but eventually logic and mathematics were brought down from the skies and put to work in clarifying the observed facts of experience. Their chief function was found to lie in guiding experiment to ever more fruitful conclusions. Hypotheses took the place of *a priori* axioms, and factual probabilities were found to be more useful than verbal certainties. The invention of the telescope and microscope extended the power of observation indefinitely in the direction of both the infinitely large and the infinitely small. An elaborate technique for checking crude observation developed. Modern science was born, something new, in extent at least, in the history of Western civilization, despite the earlier work of Alexandrian scientists.

Yet, after three centuries, when the face of the world and all our ways of living have been changed by its operations, science has not yet been taken home to our hearts. Scientific thinking is still looked upon as a special discipline with a limited application to particular fields, instead of being, as it is, the most perfect way of thinking yet discovered for dealing with *any kind of facts*.

This is evident when the general methodology of science is considered. A useful and convenient simplification may safely regard scientific processes as consisting of five separate stages, if one remembers that these processes are often carried on more or less simultaneously:

(1) Analysis of the problem to be solved
(2) Formulation of competing hypotheses
(3) Collection and classification of all relevant facts
(4) Testing of hypotheses by experiment
(5) Resultant formulation of tentative natural laws.

No methodology, of course, can entirely eliminate that bane of all thinking, the introduction of unconscious assumptions into the course of our reasoning. Scientific procedure, however, would seem to go as far in this direction as is humanly possible by directing particular attention upon the assumptions of hypotheses. Where the older mathematician said, "It is an axiom that such and such is the case, therefore so and so must follow," the modern mathematician says, "Let us assume that such and such is the case and see what follows." Such intellectual modesty, characteristic of all modern science, has had its reward in a cumulative success never before attained.

Yet the full resources of the scientific method have hardly been tapped up to the present time. In theoretic studies, in technology, and to a considerable extent in business we do utilize the exacting procedure of science. To a large degree, however, contemporary business methods rest upon rhetorical exercises and devices, much of the alleged hard-headedness of the businessman being but a rationalization of verbal exorcism. In politics, rhetoric is, as it has been for centuries, the chief expedient in maintaining the ascendancy of sects, parties, classes, and leaders. Words, in cooperation with various other forms of symbolism, serve to delude mankind into accepting the most absurd anachronisms and imbecilities.

The outlook for civilization depends mainly on whether our institutions can be brought within the realm of reason and scientific guidance, or are destined to be forever the prey of ill-disguised passions and superstitions and the lust for war and conquest. This observation logically leads us to a discussion of what is known as "cultural lag," which explains why we have thus far failed to bring our institutions and human behavior under scientific control and guidance.

V. CULTURAL LAG: THE GREAT OBSTACLE TO HUMAN WELL-BEING

As has been indicated above, the central problem of the human future is whether mankind will be able to exploit science and technology for the benefit of the human race and thus move on into an era of ever greater peace, security, prosperity, and leisure, or will use science and technology to impoverish and exterminate humanity. The solution of this problem is directly, and almost exclusively, the task of bringing social thought and institutions into harmonious relations with our dynamic and complex science and material culture. In this section we shall look into the history and nature of this problem, indicating the reasons for the so-called cultural lag, the problems that it poses, and the prospect of its solution in time to preserve, direct, and improve the course of civilization.

The most illuminating approach to the crises in contemporary civilization in the second half of the twentieth century is to be found in placing our age and its problems in the proper historical perspective. While attempts to draw direct and precise analogies with the distant past are always dangerous (for historical epochs are never exactly repeated), certain broad historical comparisons may be useful and instructive. The most significant of these analogies, perhaps, is the suggestion that we are now living during the onset of the fourth major transitional period of human history. In other words, we are now passing through the fourth great world revolution.

Our conception of a world revolution is not limited here to the violent changes which we usually associate with the word "revolution," although, thus far in human experience, war and civil violence have almost invariably accompanied the disintegration of existing social orders and the inauguration of new ones. By a world revolution we mean a fundamental change in social institutions and patterns of life, in the political and economic basis of the controls over human society, and in the dominant social values. A new type of civilization comes into being, and the basic framework of society and social philosophy is reconstructed, with new or modified social values.

The first of these revolutions began when man was still in a primitive tribal society, with a material culture based on stone implements, the crude beginnings of a pastoral and agricultural economy, and oral communication. Mankind gradually moved on into a social order founded on civil society (city-states, kingdoms, and empires), a metal material culture, well-developed pastoral and agricultural life, regional commercial relations, and a written language. This was accomplished in the ancient Near East, roughly between 10,000 and 2500 B.C.

The second world revolution took place between 300 A.D. and 800 A.D., when ancient pagan imperial and metropolitan society fell apart and was replaced by a Christian Catholic feudal social order based on an agrarian economic pattern.

The third world revolution occurred between 1500 A.D. and 1800 A.D., when Catholic agrarian feudalism was replaced by religious schisms, the national state, royal absolutism, representative and constitutional government, the rise of international commercial relations, mechanical industry, the capitalistic system, and the ascendency of the commercial middle class in the economic and political life of Western Europe.

The fourth world revolution is largely a product of the twentieth century. In this latest great critical period the main institutions that arose during the third world revolution are being subjected to the same strains, stresses, and readjustments as befell earlier social orders. We have already advanced far into the fourth great world revolution, which will either bring man into an unprecedented era of peace, plenty, and security, or will produce world chaos and return us to barbarism, if it does not exterminate the human race. The outcome will depend mainly upon our ability to bring our institutions up to date and thereby enable mankind to utilize our impressive scientific and mechanical resources for the benefit of humanity, rather than for its impoverishment and destruction.

The chief cause of these world revolutions has invariably been a discrepancy or maladjustment between material and non-material culture. Sociologists and social historians call this "cultural lag," a term which was popularized by William F. Ogburn in his book, *Social Change*.[3] At the Dawn of History, improvements in tools and weapons upset the simple life of tribal communities and started mankind on the road to conquest and the creation of larger settled societies. Later, in Greece and Rome, social and intellectual developments outstripped scientific and technological achievements, and civilization collapsed because the lagging material culture could not support the complex institutional life. As the Middle Ages wore on, the longbow and gunpowder helped to end feudalism, while better farming implements increased the crops. The mechanical fulling-machine facilitated woolen manufactures, while the horse-collar and iron-rimmed cart-

3 Viking, 1950.

wheel improved land transport. The mastery of new nautical instruments and ocean-going vessels stimulated exploration, and led to the expansion of Europe. Then, in more recent times, came the rise of science and engineering and at least five successive Industrial Revolutions which have given us contemporary energy, industry, communication, and transportation.

In all of the great world revolutions since primitive times cultural lag has been the factor which upset the existing pattern of life. And never before has there been such a gulf between technology and social institutions as exists today. We have an impressive and up-to-date equipment of science and material culture, while our institutions, mental attitudes, and social thinking are an antiquated mosaic of accretions from the Stone Age to the close of the eighteenth century. We have already entered the atomic-nuclear era which is ushering in the most revolutionary development in the whole history of the evolution of energy. We have giant turbines, a few of which can generate more energy than the entire working population of the United States. We have automatic machinery of the most amazing efficiency, controlled by thermostats, photoelectric cells, and even more complex devices which all but eliminate the human factor. We have swift jet airplanes, and are entering the rocket age. Our bathrooms would fill a Roman emperor with envy. Radio and television sets would appear miraculous to persons who died in so recent a period as the first World War. We could go on indefinitely through all the provinces of our Empire of Machines.[4]

Over against all this recent and impressive development stands our lagging institutional heritage, nearly every phase of which had taken definite shape before the year 1800. The national state system had come into being during the close of the Middle Ages, while representative government had been established on a national scale in England in the seventeenth century. Capitalism dominated urban economic life long before 1800, our ideas of the sanctity of private property were extolled by John Locke near the end of the seventeenth century, and free enterprise was praised by the leading economists of the late eighteenth century. Our system of liberal education was formulated by the Humanist scholars of the Renaissance, and the basic patterns of organization and administration of higher education can be traced back to the Middle Ages. Orthodox religious and ethical ideas date back to somewhere between the Stone Age and the beginning of the Christian Era.

Another important aspect of cultural lag lies in the fact that our urban life and new methods of transportation and communication have produced many novel social situations and social pressures for which simple agrarian life in the personal societies that have dominated human existence down to recent times has not prepared us. Cultural lag is manifest in the breakdown of our primary societies (the family, local play and cooperative groups, and neighborhoods) far more rapidly than public activity and community organization are being developed to take over their functions. This has led to a serious decline of personal and moral discipline, to social chaos, and a notable increase in crime and degener-

---

4 See Siegfried Giedion, *Mechanization Takes Command: A Contribution to Anonymous History*, Oxford University Press, 1948.

acy. Since personality and character have been molded over the centuries primarily by these simple local societies, their breakdown has led to personal as well as social disorganization.

Also important is the marked cultural lag as between institutions themselves. Certain institutions change more rapidly than others. Economic institutions, for example, can be modified more quickly than religious and moral institutions, probably because economic life is more secularized and is less enveloped in superstitions and strong emotions that resist change.

The increasingly devastating character of war has brought the problem of cultural lag into its most critical period. There seems to be no limit to the intelligence that we can apply to the technical problems and equipment of warfare, but we approach the whole institutional problem of war with emotional attitudes dating back to the period of the bow and arrow. Whatever social services war may have rendered in earlier days, it has now become a fatal anachronism. As matters now stand, our archaic institutional approach to the problem of war and peace may do little more than compel us to procrastinate helplessly until nuclear bombs and rockets, disease germs, and lethal chemicals wipe out human civilization.

This discussion of war as a crucial example of cultural lag brings us to the heart of the matter. Cultural lag has long been of great practical importance, since it has produced most of our economic waste, underconsumption, low standards of living, unemployment, crime, and much of our unnecessary disease, sickness, and death. It has brought about most of the wars in recent times, and has prevented the emergence of adequate constructive plans for peace.

In the past, despite handicaps, most of humanity could survive crises caused by cultural lag. But the development of atomic energy, new strides in aerial, rocket, chemical, and bacterial warfare and the like have introduced a new and more alarming trend into the situation. Unless we are able to bring up to date the institutions more directly involved in war and peace, it may not be long before humanity will be in large part extinguished and the remaining minority consigned to barbarism. It will avail nothing to retreat from this challenge into the fog of mysticism that is now proving so popular with those who lack the courage to face the issues with realism. Less than nothing will be gained by seeking refuge in dogmatic cults or in the mystical writings of a Spengler, a Toynbee, or a Sorokin. We must face our problems with the resolute courage of men like the late H. G. Wells, who saw that scientific and mechanical marvels could bring untold benefits to mankind if man could but learn how to utilize them to his advantage.[5]

The outlook for curbing and suppressing warfare has never been more dark and unpromising than it is today. In previous generations major wars were separated by considerable intervals: after the Napoleonic Wars, there was no major war until the Crimean War, if that can be called such, which came forty years after Waterloo. The Franco-Prussian War did not start until another quar-

5 See H. E. Barnes, *Historical Sociology: Its Origin and Development,* Philosophical Library, 1948, pp. 110-15; and H. E. Barnes, *History and Social Intelligence,* Knopf, 1926, pp. 139-44.

ter century had passed, while the first World War occurred nearly a half century later. But hardly had the second World War ended than the cold-war era came into being, and became constant and seemingly permanent. Although it has thus far been cold, there has been and is grave danger that it may turn into a universal hot war, as it did locally for a time in the Korean War. A Secretary of State of the United States all but boasted of his skill in keeping the country on the brink of war, and the masters of the Kremlin have not been lacking in provocative policies and actions.

War used to be mainly a matter of foreign affairs, but the cold-war system now thoroughly permeates domestic political and economic life. We shall now proceed to examine in more detail this menacing new development.

VI. GEORGE ORWELL, "NINETEEN EIGHTY-FOUR," AND THE COLD-WAR SYSTEM

Until fairly recently, it was a generally accepted theory that the world was moving steadily and inevitably towards happier conditions, in accordance with the theory of progress. In 1888, for example, the American publicist, Edward Bellamy, published an immensely popular and influential book entitled *Looking Backward*. The main thesis of this book was that the ever-growing efficiency of machinery would ultimately assure for mankind increased income, greater prosperity and security, more leisure, better educational opportunities, and more freedom. Bellamy's optimistic picture of the future was shared for more than half a century by most literate Americans, whether or not they had ever actually read his book.

Just sixty years after Edward Bellamy's book appeared, the brilliant British novelist and journalist, George Orwell, brought out his startling analysis and prophecy, *Nineteen Eighty-Four*.[6] This book, based upon a keen appraisal of trends in the preceding quarter of a century, sharply challenged the optimistic spirit and social prophecies of Bellamy's utopia. Orwell predicted that instead of universal prosperity, peace, and freedom for the masses, the pattern of human behavior, during an indefinite period of the future, may be perpetual war, mainly cold and phony, accompanied by permanent austerity and a rigorous regimentation of life, thought, and action.

Though it is a novel, Orwell's book is the most realistic and penetrating work produced by this generation on the current trends in national policy and world affairs. To discuss world trends today without consideration of the Orwellian frame of reference is not unlike writing on biology without noting the work of Darwin, Mendel, and de Vries, or on physics while ignoring Einstein, Planck, Bohr, and nuclear energy.

Several men had anticipated Orwell in important phases of his portrayal of current world trends. H. G. Wells, in his *The Shape of Things to Come* (1933), had emphasized the menace of war to the realization of the benefits of machinery for mankind. Lawrence Dennis, in his *Dynamics of War and Revolution* (1940), forecast the basic social patterns likely to emerge from a warring world, while

6 Harcourt, Brace, 1949, reprinted by New American Library, 1954.

James Burnham, in his *The Managerial Revolution* (1941), prepared us to think in terms of military managerialism. Numerous writers, such as Edward L. Bernays, Clyde R. Miller, William Albig, and Leonard Doob, described the methods of "emotional engineering" or propaganda which are required to build up and maintain hatred of foreign enemies, real or alleged. The rise of totalitarian governments between the two World Wars, their ideological systems, their use of propaganda, and their summary treatment of dissenters indicated the methods whereby the masses could be rigorously controlled in both their thoughts and actions. Orwell tied such ideas together in dramatic fashion, in terms of the postwar world.[7]

The main lesson driven home by Orwell's disconcerting book is that we are witnessing an ominous revolution in the whole nature and purpose of warfare. In the past, wars have been mainly the product of personal or partisan political ambition, emotional rage, national arrogance, or definite plans to conquer territory for glory, necessity, or both. They were fought against a foreign enemy with all possible vigor and the best strategy available. Victory was sought as speedily as possible, and victory meant the decisive defeat of the enemy on the battlefield.

Orwell, however, indicates that we are now passing into a period in which wars—hot, cold, or phony, but mainly cold and phony—are being used to an increasing extent as the basic instrument of domestic political strategy in order to consolidate the power of the class or party in office, to extend and retain tenure of office, to maintain prosperity and full employment and to avert depressions. The real enemy is not nations or forces outside the borders, but parties and classes within the country that are antagonistic to the party and class which hold power.

According to Orwell, there is no desire to defeat the foreign enemy quickly and decisively, for to do so would undermine the propaganda campaign of fear, curtail or end the armament boom, threaten a depression, invite social discontent, and jeopardize the existing social, economic, and political order. Basic strategy is no longer to be entrusted to vigorous military experts of the older school, but is primarily the task of the politicians, who operate through propaganda and intimidation in close cooperation with a new type of military personnel. The Korean War was the first important military conflict to be fought according to the Orwellian pattern. General MacArthur represented the holdover from the days of traditional warfare in which the foreign enemy was to be vanquished as completely and rapidly as possible. President Truman was dominated by the new Orwellian concepts of warfare that regarded warfare primarily from the standpoint of domestic political and economic considerations.

When Orwell's book was published in 1949, it was given wide publicity, but most of the comment upon it was superficial and represented the book as an ill-concealed satire on conditions of life in Soviet Russia and on possible future developments in Britain, if the Labor government continued its sway. Few commentators were sufficiently discerning and sagacious to recognize that the

7 See Christopher Hollis, *A Study of George Orwell*, Regnery, 1956; and Richard Rovere, ed., *The Orwell Reader*, Harcourt, Brace, 1956.

basic pattern of public behavior portrayed by Orwell had become the system into which all the chief countries of the world were in danger of slipping, perhaps irrevocably, unless the trend was recognized and reversed in time.

Many persons have dismissed the *Nineteen Eighty-Four* pattern of life as merely a terrifying fantasy, but the literal truth is that, in its basic pattern, it has already become well established throughout most of the "civilized" world in the guise of what we know as the cold war. The warring groups of *Nineteen Eighty-Four*—Oceania, Eurasia, and Eastasia—have already come into being. Orwell himself believed that *Nineteen Eighty-Four* was already fact, and Stephen Spender has asserted in *The New York Times* that Orwell originally intended to title his book *Nineteen Forty-Eight,* an idea which he abandoned only because his publishers thought it would cause too much reader resistance and incredulity.

Indeed, the prospect facing all the important nations today may well be far more grim than that portrayed in *Nineteen Eighty-Four,* where the perpetual war is mainly ruse and pretense, and relatively few people lose their lives in it. In Orwell's world everybody is employed and secure, even though the masses are intimidated and merely subsist on an extremely low standard of living. There seems little certainty, however, in our present world, that those who are today using the cold war to remain in power, to ward off a depression, or to increase the power and prestige of the military caste, will be successful, indefinitely, in keeping all future warfare phony and relatively bloodless.

Despite the fact that all the chief civilized nations have already entered to a dangerous extent into a pattern of life in which both political strategy and business policy are linked to a relatively permanent expanding war economy, this has rarely been the product of any consciously planned or closely reasoned ideology, such as that portrayed by Orwell in the philosophical sections of his book.[8] It has developed gradually, mainly as a result of opportunism, a favoring chain of circumstances, and the logic of events. Though all the principal nations are converging upon the same pattern, the motivation and initial developments have differed from country to country, except for the universal collective-security psychosis.[9]

Looking at the problem in a broad and general way, one can accurately say that the fundamental reason for the development of what we may call the Orwellian pattern was the frustration of institutional reforms (social, economic, and political), and behind this frustration, the wars since 1914. To a considerable extent, the wars themselves have been a product of delayed and inadequate institutional reforms. Instead of arising from any plotting or planned mendacity, the cold-war situation is the result of evasion on the part of the ruling classes; it is due to lack of resolute statecraft. The cold war itself is probably the most impressive and dangerous monument to public evasiveness in the history of the human race, for the cold-war pattern and the social system frozen by it are the current substitutes for rational institutional reforms, and the most potent ob-

8 Orwell, *op. cit.,* pp. 185 ff., 303 ff.
9 For a brief factual history of the Cold War, see Kenneth Ingram, *History of the Cold War,* Philosophical Library, 1955.

stacles to such reforms. While most acute observers have designated the existing social structure, mental orientation and public policy as the Orwellian era, it would thus be even more accurate and fundamental to christen the epoch "the Age of Evasion"—dodging the obvious responsibilities of social reconstruction while seeking to muddle through by means of the phony and cold-war substitutes for action. The longer the postponement, the more precarious the outlook for civilization. But let us turn to a brief survey of the manner in which the cold war came into being over the planet.

Soviet Russia was diverted from using the advantages of technology for the benefit of the masses as a result of the challenge of Hitler, the second World War, and the threats of war thereafter. Even before the rise of Hitler, Russia had fully established a system of psychological warfare, thought control, and espionage as a phase of revolutionary techniques and totalitarian policy. Its ministries of "Peace," "Love," "Truth," and "Plenty" had preceded the coming of the Nazis. Stalin encouraged the trend towards a cold war in February, 1946, by reviving his pre-war contention that communism and capitalism could not coexist, after having obtained all the spoils from wartime that he could gain as a result of collaboration during the war. This provided a handy excuse for the "cold warriors" in capitalist countries to step up their plans for a similar attitude and policy.

Britain, while already basically bogged down as a result of inadequate institutional reforms, was led into the *Nineteen Eighty-Four* pattern of using war for political strategy primarily because of the international political situation. The United States entered the war pattern after 1937, when political and economic opposition had paralyzed the New Deal. The advantages of the cold war in bolstering the economy, avoiding a depression, and maintaining political tenure after 1945 were quickly recognized by both politicians and economists. Professor Sumner H. Slichter, of Harvard University, the most influential economist in the United States, put the matter succinctly in an address on October 26, 1949:

> In the absence of a cold war the demand for goods by the Government would be many billions of dollars less than it now is, and expenditures of both industry and Government on technological research would be hundreds of millions less than they are now. So we may thank the Russians for helping to make capitalism in the United States work better than ever.[10]

All the main economic classes and political parties in the United States have been highly cordial to the cold-war system. The banking and industrial leaders had been very fearful of a bad business slump when the hot war was over in 1945, and labor realized the danger of the unemployment that might result from such a depression. President Truman's political rating was at an all-time low in the late winter of 1946-1947, when Winston Churchill had given his blessing to a cold war in March, 1946, at Fulton, Missouri. The material welfare of business, of the middle or white-collar class, and of labor was at least temporarily improved and Truman was reelected in 1948. And since thinking in non-material

10 *The New York Times*, October 26, 1949, p. 36.

and unemotional terms has been infrequent since the outbreak of the second World War, there has been little attention given to the less fortunate impact of the cold war on the non-material life of the peoples of the world, in general, or the citizens of the United States, in particular. While carefully avoiding any direct indication of reliance on the Orwellian analysis, the American sociologist, C. Wright Mills, has provided the best description of the progress made toward a *Nineteen Eighty-Four* social order in the United States. This is best summarized in his notable book, *The Power Elite*.[11] At the end of his administration President Eisenhower also called attention to the dangers in the merging of the powers of corporation executives, Pentagon chiefs and top defense executives, leading military technicians and scientists, and advertising moguls.

Stalin and his successors have been content with the cold war because war scares and the alleged threat of a capitalist attack have enabled the Politburo to maintain unity and prevent any threat of civil war, despite much brutal labor policy and low living standards. The cold war has also aided Soviet Russia in cementing the cordon of satellite countries more closely and firmly to Russia and for some years in assuring unity with Communist China and the revolutionary forces throughout Asia. Moreover, the Russians believe that they are winning the cold war.

The Chinese Communists have had every reason to feel highly pleased with the onset and continuation of the cold war. It notably assisted them in the conquest of China, and enabled them to consolidate their gains. It provided them with an excuse for a reign of terror at home, while the Korean War produced Russian technological and military aid and valuable military experience. Not only China but most of "Eastasia" is very congenial to the cold-war system, for it encourages and aids their rebellion against Western imperialism. The same, obviously, is true of the Middle East and Africa.

Nevertheless, no matter how well satisfied most existing parties to the cold war might seem to be at the moment, no discerning observer of world affairs can feel very contented or reassured with these developments. A cold war cannot be continued indefinitely unless it is made warmer and warmer, and the warmer it becomes the greater the probability that it will break out into a hot war. The financial burdens of the cold war upon the NATO nations of Western Europe, the knowledge that Russia had mastered the atom and hydrogen bombs, and the loss of trade, all led to some rumblings of discontent against the more rigorous phases of the cold war. This trend was intensified by the more conciliatory attitude of the successors of Stalin. Perhaps the Russians have been more concerned with leading the Western nations into ultimate bankruptcy and depression than with peace for its own sake. In any event, Russian overtures since 1956, and especially since the break with Communist China, encouraged several nations of Western Europe to demand a mitigation of the cold war. How far this trend will go cannot be foreseen at the time these lines are being written.

By 1960, there had come about a great increase in travel and in the exchange of information between Russia and the West. Great Britain had taken the lead in

11 Oxford University Press, 1956.

working for a solution of the impasse between the Iron Curtain countries and the West. On the other hand, the bitter conflict over the status and future destiny of Berlin served to perpetuate and inflame the tensions that underlay the cold war. The feverish "space war," which followed on the heels of the Russian launching of the "Sputniks" in the autumn of 1957, made it certain that these tensions could be readily perpetuated even if all the boundary and ideological controversies on the planet were settled. So long as Russia needs cold-war tensions to lessen the danger of internal revolt both at home and in satellite countries and the Western countries require them to maintain economic prosperity and political tenure for parties in power, there seemed little probability of any early end to the cold-war system or era.

It does not seem unreasonable to assume that Russia is today more agreeable to mitigating the cold war than the United States, for practical rather than idealistic reasons. Russia is less able to bear the great armament burden involved; she does not need armament industry to make her economy work; Russian citizens are in better contact with Western living conditions and demanding better living conditions; and the break with Chinese world policy would all seem to make it in the Russian interest to ease off the cold war. Short of diverting major public expenditures from armament to welfare-state activities, which is obviously not possible in the present temper of the country, there are no comparable incentives to induce the United States to wish to taper off the cold-war pattern.

Since, however, we are more concerned in this book with intellectual history than with the history of institutions, the main significance of this cold-war or Orwellian system lies in its effects on the mentality of peoples. Orwell contended that it is necessary to keep the masses at a constant fever pitch of fear and excitement and effectively to prevent them from learning that the cold-war scares are actually phony. To bring this about in *Nineteen Eighty-Four* society an elaborate development of propaganda, thought policing, regimentation, "emotional engineering," and psychological warfare was set up on an overwhelming scale. Systematic hate campaigns were developed and daily hate periods made compulsory. An all-pervading and most meticulous system of espionage was maintained, even to keeping every citizen constantly under the scrutiny of a television eye. Both past history and current news were constantly falsified and rewritten to conform to the changing daily statements and policies of those in charge of the regime. To facilitate the deception of the masses by the leaders, a new and appropriate vocabulary was provided in what Orwell calls "newspeak." The orderly logic of former days was replaced by the technique of "doublethink," which encouraged the wholesale acceptance and retention of diametrically contradictory concepts and dogmas. The department which directed propaganda and mass deception was designated as the Ministry of Truth, while all the horrible espionage, intimidation, and tortures were carried out in the Ministry of Love. The intellectual device of "crimestop" prevented the people from checking on the factual basis of official pronouncements and from analyzing public statements logically. In this manner, the masses were kept disciplined, impoverished, and sufficiently frightened so that they would not actively rebel against the grim, drab, and tyrannical mode of life to which they were condemned. They were diverted by cheap circuses, fake lotteries, and the like, while all reliable historical material was destroyed so that the masses could never contrast their present condition with earlier living conditions and become discontented.

Although no well-informed and candid person could honestly deny that the civilized world has very definitely moved toward the Orwellian pattern of public life, social motivation, and foreign policy, there are marked differences in the degree of its manifestations, especially in the rigor of social pressure. The closest approximation is to be found in the countries behind the so-called Iron Curtain, but most of their tight totalitarian controls had appeared before the cold-war system developed after the second World War.

In the United States there are some important differences in details from conditions depicted in Orwell's book. In the first place, our technological advances and productive machinery have proved far more efficient than Orwell, accustomed to England's relatively obsolescent industrial plant at the time, could well imagine. Hence, even after the enormous diversion of our industrial production into armament enough has remained for civilian consumption so that the "Proles" in the United States have so far enjoyed a far higher standard of living than those of *Nineteen Eighty-Four.* Moreover, they have been sufficiently engrossed and distracted by installment purchases of all sorts that it has not been necessary to introduce fake lotteries or public circuses. Further, even Orwell, with his wide experience in public propaganda, was unable to foresee the ease with which the American public would succumb to the most flagrant and transparent cold-war propaganda. Hence there has been no need as yet for any general introduction of the tortures of *Nineteen Eighty-Four* as administered by the Ministry of Love.

Nonetheless, it is true that all of the main mental and emotional attitudes of the Orwellian system have appeared in American public and personal reactions since the cold-war system was introduced. When he was Secretary of State, John Foster Dulles frankly stated that the American public needed to be "artificially alarmed," lest there be any relaxation in public fear. This underlying current of public fear has been the chief motivation for the rigorous security program instituted by the Federal and state governments. We have already richly developed the "newspeak" and "doublethink" semantics of the Orwellian system. Another recent contribution to our doublethink, and perhaps the most dangerous of all, is the assertion that the way to solve the problems of a society which is already in trouble mainly because science and technology are away out ahead of institutions, is to increase the emphasis on natural science and engineering in our educational curriculum, and reduce the attention given to social science and the arts. The most recent and probably the most truly Orwellian type of newspeak produced in the United States is the concept of "overkill," which refers to the fact that this country has enough nuclear weapons to destroy all human beings on the planet several times over, to say nothing of all Russians or Chinese. The most clearly Orwellian aspect of the matter is that the demonstration of and boasting about this ability to overkill was followed by the offering and approval of the most extensive military budget in the whole history of the cold war.

We have not as yet set up all the doublethink ministries of the Orwellian regime, but we have made a significant start. The War Department has been changed to the Department of Defense, and the Navy and Air Force Departments have been brought within it. The Department of Justice has not been christened the Ministry of Love, nor as yet has it deserved any such designation in extreme Orwellian terms. There is not yet any unified Ministry of Truth, primarily because all the major departments of government have their own special propaganda agencies and have not been consolidated into one single organization. But public propaganda is today the one form of activity which has attained a stature complete enough to deserve a "Nineteen Eighty-Four" ministry. It is extremely difficult to oppose or obstruct any legislation or appropriations if they can be ever so tenuously identified or associated with "defense."

The intellectual and emotional devices of doublethink, newspeak, and crimestop have permeated all classes and political groups, which is the main reason why we cannot reasonably expect any speedy relief from the system. Conservatives normally wish to protect their property and income, but are frightened by the cold-war propaganda into supporting the vast outlay for armament and for military and economic aid for nations scattered all over the globe. Liberals, if anything, outdo the conservatives in doublethink. They clamor for greater expenditures for a welfare state, while ardently supporting the cold-war financial extravagance that makes any adequate additional expenditures for public welfare out of the question.

Not only is doublethink rampant among us, but newspeak has also made great headway. In considerable part, it is protective, in the thought that the more incomprehensible the jargon the less likely it will be that any subversive thoughts or policies can be detected. We have already indicated how the social sciences, which should lead in planning a new order of peace and security, have succumbed to a professional newspeak, either the quantitative mysticism which can be understood only by those familiar with higher mathematics and the assumptions and terminology of esoteric statistical research, or to the metaphysical obfuscation almost universal with those who seek to systematize and generalize. Not even a trained FBI agent could detect subversion in either form of social science newspeak; nor could he, or anybody else, discover any guidance for a better social order.

Another mental device utilized by the leaders in *Nineteen Eighty-Four* to discourage clear and honest thinking and any logical analysis of public problems is what was called "crimestop." This means discouraging factual analysis and carrying any problem through to realistic considerations and logical conclusions. It renders basic public policies immune to analytical reasoning and any examination of their implications. To illustrate this semantic ruse by reference to current issues in the United States, it would be considered intellectual—if not political— treason for an American citizen frankly to ask what his country would do if a vast fleet of Russian submarines were assembled in the Caribbean, if there were great Russian air fields swarming with bombers carrying hydrogen bombs in Canada, Mexico, Cuba, the Bahamas, Bermuda, Panama, and Newfoundland, and large detachments of Russian soldiers, fully armed with atomic weapons, scattered about in Canada, Mexico, Central America, and Venezuela. Felix Morley and David Lawrence suggested this cogent analogy back in the early days of the cold war; they have not repeated this enlightening exercise.

On the domestic front crimestop is, perhaps, best illustrated by the public and official attitude toward inflation, which is regarded as the leading threat to the American economy. The expenditure of a few hundred millions of dollars on desperately needed housing for the nation is looked upon as dangerously inflationary, while the annual expenditure of around fifty billion dollars on armament, the outstanding inflationary item in the economy, is rarely, if ever, mentioned as a cause of inflationary trends, and suggestions to curb such expenditures would be regarded as almost treasonable. The refusal to examine the problem of armament expenditures in connection with the reality of our capacity to "overkill" is another important example of crimestop, but it frustrates any tendency to arrive at informed analysis and decisions on public affairs.

By all odds the most menacing aspect of the effect of the cold-war system on both public attitudes and the social sciences is that it increases the evasions and frustrations which, even before 1939, were making it difficult to solve the major problem of our age—and the only hope of preserving civilization—namely, bringing our institutions up to date and using our scientific and technological equipment in such a manner as to assure peace, prosperity, and security. The cold-war psychology both distracts attention from domestic problems and also makes any real attempt to solve them publicly futile and personally precarious. As the eminent commentator and critic Edmund Wilson pointed out early in 1958, there had not been a single major public reform project enacted into law since 1947; he might well have said since Pearl Harbor. Indeed, the whole Orwellian or cold-war system can be most intelligently interpreted as organized and rigorous evasion of the public responsibility to improve the social order within national boundaries. It may not always be so recognized by its proponents and custodians, but such is the reality. Hence it is not an exaggeration to describe it as perhaps the greatest threat which has ever faced the human race. On the one hand, it greatly increases the danger of a war of extermination and, on the other hand, it all but paralyzes any effort to build a social system which would justify the preservation of the human race even if peace should prevail.

VII. MENTAL CONDITIONING AND IRRATIONAL BEHAVIOR IN THE MODERN WORLD

It has been pointed out that the cold-war program and attitudes not only distract attention from a study of social problems, domestic or international, but are actually hostile to such an effort. The crimestop technique is designed to discourage or prevent any realistic examination of assumptions or thorough analysis of public procedure. Doublethink is the most powerful and complete negation of logical attitudes which has thus far appeared in human experience. Even primitive man usually drew logical assumptions from his premises, however fallacious his premises may have been.

The cold-war psychology also promotes intellectual and social docility. We have noted in many earlier chapters the past experiences of mankind relative to intellectual and other forms of tyranny. Almost invariably, these abuses provoked widespread opposition, and most of what passes for intellectual and institutional progress in the past has been the product of this resistance and of rebellion against recognized abuses.

There is little or nothing of this kind in the cold-war era that is now so well established. A main reason for this is that warfare is the one great institution and social abuse which has never been subjected to serious popular protest, and is also the one which produces the most extreme emotional reactions. Occasionally, some great humanitarian like Hugo Grotius or Emeric de Vattel might protest against the violence and misery caused by warfare, but there has been little popular resentment or opposition. Since the wars of the French Revolution and the Napoleonic era, public violence and copious and compelling propaganda have been continued and greatly increased to protect warfare against popular dissent, opposition, and factual analysis of issues right down through the second World War. Even the opposition to warfare which appeared in the intervals of peace usually vanished when a war approached, or was about to break out. An instructive example of this was the manner in which the European socialists capitulated to the war spirit at the onset of the first World War, and by 1939 had, in Great Britain and France, become the vanguard of the war party. Even in the eighteen years since the ending of the second World War, the socialists have not extensively repudiated their bellicose attitudes of 1936-1945. This is an ominous precedent, for after past wars there had usually been a period of self-examination and of remorse. Probably the main reason for the absence of any notable disillusionment and readjustment after 1945 was that there was not time enough for the process to set in. In less than two years after V-J Day the cold war was upon the world.

It is only natural that a cold war would require a far greater volume of propaganda and greater skill in its use than the propaganda which would suffice during actual wartime. Orwell outlined the extreme techniques which might be applied to produce the desired results, but outside the Iron Curtain countries the tortures which he envisaged as applied by the Ministry of Love have not been required; propaganda has sufficed.

For nearly a century after the Napoleonic period, it was generally believed that mankind has full rational control of public life. Reason and calculated self-interest were supposed to dominate in the realm of political affairs. This notion arose out of the rationalistic philosophy of the French Revolutionary period, and it was perpetuated and given a more precise and influential statement by the English Utilitarians of the first third of the nineteenth century, especially in the so-called "felicific calculus" of Jeremy Bentham, the leader of the Utilitarians. Bentham held that man guides his conduct, personal, political, economic, and ethical, by cool, calculating self-interest. This conception controlled the dominant political theory of the remainder of the nineteenth century, and upon it was founded all the major assumptions of the democratic movement. This view was first challenged by writers on crowd psychology and the nature of the mob mind around the turn of the century, chiefly French and Italian writers like Gustave Le Bon, Gabriel Tarde, Émile Durkheim, and Scipio Sighele, whose ideas were brought over into American social thought chiefly by Edward A. Ross. But the effective refutation of the Benthamite felicific calculus was the work of the English writer, Graham Wallas, who brought out *Human Nature in Politics* in 1908. Wallas clearly established the fact that rationality plays a relatively small role in either private or public behavior, as compared with the influence of emotions, which are mainly generated by habit, conventions, traditions, herd controls, the mental traits of crowds, and the like. He showed how these are fused, consciously or unconsciously, in propaganda, which plays a far larger role in public behavior than any rational considerations. But anything that Wallas knew as propaganda was simple and rudimentary when compared with that which has been developed since 1908.

Propaganda has been greatly expanded since the time of Wallas, and it has been applied in all phases of life, not only political but economic and social. It has drawn on all the resources of individual and social psychology, psychiatry, and social science. Its techniques have been given greater precision, and its applications have become ever more diversified and potent. It has even been given a more attractive and dignified name, namely, the "science of public relations," by Edward L. Bernays, who is generally regarded as the man most responsible for the foundation and development of this movement.[12]

A word might be said here about the great changes and advances in the nature and effectiveness of the physical instruments of propaganda. Down to the first World War, propaganda was carried on mainly through campaign speeches, political parades, newspaper stories and editorials, political tracts, and occasional political campaign books. By the decade of the second World War, new methods of mass communication had come into being: moving pictures, the radio, and television. These enable propaganda to be carried on far more effectively and to reach vast audiences simultaneously. Both politics and business have fully utilized the enormous advantages of these new media. It is doubtful if great radio or television networks could exist without the support of business sponsorship for the purpose of promoting the sales and prestige of their products.

These contemporary media of public information and stimulation have, by subjecting the whole population of entire countries to the simultaneous dissemination of data and indoctrination, all but destroyed the existence of any thoughtful public. At the very turn of the century (1901), Tarde made what was then a valid distinction between the public and the crowd in his *Opinion and the Crowd*. The public is made up of citizens who are dispersed in space and have time to consider and reflect in arriving at their conclusions—public opinion. Contemporary agencies for simultaneous distribution of information, almost forced into every home, have now ended the conditions that Tarde assumed. We still talk about public opinion, but it is more truly deliberately instigated and

---

12 For a comprehensive survey of this subject, see William Albig, *Modern Public Opinion*, McGraw-Hill, 1956.

directed crowd opinion, even if there is no direct physical contiguity and contact.

While politicians have used propaganda ever more widely and unscrupulously in public life to divert public attention overseas or into outer space, the most formidable utilization of propaganda has been the work of commercial advertising, which is today an impressive factor in both economic and intellectual life. In the United States alone, commercial advertising involves an expenditure of over ten billion dollars annually, and its activities are carried on by some 3,300 advertising agencies. The basic aim of advertising is to bring together products and customers, but this is no longer a simple process of announcing the availability of products and presenting their nature in an attractive visual form.[13]

As much attention is given by the larger advertising agencies to a study of human psychology as to the nature and merits of the products they desire to sell. They have set up expensive research projects, based on studies in individual psychology, social psychology, neurology, psychiatry, and various social sciences which are relevant to the task in hand. Lately, perhaps more attention has been given to a study of the subconscious mind than to methods of conscious persuasion, in order to discover the complex motivation which governs the latent desire of customers to buy products. The contemporary advertisers also try to condition customers to buy a product as automatically as Pavlov's dogs drooled when he rang the bells that they had come to associate with feeding.[14]

We need not go into any further detail as to the techniques of contemporary advertising. We are far more concerned with the manner in which advertising has entered the field of political life and brought about a situation where candidates and their policies are sold to the public by the same methods that advertisers use to market their wares. The political bosses who formerly ran campaigns are now being pushed into the background by advertising agencies. As Vance Packard reveals: "At one quite important level the presidential campaign of 1956 settled into a battle between advertising agencies: Batten Barton Durstine & Osborn for the Republicans and the smaller agency Norman Craig & Kummel for the Democrats." The effort is made to create a political image which will lure voters. This bears little relation to the actual qualities or intrinsic merits of either the candidate or his platform. The voter is led to cast his vote on the emotional level on which he would indicate his preference for a motor car, a gadget, liquor, drugs, cosmetics, or fashions.[15]

These slick and adroit techniques of contemporary advertising have now come not only to govern the conduct of campaigns, but also to guide the behavior of the successful candidate once he has taken office. The alluring, soothing, and confidence-inspiring mental image concocted and presented during the campaign must be maintained unimpaired, if possible, during the administration. This is done by the presidential press secretary, who keeps in constant contact with the advertising agency which has been engaged to supervise and guide the process. Popularity is deemed more vital to political success than constructive statecraft.

13 See Martin Mayer, *Madison Avenue, U.S.A.,* Harper, 1958.
14 See Vance Packard, *The Hidden Persuaders,* Pocket Books.
15 On advertising, public relations, and politics, see Stanley Kelley, *Public Relations and Political Power,* Johns Hopkins University Press, 1955; and Eugene Burdick, *The Ninth Wave,* Houghton Mifflin, 1956.

In crucial situations advertising experts are openly called in to direct the procedure, as when President Eisenhower brought in Eric A. Johnston and other important advertising specialists to promote his campaign for a robust foreign-aid program in the late winter of 1957-1958.

It is obvious that all this produces an attitude of restraint, caution, and passivity upon the part of both the political leaders and the public at large, and these considerations tend, at least in part, to break down the popular distinction between the "free nations" and totalitarian states.

Another factor making for irrationality in public life today has been the increase of censorship in so-called peacetime. Today, censorship, even in democratic countries, is more severe and extensive than at any time in modern history during a period generally regarded as one of peace. With the initiation of the cold war and the temporary interlude of hot war in Korea, the remnants of wartime censorship were supplemented by additional legislation, executive orders, and court decisions. This policy was justified on the ground of the necessity to insure "security," especially against the possible transmission of information, notably that related to new military technology, to enemy spies. The list of materials regarded as vitally secret became ever more extensive under the general label of "classified material." Such precautions may be necessary for public safety, but they have led to grave abuses and arbitrary extension of censorship by public officials in areas of information not at all involved in any reasonable interpretation of the needs of security.[16]

The reaction of the cold war on science has been diversified. Scientific research has been greatly intensified in lines related to military technology, and epoch-making discoveries have resulted. There have also been trends that tended to restrict scientific activities and the freedom of research. The more scientists that were lured or pushed into military technology, the fewer that remained to deal with problems directly related to civilian needs. There has also been a considerable amount of doublethink in the government attitude towards scientists employed on military technology. While some leading scientists, such as Harold Urey, Leo Szilard, and Linus C. Pauling, have favored keeping the cold war within reasonable bounds, others like Edward Teller have sometimes proved more resistant to restraint than responsible political leaders.

Censorship has also been very extensive outside of the realm of science and technology. The more important material about the causes of the second World War, beyond the captured German and Italian documents, has not been released, nor have the vital documents on American entry, notably the secret Churchill-Roosevelt exchanges. Almost frantic efforts have been made to conceal the actual responsibility for the fact that the Japanese could conduct a successful surprise attack on Pearl Harbor. The same secrecy has been observed as to much of the background and conduct of the cold war. When the Government of the United States belatedly ordered the publication of the documents bearing on the main wartime summit conferences and appropriated the funds to make this possible, there was scandalous delay in publication, and when some

16 See Walter Gellhorn, *Security, Loyalty, and Science,* Cornell University Press, 1950.

of the documents were published it was evident that they had been heavily censored and distorted. There was some publicity given to the manhandling of the Yalta documents, but when the much more vital and equally censored Teheran documents were later published there was virtually no concern or protest.

The bearing of this increased censorship is readily apparent. The first step in a rational approach to either scientific or public problems is to have the relevant data available. Until this is done, the next steps of analysis, comparison, testing, generalization, and applications cannot be carried on in a manner to command confidence as to conclusions.

VIII. EDUCATION IN THE COLD-WAR ERA

Social change can take place in a more or less automatic and planless manner—what is called "muddling through"—or in conformity with organized guidance, whether the latter be wise and successful or otherwise. Planned social change is possible only through the instrumentality of enlightened education which transmits its findings and places its trained personnel at the service of the public. The more complex the era, the greater need for training and guidance through education.[17]

There are three main types of education: science and technology, the social sciences, and what is commonly known as the arts. Scientific and technical education has, relatively, done well, and has produced the world of modern material marvels. But it has also placed society in an ever more precarious position because we have not brought our institutions up to date and so shaped them that they can divert science and technology solely to constructive goals. The only phase of education which is directly concerned with the improvement of our institutional equipment is that of the social sciences, and upon them falls the responsibility of social guidance and the avoidance of catastrophe. The third phase of education—the arts—surely represents, on the whole, the highest form of intellectual interests, but there is little prospect of being fully able to promote or enjoy the benefits of the arts so long as society totters on the edge of the abyss of impoverishment, demoralization, and extinction.

If there is to be any social future which will justify human survival, there must be a vastly greater emphasis placed on the social sciences, and they must lay the main stress on bringing our institutions up to date and making social thought competent to guide the social procession. But the social sciences today are in such a state of disunity, evasiveness, obscurity, and timidity that to give them any greater role in social guidance might actually increase the social chaos and institutional crisis of our time.

We not only need more social science; we are perhaps in even greater need of better social science. If we ever get it, its task should be: to gather all available

---

17 On education and social reform, see M. E. Curti, *The Social Ideals of American Educators*, Scribner, 1935; H. D. Langford, *Education and the Social Conflict*, Macmillan, 1936; Alexander Meiklejohn, *Education Between Two Worlds*, Harper, 1942; and J. H. Newlon, *Education for Democracy in Our Time*, McGraw-Hill, 1939.

facts relative to the existing social scene; to analyze and evaluate these facts; and, finally, to apply the conclusions in effective social planning. This is no new and revolutionary proposal; St. Simon and Comte set forth these same ideas over a century ago. The most impressive intellect among all American sociologists down to our own time, Lester F. Ward, over seventy-five years ago developed the notion of social planning, even to an Institute of Social Sciences to be set up in Washington to guide public policy and legislation.

Against this background, the present frenzied demand for more education in science and technology, and that mainly for destructive purposes, is positively appalling, and does not bode well for the future. Next to this quasi-suicidal demand, perhaps the most notable folly in recent educational discussion has been the violent and ignorant attack on the educational ideas of John Dewey, unquestionably the outstanding figure in the development of modern education, and the only educational leader who has ever offered a fairly complete program of education suitable for training children and youth for their responsibilities in a democratic social order. Dewey's conceptions were never given a fair trial in connection with mass-education and they never can be unless we are willing to spend as liberally for education as we are for armament. Their application thus far has only been a travesty on the teachings of the master.

Dewey gathered the best in the educational doctrines of the past, and combined them with the most promising contributions of contemporary psychology and pedagogy. He had the logical, if very novel, conviction that if youth is to be educated for democratic living, the educational process should be of a democratic nature in both content and method. He assumed that the American public would be willing to pay enough to support an educational system that would fit their children for a democratic society. There never has been any such willingness, and it has been quite impossible to apply Dewey's ideas even when there was any desire to do so, which has been relatively rare. It is no exaggeration to say that if Americans are ever trained to operate a democracy efficiently, it will be due more than anything else to the revival and actual application of the general education program that Dewey vainly tried to bring into general adoption.[18]

IX. THE POLITICAL AND ECONOMIC OUTLOOK

Whatever the social future may turn out to be, it is obvious that the result will depend mainly on the policy of the political system which prevails and the ability of the government to execute this policy efficiently. It should be evident that the older nose-counting democracy, which we inherited from a politically uninformed and inexperienced rural era over a century ago, is doomed as a satisfactory pattern of government in our complex, urban, industrial world civilization.

Certain improvements in our current political system are obviously desirable. If we are to operate a democracy, our citizens must be educated to this task. This is not the case today. It is no exaggeration to say that not one voter in ten thousand

18 See Max Eastman, in Edward Weeks and Emily Flint, eds., *Jubilee: One Hundred Years of the Atlantic,* Little, Brown, 1957, pp. 314-26.

is fitted by educational training to cast his ballot intelligently. The civil service and merit system should be extended to the legislative and judicial branches of the government. It is absurd to demand exacting and specialized education of a clerk in the Bureau of Standards and yet demand no educational or professional qualifications for a United States Senator. The representative system should be based on social and economic interests, rather than upon the ancient system of territorial units which have come down to us from the political aberrations of Rousseau. It would be well to revive and evaluate the reforms proposed by the Progressives of a half-century ago.

All of these suggestions, combined, might not salvage democracy, but they constitute the main avenues of hope. If they, and others which might be suggested, fail, while mankind manages to escape nuclear extermination, we may be headed for totalitarian regimes which could make Hitler and Stalin seem idealistic humanitarians by comparison.

The economic outlook is equally clear to those who are able to free themselves from prejudice. Despite all the Kremlin smears of the "capitalistic imperialists," those who make such attacks are flogging a dead horse. There is not a capitalistic country (as the term was understood by either Adam Smith or Karl Marx) in existence anywhere in the world today, nor is there any prospect that laissez-faire, free-enterprise capitalism will ever be revived. Such capitalism as exists in European NATO countries is military state capitalism, but revisionist socialism is strong in most of these countries. Military state capitalism dominates the economic scene in the United States. All the countries behind the Iron Curtain operate under a system of state socialism. They may mistakenly be called Communist, but communism is not likely to be achieved in any of these countries for generations.

Those who have regard for both liberty and economic efficiency are inclined to esteem most highly the so-called Middle Way economy of the Scandinavian countries, an economic system that has been based on experiment and empirical appraisal of results. It is founded on the assumption that competitive capitalism is preferable to any other system in those fields of economic activity where it can operate efficiently. It saves a vast amount of red tape and provides stimulus for private initiative. These countries do not base their appraisal of capitalistic operations on the propaganda of either partisans or critics. They maintain a dual yardstick: if private capitalism falls down in any sector where it has been operating, it is replaced by state capitalism or cooperation. The former predominates in the fields of public utilities, forestation and lumber, mining, and state monopolies, like matches and liquor. Cooperation is most prevalent in handling consumer goods and housing.

This Middle Way economy has proved very successful in the Scandinavian countries, even though they are relatively lacking in natural resources and operate their economic life under other scarcities and handicaps. It should be remarkably successful in countries like the United States, which are richly endowed by nature. Yet, despite some rhetorical admiration, there has been little effort to adopt it.

From what has been said in the preceding portions of this chapter, it is obvious that any prediction about the future of humanity can be no more than tentative guesswork as long as the cold war persists. There is no hope for a more secure and happier condition for mankind while this regime continues, and there is little current evidence that it is likely soon to be eased, to say nothing of being terminated. The most ominous outcome of further continuation of the cold war is a conflict leading to universal extermination. The longer such a war is delayed, the greater the probability of complete extermination. Further nuclear research and continued political irresponsibility might even result in blowing up the planet.

At best, under the cold-war system one can only anticipate gradual decline and disintegration, at least among the so-called free nations. It might be that the overwhelming manpower of the Soviet Union and Communist China, together with the natural resources that they might pool, would prevent these countries from collapsing under the burdens of the cold war. But surely the free nations could not withstand them. Already, Great Britain is showing signs of serious strain. France is still politically disturbed and in a financial crisis, and Italy faces governmental confusion and instability as well as serious population pressure. Even the United States cannot stand the drain indefinitely, and the end of the cold war would seriously undermine its economy. The slight cutback of production in military aviation in 1957-1958, because of the advances in rocket warfare, was the main cause for a sudden recession which alarmed both politicians and business men. The temporary boom which developed in 1959 furnished no basis for unqualified economic optimism. It was accompanied by increasing difficulty in marketing government bonds and by legislation raising the ceiling of the national debt. If the spending for armament under the cold-war system were drastically curtailed, the American economy would go into an immediate tailspin and would enter a period of depression far longer and deeper than that which beset the economy in 1929 and the following years. The United States has now got itself into a situation where it is damned if it does and damned if it does not. But the damnation due to persistence in the cold war is likely to be far more serious than that resulting from cessation and withdrawal.

The achievement of assured peace is the crucial desideratum for any real hope for a better era for mankind. Civilization might muddle along, even with unnecessary delays, in an era free from any threat of war. So far as scientific and technological resources and outlook are concerned, contemporary society is alerted for a veritable material utopia. But there are many intellectual and institutional deficits attached to this impressive exhibit. Our orientation is now overwhelmingly mechanical, and even here chiefly the mechanics of warfare, hot and cold.

Another factor which cannot but affect our future has been the decline of humanitarianism and humane ideals, a leading mainspring of the desire to promote human betterment. Here, the fictitious atrocities of the first World War became the authentic everyday occurrences of the second World War. Over two million civilians were killed by the so-called strategic or saturation bombing of non-military objectives, culminating in the destruction of such beautiful cities as Coventry and Dresden. Nearly 200,000 Japanese died as a result of the atom-bombing of Hiroshima and Nagasaki six months after the Washington authorities knew that the Japanese were willing to surrender on virtually the same terms that were accepted in August, 1945. More persons lost their lives in the completely needless bombing of the beautiful city of Dresden than in both of the atom-bombings of Japanese cities. The record of destruction in wartime concentration camps is well known. Civilians and war prisoners were slaughtered wholesale during the war by both the Germans and the Russians. During and after the war, tens of millions of persons were uprooted from their homes which their ancestors had in many cases inhabited since the close of the Middle Ages or earlier, and millions died in the process. Hundreds of thousands died of malnutrition and exposure in occupied countries before something like normal living conditions were restored. Millions were shipped by the Russians to slave labor camps in which life was worse than death. The Korean War was in some respects even more brutal than the second World War. Justice William O. Douglas of the United States Supreme Court, an eye-witness, had this to say of the Korean situation: "I had seen the war-battered cities of Europe; but I had not seen devastation until I saw Korea. Cities like Seoul are badly mangled, but a host of towns and villages are completely obliterated. . . . Misery, disease, pain and suffering, starvation—these are all compounded beyond comprehension."

To summarize the intellectual implications of the situation as we now move along in the second half of the twentieth century—we have at hand a vast body of new knowledge concerning nature, man and society. This knowledge could emancipate us from fear, terminate warfare, and generate enthusiasm for the creation of a new order embracing peace, security, prosperity, and leisure. We could place humanity upon that "supra-pig level" envisioned by Plato more than two thousand years ago. This would enable us to expend our energies in cultivating interests and activities that lie entirely above those of the animal kingdom. Yet, these possibilities are at present nullified by fear of war and insecurity, by general passivity in thought and action (almost reaching fatalism), by intellectual distraction from fundamental social problems, and by mechanization and standardization which tend to paralyze both intellectual and social initiative. We are in danger, as James Harvey Robinson pointed out years ago, of perishing like the hen that roosted on the edge of a bushel of wheat but refused to turn around and discover the food.

It must be admitted that the outlook is not a cheering one. But the task of an honest historian is to tell the truth as he sees and finds it, not to fabricate false cheer. We have not advanced from where we stood two generations ago when H. G. Wells correctly described the human future as a race between Education and Catastrophe. The latter has made great strides and accumulated much new momentum since Wells wrote, but Education has made little headway as a dynamic social force. It has made decisive advances only in the fields of science and technology, which, if not accompanied by a clarification and assumption of our social responsibilities, only intensify the world crisis and make any escape from impending doom that much more remote and unlikely.

SELECTED READINGS

Albig, William, *Modern Public Opinion*, McGraw-Hill, 1956.

Amory, J. A., *Around the Edge of War*, Clarkson Potter, 1963.

Armstrong, H. F., *The Chronology of Failure*, Macmillan, 1940.

Aron, Raymond, *The Century of Total War*, Beacon, 1955.

Auerbach, M. M., *The Conservative Illusion*, Columbia University Press, 1959.

Barnes, H. E., *Social Institutions*, Prentice-Hall, 1942.

—— *Society in Transition*, 2nd ed., Prentice-Hall, 1952.

Berle, A. A., *Power Without Property*, Harcourt, Brace, 1960.

Bernays, E. L., *Crystallizing Public Opinion*, rev. ed., Liveright, 1961.

—— *Propaganda*, Liveright, 1928.

Boorstin, D. J., *The Image, or What Happened to the American Dream*, Atheneum, 1962.

Brady, R. A., *Organization, Automation, and Society*, University of California Press, 1962.

Brown, Harrison, *The Challenge of Man's Future*, Viking, 1956.

Burnham, James, *The Managerial Revolution*, Indiana University Press, 1960.

Cantril, Hadley, *Gauging Public Opinion*, Princeton University Press, 1944.

Casson, Stanley, *Progress and Catastrophe*, Hamilton, 1937.

Cleveland, Harland, and Laswell, H. D., eds., *The Ethics of Power*, Harper, 1962.

Commager, H. S., *The American Mind*, Yale University Press, 1959.

Dennis, Lawrence, *Dynamics of War and Revolution*, Harper, 1940.

Doob, L. W., *Public Opinion and Propaganda*, Holt, 1948.

Ernst and Lindey, *The Censor Marches On*.

Fermi, Laura, *Atoms for the World*, University of Chicago Press, 1957.

Fleming, D. F., *The Cold War and Its Origins, 1917-1960*, 2 vols., Doubleday, 1961.

Forbes, R. J., *Man the Maker: A History of Engineering and Technology*, Abelard-Schuman, 1958.

Fortune, Editors of, *The American Advertising Business*, Simon and Schuster, 1957.

Freeman, R. E., ed., *Postwar Economic Trends in the United States*, Harper, 1960.

Gabriel, R. H., *The Course of American Democratic Thought*, Ronald Press, 1956.

Gallup, George, *Guide to Public Opinion Polls*, Princeton University Press, 1948.

Gellhorn, Walter, *Individual Freedom and Governmental Restraints*, Louisiana State University Press, 1956.

Giedion, Siegfried, *Mechanization Takes Command: A Contribution to Anonymous History*, Oxford University Press, 1948.

Goldman, E. F., *The Crucial Decade and After: America 1945–1960*, Vintage Books.

—— *Two Way Street: The Emergence of the Public Relations Counsel*, Bellman, 1956.

Guilbaud, G. T., *What Is Cybernetics?*, Criterion, 1960.

Harral, Stewart, *Patterns of Publicity Copy*, University of Oklahoma Press, 1950.

Hocking, W. E., *The Coming World Civilization*, Harper, 1956.

Hofstadter, Richard, *Anti-Intellectualism in American Life*, Knopf, 1963.

Hughes, H. S., *Oswald Spengler*, Scribner, 1952.

Ingram, Kenneth, *History of the Cold War*, Philosophical Library, 1955.

Jacobson, H. B., and Roucek, J. S., *Automation and Society*, Philosophical Library, 1962.

Jones, W. T., ed., *Library of Contemporary Thought*, 8 vols., Knopf, 1926 *et seq.*

Joyce, Walter, *The Propaganda Gap*, Harper and Row, 1963.

Key, V. O., *Public Opinion and American Democracy*, Knopf, 1962.

Kirchwey, Freda, ed., *Our Changing Morality*, Boni and Liveright, 1934.

Korol, A. G., *Soviet Education for Science and Technology*, Wiley, 1957.

Langdon-Davies, John, *A Short History of the Future*, Dodd, Mead, 1936.

Laski, H. J., *Where Do We Go from Here?*, Viking, 1940.

Lerner, Max, *The Age of Overkill: A Preface to World Politics*, Simon and Schuster, 1963.

Loeb, Harold, *Life in a Technocracy*, Viking, 1933.

Lubell, Samuel, *The Future of American Politics*, Anchor Books, 1956.

———*The Revolt of the Moderates*, Harper, 1956.

Lukacs, John, *A History of the Cold War*, Doubleday, 1963.

Lumley, F. E., *The Propaganda Menace*, Appleton-Century, 1933.

Lundberg, Ferdinand, *The Coming World Transformation*, Doubleday, 1963.

Mayer, Martin, *Madison Avenue, U.S.A.*, Harper, 1958.

Melman, Seymour, ed., *Disarmament: Its Politics and Economics*, American Academy of Arts and Sciences, 1963.

Miller, C. R., *The Process of Persuasion*, Crown, 1946.

Millis, Walter, and Real, James, *The Abolition of War*, Macmillan, 1963.

Mills, C. W., *The Power Elite*, Galaxy, 1956.

Munson, Gorham, *Twelve Decisive Battles of the Mind*, Greystone Press, 1942.

Oakeshott, Michael, *Rationalism in Politics*, Basic Books, 1962.

Ogburn, *Social Change*.

Orwell, George, *Nineteen Eighty-Four*, New American Library, 1954.

———*The Orwell Reader*, ed. Richard Rovere, Harcourt, Brace, 1956.

Packard, Vance, *The Hidden Persuaders*, Pocket Books.

Parshley, H. M., *Science and Good Behavior*, Bobbs-Merrill, 1928.

Peterson, H. C., *Propaganda for War*, University of Oklahoma Press, 1939.

Riencourt, Amaury de, *The Coming Caesars*, Coward-McCann, 1957.

Rogers, Lindsay, *Crisis Government*, Norton, 1934.

Rovere, Richard, *The American Establishment*, Harcourt, Brace, 1962.

Schlesinger, A. M., Jr., *The Vital Center*, Houghton Mifflin, 1962.

Schuman, F. L., *The Cold War*, Louisiana State University Press, 1962.

Shipley, Maynard, *The War on Modern Science*, Knopf, 1927.

Soule, George, *The Space of Tomorrow*, Twentieth Century Fund, 1958.

Spanier, J. W., and Nogee, Joseph, *The Politics of Disarmament*, Praeger, 1963.

Talbot, Daniel, ed., *Film: An Anthology*, Simon and Schuster, 1960.

Taube, Mortimer, *Computers and Common Sense: The Myth of Thinking Machines*, Columbia University Press, 1962.

Toynbee, Arnold, *Reconsiderations*, Oxford University Press, 1961.

Wallas, Graham, *Human Nature in Politics*, University of Nebraska Press, 1962.

Waller, Willard, ed., *War in the Twentieth Century*, Dryden Press, 1940.

Wells, H. G., *The Shape of Things to Come*, Macmillan, 1933.

NOTE TO INDEX-GLOSSARY

The brief definitions of terms and identifications of persons are not to be considered as complete; their purpose is to refresh the memory or provide helps. Only terms and persons occurring repeatedly are thus characterized. In the alphabetization of proper names, the more familiar form (e.g., Dante Alighieri, not Alighieri, Dante) has been used. Names to which passing reference is made are not indexed, but may be found by consulting appropriate subject heads.

INDEX-GLOSSARY

Art, *(Cont.)*
  classical Greek, 178-90
  Rbman, 252-4
  early Christian, 315-7
  Byzantine, 372-6
  early medieval, 377
  early "Renaissance," 529-44
  effect of Protestant revolt, 589
  1475-1600, 623-39
  spread of Italian influence, 638-9
  secularization of, 666
  17th and 18th centuries, 911-29
  Art-for-Art's-Sake Cult, 1022, 1033
  19th century, 1045-60
  20th century, 1276-94
  See also Architecture, Music
Arthurian romances, 448-9, 598-9
Art Nouveau, 1278, 1281
Art-song, 1065
Aryan language and race, misconceptions concerning, 21-4
Asbury, Francis, 863
Asceticism, rise of, in Christianity, 284, 291
Asclepiades of Bithynia [*Greek physician, fl. 100 B.C.*], 159, 207
Asmai, al-, of Basra, 496
Assurbanipal [*Assyrian king, c. 650 B.C.*], 94
Assyria, excavations, 64, 65, 66
Astrolabe [*early instrument for observing the positions of the stars*], 341
Astrology, 595
  Roman, 209, 227
  medieval, 427-8
Astronomical time, 3-5
Astronomy, Babylonian, 75
  Pythagorean, 152
  Dark Ages, 351, 354, 355
  Muslim, 495
  late medieval, 501
  intellectual influence of, 669
  revolution in, 676-81
  18th century, 696
  19th century, 966-7
  contemporary, 1121-40
Astruc, Jean [*French physician, critic, 1684-1766*], 816
Athanasius [*Christian father, Bishop of Alexandria, c. 296-373*], 284, 288, 320
  quoted by Bayle, 764
Atheism, early modern, 813-4, 855
  19th century trend, 989-90
Athena, 161
Athens, 118
Athletics, Greek, 180
  present-day university, 1227
Atomic conception of nature, 129-30, 159, 214, 686
  theory (chemistry), 971, 1153-6
  theory (physics), 1118-21
Atomic number [*number assigned to an element when all the elements are placed in order of increasing weight*], 1155-6
Atonality [*mus., absence of tonal center*], 1295, 1299
Atonement, doctrine of, 347
Atrium [*in church arch. See drawing, p. 318*]
Auber, Daniel F. E., 1067
Auctus, Cocceius, 209

Auden, W. H.,1261
Auenbrugger, Leopold, 702
Augbigné, Françoise de, 883
Augurs, in Roman religion, 226
Augustine, Aurelius Augustinus [*Bishop of Hippo, 354-430*], 219, 221, 285, 300-6, 358
  on clarity of expression, 310
  attitude toward classical learning, 312, 333, 335
Augustinus Triumphatus, 510
Augustus Caesar, 201-2
  renounces imperial expansion, 245
Augustus Haranguing His Troops, 253
Aurignacian period. *See* Anthropological epochs
Aurispa, Giovanni [*Italian scholar, 1369-1459*], 551, 552, 554
Ausonius, Decimus Magnus [*Latin poet, teacher, c. 310-395*], 324
Austen, Jane, 1024, 1026
Austin, John, 1008-9, 1200
Auzout, Adrien, 682
Avenzoar, 498
Averroës [*Ibn Rushd, Muslim philosopher, physician, 1126-1198*], 402-3
Avicebron, 402
Avicenna, [*Ibn-Sina, Muslim physician, philosopher, 980-1037?*], 402, 430, 498
Avogadro, Amadeo, 970
Axiology [*philos. theory of value*], 993

Babbitt, Irving, 872, 1113
Babbitt, Milton, 1297
Babel, Isaac, 1233
Babylon, morality in ancient, 85
Babylonia, 65, 66
"Babylonian captivity" of papacy, 484
Babylonian Chronicle, 100
Bach, Johann Sebastian [*German composer, 1685-1750*], 937-8
Bacon, B. W., 957
Bacon, Francis [*English statesman, writer, philosopher, 1561-1626*], 19, 217, 425, 566, 717-22
  on scholasticism, 424
  Essays, 623
  on intolerance, 757
  on progress, 826-7
Bacon, Roger [*English philosopher, natural scientist, 1214-1294*], 344, 357, 426, 486-9, 499
  opinion of contemporary learning, 406
  estimate of size of universe, 676-7
  on progress, 825
Baer, G. F., *q.,* 662
Baer, Karl Ernst von, 973
Baeyer, Adolph von, 971
Baghdad, center of culture, 401
Baikie, James, *q.,* 65
Bain, Alexander, 974
Bakunin, Michael, 952
Balakireff, Mily, 1076
Balance wheel, invention, 676
Balkhi, al-, 497
Ball, Hugo, 1286
Balla, Giacomo, 1285
Ballad poetry, late medieval, 524

Chemistry, in Dark Ages, 355
and alchemy, 429
Muslim, 496
beginnings of modern, 571
17th century, 685-6
rise of modern, 697
19th century, 970-1
20th century, 1153-9
See also Alchemy
Chénier, André, 903-4
Chesney, Gen. F. R., 64
Chesterton, Gilbert K., 1112
Cheyne, T. K., 957
Cheynell, Francis, 758
Chiaroscuro, 628
Chicago, University of, 1226-7
Chillingworth, William, 757-8
Chirico, Giorgio de, 1287
Chivalry, chivalric literature, 448-9, 599
Chladni, Ernst Friedrich [German physicist, 1756-1827], 696, 968
Chopin, Frédéric [French (native of Poland) composer, 1810-1849], 1066, 1069
Chorale [Congregational hymn of Lutheran service], 647
Chrétien de Troyes, 449
Christian Century, The, 864
Christian epic, 302, 304
Christianity, and Stoicism, 219
cultural background of, 275-7
evolution of, 278-85
persecution of, 281-2
ideas on hell, devil, 295-300
intellectual patterns of, 306-12, 1319
See also Sacramental system, Catholic church, Mystery cults, Biblical criticism
Christian Science, 987-8, 1318
Christian socialist movement, 986
Christology [in theology, the theory of the nature of Christ], 289
Christopher of Mytilene, 369
Chromaticism (music), 540, 1072
Chromosomes, 1161
Chronology, biblical, 816-7
Chronology, new conceptions of, 3-6
Chronometer, invention, 694
Chrysippus [Greek stoic, d. c. 206 B.C.], 146, 213
Chrysoloras, Manuel [Byzantine classicist and teacher, 1350-1415], 551, 554
Chrysostom, John [Archbishop of Constantinople, c. 347-407], 284
Chubb, Thomas, 793
Chuquet, Nicholas, 500
Church, Alonzo, 1199
Church and state, 390-3
medieval theory of, 435-40
See also Political theory
Church, Catholic. See Catholic church
Churchill, Winston, 1327
Cibber, Colley, 899
Cicero, Marcus Tullius [Roman orator, politician, philos., 106-43 B.C.], 146, 177, 205, 206, 213, 220-3, 232, 244, 304
Jerome's attitude toward, 321
recovery of manuscripts, 519, 555
Renaissance cult of, 554
Erasmus on, 559
on urbanity in argument, 585

Cimabue, Giovanni, 475-6
City councils, medieval, 394
City of God, 269, 285. See also Augustine
City-state, in ancient Orient, 67
in Greece, 120-2
Roman development, 254
Civilization, discussion of nature of, 1311-3
destruction of, 1313-4
Civil liberties, struggle for, 771-8
modern suppression, 779-81, 1091-2
Claudel, Paul, 1262
Clark, A. C., q., 266
Clarke, Samuel [English philos., 1675-1729], 785
Classical culture, Petrarch and, 519
late medieval study, 547
educational revival, 566-7
revival of interest, 601
Claude Lorrain [French painter, 1600-1682], 923, 1051
Claudius of Turin, 337, 345
Clausius, Rudolf, 968
Clausius of Antwerp, 572
Cleanthes [Greek stoic, c. 265 B.C.], 146
Cleland, H. F., cited, 58
Clemenceau, Georges, 989
Clementine heresy, 289
Clerestory [in church arch. See drawing, p. 318]
Clergy, in medieval times, 389. See also Catholic church, Christianity
Climate, institutional influence of, 438, 581
Clock, improvement in, 502, 508
Cloisons, 375, 378
Cluverius, Philip, 692
Cocteau, Jean, 1263, 1274
Codex, the, 575
Coinage, debasement of, 257
Coins, Greek, 188
Cold War, the, 1089-99 passim, 1314, 1326-32 passim, 1336
Colenso, John William, 957
Coleridge, Samuel T. [English poet, critic, 1772-1834], 1014-5
Collier, Jeremy, 891
Collins, Anthony [English freethinker, 1676-1729], 764-5, 789, 816
Colonate, 328
Color, in art, 1055-6
Colosseum, 251
Columba, 339
Columban, 339
Columbus, voyage of, 158, 656
Column-and-lintel [in arch. See drawing, p. 110]
Columns, use of, in architecture, 105, 181
Comedy, Greek, 172-4
Comenius, John Amos, 739
Comitatus, 387
Commercial expansion. See Expansion
Commercial paper, invention of, 72
"Commercial Revolution," 657-8
Commines, Philippe de, 621
Commodianus [Christian poet, fl. 3rd cent.], 324
Commons, John R., 1191
Communism, 952. See also Soviet Russia
Comparative ethics, 821-2
Comparative religion, science of, 664
Compass, mariner's, invented, 508
Compayré, Gabriel, q., 409
Compilations, medieval, 267, 337

MacDonald-Wright, Stanton, 1286, 1288
Macedonian heresy, 289
Macer Floridus, 357
Machiavelli, Niccolò [*Italian political philosopher, 1469-1527*], 579-80, 621, 622
MacLaurin, Colin, 695
MacLeish, Archibald, 1261
MacLeod, W. Christie, 1186
MacMurray, W. H., 1278
MacNeice, Louis, 1261
Macpherson, James, 907
Macrocosm-microcosm analogy, 314, 426, 430, 490, 574
Madison, James, 1008
Madrigal [*secular polyphonic form, fl. 16th cent.*], 541, 644, 646
Maecenas, 239, 240, 242
Maestro di cappella [*Italian equivalent of Kapellmeister*], 646, 931
Maeterlinck, Maurice, 1248, 1298
Magamát, 371
Magellan, 656
Magic, primitive religion, 47
medieval, 429-30, 595
Magna Carta, 775
Mago, treatise on agriculture, 209
Magritte, René, 1287
Mahabharata [*Sanskrit epic*], 98
Mahler, Gustav, 1075, 1079, 1295, 1297
Maillol, Aristide, 1289
Maimonides, Moses, 403
Maine, Henry Sumner, 1008
Maintenon, Madame de, 883
Maistre, Joseph de [*French statesman, social philosopher, 1754-1821*], 861, 867
Maître de chapelle [*French equivalent of Kapellmeister*], 641
Malebranche, Nicolas, 689
Malevich, Kasimir, 1286
Malherbe, François, 881
Mallarmé, Stéphane [*French symbolist poet, 1842-1898*], 1034, 1261-2, 1297
Malory, Thomas, 598-9
Malpighi, Marcello, 687
Malraux, André, 1274
Malthus, Thomas Robert [*English social philosopher, 1766-1834*], 8, 951
Ma'mun, al-, 402
Man, antiquity of, 6-8, 16, 28-30
animal characteristics of, 10-4
early types of, 28-30
Mana, 45, 224
Manassia, church at, 376
Mandeville (*pseudonym*), travels of, 655
Mandeville, Bernard, 821
Manegold of Lautenbach, 357, 358
Manet, Edouard [*French painter, 1832-1883*], 638, 1055
Manetho [*Egyptian chronicler, c. 275 B.C.*], 100
Manichaeism [*Persian mystery cult*], 224, 268, 280
Manilius, Marcus, 209
Mann, Horace, 999, 1004
Mann, Thomas [*German novelist, 1875-1955*], 1071, 1275
Mannerism (*painting*), 632-3
Manning, Henry Edward, 860
Manning, Robert of Bourne, 517

Mansur, al-, 402
Mantegna, Andrea, 627
Manuel, Don Juan, 520
Manuscripts, recovery of, 555
Manutius, Aldus, 554
Manzoni, Alessandro, 1022
Manzù, Giacomo, 1293
Maps, Roman, 208
late medieval, 503
modern, 705
Marc, Franz, 1284
Marcel, Gabriel, 1201-4 *passim*
Marcks, Gerhard, 1291
Marcus Aurelius [*Roman emperor, stoic philosopher, A.D. 121-180*], 117, 119-20
Mardini, Masawaih al-, 498
Marenzio, Luca, 646
Marett, R. R., *cited*, 45, 51, 57, 415
Maria de Novara, 501
Mariana, Juan de, 581
Mariette, Auguste [*French archaeologist, 1821-1881*], 64
Marin, John, 1286
Marinetti, E. F. T., 1262, 1285
Marini, Marino, 1293
Marinus of Alexandria, 158
Marinus of Tyre, 159
Mariotte, Edmé, 683, 684
Maritain, Jacques, 872, 1113, 1211-2
Marivaux, Pierre de, 903
Markham, Edwin, 1052
Marlowe, Christopher, 614
Marot, Clément, 602
Marriage of Philology and Mercury, 266, 330-1, 349
Marshall, Alfred, 1189-90
Marshall, Leon C., 1225
Marsiglio of Padua [*Italian political theorist, 1270-1342*], 436, 484, 511-2
Martial [*Marcus Valerius Martialis, Latin poet, A.D. c. 40-104*], 232, 243
Martianus. *See* Capella
Martin, A. J. P., 1163
Martin, Henri, 1011
Martin du Gard, Roger, 1274
Martineau, Harriet, 984
Martínez Sierra, Gregorio, 1252-3
Martyrdom, Christian, 292
Marx, Karl [*German social philosopher, 1818-1883*], 951-2, 992, 1016, 1227
Marxian socialism, 1095-6
Masaccio, 535-6
Mascagni, Pietro, 1073
Masefield, John, 1257
Maspero, Gaston [*French Egyptologist, 1846-1916*], 64
Mass, the analysis of, 383-4
music of, 544
Massenet, Jules, 1077
Massinger, Philip, 875
Masson, André, 1287
Mastaba [*arch. See drawing, p. 103*]
Masters, Edgar Lee, 1258-9
Mastery, human quest for, 1315-20
Material cause, 142
Materialism, economic, 589-91
Maternus, Firmicus, 209

Music, Greek, *(Cont.)*
    14th and 15th centuries, 540-4
    1475-1600, 641-51
    17th and 18th centuries, 929-44
    19th century, 1061-80
    American, 1080, 1302-3
    Soviet, 1076-7, 1231, 1302
    contemporary, 1294-1307
Musical instruments, 542, 1064
Musical societies, 941
Mùsica Transalpina, 650
Muslims, 271, 329, 357
    literature, 370-2
    learning, 400-5
    science, 494-9
    contribution to culture, 654
Mussatus, Albertinus, 444
Musschenbroek, Peter von, 697
Musset, Alfred de, 1021, 1038
Mussolini, Benito, 139, 1094
Muste, A. J., 1229
Muthesius, Hermann, 1281
Myron [*Greek sculptor, fl. 5th cent. B.C.*], 182
Mystery cults, 81, 164, 267-9
Mystery plays, 527-8
Mysticism, medieval, 425-6, 484, 489-90

Nadelman, Elie, 1291
Nägeli, Karl von, 973
Naevius, Gnaeus [*Latin poet, 3rd cent. B.C.*], 204, 234
Nahum [*Hebrew prophet, c. 625 B.C.*], 88
Napier, John, 569
Napoleon, Napoleonic era. *See* Romanticism
Narthex [*in church arch. See drawing, p. 318*]
Nationalism, late medieval growth, 482
    modern rise of, 548, 659-60, 1091
    and industrial revolution, 954
    in music, 1075-7
National Socialism (Germany), 1089, 1092, 1094-5
Nattier, Jean Marc, 926
Nave [*in church arch. See drawing, p. 318*], 317
Navigation, improvement of, 656
Nazism, 779, 1206. *See also* National Socialism, Fascism, Hitler
Neanderthal man, 29, 41, 55
Neckham, Alexander, 427, 435
Nemorarius, Jordanes, 500
Neoclassicism, in art, 1046-7, 1048
    in contemporary music, 1299-1301
Neolithic. *See* Anthropological epochs
Neoplatonism [*mixture of Judeo-Christian mysticism with Greek philosophy*], 119, 136, 140, 262-5, 279, 291, 308, 311, 332, 342, 490, 551, 557, 562-3
Nestorian heresy, 289
Nestorian monks, 401, 405
Neue Sachlichkeit [*"New Realism," movement in German art and poetry*], 1265, 1284
Neurath, Otto, 1199
New Criticism, the, 1273-4
New Deal, the, 1089, 1094, 1097-8
New Economic Policy, 1233
"New Humanism," the, 1112-3
Newman, John Henry [*English religious leader, 1801-1890*], 858-60, 1036
New School for Social Research, 1228

New Testament. *See* Biblical criticism
Newton, Isaac [*English scientist, mathematician, 1642-1727*], 680, 683-5 *passim,* 691, 695, 969, 1122-3
    contribution to telescope, 675
    invention of calculus, 682
    Preserved Smith's opinion of, 693
    on biblical chronology, 817
    compared with Darwin, 961
Newtonian system, 787, 844, 980
New World, discovery of. *See* Expansion
Nibelungenlied, 368, 446
Nicea, Council of, 282
Nicene Creed, 284
Nicholas II [*Russian czar, 1868-1918*], 1231, 1232
Nicholas of Cues [*Cusanus, German theologian, scholar, 1401-1464*], 436, 490, 501, 512
Nicholas of Poland, 429
Nicoll, Allardyce, *q.,* 1250
Nicomachus of Gerasa, 154
Niebuhr, Karsten [*German traveler, 1733-1815*], 64
Niebuhr, Reinhold, 1210, 1216
Niemöller, Martin, 1209, 1218
Nietzsche, Friedrich [*German philosopher, 1844-1900*], 977
Nimazi, as-, 371
Nineteen Eighty-Four. See Orwell, George
Nolde, Emil, 1283-4
Nominalism [*in medieval philosophy, the doctrine that there is no reality except in concrete examples of things*], 138, 330, 333-44, 423, 485-6, 489
Noodt, Geraert, 760
Normal schools, 999
Norris, Frank, 1267
North, Christopher, 621
Northrop, John Howard, 1162
Norton, Thomas, 613
Noumenalism, 846
Novalis, Friedrich von Hardenberg, 1019
Novara, Maria de, 570
Novel, Latin literature, 247-8
    English, rise of, 894-7
    19th century, 1023-30
    Soviet, 1233-4, 1235
    contemporary, 1266-75
Novicow, Jacques, 1006
Numbers, Pythagorean ideas of, 152

Obrecht, Jacob, 641, 643
Obscurantism, contemporary revival, 1112-3
Observatories, astronomical, 682
O'Casey, Sean, 1249-50
Occasionalists, 689
Occleve, Thomas, 524
Occultism of Humanistic period, 568
Ockeghem, Jean, 641, 642
Ockham. *See* William of Ockham
Oderic of Pordenone, 655
Odets, Clifford, 1253
Oersted, H. C., 969
Ogburn, W. F., 843, 1111, 1185, 1321
Ogden, C. K., *cited,* 53
Ohm, G. S., 970
Oil painting, invention of, 539
Old English poetry, 363-7

Pecquet, Jean, 687
Pei, W. C., 29
Peirce, Charles S., 996, 1108, 1196
Peking man, 29, 39
Pendentive [in arch. See drawing, p. 373]
Pendulum clock, invention of, 675
Penka, Carl, cited, 22
Penn, William, 759
Pepusch, John, 939
Percy, Thomas, 907
Perfectionism, 836
Pergamum, 189
Pergolesi, Giovanni, 933
Peri, Jacopo, 929, 930
Pericles [Athenian statesman d. c. 429 B.C.], 122, 183, 185, 205
Peripatetics, 144
Perotin, 477
Perrault, Charles [French writer, 1628-1703], 673, 830-1
Perrault, Pierre [French scientist, 1608-1680], 692
Persepolis, 111
Persian religion, 80
   dualism, 269, 296
   contribution to Christianity, 269, 279, 280
Persian Wars, 175
Perspective in art, 253, 536, 626
Perthes, Boucher de, 27, 1007
Perugino, Pietro, 626
Pestalozzi, Heinrich, 1003
Peter of Abano [Italian scientist, scholar, 1250-1320], 357, 435, 505
Petrarch [Francesco Petrarca, Italian humanist, poet, 1304-1374], 321, 519, 526, 551, 601, 603
Petrie, Flinders, 64, 70
Petronius, Gaius Petronius Arbiter [Roman courtier, writer, d. A.D. 66], 233, 247-8
Petrossa Treasury, 378
Petrov, Eugene [pen name of Eugene Katayev, Russian humorist, 1903-1942], 1233
Pevsner, Antoine, 1286, 1292
Peyre, Henri, q., 1268
Phenomenology, 1195-6
Phidias [Greek sculptor, c. 500-432 B.C.], 171, 183, 185, 186
Philidor [François André Danican, French composer, chess-player, 1681-1728], 940
Philistines, 80
"Philistinism," 1020
Phillips, Harold C., q., 1310
Philo [Philo Judaeus, Jewish neoplatonist, fl. 1st cent.], 119
Philology, science of, 664
Philosopher's stone, 428
Philosophes, 901
Philosophy, early Greek, 124-31
   Roman, 214-24
   in humanistic period, 562-6
   19th century, 992-7
   20th century, 1193-1204
   See also Romanticism, and names of individual philosophers
Phlogiston theory, 686, 697
Phlorius and Platziaphlora, 370
Phoenician alphabet, 90

Photius [Byzantine compiler, c. 820-891], 369, 397
Phrygian mode (music), 384
Physics, modern revolution in, 1102-7. See also Science, Mathematics
Physiology, modern, 1164-7
Piaget, Jean, 1174-5
Piano, improvement of, 1064-5
Picabia, Francis, 1286
Picard, Jean [French astronomer, 1620-1682], 682
Picaresque (novel type), 620
Picasso, Pablo, 1285, 1290, 1292
Pico della Mirandola, John [Italian philosopher and writer, 1463-1494], 553
Pictograms [pictures expressing ideas], 89, 90
Pilgrimages, medieval habit of, 457
Pindar [Greek lyric poet, c. 522-443 B.C.], 167-8
Pinel, Philippe, 702
Pinero, Arthur Wing, 1039
Pirandello, Luigi, 1253, 1306
Pirenne, Henri, q., 394
Pisano, Andrea, 532, 533
Pisano, Giovanni, 474
Pisano, Niccola, 474
Pissarro, Camille, 1056
Piston, Walter, 1301
Pithecanthropus erectus, 29, 39
Pius IX, 984, 1112, 1217
Piux X, 1217
Placental mammals, 11
Plain chant [single-voiced music of the early Catholic church], 384, 544
Planck, Max, 1106, 1117-9, 1150; q., 980
Plantin, Christophe, 578
Plato [Greek philosopher, c. 428-c. 348 B.C.], 123, 134, 135-40, 151, 153, 157, 165, 185-6, 191, 262, 398
   revival in "Renaissance," 552
   See also Neoplatonism
Plautus, Titus Maccius [Latin comic dramatist, d. 184 B.C.], 204, 234
Pléiade [16th cent. group of French poets], 168, 602
Plethon, Gemistus, 398, 552-3
Pliny [Gaius Plinius Secundus the elder, Latin compiler, antiquarian, A.D. 23-79], 186, 208, 211-2, 260, 353, 357
Pliny [Gaius Plinius Caecilius Secundus the younger, Roman politician, writer, A.D. c. 61-c. 113], 233, 247
Plotinus [Neoplatonic philosopher, in Egypt, c. 205-c. 270 A.D.], 140, 262-3
Plumbing, Roman, 248
Pluralism [philosophy, doctrine that there are many fundamental realities], 996
Plurality of worlds, Bruno's idea, 710
Plutarch [Greek biographer, moralist, A.D. c. 46-120], 184, 621, 711
Pluto, 162
Poe, Edgar Allan [Amer. poet, critic, 1809-1849], 906, 1043
Poem of Creation [ancient Babylonian epic], 93
Pösche, Theodore, cited, 22
Poetry. See Literature
Poggio Bracciolini, 551
Pointillism, 1269
Pokrovsky, Michael, 1234

A CATALOGUE OF SELECTED DOVER BOOKS
IN ALL FIELDS OF INTEREST

A CATALOGUE OF SELECTED DOVER BOOKS
IN ALL FIELDS OF INTEREST

AMERICA'S OLD MASTERS, James T. Flexner. Four men emerged unexpectedly from provincial 18th century America to leadership in European art: Benjamin West, J. S. Copley, C. R. Peale, Gilbert Stuart. Brilliant coverage of lives and contributions. Revised, 1967 edition. 69 plates. 365pp. of text.

21806-6 Paperbound $3.00

FIRST FLOWERS OF OUR WILDERNESS: AMERICAN PAINTING, THE COLONIAL PERIOD, James T. Flexner. Painters, and regional painting traditions from earliest Colonial times up to the emergence of Copley, West and Peale Sr., Foster, Gustavus Hesselius, Feke, John Smibert and many anonymous painters in the primitive manner. Engaging presentation, with 162 illustrations. xxii + 368pp.

22180-6 Paperbound $3.50

THE LIGHT OF DISTANT SKIES: AMERICAN PAINTING, 1760-1835, James T. Flexner. The great generation of early American painters goes to Europe to learn and to teach: West, Copley, Gilbert Stuart and others. Allston, Trumbull, Morse; also contemporary American painters—primitives, derivatives, academics—who remained in America. 102 illustrations. xiii + 306pp. 22179-2 Paperbound $3.50

A HISTORY OF THE RISE AND PROGRESS OF THE ARTS OF DESIGN IN THE UNITED STATES, William Dunlap. Much the richest mine of information on early American painters, sculptors, architects, engravers, miniaturists, etc. The only source of information for scores of artists, the major primary source for many others. Unabridged reprint of rare original 1834 edition, with new introduction by James T. Flexner, and 394 new illustrations. Edited by Rita Weiss. 6⅝ x 9⅝.

21695-0, 21696-9, 21697-7 Three volumes, Paperbound $13.50

EPOCHS OF CHINESE AND JAPANESE ART, Ernest F. Fenollosa. From primitive Chinese art to the 20th century, thorough history, explanation of every important art period and form, including Japanese woodcuts; main stress on China and Japan, but Tibet, Korea also included. Still unexcelled for its detailed, rich coverage of cultural background, aesthetic elements, diffusion studies, particularly of the historical period. 2nd, 1913 edition. 242 illustrations. lii + 439pp. of text.

20364-6, 20365-4 Two volumes, Paperbound $6.00

THE GENTLE ART OF MAKING ENEMIES, James A. M. Whistler. Greatest wit of his day deflates Oscar Wilde, Ruskin, Swinburne; strikes back at inane critics, exhibitions, art journalism; aesthetics of impressionist revolution in most striking form. Highly readable classic by great painter. Reproduction of edition designed by Whistler. Introduction by Alfred Werner. xxxvi + 334pp.

21875-9 Paperbound $2.50

VISUAL ILLUSIONS: THEIR CAUSES, CHARACTERISTICS, AND APPLICATIONS, Matthew Luckiesh. Thorough description and discussion of optical illusion, geometric and perspective, particularly; size and shape distortions, illusions of color, of motion; natural illusions; use of illusion in art and magic, industry, etc. Most useful today with op art, also for classical art. Scores of effects illustrated. Introduction by William H. Ittleson. 100 illustrations. xxi + 252pp.

21530-X Paperbound $2.00

A HANDBOOK OF ANATOMY FOR ART STUDENTS, Arthur Thomson. Thorough, virtually exhaustive coverage of skeletal structure, musculature, etc. Full text, supplemented by anatomical diagrams and drawings and by photographs of undraped figures. Unique in its comparison of male and female forms, pointing out differences of contour, texture, form. 211 figures, 40 drawings, 86 photographs. xx + 459pp. 5⅜ x 8⅜. 21163-0 Paperbound $3.50

150 MASTERPIECES OF DRAWING, Selected by Anthony Toney. Full page reproductions of drawings from the early 16th to the end of the 18th century, all beautifully reproduced: Rembrandt, Michelangelo, Dürer, Fragonard, Urs, Graf, Wouwerman, many others. First-rate browsing book, model book for artists. xviii + 150pp. 8⅜ x 11¼. 21032-4 Paperbound $2.50

THE LATER WORK OF AUBREY BEARDSLEY, Aubrey Beardsley. Exotic, erotic, ironic masterpieces in full maturity: Comedy Ballet, Venus and Tannhauser, Pierrot, Lysistrata, Rape of the Lock, Savoy material, Ali Baba, Volpone, etc. This material revolutionized the art world, and is still powerful, fresh, brilliant. With *The Early Work*, all Beardsley's finest work. 174 plates, 2 in color. xiv + 176pp. 8⅛ x 11. 21817-1 Paperbound $3.00

DRAWINGS OF REMBRANDT, Rembrandt van Rijn. Complete reproduction of fabulously rare edition by Lippmann and Hofstede de Groot, completely reedited, updated, improved by Prof. Seymour Slive, Fogg Museum. Portraits, Biblical sketches, landscapes, Oriental types, nudes, episodes from classical mythology—All Rembrandt's fertile genius. Also selection of drawings by his pupils and followers. "Stunning volumes," *Saturday Review*. 550 illustrations. lxxviii + 552pp. 9⅛ x 12¼. 21485-0, 21486-9 Two volumes, Paperbound $10.00

THE DISASTERS OF WAR, Francisco Goya. One of the masterpieces of Western civilization—83 etchings that record Goya's shattering, bitter reaction to the Napoleonic war that swept through Spain after the insurrection of 1808 and to war in general. Reprint of the first edition, with three additional plates from Boston's Museum of Fine Arts. All plates facsimile size. Introduction by Philip Hofer, Fogg Museum. v + 97pp. 9⅜ x 8¼. 21872-4 Paperbound $2.00

GRAPHIC WORKS OF ODILON REDON. Largest collection of Redon's graphic works ever assembled: 172 lithographs, 28 etchings and engravings, 9 drawings. These include some of his most famous works. All the plates from *Odilon Redon: oeuvre graphique complet*, plus additional plates. New introduction and caption translations by Alfred Werner. 209 illustrations. xxvii + 209pp. 9⅛ x 12¼.

21966-8 Paperbound $4.00

DESIGN BY ACCIDENT; A BOOK OF "ACCIDENTAL EFFECTS" FOR ARTISTS AND DESIGNERS, James F. O'Brien. Create your own unique, striking, imaginative effects by "controlled accident" interaction of materials: paints and lacquers, oil and water based paints, splatter, crackling materials, shatter, similar items. Everything you do will be different; first book on this limitless art, so useful to both fine artist and commercial artist. Full instructions. 192 plates showing "accidents," 8 in color. viii + 215pp. 8⅜ x 11¼. 21942-9 Paperbound $3.50

THE BOOK OF SIGNS, Rudolf Koch. Famed German type designer draws 493 beautiful symbols: religious, mystical, alchemical, imperial, property marks, runes, etc. Remarkable fusion of traditional and modern. Good for suggestions of timelessness, smartness, modernity. Text. vi + 104pp. 6⅛ x 9¼. 20162-7 Paperbound $1.25

HISTORY OF INDIAN AND INDONESIAN ART, Ananda K. Coomaraswamy. An unabridged republication of one of the finest books by a great scholar in Eastern art. Rich in descriptive material, history, social backgrounds; Sunga reliefs, Rajput paintings, Gupta temples, Burmese frescoes, textiles, jewelry, sculpture, etc. 400 photos. viii + 423pp. 6⅜ x 9¾. 21436-2 Paperbound $5.00

PRIMITIVE ART, Franz Boas. America's foremost anthropologist surveys textiles, ceramics, woodcarving, basketry, metalwork, etc.; patterns, technology, creation of symbols, style origins. All areas of world, but very full on Northwest Coast Indians. More than 350 illustrations of baskets, boxes, totem poles, weapons, etc. 378 pp. 20025-6 Paperbound $3.00

THE GENTLEMAN AND CABINET MAKER'S DIRECTOR, Thomas Chippendale. Full reprint (third edition, 1762) of most influential furniture book of all time, by master cabinetmaker. 200 plates, illustrating chairs, sofas, mirrors, tables, cabinets, plus 24 photographs of surviving pieces. Biographical introduction by N. Bienenstock. vi + 249pp. 9⅞ x 12¾. 21601-2 Paperbound $4.00

AMERICAN ANTIQUE FURNITURE, Edgar G. Miller, Jr. The basic coverage of all American furniture before 1840. Individual chapters cover type of furniture—clocks, tables, sideboards, etc.—chronologically, with inexhaustible wealth of data. More than 2100 photographs, all identified, commented on. Essential to all early American collectors. Introduction by H. E. Keyes. vi + 1106pp. 7⅞ x 10¾. 21599-7, 21600-4 Two volumes, Paperbound $11.00

PENNSYLVANIA DUTCH AMERICAN FOLK ART, Henry J. Kauffman. 279 photos, 28 drawings of tulipware, Fraktur script, painted tinware, toys, flowered furniture, quilts, samplers, hex signs, house interiors, etc. Full descriptive text. Excellent for tourist, rewarding for designer, collector. Map. 146pp. 7⅞ x 10¾. 21205-X Paperbound $2.50

EARLY NEW ENGLAND GRAVESTONE RUBBINGS, Edmund V. Gillon, Jr. 43 photographs, 226 carefully reproduced rubbings show heavily symbolic, sometimes macabre early gravestones, up to early 19th century. Remarkable early American primitive art, occasionally strikingly beautiful; always powerful. Text. xxvi + 207pp. 8⅜ x 11¼. 21380-3 Paperbound $3.50

ALPHABETS AND ORNAMENTS, Ernst Lehner. Well-known pictorial source for decorative alphabets, script examples, cartouches, frames, decorative title pages, calligraphic initials, borders, similar material. 14th to 19th century, mostly European. Useful in almost any graphic arts designing, varied styles. 750 illustrations. 256pp. 7 x 10.
21905-4 Paperbound $4.00

PAINTING: A CREATIVE APPROACH, Norman Colquhoun. For the beginner simple guide provides an instructive approach to painting: major stumbling blocks for beginner; overcoming them, technical points; paints and pigments; oil painting; watercolor and other media and color. New section on "plastic" paints. Glossary. Formerly *Paint Your Own Pictures*. 221pp.
22000-1 Paperbound $1.75

THE ENJOYMENT AND USE OF COLOR, Walter Sargent. Explanation of the relations between colors themselves and between colors in nature and art, including hundreds of little-known facts about color values, intensities, effects of high and low illumination, complementary colors. Many practical hints for painters, references to great masters. 7 color plates, 29 illustrations. x + 274pp.
20944-X Paperbound $2.75

THE NOTEBOOKS OF LEONARDO DA VINCI, compiled and edited by Jean Paul Richter. 1566 extracts from original manuscripts reveal the full range of Leonardo's versatile genius: all his writings on painting, sculpture, architecture, anatomy, astronomy, geography, topography, physiology, mining, music, etc., in both Italian and English, with 186 plates of manuscript pages and more than 500 additional drawings. Includes studies for the Last Supper, the lost Sforza monument, and other works. Total of xlvii + 866pp. 7⅞ x 10¾.
22572-0, 22573-9 Two volumes, Paperbound $10.00

MONTGOMERY WARD CATALOGUE OF 1895. Tea gowns, yards of flannel and pillow-case lace, stereoscopes, books of gospel hymns, the New Improved Singer Sewing Machine, side saddles, milk skimmers, straight-edged razors, high-button shoes, spittoons, and on and on . . . listing some 25,000 items, practically all illustrated. Essential to the shoppers of the 1890's, it is our truest record of the spirit of the period. Unaltered reprint of Issue No. 57, Spring and Summer 1895. Introduction by Boris Emmet. Innumerable illustrations. xiii + 624pp. 8½ x 11⅝.
22377-9 Paperbound $6.95

THE CRYSTAL PALACE EXHIBITION ILLUSTRATED CATALOGUE (LONDON, 1851). One of the wonders of the modern world—the Crystal Palace Exhibition in which all the nations of the civilized world exhibited their achievements in the arts and sciences—presented in an equally important illustrated catalogue. More than 1700 items pictured with accompanying text—ceramics, textiles, cast-iron work, carpets, pianos, sleds, razors, wall-papers, billiard tables, beehives, silverware and hundreds of other artifacts—represent the focal point of Victorian culture in the Western World. Probably the largest collection of Victorian decorative art ever assembled— indispensable for antiquarians and designers. Unabridged republication of the Art-Journal Catalogue of the Great Exhibition of 1851, with all terminal essays. New introduction by John Gloag, F.S.A. xxxiv + 426pp. 9 x 12.
22503-8 Paperbound $4.50

A History of Costume, Carl Köhler. Definitive history, based on surviving pieces of clothing primarily, and paintings, statues, etc. secondarily. Highly readable text, supplemented by 594 illustrations of costumes of the ancient Mediterranean peoples, Greece and Rome, the Teutonic prehistoric period; costumes of the Middle Ages, Renaissance, Baroque, 18th and 19th centuries. Clear, measured patterns are provided for many clothing articles. Approach is practical throughout. Enlarged by Emma von Sichart. 464pp. 21030-8 Paperbound $3.50

Oriental Rugs, Antique and Modern, Walter A. Hawley. A complete and authoritative treatise on the Oriental rug—where they are made, by whom and how, designs and symbols, characteristics in detail of the six major groups, how to distinguish them and how to buy them. Detailed technical data is provided on periods, weaves, warps, wefts, textures, sides, ends and knots, although no technical background is required for an understanding. 11 color plates, 80 halftones, 4 maps. vi + 320pp. 6⅛ x 9⅛. 22366-3 Paperbound $5.00

Ten Books on Architecture, Vitruvius. By any standards the most important book on architecture ever written. Early Roman discussion of aesthetics of building, construction methods, orders, sites, and every other aspect of architecture has inspired, instructed architecture for about 2,000 years. Stands behind Palladio, Michelangelo, Bramante, Wren, countless others. Definitive Morris H. Morgan translation. 68 illustrations. xii + 331pp. 20645-9 Paperbound $3.00

The Four Books of Architecture, Andrea Palladio. Translated into every major Western European language in the two centuries following its publication in 1570, this has been one of the most influential books in the history of architecture. Complete reprint of the 1738 Isaac Ware edition. New introduction by Adolf Placzek, Columbia Univ. 216 plates. xxii + 110pp. of text. 9½ x 12¾. 21308-0 Clothbound $10.00

Sticks and Stones: A Study of American Architecture and Civilization, Lewis Mumford.One of the great classics of American cultural history. American architecture from the medieval-inspired earliest forms to the early 20th century; evolution of structure and style, and reciprocal influences on environment. 21 photographic illustrations. 238pp. 20202-X Paperbound $2.00

The American Builder's Companion, Asher Benjamin. The most widely used early 19th century architectural style and source book, for colonial up into Greek Revival periods. Extensive development of geometry of carpentering, construction of sashes, frames, doors, stairs; plans and elevations of domestic and other buildings. Hundreds of thousands of houses were built according to this book, now invaluable to historians, architects, restorers, etc. 1827 edition. 59 plates. 114pp. 7⅞ x 10¾. 22236-5 Paperbound $3.50

Dutch Houses in the Hudson Valley Before 1776, Helen Wilkinson Reynolds. The standard survey of the Dutch colonial house and outbuildings, with constructional features, decoration, and local history associated with individual homesteads. Introduction by Franklin D. Roosevelt. Map. 150 illustrations. 469pp. 6⅝ x 9¼. 21469-9 Paperbound $4.00

THE ARCHITECTURE OF COUNTRY HOUSES, Andrew J. Downing. Together with Vaux's *Villas and Cottages* this is the basic book for Hudson River Gothic architecture of the middle Victorian period. Full, sound discussions of general aspects of housing, architecture, style, decoration, furnishing, together with scores of detailed house plans, illustrations of specific buildings, accompanied by full text. Perhaps the most influential single American architectural book. 1850 edition. Introduction by J. Stewart Johnson. 321 figures, 34 architectural designs. xvi + 560pp.

22003-6 Paperbound $4.00

LOST EXAMPLES OF COLONIAL ARCHITECTURE, John Mead Howells. Full-page photographs of buildings that have disappeared or been so altered as to be denatured, including many designed by major early American architects. 245 plates. xvii + 248pp. 7⅞ x 10¾. 21143-6 Paperbound $3.50

DOMESTIC ARCHITECTURE OF THE AMERICAN COLONIES AND OF THE EARLY REPUBLIC, Fiske Kimball. Foremost architect and restorer of Williamsburg and Monticello covers nearly 200 homes between 1620-1825. Architectural details, construction, style features, special fixtures, floor plans, etc. Generally considered finest work in its area. 219 illustrations of houses, doorways, windows, capital mantels. xx + 314pp. 7⅞ x 10¾. 21743-4 Paperbound $4.00

EARLY AMERICAN ROOMS: 1650-1858, edited by Russell Hawes Kettell. Tour of 12 rooms, each representative of a different era in American history and each furnished, decorated, designed and occupied in the style of the era. 72 plans and elevations, 8-page color section, etc., show fabrics, wall papers, arrangements, etc. Full descriptive text. xvii + 200pp. of text. 8⅜ x 11¼.

21633-0 Paperbound $5.00

THE FITZWILLIAM VIRGINAL BOOK, edited by J. Fuller Maitland and W. B. Squire. Full modern printing of famous early 17th-century ms. volume of 300 works by Morley, Byrd, Bull, Gibbons, etc. For piano or other modern keyboard instrument; easy to read format. xxxvi + 938pp. 8⅜ x 11.

21068-5, 21069-3 Two volumes, Paperbound $10.00

KEYBOARD MUSIC, Johann Sebastian Bach. Bach Gesellschaft edition. A rich selection of Bach's masterpieces for the harpsichord: the six English Suites, six French Suites, the six Partitas (Clavierübung part I), the Goldberg Variations (Clavierübung part IV), the fifteen Two-Part Inventions and the fifteen Three-Part Sinfonias. Clearly reproduced on large sheets with ample margins; eminently playable. vi + 312pp. 8⅛ x 11. 22360-4 Paperbound $5.00

THE MUSIC OF BACH: AN INTRODUCTION, Charles Sanford Terry. A fine, nontechnical introduction to Bach's music, both instrumental and vocal. Covers organ music, chamber music, passion music, other types. Analyzes themes, developments, innovations. x + 114pp. 21075-8 Paperbound $1.25

BEETHOVEN AND HIS NINE SYMPHONIES, Sir George Grove. Noted British musicologist provides best history, analysis, commentary on symphonies. Very thorough, rigorously accurate; necessary to both advanced student and amateur music lover. 436 musical passages. vii + 407 pp. 20334-4 Paperbound $2.75

JOHANN SEBASTIAN BACH, Philipp Spitta. One of the great classics of musicology, this definitive analysis of Bach's music (and life) has never been surpassed. Lucid, nontechnical analyses of hundreds of pieces (30 pages devoted to St. Matthew Passion, 26 to B Minor Mass). Also includes major analysis of 18th-century music. 450 musical examples. 40-page musical supplement. Total of xx + 1799pp.

(EUK) 22278-0, 22279-9 Two volumes, Clothbound $17.50

MOZART AND HIS PIANO CONCERTOS, Cuthbert Girdlestone. The only full-length study of an important area of Mozart's creativity. Provides detailed analyses of all 23 concertos, traces inspirational sources. 417 musical examples. Second edition. 509pp.

21271-8 Paperbound $3.50

THE PERFECT WAGNERITE: A COMMENTARY ON THE NIBLUNG'S RING, George Bernard Shaw. Brilliant and still relevant criticism in remarkable essays on Wagner's Ring cycle, Shaw's ideas on political and social ideology behind the plots, role of Leitmotifs, vocal requisites, etc. Prefaces. xxi + 136pp.

(USO) 21707-8 Paperbound $1.50

DON GIOVANNI, W. A. Mozart. Complete libretto, modern English translation; biographies of composer and librettist; accounts of early performances and critical reaction. Lavishly illustrated. All the material you need to understand and appreciate this great work. Dover Opera Guide and Libretto Series; translated and introduced by Ellen Bleiler. 92 illustrations. 209pp.

21134-7 Paperbound $2.00

HIGH FIDELITY SYSTEMS: A LAYMAN'S GUIDE, Roy F. Allison. All the basic information you need for setting up your own audio system: high fidelity and stereo record players, tape records, F.M. Connections, adjusting tone arm, cartridge, checking needle alignment, positioning speakers, phasing speakers, adjusting hums, trouble-shooting, maintenance, and similar topics. Enlarged 1965 edition. More than 50 charts, diagrams, photos. iv + 91pp.   21514-8 Paperbound $1.25

REPRODUCTION OF SOUND, Edgar Villchur. Thorough coverage for laymen of high fidelity systems, reproducing systems in general, needles, amplifiers, preamps, loudspeakers, feedback, explaining physical background. "A rare talent for making technicalities vividly comprehensible," R. Darrell, *High Fidelity*. 69 figures. iv + 92pp.

21515-6 Paperbound $1.25

HEAR ME TALKIN' TO YA: THE STORY OF JAZZ AS TOLD BY THE MEN WHO MADE IT, Nat Shapiro and Nat Hentoff. Louis Armstrong, Fats Waller, Jo Jones, Clarence Williams, Billy Holiday, Duke Ellington, Jelly Roll Morton and dozens of other jazz greats tell how it was in Chicago's South Side, New Orleans, depression Harlem and the modern West Coast as jazz was born and grew. xvi + 429pp.

21726-4 Paperbound $2.50

FABLES OF AESOP, translated by Sir Roger L'Estrange. A reproduction of the very rare 1931 Paris edition; a selection of the most interesting fables, together with 50 imaginative drawings by Alexander Calder. v + 128pp. 6½x9¼.

21780-9 Paperbound $1.50

AGAINST THE GRAIN (A REBOURS), Joris K. Huysmans. Filled with weird images, evidences of a bizarre imagination, exotic experiments with hallucinatory drugs, rich tastes and smells and the diversions of its sybarite hero Duc Jean des Esseintes, this classic novel pushed 19th-century literary decadence to its limits. Full unabridged edition. Do not confuse this with abridged editions generally sold. Introduction by Havelock Ellis. xlix + 206pp. 22190-3 Paperbound $2.00

VARIORUM SHAKESPEARE: HAMLET. Edited by Horace H. Furness; a landmark of American scholarship. Exhaustive footnotes and appendices treat all doubtful words and phrases, as well as suggested critical emendations throughout the play's history. First volume contains editor's own text, collated with all Quartos and Folios. Second volume contains full first Quarto, translations of Shakespeare's sources (Belleforest, and Saxo Grammaticus), Der Bestrafte Brudermord, and many essays on critical and historical points of interest by major authorities of past and present. Includes details of staging and costuming over the years. By far the best edition available for serious students of Shakespeare. Total of xx + 905pp. 21004-9, 21005-7, 2 volumes, Paperbound $7.00

A LIFE OF WILLIAM SHAKESPEARE, Sir Sidney Lee. This is the standard life of Shakespeare, summarizing everything known about Shakespeare and his plays. Incredibly rich in material, broad in coverage, clear and judicious, it has served thousands as the best introduction to Shakespeare. 1931 edition. 9 plates. xxix + 792pp. (USO) 21967-4 Paperbound $3.75

MASTERS OF THE DRAMA, John Gassner. Most comprehensive history of the drama in print, covering every tradition from Greeks to modern Europe and America, including India, Far East, etc. Covers more than 800 dramatists, 2000 plays, with biographical material, plot summaries, theatre history, criticism, etc. "Best of its kind in English," New Republic. 77 illustrations. xxii + 890pp. 20100-7 Clothbound $8.50

THE EVOLUTION OF THE ENGLISH LANGUAGE, George McKnight. The growth of English, from the 14th century to the present. Unusual, non-technical account presents basic information in very interesting form: sound shifts, change in grammar and syntax, vocabulary growth, similar topics. Abundantly illustrated with quotations. Formerly Modern English in the Making. xii + 590pp. 21932-1 Paperbound $3.50

AN ETYMOLOGICAL DICTIONARY OF MODERN ENGLISH, Ernest Weekley. Fullest, richest work of its sort, by foremost British lexicographer. Detailed word histories, including many colloquial and archaic words; extensive quotations. Do not confuse this with the Concise Etymological Dictionary, which is much abridged. Total of xxvii + 830pp. 6½ x 9¼. 21873-2, 21874-0 Two volumes, Paperbound $6.00

FLATLAND: A ROMANCE OF MANY DIMENSIONS, E. A. Abbott. Classic of science-fiction explores ramifications of life in a two-dimensional world, and what happens when a three-dimensional being intrudes. Amusing reading, but also useful as introduction to thought about hyperspace. Introduction by Banesh Hoffmann. 16 illustrations. xx + 103pp. 20001-9 Paperbound $1.00

POEMS OF ANNE BRADSTREET, edited with an introduction by Robert Hutchinson. A new selection of poems by America's first poet and perhaps the first significant woman poet in the English language. 48 poems display her development in works of considerable variety—love poems, domestic poems, religious meditations, formal elegies, "quaternions," etc. Notes, bibliography. viii + 222pp.

22160-1 Paperbound $2.50

THREE GOTHIC NOVELS: THE CASTLE OF OTRANTO BY HORACE WALPOLE; VATHEK BY WILLIAM BECKFORD; THE VAMPYRE BY JOHN POLIDORI, WITH FRAGMENT OF A NOVEL BY LORD BYRON, edited by E. F. Bleiler. The first Gothic novel, by Walpole; the finest Oriental tale in English, by Beckford; powerful Romantic supernatural story in versions by Polidori and Byron. All extremely important in history of literature; all still exciting, packed with supernatural thrills, ghosts, haunted castles, magic, etc. xl + 291pp.

21232-7 Paperbound $2.50

THE BEST TALES OF HOFFMANN, E. T. A. Hoffmann. 10 of Hoffmann's most important stories, in modern re-editings of standard translations: Nutcracker and the King of Mice, Signor Formica, Automata, The Sandman, Rath Krespel, The Golden Flowerpot, Master Martin the Cooper, The Mines of Falun, The King's Betrothed, A New Year's Eve Adventure. 7 illustrations by Hoffmann. Edited by E. F. Bleiler. xxxix + 419pp. 21793-0 Paperbound $3.00

GHOST AND HORROR STORIES OF AMBROSE BIERCE, Ambrose Bierce. 23 strikingly modern stories of the horrors latent in the human mind: The Eyes of the Panther, The Damned Thing, An Occurrence at Owl Creek Bridge, An Inhabitant of Carcosa, etc., plus the dream-essay, Visions of the Night. Edited by E. F. Bleiler. xxii + 199pp. 20767-6 Paperbound $1.50

BEST GHOST STORIES OF J. S. LeFanu, J. Sheridan LeFanu. Finest stories by Victorian master often considered greatest supernatural writer of all. Carmilla, Green Tea, The Haunted Baronet, The Familiar, and 12 others. Most never before available in the U. S. A. Edited by E. F. Bleiler. 8 illustrations from Victorian publications. xvii + 467pp. 20415-4 Paperbound $3.00

MATHEMATICAL FOUNDATIONS OF INFORMATION THEORY, A. I. Khinchin. Comprehensive introduction to work of Shannon, McMillan, Feinstein and Khinchin, placing these investigations on a rigorous mathematical basis. Covers entropy concept in probability theory, uniqueness theorem, Shannon's inequality, ergodic sources, the E property, martingale concept, noise, Feinstein's fundamental lemma, Shanon's first and second theorems. Translated by R. A. Silverman and M. D. Friedman. iii + 120pp. 60434-9 Paperbound $1.75

SEVEN SCIENCE FICTION NOVELS, H. G. Wells. The standard collection of the great novels. Complete, unabridged. *First Men in the Moon, Island of Dr. Moreau, War of the Worlds, Food of the Gods, Invisible Man, Time Machine, In the Days of the Comet.* Not only science fiction fans, but every educated person owes it to himself to read these novels. 1015pp. (USO) 20264-X Clothbound $5.00